THE ACTS OF THE APOSTLES

GIUSEPPE RICCIOTTI

THE ACTS
of THE APOSTLES

TEXT AND COMMENTARY.

TRANSLATED BY
LAURENCE E. BYRNE, C.R.L.

THE BRUCE PUBLISHING COMPANY
MILWAUKEE

IMPRIMI POTEST:

CHARLES J. WHITE, C.R.L.
Provincial Visitator and Prior

NIHIL OBSTAT:

JOANNES A. SCHULIEN, S.T.D.
Censor librorum

IMPRIMATUR:

✠ ALBERTUS G. MEYER
Archiepiscopus Milwauchiensis

August 16, 1957

Library of Congress Catalog Card Number: 57-12920

© 1958 BY THE BRUCE PUBLISHING COMPANY

MADE IN THE UNITED STATES OF AMERICA

Revisione rite peracta, facultatem facimus ut typis vulgetur opus, cui titulus: "Versio in anglicum sermonem Actorum Apostolorum Josephi Ricciotti" a R. D. Laurentio Byrne concinnatum, servatis omnibus de jure servandis.

In quorum fidem, &c. . . .

Romae, ad S. Joseph in Via Nomentana, die 30 Maii, 1956.

✠ FERDINANDUS URQUIA
Abbas Generalis Can. Reg. Later.

AUTHOR'S PREFACE

THIS book closes the series of my publications on *The History of Israel,* the *Life of Christ, Paul the Apostle,* and *The Letters of St. Paul,* which cover a period from the historic origins of the Old Testament almost to the close of the New Testament.

The present work is particularly linked with the last two mentioned above, because it deals to a large extent with the same arguments, but this time dealt with directly on historical sources. This has inevitably caused repetition which strictly could have been avoided by referring to the preceding works. However, such references would have been so frequent in the Introduction that the thread of the argument would have been lost. This, then, is the reason for the repetitions from my previous works about which the reader is therefore warned.

The method of the commentary is the same as that followed in *The Letters of St. Paul,* but with greater detail, because in the *Acts,* inversely to the former work, the historic element is greater than the doctrinal one. It is precisely the historic element which has been the chief scope of this series of which this is the last book and which I felt was most necessary for my readers. As in *The Letters,* the translation faithfully follows the Greek text and the words added for the sake of clarity are set in brackets.

It is my great pleasure here to thank Fr. S. Lyonnet, S.J., professor of the Biblical Institute, well known for his learning on this subject, who has reviewed my manuscript and suggested important improvements.

G. R.

Rome, All Saints, 1951

TRANSLATOR'S NOTE

BEING associated with Abbot Ricciotti as an English confrere of the same Order, my admiration for his works on Holy Scripture led me to hope that all his original works in Italian would eventually be made available in translations for English-speaking readers. His great trilogy of the *Life of Christ, Paul the Apostle,* and *The History of Israel* has enriched the scriptural arsenal of information in countries where scholarship in biblical works has always been in the forefront.

It was therefore with great pleasure that I undertook to translate the present work, with the humble hope that I might do justice to Abbot Ricciotti's great learning and biblical knowledge. The text is translated from the Italian, which the author rendered from the original Greek of the various codices extant today. I have preserved the insertions in brackets which, as the author says in his Preface, are added for the sake of clarity. The commentary is the author's effort to present a story which is a challenge to modern society, insofar as the life of the first Christian communities was an endeavor to be in the world, but not of it.

The reason that the Apostles Peter and Paul had such a profound effect on their world is that they lived what they talked about. They had something better to offer than the materialism they fought. The book of THE ACTS OF THE APOSTLES deals with actions as well as theories, it challenges men's living as well as their thinking. The same Holy Spirit who descended on the first Pentecost is still with the Church today, and men still have need of the assistance and guidance of the same Holy Spirit to face the world and proclaim Christ.

I must here express my deep gratitude to several of my confreres who have so ably assisted me in correcting and preparing my manuscript, and in particular Abbot A. Smith, C.R.L., who so kindly read my translation and gave me the benefit of his patient understanding. In conclusion, I would like to acknowledge my appreciation to The Bruce Publishing Company for their patience and co-operation in producing this work.

LAURENCE E. BYRNE, C.R.L.

St. Mary's Abbey
BODMIN
Cornwall, England

CONTENTS

INDEX OF MAPS

INTRODUCTION

CHAPTER ONE

THE BOOK OF THE ACTS

THE book called *The Acts of the Apostles* is placed immediately next to the four Gospels in the New Testament. This is its right place since the Gospel narrative terminates with the account of the Ascension of Jesus to heaven and the *Acts* begins with this same event and follows on with the description of the propagation of Christianity through Palestine and beyond. Such propagation, in fact, is the basic argument of the book and it can be discerned at the very beginning in those words which Jesus addressed to his Apostles before his Ascension: "You shall be witnesses for me in Jerusalem and in all Judea and Samaria and even to the very ends of the earth" (Acts 1:8).

The title of the book best attested by codices is Πράξις ἀποστόλων, viz., *Acts of Apostles*. Less authoritative are the titles *Acts of the Apostles* with the article, and that simply of *Acts*. The term *Acts,* used as a title, does not indicate, in Greek usage, a particularized historic account or a complete biography, but only a number of episodes of greater importance relative to a particular personage. Such a use of the term was already known at the time of the classics since we know that Callisthenes, a contemporary of Alexander the Great, has written the *ACTS* (Πράξεις) *of Alexander,* which certainly did not include a detailed biography of him, but only the more salient facts. The Latin expression *Res Gestae* corresponds substantially to the Greek term *Acts* inasmuch as it proffers an anthology or an incomplete summary. For that reason, therefore, in our case the more preferable title is that which is best attested, viz., *Acts of Apostles,* without the article, since the account does not refer to all the Apostles but only to a few of them, practically speaking only Peter and Paul, and even then its account of them is not complete.

The consecutive narrative regarding the two principal persons is such that the whole book falls naturally into two parts. The protagonist of the first part (Chapters 1–12) is Peter, that of the second (Chapters 13–28) is Paul. But Paul is already on the scene after the middle of the first part,

1

still as a secondary figure, so that he is already known when the second part, which is dedicated exclusively to him, begins.

Here is a summary of both parts:

Part I

Prologue; Ascension of Jesus; election of Matthias (Chapter 1).

Pentecost; the discourse of Peter; the first conversions in Jerusalem (Chapter 2).

Healing of the lame man; the discourse of Peter (Chapter 3).

Peter and John brought before the Sanhedrin; the charitable assistance among the faithful (Chapter 4).

Ananias and Sapphira; miracles of the Apostles who are imprisoned and brought before the Sanhedrin (Chapter 5).

Election of the seven deacons; Stephen is accused (Chapter 6).

The discourse and stoning of Stephen (Chapter 7).

Persecution of the community at Jerusalem with the co-operation of Saul (Paul); conversion of the Samaritans by Philip the deacon, Peter, and John; conversion of the Ethiopian (Chapter 8).

Conversion of Paul; Paul preaches at Damascus; flees to Jerusalem and then betakes himself to Tarsus (9:1–30).

Peter heals Aeneas the paralytic in Lydda; he raises up Tabitha at Joppa (9:31–43).

Cornelius the centurion; Peter at Jerusalem defends his conduct regarding Cornelius (10–11:18).

The beginning of the community at Antioch; Barnabas and Paul, famine and the alms sent (11:19–30).

The community at Jerusalem is persecuted by Herod Agrippa I; the killing of James (the Greater) and imprisonment of Peter; miraculous deliverance of Peter; death of Herod Agrippa; Barnabas and Paul return to Antioch (Chapter 12).

Part II

The first missionary journey of Paul (Chapters 13–14).

The Council of the Apostles (15:1–35).

Second missionary journey of Paul (15:36–18:22).

Third missionary journey of Paul (18:23–21:16).

At Jerusalem Paul meets James (the Less); Paul is arrested in the Temple (21:17–40).

Paul's discourse to the people; Paul in prison and then before the Sanhedrin (Chapter 22).

Discourse of Paul, plot of the Jews against him; Paul at Caesarea (Chapter 23).

Paul before Felix the governor (Chapter 24).

Paul before Festus the governor, Agrippa and Bernice (Chapters 25–26).

Paul's voyage to Rome, shipwreck, and wintering at Malta; arrival and two years' sojourn in Rome (Chapters 27–28).

As ordinarily happens in historical works which are not autobiographical, the *Acts* is usually narrated in the third person (*he . . . they*); but in four places the first person plural (*we*) is used as if the narrator had personally taken part in the events he relates. Nevertheless they are passages which appear without warning in the logical sequence of the narrative with no notice nor explanation being given for this sudden change of pronoun. These four passages in the first person plural, known in English as the "we-sections," are the following: 16:10–17; 20:5–15; 21:1–18; 27–28:16.

As is apparent they are all contained in the second part of the book. There is a "we-section" in 11:27–28 which is in the first part but this is transmitted only by the texts which reflect the Western Recension of the *Acts* of which we shall now speak.

CHAPTER TWO

THE TEXT OF THE ACTS

THE text of the *Acts* has come down to us in two principal forms which, while not conflicting with each other, are somewhat divergent and are usually called the Eastern Recension and the Western Recension. It should be noticed straightway that these two names are conventional and do not mean entirely what the terms might seem to signify. The Eastern Recension is in fact represented by testimonies of Western origin, while on the other hand, the Western Recension, though having in its favor fairly ancient documents of Western origin, is also attested by authoritative documents of Eastern origin.

The Eastern Recension. This is represented especially by the earliest and most authoritative Greek uncial codices such as *Sinaiticus* (X, fourth century), *Vaticanus* (B, fourth century), *Alexandrinus* (A, fifth century), *rescriptus Ephraemi* (C, fifth century), *Mutinensis* (H, ninth century), *Angelicus* (L, ninth century), *Porphyrianus* (P, ninth century), and other less important ones. These uncial codices do not all entirely agree with each other and each one shows individual characteristics. The codices *Sinaiticus* and *Vaticanus* are very akin and the latter can be considered to represent most faithfully the text that was published in Egypt in the fourth century as an elaboration made by the learned circles of Alexandria. A certain likeness is also found between the codices *Alexandrinus* and *rescriptus Ephraemi,* and it is possible that they received some slight influence from the Western Recension. However, notwithstanding such secondary divergencies, all the above-mentioned codices form a group which generically can be considered as representative of the Eastern Recension.

Earlier evidence is found in the Chester Beatty papyrus (pap. 45) which goes back to the third century and therefore precedes the aforesaid uncials.

Most of the Greek minuscules equally reflect the Eastern Recension and among the ancient versions we have the Copto-Bohairic (third century), the Latin Vulgate (fourth century), and the Syriac Philoxenian (sixth century).

On the same Eastern Recension depend the citations which are found in the Greek writers, Clement of Alexandria and Origen (third century), and in the majority of other writers from the fourth century onward.

The Western Recension. The codex which best represents this form, quantitatively if not qualitatively, is the Cambridge codex commonly called *Beza* (D, fifth–sixth centuries), containing as it does Greek and Latin texts. However, there are big gaps and lacunae which altogether amount to over eight chapters. Over and above the lacunae, the Latin text of this codex (*sigla d*) has particularities which are proper to it and it has certainly influenced the Greek text of this same codex, bringing about especially omissions of readings proper to the Western Recension.

Two papyri of the third century (Michigan, 1571; Florentine, 1165), which unfortunately contain only a few verses, follow the Western Recension, but even these show that it circulated in Egypt. This form is also reflected in some few Greek minuscules.

Among the versions, the Coptic-Sahidic (fourth century) partially confirms the knowledge of this recension in Egypt by means of some of its Western-style readings. This is followed in great part by the Old Latin (*Vetus Latina*—pre-Hieroniman Latin version). Little is known to us about the ancient Syriac version before the Peshitta, but from an Armenian translation of the Syriac commentary of Ephraem on the *Acts* made on such a version, it seems possible to conclude that even this version reflected the Western Recension which is thereby attested in Syria.

Two documents of particular value are the Floricensian palimpsest and the Heraklean Syriac version. The former (of Fleury) (*sigla h*) is a Latin codex of the sixth century so damaged and incomplete that it offers much less than half of the whole text, but in its particular readings it is generally in agreement with the citations of early Latin writers, Cyprian of Carthage in particular, thereby showing that it was a worthy testimony of the text that was used in Africa during the third century. The Heraklean Syriac version is not important for its text, but for the variant marginal readings (*sigla syhm*). The text is that of the already mentioned Philoxenian version, touched up by Thomas of Harkel at the beginning of the seventh century in Alexandria, while the added marginal notes display throughout the whole work divergencies which are typical of the Western Recension and cast this recension in a form which is older and freer from outside influences and concordistic preoccupations than any other document, including codex Beza.

In favor of this same recension there can be quoted almost constantly the citations of writers who lived in the West from the second century onward, e.g., Irenaeus, Tertullian, and Cyprian. Other Western writers show themselves less faithful, for example, Augustine, who seems to have followed texts which were dependent on different recensions according to the varying periods at which he wrote. John Chrysostom, himself an Eastern writer, depends sometimes on texts which bear traces of the Western Recension.

Intermediate Form. The two preceding recensions of which we have spoken are, on the whole, certain, considered as single entities apart; but, as one might expect, *a priori* there exists a kind of text which is a mixture of both, representing a fusion of the two real recensions and almost a compromise between them both, rather than a new recension in itself.

The codices *Mutinensis, Angelicus,* and *Porphyrianus,* mentioned in connection with the Eastern Recension and representing a kind of text designated by specialists as "Antiochian," already show a definite influence by the Western Recension, but it is only slight and the readings of those codices agree to a great extent with the great uncials of the fourth and fifth centuries which represent the Eastern Recension. The intermediate or mixed form, however, besides appearing in two Greek minuscules, is found much more in the codex *Laudianus* (E, sixth century) which has the Greek text alongside a Latin version (*sigla e*). The Greek text bears the stamp of the "Antiochian" type, but a great number of Western-type readings have been inserted, taken from the accompanying Latin text and translated into Greek. More important still for this intermediate form is the codex *Gigas* (Gig.), a Latin manuscript which is not earlier than the thirteenth century, but whose readings agree in a surprising manner with the quotations of Lucifer of Cagliari (fourth century) to such an extent as to give rise to the supposition that they represent the usual text of the place and time of Lucifer. It is again an "Antiochian"-type text, but one which has received notable insertions culled from the Western Recension.

The old Coptic-Sahidic versions already referred to in connection with the Western Recension, the Syriac Peshitta, the Armenian and Georgian versions, and other later ones in the Romance languages, are more or less of the intermediate form.

The quotations of early writers are of this eclectic or mixed type. Besides Augustine and John Chrysostom, already mentioned, one can with greater reason include in this category Lucifer of Cagliari, Ambrosiaster, the Venerable Bede, and others.

Characteristics of the Two Recensions. Passing over the "intermediate form" as being devoid of a specific character, the differences between the two recensions can be summed up as follows:

a) The Western Recension is regularly longer than the Eastern to the extent of 8 per cent of the whole text. Rarely, however, does the Western Recension omit small elements of the Eastern.

b) The elements added by the Western Recension usually render its text more readable and understandable than that of the Eastern in those places where the latter shows some obscurity and difficulty. But often enough the additions of the Western Recension are conceptually superfluous and do not bring new facts to the narrative. Very frequently they are clearly dictated by religious devotion and possibly by liturgical remembrances. As an example of this we have the appellative "The Lord Jesus Christ" which is more frequent in the Western Recension, even where the Eastern Recension does not employ one or even two of the three terms. Generally one notices in the Western Recension the deliberate intention of putting into particular relief the assistance of the Holy Spirit in the affairs of the Church and the work of the Apostles, particularly of Peter.

c) Besides these additions which are indifferent in themselves, the Western Recension offers others, few in number, but of greater importance since they introduce precise historic facts into the narrative which are not found in the Eastern Recension and which refer variously to chronology, geography, topography, social customs, and the like. Certainly it is not possible today to determine the accuracy of all these new historic elements, but while they frequently appear as countersigns of a complete abstract likeness, they are already known to writers of the second and third centuries such as Irenaeus, Tertullian, and Cyprian, which fact is undoubtedly in favor of their authoritativeness. Moreover, with these additions, the narrative is rendered fuller, more vivid, and fitting.

Two examples will show this. In Acts 12:10, the mention of *seven steps,* although not substantially modifying the narrative, gives it more life, while archaeologically it offers a new element which, though not confirmed, is not denied by other documents. In 19:9, the chronological limits *from the fifth hour to the tenth* are surprisingly in keeping with what we know of the usages of those times and places. Therefore, although neither case is individually confirmed, it has in its favor an inherent likelihood and fits in naturally with the contemporaneous background. This fact is so much more noteworthy inasmuch as such readings are not invented for the mere sake of inventing since, even with them, the substance of the historical narrative remains unchanged. If, therefore, they were introduced, it was because they derived from some oral or written tradition which was authoritative and fairly ancient.

There is, however, one case which goes against the authority of these additions and it is the instance of the apostolic decree (15:20–29). There the Western Recension differs notably from the Eastern Recension, both by omitting one of the prohibitions of the decree and by adding a fairly long moral prescription. Nevertheless, dealing with a unique written document, there can be only one original text and one of the two recensions must necessarily be an alteration of the other which would be the genuine one. In the case in question, the Western Recension is probably not the genuine and original one.

As a result of the preceding considerations, it would be false to regard the Western Recension as a casual mass of fortuitous alterations or of accommodations and glosses due to private readers who have revised the text of the Eastern Recension independently among themselves at different times and places. No, the Western Recension shows by itself that it is the work of one hand that worked with fairly precise aims, and whose work was rapidly diffused from its region of origin and into many other and remoter places. During this process of circulation, the Western Recension came into frequent contact with the Eastern, influencing it more or less profoundly, being influenced in its own turn and thus producing the various types of the "intermediate form."

The antiquity of the documentary evidence, especially that of the writers who knew and used the Western Recension, leads to the conclusion that it was already completed and in circulation in the middle of the second century and maybe toward the beginning of the same century. It is more difficult to know the region of its origin and while not ruling out that it could have been Egypt, it is more probable that it was Syria with its center at Antioch.

We must not forget, however, that for us today the Western Recension in its complexity is a thing of little more than academic interest, since, unfortunately, we do not possess documents which have preserved its text for us in its integrity and purity. As was seen in the paragraph devoted to this Recension, the documents in our possession which best represent it are, in the first place, comparatively few in number, especially in comparison with the many documents of the Eastern Recension, and, second, they are deficient both in completeness, since they are more or less missing in parts, and in quality, because they are more or less altered by influences of the Eastern Recension. This last reason renders particularly difficult the attempt to reconstruct the original text of the Western Recension, extracting it from the mass of variants which multiply at every step. The complicated business of action and reaction which the various types of texts have exercised throughout the centuries on the documents which have come down to us, render hopeless or at least very doubtful the assignation of a given variant to one recension rather than to the other. On the other hand, it is generally easy enough to recognize among the elements added by the Western Recension those which we noted under *b*), as due to the desire for harmony and clarity, or else to liturgical and devotional motives. Much more difficult are the additions which introduce new historic facts *c*), and these must be considered one by one.

The Origins of the Two Forms. Such being the state of the actual data, it is necessary to inquire into the relationship between the two forms. Which of them is the primitive one, which the derived? Is the Eastern form the earlier since it is shorter, so that the Western form is derived from it by means of the additions; or is the Western one more primitive since it is longer, so that the Eastern form is shorter by reason of suppressions made in it? How far do they depend upon Luke, traditionally presented as the author of the writing?

Taking the last question first, we find that Frederic Blass, a philologist of Halle, taking up and developing a hypothesis already put forward by others, proposed in 1894 that Luke himself was the author of both recensions. According to Blass, he would have written the *Acts* at Rome, first as a rough copy which was adopted by the Christian community of Rome, and that account, becoming more widespread, would be the Western form. From this Luke would later have made a new copy, revised and more precise, sending it to that Theophilus to whom the *Acts* are addressed (as was the Third Gospel), and this would be the Eastern form. In this way, both forms would come directly from Luke, the older one as a first draft, the more recent one as a careful revision of the first.[1] In support of his hypothesis, Blass cited other cases of antiquity in which one and the same writing was edited several times by its author. In fact, among other cases it turned out that there were two editions of *III Philippica* of Demosthenes, two editions of the *Accademica* of Cicero, three editions of *Contra Marcionem* of Tertullian, etc.

Although such examples do show the theoretical possibility of a repeated edition, the actual reality of such a new edition is not attested by any indication in our present case, though it ought at least to be traceable by internal evidence in a comparison of the texts. But instead we find that such a comparison leads us to reject the hypothesis of a double edition. We have seen, in fact, that the text of the Western form is usually more readable and understandable in comparison with that of the Eastern form, which contains difficulties and obscurities. Why would Luke have worsened his first edition, from the literary point of view, introducing into it defects which it did not at first possess? The more natural explanation of this is not that Luke himself is responsible for the deterioration, but that a compiler endeavored to improve the writing of Luke (the Eastern form), touching it up in several places (the Western form). We also saw that the Western form shows the tendency to put into special relief the assistance of the Holy Spirit and the work of the Apostles. How does it come about, then, that this tendency is greatly diminished in the edition made specially for Theophilus (Eastern Recension), since he had a special need to be confirmed and enlightened in his Christian faith? (Cf. Lk. 1:4.) Finally, some clear contradictions between the two recensions demonstrate that the author of the one cannot be the author of the other. The most glaring of these contradictions is in the Apostolic decree already mentioned, but other cases could be added of readings proper to the Western Recension which are clearly mistaken.

---

[1] Later (1897) Blass included in his hypothesis the origin of the Third Gospel, supposing that Luke made two rough copies of it, but he inverted the order of these, judging the Eastern form to be older and the Western more recent. This new hypothesis including the Third Gospel had a very slight following.

A further consideration of a different kind leads one to judge, at least generally speaking, that the Western Recension is less trustworthy and reliable than the Eastern one. If, as the hypothesis of Blass supposed, the Western Recension was left by the author to the Christian community at Rome, whence it was then circulated throughout the rest of the world, while on the contrary the Eastern form was destined for Theophilus, one ought to find that the Western form was the one absolutely predominant text in the manuscript transmissions which have come down to us, because it was the official text of a community as authoritative as that of the Roman Church. Contrariwise, the Eastern text should hardly be attested at all, since it was dependent on the copy destined for Theophilus, who, however important he may have been as a person, was nevertheless only a private individual. Instead, as was seen above, the great majority of codices and other manuscript testimonies is in favor of the Eastern text, while the Western Recension has something of an ephemeral nature, transmitted as it is by documents few in number, inconsistent among themselves and lost in a labyrinth of glosses and variants from which it is extremely difficult to disentangle it. An official text of the Roman Church would not cut such a poor figure in the manuscript transmissions as compared with a text prepared for a private individual.

These, and other considerations which could be added, led to the result that the theory of Blass, after an initial period in which it was acclaimed with favor by numerous learned and authoritative scholars, was eventually judged more specious than convincing, and gradually the number of its adherents dwindled.

Putting aside the hypothesis that both the recensions come directly from Luke, it could be supposed that only the Western form is from him, while the Eastern form would be the work of a compiler who revised Luke's writing, rendering it less verbose but more substantial. Some scholars took this view a century ago and some think similarly now. According to this second hypothesis, the original and genuine text of the *Acts* ought to be sought, not in the great uncial codices, but in the codex *Beza,* compared with and supplemented by the other documents mentioned above (in the paragraphs on the Western Recension and the Intermediate Form).

This suggestion has in its favor the observations we have already made on the texts of the two recensions, observations which are numerous, clear, and worthy of attention. Nevertheless, the general objections raised against the theory of Blass hold more or less against this hypothesis. If the compiler who revised Luke's writing did so only for the sake of shortening the text, he abbreviated far too little because, as we saw, the Eastern Recension prepared by him is shorter than the other by only 8 per cent, an abbreviation, therefore, which did not seem worth the labor of the undertaking. Moreover, this negligible quantitative advantage would have been paid for too dearly under the qualitative aspect, since the text of the new recension is generally less clear and readable than the other, and also less vivid and rich. For the rest, the quantitative difference between the two recensions can already be explained more easily *a priori* as an addition made to the Eastern Recension, rather than as a subtraction made from the Western. The difference between them, in fact, consists for the greater part in subordinate sentences, which add nothing to the aims of the narrative and are suggested by religious devotion or liturgical remembrances, such as the various titles added to the name of Jesus. The abundance of such material is more to be expected in a later epoch, when the ecclesiastical and liturgical organization was much more developed and when it was easy to sew around the great historic tapestry woven by Luke the small fringes of such modest additions. But on the contrary, at the time of Luke, the great tapestry was wanting and its weaving made from strictly historical materials was much more important than the accidental fringes. These latter, therefore, presuppose the former and not *vice versa*.

In conclusion, the larger content of the Western Recension, on careful examination, shows itself as a mass of retouches aimed at rendering the old text clearer and more adapted to the new times, and not at the suppression of a small ancient patrimony. However, some of the additions of the Western Recension which are deserving of special merit do not come into this category, and must therefore be examined one by one.

If we abandon the notion that both recensions come directly from Luke and, instead, maintain that the Western Recension is later than the Eastern, this latter will reflect better than any other the original work of Luke.

However, it is not a perfect reflection. Compared with the Eastern Recension, notwithstanding that this is represented by a majestic series of documents headed by the codex *Vaticanus* (B), the Western Recension has its own not inconsiderable claims. The singularity of some of its readings, their inherent probability and the antiquity of the writers who use them (cf. pp. 7 ff.), do not allow of rejecting *a priori* those of its readings which fulfill these conditions. The philologists have, in fact, noted that some of such readings contain expressions of language and style which are characteristic of Luke (although many others show opposite characteristics, thereby raising a serious prejudice against themselves). There is, then, a motive for suspecting that the Eastern Recension is not complete and that those readings proper to the Western form, which are very ancient and authoritative, can be added to its content.

Notwithstanding these conclusions based on facts, they do not allow us to determine the relationship of the Western Recension to the original writing of Luke. Here, therefore, since documentary evidence is wanting, one can only proceed by way of more or less likely hypothesis.

Adhering to the fact, then, that the Western Recension is later than the Eastern, it could have happened that an unknown compiler thought fit to introduce into a copy of the Eastern form those modifications which gave rise to the Western form. These were of two kinds: the first were modifications of little importance, namely additions which did not introduce new concepts into the narrative (see above, *b*), and these today show only that the Western Recension is a later elaboration than the Eastern one. Second, however, there were modifications which brought in new historic elements, and which modern examination shows to be authoritative and very old, and these must have been taken from some oral or written tradition accessible to the compiler.

Who was this person? We do not know and we almost certainly never shall. As we have already conjectured, he must have lived about the middle of the second century, or even a decade or so earlier. He may have been a disciple of the Apostles, who received from his masters particular information on the subject, and in fact we find Polycarp, who was a disciple of the Apostles, in one passage (Phil. 1:2) following the Western Recension in preference to the Eastern, reading ᾅδου instead of θανάτου, in Acts 2:24. The habitat of the unknown compiler could have been Egypt, but it was more probably Syria.

Compiled as it was, this editor's recension must have spread very quickly even into distant regions, but at the same time it was exposed to contaminations of various kinds. In the first place, the usual private glosses and additions found their way into it, and then the concordistic modifications occasioned by comparison with the preceding and predominant Eastern Recension, from which arose the various types of mixed and intermediate forms. It cannot be affirmed with certainty that the Apostolic decree in its Western form goes back as far as the compiler; in fact the Western Recension is most tantalizing where this decree is concerned and it shows traces of repeated touching up during the centuries, so much so that even when we have abstracted what seems the best attested reading from the collection of its variants, we have no guarantee that the early compiler of the Western Recension is responsible for any such reading.

In conclusion, in searching for the text of the *Acts* as it came from the pen of Luke, preference must be given to the Eastern Recension, especially in the form shown by codex *Vaticanus*. However, this preference should not be absolute and blindly trustful; the critic, in fact, should keep an eye open to the Western Recension with a view to rejecting indeed the maximum of useless and common readings, but even more, toward putting into the picture of possibilities those few readings that show in their favor the countersigns of authoritative criticism.

CHAPTER THREE

THE PERSON OF LUKE — THE EXTERNAL TESTIMONIES REGARDING THE ACTS

THE earliest historical testimonies, followed naturally by the mass of more recent ones, give Luke as the author of the *Acts*.

In the Christianity of the first generation, Luke is presented as a figure intimately connected with the person of Paul. Originating in Antioch, not Jewish but Greek by birth and education, Luke became a Christian before the year A.D. 50 (as early as A.D. 44, if one accepts the particular reading of the Western Recension in Acts 11:27-28). His profession is known to us from the appellation with which Paul addresses him, calling him "the dear physician" (Col. 4:14). Shortly after the year 50, we find him at Paul's side on the second missionary journey (Acts 16:10 sqq.), probably also in the capacity of physician because of the recent illness suffered by the Apostle (cf. Gal. 4:13 with Acts 16:6).

From this time onward Luke reappears as Paul's shadow in almost all the latter's travels, except for what was probably a long separation after their common sojourn in Philippi (cf. Acts 16:40 with 20:5). Joining Paul again at Philippi during the Apostle's third missionary journey about the year 57, he accompanied him for the rest of the voyage as far as Jerusalem (Acts 21:15). During the two years spent by Paul in prison at Caesarea (58-60), it seems that Luke could not stay near him, but he accompanied him on his journey to Rome, sharing the adventures of the voyage (Acts 27:1 sqq.). During Paul's first imprisonment in Rome, Luke stayed near him; later, faithful unto death, he assisted him during his second Roman imprisonment, earning from Paul in that letter which is almost the last will of the declining Apostle, the moving tribute: *Only Luke is with me* (2 Tim. 4:11).

Writing to the Corinthians in the year 57, Paul refers to *a brother whose praise is in the gospel throughout all the churches* (2 Cor. 8:18). Together with other early writers, St. Jerome believed that this unnamed *brother* was none other than Luke (*De viris illustr.* 7), and he gives the opinions of others that *every time Paul says in his letters "according to my gospel," he is referring to the volume of Luke.* This last opinion, however, is entirely untenable since Luke's Gospel was not yet written in the year 57. Besides, in the letters of Paul the term "gospel" never denotes any specific

13

writing, but only the message of the "good news" according to the etymological sense of the word. So far as the identification of the unknown *brother* with Luke goes, it would not of itself be impossible, since in the "gospel" attributed to him, one detects a reference, not to a literary composition, but to the work of one who was an "evangelist" in the original sense of that word (cf. Eph. 4:11; 2 Tim. 4:5; Acts 21:8), namely a preacher of the "good news."

This is the personage to whom is attributed the book of the *Acts* as well as the third of the canonical Gospels.

Passing over allusions or references to be found in the earliest writers which are not decisive, the explicit testimonies regarding the author of the *Acts* run parallel — as is only natural — with those regarding the author of the Third Gospel.

In the late second century, the Muratorian Fragment (a catalogue of the sacred books acknowledged by the Church of Rome, composed about the year A.D. 180, and discovered by L. A. Muratori in the Ambrosian Library of Milan) says, in its dreadful Latin (corrected to make it understandable): *Acta autem omnium apostolorum sub uno libro scripta sunt. Lucas optimo Theophilo comprehendit, quae sub praesentia ejus singula gerebantur* (lines 34–37). Here the unknown author wishes to make the point that while the deeds of Jesus are recounted in the four books of the Gospels, the deeds of the Apostles in general are narrated in only one book. The author of this book is Luke (about whom the fragment has spoken before in connection with his Gospel), and he writes for the "excellent Theophilus," relating events at which Luke himself was present.

The testimony of Irenaeus of Lyons belongs to about this same period. He frequently cites the *Acts,* giving also the title, and on a dozen occasions he explicitly attributes it to Luke. Among other things, he says: *That this Luke was the inseparable companion of Paul and a collaborator with him in the preaching of the Gospel, he himself reveals, not boasting but constrained to do so by the truth itself. In fact, he says, when both Barnabas and John, surnamed Mark, had left Paul and sailed for Cyprus, we came to Troas. . . . Sailing therefore from Troas, we directed the ship toward Samothrace. . . . We spoke with the women* (summary of Acts 15:39–16:13). *. . . Having been present at all these things, Luke put them diligently together in writing. . . . Since he was not only the disciple but also a collaborator with the Apostles, and especially of Paul (Adv. Haer.,* III, 14, 1; in Migne, *P. G.,* 7, 913–914). Also belonging to the late second century are the various Prologues, Coptic, Greek, and Latin,[1] to different parts of the New Testament, which are reproduced with amplifications by the

---

[1] Latin texts in D. de Bruyne, *"Les plus anciens prologues latins des Evangiles,"* in *Revue Benedictine,* 1928, pp. 193–214; the other text in M-J. Lagrange, *Evangile selon S. Luc,* 3 ed., Paris, 1927, pp. 13–18.

later Monarchian Prologues. Even in the earliest Prologues, Luke is mentioned as the author of the *Acts*. Usually he is already named as the author of the Third Gospel and then is added: *afterwards the same Luke wrote* the *Acts* of the Apostles.[2]

Passing to the third century, the testimonies become increasingly plentiful, both among the Latin writers (e.g., Tertullian, *De jejunio*, 10; in Migne, *P. L.*, 2, 966–1017) and the Greeks (Clement of Alexandria, *Stromata*, V, 12, 82; in Migne, *P. G.*, 9, 124; Origen, *C. Celsum*, VI, II; in Migne, *P. G.*, II, 1308 and in the quotation in Eusebius, *Hist. eccl.*, VI, 25, 14). All of them quote the *Acts* as a book of the New Testament and attribute its authorship to Luke.

To adduce any further quotations here would be unnecessary, since it is admitted by all that in the third century the *Acts* were accepted unanimously among the canonical writings and as the composition of Luke (cf. Eusebius, *Hist. eccl.*, II, 22, 1; III, 4, 1–10; III, 25, 1). It is, however, surprising to find, in a homily attributed to the well-informed John Chrysostom, the assertion that many did not know who was the author of the *Acts* and assigned it either to Clement of Rome, to Barnabas, or to Luke the Evangelist.[3]

This statement is repeated later by Photius[4] who undoubtedly depended only on the homily, since there is not the slightest evidence in antiquity that the *Acts* were in any way ever attributed to Clement of Rome or Barnabas. As for the homily itself, it is probably an adulteration of one of Chrysostom's other works and not authentic. In any case, whoever may have written this homily, must have confused the *Acts* with the *Epistle to the Hebrews,* which was actually attributed by some ancient writers to Clement of Rome or to Barnabas.

---

[2] *". . . postremo scripsit idem Lucas Actus Apostolorum."*
[3] *Hom. II in Ascensionem et initium Actorum*, 8; in Migne, *P. G.*, 52, 780.
[4] Photius, *Quaest. ad Amphilochium*, 123 al. 145, in Migne, *P. G.*, 101, 716.

CHAPTER FOUR

THE INTERNAL EVIDENCE OF THE ACTS

PASSING to an internal examination of the book, we find numerous confirmations of its close relationship with the Third Gospel and also of Luke's authorship. The Third Gospel is dedicated to a definite person, named Theophilus. It was, in fact, a mark of esteem to address one's writing to a distinguished personage, and thirty years later this custom was followed in Rome itself by Flavius Josephus, who dedicated his *Jewish Antiquities* (I, 8) and his *Contra Apionem* (I, 1; II, 1) to a certain Epaphroditus. In Luke's Gospel (1:3), Theophilus is called κράτιστε which is equivalent to our "most excellent," and this would designate the person's high degree, but that is all we know of him. Luke has addressed his Gospel to Theophilus *so that thou mayest understand the certainty of the words in which thou hast been instructed* (κατηχήθης) (Lk. 1:4). This last word shows that Theophilus was already instructed in the Christian catechesis and was probably already baptized. At any rate, in addressing his Gospel to Theophilus, Luke has not only him in mind but also those many others who found themselves more or less in his position and can therefore draw help from his writing.

The dedication must have had good effect, since we find that Luke follows the same pattern with the *Acts*. The prologue of this new book (1:1-2) is similarly addressed to Theophilus, and expressly mentions the earlier writing (πρῶτον λόγον), already sent him, viz., the Third Gospel. Moreover it also calls to mind the final episode of this writing, viz., the Ascension of Jesus into heaven, and with this same event, the new writing takes up the narrative. Hence the connection between the two is quite clear.

Besides the family likeness of the prologues, the two writings show a kinship in their general method, language, and style. When we examine the disposition of the facts related in the Gospel of Luke, it is easily noticeable that the author likes to present his material in parallel episodes, diptychs so to speak, in which one figure balances another. For example, the annunciation to Mary is joined to the announcement to Zachary (Lk. 1:2 sqq.); the episode of Simeon is placed beside that of Anna (Lk. 2:25 sqq.; and 2:36 sqq.); close upon the story of the crippled woman cured on the Sabbath, there follows the very similar one of the man with dropsy cured likewise on the Sabbath (Lk. 13:10 sqq.; and 14:1 sqq.); and elsewhere.

When we turn to the *Acts,* we find there the same stylistic preference, and it is employed much more fully. In the life story of Christ, there was only one main character and the evangelist Luke could put episodes in pairs only around that single figure, but in the *Acts,* as we saw, there are two principal characters, who occupy the center of the stage by turns, Peter in the first part of the book and Paul in the second, so that opportunities for this kind of account were more numerous and Luke could satisfy his predilection for them in greater measure.

We find, for instance, that a cripple is cured by Peter and one by Paul (Acts 3:2 sqq.; and 14:8 sqq.); Peter raises the dead Tabitha to life and Paul resuscitates the dead Eutychus (9:36 sqq. and 20:9 sqq.); Peter strikes dead Ananias and Sapphira and Paul blinds the magician Elymas (5:1 sqq. and 13:8 sqq.); the shadow of Peter is miraculous as is the linen used by Paul (5:15 and 19:12); the centurion Cornelius adores Peter as a divine being, thereby eliciting his protests, and the Lycaonians venerate Paul as the god Hermes, causing him to make similar protests (10:25–26 and 14:11 sqq.); both are miraculously freed from prison, the one in Jerusalem, the other in Philippi (12:7 and 16:26); similarly, one is scourged in Jerusalem, the other in Philippi (12:30 and 16:22); and so on through the other episodes.

This parallel series of accounts has been obtained by Luke choosing from the many episodes in Paul's life those most resembling others in the life of Peter, leaving out those not so comparable, and without doubt there were some, since we ourselves know of them as indicated to us by the letters of Paul (cf. 2 Cor. 11:23–27), about which the *Acts* tell us nothing. But even independently of the letters, Luke would have known about episodes from his long personal acquaintance with Paul. Luke was probably influenced toward the preparation of this series of parallel accounts, by what he must often have heard boldly declared by Paul, viz., that just as on Peter had been especially conferred the evangelizing of the Jews, so to him, Paul, was given in particular that of the Gentiles: *He* (namely, God) *who worked in Peter for the apostolate* (among those) *of the circumcised worked also in me in* (the apostolate among) *the Gentiles* (Gal. 2:8). This affirmation divided the field of the apostolate into two parts, one to Peter, the other to Paul, so that Luke the narrator found the argument of his narrative already divided into two, like a diptych, entirely in keeping with his own personal taste as a writer. He then painted the two pictures of the diptych which resulted in the two parts of the book.

In the *Acts* Luke shows himself an accomplished man of letters, as he had already done in his Gospel, a writer undoubtedly superior to any other in the New Testament, with the exception of the writer of the letter to the Hebrews. The expert St. Jerome had already noticed it, affirming that Luke *inter omnes evangelistas graeci sermonis eruditissimus fuit.* His vocabulary is rich, the style flowing and sometimes literary; he certainly cannot compete with the classic Greek writers, but he occupies an honorable position among his Hellenistic contemporaries. It is true that in the book there are terms which smack of Semitic influence, expressions which are not polished, constructions which are anacoluthic, but these occur especially in the first part of the book, where Luke depends more or less directly on Semitic documents and others which he sometimes seems to reproduce almost *ad litteram* with their anacolutha, particularly when they contain mnemonic points of improvised discourses. Evidently in such cases, the document is left to speak for itself.

The *Acts* and the Third Gospel are literary twin works, as is plain from the extremely detailed lexical computations made on both works and by comparison with other writings of the New Testament. As the point of departure for such studies on the *Acts,* the "we-sections" have been chosen (i.e., the passages in the first person plural which we have listed, p. 3) and the choice is right, for when the characteristics of language and style peculiar to these passages were found, the next step was to determine if they appear in the rest of the *Acts* and in the Third Gospel. According to whether they appear or not, we have a confirmation or denial that the author, speaking here in the first person, is the same as the one speaking in the third person in the rest of both works. Obviously, we are unable to reproduce here the long list of words and the interminable categories of constructions and phrases prepared by the learning and patience of scholars; and must limit ourselves to a very brief account.[1]

The *Acts* is composed of 1005 verses of which 97 are in the first person plural, representing therefore almost a tenth of the whole book. Excluding proper names and numbers, A. Harnack has counted 67 words which appear in the "we-sections" and also in the remainder of the *Acts,* but never in the Four Gospels; 43 words which occur in these same sections and reappear also in the rest of the *Acts* and in the Third Gospel but never in the other three Gospels; 20 words which occur in these sections and also in the Third Gospel, but never in the rest of the *Acts* or in the other three Gospels. To sum up, there are 63 words used in the "we-sections" and in the Third Gospel, and there are 110 words which occur in these passages and in the rest of the *Acts.* In all, there are 130 words which

---

[1] Concerning this, cf. J. C. Hawkins, *Horae synopticae,* 2 ed., Oxford, 1919; A. Harnack, *Lukas der Arzt, der Verfasser des dritten Evangeliums und der Apostelgeschicte,* Leipzig, 1906; *Die Apostelgeschichte,* Leipzig, 1908; *Neue Untersuchungen zur Apostelgeschichte und zur Abfassungszeit der synopichen Evangelien,* Leipzig, 1911; *Mission und Ausbreitung des Christentums,* I, 4 ed., Leipzig, 1924, pp. 89–107; E. Jacquier, *Les Actes des Apôtres,* 2 ed., Paris, 1926, pp. LX sqq., CLXVII sqq.

form the particular patrimony divided by the "we-sections" from the rest of the *Acts* and from the Third Gospel (always excluding the other three Gospels).

The number seems very high, especially when we consider that there are only 16 words common to the "we-sections" and the other three Gospels, and that the entire vocabulary of the *Acts* consists of about 1800–2000 words[2] of which about 450 are not found in the rest of the New Testament (always excluding the Third Gospel). Those 130 words are like so many links in a chain which joins the "we-sections" to the rest of the *Acts* and the Third Gospel, while the same chain bars the claim of any other author. It would seem to follow that the three groups of texts come from one author who has used in them his usual linguistic patrimony which, as always, is different from that of any other author.

This conclusion is confirmed by other comparisons and calculations concerning the grammatical constructions, syntax and other variations in style, but we cannot delay on these here.

On the other hand, it has been observed that the "we-sections" contain profound linguistic differences, when compared with other parts of the *Acts*. This is true. They contain in fact 111 words which do not appear elsewhere in the *Acts,* but the reason is clear. These words are used for the most part in the long account of the voyage of Paul and Luke from Caesarea to Rome and they are nautical terms. Since nowhere else in the *Acts* is there any lengthy account of this kind, we do not find these nautical technicalities.

It has also been objected that the similarity of vocabulary in the "we-sections" and the other parts of the *Acts* (as well as the Third Gospel) might be due, not to the original author's first draft, but to the skill of a later editor who copied the style of the "we-sections" and reproduced it in the other parts of the *Acts*. In the first place, however, this thesis must be demonstrated with positive proofs against the contrary possibility which undoubtedly is the more natural. An imitation of style so perfect that it cannot be discerned by the most patient modern research was an extremely difficult enterprise, and not then justified by any particular interest; or did the presumed editor perhaps fear that as soon as the book was published it would be subjected to the microscopic scrutiny that it would undergo nineteen centuries later? Finally, the better to conceal his action, this alleged editor would have had to start by eliminating the first person plural from the passages where it occurs, since this would compromise him too much as he had never been part of the group indicated by "we." Also he would have had to eliminate certain notable differences in tone which are to be

---

[2] The variation is due to the different criteria followed by different scholars in making these calculations (some count in proper names and enclitics, others do not), and also to their choice between variants in the text, and up to the additional passages in the Western text of the *Acts*.

found even today between the first and second parts of the book, as we shall see presently. The presumed editor would have been too adroit as a linguist but too inept as an imitator.

These results of the philological examination lead to the conclusion that the author of both the "we-sections" and the rest of the *Acts* (and of the Third Gospel) was one and the same person. This conclusion is confirmed by the earliest tradition which attributed these writings to no one but Luke, the physician and disciple of Paul.

The "we-sections," compared with the information gathered both from the rest of the *Acts* and from the letters of Paul, offer in another way a confirmation that Luke is the author of the whole book.

In actual fact, whoever wrote those passages must have been a person who, together with others (*we* . . .), was present when what he relates, viz., the events which occurred from about the middle of Paul's second missionary journey onward (Acts 16:10 sqq.), took place, although not without interruption. Now we know only four who were Paul's companions on his various journeys, and they are Timothy, Titus, Silas, and Luke, but all of these are ruled out one at a time as authors of the "we-sections" except Luke. Timothy is eliminated by Acts 20:4–6, since he left the group at that point, while the narrative continues in the first person plural. Titus is excluded because, although he was Paul's companion on the journey to the Council of Jerusalem (Gal. 2:3), he was not on the subsequent journey with which the "we-sections" begin. Silas is excluded by the fact that he is already in Paul's company while the narrative is in the third person (Acts 15:40), and only a little afterward it reverts to the first person plural (16:10) when the travelers reach Troas where, therefore, the narrator was. Moreover, none of these three, Timothy, Titus, and Silas, accompanied Paul on the voyage to Rome, and there the narrative is in the first personal plural. Of the four then, this leaves only Luke.

For the rest, Luke's authorship is fully consistent with the fact that his name is never mentioned in the whole book of the *Acts* (as in the Fourth Gospel the Apostle John is never mentioned), although Paul mentions him as his assistant during his first imprisonment in Rome (Col. 4:14; Philemon 24).

It cannot be proved with certainty from the mere examination of both writings that the single author of the Third Gospel and the *Acts* was a physician; but several passages seem to confirm the ancient tradition which presents him as one. Modern research has brought to light many technical terms in Luke which are also to be found in the writings of Hippocrates, Dioscurides, Galen, and other Greek physicians.[3] It is true that such

---

[3] The most extensive work on this subject is still that of W. K. Hobart, *The Medical Language of St. Luke,* Dublin, 1882. Several scholars since have reviewed the subject, some disagreeing with his conclusions, but without lessening the value of his work.

expressions may also be found in nonmedical writers who occasionally affect knowledge of medical matters (Lucianus, for example), but the case of Luke is different because he had no particular motives for introducing technical terminology save for the reason that he himself was a physician, especially as the parallel narratives of the other Gospels do not employ such terminology. On the whole, the passages in the *Acts* showing medical knowledge are neither so numerous nor so clear as in the Third Gospel. Some that may be quoted are: Acts 3:7; 4:16, 22; 9:18, 33, 40–41; 12:23; 13:11; 14:8; 28:5, 8.

Much more evident and important is the community of ideas, which links the author of the *Acts* with the spiritual world of Paul. It is highly probable that Luke in writing the *Acts* did not know, or at least did not use, the letters of Paul; nevertheless a kind of spiritual relationship binds the *Acts* to those epistles. More than a hundred words, phrases, and typical expressions in the New Testament are found only in Paul and the *Acts*. But this affinity is demonstrated less by literary style, than by concepts which in the *Acts* faithfully reflect the fundamental concepts of Paul, such as the Redemption worked by Christ, faith which justifies, without the works of the Jewish Law, the universality of Redemption, the action of the Holy Spirit, etc. Luke in fact, as Tertullian elegantly remarked, seems "illuminated" by Paul (*Adv. Marcion.*, IV, 2) in his world of concepts. All this is clear if we go back to tradition. Luke, the disciple of Paul, has gleaned from his long association with him those ideas and expressions which Paul communicated to others in his letters. The actual amount of space devoted to Paul in the *Acts,* amounting to about three fifths of the book, shows that the author was particularly well informed on the Apostle and had many things to say about him.

CHAPTER FIVE

THE HISTORICAL SOURCES

TO WRITE an account like that of the *Acts,* Luke must necessarily have availed himself of information, oral or written, which was furnished by others.

The book, in fact, embraces a period of about thirty-two years and especially in the first part deals with many events at which Luke was not present; hence he had to gather his material from various sources. Already in the prologue to his Gospel, Luke had told Theophilus that before writing he had *followed up all things very carefully from the very first* (or *for a long time*); the same care in preparation can be supposed also in regard to the *Acts* which are addressed to the same Theophilus as a continuation of the Third Gospel. This raises the question of the sources, the favorite ground of modern criticism.

How many, and which, were the sources of the *Acts?* For the second part of the book, the chief source was Luke himself, inasmuch as he was an eyewitness of the events. This is indicated by the "we-sections" examined above. These must derive from a kind of "travel diary" Luke kept for himself. Such personal diaries were not rare in antiquity; quite apart from the classical examples of Xenophon's *Anabasis* and the *Commentaries* of Julius Caesar, we have a very apt example from the Palestinian world of the time. Less than ten years after the *Acts* were written, a similar diary was written by Flavius Josephus who accompanied Titus during the siege of Jerusalem and who jotted down notes gathered from the Jewish deserters who fled from the beleaguered city or from his own direct observations (*Contra Apionem,* I, 49; cf. 55). These notes, written in Aramaic, formed the nucleus of the first Aramaic version of the *Wars of the Jews* and, later, of the subsequent Greek version.[1] A few years earlier, Luke had done the same thing. The cultured Greek physician, having already in mind, perhaps, the idea of his future historical writings (as Flavius Josephus certainly had), kept his diary, noting down the events in the first person plural.

From this diary he then took the passages we know and transferred them as they were (*en bloc*) into the *Acts.* This seems strange to us today,

---

[1] Cf. G. Ricciotti, *Flavio Giuseppe,* Vol. I, Introduzione, *Fl. Giuseppe lo storico giudeo-romano,* Turin, 1937, p. 67.

since the narrative switches from the third to the first persons without any explanation of the improvised transition, but in ancient times this was not unknown, and we have extant writings of captains, travelers, governors, and magistrates where the first and third persons are freely mingled, depending on whether the narrator was present or not at the events he is describing.[2]

For the earlier period, corresponding approximately to the first part of the *Acts,* Luke was able to gather material of all kinds from eyewitnesses. If he was not present at the founding of the first Christian community in Antioch, his native city (11:19 sqq.; 13:1-3), he certainly knew its principle members, Barnabas, Simon called Niger, Lucius the Cyrenean, and Manahen. In Caesarea, he knew Philip the evangelist (21:8), who was one of the seven deacons and well informed on the early history of the community in Jerusalem; in Jerusalem itself, he was in touch with the "elders" of that mother church, among whom was James, the "brother" of the Lord; Mnason, an "early" disciple (21:16-18); and others. Mark, the companion of Paul on his first missionary journey and author of the Second Gospel, was certainly known to Luke at Rome (Col. 4:10, 14; Philemon 23-24), and the various companions of the subsequent journeys, e.g., Timothy, Silas, Aristarchus, etc., were also companions of Luke. From all of them he could obtain basic information on the first years of Christianity in Palestine. It is, of course, superfluous to speak of Paul, who was the most important source of information for the events which had taken place since the stoning of Stephen and his own conversion.

But did Luke use written sources, in addition to this group of informants? Theoretically speaking, this would not have been necessary (except for the discourses), but certain factors lead us to think that he did use written documents. A linguistic analysis of the *Acts* shows that there was one author for the whole book; but this may be one of those instances in which a clever author does not copy the documents used word for word, but rather assimilates their content and then clothes it with his own usual literary style. On the other hand, it is a positive fact, that the first twelve chapters of the book contain many more Semitic literary elements than the second part, and the logical sequence of the narrative is thus less direct and flowing; but even this is not sufficient to argue the existence of various written sources, because the Semitisms could depend partly on the subject matter and partly on the conversations of Aramaic-speaking informants, while the slight fluctuations in the thread of the narrative could be explained by the variety of the arguments dealt with and the number of the informants whose contributions did not undergo the same editing

---

[2] Cf. E. Norden, *Agnostos Theos,* Berlin, 1913, p. 316 sqq., which cites, among other documents, the letters of Cicero, probably rewritten from official reports he had sent to the Senate about his military operations in Cilicia in 51 B.C.

process. In any case, although these points have their importance, they are not decisive and it always remains possible — probable indeed — that written sources were used.

Luke undoubtedly took the decree of the Apostolic Council (Acts 15:23–29) from literary sources and the same is to be said of the letter of the tribune Claudius Lysias (23:26–30). The discourses of Gamaliel (5:35–39), of the scribe of Ephesus (19:35–40), and of the lawyer Tertullus (24:2–8) probably depend on written notes. Then there are many Christian discourses, a fairly long one by Stephen, eight by Peter, ten by Paul, and one by James. Several of these were spoken in Aramaic, for instance Stephen's, and therefore the present Greek text must be a translation. Moreover, they are not verbatim reports, but are in summary form, giving only the highlights of the originals. Some of the speeches are presented as extemporaneous, like Paul's in Aramaic to the rioting crowd in the Temple (22:1–21). Therefore their text could not have been prepared in advance, but at best noted down afterward from memory.

These summary notes must have circulated among the early Christians who collected them and kept them with veneration, just as they did, on a higher plane, the "sayings" (λόγια) of Jesus, from which, in that period, the Gospels were evolving. But with these Apostolic "sayings," as indeed with those of the Gospels, there was no preoccupation with slavish literalism. and these various notes were employed or translated in such manner as to preserve the sense rather than the exactness of the words.[3] It is not surprising, therefore, to find in these discourses, also, some imprint of Luke. He has, as usual, clothed with his own style the ideas he took from the above-mentioned summaries. But on the other hand, it must be noted also that there are some typical expressions which link Peter's discourses to his letters (ἀθέμιτον found only in Acts 10:28 and 1 Pet. 4:3; πρόγνωσις only in Acts 2:23 and 1 Pet. 1:2), and more numerous still are the expressions which connect Paul's discourses with his epistles.

Several have affirmed, though without serious foundation, that Luke used the writings of Flavius Josephus. Even if we leave out of account the chronology of their respective writings, which does not allow a dependence of the first on the second,[4] Luke was too careful and accurate a historian to make use of such a crude and slovenly trimmer as Josephus, whose contradictions in his writings are numerous and obvious.[5] It is, however,

---

[3] This is the rule followed by the Greek translator of the Aramaic text of *Matthew*, which is confirmed by different readings of the Synoptics.

[4] For the chronology of Josephus' various writings, cf. G. Ricciotti, *Flavio Giuseppe*, Vol. I, *op. cit.*, pp. 46, 97, 157, 171.

[5] The opposite dependence, viz., that of Fl. Josephus on Luke, has been supposed by some scholars (J. Belser in *Theolog. Quartalschrift*, 1896, p. 78; Th. Zahn, *Die Apostelgeschichte*, 4th ed., II [Leipzig: 1927], pp. 214 sqq., 393 sqq., 747 sqq.). This opinion too is improbable, though less unlikely than the other, but it does not concern us here.

almost certain that Luke did not use Paul's epistles, although they were almost all of them written when he composed the *Acts*. Here, also, the complete independence of Luke's writings from those of Paul, shows the contrary opinion of some few scholars to be groundless. Not only does the *Acts* never mention Paul's letters, but it does not even make reference to certain episodes in them, which would have appeared very appropriately in the *Acts,* such as Paul's sojourn in Arabia (Gal. 1:17), his three shipwrecks which happened before that at Malta (2 Cor. 11:25), and other events. Luke was not concerned evidently with the epistles, although he had a general knowledge of their existence from the moment he had their author himself as his companion. This independence of the *Acts* emphasizes more strongly its historical value, for though it follows a different road from the epistles it never conflicts with them. The paths of the *Acts* and the epistles do not cross, but neither denies the other: *nec tecum, nec sine te.*

If it be granted that Luke used written documents, would it be possible today to recognize them and extract them approximately from his work? It is both possible and impossible. It is possible, if it is a question of a summary and generic appraisal, insofar as one can maintain that some written document on which Luke has based his narrative must underlie this account or that series of episodes, using it in more or less free style. But if anyone proposes to descend from this general viewpoint to a minute identification of periods, phrases, and even single words, with the aim of extracting and reconstructing the ancient document, he runs the risk of building his house on the sand. Very often, in fact, the criteria used in this matter are so subjective and gratuitous, that they result only in convincing one who is already convinced for other reasons, while the one who appreciates objective proof in historical research remains profoundly skeptical before such reconstructions. The greatest disproof of all this is the fact that many reconstructions of the documents underlying the *Acts* have been prepared in the past, as we shall see presently (p. 34 ff.), but they have crumbled for want of an objective basis.

CHAPTER SIX

THE SCOPE OF THE ACTS

WE HAVE seen (Chapter Four) the scope which Luke had in mind
when addressing the Third Gospel to Theophilus. Since the *Acts* is the
continuation of the historic work begun in the Third Gospel, viz., it is
the δεύτερος λόγος which closely follows the πρῶτος λόγος represented by the
Third Gospel (cf. Acts 1:1), it is legitimate to suppose that the scope of
the *Acts* was analogous to and linked with that of the Third Gospel. If,
therefore, in that first writing, Luke intended to teach Theophilus about
the facts and teaching of Jesus, he proposes in this new writing to inform
him of those things that happened after the Ascension of Jesus. In fact,
since Jesus has left the earth, there remains the institution founded by him,
i.e., the Church, which is nothing but the continuation of his own personal
work; therefore, in recounting the first developments of the Church, the
narrative of the Gospel is logically continued. In actual fact, as we have
already outlined, the main argument of the *Acts* is the propagation of the
Church, first in Palestine and then in Syria and elsewhere.

But if Christ was present at the time of the founding of the Church, he
is absent in the successive period of propagation. Nevertheless, to promote
this propagation, he has sent his "messenger," the Holy Spirit. We actually
find that the *Acts* begins with the recording of the promise made by
Jesus to his Apostles shortly before his Ascension: *You shall be baptized
with the Holy Spirit . . . you shall receive power when the Holy Spirit
comes upon you,* and therefore as a consequence of this baptism and in-
vestiture of the Spirit *you shall be witnesses for me in Jerusalem and in all
Judea and Samaria and even to the very ends of the earth* (1:5, 8). Then
follows the narration of the outpouring of this Spirit on the day of Pentecost,
with the immediate, and gradually the remote consequences of that same
outpouring. Peter, as soon as he has received the Spirit, speaks to the
crowd of Jerusalem and obtains conversions to the teaching of Jesus
(2:14 sqq.), just as, shortly afterward, he will speak *filled with the Holy
Spirit* before the Sanhedrin (4:8); the seven deacons were to be *full of
the (Holy) Spirit,* as indeed is Stephen (6:3–5); when the Samaritans
begin to be converted, Peter and John go to them and *lay their hands on
them and they receive the Holy Spirit* (8:17); as soon as Paul is converted,
Ananias goes to visit him *that he might be filled with the Holy Spirit*

26

(9:17); and as the Church *spreads through all Judea and Galilee and Samaria . . . it is filled with the consolation of the Holy Spirit* (9:31). The same may be said of the evangelization of the pagans: the conversion of the centurion Cornelius is prepared by the Holy Spirit (10:19) and then confirmed by more abundant effusions of the Spirit (10:44–47); Barnabas, who is *full of the Holy Spirit* (11:2), goes with Paul on the first missionary journey by express command of the Holy Spirit (13:2), so that they are both *sent forth by the Holy Spirit* (13:4) and the converts made during that journey *are filled with joy and with the Holy Spirit* (13:52). It would be superfluous to labor the point since the whole narrative, much more than any other book of the New Testament, is full of the interventions of the Spirit. It is evident then, that Luke's scope in the *Acts* is to recount to Theophilus the propagation of Christianity as the effect of the Holy Spirit, or, in other words, to show him the carrying out of the work of Jesus with the assistance of the One sent by him. This scope of Luke has already been pointed out by early writers who affirm with sound historical veracity that *the Gospels are the story of those things which Christ did and said, while the Acts are the story of those things which the other Paraclete said and did.*[1]

In any case, Luke is not writing only for Theophilus, but also for the many Christians whose spiritual state was similar to his. Luke sees, behind Theophilus, especially those Christians converted from paganism, belonging in great number to the churches founded by Paul and particularly those of Rome. To all of them in general, the *Acts* must show, in the light of the narrated fact, the laying down of a principle especially propounded by their accustomed teacher, Paul, viz., that *there is no distinction between Jew and Greek, for there is the same Lord of all* (Rom. 10:12), and before God *there is no Greek and Jew, circumcised and uncircumcised, Barbarian and Scythian, slave and freeman, but Christ is all things and in all* (Col. 3:11) from the moment that *the power of God is unto salvation to everyone who believes, to Jew first and then to Greek* (Rom. 1:16). This is precisely the thesis of universality demonstrated by the narrative of the *Acts* which accompanies the expansion of the Church step by step, first among the Jews of Jerusalem and Palestine, then among the heterogeneous Samaritans, afterward among the Jews of the Diaspora and at the same time among the uncircumcised of various regions, from the barbarians of Lycaonia and Phrygia in Asia Minor to the Greeks of Ionia and Achaia, finishing finally in Rome itself, the center of pagan political power.

---

[1] Thus St. John Chrysostom, *In Act. hom.*, I, 5 (in Migne, *P. G.*, 60, 21), but substantially the same thought is repeated by Ecumenius, *Arg. in Act. Apost.* (in Migne, *P. G.*, 118, 29), and later by Theophylactus, *Expositio in Act.*, in the prologue (in Migne, *P. G.*, 125, 849), who states in epigrammatic style: *The Gospels show forth the acts of the Son, the Acts those of the Most Holy Spirit.*

It may be asked whether this theological-historical thesis, which is the essential scope of the *Acts,* leaves room in Luke's purpose for any other subordinate or more practical thesis of direct and immediate advantage. An affirmative reply has been given in various ways, even to the extent of completely substituting the theological-historical thesis by other more practical ones, some of which we shall see later on; but attention may well be directed here to a particular thesis which does not entirely exclude the above-mentioned one. In 1855, M. Aberle, developing an idea already put forward by others, maintained that the *Acts* had been written to provide a defense for Paul, before Nero's tribunal in Rome.[2] Three charges had in fact been made against Paul by Tertullus, the Jewish lawyer, when the Apostle was brought before the court of Felix, the Roman procurator in Caesarea. The first was that he was a *promoter of seditions among all the Jews throughout the world;* the second, that he was a *ringleader* (πρωτοστάτην) *of the sect of the Nazarenes* (Christians); and the third, that *he attempted to profane the temple* in Jerusalem (Acts 24:5–6). The third accusation would not move Rome's judges very much, even though the Romans generally followed a policy of respect for the religious customs of the peoples they subjugated. But the first two accusations were very serious, because the charge of sedition constituted a threat to that tranquillity of order of which the Romans were so jealous, while that of being the leader of the Nazarenes overset the first by uncovering the root of the evil; the seditious were the Christians as such; consequently the new religion must be proscribed as the enemy of public order and therefore dangerous to the Roman Empire. These same accusations would be made, so this theory runs, before the emperor's tribunal in Rome, to which Paul had appealed as a Roman citizen. But during the two years Paul passed at Caesarea and the next two in Rome before the trial, Luke would have gathered the documents in defense of the Apostle to show that the charges were groundless. This would have been the origin of the *Acts,* which were therefore substantially nothing but a legal defense of Paul.

This theory is very attractive superficially, but quite shallow in substance. Other scholars were attracted to it later on, but its weakness led them to modify the general lines in various ways. As usually happens, the theory was slightly altered in detail and it was supposed that Theophilus was one of the Christians of *Caesar's household* (Phil. 4:22; cf. 1:13–14), and, together with Seneca and Burrus, a member of the imperial council before which Paul's case was brought; or even that under the pseudonym of "Theophilus," one or other of these famous personages lay hid, and suchlike poetic fancies. But the proof taken from the Muratorian Fragment is no such flight of fancy where, in line 4, it says that Paul took Luke with

---

[2] M. Aberle, *"Ueber den Zweck der Apostelgeschichte,"* in *Theolog. Quartalschrift,* 1855, pp. 173–236.

him *quasi ut juris studiosum* (almost as an expert in the law). Some have wished to correct this reading, *juris studiosum,* but it must be upheld[3] and it would therefore allude to the office of quasi-lawyer, which Luke would have undertaken and from which the *Acts* resulted.

The weakness of this hypothesis is immediately apparent, however, when we come down to the actual facts. If the *Acts* was a legal defense of Paul, the presence of at least half the events narrated there cannot be explained. Of what importance to the judges of Nero's tribunal were the Ascension of Jesus, the descent of the Holy Spirit, the long discourses filled with scriptural quotations, and so many other things, especially in the first part of the book? Then on reading the successive miracles there related, the judges would most probably have shaken their heads incredulously, quoting the words of Horace: *Credat Judaeus Apella, non ego* (Let the Jew Apella believe these things, not I). No, the *Acts,* in the form in which we have it today, could not have been either a legal defense or, more vaguely, the remains of a defense.

Nevertheless, there may be an element of truth in the theory. It is in fact obvious that the *Acts* lets no opportunity pass of showing that Paul had no trouble from the various Roman magistrates encountered in the course of his journeys, but rather that he was protected by them against the persecution of the Jews (13:6 sqq.; 16:35 sqq.; 18:12 sqq.; 19:31 sqq.; 23:23 sqq.; 25:13 sqq.; 27:3 sqq.; 28:7, 16, 31). These occasions, almost all of which are found in the second part of the book, which is devoted especially to Paul, make it appear as a kind of apologia for him, but this is simply due to the argument there dealt with. It is, however, quite possible that Luke, in treating this situation, made a special point of demonstrating this benevolent attitude of the Roman magistrates in order to dispel the malicious rumors spread by the Jews against Paul, which had reached Rome, and to help create there an atmosphere favorable to Christianity in general.

---

[3] Cf. M-J. Lagrange, *Evangile selon S. Luc,* 3 ed., Paris, 1927, p. XII.

CHAPTER SEVEN

DATE OF COMPOSITION OF THE ACTS

IT IS obvious that the *Acts* comes after the Third Gospel to which it refers, and therefore later than the years A.D. 62–63 when, as seems most likely, that Gospel was written. But there must have been a very brief interval between the two writings.

In the first place, the fact that in the *Acts* there appears no allusion, even an indirect one, to the destruction of Jerusalem and the downfall of Judaism, which took place in the year A.D. 70, already suggests that the book was written before that year. More significant still is the very brief and abrupt ending which simply says that Paul remained for two years in Rome in the house he had rented, fulfilling his ministry there unhindered (28:30–31). In this unexpected manner, the whole book comes to a close. What of the trial before the emperor? If Paul had come to Rome expressly for that trial, why not tell of its progress and conclusion, just as the events preparatory to the trial before the court of the Procurator at Caesarea had been so fully related? It can be said, in fact, that the last five chapters of the book (Chapters 24–28) tend toward one point, viz., the trial at Rome, both by recounting the trials at Jerusalem and Caesarea and by describing the journey to Rome. Why, therefore, is the natural conclusion to these five chapters wanting, namely, the Roman trial and the sentence?

Scholars have answered this question in various ways. Some have advanced the theory that Luke wrote a third work, now lost, or at least that he intended to write it and was unable to do so, in which he would have narrated the trial at Rome and what followed it. But this hypothesis, besides being gratuitous, is belied by the logical conclusion of the Third Gospel which is then taken up by the *Acts,* while in the *Acts* a logical conclusion is lacking. It has also been suggested that the ending of the original manuscript of the *Acts* suffered an accidental mutilation, or even that Luke stopped abruptly at that point, because he had no more paper on which to write. Both are fanciful and ridiculous theories. Others have thought that Luke truncated his narrative precisely so as not to refer to the tragic end of the trial which would have concluded with Paul's condemnation to death in A.D. 64. But in the first place, in the years after A.D. 64 Paul was still journeying in the West and the East and wrote letters. Even if his death sentence had taken place in A.D. 64, what motive could there be for Luke's not reporting a fact which would certainly be well known to the Christians in Rome and elsewhere? Would not the Apostle's condemnation to death have fittingly closed the narrative of the facts about him, just as the death of Jesus had worthily closed the Third Gospel (apart from the Resurrection and Ascension which had no counterpart with Paul)? It has been suggested recently (K. Lake, *Beginnings*) that the trial did not take place because the Jews did not present themselves in Rome to prefer the charges, and thus Paul was automatically set free. Even so, while admitting the possibility that Paul's Jewish accusers did not come to Rome, the trial could have been held on the basis of the written report sent by the Roman Procurator of Judea. Moreover, the question would still stand, why did not Luke allude, at least in a few words, to this unexpected close of the trial, thereby giving his book some kind of conclusion?

A theory worthy of consideration is that the trial was not finished when Luke completed the *Acts* and therefore he could not give the verdict; but that shortly after the publication of the *Acts,* between A.D. 63 and 64, the trial ended with the acquittal and liberation of Paul. According to those who consider the *Acts* as a legal defense of Paul, or at least as a relic of a defense, the book recently published by Luke would have contributed to this happy result, and it is precisely, therefore, on the abrupt ending of the book that this theory bases one of its proofs. Even so, we saw that to regard the *Acts* as such a forensic defense presents many serious problems, especially in the present case where an even greater difficulty arises from Paul's two years' imprisonment. If Luke wrote the *Acts* in defense of Paul, he should have published it in the first months of these two years so as to influence the trial and not at the end, when the trial (although it was not finished) had reached the stage when it was practically possible to foresee the decision. Two years is a very long time for the writing of a book as slight as the *Acts*. Luke, who had already gathered his material in advance, could have written it comfortably in a month or two, and then published it in the third month of Paul's imprisonment. Instead, he published it more than twenty-four months later and without the least mention of the trial and the verdict.

If, then, one does not assume that the *Acts* was a brief for the defense, one might well ask why Luke published it at the end of the two-year imprisonment, namely, when everything indicated that the trial would be over within a very short time. That being so, would it not have been better to have waited a few weeks to know the verdict of the trial and thus be able to give a worthy conclusion to the narrative of the last five chapters and to the whole book? Luke was too clever a writer to leave his writing so unfinished if there were not some serious reason for it.

In my view, this serious reason is to be found in an event which was not only of world importance but was a grave setback for Christianity and that was the burning of Rome. If Paul reached Rome in the spring of A.D. 61, the end of his two years' imprisonment brings us to the spring of A.D. 63. In July of A.D. 64, a terrible fire swept through Rome and, burning furiously for nine days, destroyed ten of the fourteen *regiones,* or districts, of the city. Immediately afterward, a persecution raged against the Christians on whom the imperial authorities put the blame for the conflagration. In consequence, the situation not only changed, but was exactly reversed: the idyl between the imperial authorities and Christianity, sketched in such a rosy and hopeful manner in the *Acts,* now disappeared forever. From now on, Rome would become for the Christians the monstrous Babylon, the great harlot sprawled on her seven hills *drunk . . . with the blood of the martyrs of Jesus* (Apoc. 17:6). Now, in the months immediately before the fire, Paul is in Rome with the faithful Luke. He is now free since the trial has concluded with his release at the beginning of A.D. 63. It is also very probable that immediately afterward, in the period between the middle of A.D. 63 and about the middle of A.D. 64, he made a journey into Spain which lasted for some months, returning to Rome in the first half of A.D. 64. There he finds Luke again, who shortly before had published his Gospel, and now with all tranquillity and care is going through his account of the *Acts,* for which he possesses the documents. He has already related the shipwreck at Malta and Paul's arrival in Rome, and he devotes quite a bit of space (12 verses, to be exact: 28:17-28) to describing the first seven or eight days of the Apostle's stay in the city. Maintaining the same proportion, he intends to give a full account of the trial and its outcome, and so to finish his book in a worthy manner.

But suddenly the fire and the persecution prevented him from writing his narrative. It was interrupted, first of all materially by the enormous confusion in urban life caused by the destruction of three quarters of the city. It was interrupted morally by the conflict that now arose between the empire of Caesar and the kingdom of Christ. What purpose would now be served in continuing the detailed narrative showing the rectitude of imperial justice in recognizing the innocence of Paul? That justice had now become supreme injustice, and the recognition of Paul's innocence was atrociously belied by the *great multitude (multitudo ingens* — Tacitus, *Annals,* XV, 44) of his brethren and disciples who were put to death. What Luke had already written could stand as a true historical testimony of a period now gone. That period was closed forever, and therefore to continue the narrative which praised the great harlot was no longer admissible. It would have meant a misrepresentation of present reality and a scorning of the *blood of the martyrs of Jesus.*

Did these considerations spring spontaneously to Luke's mind: he had already, in the Third Gospel, shown himself to be a historian of wide vision: or were they suggested to him by Paul? Possibly they occurred to both, though not necessarily at the same time. In any case, it was decided that the narrative of the *Acts* was not to continue but should be closed without a particular ending.

And so the abrupt conclusion, summing up a whole two years in about twenty words, was added to the detailed account which had got as far as relating the first days of Paul's stay in Rome. It was the testimony of a short day of sunshine which was to bring in its wake long years of storm.

CHAPTER EIGHT

THE HISTORY OF CRITICISM

MODERN criticism has hardly ever considered the book of the *Acts* by itself; its method of inquiry has been to compare it methodically with the letters of Paul. It was right to do this, for the *Acts* and epistles partly overlap and partly complete one another. In his epistles, Paul deals exclusively with contemporary facts concerning himself or the Christian communities founded by him, and only rarely does he go beyond those limits. His epistles, therefore, have no point of contact with the first chapters of the *Acts,* which refer to the days when Paul was far from following Christ. But with Chapter 7, Paul enters briefly on the scene, first as a persecutor of Christ, and then as his follower, and thereafter the account of the facts about him is included with those about Peter. From Chapter 13 to the end, the narrative is concerned exclusively with Paul, and the writing becomes in substance the book of the *Acts of Paul.*

It is clear, especially in this last part, that Paul's letters provide an excellent determining factor for the *Acts,* both for the arguments dealt with in both writings, and for those omitted by the one or the other. This determination has all the more value because, as we have already pointed out, Luke did not make use of Paul's epistles in writing the *Acts.*

In consequence of this, criticism of the *Acts* was always linked with criticism of the epistles and proceeded parallel with it. The first manifestations of this parallel criticism, about the end of the eighteenth century and the beginning of the nineteenth, are today only of an informative interest. Its first stage was the denial of the authenticity of one or the other of the three pastoral epistles (*1 Timothy, 2 Timothy, Titus*); then J. G. Eichhorn (1814) and W. de Wette (1826) denied the authenticity of all three. F. Ch. Baur, and the Tübingen School which he founded, struck at the root of the epistles as a body. After certain hesitations, Baur in 1845 declared that none of the epistles was authentic except *Galatians, Romans,* and *1* and *2 Corinthians.* He made these exceptions because in these four epistles alone, the true historical Paul appears as the opponent of the Jewish-Christian current and as entering into polemic against it. The other epistles do not show Paul in this light and are therefore not authentic.

Passing to the *Acts,* the Tübingen School applied the same touchstone;

many passages were tendentious and unhistorical because they contradicted the spirit of the four polemical epistles. From a reading of the *Acts,* said the Tübingen School, one would gather that there was perfect accord between Peter representing the Jewish-Christian current, and Paul representing the Hellenistic-Christian tendency. But that does not mean at all that there was no conflict, only that it was concealed for controversial reasons. The *Acts,* in fact, aim at reconciling the two currents and propound a pre-established thesis by artificially presenting Peter and Paul as in agreement. However, the four authentic epistles of Paul are there to show that the contrast between the two Apostles or, rather, between the two respective currents was there and, hence, that the thesis of the *Acts* is false and its plan tendentious.

In actual fact, many episodes mentioned in the epistles are passed over or changed by the *Acts.* The latter does not tell us anything at all of Paul's three shipwrecks and very little of his other adventures listed by him in 2 Cor. 11:23 sqq. It says nothing of the dispute with Peter in Antioch, nor of his Judaizing adversaries in Galatia and Corinth. Paul's journeys, related in his epistles as two, become three according to the *Acts.* The Council of Jerusalem in Acts 15 is treated as a private agreement in Gal. 2; Paul, who in the epistles proclaims the independence of his apostolate, seems in the *Acts* to have been invested with it by the elders of the community of Jerusalem. From the *Acts,* it would seem that Peter and the elders of Jerusalem took the initiative in the evangelization of the Gentiles, whereas the dispute at Antioch seems to suggest that nothing but obstacles to such evangelization came from those same elders. Moreover, the perfect symmetry between the two figures, by which every feature of Peter finds its parallel in some feature of Paul (cf. Chapter Four), places more in evidence the artificial and conventional character of both parts of the book, each being devoted to one person.

In conclusion, the historical Paul is the Paul of the four polemical epistles. The Paul of the *Acts* is by contrast a figure drawn to attract the Jewish Christians who would admire in him the devoted and subordinate co-operator of Peter in the evangelization of the pagan world. This thesis required that the *Acts* be assigned to the very late second century, because the two rival currents were not ready for fusion earlier. The other epistles attributed to Paul (except the pastorals) were written a little before the *Acts,* which could be considered as an attempt at an approach to the Jewish-Christian current.

After the first surprise produced by the Tübingen conclusions had been overcome, reflection and reaction set in, resulting in an examination of the practical value of the criterion of the Tübingen School to assess the documents (viz., the rivalry between the Jewish-Christian current of Peter and the Hellenistic-Christian one of Paul) in sorting the gold from the dross. Did it perhaps serve only to reduce everything to dross? If the *Acts* were written in the very late second century, what purpose could there be in promoting agreement between the two rival factions? What force could the Jewish-Christian current still have had and what threat did it represent to the universality of Christianity at the presumed time of the composition of the *Acts,* more than half a century after Jerusalem and the Hebrew Temple had been destroyed and the Jewish nation dispersed? Was the book of the *Acts* preoccupied with fighting corpses, or did it fear that they might come to life again? And again, were the undeniable differences between the *Acts* and the epistles so many contradictions, or were they not, rather, simple differences of exposition? Did silence about a given episode really signify its denial? Where is it implied either in the *Acts* or the epistles that either of them intended to furnish a complete biography of Paul? Could not one single fact, e.g., the Council of Jerusalem, have been reported from two different points of view, both equally objective? Could not the symmetry between the two figures of Peter and Paul in the *Acts* have been the result of a literary style employed to group together and present historic facts, a method also found in the Third Gospel, which tradition attributes to the same author as the *Acts?*

The reaction against Tübingen, therefore, induced a certain hesitancy in regard to *a priori* historic canons which were too general and instead appealed to a direct study of the documents, conducted with a certain regard for the external testimonies of tradition. Those were the days when criticism of the Old Testament engaged especially in research on five or six documents, fragments of which, when put together like a mosaic, made up the Pentateuch, and it was hoped that not only isolated phrases but even individual words of those documents could be extracted. It was natural, therefore, that a similar attempt as was being made on the Pentateuch should be made on the *Acts.*

In actual fact, attempts at research on the sources of the *Acts* had already been made long before by Konigsman (1798), Zeigler (1801), Heinrichs (1809), and others. Following their usual road, they proposed the theory that for the first part of the *Acts,* the material was furnished by an Aramaic account of the *Acts of Peter,* something like the *Kerygma Petrou,* fragments of which have been preserved for us by Clement of Alexandria. A little later, Schleiermacher and others (Bleck, Ulrich, etc.), while attributing the *Acts* as a whole to Luke, thought that the passages in the first person plural appertained to Timothy. Some attributed them instead either to Titus (Horst, Krenkel, etc.) or Silas (Schwanbeck, von Vloten, etc.). But the luxuriant flowering of documentary theories regarding the formation of the *Acts* only occurred about the end of the nineteenth and the beginning of the twentieth centuries by reason of the circumstances just outlined.[1]

These theories were so precise and exact, but also so lacking in objectivity, that it was easy to see that they would not stand the test of time, and today they are, in fact, no more than a fading memory. As an example, it will be sufficient to give one, neither too complicated nor too simple, namely the first of the theories proposed by C. Clemen.[2]

According to this scholar, the *Acts* are compiled on the basis of three principal documents. The first was a history of the Hellenist Jews (symbol: Hellen.) which related the facts about them, especially the doings of Stephen and the penetration of Christianity into Antioch. The second was a history of Peter (symbol: Pet.) which had already incorporated in it earlier documents regarding Christianity in Jerusalem, the institution of the deacons, the episode of Simon Magus, etc. The third was a history of Paul (symbol: Pa.), a kind of fusion of an "itinerary" of Paul's journeys with certain passages in the first person plural and his various missionary experiences. This fusion was accomplished by a first redactor (R-l) during the latter part of the first century. Between the years 97 and 117, a second redactor with Jewish sympathies (R-j) intervened and, working especially on the documents Pet. and Pa., revised them, joined them together, putting in new episodes favoring Peter. Between 117 and 138, the work came into the hands of an anti-Jewish redactor (R-a), who subjected it to a general revision more favorable to Paul and inserted new material, some of which was taken from Paul's epistles and some from Flavius Josephus. This, then, was the last phase of the composition of the *Acts,* which thus resulted from the material of the documents Hellen., Pet., Pa. (which incorporated other earlier documents as well as the "Itinerary"), and the successive interventions of the redactors R-l, R-j, and R-a. It was considered probable, though not certain, that the author of the passages in the first person plural was Luke, to whom, however, the whole book was attributed by later tradition.

The influence of the Tübingen School was partially reflected shortly before 1870 in E. Reuss and E. Renan. The former, nevertheless, attributed the *Acts* in great part to Luke, dating it a little after the year A.D. 70, while the latter put it between A.D. 80 and 100.

An eminent opponent of the Tübingen School at the end of the century was the conservative Protestant, Bernard Weiss, who pointed out the literary consistency of the *Acts.* For him, Luke was the author of the work

---

[1] Such an exponent of his time was A. Bludau, *"Die Quellenscheidung in der Apostelgeschichte,"* in *Bibliche Zeitschrift,* 1907, pp. 116–189, 258–281. See also in a more general sense, A. Schweitzer, *Geschicte der paulinischen Forschung,* Tübingen, 1911; A. Wikenhauser, *Die Apostelgeschichte und hir Geschichtswert,* Munster i. W., 1921; J. Dupont, *Les problèmes du Livre des Actes d'après les travaux récents,* Louvain, 1950.

[2] *Chronologie der paulinisch. Briefe,* Halle, 1893. In later works, *Paulus sein Leben und Wirken,* 2 vols., Giessen, 1904; *Die Apostelgeschichte im Lichte der neueren Forschungen,* Giessen, 1905. Clemen practically abandoned his first theory.

about the year A.D. 80, and had used earlier sources in different measure in both parts of the book.

But the most famous representative of the return to tradition was A. Harnack, who made the *Acts* one of his favorite subjects, to which he returned several times.[3] The arguments adopted by Harnack were exclusively from internal criticism, drawn from a highly detailed examination of the language and literary style both of the *Acts* and the Third Gospel. His conclusions were, that the two books were two well-connected parts of a single work, which was intended to narrate, first the personal ministry of Jesus (Third Gospel) and then the ministry of the Spirit of Jesus through the Apostles (*Acts*). Both parts of the work were by Luke the physician and disciple of Paul. For the first part of the *Acts,* Luke used written sources, two or three of which came from Jerusalem, one from Antioch, and one from Caesarea. Other information he had from Paul and eyewitnesses of the facts related. For the second part of the book, Luke himself was the witness, speaking from his own personal knowledge of the events, but even when he used written sources, he assimilated them and clothed them in his inimitable style. The language study showed that whoever wrote the "we-sections," as a result of the travel diary, had also written the rest of the *Acts,* including both the first and the second parts. As to the date, Harnack at first assigned the *Acts* to the years A.D. 78–93,[4] then to A.D. 79–96,[5] and finally he went back to A.D. 60–64.[6]

In short, the *Acts* was a work of primary historical importance, written by an alert and impartial writer — Luke — who had been a witness of the facts in the second part of the book, and had used excellent oral and written sources of information for the first part. As for the miraculous events which the *Acts* narrate throughout, Harnack rejected them, considering them as legendary distortions of natural facts. But he observed that such legends originate within a short space of time and that Luke in recording them had simply objectively reported current opinions.

In the past thirty years, works with a different approach have been published, ranging from the destructive in principle to the more cautious and guarded. *The Acts of the Apostles* edited by F. J. Foakes Jackson and Kirsopp Lake is a study of more moderate tendency, to which several scholars have contributed.[7] It is a veritable mine of scientific information, but lacks unity of judgment, since the collaborators — about a score — were left free to express their own personal opinions, which sometimes were in

---

[3] See the list of his works on p. 18, note 1.

[4] *Die Chronologie der altchristlich. Literatur,* I, Leipzig, 1897, p. 246.

[5] *Apostelgeschichte,* cited, p. 221.

[6] *Neue Untersuchungen zur Apostelgesch.,* cited, pp. 63–81.

[7] *The Making of Luke — Acts,* London, 1927.

conflict with each other; e.g., in Volume II, C. W. Emmet sides with tradition in attributing the *Acts* to Luke, while H. Windisch, who has a partial affinity for the Tübingen School, considers it a rewriting of one of Luke's writings containing contradictions of Paul's epistles, and dates it between A.D. 80 and 110. The two volumes (IV and V) of translation and commentary of the *Acts* likewise take a middle course, leaving many questions unanswered.

H. J. Cadbury, one of the chief collaborators in the foregoing work, published separately a long study of the character and "making" of both writings in his comprehensive work, *Third Gospel — Acts*.[8] The two books, he finds, are two parts of one writing by one author. Whether the author is unknown or whether he is Luke as tradition says, is of small interest to Cadbury, who in the main attributes little importance to tradition. He does think, however, that this one author is certainly a person of broad culture, a versatile *gentleman* of his day, who wrote according to the rules of historiography of the first century, and used sources varying in kind and value, but which did not include either Paul's epistles or Flavius Josephus. Even so, his statements agree in general with the data of the epistles, just as they are often confirmed by archaeological findings. The whole writing is to be considered, at least probably, as an apologia of Jesus, the Church, and Paul, compiled in a historical-expository manner and addressed to Theophilus, an important personage who could have exercised great influence on Paul's trial at the end of his first Roman imprisonment.

E. Meyer maintains a position similar to Harnack's. Like him, he accepts the "lay dogma" and therefore rejects all that is miraculous, but he also accepts, like Harnack, almost all that tradition tells us about the epistles and the Acts.[9] The latter, he holds, is the work of Luke, who was also the author of the Third Gospel and the traveling companion of Paul. It has a strictly historical value (leaving aside the miracles, for which Luke simply accepts the popular belief) and its historicity receives surprising confirmation in the epistles. The author of the "we-sections" is the same as of those in the third person, and the last nine chapters form a compact and indivisible whole. Paul's stay at Ephesus is historical fact, as is also his visit to Athens and his discourse on the Areopagus. The author of the *Acts* shows at every turn that he lived in Paul's company and assimilated his thought. The figure of the historical Paul results from the combination of features portrayed in the epistles and in the *Acts*.

From these authors, representing a relatively moderate outlook, we pass to other scholars who tend more to the left. For M. Goguel,[10] the

---

[8] *The Making of Luke — Acts*, London: Macmillan, 1927.

[9] *Ursprung und Anfange des Christentums*, III, *Die Apostelgeschichte und die Anfange des Christentums*, Stuttgart, 1923.   [10] *Le livre des Actes*, Paris, 1922.

author of the *Acts* is not Luke, but somebody who manipulated one of Luke's writings, inserting information taken from other sources. It is also possible that this rewriting was edited again by a later redactor. The sources have not been transcribed literally, but have been clothed in the author's own literary style. The *Acts* is connected with the Third Gospel, but not with Paul's epistles; indeed, in many places, it contradicts them, nor do the *Acts* rely upon the writings of Flavius Josephus. On the whole, while it is not a true historical work, the *Acts* contains much sound historical material and actually constitutes *one of the most essential foundations on which the history of early Christianity rests*. The composition of the *Acts* falls between the years A.D. 80 and 90.

The most extreme position of the extreme left was adopted by A. Loisy in his two commentaries on the *Acts*.[11] Taking up an idea already set forth by Gercke (1894), and later, more explicitly and cleverly, by E. Norden (*Agnostos Theos*, 1913), Loisy maintained that the *Acts*, together with the Third Gospel, were originally an authentic writing of Luke, but that in the second century an editor transformed it to such a degree, that today only a few fragments of the original remain, mixed up here and there with this editor's work. Luke's own writing, composed about the year A.D. 80, was worthy of the author, who was a well-informed, precise, and clear historian. Instead, the editor who worked on his writing was, so far as the *Acts* was concerned, *an unscrupulous advocate, a forger, a hoaxer, one who invents for the sake of inventing, who atrociously mutilated, cut, altered, revised, interpolated,* in a word, one who perpetrated a *continual travesty*.[12]

Even from such a ruin as this, Loisy was able to reconstruct in great part the main theme of the book, making known even parts which had totally disappeared, because suppressed by the unknown editor. The prologue, now mutilated and altered, gave a summary of the whole content of the book, which covered the period from the resurrection of Jesus to the death of Paul, and probably to the death of Peter. Then came the narrative proper: first of all, a summary of the appearances of the risen Christ in Galilee; then the return of the disciples to Jerusalem where they began to preach Christ; the formation of a group of Greek converts, directed by the seven deacons (especially Stephen), who preach the imminence of the parousia and the abrogation of the Jewish law. Stephen is stoned and the Greek Christians are driven from Jerusalem, while the Jewish Christians remain there undisturbed; the former spread their doctrine in various places and found the community of Antioch, into which many pagans were admitted. At this time, Paul is converted, also a Greek, who was not in Jerusalem at all on the occasion of Stephen's death; the former's

---

[11] *Les Actes des Apôtres*, Paris, 1920; abridged edition, Paris, 1925.
[12] These terms are found throughout the work (*Actes*, 1920).

conversion is recounted briefly (in Luke's original writing) as a purely internal and spiritual matter. Paul and Barnabas go to preach in Syria and Cilicia, which makes urgent a solution of the problem of the observance of Jewish practices, as the Jewish Christians in Jerusalem are still waiting for Christ's second coming. Those at Jerusalem then begin to entertain the liberal views of the Jewish Christians. The persecution of Agrippa I breaks out, in which James and his brother John (the Evangelist) are put to death. Peter, having taken refuge in Antioch, has the well-known dispute with Paul who then departs on his travels in Asia Minor, and subsequently to Macedonia, Achaia, and Ephesus before returning again to Jerusalem. He comes back there after the events at Ephesus, and is arrested. Then comes the journey to Rome, followed by the two years' imprisonment and his condemnation to death in the years A.D. 60–62. Probably the writing went on to describe the persecution of Nero and the death of Peter.

This, according to Loisy, was the outline of Luke's original work. Everything else we read in the *Acts* today is the tendentious and legendary fabrication of the compiler. To this category belong the accounts of the Ascension, Pentecost, Paul's conversion on the road to Damascus, the episode of the centurion Cornelius, the importance of the Twelve at Jerusalem under the primacy of Peter, the voyage of Paul and Barnabas to Cyprus, the episode of Sergius Paulus, of Gallio, a number of other incidents, and, above all, the miracles and supernatural events. In place of these falsifications, Luke's writing contained information on the Hellenist Christians, the conversion of Luke himself, the trial and death of James and John, the dispute at Antioch, and many other matters, including the trial of Paul in Rome. All this was suppressed by the compiler out of hostility.

The aim of this reviser was, in fact, to show the imperial authorities in Rome that the Christian religion was true Judaism and merited their protection. At the same time, another and more intense purpose was to magnify the Roman community, exalting Peter at the expense of Paul, and this betrays the fact that the falsification of Luke's work was desired by the Roman church, therefore that its author, namely the deceitful compiler, belonged to that church's ruling class. Once the deception was achieved, Luke's original writing was made to disappear without trace.

The imperturbable dogmatism with which Loisy presented the original plan of the *Acts,* and especially the precision with which he knew how to read the parts suppressed at the time, by the early compiler, could give the impression that by a happy coincidence he had uncovered an early copy of Luke's original writing. With this copy at hand, his confidence in pointing out the changes wrought by the compiler, and in restoring those suppressed by him, was well justified. But unfortunately, there was no copy, just as there were no documents of the Roman church to show that the compiler belonged to that church. The whole of Loisy's reconstruction was, in fact, based only on a philological analysis of the text, conducted with purely personal criteria, which were very often in opposition to the commonly accepted ones. Sometimes there was a lack of adequate knowledge of the external philological material, and an example of this lack showed from the beginning, when Loisy examined the prologue of the *Acts*. His aim was to make it appear that the destructive work of the compiler showed itself in the prologue, which served as an introduction to the rest of the book, because that part is presented in a form which seems grammatically truncated and stylistically incomplete. But this is only apparent, and if Loisy, instead of placing his faith in Norden, had made further researches, he would have found that the prologue is correct in both grammar and style. For the rest, Loisy's commentary immediately provoked many serious reservations, even among his habitual admirers, though they recognized the subtle ability with which he knew how to diminish the smallest possibilities of the text in order to favor his own preconceived thesis. This judgment has remained substantially unchanged to the present day, or, at best, further evidence has been added of this author's vivid imagination.

ACTS OF THE APOSTLES

1:1. The first account which I drew up, O Theophilus, told of all that Jesus began to do and to teach . . .

1:1 sqq. The first account is the third of the canonical Gospels, also written by Luke and dedicated to the same **Theophilus**. It is called first, πρῶτον, only because it is anterior to the present narrative of the *Acts,* but this term does not implicitly involve a series of at least three writings, as if Luke already had in mind to publish a third account after the *Acts.* Even though it be true that among classical writers πρῶτος is the first of a series of three or more, while the first of two only is πρότερος, it is also a fact that this latter term had fallen into disuse in Luke's time and was in practice replaced by πρῶτος (as is sometimes found in the classics). This **Theophilus,** who in the previous writing (Lk. 1:3) had been given the title of κράτιστε, "excellent," equivalent to our "Excellency," is certainly a real and not an imaginary person, one in authority as appears from his title, but nothing else is known about him. It has been supposed that he was a member of the imperial council before which Paul was brought as a prisoner awaiting sentence, but such a conjecture is without foundation. In any case, in addressing him Luke also intends to include other Christians in a similar position to Theophilus. — In the preceding work, **all the things** regarding Jesus were related, but **all** in the generic or systematic, not the numerical sense, since the oral apostolic catechesis was much wider than the written one (cf. Jn. 21:25). — The expression, **began to do, etc.,** can be interpreted as **from the beginning he did, etc.,** but more probably **began** stands for **he gave himself to,** and therefore the whole passage would read: **which Jesus both did and taught.** The scope of the Apostolic teaching was not only historical information but edifying exhortation, and so it transmitted first of all the example given by Jesus **(to do)** and then the teachings which were imparted **(and to teach).** This twofold class of arguments is shown in the canonical Gospels (Lk. 24:19) and the Apostolic Fathers (Papias, in Eusebius, *Hist. eccl.,* III, 39, 15).

1:2. until the day on which he was taken up, having given commandments through the Holy Spirit to the Apostles whom he had chosen.

1:2. Verse 1 relates the activity of Jesus from the beginning; in this verse, its conclusion and accomplishment is determined, that is **the day on which,** etc. The insertion of **through the Holy Spirit** can refer grammatically in Greek also to what follows, **whom he had chosen,** but it seems more fitting for it to refer to **having given,** because the general argument of the book is to expound the spread of the Church throughout the world, accomplished by the continual assistance of the Holy Spirit. — **Apostles:** the twelve disciples of Jesus, specially chosen by him, whose names Luke has already given (in Lk. 6:14–16) and which he will repeat shortly in this work (v. 13). — **Was taken up:** Luke had concluded his Gospel with a bare outline of the Ascension of Jesus into heaven (Lk. 24:51), but he will return to it again presently (vv. 9–11), thus linking up with his previous writing. — In these verses, 1 and 2, Luke gives a "recapitulation," or ἀνακεφαλαίωσις of his preceding work, as did the historians of his time when passing from one book to another of a historical account. But these same historical writers used to add to the recapitulation of their previous work a kind of summary of the subsequent book, and these two parts were usually joined together by μὲν ... δὲ, of which the word μὲν introduced the "recapitulation" and the term δὲ accompanied the summary. Here, therefore, one would expect that Luke, having introduced his recapitulation with the word μὲν in verse 1, would add the summary of the *Acts* with the usual δὲ in verse 3. Instead, there is no δὲ, and at first sight no summary of the *Acts*. This point has been investigated by several scholars: Norden (*Agnostos Theos,* 1913) gave the following explanation with a great display of philological knowledge. In Luke's original writing, the "recapitulation" of πρῶτος λόγος, i.e., the Third Gospel, was rightly followed by the summary of δεύτερος λόγος, i.e., the *Acts;* but an unknown compiler suppressed the summary with its proper term δὲ, and so the structural harmony of the entire prologue is spoiled, since all that now remains is only the "recapitulation" with its μὲν, suspended in the air and uncompleted by the requisite correlative δὲ. Norden's explanation was accepted by others, notably Loisy, who drew the most far-reaching conclusions without adducing fresh proofs. But, secondary considerations apart, the following "actual cases" are opposed to Norden's explanation. It is not surprising that the term μὲν here remains suspended and not concluded by the usual δὲ because the incidence of μὲν "by itself" is found many times elsewhere in the New Testament but always in Luke's writings or those of his master, Paul, and never in

1:3. To them also he showed himself alive after his passion by many proofs [that he was alive], during forty days appearing to them and speaking of the kingdom of God.

---

any other author. It is found fourteen times in Paul's letters in addition to two instances in *Hebrews,* once in the Third Gospel, and fourteen times in the *Acts,* including the present example (cf. 3:21; 5:41; 13:4; 17:30; 23:22; 26:4; 27:21; and elsewhere). 26:9 is of particular importance, for there, as in the present case, the term δὲ is missing and the construction is continued with the relative pronoun which is οἷς in 1:3 and ὃ in 26:10. In conclusion, therefore, the absence of the term δὲ in no way reveals an editorial suppression. The fact that the summary of the new book is omitted is not a violation of any well-established rule of the historiography of that time, for other examples are to be found. A careful and even more extensive examination than Norden's, learned as this was, of extent profane writings, has shown that it was undoubtedly usual, in ancient times, to add the summary to the "recapitulation," but that from the first century onward other means were employed, such as the "recapitulation" without the summary and vice versa. In the *Antiquities of the Jews* of Flavius Josephus, in Herodianus' *Roman History,* in the introductions of the various books of the *Anabasis* (which incidentally appear attributable not to Xenophon but to the grammarians of the Alexandrian age) the "recapitulation" of the preceding work is given, but not the summary of the work that follows. The prologue of the *Acts* is, therefore, akin to these, although it does not copy them exactly. While it is true that this prologue does not give a summary of what follows with the precise allocation of periods as do Polibius, Diodorus Ciculus, Dionysius of Alicarnasso, and other early historians, it does give it in actual fact, although in what might be called a disguised form. It will therefore be noted how, in verse 8, the diffusion of the Church, throughout the whole world by the work of the Apostles, assisted by the Holy Spirit, is already foretold by Jesus. This prophecy of Jesus, which would infallibly be fulfilled, is precisely the general argument of the *Acts* and perhaps Luke considered that such an authoritative pronouncement did not need the confirmatory evidence of the usual summary. For the whole question of the prologue, see the work of V. Larranaga, *"El proemio-transicion de Act., I, 1–3, en los metodos literarios de la historiografia griega,"* in *Miscellanea biblica,* Rome, 1934, Vol. II, pp. 311–374.

1:3. Jesus **showed himself alive,** or rather resuscitated, to the Apostles, **after his passion** of torments and death, and showed **by many proofs** that he had risen to life. Christ's Resurrection was, in fact, the cornerstone

**1:4. And taking food together [with them], he charged them not
to depart from Jerusalem, but to await the promise of the Father "of
which you have heard from me;**

---

of the Apostolic catechesis, and its historical reality was thrown into
special relief (cf. 1 Cor. 15:4-8) because **if Christ be not risen, then vain is
the preaching** of the Apostles, **vain also the faith** of the Christians (*ibid.*,
15:14). The **many proofs** are the different circumstances in which the
apparitions of the risen Christ took place, and which gave occasion to
the Apostles to see him, touch him, speak with him, eat with him, and
the like, convincing them more and more of the reality of the fact. —
During forty days is the chronological precision regarding the preceding
writing. It might be concluded, in reading the account (Lk. 24:50-51),
that the Ascension of Christ took place some hours after the Resurrection
(cf. Lk. 24:1, 13, 33, 36); but it is a résumé and therefore presents the
time element briefly. Luke possibly also intended to come back to the
point and fix it chronologically when he began the account of the *Acts*.
It is not, then, a question of uncertain or contradictory traditions, as some
have supposed, but of the only tradition contained in the Apostolic
catechesis and testified to by Paul (1 Cor. 15:5-7; cf. Acts 13:31), narrated
in summarized form (as in Luke's Gospel), or in detail as here. In the
forty days between the Resurrection and the Ascension, Christ, **appearing**
to the Apostles at intervals, speaks to them of the things **of the kingdom
of God.** They are like the final commands of a captain before he sends
his soldiers into battle, and the account of this battle and victory of the
kingdom of God on earth is precisely the argument of the *Acts*.

1:4 Taking food together with them is, in Greek, συναλιζόμενος which
seems derived etymologically from ἅλς, "salt," with the meaning of **eating
salt together** or, in general **eating together;** and almost all the ancient
versions and Greek expositors so interpret it. But there is a much less
attested reading, συναλιζόμενος, meaning **passing the time** or **conversing
together.** The former interpretation is much more authentic, since it is
reinforced by the appeal which the Apostles made to the physical reality
of the meal taken in common as proof of the Resurrection of Christ
(cf. 10:41; Lk. 24:30, 35, 41-43). Does the term contain an allusion to the
Eucharistic banquet? Such an allusion is not excluded, but neither is it
certain. — **Not to depart from Jerusalem:** it was in this city then, that the
meal in common, mentioned at the beginning of the verse, took place, and
it was unnecessary to identify this gathering with that spoken of in verse
6. The Apostles' departure from Jerusalem was necessary to announce the
kingdom of God in the rest of Palestine **and even to the very ends of the**

1:5. "for John indeed baptized with water, but you shall be baptised with the Holy Spirit not many days hence."

1:6. They therefore standing gathered together began to ask him saying: "Lord [tell us] wilt thou at this time restore the kingdom to Israel."

---

earth (v. 8); but for such an arduous mission, the Apostles did not yet possess the means necessary, which would be given to them when they were **baptized with the Holy Spirit** (v. 5; cf. v. 8). The fundamental thesis of the *Acts* is precisely this — to show the expansion of the Church in the world by virtue of the Holy Spirit. Note the improvised transition from indirect to direct speech (**of which you have heard from me, etc.**). To accentuate this abrupt transition, the Western Recension (cf. Vulgate) paraphrases it: "**which you have heard,**" said he, "**by my mouth; for, etc.**"; but cf. 23:22. — **The promise of the Father,** relating to the Holy Spirit, already made in the Old Testament (Joel 3:1-5; Isa. 44:3; Ezech. 11:19; 36:26-27; etc.; cf. Acts 2:17 sqq.), was confirmed by Jesus himself (**from me**), as the Apostolic teaching showed (Lk. 24:49; Jn. 14:16; 15:26; 16:7, 13), and is repeated in the following verse.

1:5. John is the Baptist who had baptized only in water but who foretold that after him Christ would baptize with **the Holy Spirit and fire** (Lk. 3:16). — *To baptize* is the Greek word which originally signified *to immerse* (used also of a sinking ship). Here, in the case of John, the immersion was only **with water,** while in the case which follows it had a special significance. — **Not many days hence:** the Greek has **not after many of these days,** a construction perhaps influenced by the Latin. — Peter cites these words later (11:16).

1:6. Standing gathered together, συνελθόντες: this reunion could well have been different from that of verse 4. If the two gatherings are distinct, this second one could have been prolonged for some hours, but it concluded on **Mount Olivet** (v. 12), where Bethany is situated, since this place is also referred to, in connection with the Ascension, in Lk. 24:50. In that case, the second gathering would have begun in Bethany so as to finish a little higher up on Mount Olivet from the side toward Jerusalem. If there was one gathering only, namely that of verse 4 with the meal in common, it is to be supposed that this meeting lasted a long time, because after the meal the company had to go from Jerusalem to Bethany, where, finally, the Ascension took place. — The question the Apostles put to their risen Master is one they had very much at heart, namely the restoration of a political **kingdom,** free and independent, for **Israel.** All Palestine was at that time seething with nationalistic

1:7. But he said to them: "It is not for you to know the times or dates which the Father has fixed by his own authority;

1:8. "but you shall receive power when the Holy Spirit comes upon you, and you shall be witnesses for me in Jerusalem and in all Judea and Samaria and even to the very ends of the earth."

---

aspirations, aimed above all at political independence, and the Apostles were not strangers to these widespread notions. This did not cause them to lose faith in Jesus; on the contrary, seeing him risen as the conqueror of death, they were more than ever sure that he would overcome the enemies of the chosen people (cf. Lk. 24:21) and re-establish (ἀποκαθιστάνεις) **the kingdom** for Israel. Now that the Master was risen, the restoration could begin without delay (**at this time**). The very promise of the Holy Spirit (v. 5) seemed to be a direct preparation for this great manifestation because, with such a guide, **the kingdom** would be triumphantly set up, and by spreading through the world would remain secure for Israel. Naturally, Jesus himself would sit on the throne of this kingdom, surrounded nevertheless by the Apostles (cf. Mt. 20:21; Mk. 10:37), who would therefore also be triumphant with the Master in the Messianic kingdom. This political-messianic concept of the Apostles corresponded in great part with the ideas commonly circulating at that time in Palestine (cf. 2:23 with note), of which the party of the Zealots was a typical example.

1:7-8. Jesus replied directly only to the question put by the Apostles, which was a chronological one (if **at this time**); he does not touch at all upon the manner of the re-establishment of **the kingdom**, even though that question was the more important and the one on which the Apostles most needed enlightenment. Jesus' words in reply would have done little to remove their inveterate nationalistic conviction, as had happened in the past (cf. Mt. 16:21 sqq.; 20:22; Lk. 18:31-34); that false notion had to disappear of itself when the Apostles dedicated themselves, under the guidance of the Holy Spirit, to spread the true messianic kingdom preached by Jesus. The reply to the question about when this should happen is therefore negative; the complete restoration of Jesus' messianic kingdom, and not that dreamed of by the Apostles, is in the heavenly **Father's** charge, who, as far as the time goes, **has fixed by his own authority** the gradual realization of that kingdom. It was equally reserved to the heavenly Father to know the time when the great eschatological drama would take place (Mt. 24:36; Mk. 13:32). Not knowing when that would be, the Apostles must in the meantime work for its accomplishment, showing themselves as **witnesses** of the teaching and deeds of Jesus **in Jerusalem and in all Judea and Samaria**, namely throughout

1:9. And when he had said these things he was lifted up before their eyes and a cloud received him out of their sight.

1:10. And while they were gazing up to heaven as he went, behold two men stood by them in white garments,

---

Palestine **and even to the very ends of the earth.** This far-reaching geographical extent of the messianic kingdom of Jesus corresponded somewhat to that of the kingdom dreamed of by the messianists of Palestine, who anticipated that Israel would dominate all the peoples of the earth. But the Apostles were themselves unequal to the founding of such a kingdom; the assurance is therefore given them that **you shall receive power . . . Holy Spirit.** This, as we have already pointed out, is the historic thesis of the *Acts* and the summary of its content (see also notes on vv. 2, 3, 4).

1:9. The Ascension of Jesus took place when the foregoing discourse ended; but the possibility that some time may have elapsed after Jesus had finished speaking is not thereby ruled out, since here the chronological sequence of the facts is abbreviated (see note on v. 6). — **He was lifted up:** the action is described but not the agent (God). It was also rather a slow movement, and not a sudden disappearance like that before the two disciples at Emmaus (Lk. 24:31), because the Apostles stood watching him **before their eyes** until **a cloud received him out of their sight;** and even after that, **they were gazing up to heaven as he went** (v. 10). Regarding the cloud, in the Old Testament a reverential cloud accompanied the theophanies (Exod. 14:24; 16:10; 19:9; Lev. 16:2; 1 [3] Kings 8:10; Ezech. 1:4; etc.), and even in the New Testament a cloud appeared at the Transfiguration of Jesus (Mt. 17:5 and parallel passages).

1:10. Even after the cloud had intervened, the Apostles **were gazing up;** in the Greek, the complement **to heaven** can be referred to that which follows, reading thus: **as he went (to heaven)** (cf. **going up to heaven** of v. 11). Jesus rose slowly upward enveloped by the cloud, while the Apostles followed the unexpected vision with *fixed gaze.* — As he went **(to heaven):** this is a simple description of physical appearances with no scientific-astronomical implication. **Heaven** here is that which is obvious to any spectator, and it is not one of the seven heavens of Greek cosmology, nor one of the two of Hebrew cosmology. At the Second Coming of the glorified Christ, the same course will be covered twice: once by Christ when he descends from heaven and then when he ascends again, with the elect: **the Lord himself . . . will descend from heaven . . . then we . . . shall be caught up together in clouds to meet the Lord in the air** (1 Thess. 4:16–17). — While the absorbed gaze

1:11. who said, "Men of Galilee, why do you stand looking up to heaven? This Jesus who has been taken up from you into heaven, shall come in the same way [again, namely] as you have seen him going up to heaven."

1:12. Then they returned to Jerusalem from the mount called Olivet, which is near Jerusalem, a Sabbath day's journey.

1:13. And when they had entered, they mounted to the upper room wherein they were staying, Peter and John, James and Andrew,

---

of the Apostles was directed above them, they were not aware that two men stood beside them. This again is a description of physical appearances: the two personages who appeared suddenly were in **white garments,** like those other two "men" who appeared to the women and spoke to them at Jesus' empty tomb (Lk. 24:4), and also like the two "angels" seen there by Mary Magdalen (Jn. 20:12).

1:11. Men of Galilee: the substantive **men** linked with a geographical appellative was in common use in classical Greek; later on we shall find it in the Greek joined to an appellative of relationship, **men brethren** (v. 16: 2:29, 37, etc.), but just **brethren** is also found (3:17; 23:5). — These two personages offer reassurance to the disconcerted Apostles by announcing that the departed Jesus will appear again and in exactly the same way as he left them: the manner will be the same, although inversely, because now he has disappeared by ascending, but he will reappear by descending (see the passage in *1 Thessalonians* cited in the previous note). That will take place at the Second Coming of the glorified Christ, the thing most looked for by the first generation of Christians and especially by Paul (1 Thess. 2:19; 3:13; 5:23; 2 Thess. 1:7 sqq.; 1 Tim. 6:14; Titus 2:13; 2 Tim. 1:12; 4:8, etc.); but the time of this Second Coming was not known to anyone (cf. Mt. 24:36; Mk. 13:32), and these two personages give no indication of when it will happen.

1:12. Mount called Olivet (see note on v. 6), which was as far from Jerusalem as **a Sabbath day's journey,** namely the distance that a Jew could cover during the sacred repose of the Sabbath, which was 2000 cubits (about three quarters of a mile). Bethany, on the other hand, although on the slope of Mount Olivet farthest from Jerusalem, was about 15 stadia (over a mile and a half; cf. Jn. 11:18). These indications of distance are natural in Luke since he was writing for readers for the most part unfamiliar with Palestine.

1:13. Upper room, ὑπερῷον, which occurs again in 9:37 and 39; 20:8. Note that this is a different term from that used by Luke to designate the

Philip and Thomas, Bartholomew and Matthew, James the son of Alpheus and Simon the Zealot, and Jude the brother of James.

1:14. All these were persevering with one accord in prayer, together with the women and Mary, the mother of Jesus, and with his brethren.

---

room where the Holy Eucharist was instituted, called ἀνάγαιον, etymologically "above ground level" (Lk. 22:12; cf. Mk. 14:15), and there is nothing to suggest that it was the same room. Nor is it necessary to imagine that it was a room annexed to the Jewish Temple owing to Luke's reference in 24:53, which does not actually refer to any particular part of the Temple. Mention of the dwelling place provides Luke with the opportunity to give a fresh list of those staying there, i.e., the Apostles, in addition to the one he had already given (Lk. 6:14–16) and those of the two other Synoptics (Mt. 10:2–4; Mk. 3:16–19). However, none of the four lists agrees entirely on the order of placing the Apostles' names, not even Luke's own two lists. But all four lists put Simon Peter's name at the head of the first group of four names, Philip at the head of the second group, and James, son of Alpheus, at the head of the third group of four names (which is three here, because Judas Iscariot was now dead). **Simon the Zealot** and **Jude, the brother of James,** named here, correspond to **Simon the Chananean** and **Thaddeus (Lebbeus)** of the other lists. The Apostles Andrew, Philip, Thomas, Bartholomew, Matthew, Simon the Zealot, and Jude, the brother of James, are not thereafter mentioned in the *Acts*.

1:14. While this verse gives a fleeting glance at the embryo Church, it connects up with the narrative of the earlier Gospels, particularly with that of Luke himself. **Mary, the mother of Jesus,** is named here, she who had been present at the death of her Son and was taken by the Apostle John into his house (Jn. 19:26–27), but Joseph, the spouse of Mary, is mentioned neither here nor elsewhere; in all probability, he died before Jesus. — **Women,** without the article in Greek; codex D (Western Recension), on the contrary, reads **the women,** and adds **and the children:** does this mean the wives and children of the Apostles? The women referred to here must have formed part of that group of faithful followers who accompanied and assisted Jesus, ministering to his needs during his preaching journeys in Palestine. Of these, who were very probably Luke's informants on the various episodes narrated in his Gospel, he specifically names Mary Magdalen, Joanna, wife of Chuza, and Susanna (Lk. 8:23; cf. 24:10). Special importance, in virtue of their relationship, was also given to **his brethren** (i.e., the brethren of Jesus) in this nucleus of the infant

1:15. In those days Peter stood up in the midst of the brethren (the number of persons gathered together was about a hundred and twenty) and he said:

Church. The kinship of Jesus was, in fact, extensive and comprised "brothers" and "sisters": the names of four of these "brothers" are given, namely James, Joseph, Simon, and Jude (Mt. 13:55; Mk. 6:3), but not the names of the "sisters" of whom there must have been several, since mention is made of all his sisters (Mt. 13:56). All of these in actual fact were cousins of Jesus in various degrees. Eastern custom reckoned even remote degrees of kinship, while the Hebrew language had no special word to designate male or female cousins and therefore called them generically *brothers and sisters.* It should be noted, however, that some of these kinsfolk were hostile to Jesus' ministry from the beginning, since we are told, **for neither did his brethren believe in him** (Jn. 7:5); therefore, **his brethren** referred to here by Luke were either different from those previously hostile, or those whose hostility had eventually been disarmed at seeing their kinsman's wondrous works. The life led by this group of Apostles and brethren of Christ consisted chiefly in **persevering with one accord in prayer.** It was, therefore, above all, a time of prayerful waiting: waiting for the fulfillment of Jesus' promise of the baptism in the Holy Spirit (vv. 5 and 8), which they were seeking to hasten by prayer.

1:15. Though they were waiting, they did not remain idle but sought to prepare for the day when the Apostles would have to be **witnesses** of Jesus both in Palestine and **to the very ends of the earth** (v. 8). This explains the scene that follows. — **In those days** is a vague chronological determination referring to the weeks following the Ascension but prior to the seventh week when Pentecost fell (cf. 2:1). — **Peter:** the initiative for the important decision which follows is taken by Simon Peter, the head of the Apostolic college, and he is always named first in the various lists of that college (see note on v. 13). — **Number of persons** is, literally in Greek, *multitude of names:* this use of *name* for *person* seems to be a Hebraism but is in fact found in Greek papyri of the time. — The number of those present at the gathering at which Peter spoke, was **about a hundred and twenty.** This number certainly has no allegorical significance (which would be ruled out in any case by the approximative preposition **about**), but corresponds to the actuality of the situation known to Luke, perhaps through a written source. Probably only some and not all of the hundred and twenty were Christians of Jerusalem, though they may have been in the majority. Paul (1 Cor. 15:6) speaks of an appearance of the

1:16. "Brethren, it was necessary that the Scripture should be fulfilled which the Holy Spirit declared before by the mouth of David concerning Judas, who was the guide of those who arrested Jesus,

1:17. "inasmuch as he had been numbered among us and was allotted his share in this ministry.

1:18. "He indeed bought a field with the price of his iniquity and having fallen headlong burst asunder in the midst and all his bowels gushed out;

1:19. "and it became known to all the residents of Jerusalem, so that the field came to be called in their language Hakeldamach, that is, the 'field of blood.'

Risen Christ to more than five hundred brethren at one time, which appearance certainly took place before the Ascension, but whether at Jerusalem or in Galilee is not known.

1:16. This is the first of Peter's many discourses related in the *Acts*. In view of the assiduous cultivation of memory in Semitic social life, the speeches of any important person, so far as fundamental ideas were concerned, remained impressed on the minds of attentive hearers; they were consequently able, several days later, to commit the principal ideas to writing, thereby obtaining a faithful résumé of the discourse. This first official discourse of the head of the Apostles must have followed the same pattern, and Luke probably had a written résumé of it to hand. — **Brethren:** see note on verse 11. — It **was necessary,** in the imperfect tense (not **it is necessary,** in the present, as the Vulgate and documents of the Western Recension read), because it refers to the fulfillment, already taken place, of the prophecy concerning Judas. Several weeks earlier it **was necessary** for the ancient prophecy to be fulfilled; now that it has been fulfilled, **it is necessary** (v. 21) to provide for someone to take his place. — **The Scripture . . . which the Holy Spirit, etc.,** is that quoted presently in verse 21. — **Guide,** since Judas actually led and showed the way to those **who arrested Jesus** in Gethsemani (Lk. 22:47).

1:17. Inasmuch as: this refers to the preceding **it was necessary that . . . ,** but it also paves the way for **one must** of verse 22 which declares the need for a successor to Judas. The reason is that **he . . . was allotted his share in this ministry** of the Apostles; therefore the prophecy foretelling his fall and subsequent replacement in the Apostolic ministry must be fulfilled.

1:18-19. Who is speaking in these verses, Peter still, or Luke the historian? If it is Peter, it is surprising to find that in addressing the

Jews of Jerusalem he needed to tell them that Judas' field was called by
the inhabitants of Jerusalem **in their** own **language Hakeldamach, that is,**
the "field of blood." The explanation of the name **Hakeldamach** was unnecessary, to say the least, and it must, therefore, be attributed to Luke
who wished to explain the name to his readers who did not know Semitic
languages. Even the rest of this passage, with the minute details of Judas'
end, would appear too exuberant, in Peter's discourse, to hearers who knew
only too well of the recent atrocious happening, since a single allusion to
the death of the betrayer would have been sufficient for his argument. On
the other hand, everything becomes clear and appropriate if it is Luke who
is inserting these explanations for the benefit of his non-Palestinian readers.
Similar insertions in speeches are probably to be found in John (3:16-21;
3:31-36). Luke elsewhere employs similar explanatory insertions as parentheses (Acts 1:15; 9:12?; Lk. 5:24; 23:51). — Judas' end, as described
here, shows interesting differences from the parallel accounts in Mt. 27:3-8.
In *Matthew,* the field is not bought by Judas but by the high priests who
use the thirty pieces of silver Judas received for the betrayal, and which
he threw down in the temple. Here, it is Judas who **bought** (ἐκτήσατο)
a field with the price of his iniquity. But the two narratives agree easily if
these words of Peter's are interpreted as aiming more at a moral lesson
drawn from these facts than the actual reconstruction of the facts themselves. Moreover, Peter's words are not lacking in a certain sad sarcasm
regarding Judas. They could be paraphrased thus: "Yes indeed, the traitor
made a good acquisition with the reward of his betrayal! He bought
the field in which he is buried after killing himself!" Another difference
arises in the circumstances of Judas' death. According to *Matthew,* he
hanged himself in despair. Here, however, **having fallen headlong** πρηνὴς
γενόμενος **he burst asunder in the midst and all his bowels gushed out.**
It is not necessary, in this connection, to suppose two independent or
contradictory traditions; it is sufficient that they could be two parts of
one tradition: one (part) referred to the hanging, and this alone is
reported by *Matthew* in a historical description; the other referred to
the consequences of hanging, the breaking of the rope or branch and
subsequent fall of the dead body to the ground into some ravine below,
producing the macabre results described here. The grim character of this
description impressed the popular mind, and the author of this passage
(Luke rather than Peter) records it almost as a moral comment on the
accompanying facts. A local tradition, going back to the fourth century,
seeks to identify the place of the hanging with the field of Hakeldamach,
in the valley of Gehenna to the south of Jerusalem, a place regarded from
the early times in Jewish history as cursed. — **To be called in their**
own language (own is missing in several codices) **Hakeldamach.** If it is
Peter speaking here, we must conclude that he is distinguishing between

1:20. "For it is written in the book of Psalms:
'Let his dwelling become desolate
And let no one dwell therein' (Ps. 69 [68]:26)
and
'His ministry let another take' (Ps. 109 [108]:8).
1:21. "Therefore, of these men who have been in our company all the time that the Lord Jesus moved among us,

---

the language (διαλέκτῳ) peculiar to the inhabitants of Jerusalem with which he is dealing here, and the language proper to himself and the other Galileans who are his hearers. But this is an exaggerated distinction as, although there were indeed differences of intonation and pronunciation as between the southern part of Jerusalem and the northern part of Galilee (cf. Mt. 26:73), these could not be considered to constitute different languages. If, instead, these words are introduced by Luke to clarify Peter's discourse for his non-Palestinian readers in the sense mentioned above, they offer no difficulty; just as the added translation of "field of blood" offers none, whereas for Peter's hearers it would have been a simple literal repetition of the preceding name. The Greek gives the name as Ἀκελδαμάχ (with variants, δαμάκ and δαμά), but it is a simple transcription of the two Aramaic words, *hăqel děmă,* meaning "field of blood" (Vulgate, **Haceldama**). In fact, the language usually spoken at that time in Palestine, both by the people of Jerusalem and by Galileans like Peter and his companions, was Aramaic. The form in Hebrew most resembling this Aramaic would have been *heleq dâm.*

1:20. This verse is connected, by means of the particle **for**, with verses 16–17 which it explains with regard to Judas' replacement in the Apostolic college. The proof is drawn from quotations from two different psalms, taken from the Septuagint version, somewhat modified and joined together. The authors of the respective psalms address themselves to their persecutors: Peter, in giving them a sense which is partly messianic (see also for the first of the two psalms quoted here, Jn. 2:17; 15:25; 19:28–29; Rom. 15:3; etc.), applies them to Christ's betrayer, taking Christ as the prototype of the persecuted just man. — **Dwelling,** ἔπαυλις: a country habitation: it recalls the field bought by Judas (v. 18). — **Ministry:** here the Greek has ἐπισκοπὴν, and the original Hebrew *pequddah;* from the Greek term, primitive Christianity derived the word "overseers," "superintendents" (*episcopoi*), which later became "bishops" (cf. Phil. 1:1; 1 Tim. 3:2; Titus 1:7; Acts 20:28): here it is applied to the office of apostle held by Judas; but after his betrayal, **let another take** such an office. Peter thus showed that Judas' substitution was foretold by the Scriptures.

1:22. "(from John's baptism until the day that he was taken up from us) of these one must become a witness with us of his resurrection."

1:23. And they put forward two, Joseph called Barsabbas, who was surnamed Justus, and Matthias.

1:24. And they prayed and said: "Thou, Lord, who knowest the hearts of all, show which of these two thou hast chosen

---

1:21–22. To the proof drawn from Scripture is added that demanded by the nature of the case, and it is important if we would grasp the idea that the Apostolic college had of its own office. After Judas' defection, it is necessary to replace him by choosing in his stead one of the **men who have been in our company all the time that the Lord Jesus moved among us** (a Hebraism indicating the intensity of the common life; cf. 9:28). In other words, the one to be chosen must be an eyewitness of the facts equally with the Apostles. The time of his witnessing is also specified: **all the time** in which Jesus lived in common with the Apostles, and more precisely, the period from **John's baptism** (administered by John the Baptist in preparation for the direct action of Jesus) **until the day** of Jesus' Ascension. These limitations, similarly specified by Peter in 10:37–41, conformed to the common Apostolic catechesis and appertained to the Gospels of Mark and John. The other two Gospels also include the whole of this period, and in their case it is prefaced by a brief account of Jesus' first years as a kind of *superadditum*. Moreover, in possessing this qualification of historical information, Judas' successor will be elected to **become a witness with us of** the **resurrection** of Jesus, so that Christ's Resurrection sets the seal on his whole earthly life and is the cornerstone of the Apostolic catechesis (see note on v. 3).

1:23. We know absolutely nothing of **Joseph** and **Matthias** except that as they had shown themselves eligible on the conditions laid down in the two preceding verses, they must have been companions of the Apostles and immediate disciples of Jesus. The name **Bar-sabba** is a patronymic, "son of Sabbas (*of the Old one?*)": **Justus,** on the other hand, is a Latin personal name, not an adjective, possessed by other Jews also (cf. **Titius Justus** in 18:7; **Jesus called Justus,** in Col. 4:11). Later (15:22) one **Judas surnamed Barsabbas** also appears, viz., with the same patronymic as the present **Joseph,** but it cannot be shown with certainty that they were brothers. **Matthias** is an abbreviation of the Hebrew name *Mathatias;* a Gospel and other apocryphal writings under this name were in circulation from the second century onward.

1:24–25. **Lord:** Jesus, not his heavenly Father; he must intervene in

1:25. "to take the place in this ministry and apostleship from which Judas fell away that he might go to his own place."

1:26. And they drew lots between them, and the lot fell upon Matthias; and he was reckoned with the eleven apostles.

2:1. And when the day of Pentecost was drawing to a close, they were all gathered together in one place.

---

the replacement of one of the Apostles chosen by him (v. 2) for, equally with his heavenly Father (Acts 15:8), he is the knower of **the hearts of all** (cf. Jn. 2:25; Apoc. 2:23).— **Place . . . place:** the same word is used twice, but the second time in opposition to the first. The first time, it designates the **apostleship** for which Jesus had chosen Judas (v. 2); the second use of the word refers only to the role chosen by Judas himself, in opposition to his previous status, namely that of betrayer, with its known consequences including his suicide. On the other hand, the hidden consequences following on his death, as though **his own place** (τόπον τὸν ἴδιον) alludes to Gehenna, do not seem directly intended here.

1:26. And they drew lots between them. To us today the expression does not explain the working of this election clearly. It is certain that **they drew** does not signify precisely "they extracted," "pulled out," but rather refers to the preparations for the choosing itself. We can suppose that the electors *gave* the name of the candidate of their choice, written on a piece of papyrus, to someone who put these voting slips into a small urn or vessel: one slip was drawn from this, and the name written on it was the one elected. The custom of drawing lots was common in the Old Testament, and is attested also in Lk. 1:9. There was also the feast of the Purim, or of the "lots" connected with the deeds of Esther. — He **was reckoned:** συγκατεψηφίσθη etymologically, this very rare compound signifies "collectively I decide by voting," or "I decide by voting together." The second sense seems more appropriate to the present case by implying that Matthias was coopted among the Apostles by vote. Here, they are enumerated as **eleven,** being referred to before the election of Matthias, since choosing the twelfth is being dealt with here; but the technical term for the Apostolic college was **the Twelve,** and Paul so refers to them (1 Cor. 15:5), even though he is speaking of the time when there were only eleven, as is the case here. When persons were elected to a new office, or invested with a given mission, they received an "imposition of hands" (6:6; 13:3), but no such imposition is recorded here, or any other rite, but just the election.

2:1. Pentecost: i.e., the fiftieth day, was the second of the three great

2:2.   And suddenly there came a noise from heaven as of a violent wind blowing and it filled the whole house where they were sitting.
2:3.   And there appeared to them parted tongues as of fire which settled upon each of them.

Hebrew feasts "of pilgrimage," so-called because they imposed a pilgrimage to Jerusalem on every Israelite. The first was the Pasch, the second, Pentecost, which fell "fifty days" after the Pasch, and the third, that of Tabernacles which occurred at the end of autumn. While "Pentecost" is a Greek name, the Hebrew word for the same feast was *Shabu oth,* the feast of (*seven*) Weeks, for the chronological reason given above. Here, however, the expression **was drawing to a close** refers to "fiftieth" day itself, already begun and **drawing to a close.** The hour at which the event related in verse 15 took place was before the **third hour of the day.** — **All gathered together,** in a closed place which could have been the same as that in 1:13, although it is not certain.

2:2.   The description of the event is sober but telling. While the Apostles, and others, were all **gathered together,** probably praying, **suddenly** they heard coming down **a noise** (ἦχος) **from heaven,** which was like the roar **of a violent wind blowing** and the **whole house** re-echoed with that roar. The narrative describes the outward manifestations of the phenomenon, but does not give any explanation. Nevertheless, we have here **wind,** which in the Greek is πνοή, "blowing," derived from the same root as πνεῦμα, used later to indicate the Holy *Spirit.*

2:3.   The phenomenon of sound was a preparation and attraction of the attention, followed by the phenomenon of seeing. Those gathered together, already startled by the noise, saw, unexpectedly falling from on high, many little flames in the form of **tongues as of fire.** They were **parted** (διαμεριζόμεναι) as if they had been separated, or they detached themselves from a ball one by one and **settled upon each** one of those gathered there. Here also the description presents the visual phenomenon simply and precisely, without descending to any explanation of it. As far as the symbolical and conceptual significance goes, it must be remembered that, in the Old Testament, fire was frequently an element of the theophanies (Exod. 3:2; 19:18; 24:17; Ezech. 1:13; 2 Sam. 22:9–13; 2 Par. 7:1, 3; etc.), especially as a symbol of purification (Isa. 6:6–7; Mal. 3:2–3); and even in the New Testament the difference between the baptism administered by the precursor, John the Baptist, and that of the Messias, Jesus, consisted in this, that the baptism of John was in "water" only, while that of Jesus was "in the Holy Spirit and **fire**" (Mt. 3:11; Lk. 3:16).

2:4. And they were all filled with the Holy Spirit, and began to speak in foreign tongues, according as the Spirit gave them to utter.

2:5. Now there were staying in Jerusalem devout Jews from every nation under heaven.

2:6. And when this sound was heard, the multitude came together and were bewildered because each heard them speaking in his own language.

2:4. They were all filled (ἐπλήσθησαν) with the Holy Spirit: all refers to all those gathered together of verse 1, that is, not only the Apostles but also those who were not Apostles, e.g., Joseph Barsabbas (1:23). The words were all filled express in another way the idea of you shall be baptised with the Holy Spirit of 1:5, which etymologically means, you shall be immersed. In the same way that a sinking ship fills and is saturated with water, so those gathered together were filled and penetrated with the Holy Spirit. — The first obvious effect of this fullness of the Holy Spirit was that they . . . began to speak in foreign tongues, not at their own whim, but according as the Spirit gave them to utter. These tongues were other than (ἐτέραις), or "different" from, the national language of the speakers. Which languages these were can be gathered from the full list of foreigners which follows (vv. 9–11), of whom each heard them speaking in his own language (v. 6). On the other hand, it seems certain that among the hearers were some who did not understand any of the languages spoken on this occasion, and they are the mockers of verse 13. Finally, since the language actually spoken was not chosen arbitrarily by each one, but according as the Spirit gave them to utter, it seems obvious that not everyone spoke all the languages of their hearers but only that prompted by the Spirit.

2:5–6. The scene is now transferred from the closed place (v. 1) to the city. There were staying, ἦσαν κατοικοῦντες: this periphrastic imperfect seems to emphasize the idea of a permanent dwelling place and not merely a temporary one. It is true that many Jews from all over the Diaspora made the pilgrimage to Jerusalem for the actual feast of Pentecost (see v. 1), but their stay in the Holy City was of only a few days, while here a longer residence seems to be indicated. Perhaps the allusion is to those Jews who, for reasons of study or devotion (cf. devout Jews), moved to the precincts of the Jewish Temple, although these usual residents may also include the occasional Pentecost pilgrims. The habitual residents are called devout, εὐλαβεῖς; in the present case, this description cannot mean pagans who had entered the Jewish religion, nor sympathizers with it (who, if they were still uncircumcised, belonged to the lower class called

2:7. And they were beside themselves and wondered saying: "Behold, are not all these that are speaking Galileans?

2:8. "And how have we heard each his own language in which he was born?

2:9. "Parthians and Medes and Elamites and inhabitants of Mesopotamia, Judea and Cappadocia, Pontus and Asia,

2:10. "Phrygia and Pamphylia, Egypt and the parts of Libya about Cyrene and visitors from Rome, Jews also and proselytes,

2:11. "Cretans and Arabians, [how do] we hear them speaking in our own languages of the wonderful works of God?"

---

the "pious" or the "God-fearing," σεβόμενοι or φοβούμενοι τὸν θεόν; if, however, they had received circumcision, they formed a higher class of the real "proselytes," προσήλυτοι). The **devout** mentioned here are, in fact, clearly Jews, that is, Jews by birth, since ethnically a distinction was made between Jew and "proselyte" (cf. v. 10) inasmuch as the latter was not of Jewish origin. The description, **from every nation,** has a geographical and not an ethnical significance, indicating the territories of the various nations each speaking their own language. The **Jews** by origin, born and grown up among these nations of the Diaspora, considered the language of each one of them as their own (cf. **our own languages** of v. 11). The expression **every nation under heaven,** is strictly a hyperbole, but it corresponds well to the wide distribution of the Jewish Diaspora in the territories of the Roman Empire and beyond. — **This sound** (φωνῆς) seems to refer to the **noise** of verse 2, which would therefore have been heard, by the crowd in the city, outside the house in which the Apostles and disciples were. This crowd gathered to find out what had happened and came into contact with the Apostles and disciples who were still under the immediate influence of the charism received, and each one of the polyglot crowd **heard them speaking in his own language.**

2:7. **All . . . Galileans,** referring to the majority and especially the chief ones, namely the Apostles; but among the other disciples there may have been some who were not Galileans. Evidently this question is asked by those who knew the group of Galileans in some social connection; but they were certainly not recognized as Galileans, on this occasion, by their particular pronunciation (Mt. 26:73) since, in this instance, the listeners heard them speaking in their respective tongues.

2:9-11. This list of peoples includes those from the various regions throughout which the Jewish Diaspora was spread and from which representatives were then at Jerusalem. It may well be, however, that some regions were not then represented at Jerusalem, or at least not at this event. We find, in fact, in the text we have today, that Syria, surprisingly enough, is not mentioned, although the Jews there were very numerous, and in Antioch, the capital, they had many affiliated members among the Greek population (Flavius Josephus, *Wars of the Jews,* VII, 43-45). Macedonia and Achaia are also not listed, even though there were Jewish communities there, as the *Acts* itself attests (16:10 sqq.; 18:12 sqq.). The list, therefore, does not pretend to be exhaustive with regard to the Diaspora. Moreover this list of peoples is made in accordance with a general geographical pattern, spreading from the districts of central Asia to the Mediterranean basin, but taking into account the languages spoken by the different peoples.

The **Parthians** lived to the southeast, and the **Medes** to the south, of the Caspian Sea, and they both spoke the language of the Medio-Iranic group. To the south of the Medes, along the left bank of the Tigris, were the **Elamites,** who spoke neo-Elamitan into which, by that time, many Semitic elements had crept. The **inhabitants of Mesopotamia** were those of the region between the two rivers Tigris and Euphrates, and they spoke Semitic. In the peninsula of Asia Minor were **Cappadocia,** situated to the northeast; **Pontus,** extending to the north of Cappadocia along the coasts of the Pontus Euxinus (Black Sea); **Asia** (or, substantially, the Roman province of that name), situated to the west, along the Aegean Sea; **Phrygia,** in the center of the peninsula; and **Pamphylia,** to the south, along the coasts of the Mediterranean. In all these regions of Asia Minor, there were peoples who still spoke local languages (cf., e.g., Acts 14:11) little known to us, but the Greek language was superimposed everywhere by the spreading Hellenism. Even in North Africa, in **Egypt** and in **Libya about Cyrene,** the ordinary people spoke dialects derived from ancient languages (Coptic, Berber), but in more cultured circles and in international relations, Greek predominated here more than anywhere else, and in both regions there were strong Jewish settlements. The same can be said of the island of Crete (cf. Flavius Josephus, *Wars of the Jews,* II, 103, 108), where the Cretans had already been Hellenized for centuries. The term **Arabians** seems to refer to the inhabitants of the region Paul calls **Arabia** (Gal. 1:17), which must have designated the immense half-desert territories extending from the Jordan to Syria in the north, the Euphrates to the east, and the Red Sea to the south, and Semitic was mostly spoken here.

But the list, even judged by these generic criteria, has some obscurities. The most difficult is the unexpected mention of **Judea** between Mesopotamia and Cappadocia, since there was no geographical or linguistic

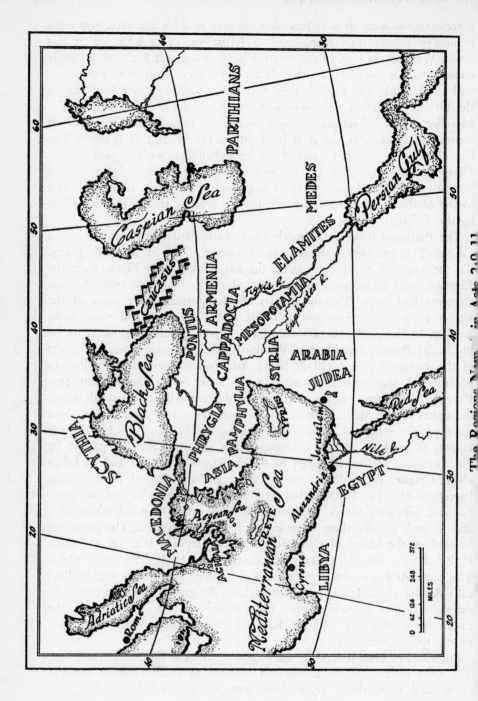

connection between these three. The present event, moreover, took place precisely at Jerusalem, the capital of Judea. The reading **Judea** is guaranteed by the codices; nevertheless, in the quotations of early writers, variants are found, such as *Jews* (Augustine), *Armenia* (Augustine, Tertullian), *Syria* (Jerome). Many modern scholars believe that it is a question either of a false addition made by some private reader, or else of a word wrongly transcribed by a copyist (it has been suggested that the reading should be corrected to *Ionia, Idumea, Yaudi, India,* etc.), but these are all abstract conjectures. In the same way the explanations of Judea itself are unconvincing (viz., that it took the place of the unnamed Syria, or to distinguish Judea from Galilee since they are both in Palestine, etc.). Strange, also, is the mention together of **Cretans** and **Arabians** who had no geographical or linguistic link and who seem to have been forgotten at first by the writer and added at the end of the list. More probably, they were so placed in a document which an unknown author had compiled, putting in writing the names which came haphazard to mind and of which Luke made use, reproducing it as it stood with the minimum of correction.

Visitors (ἐπιδημοῦντες) **from Rome:** who were they, and where did they reside? Were they Romans politically speaking, who resided at Jerusalem (cf. notes on vv. 5–6), or Jews by nationality who lived in Rome? In the former case, they were Romans of the Jewish religion who had moved to Jerusalem for a more or less prolonged stay; in the latter, they were Jewish inhabitants of Rome who had come to Jerusalem on the occasion of Pentecost. Rome, in fact, sheltered a large Jewish colony even before the year B.C. 63 when Pompey the Great, having taken Jerusalem, transferred many Jewish prisoners there and sold them as slaves (cf. Philo, *Legatio ad Caium,* 23; Flavius Josephus, *Wars of the Jews,* I, 157–158). The expression, **visitors from Rome,** can therefore be interpreted in both the senses mentioned above. Following on this explanation, we have the precisianism, **Jews also and** (τε καὶ) **proselytes.** Most probably this exact distinction refers only to those **from Rome** and not to the other races previously mentioned, so that those from Rome who were present at Pentecost, were all of the Jewish religion, but some were **Jews** by nationality, while others of different nationalities were, religiously speaking, **proselytes** of Judaism in the technical sense (see notes on vv. 5–6). — **We hear them speaking in our own languages.** How did this happen? Verse 4 shows that the charismatics spoke a language which was given to them, and chosen, not arbitrarily, but **according as the Spirit gave them to utter.** Considering, then, that the hearers spoke the many languages enumerated in verses 9–11, the scene can be reconstructed as follows: the crowd gathers at the noise it hears (v. 6), and comes into contact with the charismatics; standing there, they hear, individually or in groups, their own language spoken by one or other of the charismatics, and hearing,

2:12. And all were amazed and perplexed, saying to one another, "What does this mean?"

2:13. But others said in mockery, "They are full of sweet wine."

---

they understand perfectly, not only the actual words but also the general meaning, which is a glorification of the **wonderful works of God**. It is neither asserted nor denied, however, that some of the charismatics at a certain point changed from one language to another if **the Spirit gave them to utter** in this other language. In that case, a charismatic approached by Parthians or Medes spoke first in the Parthian or the Medean tongue, and later, if addressing a Phrygian or a Roman, in the Phrygian or Latin language. It should finally be noted that the narrative only presents the outward manifestation, without giving the inner explanation of the event, and without assigning its extraordinary character to the hearers who received the message, rather than to the speakers who gave it. It is clear, at any rate, according to the judgment both of the hearers and of the narrator relating the incident, that the speakers actually spoke the respective languages in which they were understood by their audience. To say that all the charismatics spoke one language only, and that this was understood by the audience as their own respective languages by virtue of a special charism received by each hearer, seems inadmissible.

2:12. All were . . . perplexed, διηποροῦντο: their hesitation referred, not to perceiving and recognizing the phenomenon, but to finding a satisfactory explanation of it. It shows that those present, even if they had attended pagan Corybantics, or mystagogic rites, had no knowledge of a phenomenon analogous to the one they were now experiencing. — **What does this mean?** Cf. 17:20.

2:13. Sweet wine: this cannot mean either new wine or unfermented must, because at the season of Pentecost (May–June) there were no such products from the fields, the vintage in Palestine being in August. It seems rather to allude to a special wine made with raisins and therefore sweeter and more alcoholic which more easily produced drunkenness. The mockers' words are obviously provoked by the fact that the charismatics spoke the various languages, not "calmly" but in an evident state of mental excitement, or rather of mystical exaltation. That suffices for the scoffers to judge them drunk. But who were these people, and why did they not also understand, like the others present, the languages spoken by the charismatics? The scholars who suppose that the hearers understood the languages in virtue of a charism peculiar to them (see the end of note on vv. 9–11) assert that the mockers did not understand because they had not received this charism; but much more simply and in keeping with the narrative, one may suppose that they did not understand because they had not encountered a charismatic who spoke a language known to them, and therefore they judged them to be drunk.

The question may be asked at this point whether this phenomenon of Pentecost was the same as that referred to by the *Acts* (10:46; 19:6) in the expression **to speak in tongues,** which St. Paul describes at length and is now designated by scholars as "glossolalia." Some commentators, both ancient and modern, assert that it was the same. It is, however, commonly held nowadays that it is a question of two different phenomena. The main reason for this opinion is that on the day of Pentecost, as appears from the evidence in the narrative of the *Acts* so far considered, the hearers perceived and understood immediately the charismatics who spoke the various languages; in the glossolalia, however, the charismatic who spoke in different tongues was not normally understood by the bystanders unless another charismatic, namely the "interpreter," intervened to explain the glossolalist's speech which was incomprehensible to the ordinary bystanders. For the sake of clarity it may be well to give the reader a brief statement on the glossolalia.[1]

The Glossolalia. Modern scholars now give the technical term "glossolaly" to that charism of primitive Christianity which in ancient times was called *the various kinds of tongues, tongues, to speak in tongues, to have tongues, to pray in a tongue.*

We cannot now say exactly what this charism was. It was certainly not the gift of making oneself understood at one and the same time to persons who spoke different languages as a means of accelerating and facilitating the diffusion of Christ's teaching among foreign peoples; nor was it — as several modern scholars have supposed — an outpouring of inarticulate and senseless sounds mixed at best with some conventional foreign phrase, an outburst by a person in a state of mental exaltation. On the contrary, the glossolalist spoke a real articulate and distinct language in which he expressed precise and ordered concepts, in other words, he made a real **discourse** (1 Cor. 14:9 and 19), such as a prayer to God, a psalm, a blessing, or an act of thanksgiving (*ibid.,* 14:14–17). In fact, these compositions could be exactly translated (*ibid.,* 14:5 and 27), which would obviously have been impossible in the case of inarticulate sounds with no meaning.[2]

It is also a fact that as a general rule the bystanders did not understand

---

[1] Taken from *Paul the Apostle,* pp. 175–179.

[2] The Greek grammarians used the term γλῶσσαι for archaic words either no longer in use or used with particular meanings. Quintilian is referring to these when he says: *Potest (puer) interpretationem linguae secretioris, quae Graeci* γλῶσσας *vocant, dum aliud agitur, ediscere, etc.* (*Instit. Orat.,* I, 1, 35). Some scholars have therefore considered that the charism of the γλῶσσαι consisted in impetuously pronouncing strings of words like these. The assumption is tendentious and contradicts what we know of glossolaly, chiefly by the fact that the glossolalist's discourse was organic and made sense.

the glossolalist when he spoke. Paul presupposes this more than once as, for
example, when he turns rhetorically to the glossolalist and asks: if you
speak a blessing under the inspiration of your charism, how can the uninstructed believer answer "Amen" to your blessing? **For he does not know
what thou sayest** (*ibid.,* 14:16). Paul even applies this to himself, he being
the glossolalist (*ibid.,* 14:18, Greek text) asking his faithful followers: **If
I come to you speaking in tongues, what shall I profit you?** (*ibid.,* 14:6).
He immediately explains why it would be of no advantage to them: he
would be like a flute or a harp producing confused sounds but not a
melody, or a war trumpet blowing disconnected blasts instead of the
conventional call to arms. **So likewise you — unless with the tongue you
utter intelligible speech — how shall it be known what is said? For you
will be speaking to the empty air** (*ibid.,* 14:9). Listening to a glossolalist,
therefore, was like listening to a foreigner speaking his unknown tongue,
the sounds of which could be distinguished without their meaning being
understood. **If, then, I do not know the meaning of the language, I shall
be to the one to whom I speak, a foreigner; and he who speaks, a
foreigner to me** (*ibid.,* 14:11). The reason is that **he who speaks in a tongue
does not speak to men but to God; for no one understands, though he is
speaking mysteries in the spirit** (*ibid.,* 14:2).

The glossolalist did not, in fact, speak in calmness of spirit but in an
ecstatic condition, an extraordinary psychic state, and addressed himself
to God rather than to his fellow men; nevertheless, all who heard him,
even without understanding him, felt to some degree the spiritual "con-
tagion" of his extraordinary state and, by reaction, his mystical exaltation.
Paul says that if an unbeliever or an uninstructed person should chance
to enter a Christian gathering where many glossolalists were talking at
once, he would think he had stumbled into an assembly of madmen
($\mu\alpha\acute{\iota}\nu\epsilon\sigma\theta\epsilon$: *ibid.,* 14:23).

Paul describes the glossolalist's psychic state when he says that when
the charismatic prays in a tongue, his spirit ($\pi\nu\epsilon\tilde{\upsilon}\mu\alpha$) prays, but his mind
($\nu o\tilde{\upsilon}s$) is unfruitful (*ibid.,* 14:14). This shows the glossolalist to be acting
under the impulse of the charism, that is, pervaded by the Spirit, whilst
his mind or his intellectual faculty remained purely passive and without
spiritual fruit, for when the charismatic impulse ceased, his mind retained
no clear or precise knowledge of it. Some general impression did, however, remain and when the phenomenon was over, the glossolalist's mind
remained suffused with a luminous mist which inspired delight. Paul
refers to this when he says that **he who speaks in a tongue edifies himself**
(*ibid.,* 14:4).

But the liturgical prayers of the early Christians were primarily collective and not individual. For this reason, Paul wishes the charism to benefit
not the glossolalist alone but the whole gathering, and so he prescribes that

another shall speak after him who has the charism of the interpretation of tongues, that is, the interpreter, and he is to translate into the common idiom the discourse made by the glossolalist (*ibid.*, 14:5 and 27). Where there is no interpreter, Paul commands the glossolalist to keep silence in public and speak to himself and to God (*ibid.*, 14:28) for his own personal edification.

The subtle spiritual intoxication which the glossolalist experienced in the exercise of his charism could and did lead to abuses. Sometimes, several of them spoke at once, and since those present caught some of their exaltation, the gathering (as Paul himself said) seemed quite mad; or worse still, the room resembled the court of one of the pagan temples where fortunetellers and soothsayers delivered the oracles of their deities, gesticulating and raving in a frenzy of psychic madness and communicating their excitement to the crowds watching them. Now this resemblance — however superficial — was not to be tolerated, for what harmony is there between Christ and Belial? . . . and what agreement has the temple of God with idols? (2 Cor. 6:15–16). To prevent these abuses, some believed that all public manifestations of glossolaly should be stopped. But Paul does not entirely endorse their view and says rather, Do not hinder the gift of speaking in tongues (1 Cor. 14:39); he goes even further affirming I should like you all to speak in tongues (*ibid.*, 14:5), provided that the other norms of order and decorum he prescribed were observed. These may be summed up in the following passage: When you come together, each of you has a psalm, has an instruction, has a revelation, has a tongue, has an interpretation: let all be done to the edification of all. If anyone speaks in a tongue let it be by two or at the most by three, and let them speak in turn (ἀνὰ μέρος); and let one only interpret (*ibid.*, 14:26–27).

What language did the glossolalists use? We do not know; nor do we know whether it was always the same or whether it differed from one occasion to the next. When Paul says: If I should speak with the tongues of men and of angels, etc. (*ibid.*, 13:1), he seems to be referring not only to a set of human languages but also to one of angelic tongues.[3] The quotation from Isaias (28:11 sqq.), whom Paul cites a little later, refers to a human though barbarous tongue, Assyrian, which he there compares to the language of the glossolalist (*ibid.*, 14:21). From both these instances, it seems legitimate to conclude that the "tongue" may have been at times a human language, although a very rare one, or one unknown to the

---

[3] According to the rabbinical legends there were over seventy human languages because that was the number of nations in the world (cf. Gen. 10); when the Law of Sinai was delivered, every word that came from the mouth of God divided into 70 languages (Talmud babli, *Shabbath*, 88b), and Moses also set forth the Law in 70 languages (*Genes. Rabba*, XLIX, 2). These 70 languages were taught to the Hebrew Joseph by the angel Gabriel, who knows them all, but the other angels know only Hebrew (*Sotah*, 33a; 36b). It is therefore necessary to pray in Hebrew if one wishes the angels to carry the prayer to the throne of God.

2:14. But Peter, standing up with the eleven, lifted up his voice and spoke out to them: "Men of Judea and all you who dwell in Jerusalem, let this be known to you, and give ear to my words.

2:15. "These men are not drunk, as you suppose, for it is only the third hour of the day.

2:16. "But this is what was spoken through the prophet Joel:

---

majority, for example the idiom of some still barbarous or far-distant region. In that case, if a native of such a region were present, he would understand the glossolalist even without an interpreter. On the other hand, if at times the language were some mysterious idiom known only by virtue of the charism, we have no basis for any conjecture at all.

2:14. Standing up: the stance of an orator; but here it is practically equivalent to "putting himself forward," i.e., toward the crowd. The discourse could have taken place in the Temple precincts or in the outer court (cf. v. 46). The eleven are the remaining Apostles including Matthias (cf. 1:26) who, with the speaker, formed the college of the "Twelve."

2:15. Third hour of the day: strictly speaking, it would be 9 a.m. since the period from dawn to sunset was divided into twelve hours (of varying length according to the seasons). Nevertheless, the same period was divided more loosely into four groups of hours, two groups before noon, and two after, in which case each group was determined from its first hour, so that the *first* hour comprised the first and second hours, namely until 9 a.m.; the *third* hour included the third, fourth, and fifth, i.e., until noon; the *sixth* hour, the sixth, seventh, and eighth, until 3 in the afternoon; the *ninth,* the ninth, tenth, eleventh, and twelfth (cf. the difference between Mk. 15:25 and Jn. 19:14). In the present instance, it is almost certain that the third hour should be taken in the strict sense. Some rabbis, in fact, advised against eating before this hour and much more so against drinking wine. Scripture itself contained passages interpreted in this sense (Isa. 5:11; Eccles. 10:16). From that, Peter argues that the charismatics are not drunk.

2:16-21. The passage from Joel is quoted from the Greek Septuagint which differed a little from the Hebrew. The historical background of the passage cited is concerned, first, with the great calamities that befell the people of Israel, and then with the material benefits in compensation for them, after which the prophet turns in mind to messianic times (in the last days), describing the effects by means of meteorological images. The first effect will be the outpouring of the divine Spirit upon all flesh (a Hebraism for *human race*). In applying this prophetic message to the spectacle of

2:17. "'And it shall come to pass in the last days, saith God,
that I shall pour forth of my Spirit upon all flesh,
and your sons and your daughters shall prophesy,
and your young men shall see visions,
and your old men shall dream dreams;

2:18. "'and upon my servants also and upon my handmaids
in those days shall I pour forth of my Spirit,
and they shall prophesy.

2:19. "'And I shall show wonders in the heaven above,
and signs upon the earth beneath,
blood and fire and vapour of smoke:

2:20. "'The sun shall be turned to darkness
and the moon into blood,
before the day of the Lord comes
great and manifest.

2:21. "'And it shall come to pass, that who so calls
upon the name of the Lord shall be saved.'

(Joel 3:1-5 [2:28-32])

2:22.   "Men of Israel, hear these words. Jesus of Nazareth was a

---

the charismatics, just now witnessed and admired by his hearers, Peter shows that the time of the Messias has come, beginning a new and final era which will end when **the day of the Lord comes great and manifest,** namely the parousia of the glorious Christ. — **They shall prophesy . . . see visions . . . dream dreams:** all these will be consequences of the outpouring of the Spirit. The twice-repeated expression **of** (ἀπὸ τοῦ) **my Spirit** should be noted in the partitive sense, referring to the effects of the effusion. The Hebrew text, on the other hand, both times has "I shall pour forth **my Spirit." — Wonders in the heavens . . . blood and fire . . . sun . . . moon:** meteorological images are found elsewhere in the New Testament in eschatological passages (Mt. 24:29; Mk. 13:24-25; Lk. 21:25-26; cf. Apoc. 9:2; 16:4). — **Whoso calls, etc.:** these words are quoted by Paul (Rom. 10:12-13), who applies them directly to Jesus although the Hebrew text has **Jahveh,** the personal name of the God of Israel, in place of **Lord.** But Peter does not apply this passage just yet to Jesus, because he must first counter the objection of verse 23, a most serious one for his Jewish listeners. The application, prepared in the verses that follow, is nevertheless made at the end of the discourse (v. 36).

2:22. **Men of Israel,** like **men of Galilee** in 1:11. — **Of Nazareth** is

man approved by God among you by miracles and wonders and signs, which God did through him in the midst of you, as you yourselves know.

2:23. "Him, when delivered by the settled purpose and foreknowledge of God, you have crucified and slain by the hands of wicked men.

---

in Greek *Nazareos* (Ναζωραῖος), a form corresponding to *Nazarene* (Ναζαρηνός). Luke, in the *Acts,* always uses the first form, and in his Gospel uses both forms. Both are derivations of the name of the village where Jesus grew up (cf. **Jesus of Nazareth** in 10:38); the difference between the two forms may depend on the different pronunciations of the name of the village which in Hebrew was *Nasrath,* while the Galileans who had a special pronunciation (cf. note on v. 7) pronounced it *Nasorath.* In 24:5, the followers of Jesus are those **of the Nazarene sect** (for the name "Christians," see note on 11:26). The existence of a sect of *Nazarenes* before the time of Jesus is a hypothesis of some modern scholars unsupported by serious documentary proofs. — **Approved:** the Greek text has ἀποδεδειγμένον, almost "presented with guarantees." The idea is that the messianic quality of Jesus has been **approved,** so that it ought to be accepted; and the proof provided by God is **the miracles and wonders and signs, which God did through him;** that is, they are the motives of credibility. The Apostle demands such motives of credibility (Jn. 20:25), and Paul in his turn also offered them to the faithful of Corinth (1 Cor. 15:5–12); but even before them, Jesus himself had appealed to his works as proofs of the mission given him by the Father (Jn. 5:36; 10:25).

2:23. Peter's reasoning aims at demonstrating that Jesus is the Messias foretold by the prophets to the people of Israel, but the tremendous obstacle to his hearers' acceptance of such a thesis was the fact of the sufferings and ignominious death of this Messias. Contemporary Judaism awaited a triumphant political Messias (see note on 1:6), who would never have undergone sufferings and humiliation, and this expectation was shared by the Apostles and disciples of Jesus, not only before his death (cf. Mt. 17:22–23; 20:20 sqq.; Lk. 17:25; 18:32–34), but even after his Resurrection (cf. Lk. 24:21; Acts 1:6). The speaker himself, namely Peter, felt it his duty to protest to Jesus when the Master foretold his own sufferings and death, after having approved Peter's words proclaiming him **Messias and Son of the living God.** In reply, Jesus had rebuffed him, calling him **Satan** (Mt. 16:21–23). This remark had had a good effect because Peter now defends the thesis in exact contrast to the one he had then maintained against Jesus. — **Delivered,** ἔκδοτον: does not allude

2:24. "Whom God hath raised up, loosening the pangs of death, seeing that it was not possible that he should be held fast by it.

2:25. "For David says with reference to him:
'I saw the Lord before me always,
because he is at my right hand, lest I be moved.

---

directly to the "delivery" or "betrayal" of Jesus brought about by Judas, but considers the fact in the light of the settled purpose (ὡρισμένῃ βουλῇ) and foreknowledge of God (cf. 4:28). In fact, in consequence of the divine economy of man's salvation, it so happened that God did not spare his own Son, but delivered him (παρέδωκεν) for us (Rom. 8:32). Given this divine disposition, without which nobody could have acted against Christ (cf. Jn. 10:18; 19:11), the Jews killed Christ by crucifying him. This statement could not have been pleasant for the listeners to this discourse, but Peter softens it a little by recalling that they slew Jesus by the hands of wicked men. The crucifixion was in fact carried out by the Roman soldiers, but it was at the behest of the Jews, Pilate's reluctance notwithstanding.

2:24. Whom (in the accusative), the Messias, killed by his enemies, God hath raised up. The humiliation of the Messias was according to the will of the Father (Phil. 2:8–9) and the condition of his entry into glory (Mt. 16:21; Mk. 8:31; Lk. 24:26; Acts 17:3). — The pangs of death: for pangs, the Greek has ὠδῖνας, which ordinarily signifies pains, especially of childbirth. But the whole phrase is taken from Psalm 18 (Vulgate, 17):5, which in the Hebrew has cords of death, while the Greek of the Septuagint translates it as the pangs of death. This translation depends on the exchange between the Hebrew words ḥēbel = "pang," and ḥebel = "rope" or "cord." It is certain, however, that Peter, speaking to the Jews in Aramaic, could not have quoted the defective Greek translation but the original Hebrew; therefore the introduction of the Greek reading in place of the Hebrew must be attributed to whoever compiled the résumé of the discourse (see note on 1:16), rather than to Luke who simply copied that résumé. Finally, it should be noted that, instead of pangs of death, the Western Recension (cf. the Vulgate) has sorrows of hell; this is the Septuagint reading of the next verse (6, not 5) of the Psalm quoted. For hell, see the note which follows. — The reason why it was not possible that Christ should become the prey of death, namely should be held fast by it, is contained in the passage which follows.

2:25-28. This is a quotation from Psalm 16 (Vulgate, 15). The term David could mean, in general, all the psalms (cf. 2 Mach. 2:13; Hebr. 4:7), but here it undoubtedly refers to the person of David, because the

2:26. " 'This is why my heart has made merry,
and my tongue has rejoiced,
moreover my flesh also will rest in hope:

2:27. " 'because thou wilt not abandon my soul to hell,
neither wilt thou let thy Holy One see corruption;

2:28. " 'Thou hast made known to me the ways of life,
Thou wilt make me full with mirth with thy countenance.'

(Ps. 16 [15]:8–11)

2:29. "Brethren, let me say to you freely of the patriarch David, that he both died and was buried, and his tomb is with us to this day.

2:30. "Being therefore a prophet and knowing that God had sworn to him with an oath that [a descendant] of the fruit of his loins should sit upon his throne,

2:31. "he, foreseeing it, spoke of the resurrection of Christ [by saying] that neither was he abandoned to hell nor did his flesh see corruption.

---

argument which Peter uses later presupposes David to be the author of this psalm. In the passage quoted, according to the Greek of the Septuagint, the psalmist expresses his belief that the Lord will not abandon his soul in **Hades** (which for the Greeks was the dwelling place of the dead, just as **Sheol** was for the Hebrews) and will not permit him to see **corruption**. It should be noted that the original Hebrew, instead of *in* (*Hades*), reads **to** (**Sheol**), using the preposition *to* which normally indicates the direction, the goal to be reached, or even already arrived at. Moreover, **corruption** (διαφθορά) stands in place of the Hebrew *shahath,* which can mean "corruption," "putrefaction" (root, *ŠḤT*), but can also mean "pit," "grave" (root, *ŠVḤ*).— In opposition to **Hades** and **corruption** stand **the ways of life** and **the countenance** (presence) of the Lord, which fill the Psalmist **with mirth.**

2:29–31. On the basis of the text so far quoted, Peter conducts an argument and establishes a conclusion in a similar manner to Paul in 13:35 sqq.— The patriarch David, he says, being . . . a prophet, could not foretell things which would not come about. Now he . . . died and his tomb is with us to this day (cf. Flavius Josephus, *Antiquities of the Jews,* XVI, 179 sqq.), so that David saw corruption (13:36); therefore, whatever he prophesied in the text quoted cannot refer to David himself, but to that descendant of his who should sit upon his throne, in other words to Christ, who neither was abandoned to hell nor did his flesh see corrup-

2:32. "This Jesus God has raised [him] up, whereof all we are witnesses.

2:33. "Having therefore been lifted up by the right hand of God, and having received from the Father the promise of the Holy Spirit, he has poured forth this Spirit which you both see and hear.

2:34. "For David did not ascend into the heavens, yet he says himself: 'The Lord said to my Lord: sit thou at my right hand

2:35. " 'until I make thy enemies thy footstool.'

(Ps. 110 [109]:1)

---

tion. — Brethren: see the note on 1:11; 2:22. — God had sworn to him with an oath, etc.: refers to the prophecies foretelling that the Messias would be descended from the stock of David, such as 2 Sam. 7:12 sqq.; Ps. 89 (88):4 sqq.; 132 (131):11; etc.

2:32. Whereof, referring to raised up; but it can also be translated of whom, referring to Jesus. The first translation seems the more preferable since Peter here wishes to throw into relief the resurrection of Christ (v. 31). Cf. also note on 3:15.

2:33. Jesus was lifted up by (not to; cf. 5:31) the right hand of God: it is the power of God that makes Christ rise from the dead (3:15; Rom. 4:24) and which completes the work by making him ascend to heaven (1:9). — Jesus, having received, even before the Resurrection and Ascension, the promise of the Holy Spirit, about which he had already spoken in 1:4–5. — He has poured forth, i.e., Jesus, while in verse 17 the one who pours forth is God. This, in the neuter, can refer to the Holy Spirit, but it is more probably an independent neuter referring to the scene that the hearers had witnessed, so that it can be translated he has made this effusion which you both see, etc.; but it is, of course, always in reference to the effusion of the Holy Spirit.

2:34–35. The psalm cited was attributed by Hebrew tradition to David and was considered to be messianic. Jesus had already appealed to it, discussing with the Pharisees the dignity of the Messias and comparing it with that of his forebear, David (Mt. 22:41–46 and parallel passages). Jesus had shown that if the Messias had been merely a carnal descendant of David, the latter would not have been able to call him by the honorific title of Lord (The Lord said, namely the God Jahveh, to my Lord, namely the Messias). Here Peter puts forward an argument similar both to that used by Jesus and to the one already advanced in verses 29–31; in other words, he points out that David did not ascend into the heavens because he is dead and buried (v. 29), but the Messias (my Lord) was told by

2:36. "Therefore, let all the house of Israel know most assuredly that God has made both Lord and Christ, this Jesus whom you crucified."

God to sit . . . at my right hand; since, therefore, this is fulfilled, not in David, but in Jesus, Jesus is the Messias.

2:36. This verse represents the conclusion toward which the whole of Peter's discourse had gradually led (see the end of the note to vv. 16–21), namely that this Jesus, crucified by the Jews, is both Lord and Christ. The name Christ is the Greek rendering of the Hebrew "Messias," and the psalm quoted gives him precisely this name, Lord, in treating of the Messias. The name "Lord," κύριος, dominus, was used in the Roman Empire to designate both the emperor (cf. 25:26) and other persons worthy of special deference (9:5; 11:8; Mt. 25:11; 27:63; Jn. 4:11; 12:21; etc.). In Eastern courts also the equivalent title (Mar, Maran, "Lord," "our Lord") referred to the ruler, and to other notable persons outside court circles. With the extension of emperor worship, the appellative, which had already been joined to the names of Egyptian and Eastern divinities, took on a special and sacred character among the emperor's subjects; but it was an external accident that never supplanted the original profane significance of the term, either in frequency of use or in intrinsic worth. In fact, later, at the time of Seneca (Epist. 3), it was correct to call a man "Lord" if his name were not known. Among the early Christians, however, the name as applied to Christ was used in the strictly religious sense, because it constituted the essence of the Christian belief. The Christian professed himself as such by confessing that Jesus (is) Lord (Rom. 10:9; 1 Cor. 8:5–6; 12:3; Phil. 2:11). The name "Lord Christ" must have arisen among the Christian communities converted from Judaism rather than from paganism. In fact, the religious character which the appellative "Lord" had assumed among the emperor's subjects could not but rouse revulsion among the ex-pagan Christians because of its idolatrous origin. The Christians converted from Judaism were, on the contrary, accustomed to read in Scripture that the God Jahveh was the Lord (Hebrew, adon) par excellence, yea the Lord of Lords (Deut. 10:17; cf. Apoc. 19:16), and when they read Scripture, they used, out of reverence, to substitute the title "Lord" for the personal name "Jahveh." Not only, moreover, was the Messias explicitly called Lord in the above-quoted psalm, but he was himself of a divine nature (cf. Phil. 2:6), and therefore worthy of the names which Scripture used for God, above all that of "Lord." We very often find, therefore, that what the Hebrew Scriptures had attributed to God is instead attributed to the Lord Christ. Compare he has poured

2:37. Now on hearing this they were pierced to the heart and said to Peter and the rest of the apostles, "Brethren, what shall we do?"

2:38. But Peter said to them, "Repent and be baptized every one of you in the name of Jesus Christ for the forgiveness of your sins; and you will receive the gift of the Holy Spirit.

---

forth (Jesus) in verse 33 with **I shall pour forth** (I, God) in verse 17. The case of Rom. 10:12–13 is typical among other similar cases, as already noted at the end of the commentary on verses 16–21.

2:37. Brethren: cf. 1:11; 2:22, 29. The expression here has especial value as coming from those who were **pierced to the heart** and as addressed to those producing this compunction. — The Western Recension gives this verse as follows: **All those then who had come together and heard, were pierced to the heart and some of them said to Peter and the apostles: "Brethren, what therefore shall we do? Tell us."** It is typical of this version to add words but not ideas. The only notable omission is **the rest of** before **the apostles.**

2:38. Said is omitted in many codices. — **Repent,** μετανοήσατε: etymologically (μετα-νοέω), "change of mind," namely "amend yourselves." The fundamental theme of the preaching both of John the Baptist and of Jesus had been precisely that "change of mind" (μετάνοια), which was afterward usually translated by "penance" (cf. Mk. 1:4, 15 and parallel passages). John had also preached a **baptism of penance for the forgiveness of sins** (*ibid.,* 1:4), but the baptism of which Peter speaks here is baptism **in the name of** (ἐπὶ τῷ ὀνόματι) **Jesus Christ,** and its result is to be the reception of **the gift of the Holy Spirit.** For the original meaning of **baptize,** see 1:5. The expression "to baptize in the name of Jesus Christ" recurs elsewhere with certain variations: **in the name** (εἰς τὸ ὄνομα) **of the Lord Jesus** (8:16; 19:5); **in the** (ἐν τῷ) **name of Jesus Christ** (10:48); and including the ironic use made by Paul, **were you baptised in the** (εἰς τὸ) **name of Paul?** (1 Cor. 1:13; cf. 15.) Was baptism administered with these words, or was it not rather **in the** (εἰς τὸ) **name of the Father and of the Son and of the Holy Ghost,** as Jesus himself had commanded (Mt. 28:19)? Notwithstanding the contrary opinion of some medieval theologians and some modern critics, it cannot reasonably be doubted that the liturgical form used in the administration of baptism was that which mentioned the Trinity in conformity with the prescription of Jesus. The other expression, **in the name of Jesus** (with its variants), was an exterior indication of baptism only inasmuch as it recorded the juridico-spiritual consequences of the rite and distinguished it from similar ceremonies. There was, in fact, in contemporary Judaism, a baptism administered to pros-

2:39. "For to you is the promise and to your children and to all who are far off, even to all whom the Lord our God calls."

2:40. And with very many other words he bore witness and exhorted them saying: "Save yourselves from this perverse generation."

---

elytes by which they were incorporated into Judaism, just as there was the baptism of John the Baptist which had been given until now (cf. 19:3). But these other baptisms did not carry with them the juridico-spiritual consequences of Christian baptism, i.e., incorporation into Christ (cf. Rom. 6:3 sqq.) and no longer into Moses, or John the Baptist; and the faithful **baptized in Christ Jesus** (*ibid.*) entered into a mystical union with him and therefore into his spiritual possession. Just as certain prize animals, bred with greater care, receive a stamp bearing their owner's name, so Christian baptism spiritually imprints the **name** of the Lord Jesus on the faithful, and having thus becomes his property, they are **sealed** with the Holy Spirit (Eph. 1:13; 4:30). This is the juridico-spiritual meaning of the expression to baptize **in the name of Jesus Christ** which did not, therefore, arise from the form used in the liturgy of baptism. A clear confirmation of this is found in the *Didache,* written about twenty years after the *Acts.* The correct liturgical form of baptism is twice given there with great precision: **baptise in the name of the Father and of the Son and of the Holy Ghost** (VII, 1 and 3); whereas another expression is used a little later to show the juridico-spiritual effects of baptism: "let no one eat or drink of your Eucharist if not **baptised in** (εἰς) **the name of the Lord**" (IX, 5). — **The gift of the Holy Spirit** was intimately connected with baptism **in the name of Jesus Christ,** as with that of John the Baptist, as already appears from the episode in 19:1-7. Paul also frequently reminds his neophytes of the manifestations of the Spirit proper to the Christian (1 Thess. 1:5; 1 Cor. 1:5-7; 2:4; 2 Cor. 12:12; Gal. 3:2; 4:6; Rom. 8:9; 15:19; etc.).

2:39. The **promise** of the Holy Spirit, already quoted from Joel (v. 17 sqq.), applies equally to the Jews (**you . . . your children**) and to the Gentiles, who are spiritually **far off.** It applies to the Jews in the first place (cf. Rom. 1:16; 2:9-10) since they were entrusted with the **words of God** (*ibid.,* 3:2) as the recipients of all the prerogatives of the Old Testament (*ibid.,* 9:4-5) and to them the direct and immediate mission of Jesus himself was directed (Mt. 15:24); but immediately after the Jews come the Gentiles because after the redemption wrought by Christ, **there is neither Jew nor Greek, circumcision nor uncircumcision, Barbarian nor Scythian, bond nor free, but Christ is all and in all** (Col. 3:11; cf. Gal. 3:28).

2:40. This **perverse generation** is that of the contemporary Jews (cf.

2:41. Now they who accepted his word were baptized and there were added that day [to the believers] about three thousand souls.

2:42. And they continued steadfastly in the teaching of the apostles, in the fellowship, in the breaking of bread and in prayers.

Lk. 11:29, 32) who had mostly rejected Christ and his teaching (cf. Rom. 9:1 sqq.); but despite the perverse majority, each individual could rightly follow Christ, and to these who were well disposed, Peter addresses his invitation to **Save yourselves . . . !**

2:41. Believers is implied in the text, as in verse 47, but it appears explicitly in verse 44. — **That day** refers strictly to **there were added,** but also, secondarily, to **were baptised,** because the two verbs are in fact linked together. On the other hand, it is clear that the baptism of three thousand people was not done all at one time, especially if performed by immersion and in a city like Jerusalem which has always lacked water. It may, therefore, be that the phrase, in **that day,** refers directly to the three thousand who had been converted by Peter's discourse and who were then gradually baptized on that and the following days. No description is given of any particular preparatory instructions for these new catechumens, since the all-important intention to be baptized **in the name of Jesus Christ** sufficed (v. 38). Neither is there mention of such preparation in similar cases, as, for instance, the baptism of the Ethiopian (8:36-38), of Paul (9:18-19), and the followers of John the Baptist at Ephesus (19:3-6).

2:42. Teaching of the apostles: the catechetical instructions given by the Apostles to complete the spiritual formation of the three thousand converts. A summary of the method of such instructions is given by Paul (1 Cor. 15:3-8), and includes the redemptive death of Christ, his burial and resurrection, and the various apparitions of the risen Christ. But, according to the scheme already noted in 1:21-22 (cf. 10:37-41), a résumé of Christ's life was a necessary corollary to this final phase of his activity. And this is exactly what we find later in the three Synoptic Gospels. — **Fellowship,** κοινωνία: should be understood in a general sense, whether of spiritual things (Phil. 2:1-4), or of material necessities (Rom. 15:26-27), in a word, the complete harmony that exists in any well-ordered family. — **The breaking of bread,** ἡ κλάσις τοῦ ἄρτου, with the article before each substantive. The context here shows that it is dealing not with a common action but with one of special religious value, the more so as it immediately follows the term **fellowship.** The expression is made clearer by the passage from Luke's master, Paul, in which similar expressions are used: **the cup of blessing that we bless, is it not the sharing of the blood of Christ? And the bread that we break, is it not the partaking of the body of the Lord?**

2:43. And fear came upon every soul: and many wonders also and signs were wrought by means of the apostles. . . .

2:44. And all who believed were together and held all things in common,

2:45. and would sell their possessions and goods and distribute them among all according as anyone had need.

Because (there is) one bread, we are one body (though many): all, in fact, partake of the one bread (1 Cor. 10:16–17). Paul here undoubtedly refers to the Eucharist, which he speaks of later on; but for the purpose of the present argument, it is important to note how the **fellowship** of the Christians is intimately connected with sharing the **body** and **blood of Christ.** Luke here presupposes the same historical background. The phrase **to break (the) bread** appears elsewhere with or without the article **the,** but not always with the sacramental sense referred to here. Sometimes the context clearly shows it to signify a purely secular meal, as in 27:35; on other occasions, the meaning is doubtful (cf. note on v. 46).

The **prayers,** also mentioned here on the occasion of the **breaking of bread,** are precisely those that accompanied the Eucharistic rite, as stated later in the *Didache,* IX–X, though this does not entirely exclude a secondary reference to the official **prayers of Judaism,** in which the Christians of Jerusalem still participated, since the formal break between Christianity and Judaism had not yet been effected. As the typically Christian rites, such as the Eucharist, acquired greater importance in the spiritual life of the community, less importance was given to the ritualistic prescriptions of Judaism. There is a second-century fresco, preserved in Rome in the catacombs of St. Priscilla, which depicts the scene of the **breaking of the bread** (*fractio panis*) as a fundamental Christian rite. Finally it should be remembered that the Western Recension (cf. Vulgate) links the expression **the breaking of bread** to the preceding one of **fellowship,** to read: **in the communication of the breaking of bread.** The Syriac Peshitta, without a pause, reads: "breaking **of the Eucharist.**"

2:43. Fear: like the Hebrew *jir'āh,* in the religious sense, namely fear of God, comprising reverence, admiration, and submission. The reason for this fear is immediately apparent from what follows, i.e., that **many wonders also and signs were wrought,** etc.; cf. 5:11–12.

2:44–45. The **fellowship** mentioned in verse 42 is here shown in practice. In the first place, the believers **were together,** not entirely in the strict local sense, though this was to some extent the case, but they were

2:46. And continuing daily with one accord in the temple, and breaking bread at home, they took their food with gladness and simplicity of heart.

---

especially morally united, i.e., they were always morally in agreement, and had frequent meetings. It would have been difficult in the Jerusalem of that time to accommodate more than three thousand faithful souls in one building like an enormous religious house. Second, and in consequence, the believers **held all things in common:** here the object in view was not the possession but the use of such goods as were used indifferently both by those who had owned them and those who had not. The question of possession is considered in the words which follow: **all . . . would sell . . . and distribute, etc.** The subject of these verbs is impersonal, but it certainly is not **all who believed** at the beginning of the verse, because in actual fact among them there were those who had not sold their possessions — at least not all of them — and they continued to own houses (12:12; 21:16); even Peter admitted the complete lawfulness of so doing (5:4). It was, therefore, a fact that very many fervent Christians of Jerusalem sold their own goods to meet the material needs which gradually arose among their brethren and **all . . . would . . . distribute them among all according as anyone had need.** Nevertheless they did this freely and without any legal or moral obligation, and not all of them gave up their private property in its entirety. This fervor was aroused, moreover, by exclusively religious and Christian motives, chiefly by the example and words of Jesus himself who, in regard to worldly possessions, had led a life in common with his disciples (Jn. 12:6; cf. Lk. 8:3), and had on several occasions inveighed against riches, and had exhorted his disciples, saying: **Sell what you have and give alms** (Lk. 12:33) so as to receive a reward in heaven. Another motive for the common life was Christian charity, which later moves Paul to write long exhortations to collect funds with which to help the famine-stricken Christians of Jerusalem (2 Cor. 8–9; cf. 1 Cor. 16:1–4; Rom. 15:25–31). This common sharing of goods would never, therefore, have come about without such religious motives, and these among others are precisely the chief motives differentiating the *common life* of the early Christians from the *communism* of other times and peoples. The theme of this *common life* occurs again later (4:32 sqq.; 5:1 sqq.), and new aspects of it will be considered.

2:46. Continuing daily . . . in the temple, not only because the Jewish temple, especially the "court of the Gentiles," was the great meeting place in Jerusalem, but particularly for religious reasons (see note on v. 42). —

Breaking bread: without the article "the" (see v. 42). The omission of the article does not here allow the definite conclusion that it is a question of a nonreligious meal and not the Eucharistic rite, because the article is missing in 20:7, where the Eucharistic rite is certainly intended (cf. 20:11, with the article). The recent mention of the Eucharistic rite invites us to believe that, a few lines further on, the same thing is being dealt with, but the word **food** (τροφῆς) which follows seems rather to refer to ordinary food taken to sustain life. The interpretation is therefore uncertain. — **At home,** κατ' οἶκον: in their own homes, which could be translated *house to house,* as the context requires in 5:42. Paul speaks three times (1 Cor. 16:19; Col. 4:15; Philemon 2) of a **church** (or **gathering**) **in a house** (κατ' οἶκον) of three Christians, which indicates that religious meetings were held in private houses as well as elsewhere. — **They took their food,** i.e., at an ordinary meal. If, however, the preceding **breaking bread** is interpreted as meaning the Eucharist, this meal can be considered as an addition to the Eucharistic rite intended to help the more needy. With this interpretation arises the question of the "agape," or love-feast, which is discussed in connection with the passage from Paul in 1 Cor. 11:20–21. While admitting that when Paul wrote that epistle (at the beginning of the year 56), the custom existed of holding a fraternal banquet or "agape" different from the Eucharistic rite, though connected with it, can it be concluded that the same practice was in use twenty-five years earlier, in other words at the time described here? Possibly, but the conclusion cannot be considered certain on historical grounds. — With **gladness and simplicity of heart:** habitual concepts of Paul, especially the latter (Phil. 4:4; 1 Thess. 5:16; etc.; Eph. 6:5; Col. 3:22; 2 Cor. 8:2; 9:11 and 13; 11:3; etc.). Luke, the disciple, with these expressions wishes, perhaps, to reply to the calumnies that disgraceful orgies habitually took place at Christian gatherings. Such calumnies gradually spread as time went on and included the various crimes recorded by Tertullian (*Apologet.,* 7, 1; 8, 2 sqq.; *Ad nation.,* I, 11 sqq.), Minutius Felix (*Octavius,* LX, 1 sqq.), Justin (*Apolog.,* I, 26; *Apolog.,* II, 12; *Dialog. cum Tryph.,* 10, cf. 108). In a document of A.D. 177, reported by Eusebius (*Hist. eccl.,* V, 1, 14), the origin of these slanders, at least as regards Gaul, is attributed to pagan slaves under torture. Other Christian writers likewise impute them to pagans, but Origen (*Contra Celsum,* VI, 27; cf. Justin, *Dialog. cum. Tryph.,* 108) attributes them to Jews, adding that the pagans no longer believe these stories. It is improbable that such calumnies had already been spread in Jerusalem at the time to which Luke here refers, as Christianity was much too recent and not yet separated from Judaism. But more than thirty years later, when he was writing the *Acts,* these slanders might well have been spread abroad, thereby offering him an opportunity for this veiled reference.

2:47. Praising God and being in favor with all the people. And the Lord added [to the believers] those who were being saved day by day, [joining them] together.

3:1. Now Peter and John were going up into the temple about the ninth [hour] of prayer.

3:2. And a certain man who had been lame from his mother's womb, was being carried by, whom they laid daily at the gate of the temple called the "Beautiful," that he might ask alms of those going into the temple.

3:3. And he, seeing Peter and John about to go into the temple, asked for an alms.

2:47. **Added:** re-echoes the words, **there were added,** of verse 41.

3:1 sqq. The account which begins here of the cure of the lame beggar has various resemblances to that of the man born blind cured by Jesus (Jn. 9:1 sqq.). Both narratives are vivid and immediate, and both conclude with the intervention of the Jewish leaders who cannot deny the respective miracles but who react against them. — **Peter and John,** the evangelist: two of the three specially favored disciples of Jesus (the third was John's brother, James the Greater, whose death is recorded in 12:2). Peter and John also appear together elsewhere (8:14; Lk. 22:8; cf. Gal. 2:9). — **Hour of prayer,** i.e., the official prayer of Judaism in which the Christians still participated (see note on 2:42). (**Hour) ninth,** viz., three in the afternoon (see note on 2:15). Two other official times for prayer were at sunrise (the morning sacrifice) and at sunset (the evening sacrifice).

3:2. **Gate . . . "Beautiful,"** ὡραία: this name for a gate of the Temple does not appear in any other document. Flavius Josephus (*Wars of the Jews,* V, 198–204), describing the interior of the temple, speaks of ten gates, of which *nine were completely covered with gold and silver, as were the doorposts and the architraves; one, that outside the sanctuary, was of Corinthian bronze and was far more valuable than those of gold and silver.* He also speaks of a *bronze gate* in II, 411 and in VI, 293 (this last passage corresponds to the *delubri fores* of Tacitus, *Annal.,* V, 13) and it seems to be the one the rabbis called the "gate of Nicanor." It is possible that it is the gate . . . **"Beautiful"** mentioned here. It faced east and linked the "court of the Gentiles" with the "court of the women," and across this with the "court of the Israelites." Being a busy thoroughfare, it was a most opportune place to **ask alms.**

3:4. But Peter, gazing upon him with John, said, "Look at us."

3:5. And he looked at them earnestly, expecting to receive something from them.

3:6. But Peter said: "Silver and gold I have none; but what I have, that I give thee. In the name of Jesus Christ of Nazareth, walk!"

3:7. And taking him by the right hand, he raised him up. Immediately his feet and ankles became strong,

3:8. and leaping up he stood and began to walk and he entered with them into the temple, walking and leaping and praising God.

3:9. And all the people saw him walking and praising God;

3:10. and they recognized him as the man who used to sit for alms at the Beautiful gate of the temple, and they were filled with awe and amazement at what had happened to him.

3:11. Now as he held Peter and John [by the hand], all the people ran to them in the portico called Solomon's, [and they were all] greatly wondering.

3:5-6. He looked at them earnestly, ἐπεῖχεν: used here for the word *to put upon* (someone) one's eyes or attention. — Peter had no gold or silver on him, not so much because of the *community* of goods noted in 2:42 and 44-45, as in obedience to Christ's precept whereby he was provided with purses that do not grow old, with a treasure unfailing in heaven (Lk. 12:33). He himself later curses one who had endeavored to purchase the gift of God with money (Acts 8:20). Drawing on this purse which does not grow old and which contains the gift of God, he says to the lame man what I have, that I give thee, and immediately he heals him. The cure is actually ordered in the (ἐν τῷ) name of Jesus Christ: see the note on 2:38. — Of Nazareth: the Greek has Nazareo: see note on 2:22.

3:7-8. A most vivid description (leaping up . . . he entered . . . walking and leaping and praising . . .) descriptive of the state of mind of the cured man. The description uses medical terminology (σφυδρά, "ankles," instead of the more usual σφυρά is very rare in Greek), which is not surprising in Luke the physician.

3:9-11. Here also, as in the account of the man born blind (see note on v. 1), the crowd recognized the reality of the miracle because the man who had been cured was very well known. — Portico . . . Solomon's, that which ran along the east side of the temple, from north to south along the valley of Cedron; it was a chosen place for public gatherings (5:12; Jn. 10:23). It was called after Solomon by ancient records, though

3:12. But when Peter saw it he made answer to the people: "Men of Israel, why do you marvel at this or why do you stare at us as though by our [own] power or holiness we had made this man walk.

3:13. "The God of Abraham and of Isaac and of Jacob, the God of our fathers, has glorified his servant Jesus whom you indeed delivered up and disowned before the face of Pilate when he had decided to release him.

---

the portico had actually been built entirely by Herod the Great about forty years earlier. Peter, coming out of the **Beautiful gate** which faced east, directed his steps to this public meeting place situated to the east; it was, therefore, already in his mind to give the assembled crowd the discourse which follows.

3:12. Peter has not worked the miracle by his **own power or holiness,** but **in the name of Jesus Christ;** see note on verse 6.—Several ancient documents (cf. Vulgate) have **power** instead of **holiness.**

3:13. The God of Abraham . . . Jacob: a solemn title, used earlier by Moses in the apparitions of God (Exod. 3:6; 4:5). This title with its association could not but please Peter's *Israelite* listeners (v. 12), while it allowed him to link up with fundamental facts of the Old Testament.— **His servant Jesus:** the term **servant,** παῖδα (Vulgate, **son**), had a messianic sense, having been applied to the Messias, to the "servant of Jahveh" (in Isa. 42:1; 43:10; 49:3 and 6; 52:13; etc.). It was also applied to Jesus in early Christian literature (*Didache,* IX, 2–3; X, 2; Clement of Rome, *Corinth.,* LIX, 2; Barnabas, VI, 1). It is to be found again in verse 26; 4:27 and 30.—The observation that Pilate **had decided to release** Jesus is important since it corresponds to the Gospel accounts (Jn. 19:4; 6:12), although, later, Pilate's passive complicity will be pointed out (Acts 4:27; 13:28). It should be noted, however, as the narrative of the *Acts* proceeds, how special care seems to have been taken to put the Roman authorities in a good light (cf. 5:30), especially the various judges encountered by Paul on his journeys (13:6 sqq.; 16:35 sqq.; 18:12 sqq.; 19:31 sqq.; 23:23 sqq.; 24:22 sqq.; 25:13 sqq.; 27:3 sqq.; 28:7, 16, 31), so that this remark here regarding Pilate might well seem to be the first instance of it. All this confirms the fact that when the *Acts* were written, the hope was cherished that grave differences between the Roman Empire and Christianity would not arise, and that the magistrates' benevolent attitude to Paul would continue. The *Acts* would, therefore, have been written before A.D. 64 when Nero's persecution, which began immediately after the burning of Rome, so tragically dashed that rosy hope.

3:14. "But you disowned the Holy and Just One, and asked that a murderer should be granted to you.

3:15. "But the author of life you killed, whom God has raised up from the dead; whereof we are witnesses.

3:16. "By the faith in his name, this man whom you behold and recognize, his name has made strong [in limb]; and the faith through him has given him this perfect health before you all.

3:14. The Holy and Just One: by an antonomasia. The Christians were called saints (9:13 and 32), especially in Paul's letters (Rom. 1:7; 1 Cor. 1:2; etc.), and therefore Christ, their head, is antonomastically the Holy . . . One (cf. Jn. 6:69, Greek text). Likewise, the Just One: cf. 7:52; 22:14.— Murderer: that is, Barabbas.

3:15. In contradistinction to Barabbas the murderer, Jesus is here called the author (ἀρχηγός) of life, as elsewhere, the author of salvation (Hebr. 2:10) and the author of faith (ibid., 12:2). Which life is meant? The opposition to the preceding murderer would suggest physical life, and even this interpretation has a sufficient basis in the Gospels. Christ had, in fact, on the Sabbath, healed the physical life of the man born blind, and justified himself to the Jews for this violation of the Sabbath by affirming: My Father works even until now and I work; and the Jews rightly interpreted this assertion to mean that Jesus called God his Father, making himself equal to God (Jn. 5:17-18). But over and above the reference to physical life, Peter's words can also refer to the spiritual life. In just such a sense had Jesus said that he had come so that his followers may have life and have it more abundantly (Jn. 10:10), adding that I gave them life everlasting (ibid., 10:28). Most probably, Peter is alluding to both these lives, though in different degrees.— Whereof, or of whom, refer to has raised up, as in 2:32. The chief concern of the members of the Apostolic college was to be witnesses to Christ's resurrection: see notes on 1:3 and 1:21-22.

3:16. His name (twice): namely that of Jesus, in virtue of which the miracle was commanded: see note on verse 6.— So also, faith (twice) in his name and faith through him. Who had this faith? Peter certainly, since he ordered the miracle by the faith in the name of Christ, remembering the Master's admonition according to which, having faith like a grain of mustard seed, they could move mountains (Mt. 17:20; 21:21). But, second, the lame man also could have this faith, being roused to it by Peter's air of authority, commanding in the name of Christ. This thaumaturgic name was, therefore, efficacious indeed, through the exercise

3:17. "And now, brethren, I know that you acted in ignorance, as did also your rulers.

3:18. "But in this way God fulfilled what he had announced beforehand by the mouth of all the prophets, namely, that his Christ should suffer.

3:19. "Repent therefore and be converted that your sins may be blotted out,

3:20. "in order that there may come the times of refreshment [proceeding] from the presence of the Lord, and he may send him who was appointed for you [as] the Messias, [namely] Jesus.

3:21. "Whom the heaven must receive until the times of the restoration of all things, of which God has spoken by the mouth of his holy prophets of old.

---

of faith. Jesus' teaching was similar on various occasions (Mt. 9:28–29; Mk. 9:23; Lk. 8:48 and 50; etc.).

3:17. Peter meets his fellow Israelites by affirming that both they and their **rulers** acted **in ignorance.** A similar exculpation had already been expressed by Jesus while he was being crucified (Lk. 23:24). According to Paul also (1 Cor. 2:8), **none of the rulers of this world knew** the "mystery of Christ," otherwise **they would never have crucified the Lord of glory;** but Paul sees these **rulers** as the invisible spirits of evil (cf. Eph. 6:12) who, in crucifying Christ, made use of visible responsible agents such as the members of the Sanhedrin and Pilate. At the same time Paul adduces a measure of ignorance to excuse his own early *unbelief* (1 Tim. 1:13) and that of the Sanhedrists (Acts 13:27).

3:18. All the prophets: this phrase, including the **all,** and referring to the same argument, is found in Lk. 24:27; it has a collective and not a distributive sense, that is, in the *whole* collection of the writings of the prophets, not in each one of them (cf. also **all the prophets** later in v. 24 for another argument). Luke returns elsewhere to the theme that the sufferings of Christ were foretold in the Old Testament (see 2:23; 17:2–3; Lk. 18:31–33; 24:26–27 and 46; etc.). A similar affirmation is to be found in 1 Pet. 1:10–11. The chief passages of the Old Testament foretelling the sufferings of the future Messias are Isa. 53; Ps. 22 (Vulgate, 21), cited in Mt. 27:46; Ps. 118 (117), cited in 4:11; etc.

3:19. Repent, etc.: see note on 2:38.

3:20–21. The times of refreshment (ἀναψύξεως) are those which will bring a blessed peace, after the indispensable freeing from evil (that

3:22. "Moses for his part said: 'The Lord God shall raise up for

your sins may be blotted out); they are the times of the restoration (ἀποκαταστάσεως) of all things, and they will be granted from the presence of the Lord, namely, through his will. The coming of these times of refreshment is not strictly a result of the Jews' repentance and conversion, but of God's free will. The words in order that (ὅπως ἄν, "so, that in the case") have a consecutive and not a causative value. The times of refreshment will begin when God sends him who was appointed, etc., namely, the glorious Christ who will return to the earth at his "Second Coming"; but until his appearance then, him the heaven must receive (contain, house) to which he went by his Ascension: see note on 1:11. — Who was appointed, προκεχειρισμένον, for you, Jews, in his mission as Messias. The Greek, for Messias, has Christ, and in order to retain this word it could be translated: he may send Jesus Christ destined for you. — At the "Second Coming" of Christ, the restoration of all things will take place, not only of those endowed with intelligence, but also of other things, namely, all creation. The fall of Adam had, in fact, harmful repercussions not only on the human race but also on all created nature which was subjected to the slavery of corruption by that fall. Therefore, the eager longing of creation awaits the revelation of the sons of God. For creation was made subject to vanity . . . in hope, because creation itself also will be delivered from its slavery to corruption into the freedom of the glory of the sons of God. For we know that all creation groans and travails in pain until now. And not only it, but we ourselves also who have the first-fruits of the Spirit — we ourselves groan within ourselves, waiting for the adoption as sons, the redemption of our body (Rom. 8:19-23). Christ's redemption working in precisely the opposite direction to the fall of Adam (ibid., 5:12 sqq.) effects this restoration of all things. This will happen in the fulness of time, when that re-establishment of all things in Christ, both those in the heavens and those on the earth (Eph. 1:10) will be realized. The redemption of Christ has already taken place, but its triumphant manifestation will appear at the "Second Coming." In the meantime, the period of these days (v. 24) must pass, namely, the period in which Christ's redemption will spread its effects, and groaning creation awaits the manifestation of the sons of God. Jesus himself had spoken of a regeneration (παλιγγενεσία) in which the Son of Man shall sit on the seat of his majesty (Mt. 19:28). All these things had been foretold by God by the mouth of his holy prophets of old, by means of the messianic prophecies (cf. v. 24). — Of which refers to times, rather than to things.

3:22-23. For his part, μέν, has its counterpart in the for their part, δέ, of verse 24. Two different categories are put forward, Moses, the first of

you a prophet from among your brethren, as he raised up me; to him
you shall hearken in all things that he shall speak to you.

3:23. " 'And it shall be [that] every soul that hearkeneth not to that
prophet shall be exterminated from among the people.'

(Deut. 18:15 and 19; Lev. 23:29)

3:24. "And all the prophets who for their part have spoken from
Samuel onwards, have also announced these days.

3:25. "You are the children of the prophets and of the covenant
that God made with your fathers, saying to Abraham: 'And in thy
offspring shall all the families of the earth be blessed!'

(Gen. 12:3; 22:18)

3:26. "To you first God, raising up his Son, has sent him to bless
you, that everyone [of you] may turn from his wickedness."

---

the prophets and the author of the Jewish law, and then after him the
other prophets (v. 24). — A prophet, the Messias, whom God will raise up
as he raised up me.

3:24. All the prophets: see note on verse 18. The reference there was
more particularly to the prophecies about the sufferings of the Messias,
and therefore in a more general sense to the happenings of these days (see
notes on vv. 20–21). Nevertheless, the sense here also is collective, not
distributive. The name Samuel alludes more to the writing under that
name than to the person of Samuel himself, since it was the first of the
two categories mentioned above (see preceding note). We find a messianic
prophecy in the book of Samuel (2 Sam. 7:16), but it is attributed, not to
Samuel, but to Nathan the prophet.

3:25. Children of the prophets has no technical sense as in the Old
Testament, where it designates those who were waiting and training for
the prophetic office (1 [3] Kings 20:35; 2 [4] Kings 2:3 sqq.; Amos 7:14;
etc.). Here it has a moral sense fitting in with the covenant which follows,
meaning that they are now "beneficiaries" or "heirs." — The passage cited
from Genesis should be compared with Paul's observations, also made in
a messianic sense, in Gal. 3:8 and 16 sqq.

3:26. Raising up, ἀναστήσας: this corresponds to the same verb used in
verse 22; it does not, therefore, refer to Christ's resurrection but to his
being sent (cf. has sent) by God into the world as the Messias. — The
redemption worked by the Messias is directed first to the Jews: see note
on 13:46–47.

4:1. Now while they were speaking to the people, the priests and
the officer of the temple and the Sadducees came upon them,
   4:2. being vexed because they were teaching the people and proclaiming in the case of Jesus the resurrection from the dead.

4:1-2. The subject of the plural, **they were speaking**, is Peter and
John of 3:11. The speech referred to is Peter's, though John may well
have spoken in support after Peter. The facts narrated in the preceding
chapter — the healing of the lame man, the gathering of the crowd, Peter's
discourse — had attracted the attention of the custodians of the temple who
therefore intervened at this stage. These custodians were: the **priests** on
duty in their weekly priestly function (cf. Lk. 1:8-9), **the officer of the
temple and the Sadducees.** In the place of **priests**, one might expect *high
priests* (as some codices have here) who were members of the great priestly
families to whom the office of high priest was practically reserved (cf.
Flavius Josephus, *Wars of the Jews,* IV, 148), and who were concerned
with the affairs of the temple; but the **priests**, here, can stand for those
performing their weekly functions and who had charge of the ordinary
internal course of procedure. The **officer** ($\sigma\tau\rho\alpha\tau\eta\gamma\acute{o}s$) **of the temple** was an
eminent priest especially entrusted with the general care of the temple
and with keeping order. He is mentioned again in 5:24 and 26, and it
would seem that he had other officers subordinate to him (Lk. 22:4
and 52). The **Sadducees** are named, not because as such they held the
official charges of the temple, but because the great priestly families,
mentioned above, nearly always belonged to the party of the Sadducees,
who were enemies of the Pharisees and no less hostile to the infant Church
(cf. 23:6-9). These magistrates intervened, just as had the Pharisees after
the healing of the man born blind (see note on 3:1 sqq.), **being vexed**
($\delta\iota\alpha\pi\sigma\nu\sigma\acute{\upsilon}\mu\epsilon\nu\sigma\iota$) not so much at the miracle itself as at its moral consequences, namely, that the Apostles **were teaching the people, etc.,** on the
proof of that miracle. The two Apostles were, in fact, teaching **in the
case of Jesus the resurrection from the dead,** in other words, that Jesus
had risen after his death. Now, the resurrection of the dead was not a
new doctrine, because it was taught by the Pharisees in opposition to the
Sadducees (cf. 23:8), but the resurrection affirmed by the Pharisees was
only to happen after the last day (cf. Flavius Josephus, *Wars of the Jews,*
I, 650; II, 163; III, 374) and therefore caused no difficulty; but that of
Jesus had already taken place some months before. Such doctrines,
therefore, were dangerous "innovations," especially if preached within the
temple, the nerve center of world Judaism. Roman troops had been placed
on guard along the porticoes of the temple during the feast precisely

4:3. And they set hands upon them and placed them in custody till the next day; for it was already evening.

4:4. But many of those who had heard the word believed, and the number of the men came to be [about] five thousand.

4:5. Now it came to pass on the morrow that their rulers and elders and Scribes were gathered together in Jerusalem,

4:6. with Annas, the high priest, and Caiphas and John and Alexander and as many as were of the high priestly family.

---

to prevent such innovations, and *they kept watch on the people lest they should plot "innovations"* (*Wars of the Jews,* V, 244). The Roman authorities had taken this precaution for political reasons, but perhaps also at the request and in the interest of the Sadducean custodians of the temple.

4:3. They set hands upon them: an ordinary preventive arrest while awaiting the definite decisions which could not be made there and then, **as it was already evening.** Since the two Apostles had entered the temple at the ninth hour, namely toward three o'clock (see note on 3:1), the events which happened afterward must have taken several hours, and by now the sun was setting.

4:4. From the three thousand of 2:41, the number has now reached **five thousand.** They were, moreover, previously referred to as **souls** (men and women); here, only **men** (ἀνδρῶν) are mentioned, which must therefore exclude the women.

4:5-6. The three groups enumerated here formed the great Sanhedrin, the supreme national religious council of all Judaism starting from Jerusalem. The members of the first group, who were the **high priests** (about whom, see note on vv. 1-2), are here called by the generic name of **rulers** (ἄρχ–οντες instead of ἀρχ–ιερεῖς), as if implying the **priests** of verse 1, here vaguely recalled by the adjective **their.** The second group were the elders representing the lay aristocracy and followers of the Sadducean sect. The third was that of the **Scribes** or doctors of the law, for the most part laymen and Pharisees. — **Annas,** or Annanos, was the father-in-law of **Caiphas** who was then officially the **high priest;** this title is given here, however, to Annas (also in Lk. 3:2, together with Caiphas), because of the exceptional authority he retained after his deposition, for he had five sons, as well as a son-in-law, Caiphas, as his successors in that office, so that the shadow of Annas, as the "grey eminence" of the official high priest, always loomed up behind the six relatives who succeeded him. Thus he was called *the eldest of the high priests* by Flavius Josephus

4:7. And setting them in the midst they questioned them: "By what authority or in what name have you done this?"

4:8. Then Peter filled with the Holy Spirit said to them: "Rulers of the people and elders,

4:9. "if we are questioned today about a benefit [done] to a cripple [asking us] as to how this man has been cured,

---

(*Wars of the Jews,* IV, 151) who also gives us other details about him and his family (*Antiquities of the Jews,* XX, 198 sqq.). It is a fact that both Annas and Caiphas figured in the trial of Jesus. — There are no details of **John and Alexander,** but the Western Recension has **Jonathan** in place of **John,** which would agree with the name of the third successor and relative of Annas in the office of high priest. The following are his six successors, with the dates of their tenure of office: his son Eleazarus, the years 16–17; his son-in-law Caiphas, the years 18–36; his son Jonathan, 36–37; his son Theophilus, 37–41; his son Mathias, 42–43; his son of the same name, Annas, 61. Here, in any case, it is not yet the year 36 when Jonathan became high priest.

4:7. Notice how the inquiry of the Sanhedrin does not turn on the reality of the cure of the lame man, as this is not called in question in view of the notoriety of the man who has been healed and the publication of the fact (cf. v. 16). Instead, the aim is to discover by **what authority** and by the invocation of **what name** the cure has been effected. The fear, therefore, was that the miraculous happening testified to a superior power which would not be recognized by the inquisitors (cf. v. 17). Perhaps they remembered that Jesus had reproved his adversaries for not recognizing his heavenly Father, although the wonders he worked pointed to such a recognition: **If you are not willing to believe me, believe the works, that you may know and believe that the Father is in me and I in the Father** (Jn. 10:38; cf. 5:36). The Sanhedrists with their question more or less adopt the attitude of the leading Jews who had asked Jesus, when he had driven the traffickers from the temple: **What sign dost thou show us, seeing that thou dost this** (legitimately)? (Jn. 2:18; cf. also Mk. 11:28). Nevertheless, they had not the audacity to attribute the miracle worked by Peter to **Beelzebub, the prince of devils,** as other Jews had done with Jesus (Lk. 11:15).

4:9. As to how, ἐν τίνι: could also be translated **in virtue of what,** but the Sanhedrists' question sought to discover the superior power from which the miracle proceeded; its counterpart is in the words **in virtue of this name** of the following verse.

4:10. "be it known to you all and to all the people of Israel that in the name of Jesus Christ of Nazareth, whom you crucified, whom God has raised from the dead, in virtue of this [name] does this man stand before you sound.

4:11. "This is the stone that was rejected by you the builders which has become the cornerstone.

4:12. "Neither is there salvation in any other; for neither is there another name under heaven [which is] given to men by which we must be saved."

4:13. Now seeing the boldness of Peter and John and finding that they were uneducated and untrained men, they marvelled and recognised them as having been with Jesus.

4:10. The question of the Sanhedrists receives a very clear and precise reply which, moreover, is addressed not only to them but also **to all the people of Israel.** The cripple has been healed **in the name of Jesus Christ of Nazareth,** and in case any doubt should arise, this Jesus is the one **whom you crucified,** but **whom God has raised from the dead.** Just as the mention of the crucifixion removes any doubt in identification, so the assertion of the resurrection cancels the shame of the crucifixion and is a motive of faith in the one crucified (see notes on 1:3 and 21–22; etc.).— **In virtue of this** can refer both to the name and to Jesus, but the sense is the same; it corresponds to the question **in virtue of what** in the preceding verse.

4:11. This is a free quotation in oratorical style of Psalm 118 (117):22; this passage was also quoted by Jesus and applied to himself when disputing with his adversaries (Mk. 12:10).

4:12. **Name under heaven . . . given to men:** these are words of great import which, by embracing the whole human race, by far transcend the limits of racial Judaism. When Paul, still at this time a rigid Pharisee, later insists at great length on the universality of Christian salvation without barriers of origin or social class (Gal. 3:28; Col. 3:11; 1 Cor. 12:13; Rom. 10:12), he is not originating a new idea but only developing the point he has taken from the Apostolic catechesis.

4:13. **Uneducated and untrained** (ἰδιῶται): this judgment reflects the mental evaluation of the speaker. For the rabbis, a person was **uneducated** (in rabbinical Hebrew *bur,* "a boor") if he had not studied Hebrew Law in their schools, and the unlearned were *the people of the land,* whom the rabbis heartily disliked (cf. *Pirqe Aboth,* II, 5; III, 10; etc.). The other

4:14. And seeing the man who had been cured standing with them, they had nothing to say to the contrary.

4:15. So they ordered them to withdraw from the council chamber, and they conferred among themselves

4:16. saying: "What are we to do with these men? For that indeed an evident sign has been done through them, is manifest to all the inhabitants of Jerusalem and we cannot deny it.

4:17. "But lest it spread further among the people, let us warn them to speak no more on [the authority of] this name to any man."

---

word, **untrained,** retaining its Greek form (*hedjot,* "idiot"), had come into rabbinical terminology but was used in various senses to distinguish either a private individual from a king or a magistrate (*Sanhedrin,* X, 2), an unlearned person from a learned one (*Rosh ashana,* II, 8), a professionally trained person from one who is not (*Mo 'ed qatan,* I, 8, 10), and similar cases. The Sanhedrists use it here to signify a more or less "ordinary" man, an "uncultured" person. — They **marvelled** not only at the **boldness** in speech shown by the two accused, but also at their ability to discuss the Scriptures, unlettered as they were judged to be. — **They . . . recognised them as having been** (ἦσαν) **with Jesus:** it is very unlikely that the recognition was physical, because we know that only one of them was known to the high priest (Jn. 18:15–16), and John here played a secondary role. It must, therefore, be rather a moral recognition. The **boldness** of the discourse and the independence of their conduct fitted in perfectly with their appeal to *Jesus Christ of Nazareth,* and it was sufficient to identify them as his disciples because they had been **with Jesus.** The earlier rumors about these two are now fully confirmed by what the Sanhedrists see and hear, and hence **they . . . recognised them.**

4:14. The presence of **the cured man,** who was well known in the whole city, did not allow of doubts of the reality of the miracle (see note on v. 7), and the Sanhedrists, therefore, **had nothing to say to the contrary;** but although forced to admit these indisputable premises, they wished to avoid the inevitable conclusions.

4:15–17. After sending out the two accused, the Sanhedrin continued its discussion in secret session. The theme of the discussion could have been confided to a Christian by one of the few Sanhedrists not hostile to the teaching of Jesus (cf. 5:34 sqq.; Lk. 23:50–51; Jn. 19:39; cf. 3:1). — **What are we to do . . . ?** The Sanhedrin reached an obvious impasse in being confronted with a definite happening (**we cannot deny it**) which was equally embarrassing for them. Most of them, a few months earlier, had

4:18. And summoning them, they charged them not to speak nor to teach at all in the name of Jesus.

4:19. But Peter and John answered and said to them: "Whether it is right in the sight of God to listen to you rather than to God, decide for yourselves.

4:20. "For we cannot but speak of what we have seen and heard."

4:21. But they, after threatening them, let them go (not finding any way of punishing them) because of the people, for all were glorifying God for what had come to pass.

4:22. For the man upon whom this sign of healing had been wrought was more than forty years old.

---

found themselves confronted with a similar case, that of Lazarus raised to life by Jesus, whose presence had been equally disconcerting, and therefore **the high priests planned to put Lazarus to death also, for on his account many of the Jews began to leave them and to believe in Jesus** (Jn. 12:10–11). In this new case of the cripple healed by Peter, a similar procedure is not even discussed, but all their efforts are directed to keeping quiet the news of the miracle in case it should spread further among the people. The word **spread** (διανέμω) was used by Greek physicians to indicate the progress of cancer in the human organism, and it is therefore natural for Luke to use it.

4:19-20. Whether it is right, etc.: a sublime thought. It is not surprising that the substance of this statement was repeated shortly afterward, in the year A.D. 40, by the Jews before Petronius, when they were resisting the idolatrous decrees of the emperor Caligula (Flavius Josephus, *Antiquities of the Jews,* XVIII, 270–272). It is, however, amazing to find the pagan Socrates using this same sentence almost word for word to his Athenian judges: *I have reverence and affection for you, O men of Athens; but I obey God rather than you (Apologia of Socrates,* XVII), and he expressed his intention of continuing his work of the admonition of his thoughtless fellow citizens, unless death should prevent him. This is exactly what the two Apostles are proposing to do here (cf. 5:29).

4:21-22. The words in parentheses mean literally in Greek, *finding nothing with regard to how they could punish them.* There is no question, then, of guilt on the part of the accused, but of some pretext to justify punishing them before **the people, for all were glorifying God for what had come to pass,** namely, the cure of the lame man. A moral situation was created which had arisen several times in the life of Jesus and particularly a few weeks before his death, when the people protected him

4:23. After their release they came to their companions and reported all that the high priests and elders had said to them.

4:24. But they, when they heard it, lifted up their voice with one accord to God and said: "Lord, [it is] thou who madest heaven and earth and the sea and all things [that are] in them.

4:25. "Who did say by the Holy Spirit through the mouth of David thy servant:

'Why did the Gentiles rage,

and the peoples plan vain things?

4:26. " 'The kings of the earth took their stand

and the rulers gathered together

against the Lord and against his Christ.'

(Ps. 2:1–2)

---

and the Sanhedrin had therefore not dared to take action against him: see note on 5:12–13. — He **was more than forty years old:** that is the reason why **all were glorifying God,** namely, it was a matter here of dealing with a man very well known to the people who had long been a chronic invalid. These observations — reconstructing a case history, and noting the duration of the infirmity — are characteristic of Luke as a physician (cf. 9:33; 14:8; Lk. 8:42 and 43; 13:11).

4:23. To their companions: this seems to allude, not to the Christians in general with whom they lived the common life (cf. 2:42–47), but to the Apostles and other leaders of the community; this would seem to be implied in the requests made to God in verses 29–30, which would be more appropriate from the propagators of the Gospel.

4:24. Lord: the aged Simeon in the temple used a similar expression (Lk. 2:29), one very rarely used for God in the New Testament, though among the Greeks it was the title slaves used for their masters.

4:25–26. The introduction to the quotation from the psalm differs according to the codices. Several have (**who did say**) **of our father** (referring to David), etc.; this is a violent construction, even in Greek, and in other codices it is therefore put after **mouth.** Even the expression that *God* speaks **through the Holy Spirit** is strange, since it is usually said that God, or the Holy Spirit, speaks through the prophets. Other codices suppress the words **through the Holy Spirit.** It is not improbable that these different readings, i.e., **of our father** and **through the Holy**

4:27. "For of a truth, there assembled together in this city against thy holy servant Jesus, whom thou hast anointed, Herod and Pontius Pilate with the Gentiles and the peoples of Israel,

4:28. "to do what thy hand and thy counsel decreed to be done.

4:29. "And now, Lord, take note of their threats, and grant to thy servants to speak thy word with all boldness,

4:30. "while thou stretchest forth thy hand to cures, and [make it] that signs and wonders may happen through the name of thy holy servant Jesus."

4:31. And when they had prayed, the place was shaken wherein they were gathered together, and they were all filled with the Holy Spirit and they spoke the word of God with boldness.

Spirit, are due to private glosses which have crept into the text. The psalm cited is held to be messianic in both Jewish and Christian tradition, but in the Hebrew text it is not attributed to David.

4:27-28. This is the direct application of the psalm quoted to the actual circumstances. — Whom thou hast anointed: refers to the Christ of the psalm, which in Greek (as in Hebrew) is "anointed" with the meaning of "chosen" (cf. Ps. 2:6). It alludes here to the dignity of the Messias ("Anointed," "Christ") which Jesus possesses. — The expression peoples of Israel is unusual, since Israel always means the one and only people especially favored by Jahveh. Perhaps it is an evocation of a phrase of the psalm quoted the peoples plan, etc., to signify that the people of Israel are equal to the pagan peoples in their hostility toward the Messias. — Decreed ($\pi\rho o\acute{\omega}\rho\iota\sigma\epsilon\nu$) in the sense that the sufferings of the Messias fit into the picture of human salvation established by God (see note on 2:23), and not as if Herod, Pilate, etc., were commanded to persecute him. It is a favorite term of Luke's master, Paul (1 Cor. 2:7; Rom. 8:29-30; Eph. 1:5 and 11).

4:30. This could be translated: thou stretchest forth thy hand, so that cures and signs and wonders may be wrought, etc. What Peter had done with the cripple — taking him by the hand and curing him (3:7) — God ought now to do in assisting the Apostles in their mission.

4:31. This phenomenon was not the same but similar to that in 2:2-4. In 16:26, mention is made of a real earthquake, but in different circumstances from these.

4:32. Now the multitude of believers were of one heart and soul, and not one [of them] said that anything of his possessions was his own but all things were common to them.

4:32. The situation here has already been described briefly in 2:44-45. The form of common life, moral and material, referred to there, is confirmed here and explained more precisely. The believers morally had **one heart and one . . . soul,** and materially, they had **all things in common.** Therefore, there was nobody **in want among them, for as many as were owners of lands or houses used to sell them and bring the price . . . at the feet of the apostles: and it was distributed to each according as anyone had need** (vv. 34-35). It will be seen from successive events that this was the general and spontaneous practice which allowed of an unlimited number of exceptions according to the free will of individuals (5:4). But it should be stated here that this sharing of goods was not new among the Jews, and had already been practiced by the religious sect of the Essenes, as described by Flavius Josephus: *These men are despisers of riches and the common usage (of goods) among them is admirable, nor is there any found among them who has more (than another) for it is a law* (νόμος: whereas this law did not exist among the Christians) *that those who come to them must let what they have be common to the whole order, insomuch that among them all there is no appearance of poverty or excess of riches. . . . Nor do they either buy or sell anything to one another, but every one of them gives what he has to him who wants it and receives from him again in lieu of it what may be convenient for himself, and although there be no requital made, they are fully allowed to take what they want of whomsoever they please (Wars of the Jews,* II, 122-127).

There are no historical grounds, however vague, for suggesting that the common usage practiced by the Christians was in any way modeled on that of the Essenes (on the contrary, the absence of any law about it, as has been shown, rules this out). The community of goods among the Christians was inspired instead by the example and precepts of Jesus and the other idealistic motives already mentioned (in the note on 2:44-45). The insistence and gratification with which Luke here notes this common life is typical of him, because in his Gospel also he seizes every opportunity of exalting poverty and despising riches. This common life, moreover, was still a reality in practice at the time he wrote, and it persisted for more than a century. About A.D. 57, Luke's master, Paul, recommends that he **who is instructed in the word share all good things with his teacher** (Gal. 6:6), and he certainly means material things (cf. Phil. 4:15).

4:33. And with great power the apostles gave testimony to the resurrection of the Lord Jesus, and great grace was upon all of them.

4:34. Nor was there any one in want among them, for as many as were owners of lands or houses used to sell them and bring the price of what they sold

4:35. and lay it at the feet of the apostles: and it was distributed to each according as anyone had need.

About A.D. 90, the *Didache* recommended a common life in these words: *Do not send back the needy one, but you shall put all your goods in common together with your brother and you shall not say they are your (very) own; if, in fact, you share in common those things which are of the spirit, how much more then in material things?* (*Didache*, IV, 8; cf. Rom. 15:27.) Several years afterward (about A.D. 120?), this is repeated almost word for word in the so-called *Letter of Barnabas* (XIX, 8). And even later still, in the second century a common life among the Christians is attested not only by Justin (*Apologia*, I, 14, 2; 67, 1 sqq.) and Tertullian (*Apologet.*, 39, 11), but even by a pagan, the sarcastic Lucian (*Peregrin.*, XIII). But in the later epoch, at the time of Tertullian and Lucian, it would be absurd to think of a true and perfect common use of goods, since the times did not allow of it in view of the enormous spread of Christianity in the various regions. We know, in fact, that individual Christians personally possessed goods and fell into abuses in business to the point of provoking protests from the austere Tertullian in his *De cultu feminarum*. In conclusion, it should be stated that the spirit of fraternal charity at the time of which Luke is speaking induced many Christians — so many as to seem almost all — to renounce their possessions to put them at the disposal of their needy brethren. But this renunciation was the result of a free choice, without any obligation imposed by the community. Later, however, when the first fervor cooled, these voluntary expropriations decreased more and more in number and extent, until at the close of the third century fixed contributions were imposed as of obligation to meet the expenses of the community and to succor the poor (*Didascalia apost.*).

4:33. This verse connects up logically, not with the preceding one, but with verse 31, and verse 34 then links up with verse 32, omitting verse 33. What is the basis of this irregular placing? Did an early copyist unwittingly omit the verse after verse 31, notice it later, and then copy it in here? Or is it due to the author, Luke himself, who had made use of two partly parallel sources and had recopied some from one and some from the other? These are both likely conjectures, but the latter is slightly more probable than the former.

4:36. Now Joseph who by the apostles was surnamed Barnabas [which translated is "son of consolation"], a Levite and a native of Cyprus

4:37. sold the field that he had and brought the price and laid it at the feet of the apostles.

5:1. But a certain man called Ananias, with Sapphira his wife, sold a property

5:2. and kept back for himself part of the price, with the connivance of his wife, and bringing a part only, laid it at the feet of the apostles.

4:36-37. Two examples are given to illustrate the life described above, that of Barnabas with a happy outcome, and that of Ananias and Sapphira (5:1 sqq.) with its sad consequences. As was frequently the case among the Jews of the time, Joseph the Christian had the additional name of Barnabas, which was given to him by the apostles, although we do not know on what occasion. He belonged to the Hebrew tribe of Levi and was therefore a Levite, and a native of the island of Cyprus and therefore a Cypriot, and he is referred to frequently later, especially in Chapters 11–15, and is mentioned by Paul. The insertion, which translated is "son of consolation," is unusual: modern philological science would perhaps derive it from bar-nĕbu'-āh, meaning son of prophecy, whereas son of consolation would seem to be a form of bar-nahmā' (in which, however, the b of Bar-naba is missing). Probably here, as elsewhere, it is not a strict translation in the modern sense, but simply a conceptual equivalent of the two names. Paul, in fact, says (1 Cor. 14:3) that he who speaks to men for edification has the charism of "prophet" and consolation (παράκλησις, as here), etc. (cf. Acts 15:32). Possibly here the effect (consolation) has been stated so that the cause (prophecy) might be indicated by metonymy, according to the not unusual practice of the day.

5:1-2. This, the second example, of Ananias and Sapphira, contrasts with the preceding one, and is therefore introduced with the adversative but, δὲ. The episode is important since in all its stark reality, it shows how in the midst of the general fervor of the primitive community there were some who still had all the weakness of human nature, as had Judas Iscariot among the Apostles. What was the nature of this couple's fault? It must have been something not explicitly stated in the words of the text, but only implied, while Peter's words which follow give the reason for it (vv. 3–4). Ananias, then, sold a property belonging to him, which he had

5:3. But Peter said: "Ananias, why has Satan pervaded thy heart, that thou shouldst lie to the Holy Spirit and shouldst keep back for thyself part of the price of the land?

5:4. "While it yet remained [unsold] did it not remain thine, and after it was sold, did not the money remain at thy disposal? How [did it happen] thou didst conceive this thing in thy heart? Thou hast not lied to men but to God."

5:5. And Ananias hearing these words, fell down and expired. And great fear came upon all who heard of it.

5:6. And the young men arose and wrapped him up and carrying him out, buried him.

5:7. Now after an interval of about three hours, his wife not knowing what had happened, came in.

---

no obligation to sell or to surrender (v. 4); and yet, having sold it, he brought **a part only** of the price (μέρος τι) to **the feet of the apostles.** This shows that when offering **a part only,** he declared it to be the whole amount, as Barnabas (4:37) and others most certainly had done (4:34). Therefore, it was deceit (vv. 3–4). Why this deception? It was probably, to some extent, due to avarice, but mostly to hypocrisy, so as not to seem inferior to the many other Christians who had sold their goods entirely and in all sincerity.

5:3. Here, **Peter** only intervenes and not the other Apostles. — **Satan** had **pervaded** the heart of Ananias, as he had entered into Judas Iscariot (Jn. 13:27; cf. 2). — **That thou shouldst lie, etc.:** Ananias' sin, then, was one of lying inasmuch as in giving up only **part** of the price, he had stated either explicitly or implicitly that it was the whole amount.

5:4. These very clear words afford us an historical evaluation of the whole working and character of the *common life* among the first Christians (see note on 4:32 sqq.). It was quite in order for Ananias to keep his possessions (**did it not remain thine . . . ?**) just as it was for him to sell them and keep the money (**sold, did not the money remain at thy disposal?**). — **Thou didst conceive . . . in thy heart** is equivalent to our phrase, *you had this idea in your head,* since, for the Hebrews, the heart was the seat of thought (just as the "reins" or "loins" were formerly supposed to be the seat of the affections). — Ananias' deceit is not directed against **men but God,** or rather, the **Holy Spirit** of verse 3. The other Christians, in fact, who sincerely dispossessed themselves of their goods, did it in homage to the Holy Spirit by whom their community was sustained and directed (2:4, 33, 38; 4:8 and 31; etc.).

5:8. And Peter made answer to her: "Tell me, did you sell the land for so much?" She said, "Yes, for so much."

5:9. But Peter said to her: "How [did it happen] then that you have agreed to tempt the Spirit of the Lord? Behold the feet of those who have buried thy husband [are] at the door, and they will carry thee out."

5:10. And she fell down immediately at his feet and expired. And the young men coming in found her dead and carrying her out they buried her beside her husband.

5:11. And great fear came upon the whole church and upon all who heard of these things.

5:12. Now by the hands of the apostles many signs and wonders

---

5:8. Made answer, ἀπεκρίθη: literally means "replied." In adopting this meaning, it can be supposed that the woman had just come in and asked after her husband. Peter's words were not a trap laid for the woman so that she should lie, but an opportunity for her to retract her husband's deception at which she had connived (v. 2). It was, therefore, a chance offered to her to save herself. But even on this occasion, human free will changed the chance of salvation into one of ruin. — For so much, τοσούτου: Peter must have named the exact sum, perhaps adding that it was the pile of money deposited at his feet (cf. v. 2), with the intention of discovering if that — and no more — was the price obtained. Substituting hypothetically the sum of 1,000 sicli for the so much, Peter's question then becomes: "Did you sell the land for 1,000 sicli and not for a greater sum?"

5:9. The Spirit of the Lord: namely, of Jesus (cf. 16:7): this refers to the Holy Spirit of verse 3 who also is God (v. 4) (cf. 16:6; Rom. 8:9). From an incidental note by Jerome (Epist., 130), we learn that Porphyrius, the enthusiastic apologist of paganism and embittered polemicist against Christianity, accused Peter of having caused the deaths of husband and wife. But from Luke's account it is evident that, in the narrator's mind, the sentence was pronounced and executed by the Holy Spirit to whom the couple had lied (vv. 3, 4, 9). Some early commentators (Origen, Augustine, Cassian, etc.) insist that the penalty inflicted was a temporal one so that the two culprits might escape eternal damnation (similar, though not identical, cases are to be found in 1 Cor. 5:5; 1 Tim. 1:20).

5:11. Fear: see note on 2:43.

5:12-13. Signs and wonders: see note on 2:43. — Solomon's portico: see note on 3:11. They all gathered there regularly, that is, the Apostles and

were done among the people. And they were all with one accord in Solomon's portico.

5:13.   But of the rest no one dared to associate with them, yet the people made much of them.

5:14.   And the multitude of men and women who believed in the Lord increased still more,

5:15.   so that they carried the sick into the streets and laid them on beds and pallets that, when Peter passed, his shadow at least might fall on some of them.

5:16.   And there came also together multitudes from the towns near Jerusalem, bringing the sick and those troubled with unclean spirits, and they were all cured.

5:17.   But the high priest rose up and all those [who were] with

---

the faithful. The **rest,** who dared not associate with them, seem to include not only their avowed enemies, but also the timid and the frightened, while the mass of the people openly showed them favor. It was in fact a repetition of the situation on other occasions with Jesus, both at the healing of the man born blind (Jn. 9:16 sqq.) and on the days before the last Pasch (*ibid.,* 12:42 sqq.). There were then two opposing forces, Jesus and the Jewish authorities, and between them the mass of the people who were still kindly disposed toward Jesus (see note on 4:21-22). Those who **dared not associate themselves** with the faithful refrained through fear of the Jewish authorities (cf. v. 17 sqq.) just as, in the two cases cited of Jesus, many wavered for fear of being excommunicated from the synagogue.

5:14.   Cf. 2:41 and 47; 4:4. These new **believers in the Lord** came not so much from among the diffident and fearful as from the well-wishers (see preceding note). This verse can be regarded as a parenthesis, since verse 15 links up in the train of thought with verse 13 rather than with verse 14.

5:15.   Peter's shadow works miracles in the Jewish city of Jerusalem, just as, later on, Paul's garments do, in pagan Ephesus (19:12).

5:16.   It is understood here that the multitude came from the towns (*which are*) near Jerusalem; but many codices put **in** before Jerusalem and refer it to the words **came together:** the sense is substantially the same. The fame of what was happening in the city spread with the rapidity characteristic in the East today. The same thing had happened right from the beginning of Jesus' public ministry (Mk. 1:32, 45; Lk. 6:17-18, etc.).

5:17-18.   The foregoing events provoked the reaction of the Sanhedrin

him (that is the party of the Sadducees) and being filled with jealousy

5:18. they laid hands upon the apostles and put them in the public prison.

5:19. But during the night, an angel of the Lord opened the door of the prison and leading them out said:

5:20. "Go, and standing speak in the temple to the people all the words of this life."

5:21. And when they heard this, they went into the temple about daybreak and began to teach. But the chief priest and those [who were] with him, had come and summoned the Council and the whole senate of the children of Israel, and sent to the prison to have them brought [into their presence].

(cf. v. 21), presided over by the **high priest** who was supported by the **Sadducees:** (see note on 4:1-2, 5-6).—They laid hands upon: as in 4:3. The reason for this new arrest was expedient rather than legal. The wonder-working activity of the Apostles swelled the numbers of the **believers in the Lord** (v. 14), which made the Jewish leaders full of **jealousy.** There was also a legal pretext for the persecution, since the Sanhedrin's latest order had been **not to speak nor teach in the name of Jesus** (4:18), and the Apostles were certainly working miracles by pronouncing the name of Jesus (cf. 3:6, 16; 4:10, 12), and their miracles were far more valuable for the purposes of propaganda than oral teaching.

5:19-20. The deliverance from prison is summarily described here. Another and similar liberation is narrated in detail in 12:6 sqq. Luke has a predilection, both in his Gospel and in the *Acts,* for giving twin pictures, or for recalling events with a counterpart. This first liberation had its purpose in the narrative, however, although the Apostles were soon imprisoned again, and this was to show that those **uneducated and untrained** (4:13) men were not left to themselves but protected by a mysterious power. The Sanhedrists had, in fact, asked Peter and John **by what authority** they had cured the cripple (4:7). If their question were sincere and honest, they now had their answer in this release from prison by which that *power* showed itself to be both operative and effective.—**Words of this life:** this does not mean an abstract consideration but a practical application of Christ's doctrine, whereby it becomes **the word of this salvation** (13:26). Christ is, in fact, **the author of life** (3:15; see there).

5:21. The two events, namely, the teaching of the Apostles in the temple and the convocation of the Sanhedrin, must have taken place almost at the same time, that is, **about daybreak** (ὑπὸ τὸν ὄρθρον). The

5:22. But when the officers came they did not find them in the prison; so they returned and reported

5:23. saying: "The prison we found quite securely locked and the guards standing before the doors, but on opening we found no one inside."

5:24. When the officer of the temple and the high priests heard these words, they were perplexed thereat [not knowing] what this might be.

Council could, in fact, be convened even in the early morning, especially in urgent cases, such as the trial of Jesus (Lk. 22:66), and if, therefore, the same thing happened in the present case, it was for the same reason. It is not stated, however, that the Sanhedrin was convened in the temple itself, near where the Apostles were teaching. The ordinary meeting place was the "hall of the hewn stone" (*lishkath haggazith*), which was near the southeast corner of the temple, that is, at a point farthest away from Solomon's portico where the Apostles usually gathered (v. 12; 3:11). From A.D. 30 onward, however, the Council met in another part of the temple, now unknown to us, called "tavern" (*hanuth*), just as it might meet in the house of the high priest. These various possibilities explain how, in the circumstances, the high priest could be ignorant of the fact that the accused were no longer in prison. — There is a difficulty in the phrase, **the Council and the whole senate of the children of Israel.** From what we know today, the Council or Sanhedrin (see notes on 4:5–6) should be the same as the **senate** (γερουσία), a term used in this one instance in the whole of the New Testament: the repetition "the Sanhedrin **and** the whole senate" would, therefore, be pointless. There are various explanations for this. Some say that the conjunction **and** is explicative, namely, it is intended to show that the Sanhedrin represented all the **children of Israel.** The term **Sanhedrin,** however, is used already in 4:15 without any explanation, but in that instance the explanation was superfluous after the description given in 4:5–6. Others say that the phrase is meant to indicate that this particular meeting of the Sanhedrin was larger than usual because of the very considerable number of "elders" (γέροντες, a derivation of γερουσία). Others explain it in various ways.

5:24. Officer of the temple: see note on 4:1. — **Thereat:** can refer to the **words** or to the Apostles about whom they were concerned, but the meaning is substantially the same. — **What this might be:** could also be translated, **what might come from it,** namely the consequence of the situation.

5:25. But someone came and told them: "Behold the men you put in prison are standing in the temple and teaching the people."

5:26. Then the captain went off with the officers and brought them without violence for they feared the people lest they should be stoned.

5:27. And having brought them, they set them before the Sanhedrin, and the high priest questioned them

5:28. saying: "With an injunction we commanded you not to teach in virtue of this name; and behold you have filled Jerusalem with your teaching and want to bring this man's blood upon us."

5:29. But Peter and the apostles answered and said: "We must obey God rather than men.

5:30. "The God of our fathers raised Jesus [again] whom you put to death hanging him on a tree.

5:26. For they feared the people: see notes on vv. 12–13. The Sanhedrists had a similar fear when they decided on the arrest of Jesus (Mk. 14:2).

5:28. With an injunction we commanded: a Hebrew construction which shows, here, the force of the command; it alludes to 4:18. — You . . . want to bring this man's blood upon us, namely, Jesus': an allusion to Peter's words in 2:23; 3:13–14; which must have been reported to the high priest. He does not wish to assume the responsibility for this man's blood, even though it was this same Caiphas (see note on 4:5–6) who had presided at the trial of Jesus and who, even if he had not suggested it, had certainly assented to the people's cry to Pilate of: His (Jesus') blood be on us and on our children! (Mt. 27:25.)

5:29. We must obey, etc.: see note on 4:19–20.

5:30. The Greek has raised ($\H{\eta}\gamma\epsilon\iota\rho\epsilon\nu$), but here it stands for raised again from the dead, both in contrast to the words you put to death which follow, and as a proof of Christ's redemptive mission (see note on 1:3). — You put to death: the Greek has the verb, $\delta\iota\alpha\chi\epsilon\iota\rho\acute{\iota}\zeta\omega$, etymologically, "to have in hand" or "to conduct or deal with," which in the whole of the New Testament is used only here and in 26:21. But the verb is not used here in the physical sense of killing with their own hands, but in the moral sense of wishing and causing the killing at the hands of others. In 2:23 it is in fact stated that the Jews killed Jesus by the hands of wicked men, namely the Roman soldiers, but here, and especially in 3:13, the final responsibility is attributed to the Jews and not to Pilate or the Romans.

5:31. "Him God has exalted with his right hand [to be] Prince and Saviour, to grant repentance to Israel and forgiveness of sins.

5:32. "And we are witnesses of these things and so is the Holy Spirit [witness of them], whom God has given to all who obey him."

5:33. But they, when they heard this, were cut to the heart and wanted to slay them.

5:34. But there stood up one in the Sanhedrin, a Pharisee named Gamaliel, a teacher of the Law respected by all the people, and he ordered that the men be put outside for a little while.

Once again, care is taken to put the relations of the Roman authorities with Christianity in the best possible light: see the note on 3:13.

5:31. For **Prince**, the Greek has ἀρχηγός; see note on 3:15. For **repentance**, it has μετάνοια ("penance"): see note on 2:38.

5:32. **These things:** the Greek has the Hebraism, **these words**; they are the facts recorded in the two preceding verses, namely the death and resurrection of Christ and the redemption worked by him. The Apostles are witnesses to the reality of these facts (see note on 1:3 and 21–22), as also is the **Holy Spirit** who was poured forth on the faithful (cf. 2:33 and 38); and Paul subscribes to this when he says, **the Spirit himself gives testimony . . . that we are the sons of God** (Rom. 8:16).

5:33. **Were cut to the heart** in the Greek is διεπρίοντο, etymologically, "they were sawn in two."

5:34. This is the **Gamaliel** who had been Paul's teacher in Jerusalem about twenty years earlier (22:3). In the rabbinical writings he is called Gamaliel "the Elder," and he is in fact Gamaliel I, though he is often confused with his grandson Gamaliel II who flourished about A.D. 100. Gamaliel the Elder was held in great esteem in Jewish tradition and was the first to receive the title of *Rabban*, a greater honor than that of *Rabbi*, and granted only to four or five other doctors of the Law after him. Of him it was said: *When Rabban Gamaliel the Elder died the Law ceased to be held in honour, and purity and abstinence were extinguished* (*Sotah*, IX, 15). From this account in the *Acts* we learn that he was a member of the Sanhedrin, but the rabbinical tradition that he was president of it is unfounded. He was probably the grandson of Hillel, his father being called Simon. Some later Christian writers (*Recognition. Clement.*, I, 65 sqq.; Photius, *Biblioth.*, 171, etc.) claimed that toward the end he was converted to Christianity, but it is almost certain that this conclusion is only a fantasy drawn from the fact that he afforded protection to the

5:35. And he said to them: "Ye men of Israel, bethink yourselves what you are about to do to these men.

5:36. "For some time ago there rose up Theodas, claiming to be somebody [of importance], and a number of men, about four hundred, joined him; he was slain, and all that obeyed him were dispersed and came to nought.

5:37. "After him rose up Judas the Galilean in the days of the census, and drew [part of the] people after him: he too perished and all that obeyed him were scattered.

Christians in this passage of the *Acts*. He followed in his teaching the "school of Hillel" which was generally (though not always) milder and less rigid than the opposing "school of Shammai." He protected widows against the abuses of Jewish divorce and saw to it that his fellow countrymen maintained friendly relations with the Gentiles, even to the point of studying Greek. It must not be thought, however, that Gamaliel was another Nicodemus or Joseph of Arimathea, a disciple of Jesus secretly for fear of the Jews (Jn. 19:38-39). Gamaliel was a convinced Pharisee and as such a determined opponent of the Sadducees, and as a follower of Hillel was tolerant and inclined to favor popular views. If he here recommends tolerance toward the Apostles, it is for all the above-mentioned reasons combined. By so doing, he opposed the party of the high priests and the Sadducees who were prominent in the Sanhedrin (see note on 4:1-2 and 5-6), and at the same time he ingratiated himself with the people who were well disposed toward the Apostles (cf. v. 26) and perhaps with the Roman authorities and the Gentiles in general, since they disliked severe measures taken solely on religious grounds. It should not be entirely discounted, indeed it may well be, that Gamaliel in this instance was swayed by impartiality and prudence based on experience.

5:36-37. Gamaliel gives force to his recommendation by referring to two historic episodes, that of **Theodas** and that of **Judas the Galilean;** the former was earlier than the latter and took place **some time ago,** roughly about "the beginning of our time." But since the episode of Judas the Galilean certainly took place in the years A.D. 6-7, namely about thirty years before this speech of Gamaliel, the Theodas incident must have happened before A.D. 6-7. This rebel leader, then, **rose up . . . claiming to be somebody [of importance];** and this phrase, which smacks a little of the Latin idiom, is used again more fully in 8:9. Now, who is this **Theodas** to whom Gamaliel refers? Flavius Josephus (*Antiquities of the Jews,* XX, 97-99) speaks of a rebel leader named Theodas in Jerusalem itself, but he is speaking of the years when Cuspidus Fadus was procurator of Judea (A.D. 44–46), that is, about a decade after this speech of Gamaliel. It is clear, therefore, that the speaker cannot have meant the Theodas who lived before A.D. 6–7. This discrepancy has been resolved as follows:

Gamaliel's discourse was invented, and the inventor fell into the anachronism of anticipating the episode of Theodas by more than forty years. This suggested solution lacks any positive proof, and is vitiated by Luke's historical exactness and the habitual carelessness of Flavius Josephus.

The name of Theodas might not be the original one in Josephus' text but added by a Christian amanuensis influenced by the passage in question. This is certainly a possible solution since the transmission of Josephus' text is rather complicated and it was undoubtedly modified by Christian amanuenses. Nevertheless, in the present-day text, also known to Eusebius (*Hist. eccl.,* II, 11, 1–3) the name *Theodas* is critically certain.

Flavius Josephus may have made a chronological error in postdating the episode of Theodas by more than forty years. This explanation is theoretically possible, since in Josephus, a careless compiler, numerous contradictions are found even in his own works (see G. Ricciotti, *Flavio Giuseppe tradotto e commentato,* Vol. I, Introduction, *Flavio Giuseppe lo storico giudeo-romano,* 2a ed., Turin, 1949), and other errors may therefore be legitimately presumed. In actual fact, however, any error by Josephus with regard to Theodas is not verified by documentary evidence.

Theodas, about whom Gamaliel speaks, might be one of the numerous rebels before the time of Judas the Galilean, referred to anonymously by Josephus who says that *at that time the whole of Jerusalem was filled with a war of brigands* (*Wars of the Jews,* II, 65; cf. *Antiquities of the Jews,* XVII, 285). This explanation, again, is possible, but is without documentary proof.

The same must be said, more or less, of other solutions, whether it be suggested that there were two different episodes in both of which the protagonists were called Theodas, or that there was one episode only, and that the chief character had (as was frequently the case among the Jews) two names, Theodas as mentioned by Gamaliel and one of the other Jewish names assigned by Josephus to the leaders of the insurrection (*Wars of the Jews,* II, 55–65; *Antiquities of the Jews,* XVII, 269–285). In this last hypothesis, it would be another Theodas at the time of Cuspidus Fadus.

Finally, the present state of the documents does not offer a conclusive explanation, and when it is a question of an irreconcilable contradiction between Luke and Josephus, all the general presumptions are in favor of Luke and against Josephus.

About four hundred: the Theodas referred to by Flavius Josephus was the leader of a *large multitude* (ὄχλος), which suggests far more than four hundred. Moreover, the insurgents in this case were routed and dispersed, while in Josephus' account some of them (including Theodas) were slain

5:38. "So now I say to you: keep away from these men and let them be [undisturbed]; for if this plan or work is of men, it will be overthrown;

5:39. "but if it is of God, you will not be able to overthrow it: let it never be that you find yourselves fighting even against God."

5:40. And they allowed themselves to be persuaded by him; and calling in the apostles, after having them scourged they charged [them] not to speak in the name of Jesus and let them go.

---

and some were made prisoner. But are these passages sufficient to make the two episodes different?

Much more important historically was the insurrection of Judas the Galilean, also called *the Gaulanite,* since he was a native of Gamala in Gaulanitis, of whom Flavius Josephus speaks on several occasions (*Wars of the Jews,* II, 118, 433; VII, 253; *Antiquities of the Jews,* XVIII, 4–10 and 23–25; etc.). The revolt led by him arose from the Roman census of Judea in A.D. 6–7, conducted by Caponius and Quirinus on the occasion of the annexation of the region to the Roman empire. The motive of the insurrection was religious-national, because the census was to sanction the subjection of the Jewish nation to the Romans, a situation which that people ought not *to tolerate, since it made them subject to worldly masters* (*Wars of the Jews,* II, 118). The revolt was quelled, not without force, by the Romans, but its remote consequences were very serious. The followers of Judas **were scattered,** as Gamaliel says here, but they pursued their activity secretly and thus formed the party of the Zealots which took part in the final insurrection against Rome and came to an end with the destruction of Jerusalem (cf. *Antiquities of the Jews,* XVIII, 23–25; *Wars of the Jews,* IV, 160 sqq., 355 sqq., and *passim;* VII, 253 sqq.).

5:38–39. Drawing his conclusion from the two historical episodes cited, Gamaliel proceeds from historical fact to the supreme arbiter of history, God. He openly admits the possibility that the Christian sect may come from God, and in that case nobody can stop it. The admission of this possibility shows Gamaliel's openness of mind and independence of current opinion, for it is probable that none of the Sadducees present and few of the Pharisees were disposed to admit this possibility.

5:40. Those who dissented from Gamaliel **allowed themselves to be persuaded,** perhaps for the sake of peace and in the hope that everything would quiet down. Even so, they found moral satisfaction in having the Apostles **scourged.** This was the kind of flagellation contemplated in Deut. 25:3, which allowed up to forty strokes, but was limited by the

5:41. So they departed from the presence of the Sanhedrin, rejoicing that they had been counted worthy to suffer dishonor for the Name.

5:42. And every day in the temple, and from house to house, they did not cease to teach and preach the good news of Jesus as the Christ.

6:1. Now in those days, as the number of the disciples was increasing, there arose a murmuring among the Hellenists against the Hebrews, that their widows were being neglected in the daily ministration.

---

rabbis to thirty-nine to avoid exposing themselves to the risk of exceeding the permitted number. It was frequently inflicted in the synagogues, and Paul himself testifies to having received it five times from the Jews (2 Cor. 11:24). It is hard to see the juridical reason for this punishment, since the Sanhedrists had admitted, at least implicitly, that the Christian sect could come from God; but Pilate had treated Jesus similarly: I have found no guilt in this man. . . . I will therefore chastise him and release him (free) (Lk. 23:14–16). So here, the attitude of the Sanhedrists toward the Apostles might be expressed thus: "These men may be moved by God; *therefore* let us scourge them." In both cases the *therefore* is illogical. — They charged them not to speak, etc.: a repetition of the order already given (4:18), but in vain.

5:41. Rejoicing that they had been counted worthy to suffer dishonor: the practical application of the supreme paradox contained in the Sermon on the Mount (Mt. 5:11–12); see note on 9:16 and cf. Paul's words, For you have been given the favour on Christ's behalf . . . to suffer for him (Phil. 1:29). But the most beautiful comment on this point, both poetically and historically, is that contained in *The Little Flowers of St. Francis,* Chap. VIII, "How St. Francis taught Brother Leo what is perfect happiness."

5:42. House to house: see note on 2:46.

6:1. In the fold of the Christian community itself, there is a distinction between Hellenists and Hebrews. The former were those whom we should call *Grecian,* people born of Jewish stock but outside Palestine and who spoke Greek. Hebrews, on the other hand, here indicates those of Jewish origin born in Palestine who spoke "Hebrew" (or rather, "Aramaic"; see the note on 21:40). It was natural, because of the diversity both of language and place of origin, that two groups should be formed, living

6:2. So the Twelve called together the multitude of the disciples and said: "It is not convenient that we, leaving aside the word of God, should serve at tables.

6:3. "Therefore, brethren, select from among you seven men of good reputation, full of the Spirit and of wisdom, that we may put them in charge of this work.

---

together but differing among themselves to such an extent as to affect their common life. One of the consequences was that **in the daily ministration,** namely, in the distribution of food, **the widows** of Grecian Jews **were being neglected,** though they were in fact the most needy persons in the community at that time (cf. 1 Tim. 5:3 sqq.). This neglect was due in part to the differences outlined above, but it may also have been partly because they were regarded as of lesser importance. A person not born in the Holy Land of Israel and who did not speak her sacred language had not the same dignity as a Palestinian Jew, even though the blood of Abraham flowed in his veins. It is probable that *Hebrews* were selected by the Apostles to undertake the distribution rather than *Grecian Jews.* It is clear from the following verse that there was a serious reason for the **murmuring among the Hellenists.**

6:2. The Twelve: namely, the Apostles (see note on 1:26; 2:14), do not deny the inconvenience pointed out by the Hellenists, but they explain it by saying that they themselves cannot neglect the preaching of **the word of God** to undertake personally the various distributions, beginning with food (**tables**), and probably including other necessary ministrations when everyone was gathered together at table. It is obvious from this that it was not the Apostles who were responsible for the inconvenience.

6:3. Select, ἐπισκέψασθε: almost, "inspect for choosing." — **Seven men:** why just seven is not known with certainty. **Seven** was generally a sacred number with the Hebrews, and seven members are proposed for the direction of the smaller Jewish communities. — After **Spirit,** many codices add **holy.** — **That we may put them in charge, etc.:** it must, then, have been simply a substitution of persons. Since those previously in charge of the distributions have provoked the just complaints of the Hellenists, they are to be replaced by others freely chosen by the community, so that the democratic method is followed up to this point. Nevertheless, it is the Apostles who put those chosen **in charge of this work,** and here we have the theocratic method, since the Apostles are the trustees of Christ's authority (Mt. 28:18–20; Lk. 10:16; Jn. 20:21). The Church functioned as a **democratic-theocratic** society right from the beginning.

6:4. "But we will devote ourselves to prayer and to the ministry of the word."

6:5. And the plan met the approval of the whole multitude, and they chose Stephen, a man full of faith and of the Holy Spirit, and Philip and Prochorus and Nicanor and Timon and Parmenas and Nicholas, a proselyte from Antioch.

6:6. These they presented to the apostles and [they], after they had prayed, laid their hands upon them.

6:5. The seven chosen by the multitude all have Greek names, but this is not sufficient to show that they were *Hellenists* as opposed to those who previously held office. Some of the Apostles also had Greek names (Andrew, Philip) and yet they were Palestinian Jews. However, it is likely that the majority were Greek-speaking Jews, chosen precisely to safeguard more effectively the just rights of those who had occasioned the election (see note on v. 1). — Of the seven chosen, we hear later of **Stephen** (v. 8 sqq.) and **Philip** (8:5–40; 21:8), but the other five are not referred to again, and no ancient tradition mentions them. It is said of **Nicholas** that he was a **proselyte** of Antioch — i.e., he was a pagan by birth who had embraced Judaism in its fullness, accepting circumcision and thus entering into the highest class of "proselytes" (see note on 2:5). He was believed by some ancient writers (Irenaeus, Jerome, Augustine, etc.) to be the founder of the sect of the Nicolaites (Apoc. 2:6, 15), but probably only because of the similarity of the name; others, on the contrary, reject the assertion (cf. Clement Alex., in Eusebius, *Hist. eccl.,* III, 29, 1–4).

6:6. The seven chosen by the multitude are confirmed in their office by the Apostles inasmuch as **they . . . laid their hands upon them.** The imposition of hands, already used in the Old Testament (Num. 8:10; 27:18 and 23; Deut. 34:9), is mentioned in the New Testament on several occasions, such as the conferring of offices or tasks, as here and in 1 Tim. 4:14; 2 Tim. 1:6; communicating the Holy Spirit to neophytes, as in Acts 8:16–17; 19:6; healing the sick, as in Acts 9:12 and 17; 28:8; sending off missionaries, as in Acts 13:3. Other cases, such as 1 Tim. 5:22; Hebr. 6:2, are doubtful. This ceremony of ordaining the seven to their office already suggests that it was a permanent office, and not an occasional or temporary one. The scope of this duty was actually to **serve at tables** (v. 2) when necessary, but that did not preclude a more directly spiritual duty such as the **ministry of the word** (v. 4). Later on, we find that the newly elected Stephen is in fact so devoted to the ministry of the word that he loses his life. On the other hand, we might expect that with the

6:7. And the word of the Lord continued to spread, and the number of the disciples was multiplying greatly in Jerusalem; a large number also of the priests were obedient to the faith.

election of the seven, the Apostles would dedicate themselves exclusively to the ministry of the word, but instead they are much occupied also with material things in the service of the poor. This is what Paul calls the **ministry** (διακονία) **in behalf of the saints** (2 Cor. 8:4; 9:1; Rom. 15:31), and he himself makes special journeys to collect alms (Acts 11:29–30; Rom. 15:25–31), and addresses insistent written appeals about them (1 Cor. 16:1–4; 2 Cor., Chaps. 8–9; Gal. 2:10; Rom. 15:26–28). It is with this ministry, διακονία, that the seven are entrusted here, although neither here nor later are they called *ministers,* i.e., διάκονοι. The title occurs instead in Phil. 1:1; 1 Tim. 3:8 and 12, to indicate the official hierarchical category of "deacons." Were the "deacons" of the official hierarchy a continuation of this group of seven, or — in other words — were these seven "deacons"? The fact that the term "deacons" is not used in the present brief narrative proves nothing, and for the rest, it may well be that at that time the term was not used in a technical sense. Nevertheless, although the term was not used, we find mention of various tasks of the ministry, or of the διακονία, which are its practical equivalent. Regarding the connection between the seven and "deacons" in the hierarchical sense, we find the Apostolic Fathers expressing the following judgments: the Apostles *constituted bishops and deacons* (Clement of Rome, *Cor.,* 42, 4); the deacons are those *to whom is entrusted the ministry* (διακονία) *of Jesus Christ* (Ignatius of Antioch, *Magnesians,* 6, 1); the deacons ought to be blameless *as ministers of God and of Christ, and not of men* (Polycarp, *Philipp.,* 5, 2; cf. 5, 3). The deacons, moreover, are *the ministers of the mysteries of Jesus Christ;* in fact, they *are not ministers of food and drink, but those serving the Church of God* (Ignatius of Antioch, *Trallians,* 2, 3). Such expressions cannot be explained if their authors do not intend to infer that the "deacons" of the official hierarchy were a continuation of the group of seven and connected with that group.

6:7. Luke, like the doctor he was, notes, as in a case history, the progress of the subject he is studying. The subject here is the Church whose continuing growth he here notes as he previously did in 2:41 and 47; 4:32 sqq.; 5:14; as indeed he had already done in regard to Jesus as a child and as a man (Lk. 2:40 and 52). In the note here, he records **a large number** (ὄχλος) **. . . of the priests** of the temple of Jerusalem who adhered to the Christian faith. It is probable that they did not belong to the great priestly families, or to the Sadducean sect (see notes on 4:1–2 and 5–6),

6:8. Now Stephen, full of grace and power, was working great wonders and signs among the people.

6:9. But there rose up some from the synagogue called that of the Freedmen and of the Cyrenians and of the Alexandrians and of those from Cilicia and Asia, disputing with Stephen.

---

for in that case they would have experienced great difficulty in embracing the Christian faith. It is likely that they favored the Pharisean sect (cf. 15:5); they were certainly priests of simple life, profoundly religious like the priest Zachary (Lk. 1:5 sqq.). Their adherence to the Christian faith did not in any way hinder their continuance in their priestly office, since no break had yet been effected between Christianity and Judaism.

6:8. In the unfolding of the narrative, new elements appear which are to bring most serious consequences in their train. Stephen enters the front line and propounds a radical thesis with regard to the Jewish law which occupies Luke right to the end of lengthy Chapter 7. Chapter 8 recounts a no less radical and surprising event, namely the spread of the Christian faith hitherto restricted to Jerusalem, northward among the Samaritans and to the remote south through the agency of the Ethiopian servant of Queen Candace. But Stephen, so soon to be martyred, is to have his thesis supported by Saul, who at this time, however, is working to bring about his death. After the account of the Ethiopian's conversion comes that of Saul who, in turn, is to figure as the propagator of the Christian faith in the Graeco-Roman world.— We know nothing of Stephen's antecedents, and in verse 5 he is mentioned for the first time. The style of his discourse (7:2 sqq.) points to an Alexandrian rather than a pharisaical education, and his method of dealing with the Scriptures is somewhat reminiscent of the allegorical style of Philo, the Alexandrian Jew; but no definite conclusion can be drawn.

6:9. Freedmen . . . Asia: it is not clear how many synagogues are here referred to, but three are probably in question. The first, that of the **Freedmen,** originated in Rome; the second, that of the **Cyrenians** and **Alexandrians,** came from Egypt and thereabouts; the third, that of **those from Cilicia and Asia,** came from Asia Minor. The various groups of the Jewish Diaspora were in constant relation with Jerusalem (cf. 28:21), and the wealthier ones maintained synagogal quarters at their own expense in the holy city. These quarters also served as a center and sometimes as a lodging for their members visiting Jerusalem. There was a rabbinical saying, which though legendary may have a slight foundation of truth, that in Jerusalem there were 480 synagogues, one of which was in the Temple enclosure itself. There were, in fact, at that time, many

6:10. And they were not able to withstand the wisdom and the Spirit wherewith he spoke.

6:11. Then they bribed men to say, "We have heard him speaking blasphemous words against Moses and against God."

---

synagogues supported by devout Jews of the Diaspora besides those mentioned here. The **Freedmen** were descendants of the Jewish prisoners brought to Rome by Pompey and sold as slaves after the sack of Jerusalem in 63 B.C. (Philo, *Legat. ad Caium,* 23; Flavius Josephus, *Wars of the Jews,* I, 154–158). These slaves managed by their ingenuity to redeem themselves and thus to enter the category of "Freemen" (i.e., the **Freedmen** mentioned here); they also attained a certain prosperity which allowed them to maintain their own synagogue in Jerusalem. That the Jewish **Cyrenians** were numerous is known from the fact that they formed one of four classes into which the population of the city of Cyrene was divided, and that they overflowed into Cyrenaica itself (Strabo, in Flavius Josephus, *Antiquities of the Jews,* XIV, 114–118; cf. XVI, 160 sqq.). There is no need to mention the **Alexandrians,** for Alexandria had become in many ways a more important Jewish center even than Jerusalem. Proconsular **Cilicia** and **Asia** were in Asia Minor, the former to the southeast, the latter to the west, and comprised numerous colonies of Jews attracted there by commerce. Paul, a native of Tarsus, the capital of Cilicia, met groups of his conationals everywhere on his way through Asia Minor on his three missionary journeys. The members of the synagogues named here **rose up** against Stephen whose teaching was proving very successful. Did Saul (Paul) perhaps also instigate this opposition to Stephen? He certainly had friends among **those from Cilicia** who appeared at Stephen's execution. It is quite likely, but there is no direct proof.

6:10. The discussions with Stephen, outlined in the preceding verse, must have been on several subjects and conducted on rabbinical lines, since the aim was to put the Christian propagandist to shame and to discredit him in the eyes of the people. The outcome, however, was the reverse of that expected, and the opposition's more able orators were reduced to silence. — **The Spirit wherewith** ($\check{\psi}$) **he spoke:** it can well be supposed that Stephen was a charismatic, and possessed one of the charisms especially appropriate to the exposition and defense of the Christian faith, such as that of "teacher," of the "word of wisdom," or of the "word of knowledge," enumerated by Paul (1 Cor. 12:8 and 28; 14:26; Rom. 12:7; etc.); see note on 2:13.

6:11. In the sect of the Essenes, anyone who blasphemed Moses was

6:12. And they stirred up the people and the elders and the Scribes, and [they] running together seized him and brought him before the Sanhedrin.

6:13. And they brought forward false witnesses who said: "This man never ceases speaking words against the Holy Place and the Law.

6:14. "In fact, we have heard him say that this Jesus of Nazareth will destroy this place and will change the traditions which Moses handed down to us."

6:15. Then all who sat in the Sanhedrin, gazing upon him, saw his face as though it were the face of an angel.

---

punished by death (Flavius Josephus, *Wars of the Jews,* II, 145); here, Moses and God represent a common authority.

6:12. Brought him before the Sanhedrin: this procedure was in order, since the Sanhedrin (see notes on 4:5–6; 5:21) had to judge a charge of blasphemy, and could pronounce sentence of capital punishment. Nevertheless, the sentence could not be carried out without the explicit approval of the Roman governor of Judea. Here, however, the death sentence pronounced by the Sanhedrin was executed without reference to the Roman governor for sanction or confirmation. For a further discussion of this subject, see note on 7:58.

6:13–14. The general charge of irreverent **words** is detailed here in the accusation made by **false witnesses.** The indictment, on two counts, was that Stephen had spoken **words against the Holy Place** (i.e., the Hebrew Temple) **and the Law,** in that he had foretold that **Jesus** — called here depreciatingly *this Nazarene* — **will destroy this place** (the first count) **and will change the traditions which Moses handed down** (the second count). The two accusations were, indeed, partly true and partly false. They were true insofar as they concerned the Christian faith by which the Messias Jesus has established a new spiritual economy and had abolished the function of the Hebrew Temple, and had replaced the "traditions" fundamental to the Pharisees. The charges were false, however, in the sense given by the accusers, namely that Jesus had come to destroy the material structure of the Temple, and to abolish the Law of Moses without replacing it by a higher law. It is a fact that the first charge was leveled at Jesus himself (Mk. 14:58; etc.) and also that he had rebutted the second (Mt. 5:17 sqq.).

6:15. As . . . the face of an angel: if Stephen were a charismatic (see

7:1. And the high priest said: "Are these things so?"

7:2. And he replied: "Brethren and fathers, hear me. The God of glory appeared to our father Abraham when he was in Mesopotamia, before he settled in Haran.

---

note on v. 10), this outward change in his appearance could have been the effect of his charism which on this occasion was very intense. It seems to have been usual for the charism of glossolaly to alter noticeably its possessor's behavior (cf. 1 Cor. 14:23); but Stephen's face was transfigured by the same intense joy already experienced by the Apostles when scourged by the Sanhedrin (5:41). Stephen foresaw that he would shortly be faced not by scourging but by death, and this made him supremely joyful, for thus he would bear the highest witness to his love for Christ (cf. Jn. 15:13).

7:2 sqq. This is the great discourse of Stephen who knew he was soon to die, and it continues right up through verse 53. It is, then, a spiritual testament for the future, but it is also a testimony to the past inasmuch as it recalls the spiritual history of the people of Israel. Why does Stephen reply with such a speech to the twofold accusation made against him — of having blasphemed against the Temple and the Law of Moses (6:13-14)? It is because he wishes to point out, in making an apologia for the faith in the Messias Jesus, that this faith springs from the Hebrew Scriptures, and that his contemporaries' present hostile attitude to the Messias Jesus is a continuation of that same rejection by their forefathers of the prophets of old sent by God, and of God's whole economy of salvation. In other words, Stephen intends to confute his adversaries by turning the twofold accusation back on them. Stephen's contention that the Hebrew Temple was transient, and that the Law of Moses was destined to be replaced was already to be found in the prophets of old. To quote only Jeremias, he had told that in the messianic days

they shall say no more:
"The Ark of the Covenant of the Lord,"
neither shall it come upon the heart,
neither shall they remember it,
neither shall it be visited,
neither shall that be done any more (Jer. 3:16).

The same prophet had also made the following admonition: Trust not in lying words saying: "The temple of the Lord, the temple of the Lord, it is the temple of the Lord!". . . Oh yes? To steal, to murder, to commit adultery, to swear falsely . . . and you have come before me (God), in this house in which my name is called upon and have said: "We are delivered!"

... Go ye to my place in Silo where my name dwelt from the beginning
and see what I did to it for the wickedness of my people Israel (the
sanctuary of the tabernacle in Silo had been destroyed) ... and I will
do to this house in which my name is called upon and in which you trust,
and to the place which I have given you and your fathers, as I did to
Silo (Jer. 7:4-14).

On the subject of the Law of Moses and the covenant made by God
with the Hebrew people on their exodus from Egypt, the same prophet
had foretold another Law and another covenant at the time of the future
Messias, and had expressed it thus:

Behold the days shall come — saith the Lord —
and I will make a new covenant with the house of Israel
and with the house of Juda.
Not according to the covenant which I made with their fathers,
in the day that I took them by the hand
to bring them out of the land of Egypt:
the covenant which they made void,
and I rejected them — saith the Lord —
But this shall be the covenant
that I will make with the house of Israel
after those days — saith the Lord —
I will give my law in their bosom,
and I will write it in their heart:
and I will be their God,
and they shall be my people.
    And they shall teach no more every man his neighbor,
and every man his brother,
saying: "Know the Lord!"
For all shall know me,
from the least of them even to the greatest — saith the Lord (Jer.
    31:31-34).

Many passages from other prophets could be added to those of Jeremias
to show the obdurate stubbornness of the people of Israel against the
salvific will of God. It will suffice to quote the beginning of the prophecy
of Isaias:

Hear O ye heavens and give ear O earth,
    for the Lord hath spoken:
"I have brought up children and exalted them,
but they have rebelled against me!
The ox knoweth his owner,
and the ass his master's crib:
(but) Israel hath not known me,

and my people hath not understood!"
Woe to the sinful nation,
  a people laden with iniquity,
  a wicked seed,
  ungracious children!
They have forsaken the Lord,
  they have blasphemed the Holy One of Israel:
  they are gone away backwards! (Isa. 1:2–4)

Stephen takes the complaints of these two prophets, held in veneration
by his own accusers and judges, and puts them forward in his own defense.
His long discourse was extempore but we can be certain of the report's
substantial accuracy in view of the observations made in the note on
1:16. As stated there, Semites were assiduous cultivators of their memories,
more especially the Pharisees who for centuries transmitted orally all their
immense legal material, which was later collected to form the *Talmud*.
Stephen's discourse was, in particular, almost certainly heard by the Pharisee
Saul, soon to become the Christian Paul, Stephen's spiritual heir, who
would spread throughout the world the striking and fundamental ideas of
this speech. It is natural to suppose that Luke, Paul's disciple, was assured
by his master of the accuracy of his report of the discourse.

The structure of the discourse contains no element of classical Greek
rhetoric. Relying mainly on episodes and quotations from the Bible, it is
the type of rabbinical address that a learned Jew would have made to an
equally learned Jewish audience. When, later on, Paul speaks as a Christian
to the Jews, he gives them a somewhat similar discourse (cf. 13:16–41),
but when he addresses the pagan Athenians, he gives them a discourse of
a totally different type (17:22–31). Stephen here goes to great lengths to
emphasize the historical background of his argument, while the real point
at issue (vv. 51–53) is dealt with very briefly and abruptly. The speaker
would almost certainly have developed his conclusion further if his audience, who perforce agreed more or less with his exposition of the historical
background, had not been touched in a vulnerable spot, and were therefore so enraged by his accusation that they prevented him from saying
anything further. Stephen dealt successively with the history of Abraham
and the patriarchs, Moses and the exodus from Egypt, the construction of
the tabernacle in the desert and the Temple in Jerusalem. In answer to
the accusations against himself, Stephen shows that the benefits granted
by God to the people of Israel long antedated the Mosaic Law, the construction of the tabernacle and the building of the Temple (the very
thesis which Paul is to propound more fully in Gal. 3:16 sqq.; Rom.
4:4–13 sqq.). The building of the Temple, moreover, has not enclosed or
shut God up in the building. Though Moses and the other prophets fore-

told the future Messias, the Jews for their part rebelled against Moses
and habitually showed themselves opposed to the whole plan of human
salvation intended by God. It should be noted that the main subject of
the argument, namely Jesus, is not mentioned in the whole discourse;
nor does the speaker ever refer to himself, since he is really defending
Jesus. — **Brethren and fathers:** see note on 1:11. God appeared and spoke
to Abraham when he was in Mesopotamia, before he settled in Haran.
According to Gen. 11:31-12:4, this occurred after Abraham went from Ur
of the Chaldees (Mesopotamia) to Haran, but the other text of Gen. 15:7,
must be borne in mind. This is the first of the discrepancies in historical
data to be found between Stephen's discourse and the Bible account, and
this will be explained later. Although many theories have been put forward to reconcile these discrepancies, and some may indeed be valid, others
are merely specious and most of them have no real substance. It is more
important, however, to discover the reason for these discrepancies. If
Stephen is always understood to quote directly from the Bible — whether
in the Hebrew text or the Greek of the Septuagint — some difficulties are
almost if not quite irreconcilable. If, instead, he is making direct reference,
not to the Bible, but to oral or even written traditions of the biblical
narrative, the discrepancies are still present, but they lose all force vis-à-vis
the Bible. Even leaving aside the genuine Haggadistic narratives, we find
various Bible narratives in circulation well before Stephen's time, and these
were practical and convenient substitutes for the less accessible rolls of
the Bible. Thus, according to their author, Flavius Josephus (IV, 196-197;
X, 218), the *Antiquities of the Jews* are an accurate translation of the
Bible from Hebrew into Greek, without additions or omissions; but the
modern reader knows this statement to be incorrect. These biblical narratives — which we moderns might call "Bible histories" — were usually
compiled by learned Hellenist Jews as apologetics and propaganda for
the pagans. We even know the names of some of these compilers: Demetrius, Eupolemus, Artapanus, Aristeas (the authentic one), Cleodemus,
etc., although very little of their writings has come down to us. Other
writers concentrated on poetic or philosophical arguments, always in
relation to Judaism. Yet others compiled writings of various kinds exalting
Judaism, attributing them to well-known authors to carry greater weight
(pseudo-Ecateus of Abdera, pseudo-Focilidis, *Sybilline Oracles,* etc.). All
this leads to the conclusion that on points of difference Stephen depends,
not on the Hebrew or Greek text of the Bible, but on these "sacred
stories" which his audience also accepted as practical substitutes for it.
This reliance on biblical traditions, oral or written, is found in Paul
(2 Tim. 3:8) and in Jude 14-15 (cf. the Ethiopian *Henoch,* 1, 9). Even
Jude 9, according to Clement of Alexandria, Origen, and others, depends
on the ascension of Moses. Luke, as an objective historian, gives the dis-

7:3. "And he said to him: 'Go forth from thy country and from thy kindred, and come to the land that I shall show thee' (Gen 12:1; 15:7).

7:4. "Then going forth from the land of the Chaldeans, he dwelt in Haran; from there, after the death of his father, [God] removed him into this land where you now dwell.

7:5. "And he gave him no property in it, not even a foot of land but he promised to give it to him in possession and to his posterity after him, although at this time he had not any offspring.

7:6. "And God spoke to him in this manner: 'His offspring shall sojourn in a strange land and be enslaved and ill-treated for four hundred years.

7:7. " 'And the nation to which they shall be in bondage, I shall

---

course as Stephen delivered it, leaving to him the responsibility for the historical references, just as in reporting Paul's speech at Miletus he narrates objectively Paul's personal warning that he would not come back to Ephesus (20:25), although that forecast was later contradicted by the facts (cf. 1 Tim. 1:3). This further confirms the historicity of Stephen's discourse.

7:3-4. After the death of his father: according to the figures given in Gen. 11:26 and 32; 12:4, Abraham's father must still have been alive when he left Haran, though Stephen asserts the contrary. Moreover, again according to Gen. 11:31-32, Abraham and his father left Ur of the Chaldees (which is the land of the Chaldeans mentioned here and the Mesopotamia of v. 2), and only later received God's order (Gen. 12:1) to leave Haran. — This land, i.e., Palestine.

7:5. Not even a foot of land, οὐδὲ βῆμα ποδός: a Hebraism, also found in Deut. 2:5, indicating the smallest possible space. According to Gen. 23:16-18, confirmed here by verse 16, Abraham owned the cave of Makhpelah. — But is in the Greek, καὶ, which is the conjunction and but it has an adversative sense here.

7:6. Strange land, i.e., Egypt, where the Hebrews were reduced to slavery by the Pharaoh of the oppression, who succeeded the Pharaoh who had protected them (Exod. 1:8 sqq.). — Four hundred years: the figure 430 is given in Exod. 12:40 (and in Gal. 3:17), but in the Hebrew text this refers to the Hebrews' sojourn in Egypt only, while in the Samaritan text and the Septuagint it includes the patriarchs' earlier sojourn in Palestine. Cf., later, the note on 13:20-21.

udge [it]' — said God — 'and afterwards they shall go forth and shall worship me in this place' (cf. Gen. 15:13).

7:8. "And he gave him a covenant of circumcision; and thus he begot Isaac and circumcised him on the eighth day, and Isaac begot Jacob, and Jacob the twelve patriarchs.

7:9. "The patriarchs, being jealous of Joseph, sold him [to be taken] to Egypt; but God was with him,

7:10. "and rescued him from all his afflictions and gave him favor and wisdom in the sight of Pharaoh king of Egypt, and [he] made him governor over Egypt and over all his household.

7:11. "Now there came a famine over all Egypt and Chanaan, and great affliction, and our fathers found no food;

7:12. "But when Jacob heard that there was corn in Egypt, he sent our fathers there a first time,

7:13. "and on the second visit Joseph made himself known to his brothers and the family of Joseph became known to Pharaoh.

7:14. "Then Joseph sent for his father Jacob and all his kinsfolk who numbered] seventy-five souls.

7:15. "And Jacob went down into Egypt, and he died as did our fathers:

7:16. "and they were taken to Sichem and laid in the tomb which Abraham had bought for a sum of money from the sons of Hemor in Sichem.

7:8. A covenant of circumcision: cf. Gen. 17:7 sqq. Paul frequently returns to the question of the importance of circumcision and its value in comparison with faith in Christ (Gal. 2:15 sqq.; 3:19 sqq.; 5:2 sqq.; Rom. 4:9 sqq.; etc.). — The twelve patriarchs: the twelve sons of Jacob from whom the twelve tribes of Israel were descended and after whom they were named.

7:9-10. This refers to the facts narrated at length in *Genesis*, Chapters 37, 39, 40, and 41.

7:11-14. This is narrated in *Genesis*, Chapters 42-45. — Seventy-five souls: the Hebrew text has 70 in Gen. 46:27 (cf. Exod. 1:5; Deut. 10:22), while the Greek text, which Stephen follows here, has 75.

7:15-16. According to Gen. 50:13, Jacob was buried in the cave at Makhpelah (see note on v. 5) where Abraham was already buried (Gen.

7:17. "Now as the time of the promise drew near which God had made to Abraham, the people increased and multiplied in Egypt.

7:18. "till another king arose in Egypt who did not know Joseph.

7:19. "This king dealing craftily with our race, ill-treated our fathers, by forcing them to expose their infants so that they might not survive.

7:20. "At which time Moses was born and he was acceptable to God; and he was brought up for three months in his father's house.

7:21. "But then, being exposed, Pharaoh's daughter took him and reared him as her own son.

7:22. "So Moses was brought up in all the wisdom of the Egyptians and he was vigorous in his words and in his deeds.

25:9), and not at Sichem. Also, Abraham had bought not from the sons of Hemor, as stated here, but from Ephron the Hittite (cf. Gen. 49:29–32) The cave named, moreover, was not in Sichem but much more to the south, in front of Mambre (Hebron), cf. Gen. 23:16–19. On the other hand we read in Gen. 33:19–20, that Jacob and not Abraham bought from the sons of Hemor, the man of Sichem, a field and not a cave, to put an altar there. Joseph was buried in this field, according to Josue 24:32, but there is no mention of the burial there either of his brothers or their father Jacob.

7:17. Promise: that made in verses 5–7. — Had made, ὡμολόγησεν: in virtue of a pure benefit freely promised by God to Abraham.

7:18. Another king: namely, another Pharaoh; see note on verse 6. This is followed by the events narrated in Exod. 1:8 sqq.

7:20. This is the beginning of Stephen's full and laudatory account of Moses, in which by his praise of the patriarch, he replied indirectly to those who had accused him of vilifying his works (6:13–14). — Acceptable to God, ἀστεῖος τῷ Θεῷ: in the sense of "divinely beautiful." Extraordinary physical beauty is meant here, not in actual fact, attested in the Bible, but a fact of rabbinical tradition (Midrash on Exod. 2:10; Philo, Vita Mosis 1, 3; Flavius Josephus, Antiquities of the Jews, II, 231–232).

7:22. In all the wisdom of the Egyptians: who were in fact esteemed for their learning. It was natural for Moses to be well versed in the learning of the Egyptians; but the Bible is silent on this point also, though rabbinical tradition insists on it to the extent of affirming that philosophers like Pythagoras, Socrates, and Plato culled their teachings from the wisdom of Moses, and that even poets like Hesiod and Homer partly depend on

7:23. "And when he had reached forty years of age, it came into his mind to visit his brethren, the children of Israel.

7:24. "And seeing one of them being wronged, he defended him and avenged him that was being oppressed by killing the Egyptian.

7:25. "He thought his brethren would understand that God was giving them deliverance by his hand; but they did not understand.

7:26. "The next day he came across them fighting and tried to restore peace saying: 'Men, you are brethren; why do you injure each other?'

7:27. "But the man who was wronging his neighbour thrust him aside saying: 'Who has appointed thee ruler and judge over us?

7:28. " 'Wouldst thou slay me as thou slewest the Egyptian yesterday?' (Exod. 2:14).

7:29. "At those words Moses fled and he became an exile in Madian where he begot two sons.

7:30. "When forty years had passed, there appeared to him in the desert of Mount Sinai an angel in the flame of a burning bush.

7:31. "But when Moses saw it he marvelled at the sight; but as He drew near to look, there came the voice of the Lord saying:

7:32. " 'I [am] the God of thy fathers, the God of Abraham, the God of Isaac and the God of Jacob' (Exod., 3:6). And Moses trembled and did not dare to look;

7:33. "And the Lord said to him: 'Remove the sandals from thy feet, for the place where thou art standing is holy ground.

---

him. — **Vigorous in his words:** rabbinical tradition so believed, and yet, in the Bible, Moses himself declares that he is **slow of tongue** (Exod. 4:10).

7:23. The Old Testament says nothing of this **forty years of age**; cf. Exod. 2:10 sqq. — **It came into his mind:** literally, "it came into his heart," a Hebrew expression.

7:24. Cf. Exod. 2:12.

7:26–28. Of the two quotations, the first does not correspond precisely to the Old Testament account, since in Exod. 2:13, Moses says to one of the two litigants: "Why strikest thou thy neighbor?" The second one, however, is found in Exod. 2:14.

7:29. He became an exile, i.e., a stranger in a foreign land; cf. verse 6.

7:30 sqq. The narrative from Exod. 3:1 sqq. follows on from here.

7:34. " 'Seeing I have seen the ill treatment of my people [which is] in Egypt, and I have heard their groaning, and I have come down to deliver them. And now, come: I will send thee into Egypt' (Exod. 3:5, 7–10).

7:35. "This Moses whom they had denied saying: 'Who has made thee ruler and judge?' him God sent both as ruler and judge, with the help of the angel who appeared to him in the bush.

7:36. "He it was who led them out, working wonders and signs in the land of Egypt, and in the Red Sea and in the desert, for forty years.

7:37. "This is the Moses who said to the children of Israel: 'God will raise up to you a prophet from among your brethren, as he raised up me.'

7:38. "This is he who was in the assembly in the desert with the angel who spoke to him on Mount Sinai and with our fathers: who received words of life to give to you.

7:35 sqq. After the historical introduction, Stephen begins here to argue his case. Having been accused of irreverence toward Moses, he now clearly demonstrates his greatness, a greatness far superior to that commonly acknowledged by ancient and contemporary Hebrews, and analogous to the greatness of the Messias Jesus he is announcing. Stephen has already shown in outline that from the beginning the Hebrews **did not understand** that Moses was destined to be their deliverer (v. 25), and proceeds to enlarge on this. **This Moses whom they had denied, etc.,** was indeed God's chosen one, both as **ruler and judge, etc.,** just as now the Messias Jesus, disowned by contemporary Jews, has been chosen by God to be the author of salvation (cf. 3:13–15; 4:10–12). Stephen draws this final conclusion — of decisive importance, but extremely irritating to his hearers — only at the end of his speech (vv. 51–52). In the meantime he continues his presentation of Moses and cites other incidents (**he it was . . . it was this Moses . . . this is he . . . to whom**) to show his merits. — **With the help:** literally, "together with (σύν) the hand of": a Hebraism, meaning "with the assistance of."

7:37. Cf. 3:22–23.

7:38. **Spoke . . . on Mount Sinai . . . words of life:** namely, the Hebrew Law on which the accusation against Stephen was based. That Law had been **delivered by angels, through a mediator,** that is, Moses (Gal. 3:19). The intervention of angels is also recorded in verse 53 and elsewhere (Hebr. 2:2; Flavius Josephus, *Antiquities of the Jews,* XV, 136).

7:39. "To whom our fathers would not submit, but they rejected him and they turned in their hearts to Egypt,

7:40. "saying to Aaron: 'Make us gods to go before us; as for this Moses, who led us forth from the land of Egypt, we do not know what has become of him' (Exod. 32:1).

7:41. "And they made a calf in those days, and offered sacrifice to the idol and rejoiced in the works of their own hands.

7:42. "So God turned [from them] and delivered them up to worship the host of heaven, as it is written in the book of the prophets: 'Did you offer victims and sacrifices to me in the desert for forty years, O house of Israel?

7:43. " 'But you carried the tent of Moloch,
　　　　and the star of your god Rompha,
　　　　the images which you made to worship:
　　　　and I shall send you into exile beyond Babylon.'

(Amos 5:25-27)

7:42-43. **Turned from:** as if in reply to the words **they turned** of verse 39. — **Delivered (them) up:** as into the power of an enemy. The Greek verb can also in fact signify *handed over*. — **Worship the host of heaven:** a biblical expression (Deut. 4:19, etc.): idolatrous worship of the stars. — **Book of the prophets:** the second of the three collections comprising the Hebrew Bible and explicitly called the "Prophets." It included the book of *Amos*. The quotation from *Amos* comes, not from the Hebrew but from the Greek text of the Septuagint (except for **Babylon**) which differs notably from the Hebrew as a result of ambiguities in translation and transcription. The Hebrew text reads thus:

... O house of Israel?
You have carried Sikkut, your king,
and Kijjun, your idol,
the star of your god that you made for yourselves;
and I shall send you into exile beyond Damascus.

Sikkut stands for *Sakkut,* the name of a Babylonian-Assyrian god, but this was read as *sukkot* by Greek translators and rendered as *tent*. The name **Moloch** designated the idol of the Ammonites, but it occurs here from a wrong reading of the word *melek,* "king" (Sikkut, your king). **Kijjun** stands for *Kaiwan,* the Babylonian-Assyrian name of a star-god, probably the planet Saturn (in Arabic *kaiwan,* in Syriac *kewan*): the Septuagint translation Ῥαιφάν is probably a corruption of Καιφάν. Finally,

7:44. "Our fathers had the tent of the testimony in the desert, such as he had ordered who had spoken to Moses [bidding him] to make it after the model that he had seen.

7:45. "This [tent] also our fathers inherited and brought it with them with Josue [as leader] in their taking possession of the nations whom God drove out before our fathers until the days of David.

7:46. "He found favor before God and asked that he might find a dwelling place for the God of Jacob.

7:47. "But Solomon built him a house.

---

the Hebrew and the Septuagint have **Damascus** instead of **Babylonia.** Stephen argues from this passage, dealing with the general idea without descending to details. For him, it is enough to state that **in the desert for forty years** the Hebrews did not offer sacrifices and victims to God, but practiced instead an idolatrous worship of strange gods. Stephen substitutes **Babylon** for **Damascus** primarily to recall the Babylonian exile, the severest punishment inflicted on the Hebrews for their repeated idolatrous apostasies.

7:44. During the Jews' idolatrous apostasy in the desert, there was **the tent of the testimony,** constructed a little earlier by Moses at God's command. But this command was an innovation since the patriarchs before Moses, beginning with Abraham, had no such tent. Besides, this innovation was to develop further later on with the construction of the Temple to replace the tent (v. 47). All this favored Stephen's thesis that tent or Temple could be abolished or replaced, since God's majesty was not enclosed or locked in any of these places. — **Such as he had ordered, etc.:** cf. Exod. 25:40.

7:45. In their taking possession of the nations: seems to mean *the land possessed by the nations,* or Gentiles (cf. v. 5), rather than *the act of possessing* (conquering) *the nations.* The **nations** are the Canaanites who possessed Palestine before the Hebrews.

7:46. David **asked** God to allow him to construct a permanent *building,* namely, a temple, which up to that time was lacking, but this honor was not granted him; Cf. 2 Sam. 7:2 sqq.; Ps. 132 (131):2 sqq. — Instead of **for the God of Jacob,** authoritative codices have **for the house of Jacob,** which is certainly a false reading, since the projected construction of the Temple is being dealt with here.

7:47. Stephen even makes use in his argument of God's preference of Solomon to his father David as builder of the Temple. Solomon himself,

7:48. "Yet the Most High does not dwell in what [construction] is made by hands, as the prophet says:

7:49. " 'The heaven [is] my throne,
and the earth [is] a footstool for my feet.
What house will you build me, says the Lord,
or what [shall be] the place of my resting?

7:50. " 'Did not my hand make all this?' (Isa. 66:1–2)

7:51. "Stiff of neck and uncircumcised of heart and ear, you always resist the Holy Spirit: as did your fathers, [so] do you.

7:52. "Which of the prophets did not your fathers persecute? And they killed those who foretold the coming of the Just One, of whom you have now been the betrayers and murderers.

---

in fact, eventually fell into idolatry, which showed for how little the material building of the Temple counted. In any case, the Temple in existence at the time of Stephen and his accusers was not, materially speaking, either the one built by Solomon, or that rebuilt by the Jews on their return from the Babylonian exile and which the rabbis called "the second Temple," but the one built sumptuously and entirely a few decades earlier by Herod the Great. He was not a Jew, but an Idumean, and was so little influenced by the Jewish religion that he built idolatrous temples at Caesarea, Samaria, and elsewhere. In conclusion, the God Jahveh could accept a temple built in his honor even by men who were idolaters, but he did not thereby bind himself either to the builder of the Temple nor to the building itself; the reason is explained in the following verse.

7:51 sqq. The real argument of the discourse begins here, drawing conclusions from historical premises and applying them to the present situation. As already noted above (see note on v. 2 sqq.), this section seems too brief by comparison with the preceding ones, perhaps because the audience suddenly took offense and angrily interrupted. — **Stiff of neck:** Stephen had good authority for using this expression, since it had been used in the writings of Moses (Exod. 32:9; 33:3 and 5; 34:9; Deut. 9:6 and 13; etc.); he had similar authority for the other expression, **uncircumcised of heart and ear,** also to be found in Moses and the Prophets (Lev. 26:41; Deut. 10:16; 30:6; Jer. 4:4; 6:10; etc.; cf. Rom. 2:29).

7:52. Which of the prophets, etc.?: the question was fully justified, though it was a rhetorical one and had in fact been answered in Scripture itself: **And the Lord God of their fathers sent to them, by the hand of his messengers, rising early and daily admonishing them, because he wished to spare his people and his dwelling place; but they mocked the messengers**

7:53. "[You] who have received the Law as an ordinance of angels and did not keep it."

7:54. Now upon hearing these things, they were cut to the heart and gnashed their teeth at him.

7:55. But he, being full of the Holy Spirit, looking up to heaven, saw the glory of God, and Jesus standing at the right hand of God,

7:56. and he said: "Behold, I see the heavens opened, and the Son of Man standing on the right hand of God."

7:57. Then crying with a loud voice, they stopped their ears and rushed upon him all together.

---

of God, and despised his words, and misused the prophets (2 Par. 36:15–16). With regard to the killing of prophets, Sacred Scripture records collective massacres of unnamed prophets in ancient times (1 [3] Kings 18:13; cf. Neh. 9:26); but Jewish tradition, on which Stephen depends here, also spoke of killing prophets whose writings were preserved in Scripture (Isaias, Jeremias, etc.). For the rest, it was a common saying that a prophet was marked out for death (Mt. 5:12; 23:29–37; Hebr. 11:32–38). — The coming of the Just One: par excellence, the Messias; see note on 3:14.

7:53. You who have received the Law as an ordinance of (that is, probably, by the prearranged intervention of) angels: see note on v. 38.

7:54. The speaker's last words must have been drowned by the outbreak of the storm which now burst upon him, but which, rightly or wrongly, had so far been restrained so as to preserve the formalities of the hearing. From then on, Stephen was able to say little without interruption, and he therefore abandoned his argument.

7:55–56. One of the Evangelists concludes the earthly biography of Jesus with the statement that, ascended into heaven, he sits at the right hand of God (Mk. 16:19). Here, in an ecstatic vision seen only by himself, Stephen contemplates Jesus, in the heavens opened . . . standing (ἑστῶτα) on the right hand of God. These words described a vision, but they were also a profession of faith, and the reality of the vision confirmed the foundation of that faith. These few words could be heard by the gathering in a moment of relative calm, occasioned perhaps by Stephen's transfigured appearance (see note on 6:15) which seemed to forecast some mysterious happening. But these words, although they confirmed the whole discourse, referred solely to the speaker's interior vision, and their truth was uncorroborated by any external or perceptible sign. The storm then broke in full fury on the accused.

7:57. The account here describes a real tumult provoked by the accused

7:58. And they cast him out of the city and stoned him. And the witnesses laid down their garments at the feet of a young man named Saul.

---

man's last words. The judges begin shouting, and stopping up their ears so as not to hear more blasphemies like those they had just heard. Then, **all together,** they leap from their seats and hurl themselves at Stephen. So far, then, we have a violent manifestation of the judges' feelings but no semblance of a normal judicial process.

7:58. After the tumult described in the preceding verse, we pass on to the execution of the sentence, that of stoning, in conformity with the Hebrew law against blasphemers (Lev. 24:16). Stephen had ended his discourse by accusing his judges of not observing Hebrew law; well, then, almost as if in reply, the judges wished to show that in carrying out sentence they were its most punctilious observers. Stephen was, in fact, **cast out of the city,** because the Law ordered it for blasphemers (*ibid.,* 24:14). Two or three official witnesses were also called who had to throw the first stones as the Law prescribed (Deut. 17:6–7). It is noted but as merely of minor importance that these **witnesses,** to be freer to throw their stones, **laid down their garments at the feet of a young man named Saul.** Everything, then, is perfectly in order for the execution of the sentence. But where is the sentence inflicting this penalty? The narrative says nothing about the sentence, which should have been pronounced by the high priest after regular voting on the verdict. It seems certain that sentence was passed, as in the trial of Jesus, but normal voting procedure was probably not observed because it was rendered unnecessary by the judges' tumultuous and forceful demonstration against the accused. Luke disregards this, as he does other facts with no bearing upon his narrative. But the present-day historian cannot avoid asking why the Roman procurator did not appear at the execution of the sentence passed by the Sanhedrin. It was absolutely essential (notwithstanding the contrary opinion of some modern scholars) for the representative of Rome in Judea to confirm explicitly capital sentences pronounced by the Sanhedrin, and without such confirmation they could not be carried out (see note on 6:12). This is clear at the trial of Jesus, where the Sanhedrin, although they had already condemned the accused, did not carry out the sentence until it had received Pilate's reluctant consent. Luke relates at length Pilate's intervention in Jesus' case (Lk. 23:1–25), but here in Stephen's case, he makes no reference at all to any such intervention by the Roman governor. Luke's unexpected silence may well be due to the fact that the governor did not intervene in the trial because at that time his term

7:59. Thus they stoned Stephen who prayed and said: "Lord Jesus, receive my spirit."

---

of office had actually, or legally, expired. We know, in fact, that after the trial of Jesus, Pilate remained in office until A.D. 36 when he was removed by his superior, Vitellius, governor of Syria, and sent to Rome to clear himself of serious charges made by the Samaritans. He was succeeded as governor by Marcellus (36–37), who in turn was followed by Marullus (37–41), although there is no detailed information about these two. Now, if Pilate was still governor at the time of this trial, we can be sure that he would not have allowed the Sanhedrists liberty to act since he hated them, and he would have intervened — perhaps hesitantly and by raising objections, as in the trial of Jesus — in order to command respect for his *jus gladii*. Luke, in turn, would not have failed to record, even briefly, the governor's intervention. It is, then, reasonable to suppose that the Sanhedrin astutely seized the opportunity to take action against Stephen while there was no Roman governor in Judea, as Pilate's successor, Marcellus, had not yet arrived; or if Marcellus was already there, he had only just taken over his new office a few days before, and as a *homo novus* was not well informed of the situation. A similar case occurred in A.D. 62 in the interval between the death of the governor Porcius Festus and the arrival of Albinus his successor. The high priest of that time, Ananus, *seizing the opportunity since Festus was dead and Albinus was still on the way, gathered together a meeting of judges and citing the brother of Jesus called Christ — the one called James — and others, with the charge of being transgressors of the law, he condemned them to be stoned* (Flavius Josephus, *Antiquities of the Jews,* XX, 200; also reported by Eusebius, *Hist. eccl.,* II, 23, 21–24). This James is James the Less, and the occasion of his condemnation and death — namely the absence of a governor in office — is a perfect parallel to the case of Stephen.

What has been said above about the normal voting procedure not being followed at Stephen's trial — because of the judges' action in an outburst of blind fury — is not inconsistent with Paul's words referring to the Christians he persecuted: **When they were put to death, I cast my vote** (Acts 26:10). It is certain that Paul alludes here to Stephen as the most prominent victim, but there were many others as well (cf. 8:1–3). It is, therefore, almost impossible for Paul, at this time a young man, to have been a member of the Sanhedrin, and there is no far-reaching evidence in support. Paul, in speaking of his vote, infers only a metaphorical vote, namely his own part in instigating and consenting to Stephen's condemnation and his later persecution of the Christians.

7:59–60. This describes the execution of the sentence. Stoning was

7:60. And falling on his knees he cried out with a loud voice: "Lord, do not lay this sin against them." And having said that, he fell asleep.

8:1. Saul, for his part, was consenting to his death. Now there broke out on that day a great persecution of the Church [that was] in Jerusalem: and all except the apostles were scattered over Judea and Samaria.

---

carried out as follows, according to the instructions committed to writing in the Mishna (*Sanhedrin*, VL, 1-4) long after Stephen's death. The place of execution was a kind of rampart, twice the height of a man, from which one of the two official witnesses (see note on v. 58) violently threw the condemned man to the ground so that he fell striking his chest against a rock. Then the first stone, which by law had to be very heavy, was hurled at his heart by the second witness. If with that the condemned man still did not die, a shower of stones was cast by all the people standing around the enclosure. These later instructions in the Mishna correspond substantially to those in use at the time of Stephen, but the details are to be attributed to editors who codified them later (see note on 8:2). Stephen must have been struck by the first stones while standing, as the Jews ordinarily did when praying. He directed his prayer to him whom he had shortly before contemplated in heaven standing at the right hand of God (v. 56), and he prayed: **Lord Jesus, receive my spirit!** Jesus, whom he now called Lord, had prayed the same prayer at his own death, addressing it to his heavenly Father. Only Luke, among the evangelists, records this prayer of Jesus (Lk. 23:46), as well as his other while he hung on the cross: **Father, forgive them, for they do not know what they are doing!** (Lk. 23:34.) This is also like Stephen's last prayer: **Lord, do not lay this sin against them;** they were his last words, spoken when he had already **fallen on his knees,** sinking beneath a shower of blows. With these words, **he fell asleep.**

8:1. Luke does not conclude the foregoing scene with Stephen's death, but links it to the narrative which follows by mentioning one of its principal effects. The rest of the *Acts* in fact concentrates more and more on Paul, and Luke therefore shrewdly highlights Paul's — the **Saul** mentioned here — **consenting to** the **death** of Stephen to draw attention to the fact that the blood of the martyr produced an apostle. — **For his part** — in Greek δὲ — is of particular value here. — **Now there broke out, etc.** Mention of persecution of the Christians seems a little premature here, coming

8:2. Some pious men however buried Stephen, and they made great lamentation over him.

before the account of Stephen's funeral (v. 2). This may be due to the mention of Saul who, besides **consenting to** the **death** of Stephen, was one of the chief instigators of the persecution. This **great persecution** was directed against the whole Christian body of the time, then represented only by the Church in Jerusalem. It seems from 22:5 and 26:10, that this persecution had the full support of the Sanhedrin, although the initial move appears to have come rather from those members of the synagogues who had been involved in argument with Stephen, including the synagogue of **those from Cilicia** — fellow countrymen of Saul-Paul (see note on 6:9) — than from the Sanhedrin itself. The Sanhedrin, naturally enough, was easily won over by the enthusiasm of these zealots. The persecution, the gravity of which is more fully described in verse 3, brought about an effect quite unforeseen by the persecutors, namely the spread of Christianity beyond Jerusalem to the north and south into **Judea and Samaria** (cf. v. 4 sqq.) whither the refugees fled to escape prison and death, hiding in the little villages. — **All,** using the word hyperbolically, were fugitives, or at any rate the majority, but even so **all** need not refer to the Christians in general but only to the Jewish Hellenist Christians, against whom the animosity of the instigators of the persecution, themselves Jewish Hellenists, was particularly directed. The Jewish Palestinian Christians need not have suffered serious disturbance for their attitude to the observance of the Jewish Law must have been more conciliatory than was that of the Jewish Hellenists. This explains how the Apostles were able to remain in Jerusalem. The Holy City was therefore cleared of Jewish Hellenist Christians, whom the zealots of the Law regarded as dangerous and whom they forced to return to their place of origin. But the refugee Christians, once having moved away, no longer feared these zealots and thus they increased and spread (cf. 11:19). — After the words **except the apostles,** the Western Recension adds **who remained in Jerusalem.** These words are unnecessary since this is already implied in the verse mentioning Jerusalem.

8:2. This verse is more or less dovetailed into the account of the persecution, but it would not be out of place after 7:60. It is rather the completion of what was being said but which was momentarily interrupted by the mention of Saul in verse 1. The possibility should not be excluded that the insertion depends on a source other than Luke's, but of this there is no documentary proof. There is no clue to the identity of these **pious men** who buried Stephen. It is very unlikely that they were Hellenist Christians since, according to the preceding verse, they had

8:3. But Saul was harassing the Church; entering house after house, and dragging away men and women, he committed them to prison.

8:4. Those then who had been driven away went about preaching the word.

8:5. As regards Philip, he went down to the city of Samaria and preached the Christ to them.

---

already fled and were in grave danger. Luke, moreover, would more likely than not have called them *brethren*. They may have been Hellenist Jews and friends of Stephen. The Mishna (*Sanhedrin*, VI, 4-6) prescribed that the body of a person stoned to death should first be hung up and then buried before nightfall in a special place. The remains were removed to the family grave only when they began to decompose, but no mourning was allowed by the relatives who were required to pay homage to the judges and the witnesses. As already stated (note on 7:59-60), this detailed legislation was put into writing some two centuries after the time of Stephen, and if the legislation was ancient in substance, the details were fairly recent, as was generally the case with legislation for court proceedings. Moreover, it was always possible, in one way or another, to redeem the corpse of an executed person, as was done in the case of our Lord's body. This verse, therefore, presents no historical difficulty.

8:3. After the interruption of the preceding verse, the narrative returns to the account of the persecution and to Saul. — **Saul was harassing the Church:** the verb (ἐλυμαίνετο) comes from Luke's medical phraseology, since a human body incapacitated by a serious disease was considered devastated, or *harassed*. The havoc wrought by Saul was not confined to public places, for the persecutor, **entering house after house,** dragged away not only **men** but **women** also, to put them all in prison. It was, then, a serious persecution and the responsibility for it lay principally on Saul-Paul. He himself later accepted this responsibility in admitting **beyond all measure, I persecuted the Church of God and ravaged it** (Gal. 1:13).

8:4. This links up with verse 1; *vide supra*.

8:5. This **Philip** is not one of the Twelve, for the Apostles remained in Jerusalem (cf. v. 1), but someone of that name in the group of seven: see note on 6:5, where Philip is named immediately after Stephen, just as he is mentioned here in succession to him. In 21:8-9, he is called **evangelist** (*vide infra*), and four of his daughters are mentioned as having the charism of "prophecy." — The expression **the city of Samaria** is strange, though a little later we find **of Samaria** (v. 9) and **Samaria** by itself

8:6. And the crowds with one accord gave heed to what was said by Philip, listening to him and seeing the signs which he was working.

8:7. [From] many of them who had unclean spirits, these came out shouting with a loud voice; many paralytics and lame too were healed.

8:8. So there was great rejoicing in that city.

8:9. Now a man named Simon, already had been practising sorcery in the city, bewildering the people of Samaria, claiming to be someone great:

8:10. And all from the least to the greatest listened to him saying: "This man is the Power of God, the Power called Great";

(v. 14). This seems to suggest that the name **Samaria** signifies here the district and not the city of that name. The unnamed city seems, however, to have been Samaria itself, then called *Sebaste,* in which case the simple designation of **city** would have been an antonomastic reference to the capital of the district of that name. Perhaps the name *Sebaste,* given to it by Herod when he completely rebuilt it shortly after 27 B.C., was avoided by orthodox Jews as smacking of idolatry. It was, in fact, a name given in homage to the emperor to whom the Roman Senate in the January of 27 B.C. had voted the title of Augustus (*Sebastos*); and Herod had dedicated a temple to him in the new city. It is otherwise difficult to see what other city in the region could have been sufficiently important to be designated as the city of Samaria. Neapolis, or Nabulus (Nablusa, Flavia Neapolis) did not then exist, as it was founded only in A.D. 72 under Titus and Vespasian. It should, however, be noted that other codices of lesser authority give the reading (a) **city of Samaria,** without the definite article.

8:6-7. This whole sentence is of difficult construction, as the preposition **from** is wanting in the Greek at the beginning of verse 7. It is probably an anacolutical construction following the thought rather than the words, but it had already been noted in antiquity for the codices show various corrections aimed at rendering it more grammatical. Many of the city's inhabitants took notice of Philip's preaching, being especially moved by **the signs which he was working.** But it should be remembered that several years earlier, a group of Samaritans of Sichar, situated near the site of the future city of Nabulus (see note on v. 5), had given a great welcome to Jesus and his preaching (Jn. 4:5-42). But later, other Samaritans at some unknown village were unwilling to receive him and his disciples (Lk. 9:52-56).

8:9-11. When Philip began evangelizing, he found Simon was already

8:11. And they paid attention to him because for a long time he had bewitched them with his sorceries.

(προϋπῆρχεν) there, **practising sorcery** (μαγεύων). These last two words cover charms, necromancy, and perhaps astrology — which, culled from various sources, constituted that Oriental syncretism which had prospered so much in the Roman empire. But the name *magus* often signified simply one *learned* or *wise* in the secrets of nature, and could be applied to a morally good person (cf. note on 13:6). Samaria, where an ancient residue of Jewish observance had degenerated through contact with the various rites of Syrian and Hellenist paganism, was a most fertile breeding ground for syncretistic magic. Apart from the information given here on this particular **Simon,** who has come down to us in history as "Simon Magus" (even in Dante: *O Simon Magus, O miserable followers, Inferno,* 19, 1; *There, where Simon Magus is for his desert, Paradise,* 30, 147), we have that given by Justin Martyr, a particularly authoritative source, not only because he lived between the years 100–165, but having been born at Nablus (see note on v. 5), he was thus a compatriot of Simon who was born at Gitton, a few miles west of Nablus. Justin speaks of Simon in his work, *Apol.,* I, 26 (cf. 56) and *Dialog. cum Tryph.,* 120. The story he relates (*Apol., loc. cit.*) of a statue being erected to Simon on the Tiber island in Rome with the inscription *Simoni Deo sancto* is certainly false though interesting because a statue was found on the island in 1574 and is today in the Vatican Museum. The inscription on this statue actually reads *Semoni Sanco Deo Fidio,* and concerns the Sabine deity Semone Sanco (*Semo Sancus*) to whom there was a temple in Rome. On one of his visits to Rome, Justin misread the inscription and wrongly connected it with Simon Magus. Apart from this error, Justin is worthy of credence. After Justin, Irenaeus (*Adv. Haer.,* I, 23, 1–4) and several others (Clement of Alexandria, Tertullian, Origen, etc.) speak of Simon without giving any fresh details. Only Hippolytus, *Philosoph.,* VI, 7–20, states categorically that Simon had written a work entitled *Great Pronouncement* ('Απόφασις μεγάλη), but there is no proof of this. The third-century writers refer to his followers, the Simonians, and to the reports circulating at that time about the master, rather than to Simon himself. A synopsis of the information on his person and teaching is given by Eusebius in *Hist. eccl.,* II, 13. The accounts of Simon's meetings and contests with the Apostle Peter, supposed to have taken place in Syria or Rome, are legendary elaborations, and are the imaginative basis of the pseudo-Clementine works (*Homil.,* 2, 22 sqq.; 4, 4 sqq.; *Recognition.,* 172; 2, 7 sqq.; 3, 12 sqq.), and the *Acts of Peter.*

Justin tells how Simon was accompanied on his travels by a certain

Helen, who had been a prostitute (in the city of Tyre, according to Irenaeus) and was rescued by him. These autobiographical facts form the basis of the Gnostic system which he elaborated, the fundamental points of which were the following: His followers, that is, *nearly all the Samaritans and a few even of other nations, regarded him as the first God and worshipped him as such* (τὸν πρῶτον θεόν). Helen they called *the first idea that proceeded from him* (τὴν ἀπ αὐτοῦ *Ἔννοιαν πρώτην γενομένην*) (Justin, *Apol.,* I, 26). All beings had been created by means of this *Idea* or "Ennoia," angels first of all, but Simon always remained at the head of all as *God above all Principality and Power and Virtue* (θεὸν ὑπεράγω πάσης ἀρχῆς καὶ ἐξουσίας καὶ δυνάμεως) (*Dial. c. Tryph.,* 120). The following is a résumé of the teaching of Simon as developed by Irenaeus. He taught that he appeared among the Jews as the Son, in Samaria as the Father, and among other nations as the Holy Spirit. He represented himself as being the greatest of all powers (*sublissima Virtus*), that is, the Being who is the *Father over all,* although he allowed himself to be addressed by any title men cared to use. He took with him Helen, a prostitute of Tyre in Phoenicia, whom he declared to be the first conception of his mind (*primam mentis ejus conceptionem*), by whom, in the beginning, he conceived the idea of forming angels and archangels. For this purpose, Ennoia, emanating from him (*hanc Ennoiam exsilientem ex eo*), and comprehending the will of her father, descended to the lower regions and generated angels and Powers, by whom the world was formed. But after she had produced them, she was detained by them through motives of jealousy, because they were unwilling to be regarded as the progeny of any other being (*propter invidiam, quoniam nollent progenies alterius cujusdam putari esse*). Ennoia was ill-treated by her captors so that she could not return to her father and was forced to transmigrate from the body of one woman to another down through the centuries. She became, for example, Helen, on whose account the Trojan war was undertaken, and finally became a common prostitute in Tyre. She was the lost sheep. Then Simon came to deliver her from her bonds, and to bring salvation to men by making himself known to them. Because the angels ruled the world badly, he intervened and descended into the spheres of Virtues, Powers, and angels, making himself like them, just as he had made himself like to men, although not a man, and appeared to have suffered in Judea, when in fact he had not suffered. The prophets, moreover, uttered their predictions under the inspiration of the angels who made the world, hence those who place their trust in Simon and Helen need not regard them, but live as they please.

This, then, is the summary given by Irenaeus in *Adv. Haer.,* I, 23, 1–3. Further developments could be added to this exposition, but this corresponds substantially to what Justin says and what the *Acts* here infer. Successive elaborations of the system seem to have included Castor and Pollux,

8:12. But when they believed Philip who was preaching the kingdom of God and the name of Jesus Christ, they were baptised, both men and women.

---

the two Dioscuri (cf. note on 28:11), who were brothers of Helen (*fratres Helenae, lucida sidera;* Horace, *Carm.,* I, 3, 2). In recent excavations carried out in the city of Samaria, the ruins of a temple of the first–third centuries A.D., where a cult of Helen and the two Dioscuri was probably practiced, have come to light (cf. *Revue Biblique,* 1936, pp. 221–232). Apart from these recent discoveries, which in any case belong to a later period, Simon's system corresponds exactly to the places and times to which it is attributed. It is a system elaborated in the region of Samaria and admirably adapted to religious syncretism (*vide supra*). It recognizes the authority of the two Testaments, although it undermines their foundation. It brings together Oriental dualistic concepts and Hellenistic rites, reinforcing them with magical practices flourishing at that time. Irenaeus (*Adv. Haer.,* I, 23, 2; 27, 4) presents Simon as the source of all heresies, particularly those of the Gnostics. In fact, the Gnosis, which was to develop so strongly, does show some of the characteristic and permanent traits of Simon's system, such as the inaccessible divinity, the hierarchy of eons linking the divinity with the material world, the origin of the material world by eons, the divine element imprisoned in matter and then set free by redemption, Docetism, and the like. — **Claiming to be someone great,** λέγων εἶναί τινα ἑαυτὸν μέγαν: the phrase already used without the word **great,** in 5:36. This statement is attested not only by Justin and Irenaeus, but also by Jerome who attributes the following words to Simon: *Ego sum Sermo Dei, ego sum Speciosus, ego Paraclitus, ego Omnipotens, ego omnia Dei* (in *Matt.,* XXIV, 5; in *P. L.,* XXVI, 183). — **The Power** (δύναμις) **of God . . . called Great** (μεγάλη). It may be that this word **great** is not a translation but a transcription of the Samaritan *mĕgallē,* which means "revealing," in which case, Simon was considered as the *revealing Power of God.* While this ingenious hypothesis is not impossible, it seems artificial and philologically strained. It is more likely to refer to the category of angelic beings, good or bad, called, in fact, δυνάμεις, "Virtue" (1 Cor. 15:24; Eph. 1:21; 1 Pet. 3:22); in which case, Simon would be the highest of them, the most powerful Power or "Virtue." Given the exuberance of Gnostic concepts, it is possible that a "great" Power is distinguished here from "small" ones, in relation to their emanation from the Divine Being. The expression *great Power* is found in papyri of magical writings of those days. — Verse 11 recapitulates and confirms the two preceding verses, without supposing (as some have supposed) that it is a later addition.

8:13. And Simon also himself believed and after being baptized, attached himself to Philip: and when he saw the signs and wonders being wrought, he was amazed.

8:14. Now the apostles [who were] in Jerusalem hearing that Samaria had accepted the word of God, sent to them Peter and John.

8:15. Who coming down [there] prayed for them that they might receive the Holy Spirit:

8:16. for as yet, he had not come upon any of them, but they had only been baptised in the name of the Lord Jesus;

8:17. Then they laid their hands upon them and they received the Holy Spirit.

8:13. When Simon saw the great success of Philip's preaching he also himself believed and received baptism. Moreover, he attached himself to (ἦν προσκαρτερῶν) Philip, because of the miracles he saw happening. The narrative does not say whether Simon's faith was sincere or pretended. It shows, however, that Simon, as an acknowledged magician, was impressed by seeing someone who far surpassed him in his profession and in the results obtained. The Old Testament records that the Egyptian magicians found Moses and Aaron far superior to them in the results they obtained (Exod. 7:10 sqq.); and if, as is possible, Simon knew of this biblical incident, he may have intended to become Philip's equal, not as an antagonist, like the Egyptian magicians, but as a patient learner: see note on verse 18 sqq.

8:14. Philip's success was followed with interest by the Apostles who were able to stay in Jerusalem (see note on v. 1) — Samaria here means the district rather than the city of that name: see note on verse 5. — The college of the Twelve sent Peter and John. The choice of missioners, namely, the head of the Apostles and John his companion during the recent events in Jerusalem (cf. 3:1 sqq.; 4:13 sqq.), shows the importance which was attached to the mission. Although Peter is represented as being sent by the Apostolic College, it does not mean that he was not the head of that college. When the Jews of Jerusalem in A.D. 61 sent a delegation to Nero in Rome on a question concerning the Temple, Ismael the high priest was a member of it, and he was the supreme head of all Judaism (Flavius Josephus, Antiquities of the Jews, XX, 194–195). It was a command of Jesus himself that the preachers of the kingdom of God should go not alone but in pairs (Lk. 10:1), and Peter, the chief delegate, therefore took his friend John with him.

8:15–17. The two Apostles found on reaching their destination that

8:18. But Simon seeing that the Holy Spirit was granted through the imposition of the apostles' hands, offered them money

8:19. saying: "Give me also this power, so that anyone on whom I lay my hands may receive the Holy Spirit."

Philip's converts had indeed been baptized but that the Holy Spirit **had not yet come upon any of them,** so that **they had only been** (ὑπῆρχον, in the sense of "being in the state of") **baptised in the name of the Lord Jesus.** For this last phrase of the formula for baptism, see note on 2:38. It should be noted that the article is missing in the Greek in the expression **to receive (the) Holy Spirit** (vv. 15, 17, 19), while it is present in the phrase **the Holy Spirit was granted** of verse 18. The expression without the article appears to refer especially to the effects, namely the charisms, while with the article it more directly indicates the cause, namely the Spirit. When Peter and John saw that the Holy Spirit **had not yet come upon** these neophytes, they supplied the need, and praying, **they laid their hands upon them and they received the Holy Spirit.** For the rite of the imposition of hands in general, see note on 6:6. We are dealing here in particular with a rite through which the neophyte received the Holy Spirit which so far he had not done; it was, therefore, a rite distinct from baptism and subsequent to it. Baptism also, in fact, has its virtue from the Holy Spirit, and Paul's words, among many that could be quoted, are decisive: **in** (efficient cause) **one Spirit we were all baptised for** (final cause) **one body** (the mystical body of the Church); but he at once adds: **and we were all given to drink of one Spirit** (1 Cor. 12:13). Elsewhere, Paul distinguished baptism from another rite through which **the pledge of the Spirit in our hearts** (2 Cor. 1:22) is given, and which is administered by **the imposition of hands** (Hebr. 6:2). The clearest evidence on this point is seen later in 19:5-6, where the two rites — that of baptism and of the later imposition of hands through which the neophytes received the Holy Spirit and the charisms — are explicitly distinguished: see the relevant note.

8:18-19. Simon, the new pupil who aimed at being Philip's equal (see note on v. 13), and a professional magician, observed the effects wrought by the Holy Spirit in those who received him. What visible signs indicated to Simon the presence of the Holy Spirit in the neophytes? Surely, the charisms, or at least, some of those manifestations enumerated in the similar situation of 19:6 (cf. note on 2:38). When Paul wishes to prove the genuineness of his own apostolate he records that **it was in power and in the Holy Ghost and in much fullness** (1 Thess. 1:5), in other words, **in signs and wonders and mighty deeds** (2 Cor. 12:12). Simon the magician was struck by these extraordinary events, and he hoped that by offering

8:20. But Peter said to him: "Thy money go to destruction with thee, because thou hast thought to acquire the gift of God with money.

8:21. "There is no share nor part for thee in this matter; for thy heart is not right before God.

8:22. "Repent therefore of this wickedness of thine and pray to the Lord [that he may hear thee], if by chance [it may be that] the thought of thy heart shall be forgiven thee.

8:23. "For I see thou art in gall of bitterness and in bond of iniquity."

8:24. Then Simon answering said: "Do you pray for me to the Lord, that nothing of what you have said may happen to me."

---

money he might acquire the secret of the magic wrought by the imposition of hands. The word used for this is power (ἐξουσία), found in magical writings of the period.

8:20. Thy money . . . to destruction: shows the consequences of Simon's attitude, if he does not renounce it; and in verses 22–23 he is expressly told to abandon it so as to avoid such a fate. Peter's words, then, are a warning of danger (to destruction) and a threat of impending ruin; it is, in other words, an admonition to Simon in the form of an imprecation, expressing Peter's horror at such a proposal.

8:21. There is no share nor part: a biblical expression (Deut. 12:12; 14:27; cf. Isa. 57:6), meaning "to have no concern with." — for matter the Greek has λόγος, in the sense of "affair" or "doing," referring to the charisms of the Spirit which Simon wanted.

8:22. Pray to the Lord . . . of thy heart: a halting construction here because of the implications contained in the Greek text. It could be paraphrased as pray to the Lord that it may happen that the intention of thy heart be forgiven thee (which will happen when thou hast removed the obstacles stated in the following verse).

8:23. The example of gall comes from Deut. 29:17 (18); cf. also Hebr. 12:15.

8:24. Pray . . . that nothing . . . may happen to me: these words show fear of punishment rather than a true change of heart, which is neither affirmed nor denied in our text. The Western Recension (codex D), however, states that Simon wept at length. He is not mentioned again by reliable sources, but only in legendary accounts, referred to in the note to verses 9–11.

8:25. Those [two] then, having borne witness and spoken the word of the Lord, returned to Jerusalem and preached the gospel to many Samaritan villages.

8:26. Then an angel of the Lord spoke to Philip saying: "Rise up and go south on the road descending from Jerusalem to Gaza: this is desert."

8:25. **Those [two],** namely Peter and John, of verse 14. — **They returned . . . preached:** two verbs in the imperfect expressing continual action: as they returned, they evangelized, etc.

8:26. A new episode in the expansion of the Christian faith begins here, linked up with the preceding one (see vv. 1 and 4) which described the expansion into Samaria, north of Jerusalem, whereas we now pass to the south of the city. The linking up of episodes leads us to suppose a chronological sequence in the sense that the episode in Ethiopia followed immediately or shortly after the event in Samaria. It may be, however, that Philip himself is the connecting link, the chief character in them, because after writing about Philip in connection with Samaria, Luke adds another episode about him before leaving him, although a considerable period of time separated the two events. Similar cases are found in the so-called "journey" of Jesus, also narrated by Luke (Lk. 9:51; 19:28). One scholar is of the opinion that the episode here of the Ethiopian must have taken place after that of Cornelius (Chapter 10), who was the first Gentile to receive baptism, and only received it thanks to Peter's authority. This theory is not valid because the Ethiopian was probably not a Gentile, and Philip in any case acted on the authority of an angel and with the assistance of the **Spirit** (vv. 29 and 39). **An angel of the Lord** gave the order to Philip, in what way we do not know, since Philip had almost certainly concluded his missionary journey to the north of Jerusalem (v. 25) and was in the city. When the angel orders him to **Rise up and go, etc.,** it does not follow that Philip was asleep and that he therefore received a communication in his sleep (like that in Mt. 2:13). The identical phrase **arose and went** is used by Luke speaking of somebody not asleep (Lk. 1:39, as in the following verse here). — **Southward,** κατὰ μεσημβρίαν, less well translated **about noon.** — **This is desert** refers to the *road* and not to Gaza as some have supposed. It must have been the road that went south through Bethlehem and Hebron along the edge of the desert, and not the other road from the north which ran along the Mediterranean coast. This latter route was the main highway used by caravans going to Egypt and therefore could hardly be **desert.**

8:27. And he arose and went. And behold an Ethiopian, a eunuch, a courtier of Candace, queen of Ethiopia, who was in charge over all her treasures, had come to Jerusalem to worship;

8:28. however he was returning, and sitting in his carriage, and reading the prophet Isaias.

8:27–28. *The man* described here was an **Ethiopian** and a high official of Queen **Candace, queen of Ethiopia.** The term **Ethiopian** does not necessarily refer to the man's nationality, but only to his residence or political affiliation, as he resided in the kingdom of Candace. This kingdom was Nubia, of which the capital at that time was Meroe, situated a little to the south of the confluence of the Nile and the Atbara (Astaboras) and north of the sixth and last waterfall of the Nile. The territory of this kingdom extended from about the first waterfall of the Nile (Assuan, Syene, Elephantine) to the sixth, whereas Abysinia extended still farther south. The Hebrews used to call the inhabitants of Nubia *Kush* or *Kushiti,* and this was usually translated *Ethiopia* or *Ethiopians* by the Septuagint. King Tirhaqa (Vulgate, Tharaqa) is, in fact, called in the Bible, **king of Kush** (2 [4] Kings 19:9; Isa. 37:9) because he belonged to the XXV Pharaoh dynasty which originated in Nubia. The name **Candace** was not a personal name but one common to all the queens of Meroe, rather like that of Caesar for the Roman emperors. The word is derived from the Meroitic *ḳtḳ',* equivalent to the Egyptian *ḳntḳj,* translated into Greek as κανδάκη, "candace." Graeco-Roman historians (Strabo, XVII, 1, 54; Dion Cassius, LIV, 5; Pliny, *Nat. Hist.,* VI, 35) mention several queens of that name. Strabo informs us that a *queen Candace,* ruler of the Ethiopians *a virile woman who had lost an eye* in battle, was the chief adversary of the Romans when Petronius, prefect of Egypt under Augustus, quelled an insurrection in Nubia and destroyed Napata, at that time the capital. At Meroe, in the time of Nero, another Candace received a Roman mission sent to explore the source of the Nile. Pliny too says that successive queens of Meroe were called Candace, and this is partly confirmed by Eusebius (*Hist. eccl.,* II, 1, 13) who tells us that in his day those parts were always governed by a woman. — **A eunuch, a courtier;** both terms are used, probably with a particular significance. The term **eunuch,** as in Hebrew (*saris*), was frequently used apart from its original physiological meaning, and could be used of any high official at court because of the great importance attaching to the real eunuchs who were guardians of the royal harems. Thus we find married eunuchs (the famous Putiphar in the story of Joseph: Gen. 39:1), or those who were captains of the army

(2 [4] Kings 25:19). The term **courtier** (δυνάστης) also seems to mean in particular a court functionary such as a chamberlain or minister or the like. The one described here as being in charge of **all her treasures** would be a kind of minister of finance, or of the treasury. If these meanings are accepted, the two terms *eunuch* and *minister* would be complementary, but not synonymous. — This Ethiopian **had come to Jerusalem to worship,** and as he went along **he was . . . reading the prophet Isaias,** from which we may conclude that he was either a Jew, or at least a "proselyte" of Judaism (for "proselyte," see note on 2:5–6); but from the fact that he was reading the Scriptures it seems more probable that he was of Jewish stock, notwithstanding the contrary opinion of Eusebius (*Hist. eccl.,* II, 1, 13) who says he was a pagan. We know, in fact, that although the Jews were very numerous in Egypt (see notes on 2:9–11; 6:9), they were also numerous in the south where they overflowed from Egypt. There is mention of ancient Jewish settlements at Patros, that is in the extreme south of Egypt (Jer. 44:1 and 15). According to the so-called *Letter of Aristeas,* 13, auxiliary Jewish troops fought with *Psammeticus against the king of Ethiopia,* a reference to the campaign waged by King Psammeticus II against Nubia about 590 B.C. Similarly, Philo (*in Flaccum,* 6) speaks of Jews dwelling *on the confines of Ethiopia.* Best known of all testimonies are the recently discovered Aramaic papyri which tell of a flourishing Jewish colony as early as the sixth century B.C. on the island of Elephantine (Syene, Assuan), near the first waterfall of the Nile, where the borders of Egypt and Nubia, or Ethiopia, meet. It is clear from all these documents that it was easy and of frequent occurrence for Jews living in Egypt to cross into Ethiopia. The person referred to here may well be one such case. Perhaps his forebears, or even he himself, had crossed over into Nubia, and thanks to his capacity for business, a capacity characteristic of his race, had prospered at the palace of Queen Candace to the extent of becoming her chancellor of the exchequer. Even a strict interpretation of the word **eunuch** does not preclude his being at least a "proselyte," since there seems to have been a certain remissness on this point, especially in pagan districts (cf. Isa. 56:4–5), despite the prescription in *Deuteronomy* (23:1). On his journey, the Ethiopian **was . . . reading the prophet Isaias.** He must, then, have been fairly familiar with the Hebrew Scriptures, unusual if he were a pagan. The rabbis themselves recommended the reading of Scripture when journeying alone. It seems fairly certain that he was reading Isaias, not in the original Hebrew but in the Greek version of the Septuagint, as appears from verses 32–33 which follow the Septuagint rather than the Hebrew text. He must have been reading (or was being read to by a slave in the carriage with him) in a rather loud voice, as verse 30 shows. The Jews did, in fact, distinguish two ways of reading: one for a large

8:29. Then the Spirit said to Philip: "Go near and keep close to this carriage."

8:30. So Philip running up, heard him reading the prophet Isaias and he said: "Dost thou understand perhaps the things thou art reading?"

8:31. But he said: "Why, how could I [understand], unless someone shall guide me?" And he invited Philip to come up and sit beside him.

8:32. Now the passage of Scripture which he was reading was this:
"Like a sheep he was led to the slaughter,
and as a lamb [rendered] dumb before its shearer,
so did he not open his mouth.

8:33. "In humiliation his judgment was denied him:
who shall declare his generation?
For his life is taken from the earth" (Isa., 53:7-8).

---

gathering, in which case *to read* was *qarāh* (whence the Arabic *Koran*), the other for personal use called *hagāh,* usually translated in the Vulgate as *meditari.* It would seem that mental reading was rare.

8:30. For Philip to interrupt the Ethiopian thus was quite in order. It was customary in the East for two passing travelers to greet each other, especially if they were traveling through lonely places, and these meetings sometimes lasted for quite a time (cf. Lk. 10:4; 24:15 sqq.). — **Dost thou understand:** not just the words themselves, but the **things,** namely the historical and inner meaning of the subject matter; cf. verse 34.

8:31. **Shall guide:** the more important codices give the verb in the future tense; others read the present tense, **guides** — expressing a latent desire.

8:32-33. The quotation from *Isaias* is taken from the Greek of the Septuagint, which agrees substantially with the Hebrew in verse 32, but differs profoundly from it in verse 33 where the Hebrew says, literally:
With oppression and judgment was he removed;
and who shall declare his generation?
For he was cut off from the land of the living.
The last two lines could also be translated:
and as for (those of) his generation, who considered that he was cut off out of the land of the living?
The Hebrew text is uncertain and critics endeavor to reconstruct it in various ways. The following is a probable interpretation: **With oppression**

8:34. Replying then, the eunuch said to Philip: "I pray thee, of whom doth the prophet say this, of himself or of some other?"

8:35. But Philip, opening his mouth and beginning from this Scripture, preached Jesus to him.

8:36. And as they went along the road, they came to some water and the eunuch said: "See, here is water, what is there to prevent my being baptised?"

---

and with judgment (signifying: by an oppressive judgment) he was taken (away); but (among those of) his generation who thinks that he was cut off, etc.? Or again, interpreting generation as life, it could be rendered: he was taken (away); but as for his life, who thinks that he was cut off, etc.? The divergencies in the Greek text seem to spring from faulty readings or false interpretations of the Hebrew, itself uncertain. A study of commentaries on *Isaias* is therefore recommended for this passage. We know that it belongs to the last of the four poems of Jahveh's Servant, in *Isaias,* Chapters 42–53, which deal with the future Messias and his Passion and Death. Jewish tradition (in the Targum and partly in the Talmud) gave them a messianic interpretation.

8:34. The Ethiopian's difficulty in understanding the true meaning of the passage just read (see note on v. 30) was due to the extreme repugnance of contemporary Judaism to the idea of a Messias suffering and undergoing death at the hands of his enemies; see note on 2:23. The Ethiopian's doubt here is whether Isaias is prophesying about **himself or** ... **some other.**

8:35. Philip, **opening his mouth** (a Hebraism found elsewhere: Mt. 5:2; Acts 10:34, etc.) must have given him a long instruction to prove his thesis, although it is not reported here. In his reasoning, he must have used scriptural arguments similar to those adopted by Jesus with the two disciples of Emmaus (Lk. 24:25 sqq.), and those used by Peter in his discourse (Acts 2:22 sqq.), to show that Jesus was the Messias although he had suffered and had been killed. This last theme is, in fact, common to all three. Philip, moreover, would have told the Ethiopian of the necessity of baptism if he wished to share in the remission of sins wrought by the Messias Jesus, just as Peter had already done in his discourse (2:38–39). In the next verse, we find the Ethiopian spontaneously asking for baptism, which shows that by this time he knew its effect.

8:36. The locality of **some water** here was identified in the fourth century as Ain-Dirue, situated about eighteen miles south of Jerusalem and five miles from Hebron. Later it was thought that the place was much

8:37.

8:38. And he ordered the carriage to stop, and both went down into the water, Philip and the eunuch, and [Philip] baptised him.

8:39. But when they had come up out of the water, the Spirit of the Lord took Philip away; and the eunuch saw him no more, for he went on his way rejoicing.

---

nearer Jerusalem, but neither of these traditions has any solid foundation. Of the latter this is especially true.

8:37. This verse is represented by the following words: **And Philip said: "If thou believest with thy whole heart, it is lawful."** Then (he) answering said: **"I believe Jesus to be the Son of God** (with the variant, **Jesus Christ,"** but is omitted by all the Greek uncial codices (except one — E), by many minuscules, and also by the Syriac-Peshitta, the Coptic and Ethiopian versions, and by the more important codices of the Latin Vulgate. It is, however, given by various Greek minuscules and the Vulgate, by the Heraklean Syriac version (marginal), and by the Armenian version. It was, nevertheless, known to writers of the second and third centuries, such as Irenaeus and Cyprian. Almost all modern critical editions omit this verse. It is probably a marginal note introduced into the text by a reader wishing to note the profession of faith to be made at the reception of baptism (cf. Rom. 10:9; 1 Cor. 8:6; 12:3; Phil. 2:11).

8:38. The expression **went down into the water** ($\epsilon i s$ τὸ ὕδωρ) immediately suggests baptism by immersion, which was customary (cf. Rom. 6:4; Col. 2:12); but it could have been by partial immersion, or by extensive ablution, or effusion, since baptism was also administered in this way (*Didache,* VII, 3).

8:39. **Spirit of the Lord:** without the article (cf. 5:9), like **Holy Spirit** in verses 15–17; see note. Undoubtedly, this **Spirit of the Lord** is the same **Spirit** as in verse 29, namely the Holy Spirit. In 16:6–7, the **Holy Spirit** is the equivalent of the **Spirit of Jesus.** It is certain that Luke intends to relate a miraculous happening by saying simply that the Spirit **took Philip away,** though he does not descend to the details of this marvelous removal. There is, then, no foundation for the hypothesis put forward by some that the **Spirit of the Lord** simply means *a wind divinely strong;* nor would such a suggestion eliminate the miracle, for Philip would have been smashed to bits by such a wind, whereas he **was found at Azotus** (following verse) quite safe (cf. 21:8). Others, therefore, dismiss it out of hand as a myth. — At first sight, the words **for** (γὰρ) **he went, etc.,** which refer to the preceding remark, **saw him no more,** seem strange; but the point

8:40. But Philip was found at Azotus, and evangelized all the cities through which he passed until he came to Caesarea.

9:1. But Saul, still breathing threat and slaughter against the disciples of the Lord, approaching the high priest,

9:2. asked him for letters for Damascus, [addressed] to the synagogues, that if he found any who were [followers] of that Way, whether men or women, he might bring them bound to Jerusalem.

---

here is not so much that he saw him no more as that he met him no more. It means in effect, that when Philip suddenly disappeared, the Ethiopian did not trouble to look for him, for he went on his way rejoicing at what had happened; and with that, the Ethiopian vanishes from the story. Irenaeus (*Adv. Haer.*, III, 12, 8), Eusebius (*Hist. eccl.*, II, 1, 13) and other more recent writers maintain that the eunuch became a preacher of the Gospel in his own country, and some legends venerate him as the first apostle of Abyssinia.

8:40. Was found appears to be the equivalent of **found himself,** but it could also mean that **he was found** by the people of the city of Azotus. This is the present-day Ashdod, which is near the sea, about thirty miles as the crow flies from Gaza, and further still from Ain-Dirue (cf. note on v. 36). From here, Philip turned his steps northward and resumed his missionary journey, interrupted in verse 26, and **evangelized all the cities** right up to Caesarea.

9:1-2. Up to now, our book has been pre-eminently the book of the "Acts of Peter"; with this chapter, however, Paul enters fully on the scene, but without excluding Peter who at the end of the chapter (v. 32 sqq.) is still the chief character, as indeed he is in Chapters 10–12. With Chapter 13, the book becomes practically the "Acts of Paul," and the narrative centers more and more on him, except for the account of the Apostolic Council (Chapter 15), at which, however, Paul played a significant part. — **Still breathing threat, etc.:** this links up with 8:3, where the narrative was suspended to make way for the account of Philip's activities. These latter may have been contemporary with, or perhaps later than, those of Paul which are related here. The fact that Saul, **approaching the high priest,** asked him for letters authorizing him to take strong action against the Christians of Damascus, shows that the fiery Saul was mainly responsible for extending the persecution beyond the immediate area of Jerusalem. The **high priest,** and with him the Sanhedrin (see note on 4:5–6), probably had no intention of persecuting the Christians in a district so far away as

9:3. And as he went on his journey, it came to pass that he drew near to Damascus, when suddenly a light from heaven flashed about him.

Damascus when they were satisfied that Jerusalem itself was no longer troubled. They also remembered Gamaliel's prudent warning (5:34 sqq.). There was also the danger that orders for persecution might come to nothing, for while it is true that the authority of the high priest and the Sanhedrin extended to all Jews in the Roman empire, it was more in theory than in practice, and in actual fact such authority carried little weight with Jewish communities outside Palestine and in pagan regions. This was the case in Damascus although there was a flourishing Jewish colony there. Saul was relying on the support of the Jews of Damascus. The Sanhedrin, cautious from earlier experience, distrusted the Damascene Jews, but despite this, Saul's persecuting zeal prevailed in obtaining **letters for Damascus** with full powers. No reason is given for Saul's interest in Damascus, but it is easy to suppose that as a native, not of Palestine but of the Diaspora, he closely followed the events among the Diaspora, and knew that Christianity was spreading with alarming rapidity in Damascus, a very important center of Judaism in Syria. As a zealous Pharisee then, he reacted immediately and energetically to such a threat. — The unnamed **high priest** could no longer have been Caiphas, but his son-in-law, Jonathan, the predecessor of Theophilus (see note on 4:5-6). Jonathan was deposed shortly afterward by Vitellius, the legate of Syria (Flavius Josephus, *Antiquities of the Jews,* XVIII, 123). — **Followers of that Way,** in the Greek literally **of the Way,** to be taken here in the metaphorical sense as meaning *teaching* or *doctrine,* i.e., Christianity; cf. 18:25-26.

9:3. The first of the three accounts of Saul's conversion in the *Acts* begins here, and it is Luke, the author of the book, who is speaking. In the second account, it is Saul himself speaking to his Jewish audience (22:6-16); and in the third, Saul again relates it to the Roman governor Festus and the Jewish king Agrippa (26:12-18). When matters of special importance are involved, Luke takes great pleasure in repeating himself; see note on 11:4-15. While they agree in substance, these three accounts have certain differences due to the particular nature and circumstances of each presentation. Taking Luke's present historical narrative as the starting point, we shall examine, as they occur, the particular differences of Saul's other two oratorical descriptions. — **As he went on his journey:** there were various routes from Jerusalem to Damascus; Saul's choice was probably the convenient Roman road from Jerusalem which touched Sichem (about 1¼ miles east of Nablus; see note on 8:5 and 6-7) where

9:4. and falling to the ground he heard a voice which said to him: "Saul, Saul, why dost thou persecute me?"

9:5. But he said: "Who art thou, Lord?" And he said: "I am Jesus whom thou dost persecute.

---

it turned right and, passing Beisan-Scythopolis, went up the valley of the Jordan to the lake of Tiberias. From here, going both east and west (there were two ways), it came direct into Damascus. The entire journey must have been about 144 to 156 miles, and could be done in about seven or eight days, necessarily including a Sabbath day on which a strict Jew like Saul would not travel. The journey presented no difficulty for a caravan of strong men equipped with beasts as were Saul and his companions; but the unforeseen happened toward the end when the caravan **drew near to Damascus.** This is only a general indication of nearness, but it is made more precise in verse 8 which says that Saul's traveling companions, **leading him by the hand . . . brought him into Damascus.** So the city was in sight of the travelers, and near enough for a man blinded and physically shaken as Saul was after the vision to be led into it. There is no authoritative indication of the exact spot where the incident occurred. The three or four places shown today to visitors to Damascus are doubtful, as is also the old tradition placing it at Kaukab, three or four hours' walk from Damascus along the road to Galilee. Three hours' walk would seem too much for a man in Saul's condition. As regards the time, according to 22:6 and 26:13, it happened about midday, i.e., in full daylight.

9:4. Falling to the ground: almost certainly from horseback (cf. 22:7; 26:14). On the supposition that Saul was riding a horse, no difficulty arises from the fact that presently they led him **by the hand** to Damascus (v. 8), as a mount was then more than ever necessary because of the experience Saul had just undergone. Most likely he was not in a fit state to ride by himself, and for this reason his companions helped him on to the animal as best they could (just as the Good Samaritan had done with the wounded stranger found by the wayside, in Lk. 10:34), and holding him on either side, took him into Damascus. In this case, the expression **by the hand** would have a wider meaning as referring directly to the animal which the rider could not guide by himself, and indirectly to the rider. — The **voice** spoke in Hebrew, according to 26:14 (*vide infra,* and 21:40). — After the words **persecute me,** some documents add the phrase, **(it is) hard for thee to kick against the goad;** others, including the Vulgate, add these words after **dost persecute** in the following verse. They are given in 26:14, but there is no evidence for them here.

9:5-6. Up to this point, the narrative explicitly mentions **a voice;** but

9:6. "But arise and go into the city, and it will be told thee what thou must do."

9:7. Now the men who were travelling with him were standing speechless, hearing indeed the voice but seeing no one.

---

these verses imply that a vision was manifested to Saul who, in the aura of light which flashed about him (v. 3), sees a real person — Jesus — and he asks: **Who art thou, Lord?** Later, this allows him to claim: **Have I not seen Jesus our Lord?** (1 Cor. 9:1; cf. 15:8.) Saul's question was justified, because so far as is known, he had not met Jesus before his death and therefore did not know him in the flesh (the **knowing** of 2 Cor. 5:16 is in a moral sense, not a physical sense). However, Jesus' words **dost thou persecute me** in verse 4 have already given some indication to the persecutor concerning the possible identity of the mysterious person revealed to him in a manifestation of power. An indication of Saul's state of mind is found in his use of the appellative, **Lord.** A certain solemnity may be detected in its use here, as distinct from its purely profane use as a term of politeness (see note on 2:36), because Saul is aware of the supernatural nature of the vision. — **Whom thou dost persecute** is a repetition of Jesus' preceding words with the addition of the name of the object of the persecution. As Saul had already heard the preceding words, a quick examination of conscience would show him that they were true to fact, at least in part, since he was persecuting the Christians. But these heretics were enemies of the God of Israel and therefore the zealous Pharisee was persecuting them with a clear conscience. However, he receives the answer that he is not persecuting a group of heretics, but the powerful personage who has appeared to him and who is called Jesus. There was, then, an equivalence or better, an identity between Jesus and the Christians as though the one represented the other. Later on, reflecting on the doctrinal content of these words of Jesus, Paul draws from it the teaching on the "mystical body" of Christ (Col. 1:18; Eph. 1:22–23; etc.), in which Christ is the head and the Christians are the members. Saul was utterly amazed at Jesus' words, which not only upset, but contradicted his Pharisaic principles, until the voice once more brought him out of his stupefaction: **But** (in the sense of, **well now) arise and go into the city,** etc.

9:7. Were standing, εἱστήκεισαν: can be translated simply **remained (speechless).** If, however, the notion of standing is to be retained, it must refer to the second moment of the scene, since to begin with they **fell to the ground** (26:14). Once over the first bewilderment, the others got up, while Saul still remained on the ground. — **Hearing indeed the voice,** ἀκούντες μὲν τῆς φωνῆς: whereas, on the contrary, according to 22:9, these same com-

9:8. And Saul arose from the ground but although his eyes were opened, he could see nothing; and leading him by the hand they brought him into Damascus.

9:9. And for three days he could not see, and he neither ate nor drank.

---

panions **did not hear the voice,** τὴν δὲ φωνὴν οὐκ ἤκουσαν. The two different constructions, the first with the genitive and the second with the accusative, have no influence on the meaning. It is as though the first signified perceiving only the material sound, while the second also implied understanding the sense of the words. We shall see later (22:7) the construction with the genitive, meaning an understanding of the sense of the words. While the two meanings of hearing, namely to perceive the material sound, and to understand or comprehend the sense, are implicit in the word *to hear,* one can also be said to have "heard" a speaker when one has not "understood" what he said. A comparison of the two instances in this verse, and in 22:7 sqq., clearly shows that a contrast between his companions' visual and auditory perceptions and Saul's is intended. His companions see a sudden light but see nobody, while Saul sees both the light and the apparition. In the same way, his companions were only conscious of a sound of which they understood nothing, while Saul heard it and understood. The care with which the two accounts throw into relief the part played by Saul's companions in this incident is prompted by the desire to show them as disinterested bystanders.

9:8. Were opened, ἀνεῳγμένων: indicates the state of being open, but does not imply that Saul opened his eyes only when he had finished speaking and **arose from the ground.** — **Leading him by the hand:** the distance from the city must therefore have been very small, but it was not right to expect a man so weakened as Saul, to walk even a short distance, and everything seemed to show that he could be conveyed best by being put back upon his horse; in which case, **leading him by the hand** would be in the wider sense already noted in verse 4.

9:9. The fact that Saul **neither ate nor drank** for three days was the physical result of the mental turmoil caused by Jesus' words (see note on vv. 5–6). At this decisive moment, Saul entered the mystical state he speaks of later in his epistles, and it is a fact that abstention from food and drink is common in such cases. Luke the physician would naturally not omit this important detail in his account of the incident; he even proceeds later on (v. 19) to examine his subject clinically. During this short period, Saul's whole being must have been permeated by a state of spiritual suspense. He had been told to **go into the city, and it will be told**

9:10. Now there was in Damascus a certain disciple named Ananias; and the Lord said to him in a vision: "Ananias." And he said:
"Here I am Lord."

9:11. And the Lord said to him: "Arise and go into the street
called Straight, and seek in the house of Judas for a man of Tarsus
[one] named Saul; for behold he is praying."

9:12. And he saw a man called Ananias come in and lay his hands
upon him that he might recover his sight.

---

thee what thou must do (v. 6), but with no details of how that promise
would be fulfilled. Blindness in the eyes, semiblindness in the soul! He
therefore waited, unconcerned about food and drink, but comforting himself with prayer, for behold he is praying (v. 11).

9:10-11. Of this Ananias we know only the little told us in 22:12,
namely that he was a devout Jew esteemed by his fellow men. We are
not told when he became a disciple, i.e., a Christian. It is possible, though
not certain, that he was one of the Jewish Christians who had left Jerusalem to escape the persecution (cf. 8:1 and 4). It is certain, however,
that he knew of Saul's destructive havoc and the purpose of his mission to
Damascus (vv. 13-14). — A trace of this long street called Straight still
runs through Damascus, and the name has been retained (in Arabic, Darb
al-mustaqim); it runs through the city from east to west and there are
ruins of the double row of columns which flanked it in ancient times,
although it is not as wide today as it used to be and its course is slightly
altered at certain points. The house of Judas was situated in this aristocratic
street; he was probably the best-known innkeeper to the Jews who came
to Damascus, and Saul, as the representative of the Sanhedrin of Jerusalem,
was therefore taken to him. The house of Ananias is nowadays pointed
out in the Christian quarter of the city, situated a little north of the eastern
end of the street called Straight. — For behold, he is praying: see the preceding note.

9:12. This verse is rather difficult, both for what it says and its place
in the context. So far as the transmission of the text goes, it should be
noted that while codex Floriacensis of the sixth century omits the whole
verse, other authoritative Greek codices add the words in a vision either
before or after a man; it would then be a vision (experienced by Saul) communicated during another vision (experienced by Ananias). But who is
speaking in this verse? In the preceding verse, the Lord spoke to Ananias,
and here the text goes on, and he saw (certainly meaning Saul) a man
called Ananias, etc. Now, if the Lord is still speaking to Ananias, this

9:13. But Ananias answered, "Lord, I have heard from many about this man, how much evil he has done to thy saints in Jerusalem.

9:14. "And here too he has authority from the high priests to arrest all who invoke thy name."

9:15. But the Lord said to him: "Go, for this man is a chosen vessel to me, to carry my name before nations and kings and the children of Israel.

---

mode of expression is inexplicable. If, then, the Lord is not still speaking, who is? The Latin Vulgate, by putting the entire verse in parentheses, appears to consider it an insertion dovetailed by Luke the narrator into the dialogue between Christ and Ananias. In that case, Luke uses the occasion of Saul's prayer just related to mention the vision granted to Saul during his prayer, a vision which foretold Ananias' visit related shortly afterward (vv. 17-18). One suggestion is that it is a fragment from another source, but this is unsupported by either documentary or conceptual proof. Again, this twofold vision has been thought to be a parallel to the twofold visions of the rite of initiation described by Apuleius (*Metamorphosis*, XII), but Apuleius, on the contrary, is about a century later than Luke. — **Recover his sight,** ἀναβλέψῃ: the Greek verb can also mean "to look upwards," but here and elsewhere in the New Testament it signifies "to see again" or "to recover one's sight."

9:13-14. Ananias was well informed about Saul (see note on vv. 10-11) and the progress of his mission, about which one of the Christians in Jerusalem may have informed the brethren in Damascus, so that they could make provision for their safety. Perhaps also, as the leading Christian (cf. 22:12), Ananias would have been one of the first to be imprisoned by Saul. Ananias, however, apparently did not know what had happened to Saul on the way. Ananias' words seem to be more in the nature of a request for clarification about something which to him seemed unusual. — **Saints,** the Christians, a term frequently used in Paul's letters, especially the faithful in Judea and Jerusalem (1 Cor. 14:33; Rom. 15:25-26; etc.).

9:15. Chosen vessel: literally, **a vessel of election,** a Hebrew expression for a chosen instrument. The Hebrew kĕlī, translated σκεῦος, can have a wider meaning, such as **vessel, thing, object, instrument,** etc. (in 1 Thess. 4:4, also **woman,** or even one's own **body**). The Lord's words could be paraphrased as follows: **He is the instrument that I have chosen to carry,** etc. The name **chosen vessel** later became attached to Saul-Paul in the Christian church. — Saul is to **carry the name** of the Lord before **Nations and kings and the children of Israel.** This program seems almost to summarize

9:16. "For I will show him how much he must suffer for my name."

9:17. So Ananias departed and entered the house, and laying his hands upon him, he said, "Brother Saul, the Lord has sent me — Jesus who appeared to thee on thy journey — that thou mayest recover thy sight and be filled with the Holy Spirit."

---

the remainder of the book, which might be entitled the "Acts of Paul" (see notes on vv. 1–2). The new element in the program is that Saul is to preach to the *Gentiles,* mentioned here for the first time, since Christian propaganda had until then been directed, and continued for some time to be directed, solely to the Jews (11:19). The preaching to the Samaritans (8:5 sqq.) represented a turning toward Jewish heretics, and the baptism of Cornelius (Chapter 10) takes place on the personal responsibility of Peter, the leader of the Apostles, although not without protests from the Jewish Christians (11:2 sqq.). In the light of this mission, Saul-Paul later calls himself with pride the Gentiles' apostle (Rom. 11:13), and agrees with Peter to take upon himself the apostolate of the Gentiles (Gal. 2:7–9). He will not, however, forget his Jewish fellow countrymen and will strive to save some of them (Rom. 11:14), **the children of Israel** referred to here. The **kings** are the various Roman magistrates, such as Sergius Paulus, Gallio, etc., whom Paul will meet during his missionary career. Agrippa of 25:13 sqq. was a **king** in the strict sense of the word.

9:16. The apostolate and the endurance of persecution were considered as going hand in hand, for the endurance of persecution demonstrated the genuineness of the apostolate guaranteeing the assistance of Christ. To suffer persecution was, therefore, a joy (see note on 5:41; and cf. 2 Cor. 12:10). It should be noted that Saul's vocation to the apostolate of the Gentiles, revealed here by the Lord to Ananias, is, according to the third narrative (26:16–18), communicated by Christ direct to Saul. This is simply a difference of presentation and not of idea: *vide infra.*

9:17. **Laying his hands upon him:** for the imposition of hands in general, see note on 6:6. The rite is performed here to cure Saul of his blindness, as is also stated explicitly in verse 12. A similar case is found in 28:8. The additional reason, namely, that Saul should be **filled with the Holy Spirit** is to be understood as referring to his baptism which is related forthwith, and upon which Saul was healed and filled with the Holy Spirit, whereas without baptism he would not have been able to receive this fullness. It is probable that Ananias cured Saul in virtue of his possession of the charism of "cures." Paul speaks of this charism ($\iota\acute{\alpha}\mu\alpha\tau\alpha$) later (1 Cor.

9:18. And straightway there fell from his eyes something like scales, and he recovered his sight and arose and was baptised.

9:19. And after taking some food, he regained his strength. He remained therefore, with the disciples [who were] in Damascus some days.

(2:9; 28:30); and he himself, abundantly gifted with charisms (*ibid.,* 14:18), effects a cure by the imposition of hands (Acts 28:8).

9:18-19. The account here becomes schematic and Luke the physician intends to have the lion's share of it, while passing over important details which, however, can easily be supplied. Just as the Ethiopian's instruction had been brief (see note on 8:35), so Saul, after summary instruction by his visitor, was certainly baptized during Ananias' visit. In any case, Saul may well have known from the time when he was an enemy of Christianity, the importance and significance of baptism for the followers of the Messias Jesus. It is probable also that his baptism took place in the house of the wealthy Judas (v. 11) where there would be no lack of vessels for ablutions, since Damascus has always been a city well supplied with water. Leaving all that aside, Luke speaks of the scales that fell from his eyes, of the food he took after three days' fasting (v. 9), and the sick man's consequent recovery. Is he speaking figuratively or literally when he says that **something like scales** (ὡς λεπίδες) fell from Saul's eyes? In other words, did Saul regain his sight as if scales had fallen from his eyes, or because such scales did actually and materially fall? It should be noted that the word **like** refers directly to **scales,** in the sense of "a kind of scales"; and the expression "scales (or white films) that fall" is found in Greek medical writings. It is more likely that Luke the physician, as an accurate observer of physiological phenomena, used this phrase in a figurative sense only. It is possible that the ophthalmic injury which Paul suffered may have been a consequence of the intense brightness of the vision (v. 3; and better, 26:13); at any rate, it was a supernatural cure of an injury produced by a supernatural cause. There is no basis for supposing that Saul was afflicted with chronic ophthalmia, as some have done, basing their suppositions on passages like Gal. 4:15; 6:11. — The mention of Saul's eating and regaining strength after his fast is characteristic of Luke the diagnostician who loves to follow the physiopsychological symptoms of the subjects he presents (see note on 6:7). Saul did not become a fanatic when he became a Christian; he returned to a normal mode of living. Some years later, several of his fellow countrymen, on the contrary, allowed themselves to be carried away by fanaticism to the point of swearing to remain without food or drink until they had killed Saul-Paul (23:12-14). —

9:20. And straightway he preached Jesus, [affirming] that he is the Son of God.

9:21. And all who heard him were amazed, and said: "Is not this he who used to make havoc in Jerusalem of those who called upon this name, and who had come here for this [purpose] of bringing them in bonds to the chief priests?"

9:22. But Saul grew all the stronger, and confounded the Jews who were living in Damascus, proving that this is the Christ.

9:23. But after a good many days, the Jews made a plot to kill him.

Disciples: the Christians. — **Some days** certainly indicate a short period of time, but to make it fit into the chronological sequence of events as they unfold, account must be taken of **a good many days** referred to in verse 23: *vide infra*.

9:20. The fiery Pharisee, now turned Christian, did not put away his burning zeal but used it in the service of Jesus the Messias, preaching him as being **the Son of God.** This assertion of the Divine Sonship of Jesus has not appeared before, even in Peter's catechetical discourses (3:13 sqq.; 4:27) except in 8:37 of doubtful authenticity. We shall find presently (v. 22), moreover, that the theme of Saul's preaching was that Jesus is the Christ, namely, the Jewish Messias, which was also the tenor of Peter's discourses. Everything, therefore, points to the interpretation of the term **Son of God,** not in a directly ontological sense as referring to the divine nature, but in a directly historico-messianic sense as the name of the Jewish Messias.

9:21. **Used to make havoc,** πορθήσας: Paul uses this verb twice (Gal. 1:13 and 23) in speaking precisely about his former persecution of the Church. It is true that here it is the Jews of Damascus that are speaking, but the phrase "to make havoc" may well have been adopted by Paul into his own vocabulary, and Luke possibly heard it from Paul himself.

9:22. **Proving,** συμβιβάζων: the real meaning of the word is to establish a given conclusion by a logical process. The rabbi-turned-Christian seized weapons from the well-furnished arsenal of the school of Gamaliel in Jerusalem (22:3) and used them now in the rabbinical method against a precisely opposite target to yesterday's. He had, in fact, succeeded to the spiritual heritage of Stephen, his most outstanding victim. See notes on 6:10; 7:2 sqq.; 8:1. — **This is the Christ:** see note on verse 20.

9:23. **A good many** (or days enough: ἱκαναί) **days:** in what relation do these days stand to **some days** in verse 19? The chronological sequence of

9:24. But their plot became known to Saul. They were even guarding the gates both day and night in order to kill him.

---

events must include the facts narrated in Gal. 1:16–17 which, after referring to his conversion, add: **Immediately . . . I retired into Arabia and again returned to Damascus.** This retirement into Arabia is not mentioned in the *Acts,* but the phrase, **I . . . returned again to Damascus,** implies a previous sojourn in that city. In actual fact, the two narrators speak from their own point of view and aim. Paul in his epistle does not pretend to give a complete account of the events subsequent to his conversion but only to show that when he became a Christian he had no contact with the Apostles in Jerusalem for three years (Gal. 1:18–19). So he rightly records his retirement into the solitude of Arabia, omitting mention of his first stay in Damascus since it was brief and unimportant to his theme. In any case, while the phrase, **I . . . again returned to Damascus,** explicitly posits a second stay, it implicitly suggests a first one. The *Acts* aim rather at giving a résumé of the propagation of the Gospel, so they omit the stay in Arabia and distinguish the two sojourns in Damascus — that of **some days** in verse 19, and **a good many days** in verse 23 — although they are presented as almost simultaneous. By putting Paul's retirement into Arabia between the first and second stays at Damascus, the two narratives coalesce and complete each other quite naturally. Regarding the duration of each event: the stay at Damascus for **some days** immediately followed Paul's conversion, which took place in the year 36; he then retired into Arabia which, with the second visit to Damascus, lasted **a good many days.** The words, **a good many,** can be misleading since in practice the expression is used for both "many" and "very many"; the retirement into Arabia could, therefore, have lasted many months and the second stay in Damascus must then be added to it. The entire period from Paul's conversion to the end of his second stay at Damascus certainly did not exceed the **three years** mentioned in Gal. 1:18, which brings us to the year 39. This, then, is the year in which the Jews **made a plot to kill him.** Such a plot would have been premature during his first stay at Damascus because Paul's conversion was too recent and the Jews of Damascus were still uncertain what to think of him; but after three years all doubt was removed, both by Saul's polemical activity (v. 22) and the information received meanwhile from Jerusalem.

9:24. This verse at first renders the plot less dangerous, but immediately raises another peril. The plan is no longer secret since it has become **known to Saul,** more than likely through the information of some friendly disciple not suspected by the plotters. But another danger immediately

9:25. But his disciples took him by night, and let him down over the wall, lowering him in a basket.

9:26. Now on his arrival at Jerusalem he tried to join the disciples, and they were all afraid of him, not believing that he was a disciple.

---

arises from the guarding of the gates, and this is overcome as related in the following verse.

9:25. The story of his escape is told by Paul himself in 2 Cor. 11:32-33, but there it is **the ethnarch of king Aretas** who wishes to capture him and has placed the guard at the gates, and not the Jews. It is understandable, however, and in keeping with the setting to consider the ethnarch as having been bribed by the Jews. This person must have been the local representative of Aretas IV, king of the Nabateans, against whom Tiberius, at the instigation of Herod Antipas, had waged war in the year 36. But later Caligula, who succeeded Tiberius in March of 37, entered into peaceful relations with him to the extent of voluntarily ceding Damascus to him, as appears from various sources. Since Aretas died in the year 40 and his possession of Damascus did not begin before the year 37, Paul's escape took place during this period which covers the year 39, as already suggested (cf. note on v. 23). — The most authoritative codices have **his disciples;** others have, instead, **the disciples taking him,** etc. The word **disciples** undoubtedly means the Christians (cf. v. 26) and so fits in perfectly here; but **his disciples** would be followers of Paul. Did Paul, then, barely three years a Christian, have a group of his own disciples? The question is not clear. — The escape plan was not extraordinary. Paul would have been hidden by some Christian who had a house on the city walls and, as 2 Cor. 11:33 relates, he was let down in a basket **through a window** of this house outside the guarded walls, and so escaped. Large baskets were commonly used not only for carrying quantities of miscellaneous articles, but also for bringing goods and people in through the windows or the openings in the upper stories of a building. Until recent years, visitors were carried into the monastery-fortress of St. Catherine on Mount Sinai by means of such baskets, and this is so in other places. David had made a similar escape when he was being pursued by King Saul (1 Sam. 19:12). Nonetheless, this mode of flight was undignified, and Paul writing eighteen years later in 2 *Corinthians* remembers it as a particularly worrying experience.

9:26. This was the first time that Paul had visited Jerusalem since his conversion. The purpose of this visit was, as he himself says (Gal. 1:18), **to see** ($i\sigma\tau o\rho\tilde{\eta}\sigma\alpha\iota$) **Cephas,** namely Peter, with whom he stayed fifteen days. This "interview" with Peter so occupied Paul that, as he acknowledged,

9:27. But Barnabas took him and brought him to the apostles, and he recounted to them how on his journey he had seen the Lord and the Lord had spoken to him and how in Damascus he had held forth boldly in the name of Jesus.

9:28. And he went about with them at Jerusalem, speaking out boldly in the name of the Lord.

9:29. And he spoke and disputed with the Hellenists, but they sought to kill him.

---

he did not see (any) of the apostles, saving James, the brother of the Lord (*ibid.*, 1:19). We gather from the present narrative, however, that **he tried to join the disciples** (viz., the Christians; see note on v. 25), but they suspected him. Their suspicion was not unfounded. They all remembered that three years previously he was devastating the Church in Jerusalem (8:3); news had subsequently gone around that he had been converted at Damascus, but such rumors were unreliable, for they could not be verified owing to the difficulty of communication caused by the war between Aretas and Antipas as well as by the new government installed at Damascus (see note on v. 25). This mistrust, then, was prudent but was short-lived.

9:27. This Barnabas has already been referred to (4:36), but he appears here as so well informed about Paul's conversion as to be guarantor for him to the Apostles. Since Barnabas was a Hellenist Jew from the island of Cyprus, which is immediately south of Tarsus, Paul's native city, it has been thought that they knew each other from boyhood, either at Tarsus or in Jerusalem at the school of Gamaliel, but this is mere conjecture. It is, however, certain that Barnabas' intervention removed the Christian community's suspicion.

9:28. The word **them** must refer to the **apostles** since they are the last persons to be mentioned. But Paul's remark that apart from Peter he had not seen **(any) other of the apostles, saving James** (see note on v. 26), on this occasion reduces the number of **them** to two. This difficulty can be resolved by supposing that the emphasis is not so much on the numerical strength of the Apostolic College but on the qualitative majority, since Peter was the head of that body and James was "the brother of the Lord." If this interpretation is unsatisfactory, it is suggested that the word **them** refers conceptually rather than syntactically to the **disciples** of verse 26 who had been suspicious of him; so, to mark their reconciliation, Paul is said here, to be **with them, etc.** — The Hebrew idiom "went about" — literally, "went in and went out" — has already been used in 1:21.

9:29. Events repeat themselves. Just as at Damascus Paul's dispute with

9:30. When the brethren got to know this, they took him down to Caesarea and sent him away to Tarsus.

9:31. So throughout all Judea and Galilee and Samaria the Church had peace, and was being built up, walking in the fear of the Lord, and grew through the encouragement of the Holy Spirit.

---

the Jews had only resulted in a plot against his life (vv. 22–23), so at Jerusalem he debates with them and is threatened with death.

9:30. This sudden departure from Jerusalem was certainly provoked by the danger which threatened Paul, but it must also have corresponded to a secret desire of the Christian community, who had **had peace** (v. 31) after the storm raised by Paul three years earlier. Here the former persecutor again appears on the scene, not to disturb that peace but as a defender of it. No doubt he had the best intentions, but his fiery polemics seemed out of place in Jerusalem, and it seemed preferable for the new preacher to go elsewhere to announce his message. The brethren of Jerusalem must have reasoned in some such way, and taking advantage of the danger which Paul now ran, hearing it, **they took him down to Caesarea,** and from there, probably by sea, **sent him away to Tarsus.** For several reasons Paul did not oppose this arrangement by the Christians at Jerusalem, the chief one being that during this stay at Jerusalem he must have experienced the vision in the Temple described in 22:17–21, in which the Lord commanded him to leave Jerusalem immediately because he wished him to evangelize distant peoples. We know from Gal. 1:21 that — certainly after he reached Tarsus — Paul went **into the regions of Syria and Cilicia,** most probably on a missionary venture, although the *Acts* are silent on this point.

9:31. This verse is the kind of summary delighted in by the narrator, particularly where there is a change of emphasis: cf. 2:42 sqq.; 4:32 sqq.; 5:12 sqq. — **The Church,** in the singular, is the reading given by the majority of the authoritative codices; others have **the Churches,** in the plural. The mention of Galilee as the field of the Church's expansion seems a little unexpected as there had been no previous reference to it (except in 2:7, which particularly concerns the Apostles), nor is any further reference made later. This is not significant, nor should it suggest that the word **Galilee** is an interpolation. The Gospels deplore the opposition to Jesus by the Galilean city of Corozain (Mt. 11:21; Lk. 10:13), although this is never mentioned, and the city is only referred to in this connection. It is not surprising to find a Christian community in Galilee, the Apostles' homeland, even though there is no account of its foundation. — **Had peace:** this peace also had a cause in the political conditions of Palestine in the

9:32. And it came to pass that Peter while visiting all those parts, came down also to the saints who were living at Lydda;

9:33. and he found there a certain man named Aeneas who had kept his bed eight years, being a paralytic.

9:34. And Peter said to him: "Aeneas, Jesus Christ heals thee; get up and make thy bed." And straightway he got up.

9:35. And all who lived at Lydda and in Sharon saw him, and they turned to the Lord.

9:36. Now at Joppa there was a certain disciple called Tabitha, which translated means Dorcas (gazelle): a woman full of good works and almsdeeds, which she used to practice.

---

year 39. The mad Caligula, emperor for the past two years (see note on v. 25), had decreed that the Jews, like other nations of the empire, should worship him as a god. The Jews naturally refused, and there were disturbances in Alexandria in 38, and in Jamnia and elsewhere in Palestine in 39. Caligula ordered Petronius, the legate of Syria, to take military action and to erect his statue in the Temple at Jerusalem. Petronius entered Palestine at the beginning of 40 with two Roman legions and other troops but took no action and, with great humanity, held the mad emperor in check until the latter was killed in January, 41. These dangerous events, described by Flavius Josephus (*Wars of the Jews,* II, 184–203; more fully in *Antiquities of the Jews,* XVIII, 261–309) and Philo (*Leg. ad Caium*), occupied the attention of the Jewish authorities at Jerusalem to the exclusion of the Christians and the disturbance of their peace mentioned here.

9:32. It should be borne in mind that the "Acts of Peter" are now drawing to a close and the "Acts of Paul" have already begun (see note on vv. 1–2), but we are on ground here which is shared by both Apostles. Paul, who has been to the fore in this Chapter, now retires into the background, leaving the scene to Peter; the former reappears in Chapter 13. — Saints: the Christians; cf. note on verse 13. — Lydda: a small but flourishing town on the road from Jerusalem to the port of Jaffa (Joppa), a little over ten miles from the port, and thirty miles or so from Jerusalem.

9:33. Kept his bed . . . paralytic: the usual details of interest to Luke the physician. See note on 4:22 and later in this chapter on verses 40–41.

9:35. All: in the moral sense; very many. — Sharon: not a city but the district extending northward from Joppa to Carmel.

9:36. Joppa: cf. note on verse 32. — Tabitha: the Aramaic *tebita,* cor-

9:37. But it happened, at that time, that she fell ill and died. And after washing her, they laid her in an upper room.

9:38. And as Lydda was near Joppa, the disciples, hearing that Peter was there, sent two men to him with the request: "Come to us without delay."

9:39. So Peter arose and went with them; and on his arrival, they took him to the upper room, and all the widows stood round him in tears showing him the tunics and cloaks which Dorcas used to make while she was with them.

9:40. But Peter, having sent them all out, knelt down and prayed; and turning to the body he said: "Tabitha, arise." And she opened her eyes and seeing Peter sat up;

9:41. and he gave her his hand and raised her to her feet; and calling the saints and the widows he gave her back to them alive.

---

responding to the Hebrew *sĕbī* and the Greek δορκας, "a gazelle"; a name given to women among the Greeks, after the animal admired in the *Canticle of Canticles.* — **Full of good works and almsdeeds:** Paul, in 1 Tim. 5:9–10, lays down that a woman may be included in the official class of widows in any community if she has **a reputation for good works . . .** if she has helped those in trouble, and carefully pursued every good work, qualifications possessed here by Tabitha. See note on verse 41.

9:37. At that time: referring to the foregoing narrative, namely when Peter was at Lydda (cf. v. 38). — **After washing her:** an impersonal expression; though the verb is in the masculine, it was the women who fulfilled this task, most likely those spoken of in verse 39. The custom of washing the bodies of the dead is not mentioned in the Old Testament, but is recorded in passing in the Mishna (*Shabbath,* XXIII, 5) together with that of anointing. — **Upper room:** see note on 1:13.

9:38. Lydda . . . near Joppa: see note on verse 32. — **Without delay:** probably the entreaty was made not only so as to have comfort in the distress that had befallen the community, but also because they secretly hoped for a miracle from Peter who had worked them so spectacularly at Jerusalem and elsewhere.

9:40–41. This detailed description, **opened her eyes . . . sat up . . . raised her to her feet,** reveals the trained medical observer; see the note on verse 33. — **The saints and the widows:** the **saints** are the Christians of the community (cf. vv. 13 and 32); and the **widows,** although they form part of the community, are mentioned separately for the reason given previously.

9:42. And it became known all over Joppa, and many believed in the Lord.

9:43. And it came to pass that he remained a good many days in Joppa, with one Simon a tanner.

10:1. Now there was a certain man in Caesarea called Cornelius, a centurion of the cohort called Italian.

But it would be rash to say that they constituted a special class within the community like that mentioned by Paul in the passage cited in the note on verse 36, since the Church's internal organization was still only in the initial stages. We can see here, however, the beginnings of the official class to come into existence later; in fact, Tabitha's qualifications (v. 36), her works and acts of charity while she was with those widows (v. 39), the repeated mention of all the widows and of the saints and the widows, already supply sufficient evidence for the existence of a class of widows, as prescribed by Paul, even if such a group did not as yet exist officially. We are, here, at the beginning of the year 40, while Paul is writing twenty-five years later.

It should be noted that this endearing picture of Tabitha bears out Luke's tendency to exalt womanhood, a characteristic found in many passages of his Gospel, and which appears again here further on (16:14 sqq., etc.). It may be interpreted as a reaction to the attitude to women in the depraved pagan society of that time.

9:42-43. If Peter stayed at Joppa a good many days — which can mean a month or two (see note on v. 23) — he would have done so in order to give spiritual assistance to the many who believed in the Lord. Peter is still in the house of Simon the tanner by the sea (10:6 and 32) during the events related in the next chapter. Simon the tanner must have had both house and workshop by the sea so as to have plenty of water, and also for hygienic reasons. Rabbinical prescriptions required tanneries to be not less than fifty cubits from a dwelling place because of the unpleasant smell (Mishna, Bababathra, II, 9). Although not forbidden, the tanner's trade was considered degrading because of the continual contact with the carcasses of dead animals, and a woman could divorce her husband if he became a tanner (Mishna, Ketuboth, VII, 10). In spite of this, Peter went to stay with a tanner, and such a step is a fitting preparation for the episode which follows, showing Peter's independent judgment even in the most important matters. A small mosque near the lighthouse in modern Joppa is said to have been built on the site of the house of Simon the tanner.

10:1 sqq. Up to this point, Luke has followed the spread of Christianity

in regions that were more or less Jewish: for Samaria (8:4 sqq.) belonged
to heretical Judaism, and the Ethiopian seems to have been either a Jew
or a "proselyte" of Judaism (cf. 8:27–28). Here, on the contrary, Christianity wins over a man who is not a Jew, either by birth or religion, but
a Gentile, an ex-pagan, although he was in sympathy with Judaism. The
results of a further spread of Christianity were not foreseeable, and this
first conquest among the detested Gentiles was an act of such boldness,
that much anxiety was aroused and a species of inquiry was called for
(11:1 sqq.). — The name **Cornelius** does not mean that a person of that
name was descended from the *Cornelian Gens,* one of the most illustrious
of Rome, which included many patrician families and could boast such
names as Scipio Africanus, Sulla, Lentulus, Cornelia the mother of the
Gracchi, etc. The Cornelius here, who had reached the modest rank of
centurion, must have been a descendant of one of the very many freedmen of the *Cornelian Gens* who took the name of the person who had freed
them. According to Appianus (*Bell. civil.,* I, 100) Cornelius Sulla, on one
occasion alone, bestowed the Roman franchise on 10,000 slaves. — **A centurion of the cohort called Italian:** the centurion was a junior officer in
command of a century (which did not normally number 100 men), and
it was usually the highest rank attainable by valiant and experienced
veterans who lacked theoretical training or social standing. — A **cohort**
could be "legionary," formed of Roman citizens, or "auxiliary," formed
of provincials recruited on the spot. It could also be the *Italica civium
Romanorum voluntariorum* formed, as the title indicates, of Roman citizens born in Italy. Such cohorts were stationed in the various provinces.
There were no legions in Palestine, and therefore no "legionary" cohorts;
but in addition to a wing (*ala*), or detachment of cavalry, there were five
"auxiliary" cohorts with a strength of about 3000 men. One of these was
on permanent duty at Jerusalem, and another at Caesarea, the seat of the
Roman governor. As Jews were exempt from military service, these cohorts
were recruited from among the Samaritans, Syrians, and Greeks (Flavius
Josephus, *Wars of the Jews,* II, 268; III, 66 sqq.; V, 244–245; *Antiquities
of the Jews,* XIX, 365; etc.). This **cohort called Italian** must have been
formed of Italian volunteers. The presence of an *Italian cohort* in the
province of Syria, to which Judea belonged, is testfiied in actual fact by
inscriptions from the year 69 onward, but there are none for the earlier
period (which includes the episode here), nor for Caesarea at any time.
If, however, the argument *a silentio* seems inconclusive, it should be
remembered that the account does not mention the *Italian cohort* being
at Caesarea, but only Cornelius who belonged to it (ἐκ σπείρης . . . Ἰταλικῆς).
Now, Cornelius may well have been at Caesarea on a special mission,
detached from his cohort which was stationed elsewhere in Syria. In fact,
we find the centurion Julius (27:1 sqq.), of the *Augustan cohort,* going on

10:2. He was devout and God-fearing, as was all his household, giving many alms to the people and praying to God continually.

10:3. About the ninth hour of the day, he saw clearly in a vision an angel of God come in to him and say "Cornelius!"

10:4. And he gazing at him in terror said: "What is it, Lord?" And the angel said to him: "Thy prayers and thy alms have gone up and been remembered in the sight of God.

10:5. "And now send men to Joppa and summon a certain Simon who is surnamed Peter:

10:6. "he is lodging with Simon a tanner whose house is by the sea."

10:7. When the angel who was speaking to him had departed, [Cornelius] calling two of his servants and a devout soldier from among his personal attendants,

10:8. having told them all sent them to Joppa.

---

special service around the Mediterranean far from his cohort's base (Judea or Rome).

10:2. Although a Gentile by birth, Cornelius did not practice an idolatrous religion, but was devout (εὐσεβής) and God-fearing (φοβούμενος). This last term (for which see the note on 2:5-6) shows that he was a sympathizer with the Jewish cause, although he belonged to the lowest class and not to the higher one of real "proselytes." From 11:3, we know that he was not circumcised, whereas the "proselytes" were obliged to receive circumcision. Cornelius' religious position was shared by all his household, namely, his family and servants; cf. verses 7 and 24.

10:3. Clearly: not in a dream or inner imagination, but in actual fact.— Ninth hour: three o'clock in the afternoon; cf. note on 3:1.

10:4. Been remembered, εἰς μνημόσυνον: literally, "for a memorial"; an allusion to the Hebrew liturgy of memorial sacrifice or remembrance (in Hebrew, azkarah), in which a portion of the meal offering was burned and its smoke rose up like a sweet odor to God (Lev. 2:2).

10:7. Personal attendants, or his staff (προσκαρτερούντων αὐτῷ). We may assume that they were not really soldiers but what the Romans called *calones,* namely slaves of Roman citizenship taken to war by their masters as personal servants and who were also able to take part in battle. Flavius Josephus mentions them in his description of the Roman army at the beginning of the campaign in Judea under Vespasian and Titus (*Wars of the Jews,* III, 69; cf. 125–126).

10:9. Now the next day, while they were still on their journey and were drawing near to the city, Peter went up to the housetop to pray, about the sixth hour.

10:10. And he became very hungry and wanted something to eat; but while they were preparing for him [to eat] he fell into a trance;

10:11. and he saw the heaven opened and a certain object like a great sheet, let down by the four corners onto the earth.

10:12. And in it were all the four-footed beasts and creeping things of the earth, and birds of the air.

10:13. And a voice [came] to him: "Arise, Peter, kill and eat!"

10:14. But Peter said: "By no means, Lord, for I have never eaten anything common and unclean."

10:9. **While they were still on their journey:** not a short one; Caesarea to Joppa, along the coast road, is about thirty miles, but the old Roman road wound its way zigzag and therefore made the journey longer. — **Sixth hour:** noon. If the messengers left after three o'clock in the afternoon of the day before (vv. 3, 7, 8), they covered the distance in about twenty hours, including a night's rest.

10:11. **Object,** σκεῦος: see note on 9:15. It could be translated here as **vessel,** since it contained the things listed below, but it looked like a **sheet.** — **Let down by the four corners, etc.:** the text is uncertain here and the description somewhat vague. Various documents and ancient versions add the participle **held** before or after the words **four corners,** which seems to be an explanatory gloss inserted into the text because it was considered obscure. It may broadly be said to mean that the **great sheet** was hung by its four corners so as to form a bundle; but the bundle was not let down perpendicularly, otherwise Peter, who was below it, would not have been able to see what was inside, so it must have been tilted toward Peter by two corners, or the whole of one side.

10:12. **All:** in the sense of a great number, or in bulk; it is obvious from the next verse (kill) that they were all alive.

10:14. Peter, as a good Jew, protests that he is careful not to eat meat which the Law declared **common and unclean** (*Ezechiel* makes a similar statement: Ezech. 4:14). The Law (Lev. 11; Deut. 14), in fact, contained long lists of clean animals, and of unclean animals it was forbidden to eat. We know that the observance of this law had produced martyrs among

10:15. And there came to him again a voice a second time: "What God hath declared clean, do not thou call common."

10:16. This happened three times: and then the bundle was taken up into heaven.

10:17. Now while Peter was still wondering in himself as to what the vision he had had might mean, behold the men sent by Cornelius, having inquired here and there for Simon's house, stood at the door.

---

pious Jews (2 Mach. 6:18 sqq.; 7:1 sqq.). — I have never eaten anything, etc.: this is a Hebraism for "never did I eat something, etc."

10:15. When did **God . . . declare clean** meat which was regarded as unclean by the Mosaic Law? It may possibly refer to Jesus' statement in Mt. 15:11; Mk. 7:15; and 18:18, which at the time of Peter's vision could only have been circulated by word of mouth, for our canonical Gospels had not yet been written. If this be accepted, then the voice which spoke to Peter designates Jesus the author of the declaration, by the name of God, ὁ θεός, something which Peter had not so far done. It may alternatively be interpreted that God, the author of the vision, by the fact of offering beasts indiscriminately and directing Peter to satisfy his hunger without worrying about their legal cleanness, **declared** such beasts **clean** and abolished the Law's prescriptions on this point.

10:17. Wondering in himself, etc. It was not particularly difficult to realize the immediate meaning of the vision and the words, but Peter had to reflect upon the serious consequences of the moral lesson they implied. Contemporary Judaism considered itself seated on a throne of glory placed upon the proud pillars of descent from Abraham, circumcision, laws on cleanness of food, and material and moral separation from all that was not Jewish; and these pillars were so firmly cemented together that one could not be shaken without all being shaken. Once the ritual cleanness of food was abolished, circumcision would be abolished; and then a descendant of Abraham would be on a par with anyone of another race, and by admitting this parity, a Jew would become one with the Gentiles and have to come down from his throne of glory which raised him above all the peoples of the earth (see the note on v. 34, and on 11:1–3). Peter foresaw these consequences of his vision and of the words he had heard. He was naturally disconcerted and **wondering in himself.** — **Having inquired here and there,** διερωτήσαντες: "to ask along the way," almost to seek a place step by step. — **At the door:** the Greek has **pillar,** which occurs again both in 12:13–14, where it is distinguished from

10:18. And they called out to ask if Simon surnamed Peter was staying there.

10:19. But while Peter was pondering over the vision, the Spirit said [to him]: "Behold, some men are looking for thee.

10:20. "Arise therefore, and go down and depart with them without hesitation because I have sent them."

10:21. So Peter went down to the men and said: "Behold, I am the man you are asking for. What is the reason for your coming?"

10:22. And they said: "Cornelius, a centurion, a just and God-fearing man who is given [good] testimony from the whole nation of the Jews, has received a revelation from a holy angel to have thee brought into his house and hear words from thee."

10:23. So he invited them in and made them welcome. And the next day he departed with them, and some of the brethren from Joppa went with him.

10:24. The following day he reached Caesarea. Now Cornelius was waiting for them, having called together his relatives and his intimate friends.

---

door, and in 14:13, where it is in the plural. It was the gate or porchlike construction which stood in front of the entrance (cf. Lk. 16:20).

10:18. Called out: the Greek has φωνήσαντες, meaning "to call" someone in the house. Having received a reply, **they . . . asked if Simon, etc.**

10:19. Some men: without mention of the exact number. Most ancient documents read thus; other authoritative codices have **three men;** codex Vaticanus has **two men.** These variants have the object of reconciling what is given here with verse 7. The party numbered two or three, depending upon the inclusion or otherwise of the soldier who escorted the two servants.

10:23. So he invited them into the house: they would have been in need of rest after their long journey (see note on v. 9). That Peter, the Jew, should entertain the uncircumcised was clearly an act requiring courage (cf. v. 28; 11:3). It shows that his mind was now clearing of the reasons which had made him **wonder in himself** (cf. note on v. 17), and in any case, his conscience was clear in view of the command he had received (v. 20). — Some of the brethren (Christians) **from Joppa:** six of them, according to 11:12. It was prudent of Peter to have witnesses, as he foresaw the remonstrances his action would provoke.

10:24. Relatives . . . friends: see the note on verse 2.

10:25. And when Peter entered the house, Cornelius met him, and falling at his feet did reverence to him.

10:26. But Peter raised him up saying: "Stand up, I also am a man."

10:27. And as he talked with him, he went in and found many assembled,

10:28. and he said to them: "You know it is not permissible for a Jew to associate with a foreigner or to visit him [in his house]; yet God has shown me that I should not call any man common or unclean.

10:29. "So when I was sent for, I came without hesitation. I ask therefore, why you have sent for me?"

10:25. The account is concise and does not delay to explain the coincidence of the exact timing of Peter's arrival and Cornelius' coming out to meet him. The Western Recension has supplied an explanation by changing the text as follows: **As Peter neared Caesarea, one of the servants running announced that he was approaching. Then Cornelius coming out and going to meet him falling at his feet, etc.** This text supposes that one of the servants who accompanied Peter ran on ahead to notify Cornelius of his arrival; then Cornelius went out toward him — as far as can be understood — outside the city. They then both entered the city together and finally went into the centurion's house. The compiler of this text has probably interpreted the twofold mention of "entering" in verses 25 and 27, as referring first to the entry into the city, and then into the house, and has accommodated the text accordingly. It is sufficient, however, to refer the first entering in to the moment when Peter stood in the porch (see v. 17), where he was met by Cornelius, and the second would be his actual entry into the house. — **Did reverence:** prostrating himself upon the ground; not the act of a Roman, but Cornelius wished to conform to Jewish customs as a sign of homage.

10:26. **I also am a man:** the action of Cornelius might have been interpreted as divine worship.

10:28. **You know:** as a well-acknowledged fact even among the Gentiles such as Peter's hearers. In fact, several Greek and Latin writers emphasize the spirit of segregation which animated the Jews more than other races (such writers are cited in G. Ricciotti, *The History of Israel,* II, pp. 191–195).

10:30. And Cornelius said: "Three days ago at this very hour I was praying in my house at the ninth [hour], and behold a man stood before me in shining garments

10:31. and said: "Cornelius, thy prayer has been heard, and thy alms have been remembered before God;

10:32. "send therefore to Joppa and summon Simon who is surnamed Peter: he is staying in the house of Simon a tanner by the sea.

10:33. "Immediately therefore I sent to thee and thou hast very kindly come. Now, therefore, we are all here in the sight of God to hear whatsoever has been commanded thee by the Lord."

10:34. Thereupon Peter began and said: "Now I really understand that God is not a respecter of persons,

10:35. "but in every nation, he who fears him and works justice, is acceptable to him.

10:30. Three days ago, etc.: literally in Greek, from the fourth day, but it is a difficult construction and the codices offer several variants (either by reading three days, or else adding the word fasting after the words I was; and other renderings). It seems to mean that four days before, reckoned from the moment at which he is speaking, he was praying at the ninth hour, etc. But it is not certain.

10:34. Began: the Hebrew expression means, literally, opened his mouth, as already noted in 8:5. — Respecter of persons: another Hebraism meaning, he who looks upon the face of someone. It really means to show oneself partial to somebody, preferring that person to someone else without sufficient reason. This assertion of Peter refers to God's graces in general, but to messianic salvation in particular. According to the Jews of the time — and perhaps even according to Peter himself before he followed Jesus — God could not but distribute his greatest benefits most abundantly to the chosen people of Israel before all others, and that same messianic salvation was destined directly only for the chosen nation. There had undoubtedly been a certain amount of truth in this view — which Peter now discards (I really understand that God is not a respecter of persons) — for it had been in accord with the ancient Hebrew prophecies; indeed, Jesus himself had confirmed it in his first reply to the Canaanite woman (Mt. 15:24-26). Yet, just as Jesus had granted the woman's request, so God could quite well choose those who were to be saved by Christ from all who believe in him (v. 43), irrespective of whether they were Israelites or not. Paul will return to these thoughts at length in his epistle to the Romans, Chapters 2-4; 9-11.

10:35. Is acceptable to him: not by virtue of his own righteousness,

10:36. "The word which he sent forth to the children of Israel, preaching peace through Jesus Christ: who is Lord of all;

10:37. "You yourselves know that saying which was published throughout all Judea, beginning from Galilee after the baptism which John preached,

10:38. "how God anointed Jesus of Nazareth with the Holy Ghost and with power: who went about doing good and healing all that were in the power of the devil, because God was with him.

---

but **through Jesus Christ** (v. 36), because believing in him, he will **receive forgiveness of sins** (v. 43). It is far from Peter's mind to assert that the religions of all nations are equal: for him the individuals of each nation are equally fit for admission to messianic salvation provided they predispose themselves. In short, *God is not a respecter of persons,* preferring one nation to another.

10:36-38. Peter now delivers a discourse directed at demonstrating the thesis enunciated in the preceding verse. The construction in this speech is involved and its development is halting and disconnected, especially in the first two verses. It appears almost like a collection of unfinished sentences rather than an ordered discourse. We may ask in what language Peter would have spoken to his hearers, some of whom were Romans, some Greeks? If he spoke in his Galilean dialect (see 2:7), an interpreter would have been required to translate his words into Greek, and this would help to explain why the discourse is so halting. If Peter spoke in Greek, the irregularity of the phrases could be well due to him, for he was not fluent in that language. The fact that the discourse was committed to writing does not offer any difficulty if we bear in mind the observation made on 1:16. The unique position of Peter would impress even his isolated phrases on the memory of his audience. This would be so with his Jewish Christian hearers particularly, for they, in common with other Semites, cultivated their memories to good purpose. Later, the substance of the discourse would be committed to writing and in that way it would have come to Luke who used it in his narrative just as he received it. — **The word which he sent forth, etc.:** another reading from documents just as numerous and of equal authority gives: **He sent forth his word, etc.** (see critical editions). The first reading seems preferable as a *lectio difficilior.* The unusual opening with **the word** (in the accusative), **etc.,** seems to be a *casus pendens,* frequent in Aramaic. To make grammatical sense of this verse one would have to suppose that it is preceded by some such phrase as: (all this is in conformity with) **the word, etc.** While the

10:39. "And we [are] witnesses of all he did in the country of the Jews and in Jerusalem, and they slew him hanging him on a tree.

10:40. "But on the third day God raised him up and gave him to be made manifest,

10:41. "not to all the people, but to witnesses chosen before by God, to us who ate and drank with him after he had risen from the dead.

---

word (λόγος) is followed here by **saying** (ῥῆμα), the prophecy of Jeremias in the Septuagint translation begins with **saying** followed by **word**, both being used in a kind of *casus pendens* (The saying of God which came to Jeremias . . . which was the word of the Lord to him. . . .). According to Peter, the **word** is salvation through the Messias, and God **sent** it **to the children of Israel** first of all, as Jesus had said to the Canaanite woman (cf. v. 34). This salvation was worked by Jesus **publishing the good news of peace**, which not only affected the relations between men and God (cf. Rom. 5:1 and 10; 2 Cor. 5:18-20; Col. 1:20), but also those between Jews and Gentiles by breaking down the barrier that separated them (Eph. 2:11-16). Therefore, Jesus Christ is **Lord of all** men without distinction; indeed, **there is no distinction between Jew and Greek for** (Jesus is) **the same Lord of all** (Rom. 10:12). — That **saying which was published**: a Hebraism for "that which happened." — **Beginning**, ἀρξάμενος: since this is a nominative masculine, it cannot refer grammatically to the preceding **saying**, which is neuter, nor to **Jesus of Nazareth** which comes after it and which is in the accusative. It is then an anacoluthon which must be conceptually linked with Jesus, the implied subject of the short parenthesis introduced by the word **beginning**. Here, more than ever, Luke seems to have transcribed literally the points of the discourse as they came to him. — **Beginning from Galilee, etc.**: here we have the chronological limits of the biography of Jesus within which the apostolic catechesis was ordinarily confined; see note on 1:21-22; 2:42. — **Anointed**: namely, elected (cf. note on 4:27), constituting him his "Anointed" or Chosen One (in Hebrew, **Messias**; in Greek, **Christ**). The anointing was **with the Holy Ghost**, in conformity with the messianic prophecies (Isa. 11:2; 61:1; cf. Lk. 4:18 sqq.) **and . . . power**, that the Messias should appear **a man . . . approved by miracles and wonders and signs** (see the note on 2:22) which accompanied his mission. The following verse speaks of this in detail.

10:39-41. Here are recorded the historical grounds for believing in the facts of the Messias Christ's biography (v. 39), and in his Resurrection (vv. 40-41). — **Witnesses**: cf. 1:8 and 22; 2:32. — **We . . . ate . . . with, etc.**: see note on 1:4. — It will be noted that the official "witnesses" of Christ's

10:42. "And he charged us to preach to the people and to testify that he it is who has been appointed by God to be the judge of the living and the dead.

10:43. "To him all the prophets bear witness, that through his name all who believe in him may receive forgiveness of sins."

10:44. While Peter was still speaking these words, the Holy Spirit came upon all who were listening to his discourse.

10:45. And the faithful of the circumcision who had come with Peter, were amazed, because on the Gentiles also the grace of the Holy Spirit had been poured forth:

10:46. for they heard them speaking in tongues and magnifying God.

10:47. Then Peter answered: "Can anyone refuse water that these should not be baptised, who have received the Holy Spirit just as we did?"

Resurrection are only Peter and his unnamed colleagues, namely the Apostles (cf. 1:21–22), although in order of time the first to become acquainted with the Resurrection were Mary Magdalen and the holy women. But the early Church always disregarded the testimony of the women with regard to Christ's Resurrection. The passage (1 Cor. 15:4–8) in which Paul adduces all the witnesses of the Resurrection known to him, contains no mention of the women's testimony. Paul follows the example set by Peter.

10:42. The testimony of the Apostles outlined in verses 37–41 refers to the past, namely, to the life, death, and Resurrection of Christ, but they are charged to bear witness also to the future, announcing and testifying that the Messias Jesus is both the judge **appointed** (cf. Rom. 1:4 in the Greek) **by God, of the living and the dead** (cf. 2 Tim. 4:1; 1 Pet. 4:5).

10:43. **All the prophets** (cf. 3:18), i.e., the Old Testament, the whole of which was a preparation for the New. When the risen Christ was conversing with the two disciples of Emmaus, he first of all reproved them for not believing those things **that the prophets have spoken.** He then explained to them the scriptural passages which referred to himself, **beginning with Moses and all the prophets . . . in all the Scriptures** (Lk. 24:25–27; cf. *ibid.*, 24:44). Jesus is the author of messianic salvation and therefore of the **forgiveness of sins,** and **who believe in him** will participate in this (cf. note on v. 35).

10:44–48. This passage, though connected with what has gone before,

10:48. And he commanded them to be baptised in the name of Jesus Christ. Then they asked him to stay with them some days.

11:1. Now the apostles and brethren throughout Judea heard that the Gentiles also had accepted the word of God;

11:2. and when Peter came up to Jerusalem, those of the circumcision found fault with him,

11:3. saying: "Thou didst visit [the house of] men who are uncircumcised and eat with them."

---

introduces a new element. It had been laid down that to those who were baptized **in the name of Jesus Christ . . . the gift of the Holy Spirit** was given (2:38). Also that if this held good for the Jews in the first place, it was equally the case for all those **(who are) far off, even to all whom the Lord our God calls** (2:39), namely, the Gentiles. Nevertheless, as far as the Gentiles were concerned, the matter rested in the realm of theory and nobody knew when or in what circumstances such things would come about. At any rate, the order in which things would take place was clearly outlined: first, the reception of baptism; then, and as a result of this, the reception of the Holy Spirit. But in the present case, a group of Gentiles receives the Holy Spirit before being baptized as if to show that God who had decreed that the reception of the Holy Spirit should follow baptism could reverse that order. — **The faithful of the circumcision:** namely, the six Jewish Christians that Peter had brought with him from Joppa (see v. 23), are astonished at this extraordinary happening, but they cannot cast doubt upon it for the obvious reason that **they heard them speaking in tongues and magnifying God.** This, then, was a phenomenon like that in 2:4 sqq. (see note there, and on 2:13) which, however, manifested the presence of the Holy Spirit in charismatics who were Gentiles and not yet baptized. Therefore, the explanation which Peter gave upon the former occasion also held good for this new case (see note on 2:16–21). — **Refuse water: for refuse,** the Greek has **forbid,** the word previously used by the Ethiopian when he asked for baptism (8:36). In the present passage the verb refers to the **water,** the material element of the action, before the action itself. — For the phrase **to be baptised in the name of Jesus Christ,** see note on 2:38.

11:1–3. Heard: more with amazement than with satisfaction. The reasons for their amazement are those given in the notes on 10:17 and 34. The situation was really very serious, and therefore the Jewish Christians **found fault** with the one responsible. They did not quite confront him

11:4. Then Peter beginning [to speak] explained the matter to them in order saying:

11:5. "I was in the city of Joppa praying, and I saw in a trance a vision, [namely,] a certain object like a great sheet, let down from heaven by the four corners, and it came right down to me.

11:6. "And gazing upon it, I observed and saw the four-footed creatures of the earth and the beasts and creeping things and the birds of the air.

11:7. "And I also heard a voice saying to me: 'Arise, Peter, kill and eat!'

11:8. "But I said: 'By no means Lord, for nothing common or unclean has ever entered my mouth.'

11:9. "But a voice answered from heaven a second time: 'What God hath declared clean, do not thou call common.'

11:10. "This happened three times: then it was all drawn back up into heaven.

---

with an actual *redde rationem,* but they certainly wanted to know what had prompted his action, and how he was going to face the consequences. Christians who were uncircumcised? If so, these people and the Jewish Christians would be found henceforth side by side in the various Christian gatherings (2:42; 4:32 sqq.; 5:12 sqq.; etc.), the noble descendants of Abraham duly circumcised and the ignoble "goyim" who were uncircumcised. Nay, at meals taken in common they would all *have eaten together.* This promiscuity was intolerable and altogether too humiliating for Israel, to whom the very Hebrew Scriptures themselves had reserved a position of absolute privilege and incomparable pre-eminence over all the nations of the earth. The redemption worked by the Messias could indeed extend to all the nations of the earth, but under well-determined conditions that must absolutely guarantee the privileges of Israel. Otherwise, on the absurd hypothesis of complete equality, a subversive and heretical result would follow, namely the contradiction and abolition of the Old Testament by the New. In this way the difficult problem was put, and on this occasion it received a merely temporary solution. Later, however, the matter will be raised again, and thoroughly ventilated, and this time a definitive solution will be propounded, in the main by Paul (15:1–35). Peter had opened up the pathway which Paul would transform into a main highway.

11:4-15. This is a recapitulation of the preceding narrative (10:10–44). When matters of importance are at stake, Luke does not avoid repetition,

11:11. "And behold immediately three men arrived at the house where I was, sent to me from Caesarea.

11:12. "And the Spirit bade me go with them without hesitation. And these six brethren also came with me and we entered the man's house;

11:13. "and he told me how he saw the angel in his house who said: 'Send to Joppa and summon Simon surnamed Peter,

11:14. " 'who will speak to thee words by which thou shalt be saved, thou and all thy household.'

11:15. "Now as I began to speak, the Holy Spirit fell upon them, just as it did upon us at the beginning.

11:16. "And I remembered the word of the Lord, how he had said: 'John indeed baptised with water, but you shall be baptised with the Holy Spirit.'

11:17. "If therefore God gave to them the same gifts as He gave to us who believed in the Lord Jesus Christ, who was I that I could withstand God?"

11:18. On hearing this, they held their peace, and glorified God saying: "Therefore to the Gentiles also God has given life-giving repentance."

11:19. Meanwhile, those who had been dispersed owing to the persecution that arose over Stephen, made their way as far as Phoenicia and Cyprus and Antioch, speaking the word to none except to Jews only.

---

but upon occasion, he even tells his story three times, as in the case of Paul's conversion; see note on 9:3.

11:16. This is the quotation of 1:5. Thus Peter refers back the responsibility for what happened at Caesarea to Christ himself.

11:18. They held their peace, because there was nothing to say in answer to the conclusion arrived at in the preceding verse. It was, however, an assent dictated more by deference than by inner conviction, so much so that later the question was raised again in circumstances of much deeper significance: see note on verses 1–3. — Repentance: the Greek has μετάνοια, namely, "change of mind," for which see note on 2:38.

11:19. With the case of Cornelius, the intervening wall of the enclosure

11:20. But some of them were Cypriots and Cyrenians, who on reaching Antioch, spoke the word to the Greeks as well, preaching the Lord Jesus.

11:21. And the hand of the Lord was with them, and a great number believing turned to the Lord.

(as Paul calls it; Eph. 2:14) that separated Gentiles from Jews, had been broken down, so Luke now enters the missionary field of the Gentiles and so passes to Antioch, the capital of Syria, where there were many Jews. — **Those who had been dispersed** are those previously referred to in 8:1 and 4, who now become propagators of the **word,** i.e., the Gospel. Nevertheless, they did not preach it to anyone **except to Jews only.** At first, these zealous missionaries hesitated to put Gentiles and Jews on the same level for the reasons already seen in the note on 10:17 and 34, and 11:1–3.

11:20. Cypriots: fellow islanders of Barnabas who was himself a Cypriot (4:36). **Cyrenians:** from Cyrenea, see note on 6:9. We are not given the names of these Cypriots and Cyrenians, but perhaps we can hazard a guess that they were from those named in 13:1, where Lucius the *Cyrenian* appears. — The reading **Greeks** ("Ελληνας) is given by the best documents, though many more Greek manuscripts give the alternative, **Hellenists** ('Ελληνιστάς). The first reading is better supported, and is in fact given in most critical editions. For the meaning of **Hellenists,** see the note on 6:1. The term **Greeks** could only have an ethnographic significance, but all the same it was often used in opposition to **Jews** in the religious sense, and when so used, practically amounted to *idolaters.* There are clear examples of this, both in the *Acts* (14:1–5; 16:1, 3; 21:27–28; etc.) and in Paul (1 Cor. 1:22–24; Rom. 1:16; 2:9–10; 3:9; etc.). The present passage falls into this category, for using both terms in the religious ethnical sense, the **Jews** as believers in the true God are placed in opposition to **Greeks** as idolaters. To these idolaters, then, our zealous missionaries ventured to address themselves **preaching the Lord Jesus.** Had they heard of the conversion of Cornelius? We do not know and any guess on the question would be gratuitous. It is certain that their courage was very great, and the consequences for the diffusion of Christianity were just as great.

11:21. Luke hastens to record the twofold approval bestowed upon the missionaries and their courage, first that of God and then that of men. — **The hand of the Lord:** a Hebrew expression for "power," which in this case was probably thaumaturgic, for power over devils habitually accompanied the advance of Christianity among pagans. This will be the case

11:22. Now news about them came to the ears of the Church at Jerusalem, and they sent Barnabas as far as Antioch;

11:23. who, when he came and saw the grace of God, rejoiced and exhorted them all to continue in the Lord with steadfast heart,

11:24. for he was a good man and full of the Holy Spirit and of faith: and a great multitude was added to the Lord.

11:25. And [Barnabas] went forth to Tarsus to seek Saul, and having found him, he brought him to Antioch.

11:26. And for a whole year they took part in the meetings of the Church, and taught a great multitude. And it was in Antioch that the disciples were first called "Christians."

---

at Thessalonica (1 Thess. 1:5), at Corinth (1 Cor. 2:4-5), and at Ephesus (Acts 19:11-12).

11:22-24. Barnabas returns on the scene, and if we bear in mind that he was a native of Cyprus (4:36) and an acquaintance of Paul (9:27), it will help to clarify some points of the narrative which follows. That Barnabas was sent by the Church at Jerusalem was due to the desire to offer some assistance in the new and delicate situation arising from the conversion of a great number of pagans (v. 21). The circumstances of the case involved a number of questions about ritual, organization, and the like, in dealing with which the missionaries of Antioch would have experienced serious difficulties; hence the suitability of Barnabas as an envoy. The praise here given him (**a good man and full of the Holy Spirit, etc.**) is not surprising; his admirable grasp of reality and his practical spirit resulted in the rapid spread of the Gospel, recorded in the following verse. To the **great number** of converts of verse 21 is here added a **great multitude,** and this expression will be repeated shortly afterward (**v.** 26).

11:25. The spiritual harvest that was being gathered in at Antioch was abundant indeed, but the laborers were few. Moreover, this was a harvest of a special kind because it was being gleaned among pagans. Therefore it was necessary to have laborers with special aptitudes who would go generously to those new converts without frightening them by imposing the crushing burden of Jewish legal observances. Just such a laborer existed, and Barnabas had not only the perspicacity to select him, but also the shrewdness to go personally to find him and bring him to the scene of the harvest. This worker was **Saul,** still at **Tarsus** where we left him in 9:30, toward the end of the year 39. It was now the year 43, so Saul's stay at Tarsus had lasted four years.

11:26. The length of the stay of Paul and Barnabas at Antioch was a

whole year, namely from A.D. 43 to 44, interrupted, however, by the journey described in verse 30. Probably they did not intend to stay so long in Antioch, but only to give help at first and then depart to evangelize regions farther off, as indeed they did later (13:4 sqq.). However, the amount of labor to be performed and the journey which they took to bring back the alms which had been collected (v. 30), prevented them from carrying out their original project. The Hebrew construction of the phrase — **it happened to them both to meet together . . . and to teach, etc.,** seems to allude to this unforeseen interruption of their program. — The name **Christians,** Χριστιανοί, was given for the first time to the **great multitude** of converts in Antioch. The creation of a special name shows that the great multitude was made up of persons from every walk of life, so that the whole population of the city must have known about them. This new distinctive term was certainly not given by the Jews who for a long time yet would call them *Nazarenes,* or *Galileans,* or *"minīm,"* viz., heretics. The disciples of Jesus never gave this name to themselves, since usually they called each other by such terms as *faithful, disciples, saints, elect.* It was, therefore, probably given to them by the pagans. It has been suggested that the Roman magistrates of Antioch created the name, the reason being that the suffix (*christ*)*ianòi* is of Latin origin, while a regular Greek suffix would result in the form *chrìstioi* or *christikòi.* The explanation is not entirely convincing, since there are other examples of mixed Greek-Latin forms deriving from the influence which the language of the rulers exercised on the idiom of those over whom they ruled. The name must have arisen spontaneously in the conversation of the people of Antioch talking about this new important body. It is most likely that originally it had a civil-political significance, rather than a religious one, in the sense of a "party," similar to other names such as Caesarean, Pompeian, and the like, which arose from the names of Caesar, Pompey, etc. The pagans of Antioch, seeing the **great multitude** which used *to come together* in the name of Christ for a **whole year,** called them Christians. We may ask, did the name perhaps at first have a slightly ironic and ridiculous meaning? It is hard to say either way. In actual fact, the name came from Χριστός, *christòs,* but the ordinary people may have understood it as being derived from Χρηστός, which, because of a tendency among Greeks to pronounce other vowels as *i* (itacism), was spoken as *christòs.* Now Χρηστός meant "good," "kind," but often in popular use it meant "good for nothing," "stupid" (and, apropos of this, it seems that in the Middle Ages the uncomplimentary term *cretin* derived from *Christian*). We do actually find that the form *chrestianus* is not only known to Christian writers such as Tertullian and Lactantius, but is also used by Tacitus (*Annal.,* XV, 44) reporting how the ordinary people of Rome called the followers of the new religion. On the other hand, Suetonius

11:27. Now in those days some prophets from Jerusalem came down to Antioch;

11:28. and one of them named Agabus got up and revealed through the Spirit that there would be a great famine over the whole world, which happened under Claudius.

(*Claud.*, 25) speaks of one *Chrestus,* an alleged agitator of the Jews in Rome, probably a reference to Christ of the Christians. If the term *chrestianos* in popular usage as reported by Tacitus in A.D. 64 carried an ironic and derisive meaning — as it very probably did — it is quite possible that it was used in that sense by the Jewish King Agrippa II (Acts 26:28) in the year 60. Passing from the name to the facts, it seemed that the name given at Antioch, and destined to become world-wide, typified the importance that the city would take on, in the diffusion of the new religion. Antioch will be the center of the driving force of Christianity in the Graeco-Roman world for several years, and from Antioch, Paul will depart on his missionary journeys. The headquarters of the army of the Gospel was to remain always at Jerusalem the mother Church both of the Nazarenes of Palestine and the Christians of Syria, but the advance base which supplied the spiritual forces to win the pagan world to the Gospel was Antioch. Later, following yet another advance, the powerhouse would be transferred from Antioch to Rome.

11:27. These **prophets** of the New Testament had an office similar to but not on a par with that exercised by the prophets of the Old Testament. They possessed the charism of "prophecy," and in virtue of such a gift they gave discourses of **edification and exhortation and comfort** (1 Cor. 14:3) at Christian gatherings, just as they were able **to make manifest the secrets of other people's hearts** (*ibid.,* 14:25) and sometimes foretell future events. The *Didache* says that the "prophet" *speaks in the Spirit* (XI, 7), has the right to extemporize the Eucharistic thanksgiving (*ibid.,* 10:7), and enjoys various privileges in the communities to which he belongs (*ibid.,* 13:1-6). However, some communities were without their "prophet" (*ibid.,* 13:4), and in such cases the deficiency was made good by the visits of "prophets" from other communities, and this verse describes such a visit. In view of their edifying task, the charism of "prophet" was of the highest value in the communities just beginning, and precisely because of this, Paul recommends it with particular insistence (1 Cor. 14:1).

11:28. The Western Recension represented by codex D, with a few other documents of lesser importance (see critical editions), begins this verse with the following words: **And there was very much rejoicing** (at the arrival of the above-mentioned prophets). **But when we were gathered**

11:29. So the disciples, each one according to his means, determined to send [some] relief to the brethren dwelling in Judea.

---

together, one of them named Agabus said, signifying by the Spirit, etc. If we accept the authenticity of this passage, it will be the first of the "we-sections" (the others come later: 16:10–17; etc.). From this, one would conclude that at this time, viz., in the year A.D. 44, Luke was already a Christian, and it would partly confirm the ancient tradition that he was from Antioch. But is this passage genuine? The guarantee for its transmission is very weak, as we have seen. An internal examination also leaves doubt, since even if the word **rejoicing** (ἀγαλλίασις), a favorite one of Luke's, is found there, the word **said**, which implies a direct speech to follow, is likewise used, but there is no such speech. Several scholars think that this passage comes from Luke's "Travel Diary"; others instead hold it to be an interpolation. Critical editions give it as a note to the text. In these circumstances, it seems impossible to make any judgment on it, because even if its authenticity is inherently likely, it cannot, in actual fact, be demonstrated. — **A great famine . . . under Claudius:** Claudius was proclaimed emperor on January 25, 41, and died in the year 54, but it would be wrong to think that the words **which happened under Claudius** imply that Claudius was not yet reigning when these words were spoken. Actually, famine raged more or less in various parts of the Roman empire during nearly the whole of Claudius' reign. In his first year, famine broke out in Rome (Suetonius, *Claud.,* 18; Dion Cassius, LX, 11, 1–3), viz., in 41–42, and again in the eleventh year of his reign (Tacitus, *Annal.,* XII, 43), viz., in the year A.D. 52. In Judea there was a famine under the procuratorship of Tiberius Alexander (Flavius Josephus, *Antiquities of the Jews,* III, 320; XX, 51, 101), who was in office from A.D. 46 to 48, and these years must have been very serious ones for the whole of that region, and especially for Jerusalem. It could be said with truth, then, that famine happened under Claudius in many parts of the empire, and more particularly in Judea about the year 44 (in which this prophecy was made) with special reference to the three or four following years. The expression **over the whole world** can be taken to mean the whole Roman empire, as in Lk. 2:1. — It is probable that **Agabus** here is the same one mentioned in 21:10.

11:29. According to his means: viz., material wealth, from which each made contributions to send to Judea, and especially to Jerusalem. The spiritual assistance brought by the "prophets" was now repaid with material relief, as Paul will later recommend (2 Cor. 8:14; Rom. 15:27–28), since he was particularly concerned with these alms for Jerusalem (1 Cor. 16:1–4; 2 Cor., Chaps. 8–9; Gal. 2:10; Rom. 15:27–28). It appears from the

11:30. And this they did, sending it to the presbyters by the hand of Barnabas and Saul.

---

narrative that the offerings of each one were spontaneous (**each one . . . determined,** etc.), just as Paul will require (2 Cor. 9:7). It is also clear that there was so far no voluntary community of goods practiced in Antioch as there was in Jerusalem (cf. note on 2:44–45). We have reason to suspect that the financial straits in which the Christians of Jerusalem found themselves were made worse by their reception among them of refugees from the famine, which, combined with the fact that they held their property in common, made matters worse in the long run. For as the number of the needy grew, so did the expenses, whereas the income, even including the contributions made by well-to-do converts, did not increase proportionately.

11:30. In Judea money was much less needed than food of which there was none, whereas Antioch and Syria must have been still well provided. Flavius Josephus tells how Helena, queen of Adiabene, on the occasion of this same severe famine, succored the Jews at Jerusalem who were dying of starvation, by procuring for them corn bought at Alexandria, and a cargo of figs from Cyprus (*Antiquities of the Jews,* XX, 51–52). The relief provided by the disciples of Antioch was taken by **Barnabas and Saul** on the so-called "journey of the alms," not to be confused with the journey made by them to attend the Apostolic Council (15:2 sqq.). Paul, speaking of his journeys to Jerusalem, refers to the first one he made after his conversion (Gal. 1:18), which is that narrated in the Acts 9:26 sqq., then he passes straight on to the journey which he made to attend the Apostolic Council (Gal. 2:1 sqq.), without mentioning this "journey of the alms." The reason for such an omission is clear. Paul, in treating of his journeys, does not intend to give a complete list, but only to record those which show that he received his apostolate and his mission, not from men but **by the revelation of Jesus Christ** (Gal. 1:11–12). But the "journey of the alms" did not serve in any way to demonstrate this thesis, because it was not undertaken as part of his apostolic and evangelical ministry but as a simple act of fraternal charity. It should be noted also that Paul, arrived at Jerusalem, meets the **elders** as is stated here, while the Apostles are not spoken of at all. This is another reason why this "journey of the alms" did not support his thesis, and therefore he omitted it. Who were these **elders** whom Barnabas and Saul met? Several times afterward, **apostles and elders** will be named as present jointly in Jerusalem (15:2, 4, 6, 22, 23). But here the Apostles are omitted and only the **elders** remain. Their omission is probably accounted for by the fact that, as the fury of the persecution mounted (12:1 sqq.), they were

12:1. Now about that time, king Herod put forth his hands to ill-treat some of the Church.

12:2. He slew James, the brother of John, with the sword.

---

either in prison, as will be told presently about Peter, or they had fled, as Peter did as soon as he was freed from prison; cf. 12:7.

12:1 sqq. Following upon his account of the expansion of the Church in Antioch, Luke now comes to the persecution in Jerusalem. Indeed it is his constant rule to alternate the Church's triumphs with her tribulations. The facts about Peter up until now have been a series of victories (2:41 sqq.; 4:4; 5:12 sqq.; 5:42; 8:4 sqq.; 9:31 sqq.; 11:19 sqq.) and a series of persecutions (4:3, 5 sqq.; 5:17 sqq.; 6:9 sqq.; 8:1, 3). Since Luke has almost finished recounting Peter's activities, he concludes by relating the most serious and direct danger undergone by Peter, but one which was also a triumph for him. Shortly, the acts of Paul will begin, with the further spread of the Church (13:4 sqq.) and there also we shall find this alternation of victories and persecutions. One might say that the disciple of Paul contemplates the history of the Church in the light of that principle enunciated by his master: **through many tribulations we must enter the kingdom of God** (14:22; a similar thought is found in 1 Thess. 3:3–4; 2 Tim. 3:12). — The expression **about that time** indicates, in general, a certain linking up with preceding events, like the phrase **about that time** in 19:23. However, the actual time is fixed by verse 25, from which it would seem that during the events here related, Barnabas and Saul were in Jerusalem. — This **king Herod** is Agrippa I, son of that Aristobulus who was killed in the year 7 B.C. by his father Herod the Great. He had lived an adventurous youth in Rome where he spent some months in prison. The election of Caligula was a stroke of fortune for him, as the new emperor heaped benefits upon him and named him king, giving him various territories in the north of Palestine. All the other territories farther to the south (Samaria, Judea, Idumea) were granted to him by Claudius. For other details of his life and short but successful reign, cf. G. Ricciotti, *The History of Israel,* II, pp. 382–388.

12:2. James is James the Greater, and his brother, **John** the evangelist (cf. 1:13); these two brothers, together with Peter, were the favorite disciples of Jesus. The Apostle John, unmolested as yet, together with James the Less and Peter, will be met in Jerusalem by Paul (Gal. 2:9) when the latter comes to the Apostolic Council five years later (Acts 15:2 sqq.). Despite this, some modern critics maintain that **John** was killed with his brother, though, if that had happened, it would have been easy for Luke

12:3. And seeing that it pleased the Jews, he proceeded to arrest Peter also (it was the time of the Azymes).

---

to say here *he slew James and his brother John by the sword*. These same critics suggest that originally the text read so, but that it was later altered to its present form. This hypothesis must be rejected as unhistorical, since no authoritative document is adduced as proof of it, and the testimony of Paul cited above entirely contradicts it. The real motive behind this suggestion is simply to make the Apostle John disappear from the scene before the time to which early tradition attributes the Fourth Gospel (cf. G. Ricciotti, *The Life of Christ*, pp. 136–137). We do not know the real reason why Luke, who described at length the killing of Stephen, here limits himself to giving the bare notice of the death of James the Greater. It is hardly likely that he knew no details which he could have added, but more probable that such details — perhaps of secondary importance in themselves — would distract the reader's attention from his main theme which is Peter's exposure to a very great danger and his deliverance from it.

12:3. It pleased the Jews: this is the real motive of the persecution waged by Agrippa, who personally had no animosity against the Christians. But the Sanhedrin had, because it saw that, despite its repeated interventions, the new religion was spreading, not only in Judea, but also in Samaria (8:25), Damascus (9:20 sqq.), and in faraway Antioch. Just as the news of the Christian triumphs in Antioch had reached the Church at Jerusalem (11:22), so most certainly they had become known to the watchful Sanhedrin. It was, therefore, necessary to eradicate this evil definitely by having recourse to other more drastic methods than hitherto, and for this purpose, King Agrippa could best be used. He had every political interest in showing deference to Jewish religious observances, and although before his election he had led a dissolute life, as soon as he came to Jerusalem he devoted himself to fulfilling those acts of Jewish devotion which are recorded by Flavius Josephus (*Antiquities of the Jews*, XIX, 293–302, 331). Even if the idea of persecuting the Christians, and the political advantages which would accrue therefrom, did not enter Agrippa's mind spontaneously, it would have been suggested to him by the Sanhedrin, which saw in him one who would serve their own purpose. He was an absolute monarch, and could act without reference to legal procedures or political pretexts. While no trial of James is described, we find surprisingly enough that he is killed **with the sword,** i.e., by decapitation. This gives rise to the suspicion that the condemnation was based on political reasons, because if they had been religious ones, stoning would have been the ordinary penalty, as in the case of Stephen (cf. note on 7:58 and 59–60).

12:4. After arresting him, he put him in prison, having delivered him to four quaternions of soldiers (relieved four times a day) to guard him, intending to bring him forth to the people after the Passover.

Beheading was known to rabbinical tradition (Mishna, *Sanhedrin,* VII, 1-3), but it was designated as a penalty used by *those of the government,* namely the Romans (incidentally it should be remembered that on some of the coins minted by this Agrippa, he calls himself "friend of the Romans," φιλορώμαιος). However, decapitation seems to have been applied rarely, and some rabbis maintained: *There is no death more shameful than this* (Mishna, *ibid.*). Having summarily dispatched James, Agrippa, seeing that it pleased the Jews, proceeded further to arrest Peter. This new victim was much more important, and therefore the king wished to proceed with greater formality in order to ingratiate himself still more with the Jews. Peter's arrest took place at the time of the Azymes. The Jewish Passover used to fall in the Hebrew month of Nisan, which lasted from the middle of our March to the middle of April. On the eve of the fourteenth day of that month, the Passover was celebrated, but the feast was intimately connected with that of the Azymes or Unleavened Bread which occupied the seven days following (15-21 Nisan). In practice, therefore, these eight days (14-21) were called both the Passover and the Azymes. This last name derives from the fact that from the tenth or eleventh hour of the fourteenth day of Nisan and for the seven days following, unleavened (azyme) bread had to be used, and even the smallest fragment of leavened bread was excluded from every Jewish household. Since the Passover brought great crowds to Jerusalem, Agrippa cut a fine figure before the devout pilgrims by arresting Peter. Moreover, by taking the precaution described in the next verse, he appeared as a punctilious observer of the Law.

12:4. Although Agrippa had arrested Peter during the time of the Azymes, he did not try him then, intending ... after the Passover (namely, when the days of Unleavened Bread were over) to bring him forth to the people for trial. We do not know the reason for this delay. Sitting in the tribunal on festival days was forbidden according to the rabbis (Mishna, *Besa,* V, 2), but only the first and last days of the "feast of the Azymes" were such days of rest (Exod. 12:16; Lev. 23:7-8), while the remainder were days on which work could be done. Did Agrippa want to press his observance of the Law further than its limits required, so as to appear very zealous? We do not know, but if it was so, we must not forget that this zeal of his did not prevent him from erecting statues of his two

12:5. Peter therefore was being kept in prison, but prayer was earnestly made by the Church for him.

12:6. Now when Herod was about to bring him forth, that same night Peter was sleeping between two soldiers, bound with two chains, and outside the door sentries were guarding the prison.

12:7. And behold an angel of the Lord stood beside him and a light shone in the cell; and striking Peter on the side he woke him saying: "Arise quickly!" And the chains fell from his hands.

12:8. Then the angel said to him: "Gird thyself and put on thy

daughters in Caesarea, a thing strictly forbidden by the Law, nor from ordering 1700 gladiators to fight at Beirut who were all killed (Flavius Josephus, *Antiquities of the Jews,* XIX, 336–338, 357). — **Four quaternions of soldiers (relieved four times a day):** four pickets, each of four soldiers. The night duty of Roman soldiers was divided into four *vigiliae* or watches of three hours each. In the present case a picket of four came on duty at every watch, two soldiers remaining on guard outside the cell door, while the other two went inside with the prisoner. Of these two, one was bound to the prisoner's right arm by a chain fastened upon his own left, while the other soldier was similarly fastened to the left arm of the prisoner by a chain fastened upon his own right (cf. v. 6; Seneca, *Epist.,* 5, 7; Flavius Josephus, *Antiquities of the Jews,* XVIII, 196). A very strict guard indeed, but one dictated by a prudent desire to avoid any repetition of Peter's previous inexplicable escape with which Agrippa must have been acquainted (cf. 5:19 sqq.).

12:5–6. Here we notice the literary technique of these two verses which remind one, as it were, of two armies facing each other, shortly before the final battle. One of them is now almost overwhelmed, and only awaits the final rout. Peter is practically overcome by Agrippa. Separated from his brethren, locked in a cell and guarded by soldiers, he will shortly meet the same end as James. And yet the narrator tranquilly says he **was sleeping.** What was the reason for such calmness? It has already been subtly underlined by those words with which Luke presents the army opposing King Agrippa, viz., **but (δέ) prayer was earnestly made by the Church for him.** Luke knows how to outline spiritual combats in a few phrases, just as Livy knows how to describe the battles of armies. — After the words, **kept in prison,** two codices add, **by the king's cohort.** This is true in fact, but it seems to be a gloss which is added so as to explain the above-mentioned military arrangement which was typically Roman, and therefore imitated by King Agrippa.

12:8. Gird thyself: viz, gird up the loose Oriental robe with a girdle.

sandals." And he did so. Then he said to him: "Wrap thy cloak about thee and follow me."

12:9. And he followed him out and he knew not that what was being done through the angel was real, but he thought he was having a vision.

12:10. And when they were past the first and second guard, they came to the iron gate which leads into the city, and this opened to them of its own accord. And going forth, they passed up one street and straightway the angel left him.

12:11. Then Peter coming to himself said: "Now I know for certain that the Lord has sent his angel and has delivered me from the hand of Herod and from all that the Jewish people were expecting."

12:12. When he realised [his situation], he came to the house of

---

Peter had taken off his girdle so as to sleep better, just as he had removed his sandals.

12:9. He knew not that it was real, because it was too "unlikely." It seemed, therefore, to be a vision in sleep (cf. 16:9), especially as just a few minutes before, he was sleeping profoundly (v. 6). Besides, Ps. 126 (125):1, in the Hebrew text, had spoken of those who witness extraordinary happy events like men dreaming.

12:10. The first and second (body of the) guard: i.e., probably the guards who were stationed outside the door of the cell (see note on v. 4), and then the picket at the main entrance to the prison. The prison entrance must have opened out into a yard and thence through the iron gate which leads into the city. — After the words and going forth, codex D adds they went down seven steps. If the prison where Peter was kept was in the fortress Antonia, this mention of steps is correct, because there were stairways in both wings adjoining the porticoes of the Temple (Flavius Josephus, Wars of the Jews, V, 243), and these steps are recorded also in Acts 21:35 and 40, though it is only in the present text that the exact number of seven is given. Nevertheless, it is not entirely certain that Peter was imprisoned in this fortress Antonia. It could have been in the royal palace built by Herod the Great to the west of the city; this would more easily explain the description of the iron gate which leads into the city. Wherever the prison was, the mention of the seven steps could be a gloss suggested by a comparison with 21:35 and 40.

12:12. This John who was surnamed Mark, about whom we shall hear more elsewhere under both names (v. 25; 15:37) or under one only

Mary the mother of John who was surnamed Mark, where many had gathered together in prayer.

12:13. Now when he had knocked at the gate of the porch, a maid called Rhoda came to answer it.

12:14. And recognising Peter's voice, in her joy she did not open the gate, but running in announced that Peter was standing before the gate.

12:15. But they said to her: "Thou art mad!" But she insisted that it was so. And they said: "It is his angel!"

12:16. But Peter continued knocking, and when they opened, they saw him and were amazed.

12:17. But he motioned to them with his hand to be quiet, and related how the Lord had brought him out of prison. And he said: "Tell this to James and to the brethren." And he departed and went to another place.

(13:5 and 13; 15:39; Col. 4:10; Philemon 24; 2 Tim. 4:11; 1 Pet. 5:13) is the author of the second Gospel. He was the cousin of Barnabas (Col. 4:10). Details about him are given him in G. Ricciotti, *The Life of Christ*, pp. 107–114.

12:13. The gate of the porch: the Greek has of the pillar, for which see note on 10:17. — To answer it: the Greek has "to hearken" in the sense of hearing the voice of the one who calls, so as then to fulfill the request of opening the gate, etc. — Maid, παιδίσκη: servant, slave, housemaid (cf. 16:16). — Rhoda, viz., "Rose" or commonly, Rosina.

12:15. "It is his angel!": almost as if, knowing that Peter was undoubtedly in prison, his angel had appeared in his stead at the door of Mary's house. The people gathered in the house came to this conclusion, because they were unable to admit that Peter was no longer in prison. Judaism had a well-developed belief in angels, and Jesus himself had spoken of each child having its own angel (Mt. 18:10).

12:17. Motioned to them . . . to be quiet: the Greek has beckoned to them with his hand to hold their peace. The confusion of those present, Peter's own hurry, the necessity of avoiding noise so as not to be heard at that late hour, all called for Peter's silent but forceful gesture. — James mentioned here is known as the Less, the "brother of the Lord" (Gal. 1:19), named together with Peter and John as one of those who were considered (to be) the pillars (*ibid.*, 2:9). It is not known whether he was hiding in the city or had gone away. — Went to another place, which, however, is not named. Common prudence required that the escaped Apostle should put himself outside Herod's jurisdiction, and therefore he would not remain in Caesarea, Samaria, or any such place, but would betake himself right outside Palestine. Why did not Luke name this **other place?** Certainly his reticence did not arise from any necessity to keep Peter's whereabouts hidden, for he wrote this account a score of years after the death of King Agrippa, when his kingdom had vanished and when only the memory of his persecutions and favoritism remained. Hence, no reason for concealment remained. The reason is to be sought rather in the plan of the narrative followed by Luke. With this episode, the "Acts" of Peter end, and Peter will not again appear in the narrative except incidentally (15:6 sqq.). So Luke bids good-by to Peter, leaving this **other place** unnamed, avoiding any necessity for continuing his story, even to the extent of omitting the name of his destination. In the same way the ancient playwriters used to put in their direction *exit,* when an actor's part was finished and he left the scene. Luke followed a similar method in his Gospel, 9:56, where he closes his narrative of the stay of Jesus among the Samaritans, by saying that he went to another village, without naming it. However, it is very probable that Luke knew the name of this **other place.** One cannot but recognize the vivacity of the whole of this account right down to its smallest and most insignificant details, e.g., that of the servant Rhoda, and this vivacity can be easily explained on the supposition that Luke received his information from one of those present in the house of Mary. Most likely it was Mark, her son (v. 12), who was, like Luke, a disciple of Paul, and remained at the Apostle's side during the first imprisonment at Rome. Now, it is impossible that Mark did not know the name of that **other place** where Peter went, after he left his mother Mary's house, and if Mark knew it, Luke also knew it, but did not disclose it for the reasons given above. Was this place Antioch? It may have been, and in support of this view, one could cite (though they wrote much later) the testimonies of Origen (*Homil. 6 in Lucam,* in Migne, *P. G.,* XIII, 1815) and Jerome (*De viris illustr.,* 1), who wrote of Peter as the bishop of Antioch. Could the unknown place have been Rome instead? This view cannot be ruled out, especially if we suppose that the transfer from Jerusalem to Rome was not immediate and direct, but admitted of more or less protracted stops on the way. Indeed, Eusebius (*Hist. eccl.,* II, 14, 6: cf. 17, 1) mentions Peter's coming to Rome about this time, and assigns his arrival to the beginning of the reign of Claudius (who ruled from A.D. 41–54). Jerome (*De viris illustr.,* 1) places it in the second year of Claudius, likewise Orosius (*Hist. adv. paganos,* VII, 6) who puts it at the opening of Claudius' reign. The second year of Claudius, as given by Jerome, is not tenable (in any case, the manuscript transmission is doubtful), and can only be taken as a general confirmation for the early

12:18.   Now when morning came, there was no small stir among the soldiers as to what had become of Peter.

---

years of Claudius' reign. Whether or not the journey of Peter to Rome in the first year of Claudius is accepted, an important archaeological observation cannot be overlooked. The early Christian sarcophagi of Rome reproduced the imprisonment of Peter at Jerusalem under King Agrippa with a special emphasis, so much so that there are still extant today about 60 representations of it, and in addition the scene of the imprisonment is often flanked by the baptism of Cornelius, especially from the second century onward. Sometimes the two scenes are given together (cf. G. Wilpert, *I sarcofagi cristiani antichi*, I, Rome, 1929, pp. 107, 119; also, *La fede della Chiesa nascente secondo ni monumenti dell'arte funeraria antica*, Vatican City, 1938, p. 153). From the predilection shown for these two scenes, it would seem that these sculptors represented the earliest Christian tradition at Rome, i.e., that Peter's imprisonment by King Agrippa and his subsequent departure from Jerusalem, were connected in some way with his coming to Rome; as though the baptism of Cornelius, for which Peter was responsible, represented the first Christian victory over the pagan world, crowned by his victory over Rome itself. Recapitulating, therefore, Peter leaves Jerusalem in the year 44 and goes **to another place,** which, if we accept the early evidence, could be either Antioch or Rome. It is even possible that his journey took him to Rome, taking in Antioch on his way. There is plenty of time for one or both of these stays, including traveling involved, for Peter does not reappear until the Apostolic Council at Jerusalem in A.D. 49 (15:7), and the five years which intervene provide ample time for all this. People in those days journeyed much more quickly than we moderns might think. There are many surprising examples in secular history, but we can take an instance from Aquila and Priscilla, Christians of the first generation, who leave Rome in the years 49–50 and reach Corinth in 50–51 (Acts 18:2). In A.D. 52, they are in Ephesus (*ibid,* 18:18–19), where we find them again in the year 56 (1 Cor. 16:19), but in A.D. 58, they are in Rome (Rom. 16:3–5), while later on, about the year 66, they will be back in Ephesus (2 Tim. 4:19). If, therefore, in the space of five years, Peter stayed in Antioch and Rome, he did not travel farther than did Aquila and Priscilla.

12:18.   When morning came: this seems to indicate that the deliverance of Peter took place during the fourth and last watch of the guards, viz., between three and six in the morning (see note on v. 4). If it had happened during one of the earlier "watches," the soldiers who were going off duty would have noticed the prisoner's absence and would have given the alarm long before daybreak. On the other hand, the three hours of

12:19. When Herod had searched for him and had not found him, he examined the guards and ordered them to be put to death, then he went down from Judea to Caesarea and stayed [there].

12:20. Now he was very angry with the Tyrians and Sidonians; but they came with one accord to him, and, having won over Blastus, the king's chamberlain, they asked for peace, because their country depended on him for its food supply.

12:21. So on a day appointed [for the audience], Herod having arrayed himself in royal apparel, took his seat upon the throne and addressed them;

12:22. And the people cried out: "It is the voice of a god, and not of a man!"

12:23. But immediately an angel of the Lord struck him down, because he had not given the honor to God: and he was eaten by worms and died.

---

the "watch" were sufficient for Peter to go to the house of Mary and leave again quickly.— **No small (stir):** literally, "not a little," a figure of speech for "great," "much," as is usual in Luke (14:28; 15:2; 17:4 and 12; 19:24; etc.). The fear of the guards was well founded, for they would have to answer with their lives. In Roman law the penalty of an escaped prisoner reverted to the guards who had let him escape (*Cod. Justin.*, IX, 4, 4); cf. Acts 16:27; 27:42. But in the case of Peter who was under constant surveillance, the military authorities could not explain the prisoner's escape except by the guards having abandoned their post, and this case was also punishable by death, as Flavius Josephus relates (*Wars of the Jews*, V, 482).

12:19. Then, in the Greek, is the simple conjunction, **and,** καὶ; which does not imply in Luke's manner of writing, an immediate consecutive action; so that in the present case, several weeks may have passed between the two events.

12:20–23. The death of King Agrippa is related also by Flavius Josephus (*Antiquities of the Jews,* XIX, 343–352) who wrote about it in the years 93–94, that is thirty years after the *Acts.* The two accounts agree on general lines, but Josephus does not say anything about the delegation of the Tyrians and Sidonians of verse 20, and instead he connects the event with the games given by Agrippa at Caesarea in honor of the emperor, Claudius. In fact, the emperor had returned shortly before from his expedition in Britain, celebrating the victory in Rome in the year 44. This

triumph must have been celebrated in the provinces immediately afterward and would have taken place at Caesarea between the spring and
summer of that same year. It is clear that the feast in honor of the
emperor did not prevent him from receiving the delegation of the Tyrians
and Sidonians; on the contrary, it was an opportunity to give them an
audience. Other divergencies between the two accounts are of little consequence. — This **Blastus,** about whom we have no other information, was
ἐπὶ τοῦ κοιτῶνος of the king, viz., a chamberlain (*cubicularius*) or perhaps
even an official of the Treasury. In any case, he was an important person
at court. By winning him over, the Tyrians and Sidonians who gained
their livelihood by sea trade, but had no territory which produced grain,
were sure to receive it from King Agrippa's lands, especially from the
plains along the seacoast (Shephela, Sharon) which were abundant wheat-
producing areas. — There are marked similarities between Josephus and
Luke, though the former gives a fuller account of the king's raiment and
the adulation of the crowd. Josephus, like Luke, notes that the king
neither rebuked the impious flattery of the crowd which proclaimed him
a god and one superior to mortal nature. Evidently this flattery did not
come from Jews, but from the pagans of Tyre and Sidon or Caesarea. —
An angel of the Lord struck him down: the narrative describes the action
of the angel as carrying out the Lord's commands, but does not say that
the angel was visible to the king or the people. This is a similar case
to that of the angel who exterminated the army of Sennacherib, according
to 2 (4) Kings 19:35. In the place of an angel, Josephus speaks of an
owl which suddenly appeared above the king's head. The king immediately
understood that it was a sign of ill omen, for he had seen the same
apparition some years before, and he was told on that occasion that the
first time it was a sign of good tidings, but the second time, it would
be a sign of misfortune (*Antiquities of the Jews,* XVIII, 195-202). Stories
like this were much enjoyed by the Romans for whom Josephus wrote
his work. The king was struck down **immediately** (παραχρῆμα) but it is not
related that he died straightaway. On the contrary, that which follows,
namely, that **he was eaten by worms,** which in the Greek is σκωληκόβρωτος,
evidently requires a certain interval before death. Josephus, in fact, relates
that the king was suddenly attacked by violent abdominal pains which
continued for some days, after which he died. The term used by Luke
to indicate the course of the malady is very rare in Greek writings, and
again shows that the writer was well versed in medical matters. Today,
anyone wishing to give a diagnosis of the disease would think first of
appendicitis with suppurations and consequent peritonitis, but naturally
the symptoms mentioned here are not sufficient to make such a diagnosis
certain. There are cases in ancient times of other monarchs hostile to the
Jewish or Christian religion who died in much the same way, viz., eaten

12:24. But the word of God increased and spread.

12:25. Then Barnabas and Saul, when they had fulfilled the mission [entrusted to them], returned from Jerusalem, taking with them John who was surnamed Mark.

13:1. Now in the Church at Antioch there were prophets and teachers, among whom were Barnabas and Simon called Niger, and Lucius of Cyrene, and Manahen the foster-brother of Herod the tetrarch, and Saul.

---

by worms, like Antiochus IV, Epiphanes (2 Mach. 9:5-9), Herod the Great (*Antiquities of the Jews*, XVII, 169), Galerius (Eusebius, *Hist. eccl.*, VIII, 16, 4-5; Lactantius, *De mortibus persec.*, 33). However poor the historical evidence may be for such early cases, the reality of the later ones is nowise weakened, and those few scholars who have considered the later ones fictitious are only presuming that which they ought to prove.

12:24. This is a résumé of the situation, which Luke likes to give (cf. 6:7; 9:31), and is the more fitting here inasmuch as it ends the account of Peter's activity, and the "Acts" of Paul begin; see the note on 9:1-2 and 32; 12:1 and 17).

12:25. The mission [entrusted to them]: this is reported in 11:30, where the "journey of the alms" is recounted, and which is now accomplished. This conclusion inserted here leads us to suppose that during the preceding events (Peter's imprisonment, the death of King Agrippa), Barnabas and Paul were in Jerusalem or, at least, in Judea. The reading, **from** (ἐξ or ἀπὸ) **Jerusalem** is given by most codices, but many other authoritative documents give **to** (εἰς), which, however, seems opposed to the entire context. Some codices, for clearness' sake, make an addition to the first reading by putting, **they returned from Jerusalem to Antioch.** — **John ... Mark;** cf. verse 12.

13:1. The "Acts of Peter" being completed, the Christian communities, formed of ex-Jews with their center at Jerusalem, will now be left aside, and we come to those communities formed of ex-pagans with their center at Antioch, that powerhouse of Christianity in the Graeco-Roman world (see note on 11:26). — **Prophets and Teachers:** for **prophets,** see note on 11:27. **Teachers** (διδάσκαλοι) were those who had the charism of "teaching" in a given community: Paul speaks of them (1 Cor. 12:28-29; Rom. 12:7; Eph. 4:11). Of the five persons named, **Barnabas, Simon, Lucius, Manahen, and Saul,** the first and last are already known to us, but it is possible that the others are included among those Cypriots and Cyreneans

13:2. And as they ministered to the Lord and fasted, the Holy Spirit said: "Set apart for me Barnabas and Saul for the work to which I have called them."

---

spoken of in 11:20. — We find here, in fact, that **Lucius** is a Cyrenean. The suggestion that this Lucius is our Luke has no foundation, since all the early testimonies about Luke call him an Antiochian and not a Cyrenean. — **Manahen** is a Hebrew name, but we do not know anything else about this individual. — The term **foster-brother** (σύντροφος) can have a wider meaning than its strictly legal connotation, and could signify "brought up together," "school companion." — **Herod the tetrarch** is Herod Antipas who beheaded John the Baptist. — One might venture a possible suggestion about **Simon called Niger,** that he could be Simon of Cyrene (*Simon* and *Simeon* are equivalent) who helped Jesus to carry his cross, and was the father of Alexander and Rufus (Mk. 15:21). Paul also refers to a fairly influential Christian by the name of Rufus at Rome (Rom. 16:13). The Cyreneans were dark, so his surname **Niger,** and the fact that he comes after **Lucius of Cyrene** in the list could suggest that he also was from Cyrene, in other words, that he was the Simon of Cyrene who helped Christ with his cross. This suggestion is attractive, but highly conjectural.

13:2. As they ministered, λειτουργούντον αὐτῶν. **They** refers to the prophets and teachers and the others previously named, but it necessarily includes the Christian community which participated in the liturgy. It is not stated in what the liturgy consisted, but in the episode of 20:7-11, it is specified that in the gathering at Troas, Paul **broke bread** and gave a long discourse. Everything inclines one to believe that in this meeting also at Antioch, the "breaking of bread" took place, and one or two discourses were given, probably by persons gifted with "charisms." It is important to explain that the term **liturgy** in Greek, and its derivatives (**liturgical, to follow the liturgy, etc.),** are found in the New Testament only in Luke and in the writings of his master, Paul. The liturgy here is addressed **to the Lord,** namely Jesus Christ. In fact, **the chalice of benediction . . . is the communion of the blood of Christ,** just as **the bread we break . . . is the partaking of the body of the Lord** (1 Cor. 10:16). It is worth noticing here that fasting is linked with the liturgy. — **The Holy Spirit said:** this was certainly through one of the charismatics present who spoke in the meeting, and could have had the charism of "governments" (1 Cor. 12:28) or that of "prophecy." The "prophets" of verse 1 had to exercise a general supervision so as to insure that such charismatic manifestations were genuine. — **For the work to which I have called them:** this work, as will appear in the narrative, was the apostolate among the Gentiles, and such

13:3. **Thereupon, having fasted and prayed and laid their hands upon them, they let them go.**

---

a mission had been entrusted to Saul-Paul at his conversion (see note on 9:15; cf. 22:21). So far as Barnabas is concerned, there has been no mention yet of a similar mission being given to him, since what he did for the Gentiles at Antioch (11:22-25), does not seem to presuppose a general regular evangelization. But Luke's narrative here is summary. Perhaps the mouthpiece of the Spirit replied to some collective prayer made at the meeting, or even confirmed some private revelation already received by the chosen two. Undoubtedly the fervent community had been anxious for some time to carry the Gospel to regions where it had not yet been preached, and they intermingled zealous plans with prayers to God to know his will. God made it known through the charismatic communication.

13:3. Luke continues to compress his narrative, but it is not too difficult to see some of the implications. Since the reply of the Spirit had been received, there could be no doubt about the correctness of the decision. But how was it to be put into execution? To what pagan regions should these missionaries, chosen by the Spirit, be sent? The divine command did not dispense from human prudence, and the conditions of the various regions, near or far, had to be considered, to see what Jewish communities were there, and what friendships could be counted upon in those communities, so as to give initial support to the missionaries in unknown territories. It is true that the final aim of the mission was the evangelization of the Gentiles, but the gift of the Gospel ought to be offered in the first place to Israel, the nation chosen as the depository of God's promises. If Israel refused it, it ought to be offered to the Gentiles, so that the missionaries could always say before the Jews: **it was necessary that the word of God should be spoken to you first, but since you reject it and judge yourselves unworthy of eternal life, behold we now turn to the Gentiles** (13:46; see note there). The careful considerations of the various plans were still accompanied — as in the preceding verse — with fastings and prayers **(fasted and prayed),** and finally the choice was made in favor of the island of Cyprus (following verse). The reasons for this choice are clear. Cyprus was only sixty miles or so by sea, and there were numerous acquaintances there, since some of those who had evangelized the pagans in Antioch were Cypriots (11:20) and Barnabas also was a Cypriot (4:36). It is quite possible that Paul himself, a native of Tarsus north of the island, had already visited it. The Jews of Cyprus had already heard something of the Gospel from those who fled from Jerusalem (11:19). In this island then, the missionaries would have their first experience and after-

13:4. They accordingly, sent forth by the Holy Spirit, went down to Seleucia, and from there sailed to Cyprus.

13:5. On their arrival at Salamis, they preached the word of God in the synagogues of the Jews: and they had John also [as] assistant.

---

ward they would go where the Spirit directed them (cf. 16:6–10) and where the experience gained could be put to best use. — The rite of the "imposition of hands," which was used on different occasions, was performed on the two missionaries (see note on 6:6). It does not appear in any way from the circumstances of the narrative that there was a question of conferring an office or regular task, but only a pious leave-taking at which the divine assistance was implored on the two departing missionaries. The reference to this departure given in 14:26, speaks of how the missionaries when leaving Antioch, **had first been entrusted to the grace of God for the work** they had to do. Here also, there is no reference to any office or permanent position (cf. 15:40). Jesus himself had laid his hands on children (Mt. 19:13–15) as a simple gesture of imploring the divine assistance.

13:4. The stay in Antioch prior to the mission with its accompanying discussions and the preparations for the voyage, must have taken a certain amount of time, so that now we must be at the beginning of the year 45. Thus begins the first of the three great missionary journeys of Paul known to us, about which, however, we are only imperfectly informed. In the autobiographical passage in 2 Cor. 11:23–27, events are described which are not related in the three journeys given by Luke, and which took place before the year A.D. 57, when that epistle was written. At the beginning of this first journey, the moral head of the mission is Barnabas, always named first (12:25; 13:1, 2, 7). Saul-Paul is in second place to Barnabas, but he only remains so until verse 13 where the position is reversed. According to Luke, only these two, Barnabas and Paul, are *the ones sent forth by the Holy Spirit,* as is stated in verse 2, since John Mark, their temporary assistant, eventually defected on this journey (verse 13). — **Seleucia** was the port that served Antioch sixteen miles away. — **Cyprus,** the largest island in the eastern Mediterranean: a description of it is found in G. Ricciotti, *Paul the Apostle,* pp. 31–33.

13:5. Salamis: previously known as Salamina, a city and principal port of the island facing Syria in the bay which is now called Famagusta. — **In the synagogues of the Jews:** there must have been many Jews there, especially after Herod the Great had leased the copper mines from Augustus (Flavius Josephus, *Antiquities of the Jews,* XVI, 129). This metal went all over the world under the name of *Cyprian metal, cyprium, cuprum;*

13:6. And when they had gone through the whole island as far as Paphos, they found a certain man, a magician, a false Jewish prophet, named Bar-Jesus,

---

whence it has come into our modern languages as *copper, cuivre, Kupfer.* According to Eusebius (*Chronicon,* ed. Schone, II, 164), during the revolt under Trajan, the Jews had killed 240,000 on the island and destroyed Salamis (Salamina), but these figures are certainly exaggerated. Dion Cassius states (LXVIII, 32) that so great was the hatred which the Jews drew down on themselves by this butchery, that after the ruthless Roman repression, any Jew who set foot on the island, even if he were ship-wrecked, was killed. However, these events took place 70 years after Paul's visit, and during his stay there, the Jews lived on the island undisturbed. In these **synagogues of the Jews,** the missionaries preached **the word of God** before going to the pagans, for the reason already stated (cf. note on v. 3), and in keeping with the general policy for the future. They came on the Sabbath to the synagogue, taking advantage of the common right to speak there at meetings, and endeavored to show their hearers that on the basis of the prophecies of Holy Scripture, Jesus of Nazareth was the true Messias. If their preaching had effect, at least on part of the audience, they returned the following Sabbath to perfect their work. Otherwise, they left the Jews, and addressed themselves to the pagans. A typical example of this method will be seen shortly at Antioch in Pisidia (vv. 14–49). — **John** Mark, although a cousin of Barnabas (cf. note on 12:12), plays a subordinate role to the other two missionaries (see note on v. 4). Luke presents him with the very modest term of **assistant,** ὑπηρέτης, which could also be translated as **attendant.** It almost seems to be a preparation for the unhappy news in verse 13.

13:6. When they had gone through the whole island as far as Paphos: this is a very abbreviated account, for these few words sum up a period of several months. From Salamis **as far as Paphos** is almost from the extreme east to the extreme west of the island, a distance of about 100 miles, and there must have been several villages and towns along the route where there were many Jews. This, then, is the reason why the months must have gone by rapidly, since they remained in those places only for as long as was necessary for the preaching of the Gospel on the Sabbath. We are not told the result of these months of work from Salamis to Paphos. Nevertheless, indirectly we may assume that they were not unfruit-ful, since Barnabas will revisit Cyprus later together with Mark (15:39), and this return to his native island must have been dictated not only by personal reasons, but also to confirm the good results obtained during the

Paul's First

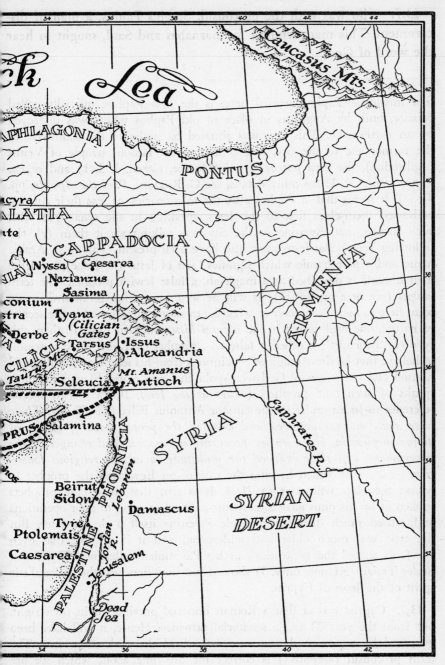

Missionary Journey

13:7. who was with the proconsul, Sergius Paulus, a man of discernment. This man, sending for Barnabas and Saul, sought to hear the word of God,

---

first mission. — **Paphos,** named here, is the new Paphos, officially called Sebaste, built by Augustus in place of old Paphos which was destroyed by an earthquake. This city was situated 60 stadia to the southwest of the former site of the city, and contained the famous temple of Venus (Aphrodite), the *diva potens Cypri* (Horace, *Carm.,* I, 3, 1) and *regina Paphi (ibid.,* 30, 1; for other details, see G. Ricciotti, *Paul the Apostle,* pp. 31–33). It seems that at Paphos also, the missionaries, as was their cutsom, addressed themselves first to the Jews, speaking in the synagogue with such success that everyone in the city was talking about them (cf. the following verse). **Bar-Jesus** must also have been present. This is an Arabic name and a patronymic which signifies "son of Jesus (*or* Josue)," and the man himself is described as **a magician, a false Jewish prophet.** The term *magus* (see note on 8:9–11), as will be seen from what follows, does not seem here to mean a sorcerer or wizard, but rather one learned in the secrets of nature, one well versed in the *natural history* of that time. If, then, this type of "alchemist" is called a **false . . . prophet** by Luke, there is reason to believe that he drew religious conclusions from his learning, and flaunted himself as a messenger of God who spoke in God's name. Flavius Josephus speaks of such false prophets (*Wars of the Jews,* II, 258) with special reference to Judea under the procurator Antonius Felix (A.D. 52–60): *These were such men as deceived and deluded the people under pretence of divine inspiration, but were for procuring innovations and changes of the government, and these induced the multitude to acts of religious fanaticism . . . ,* after which he cites the case of an Egyptian false prophet to whom the *Acts* will refer in 21:38. It is true that these false prophets spoken of by Josephus gave a messianic-political coloring to their operations and caused much disturbance inside Palestine itself a decade later. But the type was much older and widespread and it is possible that even Bar-Jesus shared the same ideals as his Palestinian colleagues. The revolt under Trajan (see note on v. 5) showed just how fiery was the nationalistic spirit of the Jews of Cyprus.

13:7. Cyprus was at first a Roman imperial province in its own right, but from the year 22 B.C., a senatorial province. Hence, it will have been governed by a proconsul who may have held the rank of praetor. The term **proconsul** (ἀνθύπατος) is correct for the time about which we are speaking, while *propraetor* would be the term prior to 22 B.C. An inscription found in Soli, a city on the northern coast of the island, gives the

13:8. but Elymas the sorcerer (for so his name is translated) opposed them, trying to turn away the proconsul from the faith.

---

name *Paul* (*pro*)*consul,* which very probably refers to this Sergius Paulus. Pliny the Elder also cites as a source of his information, probably on Cyprus, a Sergius Paulus (*Natur. hist.,* Books II and XVII, in the respective lists *ex auctoribus,* placed at the beginning), but the manuscript transmission is inconsistent, sometimes giving Sergius Paulus and sometimes Sergius Plautus. For the inscription and for Pliny, cf. G. Ricciotti, *Paul the Apostle,* pp. 252–253, footnote. Strange and uncertain is a Latin inscription (*Corpus Inscr. Lat.,* VI, 31545) which names one L. Sergius Paulus at the time of Claudius, and another found by Ramsay in 1912 at Antioch in Pisidia, which may be of a later date than this episode, naming the son of one Lucius Sergius Paulus, who could have been the proconsul. For Luke, this Sergius Paulus is **a man of discernment** (ουνετός) which corresponds to our term "cultured," "a person with an inquiring turn of mind." The proconsul, then, being a serious-minded man and anxious for information, realizing that the government of his isolated and peaceful province left him plenty of free time, filled his leisure hours with conversations with learned men, who, even if they were magicians or devotees of the occult sciences, were so much sought after at that time in the Roman empire. This explains how Bar-Jesus was **with** him. The arrival in the city of Barnabas and Saul, who must have been spoken of everywhere as learned men, was a happy occasion for the proconsul who took advantage of it immediately, and **sending for Barnabas and Saul,** he **sought to hear the word of God.** This last expression represents Luke's viewpoint rather than that of Sergius. He simply wished to know the teaching of the two philosophers of whatever kind they were, whereas, for Luke, their teaching was **the word of God.** It was said in the city that these two spoke of a certain Jesus, put to death a few years before and then risen from the dead, who had brought a new life to all men without distinction. Therefore the inquiring proconsul desired to judge for himself what there might be of importance in the teaching of the two newcomers.

13:8. Probably the encounters between the missionaries and the proconsul took place more than once, but right from the beginning they found an opponent in Bar-Jesus, who, perhaps, having heard them in the synagogue (cf. note on v. 6), realized at once that their ideas were a complete antithesis to his activity as a magician. It is also quite likely that Bar-Jesus had tried to advise the proconsul against even seeing them, but since Sergius Paulus wished to please himself, there remained nothing for the magician but to be present at the interviews as an opposing party (something which the impartial proconsul would have easily granted him)

13:9. But Saul also called Paul, filled with the Holy Spirit, gazed at him

---

and to join in the conversation, **trying to turn away the proconsul from the faith.** If Paul followed here the method preferred by him when he spoke to pagans, he would begin with the natural knowledge of the one God (14:15 sqq.; 17:22–31), and then pass on to the revelation of the Old and New Testaments. Bar-Jesus would have objected, especially to this last part of the argumentation and then a discussion would have ensued between him and the ex-rabbi on the basis of messianic quotations from the Old Testament. — The parenthesis, viz., **Elymas the sorcerer (for so his name is translated),** is difficult to understand. To what do the words, **his name,** refer? Certainly not to the name **Bar-Jesus** which has the meaning given above (in the note on v. 6). It is to be referred then to **Elymas,** and thus the whole phrase runs: **Elymas (viz.) the magician, for thus** (*magus*) **is his name** (Elymas) **interpreted.** But what is the derivation of Elymas? Many think it comes from the Arabic *alim,* "learned," whence one learned in the occult sciences was a *magus* or magician. More probably it derives from the Semitic root *LM,* "to bind," with reference to hidden powers, and thus the *magician* would be one who "binds" or dominates demoniacal forces. Nevertheless, some documents of the Western Recension (codex D, Lucifer of Cagliari, etc.) instead of **Elymas** have **Etoimas (Etimas, etc.),** which has led some to think that it refers to that magician, a native of Cyprus, who, in A.D. 54, induced Drusilla to marry the Roman procurator Felix (cf. note on 23:25; 24:24), after she had been divorced from Azizus, king of Emesa, according to the account of Flavius Josephus (*Antiquities of the Jews,* XX, 142) in which some codices give the name of *Atomos* to the Cypriot magician, though most of the authoritative ones call him Simon. It is a conjecture therefore, as can be seen, lacking even a certain chronological basis. — After the word, **faith,** the Western Recension adds, **since he listened to them very willingly.** This is simply a gloss, containing what hardly needed to be stated, and seems to be inspired by the attitude of Herod Antipas toward John the Baptist (Mk. 6:20).

13:9. Saul also called Paul: this is the first time in the *Acts* that the name **Paul** is applied to him, who until now, has been called **Saul.** It was a frequent custom among both the Jews of Palestine and the Diaspora to have a double name. There are examples as far back as the times of the Machabees, and also in the New Testament, among them being companions of Paul (**John Mark** of 12:12). The custom aimed at facilitating relations with Graeco-Romans, who easily mispronounced Semitic names. For this reason, foreign names were chosen which had some assonance with the Hebrew name. Thus in the case here, *Shaul = Paul,* though

13:10. and said: "O full of all guile and of all deceit, son of the devil, enemy of all justice, wilt thou not cease to pervert the right ways of the Lord?

13:11. "And now behold the hand of the Lord is upon thee, and thou shalt be blind, not seeing the sun for a time." And instantly there fell upon him mist and darkness, and going about he sought [someone] to lead him by the hand.

---

already at the time of the Machabees, *Jeshu'a = Jason; Eliaqim = Alkim;* etc. It must not be thought that Saul took the name of Paul on the occasion of his first spiritual conquest when he converted the proconsul of the same name, for this had not yet happened, and would be barely touched upon in verse 12. Rather are we to see in the use of the name **Paul,** which from now on will be the only one used, a literary subtlety of Luke who uses the non-Hebrew name now that Paul figures for the first time as the apostle of the non-Hebrews, which he will continue to be to the end of his life. This is the opinion expressed in antiquity by Origen (*Comment. epist. ad Rom., Praef.,* in Migne, *P. G.,* 14, 837). There is no historical foundation for the opinion, reflected in the Apocrypha, that Saul was called Paul (*paulus,* "little"), because he was short in stature.

13:10. Son of the devil: in Aramaic, it would be *Bar-Satan(a)*, in opposition to *Bar-Jesus,* the name of the magician (v. 6), but seeing that the proconsul was present, who certainly knew no Aramaic or Hebrew, Paul would surely have spoken in Greek saying, **son of the devil.** It is feasible that since the magician's name was *Bar-Jesus,* i.e., "son of Jesus (*or* Josue)," Paul used the epithet **son of the devil** by way of antithesis to this name, having Jesus of Nazareth in his mind, though this application could only be mental on Paul's part for the magician would have had no special veneration for the various individuals named Jesus or Josue in the Old Testament. Jesus himself also had accused the Jews of having the devil for their father (Jn. 8:44).

13:11. For a time: viz., not permanently. This limitation of time seems to be an exhortation to perceive that the punishment was medicinal in its nature. — **Mist:** ἀχλύς: "clouding over," or the beginning of that complete **darkness** spoken of immediately afterward. The first term, "clouding over," used only here in the whole of the New Testament, is found in the writings of ancient Greek physicians when they are treating of ophthalmic matters. — **He sought [someone] to lead him by the hand:** the exact situation in which Paul had found himself on the road to Damascus (9:8). It seems perfectly futile to have recourse to naturalistic explanations to reduce the fact to normal proportions. It has been thought that the

13:12. Then the proconsul, seeing what had happened, believed and was astonished at the Lord's teaching.

13:13. Now having sailed from Paphos, Paul and those who were with him came to Perge in Pamphylia, but John left them and returned to Jerusalem.

---

magician, being of a neuropathic constitution, was shocked by Paul's words, and remained as if hypnotized by his look (v. 9). Such explanations convince only those who are convinced beforehand, while it must be admitted by all that Luke here intends to relate a strictly miraculous event. Luke's opinion was shared in full even by the proconsul (following verse) who was the most interested of all.

13:12. The reason why the proconsul **believed** was **seeing what had happened.** The Greek also admits of the translation, **believed, being astonished, in the Lord's teaching.** Once again the theme returns that both the person of Jesus and his teaching are **approved by God . . . by miracles and wonders and signs** (2:22). These are the motives of credibility which induce acceptance of the **Lord's teaching.** — In what manner did Sergius Paulus believe? Only intellectually as a philosopher who admires a given doctrine, or in a practical way by receiving baptism, though the latter is not mentioned? The first way cannot be excluded entirely, but the second is more probable. When Luke uses the words *to believe,* he usually implies the reception of baptism (2:44; 4:44 and 32; 5:14; 11:21; 13:48). Furthermore, the purpose of Luke's narrative is not to show that the evangelical doctrine was something to be admired from the intellectual point of view, but that it was actually spread in the world, i.e., that people adhered to it by baptism. The proconsul's position as a high Roman official was not a serious obstacle to his eventual baptism, for at this time (A.D. 45), Rome showed no hostility to the new religion, and it was of no more moment that a magistrate of a province should accept Christianity than that he should be initiated into the mysteries of Dionysus. By showing the proconsul's friendly attitude toward Christianity, Luke shows again his preoccupation to present the Roman authorities favorably as he has done before (see note on 3:13; 5:30) and will continue to do when narrating Paul's activities.

13:13. The missionaries now resume their journey, leaving the island and embarking at **Paphos,** setting sail immediately northward toward Asia Minor. After a short crossing, they landed probably in Attalia (cf. 14:25), and walking on for seven or eight miles, reached **Perge in Pamphylia.** We notice, rather unexpectedly, that the party is referred to by the phrase *those with Paul,* whereas we should have expected *those with Barnabas,*

13:14. But they, passing through [the district] from Perge came to Antioch in Pisidia, and entering into the synagogue on the Sabbath day, they sat down.

---

since he was the head of the company on its arrival in Cyprus (see note on v. 4). The reason for this change is that during the stay at Cyprus, the internal disposition of the party was altered. While Barnabas was the leader at the beginning, Paul took over the leadership as their missionary activity was intensified. He was the initiator and the leader, and, as a result, the others took the second place and became *those with Paul.* As long as they remained in Cyprus, Barnabas retained a certain position of importance by virtue of being in his own country where his personal acquaintance with the Jews there was particularly useful. But this advantage had considerably diminished toward the end when they moved in the pagan circle of the proconsul at Paphos, and had ceased altogether when they left the island. All this must have been noticed with dismay by **John Mark,** the cousin of Barnabas, and his apprehension will have increased by what he saw and perceived during the brief trip from Attalia to Perge, a wild and desolate region at the foot of the Taurus mountains. Moreover, what was worse, the mountainous and more or less trackless territory was reputedly uncivilized and infested with brigands and robbers, the descendants of those who in the preceding century had given so much trouble to brave generals like Pompey, and governors like Cicero. And what made them push forward into such terrible regions? Certainly not the directives given at their departure by the community at Antioch, which had left them free to choose where they would go after Cyprus (see note on v. 3). It was Paul who wished to face this frightening adventure, and the good Barnabas had not the firmness to oppose him. Pondering over all this, John Mark was grieved, and, recalling with nostalgia the comfort of his mother's house in Jerusalem (12:12), he felt he could not go on. Hence, he **left them and returned to Jerusalem.** The unexperienced sailor returned to port at the first sign of a storm. The prudent Luke has already prepared the reader for this defection, by pointing out that only Barnabas and Paul were the real missionaries **sent forth by the Holy Spirit** (v. 4; cf. v. 2) though they had John as an **assistant.** This defection greatly displeased the ardent Paul and he remembered it for a long time (cf. 15:38). Barnabas, for his part, did not follow his fainthearted cousin this time, but remained at Paul's side.

13:14. Passing through the district from Perge they came to Antioch in Pisidia: the words are very simple, but the journey was very arduous (for the description of it, see G. Ricciotti, *Paul the Apostle,* pp. 257–258).

13:15. Now after the reading of the Law and the Prophets, the presidents of the synagogue sent to them saying: "Brethren, if you have any word of exhortation for the people, speak."
13:16. Then Paul rising up and beckoning with his hand said: "Men of Israel and you that fear God, listen.

With a journey of a little over a hundred miles, the Taurus mountains had first to be crossed, then the mountainous regions of Pisidia. Such a journey necessitated about a week of hardship and fatigue. The city of **Antioch** was called Pisidian **(in Pisidia)**, to distinguish it from the place of the same name in Syria, whence the two missionaries had set out. It was situated 3940 feet above sea level, on territory that originally belonged to Phrygia, but which was considered part of Pisidia after the Roman occupation and the consequent changes of partitions and frontiers (for the history of the city, see Ricciotti, *op. cit.*, p. 25). The Jews, attracted there by the trade in hides, must have been numerous, and the missionaries most certainly had letters of introduction to them. There was a **synagogue** to which the missionaries went regularly **on the sabbath day**, according to their practice (see note on v. 5), and **they sat down**, probably on the seats specially reserved for distinguished strangers and visitors. It should be noted that the meetings on the Sabbath day were frequented not only by those who were Jews by birth, but also by pagans who were well disposed toward the Jewish religion (cf. vv. 16 and 43).

13:15. We have here an accurate description of the procedure at meetings of the synagogue. Luke gives a similar description, though a shorter one, in his Gospel (4:16 sqq.) speaking of Jesus' last appearance in the synagogue at Nazareth. The meeting began with the recitation of the *Shema*, composed of passages from the Pentateuch, which was, so to say, an "act of faith" in the true God. Then certain prayers were said and **after the reading of the Law and the Prophets,** a discourse was given by way of instruction, usually on the passage read, explaining it and drawing practical applications from it. Any one of those present was eligible to give the discourse, though the president of the meeting used to invite those whom he considered qualified. Those who wished to offer their services voluntarily, could do so. — **Presidents:** in the plural. Strictly speaking, there was only one president in each synagogue, but the title became a kind of honorary degree which was given to persons of distinction, so much so, that in inscriptions it is found attributed to women and even to children three years old (*Corpus Inscript. Judaicarum*, I, pag. XCVIII–XCIX). These individuals sat on special seats during the meetings (cf. Mt. 23:6). — **Men brethren:** see note on 1:11.

13:16. Beckoning with his hand: the gesture habitual with pagan orators at the beginning of a speech. It will be found mentioned again in 19:33; 21:40; though it was not spoken of in the discourses of Peter and Stephen. The appeal was directed to those who were *Israelites* by birth, and the pagans *who feared God* (for this see note on 2:5-6), who were present in the synagogue (cf. vv. 14 and 43). Here begins a discourse of Paul which is of special importance because it can be considered as the typical address which this speaker used when he addressed the Jews. Evidently this time the discourse was extemporaneous, but more in form than in substance, since the ideas formed part of Paul's fundamental teaching upon which he drew when he found himself in such circumstances. Luke, who certainly was not present at the discourse, in relating the speech at length, will have touched upon that same fundamental teaching which he knew so well, since it was used by the same speaker on other occasions. Perhaps he is making use also of some general notions which he received from some member of the community of Pisidian Antioch. The ideas are typically Pauline and are surprisingly reminiscent of the epistle to the *Romans.* The opening words of the address, **Men of Israel,** correspond to the other two calls, **[Men] brethren** (vv. 26 and 38), which divide the discourse into three parts. The first part (vv. 17-25) is the historical premise, which demonstrates the preparatory plan of the redemption as outlined in the Old Testament, gradually centralized in the line of David from which the Messias Jesus had come. The second part (vv. 26-37) takes up the history of Jesus, culminating in his Resurrection. The third part (vv. 38-41) draws practical conclusions from the redemption worked by Jesus, applying them to the hearers of the discourse. The first part resembles Stephen's discourse (7:2 sqq.), though not entirely, since it differs from it by omitting his insistence upon the ingratitude of the people of Israel, but emphasizes the constant development of the divine plan for the redemption. The second part brings to mind Peter's discourse at Pentecost (2:14 sqq.), but insists more on the historical details of the events. The third part introduces the typically Pauline concept of the insufficiency of the law of Moses for justification, which is wrought only by faith in the Messias Jesus. Seeing that Paul was preaching the discourse customarily given in the synagogue which usually turned on the passages from Scripture read beforehand, some have thought it feasible to recognize these passages from the discourse. We find, in fact, that the two verbs, **nourished** (v. 18) and **gave them for an inheritance** (v. 19), are both used in Deut. 1:31 and 38. This would show that the passage read from the Pentateuch (or *parashah*) came from Deuteronomy, Chapter 1, according to the Greek text of the Septuagint. Then, we find the word, he **exalted** (v. 17), which is used in the Septuagint of Isa. 1:2, and that would indicate that the passage from the Prophets (or *haphtarah*) came from Isaias, Chapter 1. In actual fact, in the liturgy of the synagogue today, these

13:17. "The God of this people Israel chose our fathers and exalted the people during [their] sojourn in the land of Egypt, and with uplifted arm led them forth out of it.

13:18. "And for a period of about forty years nourished them in the desert,

13:19. "and after destroying seven nations in the land of Canaan he gave [them] their land for an inheritance

13:20. "for the space of about four hundred and fifty years. After that he gave them Judges until Samuel the prophet.

---

two passages (*parashah* and *haphtarah*) are found together. But in all this reconstruction, the ingenuity of those who have worked it out is to be admired more than the soundness of their conclusions, for the juxtaposition of these words could be purely a chance outcome.

13:17. Exalted, ὕψωσεν (see the preceding note): this has a particular demographic sense here of increase in numbers and power. — **Arm:** a Hebrew expression for "power." It alludes to the prodigies that accompanied the exodus from Egypt.

13:18. Nourished them, reading ἐτροφοφόρησεν, **bore them like a nurse,** as many good codices give, although many other more authoritative ones give ἐτροποφόρησεν, **bore their ways.** The expression is from Deut. 1:31 (see note on v. 16), but even in the codices of the Septuagint, both readings are found. Probably, however, the difference is merely verbal. The reading ἐτροποφόρησεν, which means **he bore their conduct** (understood as "perverse manners"), could be a substitution for ἐτροφοφόρησεν, which has two consecutive syllables begining with the aspirate φ. So as to avoid this dissonance, the first φ was substituted by the corresponding soft π. To take the sense of **he bore** with **their ways** (understood of the perverse manners of the Israelites) seems inappropriate here, since Paul wishes to avoid any allusion to the ingratitude of the Chosen People, whereas Stephen (see note on v. 16) made it his chief argument. The reading here chosen refers to the nourishment of the manna provided in the desert, but a more exact rendering of the Hebrew text might be translated **he carried them** as a father carries his child which cannot yet walk (thus is it explained in Deut. 1:31). It is an idea dear to Paul (1 Thess. 2:7).

13:19. Seven nations: those listed in Deut. 7:1. — **He gave them . . . for an inheritance:** cf. note on v. 16.

13:20–21. Here we have two precise numbers, first, **four hundred and**

13:21. "Then they asked for a king, and God gave them Saul the son of Cis, a man of the tribe of Benjamin, for forty years.

13:22. "Then having removed him, he raised up David to be their king, to whom also he said in testimony: 'I have found David, the son of Jesse, a man after my own heart, who will do all that I desire' (Ps. 89 [88]:21; 1 Sam. 13:14).

---

fifty years and then **forty years.** A few codices with certain modifications of the text, refer the number 450 to what follows and not to what precedes, but it certainly must refer to what precedes as indeed the greater number of codices show. Thus the period that extends from the conquest of the **land of Canaan** (v. 19) to the beginning of the epoch of the **Judges,** of whom **Samuel the prophet** is the last, would have lasted 450 years, and in its turn, the reign of Saul, first king of Israel, would have lasted 40 years. But neither of these figures is confirmed by the data of the Old Testament, either according to the Hebrew text or the Greek of the Septuagint. On the contrary, 450 is only one of the figures which can be arrived at on the basis of the different texts. The number 40 is frequently met with in the Old Testament as a typical number, but this is the only passage to refer it to Saul's reign. The truth of the matter is that the whole chronology of the Bible is most intricate and involves almost infinite ramifications (whoever wishes can find a summary of this in G. Ricciotti, *The History of Israel,* I, pp. 185-192, 241-242, 286), but before going into it, it would be well for the student to think over the sharp warning that the expert Jerome gave in his own day: *"Read all the books of the Old or New Testament, and you will meet with a great discrepancy of years and confusion of numbers between Juda and Israel* (i.e., between the two kingdoms), *to spend time on such questions is an occupation for those with leisure, but not for scholars"* (*ad Vital., Epist.* 71, 5; in Migne, *P. L.,* 22, 676). In any case, so far as can be seen, Paul does not depend here on the figures of the Old Testament, but on those of the tradition of his own rabbi masters (a similar case is that of 400 years in 7:6). Therefore the general observations made in connection with the biblical discrepancies in Stephen's discourse, apply here (see note on 7:2, from the middle onward). Nothing useful can be gained from the phantasmagoric chronology of Flavius Josephus, so frequent are his contradictions not only with the Bible, but even with his works, according to the sources he used. For example, in *Antiquities of the Jews,* VI, 378, he assigns 40 years to Saul's reign, as Paul does here, while later on in the same work (*ibid.,* X, 143), he assigns only 20 years to it.

13:23. "From his offspring, God according to promise brought to Israel a Saviour, Jesus.

13:24. "John having first preached before his coming a baptism of repentance to all the people of Israel.

13:25. "And when John was coming to the end of his career, he would say: 'I am not he whom you think me to be; but behold there comes one after me, the sandals of whose feet I am not worthy to loose' (cf. Mt. 3:11; Mk. 1:7; Lk. 3:16; Jn. 1:20, 27).

13:26. "Brethren, children of the race of Abraham, and those among you who fear God, to us the word of this salvation has been sent.

13:27. "For the inhabitants of Jerusalem and their rulers, not knowing him and the utterances of the prophets which are read every Sabbath, fulfilled them, by condemning him,

13:28. "and though they found no cause of death they asked Pilate that he should be killed.

13:23. These are the phrases which are found in the Pauline epistles. from the offspring of David (Rom. 1:3); according to promise (Gal. 3:29).

13:24. John is the Baptist, who had preached a baptism of penance or "repentance"; see note on 2:38; 5:31; 11:18.

13:26. Men . . . children: the new mode of address marks the second part of the discourse: see note on verse 16. — Instead of to us, other texts mostly less authoritative but greater in number, have to you.

13:27-28. The Jews who condemned Christ did it not knowing him. Their ignorance regarding the man they condemned was not material but moral, and had already been put forward as an excuse in 3:17. But this ignorance was preceded and caused by ignorance of another matter, namely the utterances of the prophets which are read every Sabbath at their meetings in the synagogue (cf. v. 15, 15:21). But even here, this ignorance was only moral, since those who heard the readings in the synagogue knew the Scriptures well enough materially but not morally as they did not comprehend that they referred to the Messias Jesus. It is one of Paul's classical thoughts that on the minds of the unbelieving Jews, a veil remains when the Old Testament is read to them, not being lifted (for them) because (that testament) in Christ is made void; but even until this day every time Moses is read, a veil covers their hearts (2 Cor. 3:14-15; cf. Rom. 11:7-8 and 25). Here Pilate appears as the intermediary

13:29. "And when they had carried out all that had been written concerning him, they took him down from the tree and laid him in a tomb.

13:30. "But God raised him from the dead,

13:31. "and he was seen for many days by those who had come up with him from Galilee to Jerusalem, who are now his witnesses to the people.

13:32. "So we now bring to you the good news of the promise made to [our] fathers,

---

in the execution of Christ, but the initial move toward his death was suggested by the Sanhedrists. He was, then, an accomplice in spite of himself, but the attenuating circumstances of 3:13 are not conceded here (cf. :27). — In the Western Recension these two verses and the one following have a somewhat different form: **And its chiefs (i.e., of Jerusalem) not understanding the writings of the prophets which are read every sabbath, and condemning him, they fulfilled (them); and not finding any cause of death in him, condemning him they gave him over to Pilate to kill him. When they had carried out all the things that were written concerning him, they asked Pilate to crucify him, and having done that again, taking him down from the tree, they laid him in a tomb, whom God raised up, etc.** It is clear that this text is simply a manipulation of the other, arising from a desire to be precise, and to distinguish the events which happened before the crucifixion of Jesus from those which happened afterward.

13:29. They laid him: Joseph of Arimathea and Nicodemus did this according to the Gospels. Therefore the subject of this verb is not necessarily the **inhabitants** and **their rulers** of verse 27, as the verb could well be regarded as an impersonal construction **(was laid),** as we find on many occasions in the New Testament. Nevertheless, if one wishes to maintain the personal construction no difficulty arises, because Joseph and Nicodemus were members of the Sanhedrin, and so were included under the heading of those who were called **their rulers.** The fact that these two were favorable to Jesus, as distinct from the rest of their colleagues, was irrelevant to Paul's discourse which attributed to the Jews generally the series of events in the trial and death of Jesus.

13:30 sqq. Paul returns to his fundamental theme, the Resurrection of Christ, and the testimony thereto given by the Apostles who were his companions; see note on 1:3 and 21–22; 2:24; 3:15; 4:10.

13:33. "[making known to you] that God has fulfilled it for their children, for us in raising up Jesus even as it is written in the second psalm: 'Thou art my Son, this day have I begotten thee' (Ps. 2:7).

13:34. "And to show that he has raised him up from the dead, never again to return to decay, he has said thus: 'I will give you the holy and sure promises of David' (Isa. 55:3).

13:35. "Because he says also in another psalm: 'Thou wilt not let thy Holy One undergo decay' (Ps. 16 [15]:10).

13:36. "For David, after having served in his own generation the counsel of God, fell asleep and was laid among his fathers and did undergo decay.

13:37. "But he whom God raised to life did not undergo decay.

13:33. There are various readings for this verse. Authoritative codices read **to our children, raising up,** etc. (cf. the Vulgate) but the greater number have the reading given here. The promise was made to the **fathers,** and its fulfillment has taken place in the generation contemporaneous with Jesus and Paul, which is represented by **their (fathers') children.** — **Second psalm:** some documents have **first psalm,** but it must be the correction of some copyist who knew that in rabbinical usage, the first two psalms were often reckoned as one, the first of the Psalter. The passage cited does not explicitly affirm the Resurrection of Christ, but only his nature as Son of God. Nevertheless, according to Paul, there is an indissoluble link between the two concepts. For him, Jesus **was foreordained Son of God by an act of power in keeping with the holiness of his spirit, by resurrection from the dead** (Rom. 1:4).

13:34. To return to decay: the word **return** could lead one to suppose a preceding state of **decay** or corruption of the body, from which Christ's body would have been freed by the Resurrection. But here also, as in 2:27, **decay** stands in general for *sepulcher, death.* And yet it is in keeping with that other phrase of Paul: **Christ having risen from the dead, dies now no more, death shall no longer have dominion over him** (Rom. 6:9). See also **did not undergo decay** in verse 37. The quotation from *Isaias* is a free rendering which also differs from the Greek of the Septuagint. Moreover, it has no direct probative force here, but serves to introduce and to serve as a frame, so to speak, for the real proof, which is given in the next verse.

13:35. This is the passage quoted more at length in 2:25-28; see there.

13:36-37. This is the reasoning already given by Peter in 2:29-31. David died and *underwent decay* in the sense of corruption of the body

13:38. "Be it known therefore to you, brethren, that through him forgiveness of sins is proclaimed to you,

13:39. "and in him everyone who believes is justified from all those things of which you could not be justified by the law of Moses.

13:40. "Beware therefore that what is said in the prophets may not prove true of you:

13:41. "Behold you despisers, then wonder and perish, because I work a work in your days, a work which you will not believe if anyone relates it to you" (Hab. 1:5).

(see note on v. 34). Therefore the psalm cited in verse 35 cannot be speaking of him. It must then be speaking of another, namely of him who was born of the **offspring of David according to the flesh** (Rom. 1:3) and who was prefigured in David: namely, the **Saviour Jesus** (v. 23). He died, but God raised him up to life, so that he . . . did not undergo decay.

13:38-39. With the repeated address, **brethren,** Paul begins the third part of his discourse in which he sums up his argument (see note on v. 16). — **From all those things of which,** πάντων ὧν: a wide and general term, but conceptually it refers to **sins,** or the totality of human faults, however many they may be. The Jews could not **be justified by** (or, **by force of**) **the law of Moses,** neither entirely nor in part. Nevertheless, Paul here only touches upon the question in general, so as to soften the blow that this teaching would have on his Jewish hearers. But in his epistles he will present it in greater detail, pointing out that the law of Moses does not bring justification, but that faith in Christ Jesus does **(in him everyone who believes, etc.):** cf. Gal. 3:11; Rom. 3:21 sqq.; 4:11 sqq.

13:40-41. The quotation from *Habacuc* is from the Greek of the Septuagint, and differs a little from the original Hebrew. The prophet (seventh to sixth centuries, B.C.) warned his Jewish hearers that, to punish them for their stubbornness, God would send a calamity upon them so great, that **you will not believe if anyone relates it to you,** namely, the terrible Chaldean invasion which would destroy everything in Judea. To what is Paul here referring in his own time when he uses this ancient prophet's threat? By comparing the analogous passages of 1 Thess. 2:16; Rom. 11:7, we can suspect that he has in view God's chastisement of Israel en masse, one which will be accompanied by material catastrophes comparable with those wrought by the Chaldeans. It is possible that when Paul delivered this warning he had in mind the eschatological discourse of Jesus (Mt. 24:4 sqq. and parallel passages), which kept the first generations of Christians in suspense (cf. also 1 Thess. 4:15 sqq.).

13:42. Now as they were going out, they asked that they would speak these words to them on the following Sabbath.

13:43. And after the synagogue had broken up, many of the Jews and the "worshipping" proselytes followed Paul and Barnabas, who speaking to them, persuaded them to continue in the grace of God.

13:44. And the next Sabbath, almost the whole city gathered to hear the word of God.

13:42-43. We have here two successive episodes. The first is when the synagogal worship was over, and the people began to leave. This seems the way to interpret the words, **now as they were going out,** namely, those present at the meeting who surely are those who **asked, etc.** Strictly, however, **they** could refer to Paul and Barnabas. The second incident is when the meeting had broken up and the people had gone outside, **many . . . followed Paul and Barnabas, etc.** As the worshipers are leaving the synagogue, the two missionaries are asked by many of the crowd to deal on the following Sabbath with the same argument, since it had interested them. Immediately after this, Paul and Barnabas are followed by **many of the Jews and the "worshipping" proselytes, etc.** Paul has already mentioned the two groups in his audience (cf. note on v. 16). The terms **worshipping** (σεβόμενοι) and **proselytes** have already been discussed (see notes on 2:5-6 and 10; 6:5), but this is the only instance of their use together. It is probable that the **worshipping proselytes** spoken of here are equivalent to the **God-fearing** of verses 16 and 26, and therefore, as usual, designate those pagans who sympathized with Judaism but were not circumcised, e.g., Cornelius (cf. note on 10:2), since only the circumcised adherents were true **proselytes.** If this be so, the more general meaning of sympathizer should be given to the term **proselytes.** Some, on the contrary, maintain that **proselytes** here has the technical sense, and they attribute a general sense to **worshippers.** It could be suspected that **proselytes** is a gloss incorrectly added to **worshippers,** but there is no proof of this in the codices. The Western Recension puts these words at the end of this verse: **and it happened that the word of God penetrated the whole city.** This is a simple observation which aims at preparing for the scene which follows.

13:44. **Almost the whole city gathered, etc.:** the news of the extraordinary happenings in the synagogue of the Jews, spread through the entire city, so that this time the pagans as well came in great numbers. Perhaps they had heard of Paul's remarkable conversion so that even they were curious to know what ideas he had. The reading **the word of God** (or **of the Lord**) is given by the great uncials and generally by documents which reflect the Western Recension. But codex D reads **. . . to hear Paul,**

13:45. But on seeing the crowds, the Jews were filled with jealousy and contradicted what was said by Paul, and blasphemed.

13:46. Then Paul and Barnabas spoke out plainly: "It was necessary that the word of God should be spoken to you first, but since you reject it and judge yourselves unworthy of eternal life, behold we now turn to the Gentiles.

13:47. "For so the Lord has commanded us, 'I have set thee for a light to the Gentiles, to be a means of salvation to the very ends of the earth'" (Isa. 49:6).

---

and adds **who gave a long discourse on the Lord.** The reading, **the word of God,** corresponds to the narrator Luke's viewpoint, which aims always at showing the spread of the Gospel, but the words **to hear Paul** are more appropriate psychologically, since they fit in more with the crowd's objective which was to hear this exceptional speaker and his new ideas, whereas they knew little or nothing as yet about **the word of God.** The addition, **who gave a long discourse** . . . does not tell us anything unusual, but it does prepare for the next verse, where we find that the Jews **contradicted what was said by Paul** on the following Sabbath.

13:45. The reason for the Jews being **filled with jealousy** is explained by the doctrine taught by Paul; see note on verses 38–39. If the law of Moses did not afford justification, and if by means of faith in Christ Jesus, a Greek, a Barbarian, or a Scythian was equal to a Jew, all those racial-religious prerogatives of which the Jews were so proud automatically collapsed (see note on 10:17, 34). From this followed the **jealousy** of the Jews toward the **crowds** of pagans who had come to hear Paul preach, and to whom he now opened the gates of salvation.— They **contradicted what was said** . . . : it is easy to reconstruct the scene. First of all there would be a heated discussion during which Paul sought to demonstrate that Jesus was the Messias foretold by the Hebrew Scriptures, and that with his death he had brought redemption to all mankind, and had abrogated the Law of Moses. While Paul was explaining all this, the Jews rejected his testimony, distorted the meaning of the biblical quotations, and did all this **blaspheming.** The Greek verb so expresses the action in the sense of "proffering insults" or "blasphemies." To whom were these outrages directed? To the heretic Paul undoubtedly, but by implication to Jesus also, the subject of the heresy, whom Paul later called **the stumbling block to the Jews** (1 Cor. 1:23).

13:46–47. At a certain point the blasphemous clamor of the Jews must have been so great that it prevented Paul from continuing his discourse.

13:48. On hearing [this], the Gentiles were delighted and glorified the word of the Lord, and as many as were destined to eternal life believed.

13:49. And the word of the Lord spread throughout the whole country.

After exchanging a few words with Barnabas, he waited until the din had subsided enough for him to make himself heard, and then proclaimed in both their names, the words given here. — **To you first:** this order of precedence, according to which the Jews had the Gospel preached to them before the **Gentiles,** was always respected by Paul, who therefore addressed himself to the Jews first. This practice was based on the words and example of Jesus (Mt. 10:6; 15:24): cf. Acts 3:26; Rom. 1:16; 2:10 (**to the Jew first, and also to the Greek**); see also note on 13:3. — **You . . . judge yourselves unworthy:** in actual fact, the Jews judged themselves not only most worthy, but the only ones worthy of that messianic kingdom and the eternal life which went with it. But for Paul, the Apostle of the Messias Jesus, rejection of the Messias was tantamount to rendering oneself unworthy of his kingdom. — The passage quoted freely from *Isaias* according to the Greek of the Septuagint is addressed by God to the Servant of Jahveh (Messias), who is to become a **light to the Gentiles** and their **salvation to the very ends of the earth.** Therefore the preachers of the Gospel who shed this light are co-operators with the Messias, so that by implication those words are addressed to them also (**has commanded us**).

13:48. The meeting of the synagogue was composed of Jews and **Gentiles** (see note on v. 44). The Jews remained hostile (v. 45); the **Gentiles** generally accepted their instructions gladly, and consequently from among them **as many as were destined** ($\mathring{\eta}\sigma\alpha\nu$ $\tau\epsilon\tau\alpha\gamma\mu\acute{\epsilon}\nu o\iota$) **to eternal life believed.** This eternal life was obtained precisely by belief in the Gospel which was preached to them. The narrator puts the position very simply by describing a particular state of mind. But the Jews and some Gentiles had not that state of mind, and therefore they did not **believe.** Other Gentiles, however, were found who showed the dispositions appropriate to those who are **destined to eternal life.** The remote and hidden causes which produced these favorable dispositions are not gone into here, but clearly, the free acceptance of the preaching of the two Apostles was the proximate and obvious cause.

13:49. A very brief description which must nevertheless imply a lot of work done. Naturally after the last meeting, Paul and Barnabas did not set foot again in the synagogue, but to make up for it, they intensified their work of evangelization among the Gentiles, holding meetings in

13:50. But the Jews incited the worshipping women of rank and the chief men of the city, and stirred up a persecution against Paul and Barnabas and drove them from their district.

13:51. But they, shaking off the dust of their feet against them, went to Iconium.

---

public or in private, as opportunity offered. Seeing that Pisidian Antioch was a busy center, both for Pisidia and in part for Phrygia, peasants, tradesmen, officials, and the like, all came there for their daily business and they would be able to take part in Paul's meetings. In turn, they would carry the teaching they had learned into their own districts, so that in this way, it **spread throughout the whole country.** This must have occupied several months, during which the Apostles would have remained in Pisidian Antioch, until the happenings occurred which are narrated in the next verse.

13:50. At Damascus, the Jews had rid themselves of Paul by having recourse to the political authorities (see note on 9:25) and here at Pisidian Antioch they do the same. They exerted pressure on the **chief men of the city** by means of the more prominent among the "worshipping" women (for this term, see note on v. 43). These pagan women affiliated to Judaism were always numerous in the city, especially when we remember that at Damascus the wives of the pagans *were all, except for a few, won over to the Jewish religion* (Flavius Josephus, *Wars of the Jews,* II, 560). In fact, in certain regions, affiliation to Judaism had become quite fashionable among the women, and even if they wished to enter the class of the true "proselytes," they were not faced with the great obstacle of circumcision. The **worshipping women** must have influenced their husbands and the **chief men of the city,** inciting them to the **persecution.** Pretexts could easily be found for this, given the privileged position that the Jews enjoyed in the Roman empire. We are given no details of the persecution, but it may well have brought on Paul and his companion some of those tribulations which he recalls later (2 Cor. 11:23–27). Maybe he received during it one of those ritual flagellations of forty stripes save one, which were inflicted in the synagogues, and of which he was the victim at least five times in his life. Perhaps during this time he was flogged by the Roman authorities, for we know that this happened to him on three occasions. Even toward the end of his life Paul will vividly recall the persecutions and afflictions suffered in Antioch and other cities during this journey (2 Tim. 3:11). The persecution ended with an uprising of hired vagabonds who **drove them from their district.**

13:51. Shaking off the dust of their feet . . . This symbolic act was pre-

13:52. And the disciples were filled with joy and with the Holy Spirit.

14 :1. Now it came to pass at Iconium that they went in the same way into the synagogue of the Jews, and so spoke that a great multitude of Jews and of Greeks believed.

14:2. But the disbelieving Jews stirred up and poisoned the minds of the Gentiles against the Brethren.

---

scribed by Jesus (Mt. 10:14) against a stubborn people. Here it signified that the fault for what had happened was due to the obstinate Jews of that city. However, the intense work of the two missionaries left its mark on the place, as is noted both in the verse which follows, and in 14:21-22, where we read that they returned to this city to tend to the seeds previously sown. — For **Iconium**, see note on 14:1.

13:52. The disciples, i.e., those who became Christians there. — **Filled with joy and with the Holy Spirit:** the first is caused by the second, but the persecution they suffered was also a reason for their joy, for persecution and joy in its acceptance as a rule went together, as we have already seen in 5:41; 9:16. The presence of the **Holy Spirit** must also have been manifested by means of the charisms which were always plentiful in these early communities.

14:1 sqq. Iconium: today Konia, was an important city assigned by ancient writers either to Phrygia (Xenophon, Pliny) or Lycaonia (Cicero, Strabo). For administrative purposes, Iconium was associated with Lycaonia, but from the ethnical viewpoint, it was considered a Phrygian city, as Luke seems to regard it in verse 6. It was a little over 80 miles southeast from Pisidian Antioch (for other details, see G. Ricciotti, *Paul the Apostle,* pp. 23 and 264). — This verse about Iconium has a certain literary awkwardness that makes one think it has been touched up. The various documents of the Western Recension take occasion to put in additions and variants to render the text more readable, but they lack critical authority. The transition from verse 2, where imminent hostility is displayed, to verse 3, where it speaks of a fruitful missionary effort which lasted for some time and presumably, without too much opposition, is very strange, more so since verse 3 would link up well with verse 1, just as verse 4 would with verse 2. Could there have been an inversion of verses 2 and 3 in the early days? We can arrive at nothing definite from the documents at our disposal. — **In the same way,** κατὰ τὸ αὐτό, i.e., "as usual"; cf. 17:2; the Vulgate has *simul* (together). Regarding this custom of Paul, see note

14:3. They stayed a long time, therefore, speaking out boldly in the Lord, who gave testimony to the word of his grace, by permitting signs and wonders to be done by their hands.

14:4. But the people of the city were divided, some siding with the Jews and some with the apostles.

14:5. But when there was a movement on the part of the Gentiles and of the Jews with their rulers to insult and stone them,

14:6. Paul and Barnabas hearing of it, escaped to the Lycaonian cities of Lystra and Derbe and the whole country round about.

14:7. And there they went on preaching the Gospel.

---

on 13:46–47.— **Greeks:** perhaps only in the ethnographical sense as opposed to **Jews,** without distinguishing whether they were "worshipping" or "proselytes" of Judaism (cf. note on 11:20; 13:42–43).

14:3. A long time: this can mean several months; see note on 9:23.

14:4. Apostles: here, and again in verse 14, this is not the title of the Twelve, but signifies those endowed with the charism of "apostolate": cf. 1 Cor. 12:28; Rom. 16:7; (1 Cor. 9:5).

14:5–6. Movement: in the Greek is ὁρμή, which ordinarily means "onset," "assault," and the like, but from what follows, we see that there was no direct attack on Paul and Barnabas, but only preparation for one. The two missionaries, warned by some Christian, forestalled the rising by leaving the city. According to a marginal note in the Heraklean Version (Western Recension) the threatened stoning took place. Besides distinguishing two different persecutions, the note concludes by saying that the two Apostles were stoned and cast out of the city. This is not only a fantastic statement, but it is in direct opposition to what Paul himself says (2 Cor. 11:25) about being stoned only once, that it was at Lystra (v. 19). In the present narrative, the *Acts* does not mention Thecla, whom various fairly ancient documents present as a distinguished follower of Paul at Iconium. Several modern scholars have thought that important historical elements are to be found in these documents (*Acts of Paul and Thecla, etc.;* see G. Ricciotti, *Paul the Apostle,* pp. 89, note; 152; 265, note).— **Lystra** was situated about 25 miles south of Iconium, and **Derbe** 30 miles southeast of Lystra. They were two small towns of Lycaonia (cf. note on v. 1). The **whole country round** spoken of here was a desolate steppe, infested with brigands, who had given Cicero so much trouble when he was proconsul in Cilicia (cf. *Paul the Apostle,* pp. 24 and 265).

14:8. And in Lystra a certain man used to sit, whose feet were crippled. He had been lame from his birth and had never been able to walk.

14:9. This man listened to Paul as he spoke when Paul gazing at him and seeing that he had faith to be saved,

14:10. said with a loud voice: "Stand upright on thy feet." And he sprang up and began to walk.

14:8-10. At Lystra, Paul does not begin his missionary activity by addressing the Jews and going into their synagogue, as he was wont to do (see note on v. 1). The reason is that although there were Jews there (cf. 16:1-3), there were not many of them and perhaps there was no synagogue. The poverty of the surrounding district and the absence of industries in small cities did not attract traders. Because of this absence of Jews, Paul directed his activity right from the beginning to the natives of the place, the Lycaonians, simple and unlettered polytheists, by preaching in the open (v. 9), and in the public places frequented by the crowds (vv. 11 and 13). — The account of the curing of the cripple of Lystra shows various likenesses, even in the choice of phrases, to the account of the cure of the lame man of Jerusalem by Peter (3:2-10). It does not follow that it is a literary invention composed on the lines of the previous account, for, prescinding from other considerations, there are several details of this episode which have no counterpart in the other, such as the lively and realistic particulars of verses 11-14. Instead, the similarities are clearly explained by the known predilection of Luke for literary diptychs portraying similar events (see *Introduction, IV*). Here also, as in the case of the lame beggar of Jerusalem, the hand of the medical writer is detected, e.g., **crippled,** ἀδύνατος, used here, is a Greek medical expression. But what is more striking is the detailed description of the symptoms, which by frequent repetition, show the condition of the patient: **feet were crippled . . . used to sit . . . lame from his birth . . . had never been able to walk.** A nonmedical writer, being less interested, would have passed over a number of these particulars. Some of the documents of the Western Recension add, here and there, small details which, in the ordinary way, do not say anything new, but which, sometimes as here, tend to stress the similarity to the account of the lame man at Jerusalem. — **To be saved:** σωθῆναι: it does not say "to be cured," but speaks of a "saving" in general, which may or may not include a physical cure. In his discourse, Paul would have spoken above all of spiritual salvation worked by Christ, although he may have spoken of him as a wonder-worker. On the other hand, it does not seem that the Apostle had worked any other miracles

14:11. Then the crowds, seeing what Paul had done, lifted up their voice saying in the Lycaonian language: "The gods have come down to us in the likeness of men."

14:12. And they called Barnabas Jupiter and Paul Mercury, because he was the chief speaker.

---

here at Lystra, and therefore he himself could not have become known as a wonder-worker. What, then, did the lame man hope for? Paul's words must have kindled in his heart, as his face showed, the great hope of participating in the "salvation" worked by Christ, which independently of physical healing surely brought happiness; and who needed happiness more than this unhappy cripple? Paul, **gazing at him,** saw reflected in his eyes the sentiments of his heart, and found that **he had faith,** in other words, he showed that he had in himself that condition which Christ had almost always demanded for a miracle (Lk. 8:48, 50; Mt. 9:28–29; Mk. 9:23; 11:22–23; etc.). Having found the condition, Paul worked the cure.

14:11–12. Paul had spoken in Greek which had come into the country with Greek culture and had become an international language, though the local people usually spoke Lycaonian, some fragmentary inscriptions of which are still extant. It is to be expected that the people here should use their own native Lycaonian language to express their surprise. But Paul and Barnabas did not understand it and at first they did not grasp the fact that they had been mistaken for **gods . . . in the likeness of men.** The two gods were immediately identified as *Zeus* or **Jupiter** in the person of Barnabas, while Paul was *Hermes* or **Mercury.** This identification with the two gods was not prompted by physical appearances, for Barnabas was robust and elderly, and Paul slimmer and younger. It was because Mercury was the god of eloquence and the messenger of the gods, and therefore rightly represented by Paul who was the **chief speaker** of the two, since only he had spoken. Barnabas, on the other hand, who had kept a majestic silence, naturally called to mind the Olympic father of the gods. The Greek names of the two divinities had been brought into Lycaonia by Hellenism which, as usual, had transformed the local divinities, probably nature gods, fusing them with the Greek deities and giving them Greek names. The Lycaonians also knew the legend—of Phrygian origin—related by Ovid (*Metamorph.,* VIII, 620 sqq.), in which Jupiter and Mercury are said to have wandered on earth and to have received hospitality from the aged couple Baucis and Philemon, who were rewarded with immortality. The memory of this legend would have made the identification of the two unknown strangers easy. Up to this point, all

14:13. And the priest of Jupiter which stood at the entrance to the city, having brought oxen and garlands to the gateways, would have offered sacrifice along with the people.

14:14. But on hearing [of this], the apostles Barnabas and Paul, tearing their garments, rushed into the crowd crying out:

---

went smoothly, since the Apostles did not understand the language. The people assumed that the two gods, by their silence, were glad to have been recognized and acclaimed. But the scene changed when the acclaim was followed by action.

14:13. This verse is obscure. Instead of **the priest**, the Western Recension has **the priests,** which would seem more in accordance with the evidence of inscriptions found in Asia Minor, and particularly in the region of Lystra, which show that there were temples served by colleges of priests. — Of Jupiter . . . stood at the entrance to the city, τοῦ Διὸς τοῦ ὄντος πρὸ τῆς πόλεως: this may have a locative meaning thus: *of Jupiter (whose temple) stood at the entrance to the city,* or a figurative meaning, viz., *of Jupiter who protects the city.* But codex *Beza* (Western Recension) reads τοῦ ὄντος Διὸς πρὸ πόλεως, which would seem to suggest an appellative understood either in the material sense ("Jupiter standing before the city") or in the figurative sense ("Jupiter protecting the city"). The locative and material meaning, which, in any case, can be linked up with the figurative sense, seems the more likely. — Nor is the word **gateways,** πυλῶνας, clear. Are they the entrance gates of the temple, or of the city, or even of the house where Paul and Barnabas were lodging? The word **entrance,** "porch," has already been seen in 10:17 (see there) and in 12:13–14, but always in the singular. Here, however, it is in the plural **gateways.** Possibly the reference is to the gateways of the temple where an altar would be permanently or temporarily erected in the porch. Nevertheless, verse 14 contains indications which would seem to suggest that the house where the Apostles lodged is meant.

14:14. When they realize what is contemplated, the Apostles cease their passive acquiescence. But how did they know about it? The expression, **on hearing [of this],** ἀκούσαντες, seems to exclude any visual sign since the Greek verb does not mean this in any way; therefore they must have "heard" from someone about the preparations being made, without "seeing" them. The expression **rushed into,** or **sprang out,** ἐξεπήδησαν should be noted as implying that they were in a closed place from which they rushed "out." Did they rush out of the house where they were lodging or out of the city, before which the temple stood? It is difficult to say

14:15. and saying: "Men, why are you doing this? We also are mortals, human beings like you, bringing to you the good news that you should turn from these vain gods to the living God who made heaven and earth and the sea and all things in them.

---

see the preceding note. However, it should be known that some few codices of lesser authority read εἰσεπήδησαν, **they rushed inside.** — If Barnabas is named before Paul here, it is because of verse 12, where Barnabas is represented as Jupiter, and is put before Paul who is represented as Mercury. — **Tearing their garments:** the customary dramatic gesture of the Jews on an occasion of great misfortune: cf. Mt. 26:65. — The zeal with which the two missionaries **rushed** out to prevent an act of idolatry shows clearly the profound aversion they had for the worship of false gods in any form, an aversion natural in those born and brought up in strict Jewish orthodoxy. This serves to show that there is no foundation for the opinion of some modern scholars who wish to maintain that much of Paul's theological thought depends on idolatrous mystery religions. This is so, even if we disregard chronological considerations which would suggest an inverse dependence.

14:15. This is a short résumé of the speech probably made by Paul, since he was the **chief speaker** (v. 12), aimed at preventing the people from offering the sacrifice. Directed as it was to a people used to nature worship and of little culture, the speech does not appeal to biblical arguments and facts, nor to complicated ideas like those which are used in the speech to the learned idolatrous Areopagites (17:22 sqq.). Here, the fundamental notion is that God, the author of nature, can be known through nature. Nonetheless, past generations have not known God, even though they have enjoyed the benefits which God has given them through nature. These ideas will be developed more fully by Paul in Rom. 1:18 sqq. — **Human beings like you:** this is the sense of the Greek, ὁμοιοπαθεῖς, meaning "those who undergo the same things," being exposed to the same vicissitudes of body and spirit. If the Apostles were gods, they would enjoy divine attributes such as ἀπάθεια, "impassibility." — **Bringing to you the good news:** the Greek has **evangelising you** with reference to the **good news** or "Gospel" of Christianity. — The Greek word **these** can be either masculine or neuter. In which case, it can mean first **vain (gods)** in opposition to the **living God,** or it could refer to *these vain things,* namely the things made ready for sacrifice. — **Who made heaven and earth, etc.:** cf. Ps. 146 (145):6. For the method of arguing from created things to a Creator, cf. Ps. 8:2–5; 19 (18):2–6; Wisd. 13:1 sqq.; and the passage cited in *Romans.*

14:16. "Who in past generations let all the nations follow their own ways.

14:17. "And yet he did not leave himself without testimony, bestowing benefits, giving rains from heaven and fruitful seasons, filling your hearts with food and gladness."

14:18. And even with these words they could hardly restrain the crowds from offering sacrifice to them.

14:19. But some Jews arrived from Antioch and Iconium, and after winning over the crowds, they stoned Paul and dragged him outside the city, thinking that he was dead.

14:16. Nations: pagans, as distinct from the people of Israel, who had the law of Moses to guide them.— Their own ways: ways which led them away from God.

14:17. Testimony of his existence and goodness.— Bestowing benefits means all that evidence which could be read by reason in the book of nature, even by such nature worshipers as the Lycaonians. The Jews, however, over and above this testimony of nature, had supernatural evidence contained in the law of Moses. Paul treats the comparison of the two kinds of testimony at some length in Rom. 2:9 sqq.— That their hearts should be filled with food as well as gladness is a figure of speech, but it is likely that the two ideas arise from the customary sacrificial banquet at which eating and merrymaking went together; cf. 1 Cor. 8:9 sqq.; 10:18 sqq.

14:19. There is obviously a gap in the succession of events, since some time must have elapsed between the attempted sacrifice and these new facts, but Luke is silent about it. The prohibition of the sacrifice must not only have lessened the regard in which the Lycaonians had held the two missionaries, but must also have given them grounds for suspicion. From the moment when the Apostles had declared that they were men like the rest, it was clear that they worked miracles through magic, like so many other preachers wandering around at that time. They must be left alone, therefore, but at the same time it was necessary to keep an eye on them, because one day they might use their mysterious powers to harm or trick the people. So, for an indefinite period, Paul and Barnabas continued their preaching in the city and roundabout, making disciples (who, incidentally, are not mentioned until v. 20), until their success was heard of in Antioch of Pisidia and Iconium, arousing the fury of the Jews there. These Jews came to Lystra, and after working secretly for some days to gain influential friends, just as they had done before at Pisidian Antioch

14:20. But the disciples gathering round him, he got up and re-entered the city. The next day he set out with Barnabas for Derbe.

(cf. 13:50), persuaded the crowd that the missionaries were common tricksters (certain Western Recension documents give additions in this sense). Then, after winning over the crowds, they gave the final blow. How they worked up the people to this radical change is not told, but the fact that Paul was stoned leads us to think that local Jewish authorities were responsible for this sentence, since it was a typically Jewish punishment passed on blasphemers (see note on 7:58).

Something like the following must have happened. The Jews from outside challenge Paul (Barnabas never appears in the whole incident) to a public debate, just as in the case of Stephen (cf. 6:9 sqq.) and for which the audience is hand-picked and comprised those who had been won over by the Jews. At a certain point, the audience begins to cry out against Paul, the Jews accusing him of blaspheming against Moses, and the Lycaonians charging him with having disturbed the peace of their city. Sentence of stoning is pronounced and immediately executed by the Jews in virtue of the prescription of Lev. 24:14–16. However, that prescription laid down that stoning should take place outside the city, as happened in the case of Stephen, but here it takes place inside the city. Moreover, it was done in the territory of a Roman colony and on a Roman citizen: two flagrant violations of the prevailing civil law. The Jews hope that the magistrates who had been won over by them will keep quiet on that point, and that the secrecy which accompanied the stoning will secure them from detection. So, when Paul faints under the blows of the stoning, they drag him out of the city, thinking he is dead. There, in the open, dogs and vultures will ensure the disappearance of the evidence in a short time.

14:20. At nightfall, the disciples go out to care for his body, and instead they find Paul alive, so much so that he is fit to get up and re-enter the city, and the next day he made the journey to Derbe with Barnabas. The events are presented in rapid succession by Luke the physician, who, however, does not speak of a miracle, though he does not exclude one. We have, in fact, a man subjected to stoning similar to that described in the note on 7:59–60 (see also note on 8:2). The expert executioners examine the body and, judging him to be dead, drag the corpse (ἔσυρον) along the ground and cast it from the city. There it remains for some hours alone; then a short time afterward, on being found by his disciples, this victim of stoning gets up, re-enters the city, and the following day makes a journey to Derbe, a distance of about 30 miles from Lystra. The subtle Luke does not speak of a miracle, but gives his readers the facts,

14:21. After preaching the gospel to that city and making many disciples, they returned to Lystra and Iconium and Antioch,

14:22. reassuring the disciples, and exhorting them to continue in the faith, and [reminding them] that "through many tribulations we must enter the kingdom of God."

---

so that they can judge for themselves. It is quite likely that, the night before his departure, Paul recovered in some house nearby, perhaps that of Timothy (see note on 16:1) where this disciple's grandmother and mother dressed his wounds. It is likewise possible that he went to Derbe on a beast lent by the anxious disciples, but all this would by no means render Paul fit to take up his missionary work immediately. How, this happened, therefore, Luke does not say. Nevertheless, Paul retains a lasting memory of this stoning at Lystra, since he not only mentions it specifically in the long list of his tribulations (2 Cor. 11:25; cf. 2 Tim. 3:11), but probably also alludes to it when he refers to **the marks of the Lord Jesus** on his body (Gal. 6:17). Just as captured fugitive slaves were branded with the mark of their owners, so Paul is branded as a slave of Christ by the scars of the blows received in this stoning. At Paul's departure, Barnabas, who had probably hidden himself during the commotion, now reappears. The immediate leave-taking is prompted by the desire to avoid exposing the Christians of Lystra to further persecution.

14:21. The narrative here is very summary, merely giving a list of the places visited by the two missionaries. They first stopped at Derbe, a small Lycaonian city (see G. Ricciotti, *Paul the Apostle,* p. 24), where they must have remained for some time, since they made **many disciples.** Then they retraced their steps, passing through the same towns as before, Lystra, Iconium, and Pisidian Antioch. Wishing to return to Antioch in Syria (v. 26), they could cross the Taurus mountains at the Cilician Gates and descend to Tarsus, Paul's birthplace. From there the journey to Antioch was much easier and more direct. But the two missionaries were anxious to see once more the communities they had founded for the reasons explained in the following verse, since they had undoubtedly received news from time to time about them, and were convinced that a visit would be useful. Moreover, to reappear in places whence they had been forced to flee because of persecution no longer presented the same dangers, since time had passed and most of the local magistrates had changed, so that with a little prudence any difficulties could be overcome.

14:22. Here we are told the general purpose of the return visits. — **Reassuring,** ἐπιστηρίζοντες: viz., "strengthening" or "confirming," in the sense of "placing securely upon," as of a column which has a solid base.

14:23. And when they had appointed presbyters for them in each church, with prayer and fasting, they commended them to the Lord in whom they had believed.

Because of the word **we** which is used, the quotation is held to be the actual words of the Apostles. The thought here expressed is one which is found again in Paul (see the quotations referred to in the note on 12:1).

14:23. After the general purpose of the return journey has been indicated in the preceding verse, we now have the special reasons for the visits, namely to establish a stable organization for the places which the Apostles had evangelized. After the departure of their founders, these groups of neophytes had been isolated except for occasional letters they may have received from Paul and Barnabas. Separated now from the local synagogues, the new converts gathered to pray in private houses, and found solace in the charisms with which they were generously endowed. But they were bereft of leaders to direct their communities. To remedy this situation, the two founders take the necessary steps to provide such leaders: **and when they had appointed presbyters for them, etc.** The verb, χειροτονήσαντες, etymologically signifies "to stretch out the hand" for the purpose of designating somebody to an office. Usually it means "to choose by a show of hands," which then becomes synonymous with "to elect" independently of any raising of hands (it is found applied to God in choosing a king, and to a monarch choosing a magistrate, etc., situations which obviously did not require a show of hands). Here the verb is in the active aorist tense and refers to the two Apostles, thereby making them the electors. Moreover the verb is followed by the dative of use, αὐτοῖς, which shows for whose benefit the action is performed, viz., **for them,** i.e., the **disciples** of verse 22, or the communities listed previously. The same verb is followed by the objective complement, **presbyters,** referring to those chosen by the two Apostles. In 11:30, **presbyters** dwelling at Jerusalem were spoken of (see also note on 15:2). In this particular case, following the custom of the mother Church, the presbyters are ordained for each community (**in each church**). The elections were not solely juridical, but were accompanied by religious rites: **with prayer and fasting, etc.** It should be noted that the same expression **with prayer** was used in 6:6, where the election of the seven deacons is spoken of, with the additional remark that the Apostles **laid their hands upon them** (for the different uses of this phrase, see note on 6:6). It is natural, therefore, to conclude that here too the rite of the imposition of hands was performed by the two Apostles (cf. 13:3), so much so, that later on Paul will remind his disciple Timothy who was from Lystra, that he performed this rite on him,

14:24. Passing through Pisidia, they came to Pamphylia

14:25. and after speaking the word in Perge, went down to Attalia.

14:26. From there they sailed down to Antioch, where they had first been entrusted to the grace of God for the work which they had now finished.

14:27. On their arrival they called the church together and reported all that God had done with them, and how he had opened to the Gentiles a door of faith.

14:28. And they stayed no little time with the disciples.

15:1. But some came down from Judea and began to teach the brethren saying: "Unless you be circumcised after the manner of Moses, you cannot be saved."

---

though he does not say when he did it (2 Tim. 1:6; cf. 1 Tim. 4:14; the case in 5:22 is doubtful). By this rite, those elected became the leaders of their respective communities, with authority to preside over the gatherings and to conduct divine worship.

14:25. Perge: this city was passed through on the outward journey but not evangelized (13:3). — **Attalia,** today called Adalia, a delightful little city with the only harbor in the region.

14:26. Antioch in Syria, from whence the missionaries had set out, 13:1-3.

14:27. Opened to the Gentiles a door of faith: a metaphor akin to that used by Paul who speaks three times of a door open for the evangelization of the Gentiles (1 Cor. 16:9; 2 Cor. 2:12; Col. 4:3). It is precisely before this door that the great battle, which is recounted in the following chapter, is staged.

14:28. No little or **not a little:** the usual figure of speech used by Luke for saying **much** or **a long time;** see note on 12:18. — So finishes the first missionary journey which began at the opening of the year A.D. 45 (see note on 13:4). By adding this stay of *some considerable time* at Antioch (probably several months) we arrive at the end of the year 49, or the beginning of 50. The Council of Jerusalem which follows is related in the next chapter. For the historical basis of this chronology, see G. Ricciotti, *Paul the Apostle,* pp. 124-125.

15:1. Hitherto, Luke has related the progress of the Gospel in pagan regions and the obstacles overcome there. But one very serious difficulty still remained in the region whence the Gospel had come, viz., Judea, and among the people to whom it had first been preached, viz., the Jewish nation. The Jews had a great attachment to the privileges of their nation, chosen as it was by God, an attachment which we already saw tested in the Apostle Peter (see note on 10:17, 34; 11:1 sqq.). Now, many Jews had accepted Christianity, recognizing in Jesus the Messias foretold in their Scriptures, and they were prepared to admit that the redemption worked by him was intended for all the peoples of the earth without distinction. All that was true. But it was also true that the promises made by God to the Hebrew patriarchs and to the Chosen People could not fail, and the institution established by God in the Old Testament could not be reduced to nothing. Had not Jesus himself declared that he had come to fulfill and not to abrogate the law of Moses? (Mt. 5:17.) Had he not directed his preaching to the Jews alone, specifically excluding non-Jews (Mt. 15:24 and 26)? Consequently, pagans could indeed become followers of the Messias Jesus, provided they were incorporated into the chosen nation of God by accepting circumcision and the other prescriptions of the Mosaic Law. For them to refuse to do so would be tantamount to a declaration that God's promises of old were of no avail and that the divine law was abrogated, all of which would be the equivalent of blasphemy. True, there had been the case of the centurion, Cornelius, who was received into the Church although he was an uncircumcised pagan; but his case was the exception and not the general rule, for Peter himself had had to justify his action before the general meeting (see note on 11:1–3). Undoubtedly, these were the sentiments of the majority of the Palestinian Jewish Christians, nevertheless, the most ardent exponents of such views were those Jewish priests who had been received into the faith (cf. 6:7), and the converted Pharisees referred to later (v. 5). The ideas of the Hellenistic Jews were very different (see note on 6:1), especially of those who came from paganism. For them, the account of the two missionaries just returned, telling **all that God had done with them, and how he had opened to the Gentiles a door of faith** (14:27), revealed a hopeful vision of the future in which innumerable peoples would be united with the nation of Israel, all becoming brothers solely by faith in the Messias Jesus. How could circumcision and the other Jewish prescriptions which the Jews themselves judged intolerable (v. 10) be imposed upon these pagans? That would be like closing the *door of faith* in the face of those who knocked, and in actual fact, Jewish propaganda in its efforts to attract pagans to Judaism had learned by experience that candidates for the highest class of the true "proselytes" (see note on 2:5–6) were extremely rare, because of the obstacle of circumcision. By all means let Jewish-born converts continue with some Jewish ritual observances, if they were so inclined (were these the **weak ones** of 1 Cor. 8:9; Rom. 14:1 sqq.?), but

15:2. And when no little objection was made against them by Paul and Barnabas, they decided that Paul and Barnabas and certain others of them should go up to the apostles and presbyters at Jerusalem [to consult them] about this question.

---

they must not presume to impose them on converted pagans who had never observed them. This solution, founded on a sound psychological basis, was being opposed by **some** who **came down from Judea,** which in practice meant Jerusalem (cf. v. 24), and who had presented themselves at Antioch, requiring Jewish circumcision as an essential prerequisite for participation in Christian salvation **(you cannot be saved).**

15:2. The Antiochenes reacted very strongly against these Jews of Judea. The term **no little** is Luke's figure of speech for *great* (see note on 12:18; 14:28). When no agreement was reached, the question was referred to the mother Church at **Jerusalem** where some delegates were sent expressly to consult **the apostles and presbyters.** These **presbyters** or **elders** have been mentioned already in 11:30 (see there, and note on 14:23), but by themselves. Here, however, they are named together with the **apostles,** as they will be in future (vv. 4, 6, 22, 23, etc.). It might be asked, what was the hierarchical position of these **presbyters,** especially in relation to the **apostles?** Certainly the significance of the term **presbyter** or **elder** differs here from its etymological meaning (πρεσβύτερος, "an older person," "senior"), just as do the terms *senator* and *senate* in the Roman empire. In both cases they were titles of an office or a dignity. Certain officials in the towns were called *elders* by the Greeks in Egypt and Asia Minor, and the title *priest elders* (πρεσβύτεροι ἱερεῖς) is found several times in papyri (A. Deissman, *Bibel-Studien,* p. 153 sqq.; *idem, Neue Bibel St.,* p. 60 sqq.). There was a group in the Sanhedrin at Jerusalem composed of **elders** (see note on 4:5-6), and we have seen how Paul and Barnabas, in imitation of the organization of the mother Church at Jerusalem, placed **elders,** who were chosen and appointed by them, in charge of the communities which they founded in Asia Minor. The **elders** or **presbyters** of the mother Church, probably on the pattern of the Sanhedrin, formed a college or senate which assisted the Apostles in the government of the community; cf. 21:18 sqq. The procedure of Paul and Barnabas when they inducted these **presbyters** in Asia Minor, demonstrates that the hierarchical authority of these **presbyters** of Jerusalem was conferred on them directly by the Apostles. This does not rule out the possibility that the presbyters were proposed by the community, as happened at the election of the seven deacons, where the theocratic-democratic method was followed; see note on 6:3, 6.

15:3. So they, sent on their way by the church, passed through Phoenicia and Samaria, relating the conversion of the Gentiles, and they caused great rejoicing among all the brethren.

15:4. On arriving at Jerusalem they were welcomed by the church

---

The leaders of the delegation sent from Antioch to Jerusalem were Paul and Barnabas, recently returned from their missionary journey and full of practical experience; but **certain others of them** also went, among whom was Titus (Gal. 2:3), who is, however, never mentioned in the *Acts*. Several manuscripts of the Vulgate read **some others of the other side,** which would refer to those who thought differently from Paul and Barnabas and went to Jerusalem to put forward their views. Theoretically it is quite possible that this was so, and perhaps these Judaizers were, in the event, the **false brethren brought in,** referred to by Paul in Gal. 2:4 (see the note presently on v. 6). But it could be a simple writer's error (*quidam alii ex aliis,* instead of *quidam alii ex illis*). The Western Recension, here and later, abounds in variants lacking any authority. Of the present verse it says: **. . . against them by Paul and Barnabas. In fact, Paul said that things should remain as they were according to the faith as it was received, insisting strongly (on this). But those who came from Jerusalem, insisted that Paul and Barnabas and some others should go up to the apostles and presbyters in Jerusalem, so that they might be judged by them about this question.** This reading would almost turn the envoys into defendants, summoned before the tribunal of the Apostles, and so falsifies the facts that one is led to suspect that it is from the pen of some remaining supporter of the Judaizing view.

15:3. As has already been stated (in 11:30), this is not the "journey of the alms" which took place in the year 44, but that other journey mentioned by Paul in Gal. 2:1 sqq. By referring to his conversion, this journey can be fixed as having taken place *fourteen years later,* i.e., in the year 50, as in Gal. 1:18 (cf. note on 14:28). There Paul speaks of having gone to Jerusalem **according to a revelation** (Gal. 2:2), but this does not conflict with Luke's statement that he was sent by the community of Antioch. Luke merely reports, as by way of routine, that the community appointed its representatives including Paul; Paul himself is recalling his own mystical experiences, which at decisive moments in his life affected him, and his being chosen to go up to Jerusalem was one of them (Acts 16:6, 7, 9; 18:9; 20:23; 22:17; etc.). The revelation to Paul preceded or followed very soon after the appointment by the community, thereby confirming it.

15:4. The delegates were received at Jerusalem with marked respect and the apostles and the presbyters, and they proclaimed all that God had done with them.

15:5. But some of the Pharisees' sect who had accepted the faith, got up and said: "They must be circumcised and also told to observe the law of Moses."

15:6. So the apostles and the presbyters met together to see about this matter.

---

by the general assembly of the faithful, **the church,** comprising the two leading groups of the **apostles** and the **presbyters** (for these last, see note on v. 2). Present among the Apostles were *James,* the "brother" of the Lord, *Cephas* (Peter), and *John* (the future evangelist). These were considered the **pillars** of the Church (Gal. 2:9). To this assembly, the delegates reported **all that God had done with them,** namely the excellent results of their labors in Asia Minor. Moreover, they spoke about the specific purpose of their visit, namely, the question of whether Jewish observances should be imposed on pagans who became Christians. From the cordial reception they received, it would seem that the opposition were in a minority, and that the greater part of the assembly shared the view of Paul and Barnabas.

15:5. The Western Recension deviates in this verse also by giving the following reading: **Those, then, who had commanded them to go up to the presbyters stood up, some from the Pharisees' sect who had accepted the faith, saying: "They must, etc."** Clearly this is an artificial combination of elements of verse 2 (according to the Western Recension) with others of verse 5 (according to the Eastern Recension). — No sooner is the subject of controversy raised, than the Jewish Christians belonging to **the Pharisees' sect** rise up and maintain their view that **they must be circumcised, etc.** As Pharisees of long standing, they were former colleagues of Paul.

15:6. The events of the preceding verse must have taken place at the general assembly which had been held to receive the delegates, but besides this first open public meeting, a secret session was held, about which Paul informs us, and which is here outlined by the words: **so the apostles and the presbyters met together, etc.** The two chief groups considered the matter in private without the ordinary faithful being present. They must have had more than one discussion on the matter as is seen from verses 4, 6, 7, 12, 22, to which may be added what Paul himself says: **I communicated to them** (the community in general at Jerusalem) **the gospel which I preach among the Gentiles, but separately** (I expounded it) (κατ' ἰδίαν) **to the men of authority** (Gal. 2:2), namely, the Apostles whom he names shortly afterward (see note on v. 4). Independently of the *Acts,*

15:7.   And after a long debate, Peter got up and said to them: "Brethren, you know that in the early days God made choice among you that through my mouth the Gentiles should hear the word of the gospel and believe.

---

therefore, Paul refers to the public and private consultations, which may well be the same as those mentioned here. But the matter was not yet concluded, since both sides held tenaciously to their views. Paul tells us how the upholders of the Jewish observances demanded that his companion Titus should be circumcised, but that he energetically refused (Gal. 2:3 sqq.). A hint of such a request can be seen in the words of these ex-Pharisees in verse 5, **they must be circumcised,** which may have been intended to apply to the particular case of Titus and as a general principle thereafter. The demand of these ex-Pharisees was supported by another group, which Paul refers to as being formed from **false brethren who were brought in secretly** (παρεισάκτους) **who slipped in** (παρεισῆλθον) **to spy, etc.** (Gal. 2:4). These phrases bring to mind the Judaizers who had infiltrated into the community at Antioch, and then presented themselves at the Council of Jerusalem, where they would strongly support the ex-Pharisees to attain their common purpose. On documentary grounds this hypothesis finds support in a reading of verse 2 given in the manuscripts of the Vulgate, viz., **some others of the other side.**

15:7. Is this meeting at which Peter speaks the same one as in the preceding verse? It would not seem to be, for, in fact, only **the apostles and presbyters** appear in the former, whereas in this latter which goes on for a long time, **the whole multitude** appears also (v. 12), and more explicitly **the whole church** (v. 22). There were then three meetings, first, the public one to receive the delegates (v. 4), then a second one which was private with the Apostles and presbyters (v. 6), and finally this one in public in which the decisions were taken (v. 7 sqq.). Luke's wish is to describe the general sequence of events rather than what happened at each meeting, and so he simply relates, without separating them, how the private session of the Apostles and the presbyters was followed by the final public meeting. From the literary point of view, the position is made clear if we understand a parenthesis at the beginning of this verse, which would then read as follows: **after a long debate** (*in another meeting of the whole church*), **Peter . . .** While **the whole church** is explicitly spoken of in verse 22, its presence is implicitly required by the **long debate** mentioned here, since it would be an exaggerated expression if applied to the Apostles and presbyters only.— Peter's discourse, given to us only in outline, is noteworthy for its balance and realism. The question proposed by the

15:8. "And God who knows the heart, bore them witness, by giving the Holy Spirit just as he did to us;

15:9. "and he made no distinction between us and them, cleansing their hearts by faith.

15:10. "Now therefore, why do you tempt God by putting on the neck of the disciples a yoke which neither our fathers nor we have been able to bear?

15:11. "But we believe that we are saved through the grace of the Lord Jesus Christ just as they are."

Judaizers had to be solved in conformity with the facts, and these were, first, that the evangelization of the Gentiles had already begun some time ago. Second, that earlier converts had received the Holy Spirit, just as the converted Jews. Third, that the law of Moses was an intolerable burden which the Jews themselves had not borne in its entirety. Against all this, he set the grace of the Messias Jesus, which alone could bring salvation to both pagans and Jews without distinction. — In the early days, i.e., relatively to the spread of the Gospel. Since here we are in A.D. 50, and Jesus had died in A.D. 30, this period of diffusion was about twenty years. Therefore the expression early days refers to a time not later than the first half of that score of years, i.e., from about A.D. 30 to 40. What is Peter referring to when he says that the Gentiles heard the Gospel through my mouth and believed? Interpreters commonly see an allusion to the conversion of the centurion Cornelius, which, in the present state of our knowledge, seems the most plausible opinion (see also note on v. 8), but there remains the difficulty of the early days. It is true that we know nothing precise about the date of Cornelius' conversion (see note on 8:26), but from little we do know, it would seem difficult to assign it to the early days mentioned above. At the earliest, it could be put only five or six years before this discourse of Peter. On the other hand, if we do not accept the reference to Cornelius, we do not know of any other episode between the years A.D. 30 and 40 in which Peter figures as an evangelizer of the Gentiles. It is one of those cases where the scarcity of information does not allow a sure conclusion. — Among you: some codices have among us.

15:8. Giving (various codices repeat the words to them) the Holy Spirit: this seems a clear allusion to the conversion of Cornelius; see note on 10:44. For the manifestations of the presence of the Holy Spirit, see notes on 2:4, 13.

15:10-11. The first of these two verses is negative regarding the Jewish

15:12. Then the whole multitude [quieted] down, and listened while Barnabas and Paul told what great signs and wonders God had done among the Gentiles through them.

15:13. After these had finished speaking, James made answer saying: "Brethren, listen to me.

---

law, the second is positive regarding the salvation brought by the Gospel. The word **but,** which joins the two sentences, shows the contrast. — **Neither our fathers . . . to bear,** the point Stephen had made (7:53) and Paul (Rom. 2:21 sqq.). — **We believe that we are saved,** not by the Jewish law, but by the **grace of the Lord Jesus Christ,** which is the **faith** spoken of in verse 9. A typical Pauline concept, though not exclusive to him, which must have come into Peter's mind on the occasion of the famous contest at Antioch (Gal. 2:14 sqq.; cf. also Rom. 3:21 sqq.).

15:12. **The whole multitude:** namely, the general assembly (cf. note on v. 7) quieted down by reason of having no more protests to bring forward. Peter, the head of the Twelve, having spoken, any argument to the contrary was out of place. But the two recently returned missionaries, **Barnabas and Paul,** did not keep silent (note how, as in 14:4, Barnabas is put before Paul, probably because Barnabas was better known at Jerusalem than Paul), and grasping the opportunity, they spoke of the fruits of their labors among the Gentiles, thus adding further weight to Peter's thesis.

15:13. **James** is known as the Less, "the brother of the Lord"; see note on 12:17. Because of his relationship to Jesus and his position as an Apostle, he enjoyed the highest authority in the Christian community at Jerusalem, and he was also held in great esteem by the pious Jews (Flavius Josephus speaks of him, *Antiquities of the Jews,* XX, 200–201; Hegesippus, in Eusebius, *Hist. eccl.,* II, 23, 10–18). A phrase of Paul (Gal. 2:12) seems to infer that a group of Judaizing Christians centered about James, and perhaps used his name in order to advance their own ideas. On this particular occasion, the one slight hope of the Judaizing party was James. If he spoke, he would perhaps save something of their position, which had just been demolished by Peter. And James did speak, as reported here, but this speech disappointed the secret hopes of the Judaizers. This has led some radical scholars to regard his discourse as of doubtful authenticity, but this is simply because they have built up a false idea of James's position, an idea which is utterly opposed to the historical evidence. James's view is in complete accord with that of Peter, namely that the pagan converts ought not to be troubled with the Jewish prescriptions. But as a zealous Jew, James is concerned about his fellow countrymen, and asks that the

15:14. "Simon has told you how God first visited the Gentiles to take from among them a people to bear his name.

15:15. "And with this the words of the Prophets agree, as it is written:

15:16. " '. . . after these things I will return
and I will rebuild the fallen tabernacle of David,
and the ruins thereof I will rebuild
and I will set it up once more,

15:17. " 'that the rest of mankind may seek after the Lord
and all the nations upon whom my name is invoked:
[thus] saith the Lord who doth these things'

(Amos 9:11-12).

---

converts from paganism should show a certain regard for the converts from Judaism, by abstaining from certain practices to which the pagans attached no importance, but which were repugnant to the Jews. — [Men,] brethren: see note on 1:11.

15:14. Simon: Peter. — **First,** i.e., *for the first time,* πρῶτον: this corresponds to the words, **in the early days,** of verse 7. — **Visited:** the Greek has (ἐπεσκέψατο) which means **visited,** but it is a Hebrew expression (*paqad*) used before (see note on 6:3), and here in particular it is used to express the benevolent character of him who investigates before making a choice in favor of another.

15:15. Prophets: see note on 7:42.

15:16-17. This quotation is from the Greek text of the Septuagint and is freely quoted in the first verse. The Septuagint differs notably from the Hebrew text which reads: **In that day I will raise up the tabernacle of David that is fallen, and I will close up the breaches of the walls thereof, and repair what was fallen, and I will rebuild it as in the days of old that they may possess the remnant of Edom and all nations, because my name is invoked upon them saith the Lord who doth these things.** The general idea of the Hebrew text (which seems to have been the one used by James, while Luke has used the Greek) is that God, in the days of the Messias, will restore to new glory the house of David — now in decadence — and will make it rule over Edom and all the pagan nations on whom the name of the true God Jahveh will be invoked. James quotes this text, which foretells the extension of the Messias' spiritual kingdom to the pagan Gentile nations, to support Peter's view. The renewal of the house of David from which the Messias came is thereby connected with the extension of his spiritual dominion over all nations.

15:18. "known from of old.

15:19. "Wherefore my judgment is not to disquiet those among the Gentiles who are turning to God;

15:20. "but to send them written instructions to abstain from anything that has been contaminated by idols, from immorality, from anything strangled and from blood.

15:18. These words are not in the Hebrew text nor the Septuagint. They are given, however, in the more important codices. Others read: **known from of old to God are his works.** Still others read (cf. Vulgate): **To the Lord was his own work known from the beginning of the world.** It seems to be a reflection inserted by James into the passage which he quoted.

15:19. Not to disquiet: by imposing the observance of the Jewish law. Hitherto James is in complete agreement with Peter, but in the following verse he goes further than Peter by requiring that a certain regard should be paid to the prejudices of his fellow countrymen; see note on verse 13 sqq.

15:20. There are four abstentions here required by James, and they deal with **anything that has been contaminated by idols,** i.e., eating meats sacrificed to idols (called **things sacrificed to idols** in verse 29); **immorality; anything strangled,** namely the flesh of animals which had not been previously bled; and **blood** taken as food. To eat the meat of animals sacrificed to idols was considered as participation in the idolatrous sacrifice itself (the question will be dealt with at length by Paul in 1 Cor. 8–10). The term **immorality** (πορνεία) means sexual intercourse between unmarried persons (cf. 1 Cor. 7:2). It does not seem to refer to marriage contracted within certain degrees of kinship forbidden by Jewish law, as some scholars have thought, among them J. Bonsirven (*Le divorce dans le Nouveau Testament,* Paris, 1948). The suggestion that instead of πορνεία (*fornication*) the word πορκεία, *pig* (*meat*), is meant, is not worthy of consideration since this expression is never used even in profane Greek writings. With regard to eating **anything strangled** and **blood,** it was forbidden because of the very ancient belief among the Semitic people, accepted also by the Mosaic law (Gen. 9:3–4; Lev. 17:10–14), that the blood was the seat of the soul, and, by eating it, one absorbed the soul of the animal with all its brutish qualities. The Jews attached such importance to the prohibitions against eating *the meat of animals sacrificed to idols,* the meat of animals butchered without having been previously bled (i.e., *strangled*), and *blood* that they were included in the seven precepts of the sons of Noah ("Noachic precepts"), which, according to rabbinical legislation, had to be observed

15:21. "For Moses from early generations hath in every city them that preach him in the synagogues, where he is read every Sabbath."

15:22. Then it seemed good to the apostles and to the presbyters together with the whole church — after having chosen [some] men from among them — to send them to Antioch together with Paul and Barnabas, [namely] Judas surnamed Barsabbas and Silas, leading men among the brethren.

15:23. They sent, by their hands, this message in writing: "The brethren who are apostles and presbyters send greetings to the brethren of Gentile origin in Antioch and Syria and Cilicia.

---

even by non-Israelites living in Israel territory (*Sanhedrin*, 56, 6). For the precise number of these prohibitions and the reason for their imposition, see notes on verses 28–29.

15:21. **For** introduces the consequential reason of the preceding verse. These abstentions must be imposed on the converts from paganism because the Mosaic law (**Moses**) which exacts them is read **in the synagogue** . . . **every Sabbath** (see note on 13:27) from **early generations in every city** (see note on 2:9–11) and its prescriptions are known, in great part, even by pagans (cf. 10:28). This being so, the violation of these prohibitions by the ex-pagan Christians would be a scandal to the Jewish Christians, who had a long-standing repugnance for such practices, and they would cause wonder even among the pagans, who knew well how far Christianity depended on Judaism.

15:22. **It seemed good,** ἔδοξε: from the verb δοκέω, from which *dogma,* "decree," is derived, a word which will be used in 16:4 referring to the facts related here.—**Apostles . . . presbyters . . . the whole church:** the whole public assembly; see note on verse 7.—**Judas surnamed Barsabbas:** see note on 1:23.—**Silas** will appear later as the companion of Paul on his second missionary journey (15:40; 16:19, etc.), and seems to be the same person who is called **Silvanus** in the letters of Paul (1 Thess. 1:1; 2 Thess. 1:1; 2 Cor. 1:19). He and Judas were **leading men,** both endowed with the charism of "prophet" (v. 32).

15:23. **By their hands, this message in writing:** thus the Greek reads, but the sense is **this message in writing** (viz., the following letter which was sent) *by them.*—**And presbyters who are brethren:** the more authoritative codices give this reading, while others have **and presbyters and brethren.** This latter is a false reading, probably influenced by verse 22 where, after **apostles and presbyters,** is added **the whole church.** Here it

15:24. "As we have heard that some of our number who went from [here] have disturbed you with their teaching unsettling your minds, to whom we gave no mandate,

15:25. "It hath seemed good to us, and we have come to one accord [therein] after having chosen out [some] men to send them to you with our beloved Barnabas and Paul,

15:26. "[who are] men who have pledged their lives for the name of our Lord Jesus Christ.

15:27. "We have sent Judas and Silas who themselves also by word of mouth will give you the same message.

15:28. "For it hath seemed good to the Holy Spirit and to us to lay no further burden upon you, other than these necessary things:

---

is a question of a doctrinal discussion for which the responsibility rests on the Apostles and the presbyters alone. — Antioch and Syria and Cilicia are the places concerned in the question now being discussed before the Council. The places evangelized by Paul and Barnabas on their recent missionary journey are not named, but Paul will let them know too of the apostolic decree: cf. 16:4.

15:24. Some of our number: these are those who **came down from Judea** of verse 1. — Some codices omit **who went from here:** whether or not this clause is maintained, it is certain that the Christians referred to came from Jerusalem and belonged to those groups which were associated with the Apostles. Shortly afterward, Paul refers to other Christians who presented themselves at Antioch as coming **from James** (Gal. 2:12). This is James of verse 13, and those who were his followers used his name to spread their Judaizing ideas. But the repudiation of any order having been given to these false representatives of the Apostles is clear: **to whom we gave no mandate.**

15:26. After the repudiation of the Judaizers comes praise for the anti-Judaizers: **Barnabas and Paul** (Barnabas is again put before Paul as in verse 12) are called **beloved** ἀγαπητοί: as Paul calls the physician Luke in Col. 4:14), and it is put on record that they **have pledged their lives** for the Gospel of Christ on their recent missionary journey. In doing all this, the Apostles and presbyters are in **one accord.** Such unanimity on the part of James and Cephas and John in this regard is confirmed by Paul both in the field of doctrine (Gal. 2:6), and the field of practical evangelization (*ibid.*, 2:9).

15:28. It hath seemed good: as in verse 22. — Not only to the **Holy**

15:29. "namely, that you abstain from things sacrificed to idols and from blood and from what is strangled and from immorality. Keep yourselves from these things and it shall be well with you. Farewell."

Spirit, but also **to us:** the former gave the **power** (1:8) according to Christ's promise; the latter brought their human experience and their Jewish character which had great influence on the present question. Neither God without men, nor men without God, but both agree and concur in the decision or "dogma" which results therefrom **(it . . . seemed good to the Holy Spirit and to us).** — These necessary things are those listed in the following verse, all of which, except the last, are not rendered necessary by the permanent prohibition of the Mosaic Law, but insofar as they are imposed by the new law of the Gospel, which is charity. The question is concerned with abstention from three kinds of things (*meats sacrificed to idols, blood, and things strangled*), which while indifferent in themselves, were abhorrent to the Jews, even when they became Christians. Thus out of Christian charity, the converts from paganism must respect the conscience of the convert Jews (cf. note on v. 21), especially when meals were taken together, whether at Jerusalem (2:46; 6:1) or at Antioch (Gal. 2:12). This charitable tolerance which did not in any way weaken the principle of the abolition of the Mosaic Law, was expressly defended later by Paul, who figures here among the stanchest supporters of that abolition. He says: **Now food does not commend us to God: for neither shall we suffer any loss if we do not eat, nor if we do eat, shall we have any advantage. Still, take care lest this right of yours become a stumbling block to the weak . . . and through thy knowledge the weak one will perish, the brother for whom Christ died. Now when you sin thus against the brethren and wound their weak conscience, you sin against Christ. Therefore if food scandalises my brother, I will eat flesh no more forever, lest I scandalise my brother** (1 Cor. 8:8–13; cf. Rom. 14:1–21).

15:29. The four prohibitions are the same as those in verse 20, though in a different order, with **immorality** placed last. They appear again in 21:25. There is a textual difficulty for all three quotations of this passage which is most complicated when the Eastern and Western Recensions and the other mixed secondary forms are compared with one another (see "Introduction," II). The Eastern text is the one we have given in all three quotations of this passage, and it is represented by the Greek uncial codices (except codex *Beza*), the majority of Greek minuscules, those of the Latin Vulgate, some of the *Vetus Latina,* besides ancient versions and Greek writers. The Western form gives only three prohibitions, omitting that of **things . . .**

strangled, but adds what is commonly called the "golden rule" of charity expressed by these words, **whatsoever you would not have done to yourselves, you should not do to others.** This is given by codex *Beza,* a Greek minuscule, and in quotations of Irenaeus and Cyprian. Then there are the mixed types, which partly reflect one or other of the two chief recensions (critical editions should be consulted for the documentary evidence for each of the three above-mentioned passages). For example, in Tertullian, Ephraem (?), Pacianus, Jerome, Augustine, Ambrosiaster, etc., we find three prohibitions listed, without mention of **things strangled** or the "golden rule." Again, the four prohibitions are given with the "golden rule" in some Greek minuscules, some Latin codices, in Coptic-Sahidic versions, and in the Ethiopian and Heraklean Syriac versions. The important Papyrus 45 (third century) follows the Eastern Recension in verse 20, but leaves out **immorality.** The mixed forms are hardly worthy of attention, since they are obviously derived from the two principal recensions. These two chief forms in their turn, are both supported by testimony from the second century (the Western, by means of quotations of Western writers), but the Eastern Recension has far more documents in its favor than the Western Recension. What is the reason for the differences between them, which turn mainly on the suppression of **things . . . strangled,** and the addition of the "golden rule"? Considering both the addition and the suppression in relation to the times at which they appear, it would seem that they are due to the desire to render the Apostolic decree adaptable to the existing state of things, serving as a little moral code or catechism for the new Christians. In fact, at first sight, the "golden rule" ought not to be there, since it is contained (in a much nobler, because positive form) in Mt. 7:12, and had not been raised at all in the discussion, whence there was no reason for citing it in the decree. As far as the question of **things strangled** went, the progressive abandonment of Jewish practices as Christianity spread in pagan regions rendered this part of the decree rather useless and outdated, even if it did not contrast with the large-mindedness of Paul on this point (cf. 1 Cor. 8:8; Rom. 14:17; Col. 2:16; 1 Tim. 4:3). Consequently, that prohibition (**things strangled**), which would be out of place in a Christian moral code, was suppressed. It is true that there still remained the two Jewish abstentions from **things sacrificed to idols** and **blood,** but these could be retained since they were sublimated and given a more spiritual sense. The abstention from **things sacrificed to idols** now stood for the rejection of everything connected with idolatry, and the abstention regarding **blood** was interpreted as a command not to shed human blood, namely the forbiddance of killing (Tertullian refers to it in this sense, *De Pudicitia,* 12). **Immorality,** in any case, was more strictly forbidden by the law of the Gospel than by the Mosaic Law. Thus the moral codex was complete, since it included duties toward God (the prohibition of idolatry), toward one's neighbor (the prohibition of killing), and toward oneself (the prohibition of immorality). But the whole would be fittingly bound together with the mention of the greatest precept of Christianity, that of charity represented by the "golden rule."

All of this clearly shows that the text of the Apostolic decree as given by the Western Recension is a modification of the Eastern Recension, and is of later origin.

It now remains to explain why the authors of the decree not only listed the three Jewish prohibitions on which the discussion had effectively turned, but had added the prohibition of **immorality** which had not been called into question, and, in any case, was already forbidden by the natural law. The word **immorality** or **fornication** appears in all three passages. Here and in 21:15 it comes last after the other three, while in James's discourse (v. 20), it is placed second. Its authenticity cannot be doubted, since the only document that has not got **immorality** is the above-mentioned Papyrus 45, which omits it in James's discourse (the only exception there), while the uniform transmission of all the codices of both Eastern and Western Recensions and the citations of early writers all support it. We have already said (v. 20) that **immorality** here has no other meaning than that usually associated with it, the meaning which the converts from paganism, to whom the prohibition was addressed, would have attached to it. This is precisely the reason why this fourth prohibition was added, viz., the prevailing mentality of the pagan world regarding this matter. Fornication was commonly accepted among pagans as something indifferent, nay even ordinary and therefore lawful, since it corresponded to natural instincts. Such a criterion was so widespread that it was regarded lightly on the grounds that it was the common practice (cf. Horace, *Satires,* I, 2, 31 sqq.; Terentius, *Adelph.,* 101; Seneca, *Controv.,* 2, 4 (12), 10; Quintilianus, *Instit. Orat.,* 8, 3, 48; etc.; besides the entire *Satyricon* of Petronius Arbiter), and men like Cicero undertook to defend it by appealing to ancient practice (pro M. Coelio, 20: . . . *When has this not been done? When has it been reproved? When has it not been permitted? In short, when has it happened, that a thing which is licit is not licit?*). Moreover, such an outlook was so deeply rooted among pagans that it constituted a real difficulty for those who embraced Christianity, even after their baptism (cf. 1 Cor. 5:1 sqq.; 6:9 sqq.). Even after four centuries of Christianity, it kept back from baptism a young catechumen, the son of a fervent Christian mother, as we know from the *Confessions* of St. Augustine. Besides, fornication had penetrated many pagan cults as an ordinary adjunct and thus received an almost religious legitimacy. Bearing this pagan background in mind then, it is easy to understand why the authors of the Apostolic decree considered it opportune to record, after

15:30. So they, upon being dismissed, came down to Antioch, and gathering the multitude together, they delivered the letter.

15:31. And they having read it, were delighted with the encouragement it gave them.

15:32. Moreover, Judas and Silas, being themselves prophets, exhorted the brethren with many words and strengthened them.

---

the three prohibitions which were discussed, the prohibition of **immorality** which had not been discussed, of whose intrinsic unlawfulness it was necessary to remind the ex-pagan converts.

This decree, then, decided the question of Jewish observances which it had been hoped to impose on the converts from paganism, declaring that they were exempt in principle, but obliging them to certain observances provisionally and for practical reasons. So great, however, was the authority of this decree that its provisions were respected for a very long time in the Church, even after the danger of scandal which raised it had disappeared. Not only in the year A.D. 177 did the martyrs of Lyons declare that as Christians they could not eat blood (in Eusebius, *Hist. eccl.*, V, I, 6), but even in succeeding centuries down to the Middle Ages, we encounter unexpected echoes of this early "abomination," due unquestionably to the decree as well as to well-nigh ineradicable customs. In conclusion, the decree had been, in substance, a victory for Paul who at that time proposed the complete separation of the Church from the Synagogue, as he later vigorously urged in his letters to the *Galatians* and elsewhere. Yet in his epistles, Paul never alludes to the decree, even when he is treating subjects connected with it, even though it was the memorial of his victory. Was this humility? Perhaps not. Does it imply a hidden disagreement with the first three prohibitions? It is possible, but it is more probable that it is the effect of Paul's strong desire to show that he is an **apostle (chosen) not from men nor by men, but by Jesus Christ and God the Father** (Gal. :1) and that **the gospel preached by him was not received by me from men, nor was I taught it, but I received it by a revelation of Jesus Christ** (*ibid.*, 1:12). To show this, he refers to the meeting he had in Jerusalem with the Apostles (pillars) who **laid no further burden** (οὐδὲν προσανέθεντο) on the Gospel preached by him (*ibid.*, 2:6). This phrase must mean the Jewish prescriptions with which he is dealing when writing to the Galatians.

15:31. The subject of this verse now changes to the Christians of Antioch. The **encouragement** is that gained from the letter which announces their freedom from Jewish observances.

15:32. Prophets, in the charismatic sense, in virtue of which they gave

15:33. After spending some time there, they were dismissed wit peace by the brethren to those who had sent them.

15:34.

15:35. But Paul and Barnabas stayed on in Antioch, teaching an preaching the word of the Lord, with many others.

15:36. Now some time after, Paul said to Barnabas, "Let us retur and visit the brethren in all the cities where we have preached th word of the Lord [to see] how they are doing."

---

the long discourse of **many words** (see note on 11:27). — **Strengthened** see note on 14:22.

15:34. This verse, where it is found, reads thus: **But it seemed goo to Silas to remain there: and Judas departed alone.** It is not found in th greater number of codices. The first part of it (as far as the words — **t remain there**) is given in codex C, codex *Beza,* and certain Eastern version The remainder of the verse is found in codex *Beza* and in a few othe documents. The Vulgate in the Sixto-Clementine edition (though not i the best codices) gives both parts. The critical authority supporting thi verse is almost completely lacking. Probably it is an addition made in th Western Recension to explain the presence of Silas in Antioch, as relate in verse 40. But Silas could very well have gone to Jerusalem and returne to Antioch when Paul called him back there. In fact, we find Mark als at Antioch (vv. 37 and 39) whom we left in Jerusalem (cf. 13:3). Perhap Mark followed Silas when the latter returned to Jerusalem from Antioch

15:36 sqq. **Some time after:** this can mean several weeks according t Luke's way of writing, but it certainly was a brief period (cf. 9:19) Nevertheless, in this short time, an important event took place, namel Paul's stand against Peter at Antioch, provoked by Jewish observance which Paul alone relates in Gal. 2:11 sqq. It is obvious that it happene during this interval, i.e., immediately after the Council of Jerusalem, bot because of the sequence of events narrated in *Galatians,* and from th presence of Paul and Barnabas at Antioch at that time, as *Galatians* an the *Acts* here show. Both these missionaries were preparing for a nev journey which they planned to undertake together, as the present vers shows, but which was to break up into two enterprises, one of Paul, th other of Barnabas, as verses 39–41 will relate. After this stay together a Antioch, we do not know if Paul and Barnabas ever met again, sinc Barnabas disappears from the *Acts,* and from the story of early Christianit Therefore it was undoubtedly upon this occasion that this incident betwee Peter and Paul occurred. There is no reason to doubt that Luke knev of it. He was from Antioch, and belonged to the community there who would remember this event for a long time, since it happened in their midst. Again, Luke remained for many years with Paul, who no doubt told him of it more than once. Notwithstanding all that, no reference is made in the *Acts* to the incident. This silence on the part of Luke must have been inspired by veneration for the leader of the Apostles, and from a sense of discipline in the Church, though Paul himself may well have suggested it.

Peter had done an unwise thing. Shortly after the Council of Jerusalem, he had gone to Antioch and there had partaken of a meal with convert pagans at which no one worried about the Jewish prescriptions regarding forbidden foods. This was fully in keeping with the decisions of the Council. But along came some Judaizing Christians from Jerusalem, who, when they saw what was happening, protested at the scandal. Peter, being alarmed at the clamor, withdrew, and thenceforth refrained from such meals. For this, Paul openly withstood Peter in the name of that charity which — as St. Augustine says — was *libera in Paulo ad arguendum, humilis in Petro ad obediendum.* Undoubtedly, Peter had committed an error, even if with the best intention (cf. *Paul the Apostle,* pp. 283-284), but as Tertullian says, *conversationis fuit, non praedicationis* (*De praescript.,* 23), an error of conduct, not of doctrine. Would it have been proper to divulge in a work like the *Acts* an error committed in good faith by Peter? Luke thought not. He wrote the *Acts* about fifteen years after the incident had taken place, and when the Judaizing Christians were diminishing in number or withdrawing from the Church altogether. Therefore the opposition between Peter and Paul meant little when he wrote. On the other hand, to retell it now would offer ammunition to the new enemies of the Church and its hierarchical constitution. It is true that, as a historian, Luke had his obligations, but an objective historian is not bound to give all the facts known to him if these do not fall within the general framework of his story. The framework of the *Acts* was the diffusion of the Church in general, and not the detailed chronicle of its diffusion, much less the various methods used to spread the Gospel, adopted by this or that Apostle. Thus the episode at Antioch was irrelevant to Luke's theme, and he could omit it without prejudice to his objectivity and truth as a historian. The Hebrew Scriptures themselves offer a far more striking example of such an omission. The books of Chronicles (*Paralipomenon*) omitted from the story of King David the adultery and the subsequent murder he committed, although both these crimes had already been narrated in the books of *Kings.* As the author of *Chronicles* passed over these two unsavory deeds out of respect for the great king of Israel, so Luke quietly omitted the weakness of Peter out of *respect for the high keys* (Dante, *Inferno,* 19, 101). It would be satisfying to

15:37. But Barnabas wanted to take [with them] John also, who was surnamed Mark;

15:38. but Paul deemed it not convenient to take [with them] him who had withdrawn from them in Pamphylia, and had not gone with them to their work.

15:39. And there arose a sharp contention, so that they separated from each other, and Barnabas taking Mark sailed for Cyprus.

15:40. But Paul choosing Silas set out, the brethren commending him to the grace of the Lord.

15:41. And he passed through Syria and Cilicia strengthening the churches.

---

imagine that this silence of Luke, over and above his own personal reflections, was suggested by an explicit recommendation of Paul.—In all the cities where we have preached, etc.: This refers to the first missionary journey made by Paul and Barnabas (13:4 sqq.).

15:37-38. John here is John Mark who had left them on their first missionary journey (13:13).

15:39. Sharp contention: this is, in the Greek, "paroxysm," a term frequently used in Greek medical writings to indicate a violent attack of fever. Luke the physician finds it the appropriate term to describe the state of mind (used again in 17:16) of these two, which was certainly a state of exasperation accompanied by lively disputes which, instead of composing their differences, ended in their parting company. This is a lifelike picture of human nature, corresponding to the character of Paul as shown in the letters to the *Corinthians* and *Galatians*. But the separation left no rancor. Later on, Paul remembers Barnabas with respect (Gal. 2:9; 1 Cor. 9:6), and abandons his mistrust of Mark which he shows here, and accepts him in his company (Col. 4:10; Philemon 24; 2 Tim. 4:11). Of Barnabas, we hear no more (see note on v. 36) after this voyage to his native Cyprus, undertaken for missionary motives.

15:40-41. For Silas, see note on verse 34.—In Syria and Cilicia, Paul himself tells of his having been there a few years after his conversion (Gal. 1:21), certainly for missionary purposes, and Christian communities in these regions are referred to in verse 23. It suffices to remember that the capital of Syria was Antioch, the great center of Christian propaganda among the pagans (13:1 sqq.), and the capital of Cilicia was Tarsus, Paul's native city, where he dwelt for some time after his conversion (cf. 9:30 with 11:25). It is not stated, however, that the churches mentioned in these

16:1. And he reached Derbe and Lystra. And behold a certain disciple was there named Timothy, son of a believing Jewess, but of a Greek father:

16:2. who was well thought of by the brethren in Lystra and Iconium.

16:3. This man Paul wished to go forth with him and he took and circumcised him on account of the Jews who were in those parts, for they all knew that his father was a Gentile.

---

places were founded by Paul. Luke here records them as being already in existence without saying how they began. This fact shows that the silence of the *Acts* on some matters does not in any way prejudice the reality of the facts themselves. — Strengthening: cf. note on 14:22.

16:1-3. We are now in the first months of the year A.D. 50, and the second missionary journey of Paul begins. As will appear from verses 6-10, he had no definite geographical plan for this journey. He aimed, in general, at pagan regions not yet evangelized. The excursion into Syria and Cilicia (15:41) must have served merely as a preparation for his next real missionary effort. Here, then, he visited the places already evangelized on the preceding journey (Derbe, Lystra, etc.) which he and Barnabas had decided to do before they separated (15:36). To reach Derbe, Paul, who departed from Cilicia with his companion, had to cross the range of the Taurus mountains at the Cilician Gates, which was a far more arduous climb than that of the Taurus in Pamphylia accomplished on the previous journey (13:13-14). Then they had to cross the endless plain of Lycaonia which involved great difficulty, since in springtime it was a great marsh. After about ten days of travel and danger, Paul and Silas arrived at Derbe. From there they went to Lystra where Paul had been stoned (14:19-20) and here **Timothy** appears on the scene for the first time. Called a **disciple**, Timothy had been a Christian from the time Paul had passed through Lystra on the first occasion. His father, who must have been dead by now, had been a **Greek** (Ἕλλην) which was equivalent to a pagan (cf. note on 11:20), and in fact the young man was uncircumcised. Brought up by his mother Eunice and his grandmother Lois, both fervent Jewesses, he reflected this pious and feminine upbringing. He was an affectionate, delicate, almost timid, and very devout youth (2 Tim. 1:4 sqq.), and of a weak constitution (1 Tim. 5:23). At this time he would have been hardly more than an adolescent, barely twenty, since fifteen years later, Paul says that he was still in his **youth** (1 Tim. 4:12; cf. 2 Tim. 2:22). During the

16:4. And as they passed through the cities they delivered to the brethren for their observance, the decrees enacted by the apostles and the presbyters at Jerusalem.

Apostle's absence between the first and second missionary journeys, Timothy had been active in keeping alive the faith in his own city and its environs, so that he **was well thought of by the brethren in Lystra and Iconium.** His good standing made Paul see in him a good co-worker, and on his departure he took him without hesitation. From then onward, Timothy was one of Paul's most assiduous companions. It should cause no surprise that Paul had Timothy circumcised, although he flatly refused to circumcise Titus (see note on 15:6). The cases were different. Previously, it had been a question of principle, as to whether it was a necessary rite to obtain salvation in Christ. Here, the rite was performed **on account of the Jews,** namely, to avoid the usual difficulties that would have been raised by the Jews to whom Paul always preached first (see note on 13:46). But this concession did not imply that it was a matter of obligation. The decree of the Apostolic Council had exempted from the rite those pagans who entered the Church, but it did not forbid it to the sons of Jews (Timothy's mother was Jewish) who willingly accepted it. Tolerance in some cases, by all means, but never obligation in all cases, for the general reason that **in Christ Jesus neither circumcision availeth anything nor uncircumcision** (Gal. 5:6). Paul, who later practices Jewish rites on himself (cf. 18:18; 21:26), induced Timothy to be circumcised, not for doctrinal necessity, but for practical reasons of charity, according to his principle of **becoming to the Jews a Jew that I might gain the Jews** (1 Cor. 9:20) to Christ. It is likely, though not certain, that Paul alludes to this case of Timothy when he says that **he yet preaches circumcision** (Gal. 5:11). He would be alluding to his preaching with deeds and not with words.

16:4. They delivered, παρεδίδοσαν: the same root from which comes the word, *tradition,* παράδοσις. Just as there was a Jewish tradition to which the Pharisees adhered, so a Christian tradition was in the process of being formed. This could transmit **the decrees** (the Greek has **dogmi;** see note on 15:22) of the rulers of the Church, as was the case here, or norms of faith or morals or liturgy. The term "tradition" was already used by Paul (2 Thess. 2:15; 3:6; 1 Cor. 11:2) and the collection of these norms constituted a **deposit** (1 Tim. 6:20) to be handed down (2 Tim. 2:2). In this case, Paul is one of those who guards and delivers the decrees (as in 1 Cor. 15:3), but the Western Recension seems to consider this office too modest, and therefore presumes to add to the text, by presenting the two missionaries as preaching on their own behalf. This is what it says: **Passing**

16:5. So the churches were strengthened in the faith and increased in numbers from day to day.

16:6. Now they passed through Phrygia and the Galatian country, having been forbidden by the Holy Spirit to speak the word in Asia;

16:7. And when they were come to Mysia they tried to get into Bithynia and the Spirit of Jesus did not permit them;

16:8. so passing by Mysia, they came down to Troas.

---

therefore through the cities, they preached (and delivered to those there) with all boldness, the Lord Jesus Christ, delivering also the precepts of the apostles, etc. The parenthesis is rightly omitted from the margin of the Heraklean Syriac version.

16:8. These three verses are one of those summary accounts which nevertheless cover the work and important activities of several months. Paul, having visited the communities founded by him on his previous journey (vv. 1-5), now proposed, with Silas and Timothy, to turn his steps to **Asia,** namely, those various districts included in the Roman province of Asia which had its capital at Ephesus. This was an area ripe for a spiritual harvest, but the three missionaries were **forbidden by the Holy Spirit** to go there. Just what the nature of this prohibition of the Holy Spirit, as well as that of the **Spirit of Jesus,** was we do not know. It could have been a charismatic communication of Silas who was a "prophet" (cf. 15:32), or of some other charismatic (cf. 11:27-28; 21:10-11) just as it might have been an incident which was interpreted as a providential warning. In view of this prohibition, the three missionaries, instead of turning westward, went north, and crossed **Phrygia and the Galatian country** (cf. inversely in 18:23), the one northeast of the other. The expression **Galatian country** indicates the zones where, already in the third century B.C., the immigrant Galatians had settled, and so it means Galatia proper, and not the Roman province of Galatia, which besides the **Galatian country** comprised other territories (Lycaonia, Pisidia, etc.). It should be noted that the missionaries were already in the Galatian province during the events narrated in verses 1-5 and therefore when entering into the **Galatian country,** they did not enter another province, but another region of the same province. The stay of the three missionaries in Galatia was prolonged for some months because Paul, overtaken by a sudden illness, had to stay among the Galatians until he recovered after which he evangelized them **for the first time** (Gal. 4:13-15). Luke merely mentions this first stay in Galatia and also the second (Acts 18:23), probably because he was anxious to present Paul's entrance into and activity in Europe (v. 11 sqq.). Having terminated their stay and mission among the Galatians,

16:9. And Paul had a vision one night; a Macedonian was standing, appealing to him and saying, "Come over into Macedonia and help us."

16:10. As soon as he had the vision, straightway we made efforts to set out for Macedonia, being sure that God had called us to preach the gospel to them.

---

the three set off westward again, with the idea of skirting Mysia and then going up into neighboring Bithynia. But at this point there was another mysterious communication, this time from the **Spirit of Jesus.** This new expression, which equals the previous one of the **Holy Spirit** has only one counterpart in the New Testament in Phil. 1:19 (but cf. also Acts 5:9). The reasons for both prohibitions to enter **Asia** and **Bithynia** are unknown to us. It could be supposed that there already existed Christian communities there and therefore it did not fit in with Paul's rule of not entering fields plowed by others, but of working new ones himself. Later, however, perhaps because of the change of circumstances, he will enter **Asia,** establishing himself in its capital at Ephesus (19:1 sqq.). Finally, at their third attempt, going westward again they came to the sea at **Troas.** This was the name of the city and the nearby surrounding countryside. The city, Alexandria Troas, was about 12 miles from the Troy of Homer, a Roman colony which had received every kind of privilege from the imperial descendants of the *Gens Julia,* which associated its own legendary origins to the Troy of Homer. Its port was a source of active commerce with near Europe (for all these geographical features, see G. Ricciotti, *Paul the Apostle,* pp. 11 sqq., 292 sqq.).

16:9. The Western Recension adds unnecessary details thus: **And a vision was seen by Paul at night as of a certain Macedonian standing before him,** etc. A third message is now added to the two previous mysterious communications which had only offered obstacles; but this one indicates the new field of labor. Since the **vision** took place at **night,** one naturally thinks of a dream like that of Joseph in Mt. 1:20, 24. It is possible, however that it was a vision that Paul had while he was praying during the night. The man who appeared was recognizable as a Macedonian, both from the words he spoke and from his appearance in a full cloak and broad-brimmed hat, like those worn by the Macedonian merchants whom Paul had already seen in the streets and down at the harbor of Troas during the days of waiting.

16:10. The wait in Troas was brightened by the meeting with Luke. From the use in the narrative of the first person plural (**we made efforts**),

16:11. So sailing from Troas we ran a straight course to Samothrace, and the next day to Neapolis,

16:12. and thence [we passed] to Philippi which is the first city
of the district of Macedonia, a colony: and we stayed some days in
this city.

---

we may conclude for the first time with certainty that Luke was present
(the previous "we-section" is rather doubtful: see note on 11:28). We do
not know for what purposes Luke was in Troas, but there are various
possibilities. He may have been on his way to Philippi where he left Paul
(in v. 40, where the narrative is continued in the third person) and may
have had business in connection with his profession as a physician. Perhaps also, having learned that Paul was seriously ill in Galatia (Gal. 4:13–
14), he set out to look for him, catching up with him in the country
around Troas. Learning that Paul had plans to evangelize new territories,
it is probable that Luke himself suggested Macedonia, as he already knew
it. On such a hypothesis, Paul's vision officially confirmed Luke's suggestion.

16:11. From **Troas** to **Neapolis** is a sea journey of about 175 miles
with the island of **Samothrace** about halfway between, and there the
voyagers made a short stop. The voyage was without incident and the
distance was covered in two days only, whereas later, on the return, it
took five days (20:6). **Neapolis,** the present-day Kavalla, was actually in
Europe. The Egnatian Way across Macedonia connected it with Durazzo,
opposite the Adriatic port of Brindisi, which marked the end of the
Appian Way from Rome.

16:12. Philippi was about ten miles north of Neapolis. This city was
founded by Philip of Macedon on the site of an ancient village previously
called Krenides ("Fountains") which achieved fame in the year 42 B.C.
because, on the surrounding plain where the river Gangites ran, two
battles took place which marked the end of the republican party of Rome.
The first battle was won more by Antony than by Octavianus, and right
from the beginning Antony founded there a colony of his veteran
legionaries. After the defeat of Antony at Actium (31 B.C.), Octavianus
sent to Philippi many of the former partisans of Antony whose properties
had been confiscated and given to the emperor's veterans. Thus a Roman
"colony" arose called *Colonia Augusta Julia (Victrix) Philippensium,*
favored with many privileges by Augustus (Octavianus), where those
from Italy introduced the Roman language and customs which they
imposed on the previous local population (for other details, see G. Ricciotti,
Paul the Apostle, pp. 34-35, 296 sqq.). — The phrase in apposition to

16:13. And on the Sabbath we went outside the gate to the bank of the river, where we supposed there was a place of prayer, and sitting down we spoke to the women who had gathered [there].

Philippi is very difficult to understand, viz., **which is (the) first city of the district of Macedonia, a colony.** Codex *Beza* (Western Recension) followed by the Syriac Peshitta reads: **which is the capital of Macedonia.** This, however, is historically untrue, since Thessalonica was the capital where the governor of the Roman province of Macedonia resided. Other codices have **which is the first district,** etc., or other variants. Some interpreters see in the adjective **first** (πρώτη) a Greek term of honor, almost like "outstanding," "noteworthy." Others, following certain Vulgate manuscripts, correct the phrase to **city of the first district,** etc., by reading πρώτης instead of πρώτη τῆς, which would refer to the ancient division of Macedonia into four districts made by Paul Emilius in 168 B.C. (cf. Titus Livy, XLV, 29). Still others suggest different corrections. The whole thing is uncertain. — **Colony:** the Greek has the Latin word which is found in the papyri, but not elsewhere in the New Testament. — **We stayed:** the Greek gives this in a periphrase. — **Some days** must have been spent looking around the district, and from the following verse (**Sabbath**), it appears that this time was not more than a week.

16:13. As always, Paul preaches first to the Jews (see note on 13:46), but at Philippi there were so few of them that they did not have a building for a synagogue. On the **Sabbath,** they gathered in the open air **outside the gate** of the city on **the bank of the river.** This stream could have been the Gangites, or more probably one of the many springs which had given the city its ancient name, Krenides ("Fountains"; see preceding note). In any case, the place was chosen near the water because this was necessary for the ablutions prescribed by the Mosaic Law. The meeting place here is called an "oratory," προσευχή, which designation was known to Roman writers (*In qua te quaero proseucha?* Juvenal, *Sat.,* III, 296), but ordinarily it signified the building used as a synagogue. — **We supposed,** ἐνομίζομεν: the Western Recension has **it seemed;** other majuscule codices and quite a few minuscules have ἐνομίζετο, in the sense of "it was customary." It would appear from the circumstances that the missionaries did not know much about the meeting place. There, it seems, they found only **women** present, which was a sign of the fewness of the inhabitants in the place. But that did not dismay the missionaries who, **sitting down** on a bench or step, did not formally preach, but rather conversed in a friendly way (**we spoke**) with the women by way of introducing themselves. Most of these women must have been pagans by birth, but affiliated to Judaism as Lydia was, about whom the following verse speaks.

16:14. And a certain woman named Lydia, a seller of purple from the city of Thyatira, who worshipped God, was listening; and the Lord touched her heart to give heed to what was being said by Paul.

16:15. And when she and her household had been baptised, she appealed to us and said, "If you have judged me to be a believer in the Lord, come into my house and stay [there]." And she insisted upon our coming.

16:14. **Lydia** here does not seem to be a personal name, but rather a surname, i.e., "the woman from Lydia" (like the *Roman,* i.e., from Rome; the *Venetian,* i.e., from Venice) because she was **from the city of Thyatira,** which was in Asia Minor in the province of Mysia, but near the borders of Lydia, whence Thyatira was often assigned to the region of Lydia. It was a colony of Macedonians famous for the manufacture of purple, which accounts both for the woman's presence in Macedonia and for her occupation. — **Worshipped God:** she was one of the "devout" proselytes, and therefore not a born Jewess; see note on 13:43 and 50.

16:15. The narrative is again summary. It omits to mention the time necessary for preparing Lydia for baptism, just as it does not give us particulars about **her household.** Since she figures as the head of her family, it can be supposed that she was a widow. She must also have been wealthy, because the trade she engaged in was a lucrative one. She herself was baptized first, and then her whole household, namely her servants and eventually her children who would follow the example set by their mother. The spiritual benefit received by Lydia caused her to reciprocate it with a material offer to the missionaries. Having a well-appointed and comfortable home, it did not seem right to her that the missionaries should stay in some humble merchant's inn. With a woman's delicate intuition, she felt that those who had introduced her into the spiritual house of the Lord, might, in their turn, be given decent accommodation in her house, and so she insisted on their staying there. The verb **insisted,** παρεβιάσατο, is not exaggerated, for Paul in principle did not accept material help from anybody, much less from those he evangelized (cf. 20:33–35; 1 Thess. 2:9; 2 Thess. 3:8; 1 Cor. 9:15 sqq.; 2 Cor. 11:7 sqq.). Nevertheless, he made an exception in the case of the Philippians, from whom he accepted material assistance which was sent to him at Thessalonica, Rome, and Corinth (Phil. 4:10–18; 2 Cor. 11:9), and it is easy to recognize as the principal contributor, the wealthy Lydia. At all events, on this first occasion, she had quite a task in overcoming the reluctance of Paul and his companions to accept her hospitality. This she eventually did, because **she insisted.**

16:16. Now it came to pass as we were going to the place of prayer that a girl met us who possessed a divining spirit, and brought her masters much profit by soothsaying.

16:17. She followed Paul and ourselves, and kept crying out saying: "These men are servants of the most high God and they proclaim to you a way of salvation."

16:18. This she did for many days; until Paul, being very much grieved, turned and said to the spirit, "I order thee in the name of Jesus Christ to go out of her." And it went out that very moment.

16:16. Again the narrative is brief, as in the preceding verse, but it is obvious that the episode recounted here, and which ended the stay of the missionaries at Philippi, must have happened quite a time after the events related in the two preceding verses. During this time, the activity of the missionaries must have been intense, since the flourishing Christian community which is spoken of in the letter to the Philippians could not be otherwise explained (1:8, 26 sqq.; 2:12; 4:1 sqq.). This episode gives rise to the only persecution which Paul encountered at Philippi, and this time it was not caused by the Jews, which fact tends to confirm the view that there were not many Jews there. — Girl, or slave, as in 12:13. She was one of the many women fortunetellers common in pagan religions who were perhaps possessed. This one at Philippi **possessed a spirit,** i.e., Python, πνεῦμα πύθωνα (not **a spirit of Python,** as some codices put it). According to mythology (Ovid, *Metamorph.,* I, 443 sqq.) Python was the serpent who in ancient times pronounced the oracles at Delphi, but Apollo killed him and gave the oracles in his stead. This is the origin of the epithet Pythian applied to the god, and the name Pythia given to the priestess of Apollo at Delphi who kept up the practice of divining, seated on a three-legged stool covered with the skin of the serpent. Greek writers also called a ventriloquist "python," viz., εγγαστρίμυθος, but originally this word (*in-ventre-loqui*) referred more to the power which produced the words, than to the word itself, and therefore the divining soothsayer was considered pregnant with power (in conformity with the usual Greek expression *in ventre habere* to signify pregnancy). Augustine (*De civit. Dei,* II, 23) thought that this girl was a ventriloquist, and certainly she performed extraordinary acts which accompanied pagan divinations, and aroused such belief among learned and unlearned alike. By divining in this manner, the girl **brought her masters much profit.**

16:17-18. The repeated cries of the soothsayer could have seemed favorable to the **servants of the most high God** but Paul who did not believe

16:19. But her masters, on seeing that their hope of profit was gone, laying hold of Paul and Silas dragged them to the market-place before the rulers.

16:20. And bringing them to the magistrates they said: "These men are making a great disturbance in our city; they are Jews,

16:21. "and are advocating practices which it is not lawful for us to accept or practice since we are Romans."

---

in Python, but believed in the devil, did not think so. He remembered that the unclean spirits had been obsequious to Christ by declaring: **Thou art the Son of God!** and yet Christ had driven them out (Lk. 4:41; Mk. 3:11-12). Paul, therefore, does the same by his charismatic power because he was *grieved*, διαπονηθείς, i.e., worn out with vexation, at these noisy protestations. — The appellation, **the most high God** is used in exactly the same way by the evil spirits in the Gospels (Mk. 5:7; Lk. 8:28) and is a translation of El Elyon which is used as the name for the god of the Canaanites (Gen. 14:18 sqq.; cf. Hebr. 7:1) as well as for the god of the Phoenicians (Ἐλιοῦν καλούμενος Ὕψιστος: in Philo of Byblos, in Eusebius, *Praepar. evang.,* I, 10). The adjective, **most high,** by itself, could mean God, both among the pagans, like Balaam (Num. 24:16), as well as the Hebrews (Deut. 32:8; 2 Sam. 22:14, etc.).

16:19. Was gone: the same verb in the preceding verse refers to the devil who was the cause of the hope spoken of here. — **The market-place** was the equivalent of the forum of the Romans, the business center, and site of the tribunal. The **rulers** or "archons" are the same as the magistrates who are called *strategoi* in the following verse. They were actually duumvirs, elected by an assembly of citizens, who ruled the Roman colony and had the right to be preceded by lictors carrying the fasces. It should be noted that the crowd seized only Paul and Silas, although, when Paul exorcised the girl, Luke and Timothy were present. But some time must have elapsed between this and the preceding verse, so as to allow the girl's masters to realize that they had lost **their hope of profit.** Once they learned how this had come about, they seized the two leaders of the group, **Paul** and **Silas.** It may also be that Luke and Timothy were not present when their two companions were captured. A similar case is related in 19:29-31, where Paul is not taken.

16:20-21. The accusation, covering up the real motive of their lost gain, brings forward several reasons together; the disturbance of public order, Jewish propaganda, and the nonobservance of Roman customs. A veiled antithesis between **Jews** and **Romans** can be detected here.

16:22. Then the crowd joined in the attack against them, and the magistrates tore off their clothes and ordered them to be beaten with rods;

16:23. and after inflicting many strokes upon them, they cast them into prison, charging the jailer to keep them safely:

16:24. who, on receiving such orders, cast them into the inner prison and fastened their feet in the stocks.

16:25. Now about midnight, Paul and Silas were praying, singing hymns to God: and the prisoners were listening to them;

16:22-24. The pretexts of the accusation, as cunning as they were groundless, made an impression both upon the crowd and the judges, since all were intent on maintaining the peace in their colony. So, as soon as the charge was made and the discussion of the case began, **the crowd joined in the attack against them.** The judges allowed themselves to be swayed by the general excitement, and deemed it opportune to take summary action, foregoing the formalities of a trial. They considered that the two accused were good-for-nothing troublemakers, who came disturbing a Roman colony, and it was best to take severe measures against such mischief-makers forthwith. So, before the session was over they ordered the punishment of scourging. The traditional commands rang out: *Submovete* — "Push back the crowd." *Despoliate* — "Strip the condemned." *Verberate* — "Strike them with the rods (taken from the fasces of the lictors)." Certainly the two accused would have tried to speak both to protest their innocence and to claim their Roman citizenship (cf note on vv. 37-39), but the shrieks of the mob drown their voices, convinced, as they were, that the accused were uttering the usual pleas of those condemned to the rod. After the scourging, which was inflicted with severity (**many strokes**), the judges, so as to be on the safe side, had them put in prison under special custody. The jailer, carrying out the order with care, locks them in an inner cell of the prison, and in addition fastens their feet in the stocks. A prisoner thus bound could only lie on the ground, or at best sit up, and in the case of Paul and Silas, their bleeding bruises, resulting from the scourging, aggravated their condition. Later on, Paul with Silas as his amanuensis, writing to the Thessalonians will recall that both of them, **having previously experienced suffering and shameful treatment at Philippi,** had the courage to evangelize the recipients of the letter immediately afterward (1 Thess. 2:2).

16:25. The moral reason which caused the two missionaries **to pray and sing hymns to God,** even though they were reduced to their present state

16:26. and suddenly there was such a great earthquake that the foundations of the prison were shaken: and at once all the doors flew open and everyone's chains were unfastened.

16:27. And the jailer, roused out of sleep and seeing that the doors of the prison were open, drew his sword and was about to kill himself, thinking that the prisoners had escaped;

---

was the same as that referred to in similar circumstances in the note on 5:41. But the reason for their so acting at this particular time was probably that about that hour (**midnight**), they were due to participate in a Christian gathering, perhaps in Lydia's house *to break bread* (cf. 20:7), and to pray, singing those poetic compositions recorded by Paul (Col. 3:16; Eph. 5:19), and also by Pliny the Younger about the year A.D. 112 in his letter to Trajan (*Epist.,* X, 96). Although their bodies lay in prison, their spirits were united with their brethren through their prayers and hymns. Their strange behavior must have subdued the other prisoners who were common malefactors, used only to uttering oaths and blasphemies instead of prayers. Stupefied by what they heard, they did not dare to disturb the strangers, but simply listened without seeing anything, because the prison was in darkness (cf. v. 29). Perhaps, with their pagan mentality, they imagined that these two mysterious prisoners had a relationship with some powerful spirit whom they now invoked with their hymns to come and free them. If the spirit they invoked were really to appear, there might be some chance for them also.

16:26. The vague expectation of the other prisoners was quickly realized. A **great earthquake** caused what is here related. Earthquakes are not infrequent in the Balkan peninsula, but neither there nor elsewhere does an earthquake open barred prison doors, much less unfasten prisoners' feet from the stocks. It is, therefore, indisputable that the narrator's intention here is to recount a miracle in the true sense of the word. But since a miracle is impossible for the Rationalists they explain it either by supposing that the narrative exaggerates some small consequences of the earthquake, such as the crumbling of a small wall, or the displacement of a door (though today, this method of explanation is almost abandoned), or they say that the whole account is based upon a legend. Anyone who is satisfied to accept such explanations is free to do so; but when one remembers that the narrator was present in the city, and anxiously followed the fate of his two beloved friends in prison, and moreover, that this witness is Luke, whom the earliest tradition regarded as an objective and impartial historian, these explanations prove to be historically absurd.

16:27-28. The terror which drove the jailer to attempt suicide was not

16:28. but Paul cried with a loud voice saying, "Do thyself no harm for we are all here."

16:29. Then calling for a light, he ran in and trembling for fear fell down at the feet of Paul and Silas;

16:30. and bringing them out he said: "Sirs, what must I do to be saved?"

16:31. And they said: "Believe in the Lord Jesus, and thou shalt be saved and thy household."

16:32. And they spoke the word of the Lord to him and to all who were in his household.

16:33. And he took them at that very hour of the night and washed their wounds; and he and all his family were baptised immediately.

---

without foundation, since the responsibility of one who allowed prisoners entrusted to him to escape was most serious (see note on 12:18; 27:42); and seeing that the doors of the prison were open, he naturally thought that all the prisoners had escaped. Everything was in darkness, but it was easy to guess from the jailer's cry what his intentions were. In any case, he came in from outside where there was probably a lantern to light up the entrance to the cells (cf. the following verse), and Paul from inside could see him outlined against the lighted courtyard.

16:29-33. How was it that the jailer changed his attitude toward Paul and Silas so suddenly? Undoubtedly, the earthquake was one reason which made the missionaries seem more than other men. Moreover, a change of feeling was probably prepared for by the fact that he may have known that Paul and Silas were preaching a new religion. Perhaps he had heard, more than once, the slave girl announce in the street that they were proclaiming a way of salvation (v. 17). The earthquake opened his eyes and he now asked these two mysterious beings what he must do to be saved, and humbly addressed them as Sirs (literally, Lords) (see note on 2:36; 9:5). Then, almost as if in reply to this title, the two missionaries urged him to believe in the Lord Jesus as a condition of the salvation which he sought. The formula of Christian belief consisted in confessing that Jesus is the Lord (cf. Rom. 10:9; Phil. 2:11). Naturally this formula had to be explained, at least briefly, to the jailer and his family, as is stated in the words they spoke the word of the Lord, etc. Most probably, this was done shortly afterward while the jailer tended their wounds. There was a close link between those wounds and that baptism which followed immediately.

16:34. And taking them into his house, he set food before them, and rejoiced with all his household over his faith in God.

16:35. But when day came, the magistrates sent the lictors with the instructions: "Let these men go."

16:36. And the jailer reported these words to Paul: "The magistrates have sent word that you are to be released; now therefore come forth and go in peace."

16:37. But Paul said to the lictors: "After having beaten us publicly and without trial, we who are Romans, they threw us into prison and now they cast us out secretly. By no means, but let them come themselves and take us out!"

16:34. The meal, which was welcome to the hungry and exhausted missionaries, did not mar but rather strengthened the spiritual joy of the occasion. This is a thought which is dear to Paul and Luke (see note on 2:46). It cannot be ruled out that the meal served also to introduce the neophytes fully into the Christian way of life, by enabling them to participate in the principal action of the liturgy, the Eucharist, which Paul may have celebrated (cf. 20:7 sqq.), but this cannot be affirmed with certainty (cf. 27:35).

16:35. If the magistrates sent this order, it is clear that they were not quite at ease about what had happened the previous day. The Western Recension adduces the earthquake as the reason for their change of heart, and psychologically, this might well have been so, just as the jailer was moved to conversion by it. But apart from the doubtful authenticity of this addition to the text, other reasons must have influenced the magistrates. Thinking over what had happened, they must have realized that their procedure in judging the two strangers had been altogether too hasty, and might lead to very unpleasant consequences for them. In the meantime, they may have received information favorable to the two accused, which might well have been sent or even brought personally by Lydia herself, who since she was a person of some standing, had the influence to make the magistrates listen to her. In the end, they must have seen themselves in danger, because if the two accused had recourse to the Roman authorities of the province, they could show that they had been condemned contrary to all Roman law. As they seemed to have a certain civil standing, the Roman authorities might take their side and punish the magistrates. By releasing them, therefore, everything would be all right. At this point however, the unexpected happens.

16:37–39. The two missionaries were **Romans,** i.e., they enjoyed Roman

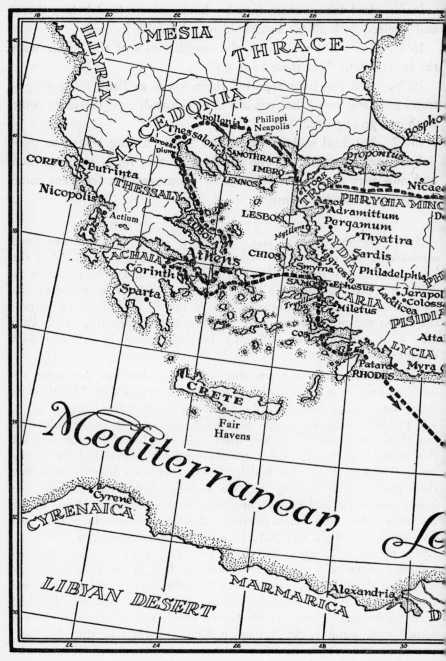

The Second

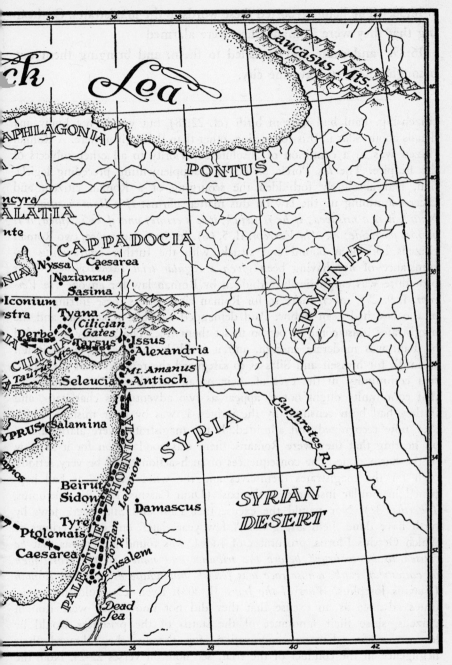

Missionary Journey

16:38. The lictors reported these words to the magistrates. On hearing that they were Romans, they were alarmed

16:39. and came and appealed to them, and bringing them out, besought them to leave the city.

---

citizenship. Paul had it from birth (cf. 22:28), but we do not know any details about Silas in this connection, other than those given here. A Roman citizen was in a condition of absolute superiority to all other subjects of the Empire. The *lex* Porcia of 248 B.C., supplementing preceding legislation, had absolutely forbidden the scourging of a Roman citizen, and Cicero summing up the law on this matter affirms: *If a Roman citizen is bound, it is a misdeed; if he is struck, it is a crime; and if he is killed, it is almost parricide; etc.* (*in Verrem,* II, 5, 66). In the present case, two Roman citizens had been bound and struck, with the further aggravating circumstance of *not* having been *given a regular trial* (ἀκατακρίτους). This procedure was emphatically forbidden by Roman law for anyone (*in Verrem,* I, 9, 25), much more so for Roman citizens. As these infringements of the law had been public, Paul demanded a public reparation, and the magistrates must come in person to set them free. The apology demanded by Paul was moderate enough, and it is likely that he requested it not so much for himself and Silas as to safeguard the reputation of the Christian community in the eyes of their pagan neighbors. The founders of that community ought not to appear as two adventurous charlatans, and if they had been censured by the judges, it was by their mistake which they now recognized and admitted. If the magistrates **were alarmed . . . on hearing that they were Romans,** there was good reason for it in view of the harm done. The consequences of such action could be very serious, both for the magistrates themselves and the whole colony, as had happened in similar instances in the past (Dion Cassius, LX, 24; Suetonius, *Tiberius,* 37). Nor would the excuse that Paul and Silas were Jews by birth have done them any good. A few years later, one of the crimes of which Gessius Florus, procurator of Judea, was found guilty was that *he caused to be scourged before the tribunal and nailed to the cross, men of equestrian rank, whose race was Jewish, but whose dignity was Roman* (Flavius Josephus, *Wars of the Jews,* II, 308). Even less could the magistrates advance as an excuse that they did not know they were Roman citizens, since their ignorance of the status of the prisoners would be less an excuse than an aggravation, for thereby they showed their negligence in the conduct of the trial; see note on verses 22–24. Note the repetitive sense of the phrases — **they threw us . . . they cast us,** both times in a scornful manner.

16:40. And leaving the prison they went to Lydia's house, and after seeing the brethren and encouraging them, they departed.

17:1. Now after passing through Amphipolis and Apollonia, they came to Thessalonica, where there was a synagogue of the Jews.

17:2. And Paul, as was his custom, went into them, and for three Sabbaths discussed with them, [reasoning] from the Scriptures

17:3. explaining [their sense], and showing that the Christ had to suffer and rise from the dead [affirming]: "This is the Christ, Jesus whom I preach to you."

16:40. The appeal of the magistrates was accepted *pro bono pacis,* and the departure took place at once or almost at once. From the fact that the narrative is at this point again related in the third person plural (**they departed**), we gather that Luke did not leave the city. Probably Paul left him at Philippi where he was well known, and entrusted him with the care of the new community, and he will rejoin Paul later (20:5–6). As for Timothy, although he is not mentioned in this departure, he probably left with the other two. Not only do we find him with Paul later on in Beroea (17:14), but from the salutations in the epistles to the **Thessalonians,** he seems to be well known to them, and therefore it is likely that he was one of the founders of that community, for Paul was now departing for Thessalonica.

17:1. Traveling along the Egnatian Way (cf. note on 16:11) and passing through the two small centers of **Amphipolis** and **Apollonia,** Paul and his companions reached **Thessalonica** after a journey of about 100 miles. Situated at the head of the Thermaic gulf, and linked by secondary roads to the hinterland, the city was populated by a mixture of races, with Greeks in the majority, but Jews were also very numerous there. It was the seat of the governor of the Roman province of Macedonia. Paul had a hard time during the first day of his stay there. Having found a lodging with a certain Jason (v. 5), he sought at once to exercise his trade as a weaver, so as to earn his living, since he did not eat **any man's bread at his cost, but working night and day in labor and toil so as not to burden anyone** (2 Thess. 3:8; cf. 1 Thess. 2:9). Nevertheless, his manual work, together with his preaching, and hindered by ill-health, did not yield much, so that he found himself in such financial straits that twice he had to accept material help from the faithful at Philippi (see note on 16:15).

17:2–3. As was his custom: viz., to address himself first to the Jews; see notes on 16:13; 13:46. — These **three Sabbaths** do not cover the whole

17:4. And some of them believed and joined Paul and Silas, along with a large number of the "God-fearing" and of the Greeks and of the Gentiles and not a few women of rank.

17:5. But the Jews being moved with jealousy, gathering some base loafers and forming a mob, set the city in an uproar; then besetting Jason's house, they sought to bring them out before the [assembly of the] people.

17:6. But not finding them, they dragged Jason and certain brethren before the city magistrates shouting: "These men who have set the world in an uproar, have come here too,

17:7. "and Jason has given them hospitality. All these are acting contrary to the decrees of Caesar, saying that there is another king, Jesus."

---

period that Paul stayed at Thessalonica, since he must have remained there some months, but they refer to the attempts he made to convert the Jews. Rejected by them, he turned to the pagans as he had done at Pisidian Antioch (13:46), and will do later at Corinth (18:5-7), and at Ephesus (19:8-9). — The object of his preaching to the Jews was to show that the Christ (namely, the Messias awaited by them) had to suffer. This was, in fact, the great obstacle to their conversion; see note on 2:23.

17:4. The Jews who were persuaded (believed) must have been few, since those to whom Paul addresses the two letters to the Thessalonians seem to be in the majority ex-pagans. — And joined, προσεκληρώθησαν (were allotted to the part): this word is used only here in the whole of the New Testament; the lot (or part) is that of the Gospel preached by Paul and Silas. — God-fearing: see notes on 13:43 and 50. The conjunction and after God-fearing occurs only in a few codices, but conceptually it is the better reading. For Luke, Greeks are pagans or idolaters (see note on 11:20), so that if the conjunction and was left out, it would read the God-fearing idolaters, which would be absurd. — Not a few: Luke's customary figure of speech for many; see note on 12:18.

17:5-7. But the Jews being moved with jealousy, etc.: the events at Pisidian Antioch are more or less repeated here (cf. 13:45 sqq.). This time, to attain their end, the Jews have recourse to the rabble, ἀγοραίων, namely, those loungers who hung around the market place or forums without any fixed occupation, and applauded or heckled according as they were paid to do so. Cicero gave them the picturesque epithet of subrostrani, for they invariably gathered about the rostrum where an orator was speaking and

17:8. And they stirred up the people and the magistrates who heard this;

17:9. and taking bail from Jason and the rest, they let them go.

---

decided the success or failure of his discourse. At Thessalonica, these loafers put themselves at the disposal of the Jews who had paid them. First of all, **forming a mob,** they **set the city in an uproar,** perhaps with acclamations for Caesar and maledictions against foreign enemies of the city. Then they gathered together in front of **Jason's house** where Paul and Silas were lodging, crying death to the traitors, and **they sought to bring them out before the [assembly of the] people.** We know nothing of Jason. Probably he was a Jew of Thessalonica who had changed his original name of Jesus (Josue) to that of Jason. **The [assembly of the] people** was that body which presided over the internal affairs of the city, and had at its head five or six magistrates, to whom Luke gives the name, *politarchs.* It was the technical name for magistrates in Macedonia and its confines, as confirmed by various inscriptions. The quarry the mob sought, Paul and Silas, were not in the house, probably because they had been warned in time by friends and conducted elsewhere (a similar case happens in 19:29–31), and so the crowd gives vent to its anger by seizing **Jason and certain brethren,** namely, other Christians. The house, therefore, must have been a Christian meeting place. But Jason, a resident of Thessalonica, could not be accused before the magistrates of things which the strangers, Paul and Silas, had done. Nevertheless, he was involved in the charge, since he had sheltered them, and that showed that he was in league with them and shared their ideals. The accusation was that they had **set the world in an uproar** (see note on 11:28), and had acted **contrary to the decrees of Caesar, saying that there is another king, Jesus** (Jn. 19:12). The charge was cleverly framed, being based on political grounds and making much of public order and loyalty to Caesar of Rome. The force of this charge indirectly reveals that those who contrived it were Jews, since they could know well that Jesus himself had declared before Pilate that he was a **king** (Jn. 18:36–37), just as their Jewish forebears who had accused Jesus (Jn. 19:6) proclaimed solemnly before the same Pilate that they had no king but Caesar (Jn. 19:15).

17:8–9. The magistrates of Thessalonica were not so impulsive or precipitous as those of Philippi (cf. note on 16:22–24), because they knew from long experience the insincerity of those scheming *subrostrani,* and how much their zeal for public order and Caesar of Rome was worth. However, the charge in itself was serious because it amounted to *crimen laesae majestatis* or high treason, and the magistrates could not seem to be

17:10. But the brethren straightway sent Paul and Silas away by night to Beroea, and on their arrival there, they went into the synagogue of the Jews.

17:11. Now these were of a nobler character than those of Thessalonica, and they received the word with great eagerness, studying the Scriptures every day [to see] whether these things were so.

17:12. Many of them became believers, and not a few prominent Greeks, women and men.

17:13. But when the Jews of Thessalonica found out that in Beroea too the word of God had been preached by Paul, they came there also to stir up and excite the multitude.

17:14. Then straightway the brethren sent forth Paul to go as far as the sea, while Silas and Timothy remained there.

17:15. But those who escorted Paul took him as far as Athens, and receiving instructions from him for Silas and Timothy to rejoin him as soon as possible, they set out.

---

indifferent to that. To save appearances, therefore, they let the accused *go free* after **taking bail** from them. Just what the bail (τὸ ἱκανόν) was, we do not know, but it must have been either a sum of money or a pledge that they would not be implicated in such matters in the future.

17:10. The haste with which they departed was certainly due to the fear of further hostilities, since the Jews could have been by no means satisfied with the magistrates' decision. — **Beroea,** today Veria, was a little "out-of-the-way" city, as Cicero described it (*in Pisonem, 36*), three days' journey on foot, southwest of Thessalonica. Paul's stay at Beroea was short, probably only a few weeks, but it was not stormy like the preceding ones. The time must have been the beginning or the middle of the year 51. — **Into the synagogue:** Paul's usual practice (cf. note on v. 2).

17:11. Nobler character: because they were of nobler birth. They were also conscientious and keen, since they examined **the word** of the Gospel preached by Paul eagerly, **studying the Scriptures every day . . .**

17:12. Cf. verse 4.

17:13. This is a group similar to that which drove Paul from Lystra: 14:19.

17:14. For the presence of **Timothy** at Beroea, see note on 16:40.

17:15. After the word **Athens** the Western Recension adds: **But he**

17:16. Now while Paul was waiting for them at Athens, he was exasperated to see how the city was full of idols.

---

traversed Thessaly, since he was prevented from preaching the word among them. The second part of this addition is traced back to 16:6. The crossing of Thessaly is possible from a geographical point of view, since Thessaly extends south of Beroea from where Paul came, and whoever went to Athens overland, had to cross it. But did Paul choose the overland route, or did he go by sea? The latter is more likely since thus he could reach Athens in three or four days, while the journey down through Thessaly would have taken about twelve days. Probably he embarked at the port of Dium which was about thirty miles south of Beroea, and sailing down the eastern coast of Greece, arrived at Athens. But why did his conductors take **him as far as Athens,** and return immediately to the place they had come from, and not simply accompany him to the boat, thus relieving themselves of any further trouble? It has been conjectured, with every likelihood, that Paul had recently suffered an attack of his chronic illness — not the one which afflicted him during his stay among the Galatians (see note on 16:6-8), but that mysterious one referred to in 2 Cor. 12:7-9 — and therefore it was not proper to leave him by himself. — **Receiving instructions** (given by Paul) **for Silas and Timothy . . . :** we find, in fact, that these two coming from Macedonia rejoined Paul later, not at Athens, however, as the present order required, but at Corinth (18:5). How did all this happen? First of all it should be noted that Paul's stay at Athens covers the journey made by Timothy whom Paul had sent to Thessalonica to visit the communities there, and during that time, Paul remained **at Athens alone** (1 Thess. 3:1-2), that is, without even Silas. Among the various explanations offered to reconcile these facts, the most natural seems to be that Timothy and Silas joined Paul immediately in Athens, as he had requested. Then Timothy was sent to Thessalonica, and Silas elsewhere (perhaps to Philippi), and when their missions were completed, they both joined Paul again, this time at Corinth.

17:16. Paul's stay at Athens is a page full of vivid description and historical interest. Moreover, there is a certain Greek coloring to the style due to the lively participation of the narrator as he deals with a new situation. At this time, Athens was a city that lived on the glories of its past, abundantly rich in monuments, unique throughout the world, frequented by foreign young men who were devotees of culture. It languished contentedly among the relics of ancient glories without producing anything new. Horace (*Epist.,* II, 2, 81) called it *empty Athens,* meaning not only "empty," but "inert," "dormant." On their visits to Athens, Cicero, Horace,

17:17. He had discussions therefore in the synagogue with the Jews and those who worshipped God, and in the market place every day with those who were there.

17:18. And some of the Epicurean and Stoic philosophers debated with him; and some said, "What is this babbler trying to say?" But

---

and other Roman notables regarded the city from their viewpoint as philosophers, politicians, or aesthetes. Paul naturally contemplated it with the eyes of an ex-rabbi become a Christian apostle. But in both roles he experienced a profound traditional aversion to the idolatry he saw represented by the temples, statues, and images of every sort which were admired by cultured Romans who visited Athens. For Paul, all those things were not the simple artistic creations they appear today, when they no longer have any religious significance; they were testimonies of triumphant idolatry and the impieties of idolatrous worship. And so **he was exasperated** (the Greek has, **he was in a paroxysm,** for which see note on 15:39) as he walked around the streets of Athens, where at every turn he saw things which wounded his conscience, both as an ex-rabbi and as an apostle. The extraordinary number of these objects in Athens, indirectly confirmed by verse 22, is attested by various writers of the time (Titus Livy, XLV, 27; Pausania, I, 17, 1 etc.; but the judgment of Petronius, *Satiric.,* 17, which has often been cited in this connection, viz., *Our country is so full of divinities, that in it you may more easily find a god than a man,* does not necessarily refer to Athens).

17:17. The Jews were not numerous at Athens, but they had a **synagogue** there in which Paul, as usual, addressed them first. — **Those who worshipped God:** see note on verse 4. — The reception given to Paul by his fellow countrymen was cold, and so he turned to the pagans and had discussions with those who frequented the market place. In Athens there were several agoras, each known by a special name, but the chief one called the Kerameikos or "Ceramic" was the one which stood at the foot of the Areopagus near the Acropolis. There, all types came together, citizens, foreigners, merchants, politicians, charlatans, and philosophers, all spending much time there. Paul first threw his net into this *mare magnum* by speaking of the Messias Jesus to a group of bystanders. But even here he seems to have made very little impression as he was probably considered to be one of those Orientals — and his manner of speaking did not belie it — who presented themselves to the crowd to announce the power of some unknown Oriental god, or the secret efficacy of some unknown rite.

17:18. The only ones who through sheer curiosity were in any way

others: "He seems to be a herald of strange gods," because he pro-claimed to them Jesus and the Resurrection.

---

interested in Paul were **some . . . Epicurean and Stoic philosophers.** The latter held meetings in the *Stoa poikile* (from which they got the name "Stoics"), which was on the outskirts of the market place. The Epicureans, on the other hand, met in gardens inside the city. Followers of other schools like the Peripatetics of Aristotle, or the Academians of Plato, are not recorded here by Luke, because Paul probably did not meet any of them (in any case, at this time they were few, and lacked influence). Perhaps also because only the Epicureans and Stoics corresponded to the similar Jewish groups of the Sadducees and Pharisees (cf. Flavius Josephus, *Wars of the Jews,* II, 119 sqq.; *Antiquities of the Jews,* XVIII, 11 sqq.). Needless to say, both the Epicureans and the Stoics could not but be hostile to Paul's teaching, though for different reasons. Both schools acknowledged a Divinity, but the Stoics had a pantheistic notion of God, considering him to be the soul of the world and material nature. The Epicureans equally admitted the existence of gods, imagining them to be formed of more subtle and ethereal atoms than those of men. It is clear such doctrines were a complete antithesis to the spiritual Hebrew Christian idea of the Deity which Paul taught, even leaving out of con-sideration all the other differences which existed between them. — **And some said:** if these words refer to the foregoing **Epicureans and Stoic phi-losophers,** the first observation can be attributed to the Epicureans, the second to the Stoics. But these same words can have an impersonal sense, *they said,* referring to the Athenians of the market place. — **Babbler** or *prater* is in Greek σπερμολόγος, meaning, etymologically, *gatherer of seeds.* It was originally an epithet of the crow and the magpie because of their habits, and later of beggars who gathered up the kernels of grain spilled in the market place. It then came to be used figuratively to mean "a gatherer of words," a talkative person, one who, by means of the ideas he has picked up, wishes to appear a philosopher. Paul, then, in this present text, at no particular loss for words, seemed to be such a philoso-pher. — **Strange gods,** ξένων δαιμονίων: even Socrates, in Athens itself, had been accused of believing in *other new divinities,* ἕτερα δαιμόνια καινά (Plato, *Apolog. of Socrates,* XI), but undoubtedly the observation is made here, not as an accusation, but as a statement of fact. These **strange gods** preached by Paul would have been **Jesus and the Resurrection,** regarded by his hearers as a normal pair of gods, male and female. Since there were, in Athens, shrines in honor of personified abstract ideas such as Compassion, Modesty, Victory, and even Insult and Impudence, those citizens did not wonder that a foreign preacher should come and speak

17:19. And taking him, they brought him to the Areopagus, saying: "May we know just what is this new doctrine which thou teachest?

---

of a goddess named **Resurrection,** probably the wife or daughter of **Jesus.** Later on, Mohammed fell into a similar misunderstanding when he heard Christian preachers teach the Divine Trinity of the Father, Son, and Holy Spirit. In Arabic, the word "spirit" (*ruḥ*) is feminine, and Mohammed thought it designated a woman, the wife of the Father, and mother of the Son, whom he then identified with the Virgin Mary (Koran, *surah,* 5, 116; cf. 5, 77; 4, 169). In the Western Recension (codex *Beza* and *Gigas*), the words **because he proclaimed to them Jesus and the Resurrection** are omitted, but such an omission can be explained as a suppression intended to avoid including the name of Jesus in the category of pagan gods, δαιμόνια, just spoken of. The idea expressed here, however, fits in with what we read in verse 32. Paul's hearers interpreted the word **Resurrection** in a causative sense as if it were a deity particularly concerned with "raising" the dead.

17:19. Taking him with them (ἐπιλαβόμενοι), not in the sense that violence was used, but merely that they accompanied him. — **The Areopagus** named here could designate either the hill to the west of the Acropolis, or the tribunal which took its name from the place where it met. Legend interpreted the name to mean "hill of Ares," the god of murder and of war, equivalent to the Roman god Mars. Legend also said that on that hill, Ares had been judged by the other gods for a murder. In actual fact, the name had originally meant "hill of the Arai" or the Eumenides, for on its slope there was a temple dedicated to them, where those acquitted by the tribunal on the top of the hill offered sacrifice (Pausania, I, 28, 6). Later, the name Areopagus clung to the tribunal itself, even when it no longer met on the top of the hill, but in the market place in the Royal Portico (*Stoa basileios*); cf. Cicero, *ad Attic.,* I, 14, 5; Seneca, *De Tranquill.,* 5. In Roman times, it seems that this tribunal safeguarded the ancient traditions of the city, and passed judgment on religious, moral, and cultural questions, as we know from the intervention of Cicero with the Areopagus in favor of the philosopher Chratippus, narrated by Plutarch (*Cicero,* 24). In the present case, does the **Areopagus** mean, topographically, the hill or, juridically, the tribunal? It is most probable that it means the hill. There is no hint in the entire episode that Paul was officially questioned by a tribunal and much less that a "writ of impiety" had been presented against him like that proffered against Socrates in the same city 450 years before. Just as there is no accusation,

17:20. "For thou bringest certain strange things to our ears; we wish therefore to know what these things mean."

17:21. Now all the Athenians and the visitors there from abroad used to spend all their leisure telling or listening to something new.

17:22. Then Paul standing up in the midst of the Areopagus said: "Men of Athens, I see that in every respect you are extremely religious.

---

no cross examination, so there is no discussion, no defense, no sentence, nor any hint of a trial. Paul does not speak as a defendant before judges, but as a private citizen to other private individuals on a given religious topic, until his hearers dismiss him because they are bored and disappointed. Paul, therefore, was taken to the **Areopagus** (ἐπὶ τὸν), i.e., the hill, because it was a quieter place for a discussion than the crowded and noisy agora. On the top of the hill there were steps cut in a semicircle, intended — when the tribunal was sitting — for the judges, while the two speakers, the defendant and the plaintiff, used to take their places on two stones opposite them. So on this occasion the philosophers sat on the steps, while Paul spoke to them, **standing up in the midst of the Areopagus** (v. 22). For the rest, we can gather from the narrative that the philosophers who had invited Paul to this discussion were few in number, probably little more than ten. They did not take the matter too seriously, but were moved more out of a curiosity not lacking in irony. This appears in a disguised manner in the question they put to Paul: **May we know, etc.,** rather like that famous question put by Cicero: *Possumus hoc quoque ex te audire?* (*pro Quinctio,* 79; cf. Plautus, *Amphitr.,* 346.)

17:20. The subtle irony continues. **Strange things,** ξενίζοντα: such as cause wonderment because of their singularity; but already those philosophers considered them as the idle tales of a charlatan. — **We wish,** βουλόμεθα: the Greek word here is best translated by its original meaning of "deciding after deliberation"; the matter was of such importance, in the ironic sense, that it deserved mature deliberation. — **What these things mean:** a similar phrase to that of 2:12 (there in the singular). This is still probably said ironically and needed only the addition of *which are so important* to complete the irony.

17:21. The curiosity and the levity of the Athenians was known also to Greek writers; cf. Thucydides, III, 38, 5; Demosthenes, IV, 10. — **Visitors . . . from abroad:** cf. note on 2:10. These were the young men and students who came for cultural reasons rather than the merchants, but even these foreigners were infected with the moral epidemic of that city.

17:22. This discourse of Paul, given here only in brief, is entirely

different from his talks to the Jews, for example, that in the synagogue of
Pisidian Antioch (13:16 sqq.). Seeing that he is speaking here to pagans, he
makes no reference to the Bible, but quotes instead a pagan poet (v. 28).
He does not allude to the revelation of the Old Testament, but speaks
instead of the knowledge of God attained by human reason, as various
Greek philosophers had done, and as — in almost the same place — Socrates
had testified at his death. Many modern critics, among whom the most
learned was E. Norden (*Agnostos Theos,* Leipzig, 1913), have denied that
the discourse is Paul's. On the other hand, many others, including non-
Catholics, have defended its authenticity, among them Harnack (*Ist die
Rede des Paulus in Athen ein ursprunglicher Bestandeil der Apostelgeschicte?* in *Texte u. Untersuch.,* XXXIX, 1, Leipzig, 1913) who particularly examined the proofs adduced by Norden. According to a note of
E. Meyer, *Ursprung u. Anfange des Christentums,* III, Stuttgart, 1923,
p. 92, Norden abandoned his previous opinion, admitting that Luke had
faithfully reproduced the content of Paul's discourse. Loisy, taking up
Norden's original opinion, adduced no new proofs, but only assertions
based on the requirements of his theory and personal feelings. According
to Norden, the discourse was invented at the beginning of the second
century, and its author was inspired by a piece of information in Philostratus' life of Apollonius of Tyana (VI, 3), and a discourse (διαλέξις) on
sacrifices (περι θυσιῶν) given at Athens by Apollonius, of which only a
fragment remains (in Eusebius, *Praepar. evang.,* IV, 13). In the fragment
of the discourse at Athens, no reference is to be found to altars in honor
of unknown gods, while they are mentioned in the biography, as being
not at Athens, but in Upper Egypt. With all that, Norden supposed that
the discourse at Athens contained a reference to altars, just as Paul's
discourse mentions the altar "to the unknown god" (v. 23). Therefore,
concluded Norden, the author of the account as given here in the *Acts*
based Paul's discourse on the lines of that of Apollonius, adding ideas
taken from contemporary Stoicism. It is clear that Norden's construction,
despite its cleverness, is without foundation. On the other hand, Harnack
and other scholars have collected expressions and words from which it
can be seen that the vocabulary used in the discourse here is found wholly
in the rest of the *Acts,* thereby showing the identity of the author. As for
the ideas contained in the discourse, they show a substantial likeness to
the letters of Paul; thus, e.g., the knowledge of God by human reason
(vv. 27–28) cf. Rom. 1:19 sqq.; the importance of Christ's Resurrection in
the preaching of the Gospel (v. 31), cf. 1 Cor. 15:14–15; the supreme
dominion of God over all material things connected with worship (vv.
24–25 and 29), cf. 1 Cor. 8:4–6, and other minor parallels. The fact that
the discourse may have some ideas and even some phrases in common

17:23. "For as I was going about and observing objects of your worship, I found also an altar with this inscription 'To the unknown god.' What therefore you worship in ignorance, that I proclaim to you.

---

with Stoicism is possible, but that simply confirms Paul's principle of **becoming all things to all men** as much as he could for Christ (1 Cor. 9:22). If the Stoics, with their speculations, had arrived at any truths, Paul would not have rejected them, since he was prepared to accept good from whatever quarter it came (cf. Phil. 4:8). On the contrary, speaking to the Stoics, he would have availed himself by preference of those very truths, in order to approach their mentality as much as possible. — In accordance with the practice of the orators of his time, Paul's discourse begins with a *captatio benevolentiae,* praising them for being **extremely religious,** ὡς δεισιδαιμονεστέρους. The adjective here, the only example of its use in the whole of the New Testament, can have either a derogatory meaning, equivalent to *superstitious,* or a good sense as here. The abundance of the religious manifestations of the Athenians is confirmed by many Greek writers (Sophocles, *Oedipus,* Col. 260; Pausania, 1, 17; Elianos, *Var. hist.,* who attributes to the Athenians this religious sense), as well as by Flavius Josephus (*Contra Apion.,* II, 130).

17:23. Paul takes the opening of his discourse from the altar he saw when **going about** the streets of Athens. This reference to an actual fact was in accordance with the oratorical customs of the time. Much discussion has taken place on the inscription on the altar, viz., **To the unknown god.** An altar with this precise inscription to only one unknown god in the singular has not been found, but this proves nothing. In favor of it, we have the attestations of ancient writers and the results of modern research which cannot be overlooked. Philostratus records the existence of altars in honor of unknown gods erected at Athens (see preceding note), and Pausanias (I, 1, 4; cf. v. 14, 8) attests that along the streets from the harbor of Phalerus to Athens there were various altars dedicated to unknown gods. But the dedications are in the plural, while Paul speaks of it here in the singular, and then reasons from this in a monotheistic sense. Some early writers supposed that Paul actually read it in the plural (Tertullian, *Ad nation.,* II, 9; cf. *Adv. Marcion.,* I, 9; Didymus the Blind, in Mai, *Nova Patrum Bibl,* IV, 2, p. 139), and Jerome states definitely that Paul quoted it in the singular for the sake of his argument: *The inscription on the altar was not as Paul stated "to the unknown god," but "to the gods of Asia and Europe and Africa, to unknown and foreign gods," but be-*

cause Paul did not need several unknown gods, but only one, he used the word in the singular so that he might teach that this was his God whom the Athenians had noted by the title on the altar, and rightly knowing him they ought to worship the one they venerated, and of whom they could not be ignorant (in Titum, 1, 12). From what source Jerome took this statement we do not know; it may have been from Origen or some other writer who knew Athens well. Later, it is repeated, again from an unknown source, in Ecumenius (Migne, *P. G.,* 118, 237), Theophylactus (*ibid.,* 125, 1000 and 1109), and pseudo-Euthalius, all with variants. Much more authoritative is the statement of Diogenes Laertius (Epimenides, I, 10, 110) according to which some sheep were let loose to free Athens from the plague, and where they rested they were killed and sacrificed to the tutelary deity of that place, so that *even now anonymous altars can be found along the streets of Athens in memory of the ceremonial sacrifice which then took place.* It is clear that these altars were "anonymous," because being dedicated to an unknown god, they did not bear the name of any local deity, but they must have had some inscription which connected them with the propitiatory sacrifice. It may be, then, that, later on, the custom spread of designating these memorials collectively as *the altar to the unknown gods,* since it was a question of altars raised for a common purpose. This would account for the difficulty in which later visitors to Athens would find themselves, in thinking that every single altar was dedicated to several *unknown gods* together. In such a case, Paul's reading of the inscription was correct. Besides, there were in other places dedicatory inscriptions to one god, who for some reason or other had not been identified. Such an altar is extant on the Palatine hill in Rome today. The text of the inscription on this altar is as follows: *Sei Deo Sei Deivae Sac(rum) — C. Sextius C(aii) F(ilius) Calvinus Pr(aetor) — De Senati* [sic] *Sententia — Restituit.* The letters of the inscription indicate that it belongs to about 100 B.C. The present altar is a restoration of, or substitution for, the previous altar, made by order of the Senate, which was dedicated in Republican times to a single deity for reasons we do not know, just as those who dedicated it did not know whether it was a god or goddess, in other words, an *unknown god.* A quotation from A. Gallio (II, 28, 3) seems to come close to the Roman inscription: *Si deo si deae immolabant, idque ita ex decreto pontificum observatum esse M. Varro dicit, quoniam et qua vi et per quem deorum dearumve terra tremeret, incertum esset. —* The reading, **What . . . that,** in the neuter, is given by the best codices. Others have the masculine, **he whom . . . him,** but it is a correction. Paul, abstracting from the true or false god, refers to the object of the Athenians' worship.

17:24. "God, who made the world and all [that is] in it, since he is Lord of heaven and earth, does not dwell in temples built by hands;

17:25. "neither is he served by human hands [as though he were] in need of anything, since it is he who gives to all men life and breath and all things.

17:26. "And from one man he has created the whole human race, to dwell upon the whole face of the earth, having determined their appointed times and the boundaries of their habitation,

---

17:24. These are the same ideas as those in Stephen's discourse, 7:47 sqq.

17:25. The thought that God is not **in need of anything** is one expressed also by pagan writers: *God has no need, if he is really God, of anything* (Euripides, *Heracles*, 1345); *Divom natura . . . nihil indiga nostri* (Lucretius, II, 650); cf. also Plato, *Timeus,* 33 D, 34 B; etc.— **He who gives to all men life, etc.:** cf. 14:15–17, where Paul speaks to pagans, but uncultured ones. This idea also, taken here from the O. T., is frequently found in pagan writers: Orpheus, fragment 164 (298); Diogenes Laertius, VII, 147, etc.

17:26. One: some codices add **blood.** It is sufficient to understand **man,** resulting in the human race; cf. Rom. 5:12.— **Appointed times** (καιρούς): this does not seem to mean the succession of *seasons,* as in 14:17, but, by being linked up with the **boundaries** of nations, refers to the periods of their prosperity or decay. Just as the Stoics perceived in history a (θεια) πρόνοια, or (*divine*) *providence,* so Paul sees it in the **times** and **boundaries** assigned to each nation's history. But he says this only in a general way, without mentioning individual nations. Elsewhere, he shows his concern for the nation of Israel (Rom., Chaps. 9–11), which was not to his purpose here. So far as other nations are concerned, he knows that there is a **mystery which has been kept in silence for eternal ages, which is manifested now . . . to bring about obedience to the faith to all the Gentiles** (Rom. 16:25–26; cf. 1 Cor. 2:7; Col. 1:26–27; Eph. 3:4–9), and this "mystery" consists in **re-establishing all things in Christ** (Eph. 1:10), including the pagan nations. Since Paul is here speaking to pagans, he limits himself to the (*divine*) *providence* believed in by the Stoics, but he has in mind this "mystery," namely the economy of salvation by Christ. It must be remembered, nevertheless, that Paul knew the general outlook on the destiny of nations, as given in the Old Testament (cf. Deut. 32:8; Job 12:23; Dan. 2:21; 4:17; etc.).

17:27. "that they should seek God — and perhaps grope after him and find him — though he is not far away from any one of us.

17:28. "For in him we live and move and have our being, as indeed some of your own poets have said: 'For we are also his offspring' (Aratus, *Phenomena*, 5).

17:29. "If therefore we are the offspring of God we ought not to imagine that the Divinity is like to gold or silver or stone, to an image graven by human art and thought.

17:27. **Grope after him,** ψηλαφήσειαν: "feel," "grope." Here it is used rather as of one plunged into total darkness, seeking someone who stands perfectly still and quiet nearby. — **He is not far, etc.:** even here there are parallel passages both in the Old Testament (Ps. 139 [138]:5-13; 145 [144]:18; Jer. 23:23-24), and in Stoic writings, though these latter give a pantheistic description according to their philosophy (*Prope est a te Deus, tecum est, intus est:* Seneca *ad Lucil.,* IV, ep. 12, 1; likewise Dion Chrysostom, *Orat.,* XII, 28).

17:28. **In him we live and move and have our being:** the Hebrew-Christian point of view is opposed to the Stoic-pantheistic view of God as the supreme mover of the universe (already outlined in Plato, *Timeus,* 37 C). At first sight, it would seem that the threefold assertion of **living, moving and having our being,** corresponds to the terms **life and breath and all things** in verse 25, but it is actually a quotation from the poem on Minosses written by Epimenides of Crete in the sixth century B.C. This is attested in the eleventh century by the Syriac commentator, Isho'dad (Jesudad) of Merw (cf. M. Dunlop Gibson, *Horae Semiticae,* Cambridge, X, p. 29) who probably depends on Theodore of Mopsuestia. This passage from Epimenides consisted of four verses, of which this was the last, while the second verse was the quotation given by Paul in Titus 1:12 (other early expositors attribute this sentence, partly at least, to Callimacus). — The plural **some** should be noted, since, in fact, the verse is found substantially in two poets of the third century B.C., Aratus of Soli in Cilicia (therefore a fellow countryman of Paul) and Cleanthes of Assos in Troas, both Stoics (Aratus, *Phenomena* 5; Cleanthes, *Hymn to Jupiter,* 5). Paul, quoting these expressions of pantheistic thought, uses them in his own monotheistic sense.

17:29. The Divine nature — or as the Greek has **the Divinity** or **Godhead** (in the neuter) — cannot be likened to an image of gold or silver which is lifeless and without movement, whereas God is the One who **gives to all men life and breath and all things** (v. 25).

17:30. "God indeed, having overlooked the times of ignorance, now calls upon all men everywhere to repent.

17:31. "Because he has fixed a day on which he will judge the world with justice by a Man whom he has appointed [for that end], whom he has guaranteed to all by raising him from the dead."

17:32. Now when they heard of a "resurrection of the dead" some began to sneer, but others said: "We will hear thee again on this matter."

17:30. Having overlooked: thus the Greek, ὑπεριδών, the only instance of its use in the New Testament. The sense is "to disregard with a glance," "to pretend not to see." God has pretended not to see, so as not to punish them as they deserved for the errors which they committed in **the times of ignorance,** namely, those times during which men did not know the God whom they were blindly seeking (v. 27). This idea has already been expressed in 14:16, and will be repeated again in another form in Rom. 3:25–26.— **All men everywhere,** πάντας πανταχοῦ: a play on words as in 24:3. — **To repent:** the Greek expression for *doing penance;* see note on 2:38. With these words, Paul now leaves the field of natural reason and enters that of the Gospel.

17:31. The world: not only the Roman Empire, as in 11:28; 17:6, but the whole human race dwelling on earth.— **A Man** (Jesus) **whom he has appointed:** the same thought is that expressed in 10:42.— Why should *all men* be sure that God will judge them **by a Man** appointed for that end? Because God provided him with fitting credentials (the thought of 2:22), **guaranteeing to all** *the* basis of the *faith* to be placed in this Man, inasmuch as he has raised him from the dead. For the importance of Christ's Resurrection in the Apostolic catechesis, see note on 1:3. In its turn, Christ's Resurrection is the forerunner and guarantee of the resurrection of all men, whom Christ himself will judge.— Note the words here, "raising **from** the dead," while in the next verse, "resurrection **of** the dead" is used.

17:32. Paul's discourse had already begun to disconcert his hearers by his reference to God's calling men to repentance, and to the judgment of all men by a Man. But what really caused the final dismissal was the mention of the **resurrection of the dead.** Such fantasy could not be taken seriously by a Greek, and Paul's audience was convinced that it was a waste of time to listen to such a charlatan. Therefore, **some began to sneer** and burst out laughing. These were probably the Epicureans. Others, most likely the Stoics, preserved the appearance of good manners and, with a courteous dismissal, said they would hear him on another occasion. So

17:33. So Paul went forth from among them.

17:34. Certain men however joined him and became believers, among whom was Dionysius the Areopagite, and a woman named Damaris and others with them.

18:1. After this he departed from Athens and came to Corinth.

---

they all went away, leaving Paul in the midst of the Areopagus. Perhaps Paul was thinking of this scene when later he writes that **the Greeks look for wisdom, but we for our part preach a crucified Christ . . . foolishness to the Gentiles** (1 Cor. 1:22–23). He had, in fact, attempted to preach that "foolishness" in Athens, seat of that "wisdom" of the Greeks, and he had been judged foolish.

17:34. On the whole, the preaching of Paul at Athens was a failure. The few persons, here noted as won over to the Gospel, were a handful of seed for the future, which sprouted slowly and with difficulty. From the information we possess, it seems that Paul afterward made no further attempt to convert the Athenians. It is certain that in the fourth century Athens was still for the most part pagan. **Dionysius,** here mentioned as **the Areopagite,** must have been a member of the tribunal of that same name (see note on v. 19), but we know nothing else about him. In the second century, Dionysius of Corinth states that his namesake, the Areopagite, was the first bishop of Athens (in Eusebius, *Hist. eccl.,* III, 4, 10; IV, 23, 3). A later legend identifies him with the bishop of Paris martyred in A.D. 250. Toward the end of the fifth century, an unknown but clever writer published several writings under the name of the Areopagite, and quite skillfully sustained the fiction. These works were widespread during the Middle Ages, largely because of the attribution to the Areopagite. — We know nothing of **Damaris,** a name which does not appear anywhere else, though the names *Damares* and *Damalis* are found. John Chrysostom (*De Sacerdotio,* IV, 7) calls her the wife of Dionysius. On the other hand, codex E reads instead of simply **woman,** the title of **honorable woman.** This addition (which is reflected also in codex *Beza*) is perhaps intended to safeguard Damaris' reputation, since respectable women did not take part in public gatherings in Athens.

18:1. Passing from **Athens** to **Corinth,** only a short journey, Paul now changed his field of activity, but found the new conditions worse than the old. He left behind the frivolous surroundings of the philosophers of the Areopagus and now entered the society of Corinth, where nothing was thought of but the making of money by commerce, and the worship

18:2. And finding a certain Jew named Aquila, a native of Pontus, who had recently come from Italy, with his wife Priscilla (because Claudius had ordered all Jews to leave Rome), Paul visited them.

---

of the goddess Aphrodite by the worst kind of corruption and vice. The temple of this goddess on the summit of the Acrocorinth was served by more than a thousand prostitutes, while down below, practically the whole city was devoted to this worship, so that the goddess truly merited the title of *Pàndemos,* i.e., "of all the people." (Other details on Corinth are to be found in G. Ricciotti, *Paul the Apostle,* pp. 38–41, 324–325.) Moreover, Paul must have been discouraged and tired by his failure at Athens. His continual moving about during the past few months had not allowed him to work to gain his livelihood, and probably his chronic illness had partly prevented him (see note on 17:15). Consequently, he found himself in economic straits and suffered hunger (cf. 1 Cor. 4:11). Besides, he had been alone in Athens, since he had sent Silas and Timothy into Macedonia (cf. note on 17:15), and had not received the expected news of his beloved converts of Macedonia, whom he knew were exposed to persecution. He himself reveals his state of mind on entering Corinth, in these words: **And I brethren, when I came to you, did not come with pretentious speech or wisdom, announcing unto you the witness to Christ. For I determined not to know anything among you, except Jesus Christ and him crucified. And I was with you in weakness and in fear and in much trembling. And my speech and my preaching were not in the persuasive words of wisdom** (like that attempted on the Areopagus, with such poor results), **but in the demonstration of the Spirit and of power** (especially by means of the charisms), **that your faith might rest, not on the wisdom of men, but on the power of God** (1 Cor. 2:1–5).

18:2. This couple, **Aquila** and **Priscilla,** are mentioned later (vv. 18 and 26), and in the letters of Paul (1 Cor. 16:19; Rom. 16:3; 2 Tim. 4:19). **Priscilla** is the diminutive of *Prisca,* which latter form is the one used by Paul in his epistles. Since Aquila was **a native of Pontus,** he came from the same province as that other Aquila, born at Synope in Pontus, who translated the Old Testament into Greek at the time of Hadrian. A few documents of the Western Recension here add the information that he was **of the same tribe** as Paul. These two traveled extensively, perhaps for business reasons (the various places they visited are enumerated in the note on 12:17). From the information in 1 Cor. 16:19, it seems that they were wealthy, since their dwelling at Ephesus was large enough to serve as a meeting place for the Christians, as also was their house later in Rome (Rom. 16:3–5). There seems to be no foundation for the view

18:3. And, as he was of the same trade, he stayed with them and he set to work (for they were tentmakers by trade).

---

expressed that there are references to these two persons in the catacombs of Rome. In the hypogeum of the senatorial family of the Acilii in the catacombs of Priscilla, we find the following inscription: *M. Acilius V(erus?) c(larissimus) v(ir)* . . . *Priscilla c(larissima femina)*. But since the inscription belongs to the second century A.D., and the name *Acilius* can hardly be linked with that of *Aquila* ('Ακύλας), we cannot discover, in the *clarissima femina,* any relationship to the wife of the tentmaker of whom Luke here speaks. The idea that they were household servants of a senatorial Roman family also seems excluded by the fact that Aquila was a Jew from Pontus, like his namesake who translated the Bible. — The expulsion of the Jews from Rome, referred to here, is attributed to Claudius by Suetonius (*Claud.,* 25), who gives as the motive the Jewish tumults in Rome at the instigation of one *Chrestus.* Today it is commonly held that *Chrestus* stands for *Christus,* in whose name the disturbances had arisen, since the Jews tried to prevent the spread of Christianity in the capital of the empire. The edict must have been only blandly enforced, or it only forbade meetings, as we see from Dion Cassius (LX, 6; cf. XXXVII, 17). It is certain that, shortly afterward, Jews including Aquila and Priscilla were back again in Rome. Suetonius does not give the year of the expulsion. Orosius (VII, 6, 15), on the other hand, gives it as the ninth year of Claudius, i.e., between A.D. 49 and 50, basing his information on (Flavius) Josephus. But since we do not find any such data in the extant writings of this historian, the date given by Orosius is not certain. In any case, it fits in well with other chronological data we possess, so that if Aquila and Priscilla were expelled from Rome in A.D. 49, they could make the journey to Corinth by 50 or 51, even allowing for the frequent stops which their business may have necessitated, and there, a little later, they met Paul.

18:3. The narrative does not tell us that this couple were already Christians, but it is easy to read between the lines. They were energetic and active (Rom. 16:3-4), and probably had more than average culture, and Paul would not have formed such a warm friendship with them so easily if they had not been followers of Christ. Besides the comfort of their company, Paul found lodging and work which gave him new life. They were **of the same trade** (ὁμότεχον: a term which also expresses the liberal arts), namely, **tentmakers,** σκηνοποιοί: a calling very widespread in Cilicia, Paul's homeland, where large herds of mountain goats were raised with thick, shaggy coats from which was woven a stiff rough cloth, suitable for tents and similar coverings. This rough haircloth took its name from

18:4. And he would preach in the synagogue every sabbath and try to convince Jews and Greeks.

18:5. But when Silas and Timothy came from Macedonia, Paul was wholly occupied with [the ministry of] the word, emphatically assuring the Jews that Jesus is the Christ.

18:6. But as they contradicted him and blasphemed, he shook his garments in protest and said to them, "Your blood [be] upon your own heads; I am innocent of it. Henceforth I will go to the Gentiles."

18:7. And departing from there he went into the house of a man

---

the region, and was called *cilicium*. Paul had learned this trade as a boy, perhaps in his father's house, where probably there was such a workshop. As some manual trade or craft was nearly always practiced by the doctors of the Law, so Paul thought it right to continue to exercise it, even when he had dedicated himself entirely to preaching, and also to avoid being a burden to the faithful (cf. G. Ricciotti, *Paul the Apostle*, pp. 186–187).

18:4. Here we have Paul's usual method of preaching, first, in the synagogue to the **Jews** (cf. 17:2 and 17). These were very numerous in Corinth, attracted there by commerce, and their synagogue was frequented also by pagan **Greeks,** namely, the usual "devout" (cf. note on 17:4) of whom Titius Justus of verse 7 was one.

18:5. Silas and Timothy came from Macedonia: see note on 17:15 for their itinerary. The arrival of the two beloved disciples helped greatly to raise Paul's spirits, especially as they brought good news and good things. The good news in general was about the Christian communities at Thessalonica, though there were reports which were not so good and which occasioned the two letters to the Thessalonians written by Paul at this time from Corinth. The good things were the financial assistance sent by the Christians of Macedonia (cf. 2 Cor. 11:9) and especially from Philippi (cf. note on 16:15). This financial help freed Paul a little from manual labor and allowed him more time for preaching, so that he **was wholly occupied** in it. For this last expression, the Greek uses the word συνείχετο, viz., "he was in the midst of," "tied to," "constrained," "totally dedicated to" his preaching.

18:6. The scene at Pisidian Antioch is repeated here (13:45–51) with the difference that Paul shakes his garments while there he shook the dust from his feet; but the moral significance of the gestures is the same. Nevertheless, here is added a severe imprecation.

18:7. Already in 1:23 there has appeared a Joseph Barsabbas **who was**

named Titius Justus, "a worshipper of God," whose house adjoined the synagogue.

18:8. But Crispus, the president of the synagogue, believed in the Lord and so did all his household, and many of the Corinthians heard Paul, and believed, and were baptised.

---

surnamed Justus, and in Col. 4:11, we read of Jesus called Justus, but they are both Jews. Titius Justus, however, is a typical Roman *name* and *surname,* suggesting that this individual was a Roman living at Corinth. He was also one of the "devout"; cf. note on verse 4. The fact that the house of Justus adjoined the synagogue was convenient for those who were already interested in Paul's discourses in the synagogue. In fact, Paul removed to Justus' house after he left that of Aquila, but for the purpose of holding meetings and not to take up residence, as the Western Recension wrongly supposes.

18:8. This Crispus is certainly the person recorded by Paul in 1 Cor. 1:14 as one of the few baptized by him personally at Corinth. For his title of president of the synagogue, see note on 13:15.— The many . . . Corinthians who were converted had been mostly pagans from the lower classes, or slaves, who were very numerous in Corinth (1 Cor. 1:26; 7:21). We know the names of some of them incidentally: a certain Stephanas and his family were the first-fruits of Achaia (*ibid.,* 1:16; 16:15) and were baptized by Paul himself, as was Gaius also (*ibid.,* 1:14) with whom Paul afterward lodged in Corinth (Rom. 16:23). Also mentioned are a certain Fortunatus and Acaicus (1 Cor. 16:17), and among those of better social position we have Erastus, the city treasurer (Rom. 16:23). Two Roman names appear, a certain Quartus (*ibid.*) and Tertius who was Paul's amanuensis when he dictated the epistle to the Romans from Corinth (*ibid.,* 16:22). Among the women converts, we have the wealthy Chloe, whose servants went to Ephesus (1 Cor. 1:11); then there is Phoebe, the deaconess of the community founded in the eastern Corinthian port of Cenchrae, who in all probability took Paul's epistle to the Romans from Corinth, and who assisted many, including myself (Paul) (Rom. 16:1–2). It would be a great mistake to imagine that these converts became models of perfection overnight. The corruption of the city (see note on v. 1) and the base instincts of the majority explain how evil habits remained, forcing Paul, some years later, to give them warnings like the following: Do not err; neither fornicators, nor idolaters nor adulterers, nor the effeminate, nor sodomites, nor thieves, nor the covetous nor the evil-tongued nor the greedy will possess the kingdom of God. And such were some (of you), but you have been washed . . . (1 Cor. 6:9–11). Undoubtedly,

18:9. And one night the Lord said to Paul in a vision, "Do not fear, but speak and do not keep silence;

18:10. "because I am with thee, and no one shall attack thee or injure thee, for I have many people in this city."

18:11. So he settled there a year and six months, teaching the word of God among them.

---

to **wash** such a sordid flock was hard work for Paul, especially as he had to contend at the same time with the hostility of the corrupt pagan surroundings, and the opposition of the nearby **synagogue** (v. 7) which had lost its president Crispus, and saw with jealous hate Paul's followers increase. It is not surprising, therefore, that finding himself in this situation, Paul drops a veiled hint of **all our trials and tribulations** (1 Thess. 3:7). Luke, on the contrary, does not say anything here about this state of things, but lets it be seen indirectly from the remedy spoken of in the following verse.

18:9–10. Without the consolation afforded by this vision, Paul would probably not have continued in Corinth. But this vision, in its turn, demanded great faith in the one who received it because, judging by human standards, it was impossible to see how **many people** could be gained to Christ in a city so wicked and so hostile to Christ. Nevertheless, Paul imitated his ancestor Abraham, of whom he himself says that **hoping against hope he believed** (Rom. 4:18), and like him, Paul became the spiritual father of **many people.**

18:11. This **year and six months** was from about the middle of A.D. 51 (see note on v. 2) to the close of 52, but during this time, other events took place which Luke omits. In the first place, Paul's activity reached beyond Corinth since the foundation of a community at Cenchrae, about eight miles from Corinth, must certainly be attributed to him (cf. note on v. 8). Less definitive is the information that there were Christians throughout **all Achaia** (2 Cor. 1:1; cf. 11:10), of which Corinth was the capital. This allows us to suppose that, as happened later at Ephesus (19:10), Paul's activity radiated from the capital to the rest of the province. Over and above all that, he anxiously followed the fortunes of the communities already founded by him, which he calls **my daily pressing anxiety, the care of all the churches** (2 Cor. 11:28). It was precisely during this stay at Corinth when he received disquieting news from Thessalonica, that he wrote the two epistles to the *Thessalonians,* with a short interval between the first and the second.

18:12. But when Gallio was proconsul of Achaia, the Jews made a concerted attack upon Paul and took him before the tribunal,

---

18:12. The title of **proconsul** (ἀνθύπατος) given here to **Gallio** is correct, since the province of Achaia which first was of senatorial rank and then became an imperial province (see note, 13:7) again became a senatorial province in A.D. 44 (Suetonius, *Claud.*, 25). Such it was during Paul's stay there at this time, and therefore its governor was a **proconsul**, and not a *propraetor* as in the imperial provinces. This proconsul was originally named Marcus Annaeus Novatus and was the older brother of the philosopher Seneca (Lucius Annaeus), who speaks of him in a letter (epist. 104). But afterward he took the name of Gallio from the orator Junius Gallio, by whom he was adopted. The date of his proconsulship is important for the chronology of Paul, since they met in Corinth when Paul had been there eighteen months (v. 11). When exactly, therefore, did the year of Gallio's proconsulship fall? A somewhat mutilated inscription found at Delphi is of great help in this question. It was published by E. Bourguet (*De rebus Delphicis imperatoriae aetatis,* Montpellier, 1905), who seems to have been unaware of its extraordinary importance, but it was soon studied by other scholars. The inscription consists of twelve incomplete lines, and reproduces a letter written by the emperor Claudius to the city of Delphi, and from it we gather the following data. The letter was written while Gallio was in office as proconsul, since the sixth line reads: (*Ju*)*nius Gallio my friend and proconsul of Achaia.* Also, it was written after Claudius had been proclaimed emperor for the twenty-sixth time (second line). This twenty-sixth proclamation took place before the first of August in A.D. 52, since we learn from other documents that the next imperial proclamation (the twenty-seventh) also took place before this, and therefore the twenty-sixth recorded in this inscription was anterior to it. We also know that the twenty-fourth proclamation had occurred not long before January 24, A.D. 52. Although we know nothing of the twenty-fifth, there can be no doubt that the twenty-sixth acclamation took place between January and July of 52 . Some time within these few months, therefore, Claudius wrote the letter reproduced in the inscription, and at that time Gallio was proconsul of Achaia. But when did the latter begin his year of office? It seems that proconsuls at the time of Claudius had to leave Italy and be in their respective provinces by April (Dion Cassius, LX, 11, 6). This rule, however, was for proconsuls chosen by vote (κληρωτοί), and did not affect those chosen by the emperor (αἱρετοί), as Gallio seems to have been. He was then in office as proconsul of Corinth in the period from April to July of 52, and Paul was brought before his tribunal by the Jews. It is quite probable that Gallio had been only a

18:13. saying: "This fellow is persuading men to worship God contrary to the Law."

18:14. But as Paul was about to open his mouth, Gallio said to the Jews, "If there was some [question of] misdemeanor or serious crime, O Jews, I should with reason bear with you.

18:15. "But if these are questions of doctrine and of titles and of your Law, look to it yourselves: I have no wish to decide such matters."

---

hort time in office, so that the Jews thought to profit by the inexperience of a "new man" (the *homo novus*), although Paul had already been in Corinth for eighteen months. Later, the Jews at Jerusalem will try the same trick, attempting to work on the *homo novus,* Porcius Festus, who had been in office only a few days (25:2 sqq.).

18:13-15. **Contrary to the Law:** the Jewish accusers did not state definitely which law they meant, the Jewish or the Roman law, hoping thereby to make a bigger impression on the proconsul whose immediate concern was with the Roman law. But they undoubtedly meant the Jewish law, and Gallio also understood it as such (cf. the words of your Law). It is true that the Roman law recognized and protected the Jewish religion as a lawful religion (*religio licita*), but the Empire did not thereby take to itself the solution of internal questions of Judaism. At that time also, in the eyes of the Roman authorities, Christianity figured only as a particular current of the mainstream of Judaism. Gallio replied in this strain, declaring that he was prepared to punish any common misdeed, but explicitly stating his juridical incompetence in religious matters. So as to specify what these religious matters were, Gallio contemptuosly numerates them, viz., **questions of doctrine** (λόγου, without the article) and titles, almost opposing them to concrete facts, which are the only things about which he is prepared to give judgment. All these abstract names and words come from **your Law,** and not from that of the Roman legislator. is not possible to discern exactly what Gallio alludes to, by referring to questions of doctrine and titles, but most probably they were connected with accusations formulated by the Jews against Paul's preaching. Porcius Festus displays an outlook similar to Gallio's in relation to the Jews and Paul (25:18-19). From the juridical viewpoint, Gallio's position was unassailable, and he realized it and took his stand as soon as the Jews had made their accusations against Paul, and even before Paul could open his mouth to defend himself. But he was also driven to this stand by his aversion to the Jews, common among Roman patricians, which he

18:16. And he drove them from the tribunal.

18:17. Then they all seized Sosthenes, the president of the syna
gogue, and beat him in front of the tribunal; but Gallio paid no
attention to it.

18:18. But Paul, after staying there for some time longer, takin
leave of the brethren, sailed for Syria with Priscilla and Aquila, hav
ing had his head shaved at Cenchrae because of a vow he had made

---

showed forthwith by his action (cf. the following verse) which was af
proved of by his brother Seneca, as seen from his bitter judgment on th
Jews, pointed out by St. Augustine (*De civitate Dei,* VI, 11).

18:17. Who are all spoken of here? The better codices use this word b
itself, referring to all those present. A very few documents add **the Jew**
but it is very unlikely that the Jews would beat the president of thei
synagogue in public. On the other hand, the Western Recension add
the Greeks, and historically it seems more likely, because even at Corint
the Jews could not have enjoyed widespread sympathy. This reading
however, has every appearance of being one of the usual explanator
glosses, and of not belonging to the original text. — **Sosthenes, the presider
of the synagogue** must have been either the successor in that office o
Crispus of verse 8 who became a Christian, or a contemporary colleagu
since there could be several presidents at one time (see note on 13:15).
the mob gave vent to its ill feeling by attacking him, it was probabl
because he had been the instigator of the Jewish action against Paul. Lat
on, Paul writing to the Corinthians from Ephesus (1 Cor. 1:1) names or
Sosthenes our brother. The only argument which identifies him wit
this person is the fact that they both bore the same name, not of itse
very convincing. If it were established that the two persons named we
in fact the same one, it could be supposed that this misfortune ha
brought him to Christianity, perhaps because of the interest Paul took i
him after the beating. — While all this uproar was taking place, **Gall
paid no attention to it,** which shows the contempt he had for the Jev
(cf. preceding note).

18:18. To establish the length of Paul's stay at Corinth, **some tim
longer** must be added to **the year and six months** of verse 11. From th
verse to verse 23, Luke's narrative is a very concentrated summary, whic
includes facts and events that are barely touched upon. In the first plac
the rest of Paul's stay at Corinth is quickly dismissed, though it may we
have lasted a month or two, during which time Paul continued his activi
undisturbed by the Jews. Perhaps he and Gallio did not meet again, b

18:19. They arrived at Ephesus and there Paul left them; but he himself entered the synagogue and had a discussion with the Jews.

---

both became victims to Nero, for Gallio was involved in the conspiracy of Piso, and was forced to kill himself shortly after the suicide of his brother Seneca (Tacitus, *Annal.,* XV, 73; XVI, 17). Deciding that the community at Corinth could manage on its own, Paul departed, but he followed its progress anxiously for some time. He sailed for Syria with the intention of going to Antioch (v. 22). With this in view, he disembarked at the port of Cenchrae (see notes on vv. 8 and 11) in company with the indefatigable travelers **Priscilla and Aquila** (see note on v. 2) and again set off after **having had his head shaved . . . because of a vow he had made.** Who had made the vow? Aquila or Paul? Grammatically, the phrase may apply to Aquila who is the last named in the text, but from the context it would seem that Aquila's share in these events was unimportant, and therefore the reference is more probably to Paul who is the subject of the narrative. This vow was probably a mitigated form of that associated with the ancient Hebrew rite of the "Nazarite" (Num. 6:2–21). Even Queen Bernice, whom Paul met later (25:13), *had come to Jerusalem to fulfil a vow to God, since there is the custom that those suffering from some illness or other trial, take a vow thirty days before the day on which they are to offer sacrifices to abstain (during this time) from wine and to shave their hair* (Flavius Josephus, *Wars of the Jews,* II, 313). The Mishna (*Nazir,* III, 6) also prescribed the thirty-day period for those entering Palestine from abroad. It should be noted, however, that while the "Nazarite" vow required that the hair should be cut at the end of the period of the vow, Bernice and — as far as can be seen — Paul, also, had their hair cut at the beginning. Later, Paul actually came to Jerusalem (v. 22), where those who had taken the real "Nazarite" vow had to present themselves to complete the vow by having their hair cut. The narrative gives no indication of Paul's motive in taking the vow, and all the suggestions put forward are without foundation. It is important, however, to note that, though he asserted the Christian's independence of the Jewish Law, he still practiced some of its observances. But he did this by his own personal free choice, and did not thereby establish a general rule which would oblige the converts from paganism; see note on 16:1–3. Another similar episode takes place in 21:23 sqq.

18:19. It is surprising that Paul, who embarked for Syria, landed at Ephesus, which is in Asia Minor opposite Corinth, much higher up than Syria. We must suppose, therefore, that Paul, not finding a ship that was going direct, took advantage of one that was going past Ephesus. — The

18:20. But when they besought him to stay some time longer, he did not consent,

18:21. but bidding them farewell and saying: "I will come back to you, God willing," he put to sea from Ephesus,

18:22. and landing at Caesarea, he went up [to Jerusalem] to pay his respects to the church, and then went down to Antioch.

Western Recension gives a reading in this and the following two verses which is substantially the same, save for one or two additions and changes Aquila's departure, expressly mentioned, takes place after the visit to the synagogue. Moreover, Paul expresses the firm intention of keeping the next feast at Jerusalem (probably in imitation of 20:16), and the Sabbath is mentioned as the day for the visit to the synagogue. These are variants which have the clear mark of a re-editing.

18:20. His stay was short, perhaps because the ship, having unloaded and reloaded, set sail again for Caesarea.

18:22. He went up, ἀναβάς: more literally, "having gone up"; this phrase is almost the official expression to signify a journey to Jerusalem (Lk 18:31; Mk. 10:32-33; etc.), therefore the name of the city is not mentioned The designation of **the church** also naturally suggests the mother Church at Jerusalem, since there is no reason to refer it to Caesarea. Paul most certainly could have visited the brethren at Caesarea since he was in that city, but it would have been purely a fraternal visit as he had no particular bond with that community which had been founded by Peter (10:1 sqq.). On the other hand, his visit to the mother Church at Jerusalem had a special significance, and was for the purpose of giving an account of his missionary journey which was now finishing, just as he had reported there after his first missionary journey (15:4). Nevertheless, the visit to Jerusalem was brief, not only because of the speed at which Paul journeyed, but perhaps also on account of a certain coolness in the reception given him by the Judaizing Christians of that city. Actually, the Judaizers had not yet got over the victory won by Paul at the Apostolic Council, and they were not at all satisfied with the crowds of uncircumcised pagans that he brought into the Church. Later, they will attempt something in the nature of an insurrection (cf. 21:20 sqq.), but for the moment they bided their time. Paul knew their attiude of mind well, so much so, that the next time he was due to come to Jerusalem he was afraid, not so much of his openly avowed enemies (20:22-23), as of deceitful brethren (Rom. 15:30-31). Paul must have felt ill at ease among these narrow-minded Judaizing Christians, so, in order to avoid the old contentions

18:23. After spending some time [there] he departed and traveled through the Galatian country and Phrygia in turn, strengthening all the disciples.

---

about the observance of the Jewish Law, he promptly left for Antioch. This fervent missionary center, which was to be the hub of Christian activity to the pagan world (see note on 11:20 sqq.; 13:1-2), suited Paul much better than the Judaizing circles of Jerusalem.

18:23. This verse concludes Paul's second missionary journey, begun at Antioch (15:35 sqq.; see note on 16:1-3), and immediately the third missionary journey begins. Here Luke's narrative is the very soul of brevity, the few words of this verse covering a period of several months. If Paul began his third journey in the spring of A.D. 53, this verse comprises the rest of this year and part of 54, after which Paul reached Ephesus (19:1), where Apollos already was before him (18:24). But for Luke, Ephesus is new territory for the preaching of the Gospel (since the brief reference of vv. 19-21 serves merely as a preparation for it), while **the Galatian country and Phrygia** are regions already visited on the preceding journey. Therefore the narrator passes over the regions previously visited, as in this verse, and dwells at some length on the sojourn in the new region of Ephesus. The designation, **the Galatian country and Phrygia,** has already been used in inverse order in 16:6; see there. Going directly from Antioch to **the Galatian country,** Paul would have had to cross the Taurus mountains through the Cilician Gates as he did on the previous journey (see note on 16:1-3), but thereafter, instead of preceeding west in the direction of Derbe, as on the previous occasion, he headed north and entered the Galatian country from the east. This second visit to Galatia is deduced from his epistle (Gal. 4:13), where Paul says that he evangelized them **the first time,** το πρότερον, on the occasion of his illness. But the expression "the first time" necessarily entails a "second time," and this present visit is just that. In fact, even when Paul had left the Galatians after his first visit, he followed the life of that community with concern, because he knew that the usual Judaizing Christians were trying to win them over to their teaching. There was good reason, therefore, to fear for these new converts, when account is taken of the fact that their fickleness was proverbial (Caesar, *De bello gallico,* II, 1; III, 10; IV, 5). Paul's present visit was directed at **strengthening** their faith so as to prevent their defection. For the time being this was achieved, but later the danger again threatened much more seriously, and then Paul wrote his epistle to the *Galatians.* — From **the Galatian country** Paul turned southwest and came into Phrygia. This region cor-

18:24. Now a certain Jew named Apollos, a native of Alexandria, came to Ephesus. He was an eloquent man, and mighty in the Scriptures.

18:25. He had been instructed in the Way of the Lord, and being fervent in spirit, used to speak and teach carefully whatever had to do with Jesus, though he knew of John's baptism only.

18:26. This man therefore began to speak confidently in the synagogue, and on hearing him, Priscilla and Aquila took him home and expounded the Way of God to him more precisely.

---

responded to **the upper districts** of proconsular Asia mentioned in 19:1, which Paul passed through to arrive at Ephesus. It seems that even at this time there may have been **disciples** in Phrygia, but we do not know for certain.

18:24. Before recounting the evangelization of Ephesus, Luke recalls an earlier episode, partly connecting it with what he has already told about Paul's previous very brief stay in that city (vv. 19–21). He had left Aquila and Priscilla there, but during Paul's absence, a certain person, hitherto unknown to us, namely Apollos, arrived there, and Luke presents this man and his activity. The Greek name Ἀπολλῶς is an abbreviation of Apollonius or Apollodorus. He is met with again in 1 Cor. 1:12; 3:4 sqq.; 16:12; Titus 3:13. Being a Hellenist Jew, born in Alexandria, he may have been a disciple of Philo, and even if he was not, he must have followed his exegetical school of Scripture, which, using an allegorical method, tried to reconcile Greek and Hebrew thought. It is in this sense that Apollos is here presented as **mighty in the Scriptures.** He was also a convincing and successful speaker, **an eloquent man** (λόγιος), and these accomplishments will gain him great successes among the Christians of Corinth, to the extent that some of them will form a group about him in preference to Paul himself: **I am of Paul! (but) I am of Apollos** (1 Cor. 1:12).

18:25–26. **The Way of the Lord:** like the **Way of God,** used later, means the teaching of the Gospel; see note on 9:2. After the word **instructed** the Western Recension (codex *Beza*) adds, **in his native city,** namely, in Alexandria, where Apollos would have heard for the first time **whatever had to do with Jesus.** This shows that the Gospel was already introduced into Alexandria at this time. However, this addition may be a mere inference drawn from the preceding references to his being **a native of Alexandria,** and his coming to **Ephesus.** The compiler of the Western Recension must have thought that since Apollos was

18:27. And as he wanted to go into Achaia, the brethren encouraging him wrote to the disciples to welcome him. On his arrival there, he was of great service by his eloquence to those who had believed,

---

already instructed when he arrived at Ephesus, he must have received such instruction in Alexandria. — **Fervent in spirit:** i.e., an ardent character with an active temperament. — **He ... used to teach carefully,** ἀκριβῶς: viz., he communicated to others with care and diligence what he knew of the Messias Jesus. But that does not mean that he taught all that was known of him. What he taught was true, but he did not possess the whole truth of the Christian teaching. The reason for this lack of complete knowledge was that **he knew of John's baptism only.** This fact is important and throws light on certain passages of the fourth Gospel. **John's baptism** was the rite practiced by John the Baptist which had great success in Palestine, spreading thence throughout the Diaspora. There is even greater evidence of this in the fourth Gospel, the first chapters of which underline more than once the full accord between John the Baptist and Jesus, showing the former's frank and open submission to Christ (cf. Jn. 1:15 sqq.; 3:26 sqq.; 5:33 sqq.; 10:41–42). This indicates that at the end of the first century when this Gospel was written, its author was still concerned with disciples of John the Baptist who were dissenting from the Messias Jesus, or at least were unaware of him. He was anxious, therefore, to call them to follow the Messias. Apollos was one of these. It seems that his knowledge of Jesus was limited to a very few facts about his life, though he knew more of the Old Testament prophecies *about Jesus* as the Messias. These were the prophecies to which Peter, Stephen, Philip, and Paul appealed in their discourses (2:16 sqq.; 3:12 sqq.; 7:51 sqq.; 8:32 sqq.; 13:22 sqq.; etc.). This explanation of a difficult passage seems to be supported by verse 28, according to which Apollos at Corinth showed according to **the Scriptures** that Jesus was the Messias. — Animated, therefore, by his ardent fervor, Apollos **began to speak confidently in the synagogue** at Ephesus, as Paul had already done (v. 19). But here he was heard by Priscilla and Aquila, who noted the accuracy of what he said, but also the lack of full knowledge in his teaching. They therefore supplied his deficiency, and **expounded ... to him** the Gospel teaching more precisely, i.e., with greater fullness.

18:27. The brethren encouraging him wrote ... : the phrase is not clear. The subject of **encouraging** is the Christians of Ephesus (**the brethren**), but the object can be Apollos himself, or the **Disciples** of Corinth. In the first case, the sense would be, they *encouraged* (*him*), namely, to go to Achaia. In the second case, it would mean that *the brethren wrote to*

The Third

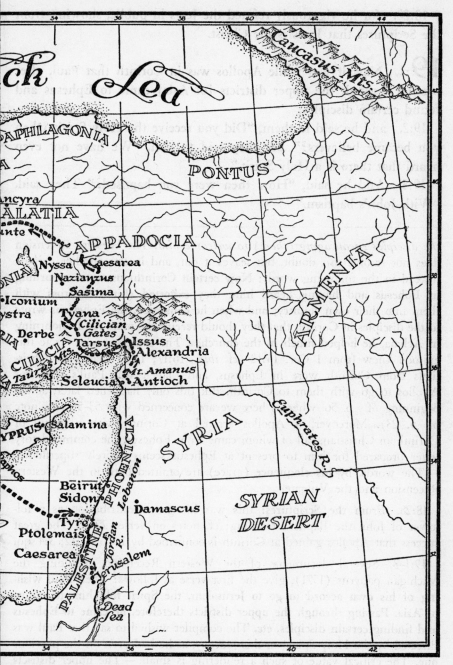

Missionary Journey

18:28. for he vigorously refuted the Jews in public, showing from the Scriptures that Jesus is the Christ.

19:1.

Now it was while Apollos was in Corinth that Paul, after passing through the upper districts [of Asia] came to Ephesus and found certain disciples;

19:2. and he said to them, "Did you receive the Holy Spirit when you became believers?" But they said to him, "We have not even heard that there is a Holy Spirit."

19:3. And he said, "How then were you baptised?" They said, "With John's baptism."

---

the disciples encouraging (them) to welcome him. The Western Recension does not resolve this doubt, but leaves it out, and inserts another episode instead in the following words: **Now certain Corinthians were sojourning in Ephesus and having heard him, they exhorted (him) to cross with them into their own country; and when he consented, the Ephesians wrote to the disciples in Corinth that they should receive the man. And sojourning in Achaia, he helped much in the churches.** The compiler who wrote this episode knew from 1 Cor. 16:12 (cf. *ibid.*, 16:17; 1:11) that some Christians from Corinth were in Ephesus, and that it was Paul's wish for Apollos to go with them to Corinth. But this only happened later, at the beginning of A.D. 56, whereas here we are concerned with 53–54 (see note on v. 23). Moreover, if Apollos arrived at Corinth with a group of Corinthian Christians, all of whom came from Ephesus, the commendatory letter prepared for him to present at Ephesus seems entirely superfluous. — The words, **by his eloquence** (grace) are omitted both in the Western Recension and the Vulgate.

18:28. From the Scriptures: this was his great contribution as a follower of John the Baptist's teaching; cf. notes on verses 25–26. The great success that Apollos gained at Corinth is confirmed by 1 Cor. 1:12; 3:4 sqq.

19:1-3. Several documents of the Western Recension, including the Michigan papyrus (1571), give the first verse as follows: **Then Paul wishing of his own accord to go to Jerusalem, the Spirit told him to return to Asia. Passing through the upper districts therefore, he came to Ephesus and finding certain disciples, etc.** The compiler wished to say that Paul was directed by the Holy Spirit on this journey, as he had been on the previous one. The critical value of such a rendering is small. — The **upper districts** are those of proconsular Asia of which Ephesus was the capital. In ancient times, the "upper districts" of a region were those inland, as opposed to

19:4. Then Paul said: "John baptised the people with a baptism of repentance, telling them to believe in him who was to come after him, that is, in Jesus."

19:5. On hearing this, they were baptised in the name of the Lord Jesus;

---

the "lower districts" which lay along the coast, where Ephesus actually was. The **upper districts**, then, are Phrygia (cf. note on 18:23). The preceding events took place while Paul was staying in Galatia and Phrygia. Paul came to Ephesus only after Apollos had left there for Corinth. Ephesus, which is now a scene of desolation, was in those days, commercially and politically, the chief city of Asia Minor. Its shrine of Artemis or Diana (19:24 sqq.), which was one of the most famous of the Roman Empire, gave it a special importance among the pagan worshipers. (For a description of the city and the recent archaeological discoveries, cf. G. Ricciotti, *Paul the Apostle,* pp. 12–16, 344 sqq.) Paul found **certain disciples** in this city, *viz.,* those who had accepted the faith (πιστεύσαντες) and become believers. These are the terms Luke usually uses for faithful Christians. But these disciples at Ephesus had not received Christian baptism, and did not even know of the existence of the Holy Spirit. They had only received **John's baptism.** They were, therefore, in the same condition as Apollos had been when he first came to Ephesus (cf. note on 18:24–26), and they had probably been his companions and disciples. They were, then, only half Christians as it were, on their way toward Christianity, and we must conclude that Luke calls them **disciples** in this wide sense, and says that they had *accepted the faith.* John the Baptist had actually prepared for the coming of Christ, and anyone who sincerely accepted the teaching of John, implicitly accepted that of Jesus (cf. v. 4). It is to be noted that Paul asks them if they had received (the) **Holy Spirit** (without the article), to find out if they were Christians. The possession of the charisms given by the Holy Spirit was the distinctive note of anyone who had been incorporated into Christ's Church (see note on 2:38; 8:18–19).—The reply of those questioned is surprising. They do not know **even** if **there** is (ἔστιν) a Holy Spirit. This answer must have seemed irreverent or otherwise unbefitting to some compilers, since these words are substituted in some documents of the Western Recension by the following: "We have not even heard that **such receive** the Holy Spirit."— **How then (in what),** εἰς τί: in the neuter; the word **name** (neuter in Greek) is to be understood in connection with verse 5; thus it would read: **in what name,** etc.

19:4. Cf. 1:5; 11:16; 13:24–25.

19:5-6. For the formula, "to baptize **in the name of Jesus Christ,**" see

19:6. and when Paul laid his hands on them, the Holy Spirit came upon them, and they began to speak in tongues and to prophesy.

19:7. There were about twelve men in all.

19:8. Now for three months he used to go to the synagogue and speak confidently, holding discussions and trying to persuade them about the kingdom of God.

19:9. But when some were obstinate and refused to believe, speaking evil of the Way [of the Lord] before the community, he left them and withdrew his disciples from them, and held daily discussions in the school of one Tyrannus.

---

note on 2:38. Two distinct rites are described here. The first is the administration of baptism (v. 5), then Paul lays his hands on those baptized, and **the Holy Spirit came upon them,** with the consequent manifestation of glossolaly and the other charisms (v. 6); see note on 8:15-17. We are not told who administered the baptism. Probably it was not Paul, who baptized only on rare occasions (cf. 1 Cor. 1:14-17), but one of his assistants who were with him at Ephesus, such as Timothy and Erastus (v. 22), or Gaius and Aristarchus (v. 29), or Sosthenes (1 Cor. 1:1). Here, too, the Western Recension has seen fit to add the words, **for a remission of sins,** after the name, **the Lord Jesus.** Perhaps it was intended to show that only the baptism of Jesus, and not that of John, remitted sin.

19:7. About twelve men, ἄνδρες: probably excluding women and children.

19:8. The **synagogue** is the one mentioned before (18:19-20), where he had received a welcome.

19:9. The **Way [of the Lord]:** see note on 18:25-26. Just as, in Corinth, Paul had left the synagogue and moved into the house of Titius Justus (18:7), so here in Ephesus he established a center for his activity, *withdrawing* the disciples he had made *to the school of Tyrannus,* holding discussions there *every day.* The name **Tyrannus** and **school** (σχολή) are typically Grecian, and make one think of a man and an institute of Greek origin rather than Jewish. The Greek "school" was a place for imparting regular instructions, or for passing free time in intellectual pursuits. Tyrannus may have been a Greek rhetorician who gave regular lessons in the morning in a "hall," or school, which was then free in the afternoons. He, therefore, let Paul have the use of it, either gratis or for payment, for his meetings in the afternoons. The Western Recension, in fact, adds after the name **Tyrannus: from the fifth to the tenth hour,** which would be from about eleven in the morning until four in the afternoon of our time.

19:10. Now this went on for two years, so that all who lived in the province of Asia, both Jews and Gentiles, heard the word of the Lord.

This information may well be authentic, and in any case is inherently likely. The ancients were very early risers, and they began the day's business at dawn and continued until near noon. The afternoons were reserved for leisure, amusement, rest, and recreation, including the frequenting of a "school." Paul, instead, did twice as much work. In the mornings he worked at the weaver's loom to earn his living. In the afternoons he went to the hall of Tyrannus to speak there about the Messias Jesus, and to debate in public with those who chanced to listen to him.

19:10. This hard life, further burdened with the anxiety for all the churches he had founded (2 Cor. 11:28), and with which he maintained close contact by letters, lasted **for two years,** viz., from about the end of A.D. 54 to the end of 56. By adding to this the three months spoken of in verse 8, and the other unspecified time of verse 22, we arrive at a total of about **three years** fixed by Paul as the length of his stay in proconsular Asia (20:31; cf. 18). Moreover, Paul records how during this time he suffered **trials that befell me because of the plots of the Jews** (20:19), who never forgave him for his secession from the synagogue. We have no particular information on these plots, but it can easily be gathered from the veiled allusions in 1 Cor. 15:32; 2 Cor. 1:8-9; Rom. 16:3-4, that they were of a serious nature. Notwithstanding his long experience of hostility of every kind and his fortitude in facing it, Paul at a certain point felt very desperate. In the autumn of A.D. 57 he recalls **the affliction which came upon us in Asia. We were crushed beyond measure — beyond our strength, so that we were weary even of life** (2 Cor. 1:8). Even before that, writing from Ephesus to the Corinthians in the spring of 56, he draws this picture of his apostolate: **To this very hour we hunger and thirst and we are naked and buffeted and have no fixed abode. And we toil, working with our own hands. We are reviled and we bless, we are persecuted and we bear with it, we are maligned and we entreat, we have become as the refuse of this world, the offscouring of all, even until now** (1 Cor. 4:11-13). Despite all this, his apostolate was most fruitful and the Christian message reached **all** the inhabitants of proconsular Asia. This agrees with what Paul writes from Ephesus to the Corinthians: **For a door has been opened to me, great and evident,** yet immediately he adds that **there are many adversaries** (1 Cor. 16:9). The Christian message spread from Ephesus, the capital of the province of Asia, to the 500 cities throughout the country.

19:11. And God worked miracles of no ordinary kind by the hands of Paul,

19:12. so that handkerchiefs and aprons which had touched his body were taken away [to apply] to the sick, and their diseases left them, and the evil spirits went out.

19:13. But certain itinerant Jewish exorcists also attempted to invoke the name of the Lord Jesus over those who had evil spirits in them, saying: "I adjure you by the Jesus whom Paul preaches."

People came to Ephesus from these cities on their business and there by chance heard Paul in the hall of Tyrannus. Many were convinced by his teaching, and returning home spread what they had learned. It was Paul's plan to foster the development of these first contacts, sending to these places this one or that of his companions (named in the note on vv. 5-6). He met other occasional helpers when they came to Ephesus. In this way communities arose in the country along the river Lycus, i.e., at Laodicea, Colossae, and Hierapolis. Paul himself had never been to these places and was personally unknown there, although he sent letters to those communities. The chief propagator of the Gospel in those regions was Epaphras, a wealthy Greek of Colossae, who had probably known Paul at Ephesus in the school of Tyrannus, and had been converted by him. The same may have happened to Philemon who was also from Colossae, and to whom Paul addressed the short epistle which is still extant.

9:11-12. No ordinary kind: one of Luke's expressions for *extraordinary*: he uses it again in 28:2. Paul's apostolate was accompanied and favored by miracles, as had already happened to the Apostles in general, and to Peter in particular (2:43; 5:12-16). These **handkerchiefs** were large ones, used in the East for wiping the forehead or covering the head, rather like those used today by the peasants of the Roman countryside. The **aprons** were those strips of cloth which covered the front half of the dress, whence the name in Greek — which is taken from the Latin — of *semicinctium*. Workmen also used them to protect their clothes while they worked, and so Paul too must have used one, working at the loom. Those who sought these objects of Paul must have been not so much the Christians, who were still only few, but rather the pagans, prompted by the undoubtable benefits which they received from them. Thus they anticipated, in a certain sense, the cult of relics, which developed later in the Church.

19:13. While Paul's fame as a wonder-worker make him known in and around Ephesus, thereby gaining him the friendship of some distinguished citizens (cf. v. 31), his miracles made him appear in the eyes

19:14. There were seven sons of a certain Sceva, a Jewish high priest, who were doing this;

---

of the pagans as somebody surrounded by an aura of mysterious power, just like Peter and John before Simon Magus (cf. 8:18 sqq.). Simon's attempt to acquire the Apostles' power was repeated here at Ephesus in another way, by **itinerant Jewish exorcists.** An exorcist was one who freed a possessed person from the devil using special formulas. Jesus himself had been accused by the Pharisees of casting out devils by Beelzebub, the prince of devils, and in reply pointed out that there were exorcists among the disciples of the Pharisees (Mt. 12:24–27; Lk. 11:15–19). Moreover, the practice of exorcising among the Jews is widely attested in Jewish writings. According to Flavius Josephus, Solomon had left efficacious formulas for exorcism against the devils, and Josephus himself witnessed their efficacy in several cases of possessed persons cured in the presence of Vespasian (*Antiquities of the Jews*, VIII, 45–48). The same historian speaks of a special root that grew in the neighborhood of Macherontes which was much sought after, because *the so-called demons, which are no other than the spirits of the wicked that enter into men that are alive, and kill them, unless they can obtain some help against them, are quickly driven away by this root, even when it is only brought to sick persons* (*Wars of the Jews*, VII, 185). The Talmud gives formulas of conjurations as follows: *Lul, Shaphan, Anigron and Anirdaphon, I sit among the stars, I walk among lean men and fat men.* For individual cases, like that against Shabriri, the demon of blindness, there existed the formula: *My mother said to me: Guard thyself from Shabriri, Briri, Riri, Iri, Ri* (by repeating the name of the demon and leaving out one syllable or letter of his name every time, it was believed that the demon himself gradually vanished). Other formulas have been found in papyri and prayer tablets which contain isolated words (φρίξ, φρόξ, ἄσκιον, κατάσκιον, BESCU, BEREBESCU, etc.), probably derived from the *Ephesia grammata* (see note on vv. 18–19). Obviously, in practice, the step from exorcism to magic was a short one, and often the exorcist acted as a magician (cf. notes on 8:9–11; 13:6). These **Jewish exorcists** were **itinerant** (περιερχομένων) since they went from place to place practicing their art, and had come to Ephesus, a place much favored by magicians (cf. v. 19). Knowing and seeing Paul's power over demons, they imagined that he was one of their profession, though much abler than they, and so they **attempted** to steal and use his secret. As the name of the deity in virtue of which exorcisms were performed was a most important element, they used the name of that celestial being, Jesus, preached by Paul, with the words: **I adjure you by the Jesus whom Paul preaches.**

19:14. This **Sceva** (Σκευᾶ, in the genitive) seems to be a name derived

19:15. but the evil spirit answered and said to them: "Jesus I acknowledge, and of Paul I am aware, but who are you?"

19:16. And the man in whom the evil spirit was, sprang at them, and mastering both of them overpowered them, so that they fled from that house naked and wounded.

---

from the Latin, *scaeva,* "a lefthanded person," from which comes the diminutive *Scaevola,* the surname of the famous Mucius Scaevola. Since we are dealing here with proconsular Asia, it should be remembered that there was a governor of Asia named Q. Mucio Scaevola, who left such a pleasant memory that the inhabitants of those parts instituted the feast "Mucia" in his honor. On the other hand, we do not know of any **Jewish high priest** of that name, but this can be explained by supposing that he belonged to a high-priestly family, and the honorary title was extended to all the members of the family. There were **seven sons** of Sceva (this number does not appear in the Western Recension). The following coincidences should be noted, even though they are purely fortuitous. *Seven* in Hebrew is *seba;* the father's name is *Sceva,* which therefore could represent the pronunciation of *sceba* (the letter *b* and *v* were often interchanged, i.e., cf. the name *David,* written Δαυίδ and sometimes Δαβίδ). The Hebrew verb "to perform exorcisms," *nīsbʿa,* is derived from the numeral *seven,* almost as if it meant "septenate." The Western Recension greatly amplified this verse which, with a minimum of variants, can be rendered as follows: **Among whom the sons of a certain priest Sceva also wished to do the same — they were accustomed to exorcise such persons — and going in to the possessed, they began to invoke the name saying: We command you in Jesus, whom Paul preaches, to go out, etc.** Substantially this is simply an arbitrary application of the preceding verse to a single case, but the number **seven** and the words, **Jewish high** (priest) are suppressed. It can be supposed that the author of this text, being scandalized at the thought of a Jewish high priest whose seven sons practiced magic, attempted to portray him simply as a pagan priest, like the one of Lystra (14:13). If he had such a scruple, he must have falsely supposed that Sceva's seven sons were not included among the **Jewish exorcists** of verse 13.

19:16. Both (ἀμφοτέρων) refers to the exorcists. Taking it in the numerical sense, it would seem that only two of the seven brothers tried to exorcise the possessed man. But there are examples in the papyri from the second century A.D., in which *both* is used for four or five persons, thus losing the exact numerical significance, and meaning more a totality. Such seems to

19:17. And this became known to all the Jews and Greeks who dwelt in Ephesus, and fear fell on them all, and the name of the Lord Jesus was magnified.

19:18. And many of those who believed came confessing and declaring their practices;

19:19. and many who had practised magical arts, having collected their books together [in one place], burned them publicly: and they reckoned up their value, and found that [it amounted to] fifty thousand silver pieces.

---

have been the case here, for the Syriac version translates it by all, referring to the seven brothers: perhaps there is a similar case in 23:8.

19:17. Fear: see note on 2:43; (5:11).

19:18-19. The foregoing episode made an impression on the neophytes (those who believed) of Ephesus also, who before their conversion, had followed magical practices (περίεργα), which flourished greatly in that city. These now openly repudiated (confessed by surrendering) their magical arts (πράξεις, a technical term found in the papyri) and since they had still kept many of these superstitious objects on their persons or in their homes, they now gathered them all together and destroyed them. Such objects are here called **books**, but actually they were leaflets or little scrolls, known in ancient times as the *Ephesia grammata*. They contained little combinations of letters of the alphabet, or words, or special formulas which were considered to have magic powers in cases of illness, gambling, love, and the like. At first, they were probably imitations of the inarticulate and meaningless sounds given forth by the soothsayers of the temple. Then gradually there grew up a whole trade in these texts which, when worn on the body or kept in the house, could be helpful in numerous situations in daily life. Magicians especially recommended them to the possessed, as Plutarch relates (*Sympos.*, VII, 5, 4). Clement of Alexandria records a few brief examples (*Stromata*, V, 8, 42). The wholesale destruction of them recorded here was not a unique case; elsewhere in ancient times, similar public bonfires of obscene and filthy literature took place (Titus Livy, XL, 29; Seutonius, *Divus August.*, 31). — The sum of **fifty thousand silver pieces** (drachmas) is reckoned as having a present-day value of about £1,800–2,000 ($5,000–$6,000), an enormous sum for those times, but one must bear in mind that quite apart from the mere quantity of the books destroyed, the bonfire was a most expensive one, involving the destruction of possessions which were valued both for sentimental reasons as well as for the precious materials from which they were made.

19:20. Thus mightily did the word of the Lord spread and prevail.
19:21. After all this, Paul made up his mind to go to Jerusalem,
passing through Macedonia and Achaia, saying: "After I have been
there, I must also see Rome."
19:22. So he sent two of his assistants, Timothy and Erastus, into
Macedonia, while he himself stayed on for a while in Asia.

19:20. This is one of those characteristic summaries of the situation, so
dear to Luke; see 6:17; 12:24.

19:21–22. Luke, who has narrated the events at Ephesus up to the end
of A.D. 56 (see note on v. 10), now relates in these two verses the episode
which provoked Paul's departure from that city. But as he does not intend
to give a detailed account he leaves out certain events, which, however, we
can partially supply from the information found in the two epistles to
the Corinthians. Already toward the end of A.D. 55, Paul had received disquieting news about the community at Corinth, which induced him to send
Timothy there from Ephesus (1 Cor. 4:17; 16:10). This mission of Timothy
is different from that related here in verse 22. The first time he was sent to
Corinth was at the end of A.D. 55. His mission to Macedonia was at the end
of 56 (1 Cor. 16:5–6). In the spring of 56, Paul sent the *First Epistle to the
Corinthians* to help Timothy in his work at Corinth. Toward the autumn
Timothy returned to Ephesus, bringing bad news from Corinth where
things were deteriorating so much that only Paul's presence could remedy
the situation. Paul, therefore, made a very quick visit to Corinth, which
is implicitly but clearly attested in 2 Cor. 12:14; 13:1–2 (Greek text), though
it is not mentioned in the *Acts*. At the end of A.D. 56, Paul, having returned
to Ephesus, sent Timothy into Macedonia as narrated here in verse 22
and also another letter, the one written **with many tears** (2 Cor. 2:4; 7:8)
which has not come down to us. Toward May of A.D. 57, the riot of the
silversmiths, described here by Luke, took place. This forced Paul to leave
Ephesus. Having reached Macedonia in the summer of this same year, he
met Titus who had returned from Corinth with good news, and shortly
afterward Paul wrote the *Second Epistle to the Corinthians*. (For the
whole of this intricate question, see G. Ricciotti, *Paul the Apostle*, pp.
363 sqq.) — Paul's plan here was first of all to make a visit of encouragement to the communities founded on his second missionary journey in
Macedonia and Achaia, then one to **Jerusalem**, and finally a journey to
Rome. For many years he had had the desire to visit Rome (Rom. 15:23)
and he hoped to combine it with a visit to Spain (*ibid.,* 15:24). Beginning
with the most recently founded communities, Paul sent **Timothy and
Erastus** into Macedonia to prepare for his coming. The first named had

19:23. Now about that time there arose no small disturbance in regard to the Way of the Lord.

19:24. For a certain silversmith named Demetrius, who used to make silver shrines of Diana and provided no little business for the craftsmen;

19:25. having gathered them together along with the workmen of like occupation said: "Men, you know that our wealth comes from this trade,

---

returned from Corinth about a year previously. Erastus does not appear to be the same person as the one named in Rom. 16:23, and in 2 Tim. 4:20, but a namesake of his of whom we know nothing else. We do not know precisely how long Paul prolonged his stay **for a while** in proconsular Asia, but it could not have been for very long (see note on v. 10). At the end of it, took place the riot of the silversmiths, which Luke now relates.

19:23. This episode is one of the most vivid and colorful in the *Acts.* Even today, the archaeologist with the text in his hand can follow the route followed by the mob. If the crowd was collected by Demetrius in the Roman market place, as seems most likely, in order to reach the *theater,* it must have gone along the road still existing which was later called the Arcadian Way. Historically speaking, the social setting of the episode is that of a city of Asia Minor which lived on its commerce and its traditional institutions. But the description of the behavior of the crowd, impulsive, irresponsible, and changeable, like all mobs of all times and everywhere, is most striking and characteristic of crowd psychology. Luke is not speaking here as an eyewitness of the event, for he was not in Ephesus at that time, but he would have been told of it by those who were present, perhaps by **Aristarchus** spoken of in verse 29, who later sailed with him to Rome, or by Paul himself, or by **Gaius** of verse 29, or others not named. — For the expression, **about that time,** see note on 12:1. — The disturbance was **no small** one, Luke's usual way of saying "great"; see note on 12:18. — The **Way (of the Lord):** see note on 18:25–26; 19:9.

19:24. This **Demetrius** was not only a **silversmith** himself, but was also at the head of a number of **craftsmen** for whom he provided **no little** (the customary litotes for "much") **business.** Such associations of workers are mentioned several times in inscriptions with the name of συνεργασίαι ("co-operatives"), and they had great influence in the social and political life of Greek cities. Demetrius addresses both the craftsmen (τεχνῖται) and the workmen (ἐργάται). The former were probably the more skillful workers

who put the finishing touches to the objects fashioned from precious
metals, while the latter were the ordinary unskilled workers. At any rate,
both classes depended on Demetrius who, like a large-scale contractor,
collected orders and then distributed them, with profit for himself, to his
various dependents. His industry consisted in making silver shrines
(ναοὺς ἀργυροῦς), namely, models of the temple of Diana at Ephesus, reproduced in miniature with a little statue of the goddess inside. Such reproductions or "little temples" (ναΐσκοι, or aediculae; cf. Amianus Marcellinus,
XXII, 13; Dion Cassius, XXXIX, 20) were very popular with pilgrims.
They were also made in such cheap materials as stone or terra cotta, as
well as in precious metals as were those produced by Demetrius. Excavations at Ephesus have brought to light several of the cheaper kind, but
none made from precious metals, since they must certainly have been
stolen in ancient times because of their intrinsic value. The large models
and those of stone or common material could be set up outdoors, while
the smaller ones served as offerings (ex-votos) for the temple of the
goddess in Ephesus, or were kept at home for private devotion. The
temple was also inscribed on coins and medals, and even at the time of
Valentinian I (fourth century) such coins were minted, some of which
are still extant. — The publisher of the Greek inscriptions of the British
Museum, Hicks, identified the Demetrius mentioned here with one named
in an inscription from Ephesus of the second half of the first century A.D.
as νεωποιός, which was the title of the magistrates entrusted with the care
of the temples. Such magistrates are also recorded in inscriptions from
Delos, Halicarnassus, Magnesia, Sardis, and elsewhere. Proceeding further,
Hicks suggested that the present account comes from a misinterpretation
by Luke who considered that Greek term as designating one who exercised
the art of making these "little temples." But Hick's hypothesis is very
doubtful on documentary grounds, because the inscription on which he
bases it is damaged, and only the first letter of the word which he
restores to Ν(εωποιός) remains. In actual fact, it could be restored with
the names of other magistrates beginning likewise with the letter Ν.
Moreover, while the name Demetrius does not prove anything since it was
a very common name, the speech he makes to the workmen has no connection with the magistrature of the νεωποιός, whereas it contains several
references to the industry of the "little temples," and the existence of
this industry is entirely confirmed both by early historians and archaeological discoveries. — Diana (or Artemis) was the goddess of the great
temple of Ephesus, the Artemision, regarded by the ancients as one of
the seven wonders of the world. Its origins are legendary. When in 559 B.C.
Croesus captured Ephesus (Herodotus, I, 26), he was responsible for the
complete remodeling of the temple which emerged as a building of very
great splendor. But in the year 356 B.C., it was burned down by Erostratus

19:26. "and you see and hear that not only at Ephesus, but almost over all [the province of] Asia, this man Paul has persuaded and

---

on the night of the birth of Alexander the Great, while the goddess was busy assisting at the birth. Immediately, reconstruction was begun which proceeded very slowly, but eventually resulted in a building two thirds the size of the basilica of St. Peter's in Rome. According to Pliny's description (*Nat. hist.,* XXXVI, 21) it contained 127 columns presented by as many kings, each column being 60 feet high, and 36 of them adorned with sculptured bas-reliefs. The best Greek artists, Polycletus, Praxiteles, Scopas, had contributed to the magnificence of the temple with their master-pieces. Later, cults of foreign divinities were introduced. The Romans, who bestowed favors on the temple, introduced there the cult of the goddess Roma and that of the emperor. Originally the goddess worshiped in the temple was certainly not the Artemis or Diana of Greek mythology, the young virgin huntress, daughter of Latona and Jupiter, but — as Jerome pointed out (*Prol. in Epist. ad Ephesios*) — this goddess was a divinity of an entirely different kind, one with multiple breasts (*multimammia,* πολυμαστός), which showed her distinctive characteristic, viz., *bestiarum et viventium esse nutricem* ("the nurse of animals and living things"). This must have been a primitive fetish which the popular fancy decided had fallen from heaven (v. 35), and the statue of it was copied in several reproductions which went far afield from proconsular Asia, and some have even come down to us today. The numerous breasts show that the goddess belonged to the group of nature divinities, and personified fecundity. Many feasts were celebrated in her honor throughout the year. In the shrine of Ortygia, a little south of the city, special mysteries were celebrated to commemorate the birth of the goddess as Diana. The principal role in these mystery rites seems to have been played by the college of Curetes. At the time of Paul, the worship of the goddess was no longer presided over, as it had been in the past, by a eunuch high priest (called the Megabyzos), but was entrusted to the priestesses who had to remain virgins throughout their term of service. This was a purely legal reminder of the "virgin goddess" Diana, since the various rites of the cult comprised obscene orgies and sexual depravity. The temple enjoyed the "right of asylum." Evildoers of all kinds took refuge in its enclosure to escape justice or wandered around the city, ready to flee to it when they were pursued. At the time of Tiberius, an attempt was made to abolish this troublesome privilege, but a delegation of Ephesians hurried to defend the rights they had acquired in this matter (Tacitus, *Annal.,* III, 60–61).

19:26. In the Greek there are two genitives, **of Ephesus . . . of all Asia,** but they refer to the **multitude (numbers of people)** which follows. It turned away numbers of people, saying, 'Gods made by human hands are not gods at all.'

19:27. "It is not only that this branch [of our industry] runs the risk of being discredited, but also that the temple of the great goddess Diana [is in danger] of being regarded as nothing, and she would even be deposed from her magnificence, whom all Asia and the world worships."

19:28. On hearing this they were filled with wrath, and cried out, saying, "Great [is] Diana of the Ephesians!"

19:29. And the city was filled with confusion, and they rushed by a common impulse into the theatre, dragging along the Macedonians Gaius and Aristarchus, Paul's fellow-travellers.

19:30. But when Paul wanted to go before [the assembly of] the people, the disciples would not let him;

19:31. and some of the Asiarchs who were friends of his, sent to him and begged him not to venture into the theatre.

---

does not seem likely that they are to be understood in the locative sense. Demetrius' denunciation of Paul's successes confirms this statement in verse 10. — Are not gods: this remark of Demetrius is correct, since Paul both as a former rabbi and a Christian Apostle could not but reprove the idolatry of which the worship of Diana was a glaring example.

19:27. Branch is in the Greek portion or share, and refers surely to the trade of the silversmiths, and as a consequence, to their threatened profit (cf. v. 26). But Demetrius very cleverly passes over this mundane consideration and rises to lofty religious motives (the temple of the great . . . Diana), and patriotism (all Asia, etc.). He was speaking chiefly *pro aris et focis.* — The world: cf. note on 11:28; 17:6. Demetrius' remark was not an exaggeration. Not only ancient writers attest that Diana of Ephesus was worshiped everywhere, but recent excavations have shown the existence of her cult in many regions of Asia, Africa, and Europe.

19:28-31. Here we have the typical behavior of a mob which gets aroused at the first incitement, without considering the motives of it, and immediately lets off steam by shouting and getting worked up (confusion) for no special reason. The town clerk later draws the crowd's attention to this impulsive behavior (v. 36 sqq.). The meeting of the silversmiths probably took place in the Roman market place, but as the disturbance spread through the city, and the crowd grew bigger, they went into the theatre (cf. note on v. 23), which was used for meetings, to decide on their action. In the meantime, the crowd's indignation had received partial satisfaction from seizing **the Macedonians Gaius and Aristarchus, Paul's fellow-travellers,** and dragging them to the theater. Some of the rioters, who were probably better informed, had gone to Paul's lodging, but not finding him there, either because he was absent or for some other reason (see later in this note), had therefore captured his two companions. In 16:19, the reverse happened, viz., Paul was captured and his companions escaped. **Aristarchus** is undoubtedly the future companion of Paul on his journey to Rome and during his Roman imprisonment (27:2; Col. 4:10; Philemon 24), and his nationality as a **Macedonian** is confirmed in 20:4, where he is called a **Thessalonian.** As for **Gaius,** since he was a **Macedonian** also, he cannot be the Gaius of Corinth (see note on 18:8), nor the Gaius spoken of in 20:4, who, according to the greater number of readings given by the codices, was from Derbe in Lycaonia (cf. 14:6 and 20–21; 16:1). In any case, Gaius was a very common name. Another person of the same name is mentioned in 3 Jn. 1. If these two were captured in the house where Paul was lodging, as we are led to believe, it can well be supposed that this was the hospitable dwelling of Aquila and Priscilla (cf. 18:18, 19, 26). This suggestion seems to be borne out by Paul's remark, when at the beginning of A.D. 58, writing to the Romans, he bids them salute **Prisca and Aquila, my helpers in Christ Jesus, who for my life have risked their own necks** (Rom. 16:3–4). This last phrase which is found in the papyri, and is similar to that of **giving one's eyes for someone** (Gal. 4:15), shows that this couple deliberately risked death to save Paul's life. We do not know the time nor the place in which this act of courage occurred, but one's mind naturally turns to the riot of the silversmiths, when by some ingenious though risky plan, these faithful friends saved their guest Paul from the fury of the mob. As he left Ephesus immediately after the riot, so they departed shortly afterward, making their way to Rome. — Two acts of generosity are then described, one on the part of Paul, the other on that of the **Asiarchs.** Paul, finding himself safe, but knowing that his two companions were in immediate danger, wished to save them also by appearing in person before the crowd in the **theatre.** It is true that in a city like Ephesus, ruled by Roman laws, he was safe-guarded by his Roman citizenship, but on this occasion rather more in theory than in practice, for the outcome would have been the same as at Philippi (16:19 sqq.), such was the fury of the mob. The Christians (disciples) knew this only too well, and therefore prevented his attempt. The same advice was given by means of a messenger by **some of the Asiarchs who were friends of his.** The office of Asiarch was connected with the "Asiatic assembly" (κοινὸν Ἀσίας), an ancient religious institution which from the time of Augustus had acquired particular importance, since it provided for the worship of the goddess Roma, and later that

19:32. Meanwhile, some were shouting one thing and some another; for the assembly was in confusion, and most of them did not know why they had gathered together.

19:33. Then [some] of the crowd called upon Alexander, as the Jews were pushing him forward; and Alexander, motioning with his hand, wanted to give an explanation to the people.

19:34. But as soon as they saw that he was a Jew, one cry broke out from all, and for about two hours they continued shouting: "Great [is] Diana of the Ephesians."

---

of the emperor. This assembly, to which every principal city sent delegates, met at intervals to discuss administrative questions, and it was accompanied by religious festivals and games. The president had the title of **Asiarch.** It appears also, though it is not certain, that he was given the title of "high priest of (proconsular) Asia," because of the religious character of the assembly. As the number of cities which erected their own temples to emperor worship increased — following the example of Pergamum — so the number of Asiarchs multiplied. Even those who had relinquished office continued to hold this honorary title, just as in the case of the office of high priest among the Jews at that time. Similarly, in other provinces, there were Bithyniarchs (for Bithynia), Galatarchs (for Galatia), and so on. These Asiarchs of Ephesus, money-loving and ambitious, were almost certainly not Christians, and yet they were **friends** of Paul, and had his safety at heart. This confirms his great fame and the prestige he enjoyed (vv. 10, 17, 26).

19:32. A simple but very telling description. It constitutes what we might call a picture of a madding crowd. Nor is irony missing **(most of them did not know why they had gathered together).**

19:33-34. This is an obscure passage, both as regards the words and the facts. — **Called upon** is in the Greek, συνεβίβασαν, the reading given by the best codices. Other documents give προεβίβασαν, **brought forward;** codex *Beza* gives κατεβίβασαν, **made him descend,** cf. the Vulgate, *detraxerunt* **(drew forth).** The subject of the verb is [some] of the crowd, who induced **Alexander** to put himself forward to speak to the people. Seeing that Alexander was a Jew, the **some** who put him forward must also have been Jews, and they did it in their own interest. Therefore, if Alexander wished to speak to the crowd in the theater, it was because he wished to give an explanation and defense for his own Jewish co-religionists. We know nothing about this Alexander other than what is related here, just as the information on Jason (17:5-9) and Sosthenes (18:17) was like-

19:35. But when the town clerk had quieted the crowd, he said: "Men of Ephesus, what man indeed is there who does not know that the city of the Ephesians is temple-warden of the great Diana and of the statue which fell down from Jupiter?

19:36. "Since therefore these things are beyond dispute, you ought to be quiet and do nothing rash.

---

wise brief. The Jews at Ephesus, having the right of citizenship, were able to take part in public meetings, but certainly not in idolatrous worship in honor of Diana or any other pagan divinity. This put them in a bad light with the pagans since, in the Hellenistic mind, the worship of the city deities was an integral part of civic duty. Probably those who **called upon** Alexander wished him to show in his speech that the Jews of Ephesus were not responsible in any way for the anti-idolatrous preaching of Paul, and therefore the fury of the crowd should not be directed against them. But the project failed. Alexander, **motioning with his hand** for silence (cf. 13:16), could hardly begin to speak before the crowd recognized **that he was a Jew.** It was like adding fuel to a fire, for though Paul's preaching against idolatry was recent, the aversion of the Jews to any idolatrous worship was well known long before. Not only, therefore, did they not allow him to speak, but they forestalled him by shouting **for about two hours, "Great [is] Diana of the Ephesians!"** The cry must have been commonplace among the Ephesians (cf. vv. 27, 35), and the title of **great** is also found attributed to Diana in inscriptions. After shouting at the top of their voices for two hours, the stupid crowd began to quiet down, if only because they were weary and so became more amenable to reason.

19:35 sqq. The *Scribe* (γραμματεὺς) of the people, or **town clerk,** was a high official, a kind of recorder, chancellor, or secretary-general who had great influence in civic matters, and sometimes was an Asiarch (v. 31). The title is found in inscriptions. This town clerk, an expert man of affairs gifted with good sense, acted and spoke very ably. He first of all calmed the weary crowd, so that they ceased from their monotonous cry. Then he settled their apprehensions regarding the temple of Diana, pointing out that the position of Ephesus in the cult of Diana was too secure to need such vindication. In any case, if Demetrius and his workmen had any grounds for complaint, they could take proper legal steps, whereas such rioting as they had begun would irritate the Roman authorities of the province who might suspect political motives. — **Temple-warden:** the Greek has νεωκόρον: **(of a) temple-keeper,** equivalent to the Latin *aedituus,* a "custodian" or "superintendent" of the temple, or even "priest" (in earlier

19:37. "For you have brought these men [here who are neither] guilty of sacrilege nor blasphemers of our goddess.

19:38. "Therefore, if Demetrius and the craftsmen with him have a complaint against anyone, court-days are kept [for such purposes], and there are proconsuls: let them take action against one another.

19:39. "And if you require anything further, it shall be settled in the lawful assembly.

---

times it meant a verger, "temple sweeper"). At the time of Paul it was a title connected with the cult of the emperor (cf. note on vv. 28–31), designating those cities which had erected a temple in his honor. In Asia, it was very widespread as a title granted officially by senatorial decree, and it could be conferred more than once according to the number of temples built to the emperor by the cities. But the term could also be used independently of emperor worship. Ephesus was called **temple-warden** of Diana, not only here, but also in inscriptions and on coins. Flavius Josephus (*Wars of the Jews,* V, 383 and 389) uses the expression twice applying it to the Jews as worshipers of Jahveh; the first time, before the Temple was built and there was only the Ark of the Covenant; the second time, when neither existed, since they had both been destroyed. — **Fell down from Jupiter** (διοπετοῦς), i.e., from heaven. The Vulgate rendering of **Jupiter's offspring** must have resulted from reading, or at least interpreting διόπαιδος, which was an epithet applied to Apollo, the brother of Diana. The statue (cf. note on v. 24) was supposed to have fallen from heaven, like the Palladium of Troy and other sacred objects of paganism. It was made, not of stone, as a meteorite would be, but of wood. Shortly before the time of Christ, Vitruvius (II, 9, 13) records that it was made of cedar wood; seventy years later, Pliny the Elder (*Nat. Hist.,* 16, 79) reports the opinions of others, according to which it was made of ebony or the wood of the vine (*vitigineum*).

19:37. **These men:** Gaius and Aristarchus of verse 29 had not treated the goddess Diana with contempt, either by deeds (**guilty of sacrilege,** ἱεροσύλους; cf. Rom. 2:22) or by words (**blasphemers**).

19:38. **Proconsuls:** in the plural, although, as in all senatorial provinces, and Asia was such a province, there was only one (cf. note on 18:12). But seeing that the proconsul was changed every year, the town clerk here refers in general to the series of these magistrates (a "plural" of category).

19:39. The **lawful assembly** was convened with due formality, and not in the riotous manner which characterized the present assembly.

19:40. "For we are even in danger of being accused of riot over today's uproar, since there is no reason which we shall be able to offer in explanation of this concourse." And with these words, he dismissed the assembly.

20:1. Now when the tumult had ceased, Paul sent for the disciples and exhorted them, and having taken leave of them, he departed to go into Macedonia.

19:40. The town clerk, an experienced and practical man, dealt with the probable consequences of the crowd's behavior by uttering veiled threats against the rioters. The Roman authorities were not to be trifled with, and although they allowed a limited autonomy to Greek cities, they suspected popular gatherings which were disorderly and illegal, of sedition, against which very severe penalties, even collective ones, were prescribed. — The better codices put **not** with the words **we shall be able,** but this must be a repetition of the preceding **not** (περὶ οὗ οὐ); by suppressing it, as other documents do (cf. the Vulgate), the sense is clear.

20:1. The riot of the silversmiths caused Paul to leave Ephesus, which he did so as not to expose the Christians of that community to further troubles, and he now undertook his journey into **Macedonia** (cf. 19:21). He left about the May of A.D. 57 (see note on 19:21–22). But Luke's narrative, which is summary, leaves out facts indicated in Paul's own writings. The passage in which he says that he was on the point of being **weary even of life** (given in the note on 19:10) was written in the autumn of 57 from Macedonia, viz., after he had left Ephesus, and this may well refer to the riot of the silversmiths. But this was only the last link in a long chain of trials of increasing severity which afflicted him during the whole of his stay at Ephesus. Another grave though obscure reference is contained in the words **(speaking) as men do, I fought with beasts at Ephesus** (1 Cor. 15:32). This was written in the spring of 56, about a year before the riot at Ephesus, and consequently it cannot refer to this incident. These words undoubtedly have a metaphorical sense, and the beasts symbolize the enemies of the Apostle, very likely the Jews who, toward the end of the year 55, subjected him to a severe persecution; but more than this we do not know. Some early writers, relying upon the apocryphal *Acts of Paul,* believed that Paul was actually exposed to wild beasts in the arena at Ephesus. But they left out of account the fact that Paul by his Roman citizenship could not be thrown to wild beasts, certainly not in the city where the Roman proconsul of Asia resided. The same

20:2. After traveling through those parts and giving them much encouragement, he came to Greece;

20:3. and after spending three months there, a plot was laid against him by the Jews as he was about to sail for Syria, so he decided to return through Macedonia.

---

metaphor of "fighting wild beasts" (θηριομαχεῖν) was used a few decades later by Ignatius of Antioch (*Romans,* V, 1), who alludes to the ten soldiers escorting him as a prisoner, as ten leopards. A possible reference, though even more obscure, is found in the epistle to the Romans (16:7), written at the beginning of A.D. 58, in which Paul bids them greet **Andronicus and Junias . . . my fellow-prisoners** (συναιχμαλώ τους). These two were probably husband and wife. We know nothing of Paul being in prison with them, or indeed with any woman. Until the year of the epistle to the Romans (58), the only imprisonment of Paul we know of was that at Philippi (16:23), which lasted only a few hours, and cannot enter into the question. The only remaining possibility is an imprisonment at Ephesus, but this is mere conjecture without any sure foundation. If he was imprisoned there, it could not have been for long, otherwise Luke would hardly have left it unmentioned.

20:2. Here, also, Luke travels like a bird on the wing. First, Paul visited **those parts** of Macedonia (Philippi, Thessalonica, etc.), exhorting the communities founded there by him, and in the meantime wrote the *Second Epistle to the Corinthians* which brought about the reconciliation of the Apostle with that community. At this time he must have gone near Illyria. In the epistle to the Romans (beginning of A.D. 58), he says that he preached the Gospel **from Jerusalem round about as far as Illyricum** (Rom. 15:19). Whether Paul went no farther than the borders of Illyricum (which corresponds roughly with modern Dalmatia), or whether he proceeded into the interior, there is no occasion other than this when a mission into that country could be fitted into the geographical and chronological scheme of his journeys. This verse, then, gives no more than a glimpse of a very active period lasting from May to the winter of A.D. 57. — **Greece:** this is the only instance in the New Testament of the use of this name in place of the usual name of Achaia.

20:3. These **three months** comprise the winter months between A.D. 57 and 58, and were passed at Corinth as Paul had planned (1 Cor. 16:5–6). There the epistle to the Romans was written. After this, Paul prepared to make the voyage by sea **(to sail) for Syria.** It is likely that the ship he chose was bound for Seleucia, the port which served Antioch and the whole of Syria (cf. note on 13:4), but his final goal was Jerusalem. There he was

20:4. And there accompanied him Sopater of Beroea, [son] of Pyrrhus, and of the Thessalonians, Aristarchus and Secundus, and

---

going principally to take the alms which he had collected over a long period in many places such as Corinth, Galatia, Macedonia (cf. 1 Cor. 16:1 sqq.; 2 Cor. 8:1 sqq.; Rom. 15:25 sqq.) and which was intended for the relief of the poor of the mother Church. It must have been a considerable sum. But while he was preparing to set sail, he got news that **a plot was laid against him by the Jews.** Certainly some Christian had learned of it and in his anxiety for the Apostle's safety had told him of it. It must not be thought that the plotters intended to steal the money which Paul had with him. Such thefts would not have been thought of by the Jews of the Diaspora, especially if it involved violence and the murder of a fellow countryman. But if robbery were not the motive, it could well have been fanaticism. Just at that time, a section of the Zealots called Sicarii were multiplying attacks against individuals and groups which stood in the way of the fulfillment of their religio-nationalistic program (see note on 21:27–29). Paul was an excellent target, inasmuch as he was **a pest, a promoter of seditions among all the Jews throughout the whole world, and a ringleader of the sedition of the Nazarene sect** (24:5). To get rid of such a one was worth far more than to take the money he had with him. Probably the Jews who had been hostile to Paul, both at Corinth and at Ephesus, had been in touch with some Zealot leader in Judea, who had his emissaries abroad, and the plot was suddenly decided upon as a very good opportunity now presented itself. The Hebrew Pasch was approaching, and the ships sailing for Syria from the various Mediterranean ports were loaded with Jewish pilgrims en route for Jerusalem, A well-directed knife thrust at night in some dark corner of the ship, while accomplices kept watch, would get rid of the renegade whose body could be thrown into the sea forthwith. But as happened later in another plot (23:16), this time the would-be assassins' secret leaked out, probably because there were too many of them, and Paul knowing about the plot gave up his plan to go by sea and **he decided to return through Macedonia,** viz., by the overland route. This was much longer, and prevented him from being in Jerusalem for the Pasch. — In this verse, also, the Western Recension presents the facts differently. It supposes that Paul's departure from Corinth was decided upon after the discovery of the plot, and that the decision to journey through Macedonia was due to a message from the Spirit. These are clearly later elaborations.

20:4. Paul appears here surrounded by a goodly company. We do not know whether **Sopater** here is the same person as Sosipater mentioned in

Gaius of Derbe, and Timothy, and of the province of Asia, Tychicus
and Trophimus.

20:5. These having gone in advance, waited for us at Troas;

20:6. but we ourselves sailed from Philippi, after the days of the
unleavened Bread and five days later joined them at Troas, and there
we stayed seven days.

Rom. 16:21 as a kinsman of Paul. **Aristarchus** has already been spoken of in
19:29, but **Secundus** is named nowhere else. As for **Gaius,** since he was
from **Derbe,** he cannot be Gaius the Macedonian spoken of in 19:29 (see
note there). Codex *Beza* has Δουβέριος, instead of Δερβαῖος, which has been
linked with Δόβηρος, *Doberos,* a city of Poenia in northern Macedonia, and
with the Δόβηρες, the *Doberi,* the inhabitants of the place. According to
this reading, this Gaius would be a Macedonian, like the one in 19:29, and
consequently the same person. However this reading of codex *Beza* is not
trustworthy, both because it stands alone with this reading against all
other codices, and also because it has the appearance of being a corruption
of the name **Derbe,** which cannot refer to the city of Doberos. For **Timothy,**
see note on 16:1. — **Tychicus** and **Trophimus** were *Asians,* or from proconsular Asia (Ephesus). The former is mentioned by Paul in Col. 4:7;
Eph. 6:21 (which epistles were entrusted to him to bring from Rome to
their recipients); Titus 3:12; 2 Tim. 4:12. The latter is spoken of later
(21:29), and in 2 Tim. 4:20. This body of men representing the various
districts was for the purpose of witnessing and guaranteeing that the alms
which Paul carried were honestly administered. Paul attached great importance to this public control of monies collected as alms (cf. 2 Cor. 8:20–21).

20:5–6. The narrative here is not clear, since many good codices read
they having come to meet us, instead of **having gone in advance.** It is not
quite clear who were the ones who left the main body to go on ahead
and wait at Troas, or who, coming from some undetermined place,
waited for the others at Troas. It should be noted, however, that besides
Paul and his seven companions named in the preceding verse, Luke the
narrator is also present, since the first person plural reappears in the
narrative (these . . . waited . . . we ourselves sailed . . .). It is obvious that
Luke joined the party, or at least joined Paul in **Philippi,** the place where
he was last with them (see note on 16:40). The group must have divided
up at Philippi after Luke had rejoined it. Those who "went on ahead"
(this reading is preferable to the one "those who came to meet us") may
have been all the seven named, or only the last two. Paul and Luke
remained at Philippi, which accounts for the "we-section." Finally, they
were all reunited at Troas. — **The days of the Unleavened Bread:** the

20:7. And on the first [day] of the week, when we had met for the breaking of bread, Paul addressed them, as he was to leave the next morning, and he prolonged his address until midnight.

---

seven days from the fifteenth to the twenty-first of the month of Nisan, which followed the Hebrew Pasch (14 Nisan). — The crossing from **Philippi,** namely from the port of Neapolis to **Troas,** lasted this time **five days,** probably because of a rough sea. Previously it had only taken two days: see note on 16:11.

20:7. The first [day] of the week: A Hebrew expression which corresponds to what we call Sunday or the *Lord's Day.* The custom of calling Sunday the Lord's Day (*Dominica*) goes back to these early Christians in memory of Christ's Resurrection on the first day of the week. It was also the practice to hold a liturgical gathering on that day (cf. 1 Cor. 16:2; Apoc. 1:10; *Didache,* XIV, 1; Ignatius of Antioch, *ad Magnesios,* IX, 1). The gathering was held for the purpose of the **breaking of bread.** Here the phrase has not the article *the* before the word **bread,** while in verse 11 the phrase is used with the article. In both cases, it is certain that the Eucharistic rite is meant (see note on 2:42, 46; 16:34; 27:35). — The phrase **the next morning,** or the morrow, raises the question of the time of the evening meeting, i.e., whether it took place on the night between Saturday and Sunday, or the night between Sunday and Monday. The Hebrews reckoned the day from the evening of one day to the evening of the next. The Romans reckoned the days from one midnight to another for legal matters (debts, etc.), but they counted the hours of the day from sunrise to sunset, and those of the night from sunset to sunrise. If here, therefore, we follow the Hebrew method of reckoning, the gathering took place on Saturday night, and Paul departed at daybreak on Sunday morning (v. 11). If, instead, we adopt the Roman way, the meeting took place on Sunday, night, and Paul left at daybreak on Monday morning. We cannot say with entire certainty from what Luke tells us, just when it took place. In other instances, he follows the Roman reckoning of time (4:3-5; 23:31-32), and it is probable that this was followed by the community at Troas which was mainly composed of convert pagans. On the other hand, Christ's Resurrection had taken place on the night between Saturday and Sunday (Mt. 28:1-2; Jn. 20:1). Likewise, the institution of the Eucharist took place on the evening between Thursday and Friday. Pliny the Younger in his letter to Trajan, written about the year 112 (*Epist.,* X, 96) speaks of these Christian gatherings at night, but he does not say on what day, simply saying that the meetings took place on a "fixed day" (*stato die ante lucem*).

20:8. Now there were many lamps in the upper room where we had assembled.

20:9. And a young man named Eutychus, who was sitting at the window, being overcome with drowsiness while Paul addressed them at great length, went fast asleep and fell down from the third floor to the ground and was picked up dead.

20:10. Then Paul went down to him and laid himself upon him and embracing him said: "Do not be alarmed, life is still in him."

20:11. Then he went up and having broken the bread and eaten, and having spoken to them a good while, even till daybreak, so he departed.

20:12. And they took away the boy alive, and were not a little comforted.

20:8. The upper room (ὑπερῷον) was on the third floor (v. 9). It will be remembered that the Eucharist was instituted in an upper room ("a room above ground") (see note on 1:13).

20:9–12. The crowded room together with the increasing fumes from the lamps made Eutychus seek a seat on the window sill which had no bars. While Paul, transported by fervor, was long preaching, Eutychus nodding with sleep, gradually swayed toward the opening of the window, until, at a certain point, he fell out. Luke, who makes no pretense of literary description, does not delay here to describe the confusion and cries which arose in the upper room when Eutychus fell out, but simply limits himself to saying that he was picked up dead from the place where he fell. Some modern scholars have supplied the deficiency of this brief account of the historian who was a doctor and an eyewitness, by adding that the young man died of a fracture of the base of the skull, or suchlike injuries. According to others, he did not die at all, but only fainted. Anyone who wishes to satisfy himself with one or other of these explanations is free to do so. Paul, however, going down below with the others, laid himself on the dead youth, embracing him. This was the gesture that Elias and Eliseus had used when they raised the dead; cf. 1 (3) Kings 17:21; 2 (4) Kings 4:34. The cry of the crowd can be imagined from Paul's exhortation, do not be alarmed. The words which follow and justify this assurance are limited simply to relating the fact that life is still in him. These words are completely contradictory to the previous condition of the youth, viz., that he was dead. He was dead first, and now instead he is alive again. Luke does not give any explanation of how this happened, but rather, by giving Paul's words, he implicitly invites the

20:13. But the rest of us had already embarked and set sail for Assos, intending to take Paul on board there: that was the arrangement he had made as he intended to travel there by land.

20:14. So when he met us at Assos, we took him on board, and came to Mitylene.

20:15. From there we arrived on the following day off Chios, the next day we made Samos, and the day after we reached Miletus.

---

reader to ask Paul himself for the explanation. It is to be noted that the narrative attaches little importance to the entire episode, which figures merely as an incident which interrupts the Eucharistic rite. It is only a slight interruption, so that as soon as the dead youth is resuscitated and the others are reassured that all is well, Paul returns to the upper room, and having **broken the bread** (here the article is used; cf. note on v. 7), he finishes the celebration and renews his address which continues **till daybreak.** For him, it was as though nothing untoward had happened. The important thing was the rite and the address which accompanied it. Meanwhile, the youth had probably been laid on a bed in another room as a precaution. No doubt he tried to remember how the whole thing came about. He was called **Eutychus** or "Bona-ventura" ("good fortune"), and if the significance of his name was not verified at the beginning of the incident, it certainly was at the end!

20:13. On the morning when all this had happened, the party divided into two groups and set off again on another voyage. The party of Luke the narrator left first, and coasted around the promontory south of Troas, thus reaching Assos after a voyage of about 35 miles. The other group, that of Paul and most certainly some Christians of Troas, followed the land route cutting across the base of the triangle of the promontory and reached Assos some twenty or so miles away. We do not know why Paul chose to go by land, perhaps because of his chronic illness, a recurrence of which would have prevented a sea voyage, but this is only a conjecture. When the text speaks of **making a journey by land** this does not rule out the use of a carriage or horse, as appears from numerous examples in classical writers.

20:14-15. From Assos southward the voyage was a coasting trip which can easily be followed on a map. Even today the navigation of the Dardanelles toward the western coast of Asia Minor follows more or less the same route. — After **Samos,** codex *Beza,* confirmed by various codices and versions, adds the words **and after tarrying at Trogyllium came on the day after . . .** This addition could be part of the original text and is quite

20:16. For Paul had decided to sail past Ephesus, lest he should be delayed in the province of Asia; for he was hastening to be in Jerusalem, if it were possible for him, by the day of Pentecost.

20:17. From Miletus, however, he sent to Ephesus for the presbyters of the church;

20:18. and when they had come to him he said to them: "You know in what manner I have lived with you all the time since the first day that I came into the province of Asia,

20:19. "serving the Lord with all humility and with tears and in trials that befell me because of the plots of the Jews;

---

likely. Trogyllium, the present-day Santa Maria, lies on the mainland opposite the island of Samos, and forms the most westerly point of the promontory of Mycale, where the famous victory of the Greek fleet over the Persians took place in 479 b.c. This possible stop at Trogyllium, in any case a very brief one, must have been caused by a wind which was either insufficient or contrary.

20:16–17. The clause that **Paul had decided to sail past Ephesus** could lead one to suppose that he decided on the ship's course, as though he had hired the ship for his company, but such a supposition is not necessarily true, and the expression can mean that when Paul embarked at Troas, he chose a ship that was not calling at Ephesus. Paul had left his heart at Ephesus, and he was so well known there that he realized that a call would inevitably be prolonged into a long stay, whereas he was in a hurry for the reason given. He made up for it, therefore, by a reunion at Miletus, so as not miss the chance of seeing his converts again and speaking with them. The ship must have tarried at Miletus for several days. The distance from Miletus to Ephesus, as the crow flies, is about 35 miles across the gulf of Latmicus, so that it would take not less than three full days to send a messenger **from Miletus . . . to Ephesus** to summon **the presbyters** there, and bring them to Miletus so as to hold a meeting at a convenient hour. — **Miletus,** the chief city of Caria, and among the most famous of all Ionia, had a flourishing maritime trade because of the ports along the gulf of Latmicus, where the river Meander entered the sea. But in the course of centuries this muddy river silted up its harbors, cutting off the city from the sea, and causing its rapid decline. — For the term **presbyters,** see note on 11:30; 14:23; 15:2. It should, however, be noted that these **presbyters** are called **bishops** (overseers) in verse 28: see note there.

20:18 sqq. The speech which begins here is, first of all, an apologetic

20:20. "how I have kept back nothing that was for your good, but have declared it to you and taught you in public, and from house to house,

20:21. "urging Jews and Gentiles to turn to God in repentance and to believe in our Lord Jesus Christ.

20:22. "And now, behold, constrained in spirit, I am going to Jerusalem, not knowing what will happen to me there;

20:23. "except that in every city the Holy Spirit warns me that imprisonment and persecution are awaiting me.

---

account of the speaker's conduct in the past, and then an admonition to the assembly about the future. The historical links with Paul's epistles to the *Corinthians,* the similarity in tone of its exhortatory part with the Pastoral Epistles (*Timothy, Titus*), confirms its Pauline authorship (equally relevant here are the observations already made on other discourses: 1:16; 7:2 sqq.; etc.), in substance at least, since here also we are dealing with a summary account. It should be remembered, likewise, that Luke himself heard this discourse as he was in Paul's company (see the "we-section" in v. 15, and again in 21:1). — In this and the following verse, the historical circumstances of Paul's ministry in proconsular Asia are recorded; see notes on 19:10; 20:1.

20:20. Cf. verse 27. — House to house: for this expression, see notes on 2:46; 5:42.

20:21. Urging Jews and Gentiles: the expressions used here express ideas dear to Paul. For the verb **urging,** cf. 1 Thess. 4:6; 1 Tim. 5:21; 2 Tim. 2:14; 4:1. For Jews . . . Greeks (Gentiles), cf. 1 Cor. 1:24; Rom. 1:16; 2:9-10; 3:9. — Repentance, viz., penance; see notes on 2:38; 11:18.

20:22-23. Constrained in spirit: this does not refer to the Holy Spirit, but to the human spirit, as on other occasions in Paul's writings (1 Cor. 2:11; 5:3-4; Rom. 1:9; 8:16; etc.); it corresponds to being *spiritually compelled.* — Not knowing, precisely and exactly, but in a general way, expecting **imprisonment and persecution** (literally, *chains and tribulations*). The close of the epistle to the *Romans,* written shortly before, reveals that Paul's preoccupations referred as much to **unbelievers in Judea,** namely his fellow countrymen, who persecuted him as a renegade, as to the possibility that his **ministry for those in Jerusalem** might not be **acceptable to the saints,** viz., that the Jewish Christians of Jerusalem might scornfully refuse to accept the offerings which he brought with him (Rom. 15:31). Such forebodings, he says here, were testified to him by the **Holy Spirit . . .**

20:24. "But in no way do I hold my life dear unto myself, in order to complete my course and the ministry which I received from the Lord Jesus to testify to the gospel of the grace of God.

20:25. "And now, behold, I know that all of you among whom I went about preaching the kingdom of God, shall see my face no longer.

20:26. "Therefore I call you to witness this day that I am innocent of the blood of all;

20:27. "for I have not shrunk from declaring to you the whole counsel of God.

---

in every city, as he neared his goal at Jerusalem. These attestations of the Spirit are not explained to us, but in 21:4, 10 sqq. we have two examples due to the charisms of fellow Christians, to which can be added the charismatic communications received by Paul himself.

20:24. The first part of this verse is a little difficult, and the text presents various readings due certainly to the desire of copyists to clarify the sense. The translation given is in conformity with the reading of the more authoritative codices. Other readings are: **in no way do I count nor hold life,** etc. Codex *Beza* reads: **in no way do I hold, nor do I count my life dear unto myself.** The Vulgate rendering is singular: **I fear none of these things, neither do I count my life more precious (?) than myself.** Perhaps the primitive text simply had: **in no way** (viz., **of no account**) **do I count life,** which was then altered by additions and glosses. — **To complete my course:** Paul had a predilection for this metaphor, taken from the games in the stadium; cf. 1 Cor. 9:24–26; Gal. 2:2; Phil. 2:16; 3:12–14; 2 Tim. 4:7. Here it symbolizes the apostolic ministry (the same term is used in Rom. 11:13), which Paul had received direct from the Lord Jesus, as he also strongly affirms in Gal. 1:12.

20:25. This prediction is a personal conjecture on the part of Paul which proved incorrect, because he did return to Ephesus later on (cf. 1 Tim. 1:3; 2 Tim. 1:18), as well as to Miletus, where he is now speaking (2 Tim. 4:20). He is moved to such dark forebodings by his state of mind (vv. 22–23). The lack of any basis for this prediction shows clearly that Luke wrote the summary of this discourse and the *Acts* before the Pastoral Letters were written, which tell us that Paul did return to Ephesus, and which were dictated while Luke was with Paul (2 Tim. 4:11). We may be sure that if Luke had known the Pastoral Letters when he wrote this discourse, he would have omitted Paul's mistaken prediction.

20:26–27. Just as Samuel, on the day he laid down his ruling power,

20:28. "Take heed to yourselves and to the whole flock in which the Holy Spirit has placed you as bishops, to rule the Church of God, which he has purchased with his own blood.

---

examined his conduct before the people, showing that he had no material responsibilities toward anyone (1 Sam. 12:2-5), so here Paul affirms that he has no responsibility for the eventual moral ruin (**blood**) of anyone. He himself has done everything to prevent such ruin; verse 27 repeats the idea of verse 20.

20:28. The presbyters, to whom Paul is speaking (v. 17), receive here the name of **"bishops,"** overseers, so that at the time of this discourse, viz., in A.D. 58, the two names were practically synonymous. In his epistles, Paul uses the word **bishops** in Phil. 1:1; 1 Tim. 3:2; Titus 1:7. In the first of these passages, the **bishops** are distinct from the **ministers** or "deacons" (see note on 6:6). In the last passage, the same person is called first an **elder** or "presbyter," and then a **bishop** (cf. Titus 1:5-6 with 7). The practically synonymous use of **bishop** and **elder** witnesses to a period of organization and a hierarchy as yet in its early stages, for fifty years later — as we see from the letters of Ignatius of Antioch — there is a clear distinction of terms, and the **bishop** stands at the head of a fixed hierarchy, with the **elders** or "presbyters" (priests) under him, and last of all the **ministers** or "deacons." For this question, see G. Ricciotti, *Paul the Apostle,* p. 489. — These **bishop-overseers** have been placed by the **Holy Spirit** at the head of **the whole flock,** viz., **to rule the Church of God.** — The reading of the **Church of God** is that given by the more authoritative codices, and corresponds to the wide use that Paul makes of this expression in his epistles (1 Thess. 2:14; 1 Cor. 1:2; 10:32; 11:16, 22; 15:9; 2 Cor. 1:1; Gal. 1:13; etc.). Other codices and some early writers give the reading **Church of the Lord,** but in Paul's epistles the expression **Church of Christ** occurs only in Rom. 16:16. The readings which give, **of the Lord and of God,** or **of the Lord God,** are simply attempts to reconcile both versions and are less well attested. The first reading is rightly preferred in critical editions as being more trustworthy and characteristic of Paul. The second reading, **Church of the Lord,** can cleverly be explained as a substitution called for by the phrase which follows, viz., **with his own blood,** which would be equivalent to "blood of God," and therefore was irksome to some reader. But just as the idea that Christ **bought** the faithful of his Church (cf. 1 Cor. 6:20; 7:23; Eph. 5:23 and 25) is typically Pauline, so also does the idea of the redemptive power of the **blood** of Christ belong to Paul (cf. Eph. 1:7; 2:13; Hebr. 9:12-14). It is obvious that here "blood of God" signifies "the blood of Christ"; therefore, according to Paul, Christ

20:29. "I know that after my departure fierce wolves will get in among you, and will not spare the flock.

20:30. "And from among your own selves men will rise speaking perverse things, to draw away the disciples after them.

20:31. "Watch, therefore, and remember that for three years, night and day I did not cease with tears to admonish every one of you.

---

is God. It has been suggested that in translating the phrase **his own blood,** which in Greek has two genitives, the second genitive should be subordinated to the first, and by supplying the word **son,** it should be made to read, **by means of the blood of his own (son).** But apart from the fact that this explanation renders obscure what is clear, there is not one example in the New Testament where the word **son** is to be implicitly understood, while there is an apposite example in Paul's own writings, according to which **God did not spare his own son, but delivered him for us all** (Rom. 8:32), where the **son** is explicitly mentioned.

20:29. For **departure,** the Greek has ἄφιξιν, which ordinarily means "arrival," seldom "going away." The Vulgate translates it **post discessionem meam;** the Syriac Peshitta gives **after I shall have gone.** This last rendering agrees better with the context. — These **fierce wolves** (the Greek has "grievous," "tiresome") **will get in** the flock. They will come from outside, therefore, and not from within the flock itself like the **men** denounced in the following verse. They are probably the Judaizing Christians whom Paul had already denounced, both in his epistle to the *Galatians,* written probably a few months before this discourse (at the end of the year 57), and in the previous epistles to the *Corinthians,* and very likely also in the epistle to the *Romans* (16:17 sqq.). These Judaizers practically dogged Paul's footsteps, and wherever he founded a Christian community, they turned up a little while after to do the work of **fierce wolves.** Paul's past experience allowed him to foresee the future at Ephesus.

20:30. Besides the danger of wolves from outside, there will be the internal risk of men who **from among your own selves will rise . . . speaking perverse things** and trying to make **disciples.** We do not know what persons Paul had in mind when speaking of this internal dissension. Later, however, he will insist at length to Timothy, whom he left behind in Ephesus, that he must beware of innovators and heretics, naming as such Alexander, Hymeneus, Philetus, etc. (1 Tim. 1:20; 2 Tim. 2:17; 4:14). Ephesus, a city where the most divergent races and beliefs were all mingled together, was indeed a most fertile breeding ground for the growth of such heterodoxy.

20:31. For the reckoning of this **three years,** see note on 19:10.

20:32. "And now I commend you to God and to the word of his grace, who is able to build up and to give the inheritance among all the sanctified.

20:33. "I have coveted no one's silver or gold or apparel.

20:34. "You yourselves know that these hands of mine have provided for my needs and those of my companions.

20:35. "In all things I have shown you that by so toiling you ought to help the weak and remember the word of the Lord Jesus, that he himself said: 'It is more blessed to give than to receive.'"

20:36. Having said this, he knelt down and prayed with them all.

20:37. And there was much weeping among them all and they fell on Paul's neck and kissed him,

20:38. being grieved most of all at his saying that they would no longer see his face. And they escorted him to the ship.

20:33–34. Paul, continuing his account of his conduct (cf. note on v. 18), now comes down to material things, just as Samuel had done (cf. notes on vv. 26–27). When it was a question of material means, Paul was so scrupulous and exacting as to appear oversensitive, and never let an occasion pass to point out that he gained no material reward from his apostolic ministry, but provided for his necessities by manual work. He thereby wished to differentiate himself from his Jewish adversaries who were money-lovers and self-seekers (cf. 1 Cor. 9:11–18; 2 Cor. 8:20–21; 11:8–12; etc.) — These hands, which were probably calloused by his daily task of weaving (see note on 18:3); perhaps while he said this, he showed them his palms, so that they might see for themselves. It is to be noted that by his manual labor Paul provided not only for himself, but also for others who were his companions, e.g., Timothy, his helper, who was delicate and infirm (1 Tim. 5:23).

20:35. The weak (ἀσθενούντων), not in the moral sense of one who is weak in the faith (Rom. 14:1), but in the material sense, though not referring so much to physical weakness as to the social aspect of being needy, poor; what the Romans called tenuiores. Such weak ones must be succoured by so toiling (viz., as Paul had done). A similar thought is found in Eph. 4:28, and cf. 2 Thess. 3:7 sqq. The final word is a logion (saying) of Jesus, not reported anywhere else, which Paul must have got from the apostolic catechesis. The way in which he quotes it, and remember . . . , would suggest that his hearers knew of this saying, probably from Paul himself at Ephesus. Other similar "sayings" of Jesus, of more

21:1. And when we had parted from them and had set sail, we made a straight course and came to Cos, and the next day to Rhodes, and from there to Patara.

21:2. There we found a ship crossing over to Phoenicia, and we went on board and set sail.

21:3. After sighting Cyprus and leaving it to the left, we sailed for Syria and landed at Tyre, for there the ship was to unload her cargo.

21:4. Having looked up the disciples, we stayed there seven days. And they told Paul through the Spirit not to go to Jerusalem.

---

or less historical authenticity, are given by the Apostolic Fathers, by writers of the first centuries, and by papyri (cf. G. Ricciotti, *The Life of Christ,* p. 87 sqq.).

21:1-3. The coasting voyage begins again: cf. note on 20:14-15. **Patara,** directly east of Rhodes, was on the west coast of Asia Minor. It was a fair-sized port, opposite the islet of Castelrosso, and there they changed ship. The Western Recension after **Patara** adds the words **and Myra,** which was slightly eastward of Patara and was the capital of that region of Lycia (cf. 27:5). The addition was probably made because of the copyist's surprise that Patara should be preferred to the capital which was not even mentioned. After Patara, the coastal journey came to an end, and the voyage now lay across the open sea with the course set for **Tyre** in **Phoenicia.** The reason why the text gives **Syria** as the goal is because politically Phoenicia was a part of the Roman province of Syria. The island of Cyprus was passed **to the left,** since the ship sailed south of it. A favoring northwest wind, therefore, must have helped the ship along toward the coast of Phoenicia. On the next outward-bound voyage the same northwest wind was blowing, but on that occasion it proved a hindrance, and the island was passed on the eastward side so as to gain shelter from the wind (cf. note on 27:4).

21:4. These Christians (**disciples**) of Tyre must have been converted when the Gospel was preached in Phoenicia on an earlier occasion (cf. 11:19).— The stay of **seven days** at Tyre was rather a long one, given Paul's hurry (cf. 20:16) in traveling, but it must have been because the ship needed attention.— **Through the Spirit,** i.e., by means of a charismatic communication (cf. note on 20:22-23). Such communications had revealed to these charismatics of Tyre the same **imprisonment and persecution** prepared for Paul which had been revealed to him (20:23). But by going

21:5. But when our time was up we left there and went on, and all of them with their wives and children escorted us till we were out of the city, and we knelt down on the shore and prayed.

21:6. And having said farewell to one another, we went on board the ship and they returned home.

21:7. After completing the voyage from Tyre, we landed at Ptolemais where we greeted the brethren and spent a day with them.

21:8. The next day we departed and came to Caesarea, where we went to the house of Philip the evangelist, who was one of the seven, and stayed with him.

21:9. He had four daughters, virgins, who had the gift of prophecy.

---

to Jerusalem to meet these trials, he was obeying the Spirit, while they, by dissuading him from going, were obeying a dictate of Christian charity. The two communications were not contrary, rather they completed each other, but since charity was subordinate to the dictates of the Spirit, Paul obeyed the Spirit; see note on verses 12–14.

21:5. **Our time was up** (literally, **we had completed, etc.**). The verb in Greek is ἐξαρτίζω, which means "to adapt," "to complete," "to accomplish," "to furnish," from which comes the verb "to bring to an end" as in the old Italian (Petrarch says of the old man about to die, that *he had his age completed,* i.e., his time was finished).

21:7. **Ptolemais,** in the bay at the foot of Mount Carmel, was in Palestine, although it still belonged to Phoenicia. The presence of a Christian community there (**brethren**) can be explained in the same way as at Tyre (cf. v. 4).

21:8–9. **Philip** was **one of the seven** (cf. note on 6:5; 8:5 sqq.) and an **evangelist.** This last term did not mean that he had written a biography of Jesus, but rather that he was endowed with that special charism named by Paul immediately after that of **apostle** and **prophet** (Eph. 4:11; cf. 2 Tim. 4:5). The work of an "evangelist" was in particular the proclaiming of the good news, viz., the Gospel, delivering the account and witnesses of the doings and teaching of Jesus. An "evangelist," therefore, together with an "apostle" held a place of honor in the Christian teaching. At the time of Eusebius of Caesarea, the charism of "evangelist" had disappeared, nevertheless he describes his mission — probably on the basis of early documents — in the following manner: *They occupied the first place among the successors of the Apostles. And they also, being illustrious disciples of such great men, built up the foundations of the churches which had been*

21:10. And while we were staying on there for some days, there came down from Judea a certain prophet named Agabus,

21:11. and coming to us and taking Paul's girdle, he bound his own feet and hands, and said, "Thus says the Holy Spirit: The man whose girdle this is the Jews will bind like this at Jerusalem, and they will deliver [him] into the hands of the Gentiles."

---

laid by the Apostles in every place, and preached the Gospel more and more widely, and scattered the saving seeds of the kingdom of heaven far and near throughout the whole world. . . . *And when they had only laid the foundations of the faith in foreign places, they appointed others as pastors, and entrusted them with the nurture of those that had recently been brought in, while they themselves went on again to other countries and nations, etc.* (*Hist. eccl.,* III, 37). Philip is here presented precisely in this very role for he had evangelized Samaria (8:5 sqq.) and other regions. — The **four daughters** of Philip were **virgins.** Most probably they were such by choice, in keeping with the principles already diffused among the various Christian communities, and which Paul barely two years previously had recommended in writing (1 Cor. 7:25–40). Moreover they **had the gift of prophecy,** i.e., they had the charism of "prophecy" (see note on 11:27), just as in the Old Testament there had been prophetesses. Since the charism of "prophecy" was especially used for speaking at public gatherings of the community, these prophetesses would also have spoken in virtue of their charism. In fact, we find that Paul considers the case of the woman who prays and prophesies (1 Cor. 11:5), although shortly afterward he himself commands: **In all the churches of the saints, let women keep silence in the meetings, for it is not permitted them to speak** (*ibid.,* 14:33–34; cf. 1 Tim. 2:12). But with this prohibition, Paul refers only to public gatherings, while neither here nor elsewhere does he forbid women to use the charism of "prophecy" in private, or before a few acquaintances, especially in the company of women. Perhaps the deaconesses, such as Phoebe (see note on 18:8) were also prophetesses.

21:10–11. It is possible that this **Agabus** is the same as the one mentioned in 11:28, but it is not certain. The fact that he is referred to by the words, **a certain** (τὶς) **prophet,** as though he had not been spoken of before, presents no difficulty since it is probably due to the fact that Luke is transcribing his source of information literally. This was his "travel Diary," written when he did not yet know Agabus, and therefore he designates him here in this manner. Because Agabus had the gift of "prophecy" like the daughters of Philip, he performed one of those symbolical actions which were frequently used by the Hebrew prophets of old, especially Ezechiel.

21:12. On hearing this, we ourselves and the people there begged him not to go to Jerusalem.

21:13. Then Paul answered and said, "What do you mean by weeping and breaking my heart? For I am ready not only to be bound but even to die at Jerusalem for the name of the Lord Jesus."

21:14. And when we could not persuade him, we acquiesced and said: "The Lord's will be done."

21:15. After this we made our preparations and went our way to Jerusalem.

21:16. And [some] of the disciples from Caesarea went with us, bringing us to Mnason, a Cypriot, an early disciple, whose guests we were to be.

The Semites, generally speaking, were inclined to accompany their words which expressed a given idea, with actions that emphasized their meaning. Agabus then performed such an action and pronounced the words here narrated with an obvious significance. His prophecy agreed with that of the charismatics of Tyre (v. 4).

21:12-14. The contrast already noted in verse 4 returns. On the one hand a charismatic points out the danger, and the faithful beg Paul, through Christian charity, to avoid it. On the other hand, Paul, by his own charismatic power conscious of the danger (cf. 20:23), decides that it is his duty to face it. The internal conflict in Paul is great and he feels "his heart breaking." But when it is a question of **the name of the Lord Jesus,** he is **ready not only to be bound but even to die.** The faithful, therefore, realize that it is **the Lord's will,** and surrender to it by refraining from entreaties which their affection for the Apostle dictated. **The Lord's will be done.**

21:15. **We made our preparations,** ἐπισκευασάμενοι: the codices give variant readings, such as, **having packed our baggage; taking our leave,** etc. The special mention of these preparations is not without significance. The distance from Caesarea to Jerusalem was about 55 miles, so that it would almost certainly be necessary to sleep more than one night on the way. Besides, the company carried the alms collected by Paul for Jerusalem (cf. note on 20:3) which must have consisted of clothes and money, and thus the transport of these things necessitated some preparation.

21:16. The text here, which is extremely condensed and offers difficulties, is interpreted in different ways by the early versions. According to the Vulgate, with which the Syriac Peshitta substantially agrees, the disciples

21:17. On our arrival at Jerusalem, the brethren gave us a hearty welcome.

21:18. On the next day, Paul went with us to James, and all the presbyters came in.

21:19. After greeting them, he related in detail what God had done among the Gentiles through his ministry.

---

of Caesarea who are accompanying Paul, bring along with them — from Caesarea, as far as one can judge — **Mnason,** who is to be Paul's host. The Western Recension goes even further by saying: **these** (the disciples of Caesarea) **led us to those with whom we were to lodge; and arriving at a certain village, we stayed with a certain Mnason, a Cypriot, an early disciple: and going forth from there, we came to Jerusalem.** In this reading, which is simply an amplified statement of the original text, Mnason is neither at Caesarea nor at Jerusalem, but at some point halfway, **a certain village,** where the travelers stayed the night as Mnason's guests. The original text, however, despite its obscurity and brevity, does not warrant such interpretations. Mnason entertained the travelers at Jerusalem and was already there, without coming specially from Caesarea. Luke had no reason to speak of him if he had already entertained the company on the way during the journey, whereas he would have cause to record precisely who was their host in Jerusalem, since the offer of hospitality would show their host's feelings toward them. Mnason was a **Cypriot** — and therefore a fellow countryman of Barnabas — and as his Greek name shows, a Hellenist Jew, wherefore his house at Jerusalem was considered the most convenient lodging for Paul's group among whom were certainly some who were uncircumcised. Such guests would not have been readily received in the houses of Judaizing Christians (cf. note on 11:3), and severe quarrels might have ensued. — The description of Mnason as an **early disciple** could be linked up with the mention of the early days in 15:7 (see there), though no certain conclusion can be drawn from it. We have no other information about Mnason since he is not spoken of elsewhere in the New Testament. — This was Paul's fifth visit to Jerusalem, of which we know, since his conversion.

21:17-19. To appreciate this meeting of Paul with the community at Jerusalem, it must be remembered that he was greatly preoccupied as to how he would be received (see note on 20:22-23). He had every good reason to fear a cold reception or even an openly hostile one on the part of some of the members of that community. The narrative shows almost a twofold reception. The first is cordial and warm (vv. 17-19). The second is reserved from dissatisfied people who immediately question Paul (v. 20 sqq.). The brethren who received the company with a hearty welcome were the Hellenist Christians, who, as soon as they heard of their arrival, went to greet the missionaries to the Gentiles, who had reaped such fruit among the pagans. But alongside the Hellenists were the Jewish Christians who were the more numerous and powerful at Jerusalem, and who were not pleased to see all these uncircumcised converts admitted into Christ's Church. For these Jewish Christians, the Apostolic Council and its decree (15:1 sqq.) were not meant to have much practical value. Over and above these two groups were the supreme rulers of the community, James and Cephas and John who were considered the pillars of the Church (Gal. 2:9), who endeavored to keep both groups in agreement, at least in practice, so that divisions should not arise (1 Cor. 1:10). To this end, they sought to obtain, now from one side, now from the other, some concession or practical renunciation of their own predilections, so as to keep them together. Of these supreme rulers, only James is mentioned here as being present, probably because the other Apostles were absent from Jerusalem. Even here, James continues his conciliatory work which he had already performed in the Apostolic Council (cf. note on 15:13 sqq.). The presbyters are recorded as being present together with James, about whom see note on 15:12. The sequence of events must have been somewhat as follows. The recently returned missionaries must have been joyously welcomed back by the Hellenist Christians (v. 17). The news of their arrival spread throughout the community, and word came to the leaders that the new arrivals wished to be received officially by them, in order that they might deliver to them the sums of money they had collected. The next day having been fixed for the meeting, Paul with his companions present themselves at the reception, where he relates in detail what God had done among the Gentiles through his ministry (vv. 18–19). But in the interval between the arrival and the interview, there must have been animated discussions which Luke does not relate, but the consequences of which can be perceived. The more rigid Jewish leaders probably proposed that the alms collected among the uncircumcised be rejected outright, as Paul himself feared (Rom. 15:31), and that Paul's method of evangelizing the pagans be openly repudiated. Others less fiery would have suggested that the offerings be accepted, but that at the same time Paul be required to impose on his pagan converts at least the fundamentals of the Jewish Law. But in the discussion between the two groups, someone who was superior to both intervened, viz., James, who managed to make an arrangement whereby both sides could be more or less accommodated. This is the agreement proposed in verse 20 sqq. by an unnamed speaker who was most probably James himself, or at least one who spoke on his behalf.

21:20. They praised God when they heard it and they said to him: "Thou seest, brother, how many thousands of believers there are among the Jews, all of them zealous upholders of the Law.

21:21. "Now, they have been informed about thee that thou dost teach the Jews who [live] among the Gentiles to depart from Moses, telling them they [should not] circumcise their children nor observe the [Jewish] customs.

21:20 sqq. All without exception **praised God,** even the Jewish Christians, who were certainly glad to hear of the expansion of the Church even though they had serious reservations to make about the manner of that expansion. At any rate, the offerings were accepted. The admission of the uncircumcised into the Church was left undecided, but some sign of respect for the Jewish rites was required of Paul. To facilitate its acceptance, the proposal was put to him, not as a personal request by the one who spoke, but in the name of **thousands of believers** in the Messias Jesus, who were Jews by birth and **zealous upholders of the Law** of Moses. It was about the time of the feast of Pentecost (cf. 20:16), which attracted many Jews to Jerusalem, especially those of the Diaspora, since it was a good time for making long journeys, especially by sea. Thus, among these pilgrims, there were many who had become Christians but still continued to observe the great Hebrew feasts. If these Jews, precisely because they were **zealous for the Law,** should see Paul performing some act of respect to the rites of that Law, they would reverse the unfavorable judgment they had formed of him. The authority of these *zealots for the Law* had to be reckoned with, if only because they were so numerous, as a countermeasure to the many pagans Paul had converted. The proposal made to Paul was by way of being a charitable *quid pro quo.*

21:21. Thou dost teach . . . to depart from Moses: in actual fact, Paul had not taught such apostasy, but only adherence to Christ Jesus, and this the Jewish Christians also accepted. If the consequence of adhesion to the doctrine of Christ was that the Law of Moses was superseded, this did not depend on Paul, but on Christ. In any case, in practice, Paul taught that the pagans who became Christians were not bound to Jewish observances, but he left Jewish converts free, according to their consciences, to continue or not in these observances, declaring that the Law of Moses had been abolished with the coming of the Messias Jesus, and that as a consequence, these observances were useless (cf. note on 16:3). As a wise psychologist, Paul knew how much it cost a man to give up his ancient and revered traditions, and it was with this human consideration in mind that he treated his compatriots.

21:22. "What then? They will certainly hear that thou hast come.

21:23. "So, do what we tell thee. We have four men who are under a vow;

21:24. "take them and sanctify thyself along with them, and pay for them that they may shave their heads; and all will know that what they have heard of thee is false, but that thou thyself also observest the Law.

21:25. "But as for the Gentile believers, we ourselves have written our decision that they abstain from idol offerings and from blood and from what is strangled and from immorality."

21:22. After the word **certainly** (literally, **in every case**), several authoritative codices (see critical editions) add, **the multitude must needs come together** (in the sense **it will certainly assemble**) **for it will hear,** etc. This is a noteworthy variant but it can be taken as understood. A crowd of the above-mentioned Christians would assemble to observe Paul's conduct in relation to the Jewish observances.

21:23-24. The words **we have** show that the speaker had a certain interest in the **four men,** and therefore that they were Christians. The vow they had taken was that of the "Nazarite," for which see note on 18:18. — **Pay for them,** etc. It often happened that poor Jews who had taken the "Nazarite" vow could not meet the considerable expense involved in performing the sacrifices prescribed when the time of the vow was over, and which consisted in a lamb, a sheep, a ram, etc., for each one who had taken the vow (cf. Num. 6:14 sqq.). In such cases, wealthy persons gained merit by offering them the means of paying for the sacrifices, after which they could shave their heads and be free from the vow. Flavius Josephus (*Antiquities of the Jews,* XIX, 294) recounts such an action being performed by Herod Agrippa I. Here the same act of generosity is proposed to Paul. The elders chose this act because they had probably heard that Paul, of his own initiative, had taken such a vow at Cenchrae five years earlier (18:18). That which he had then done from personal devotion, let him now do with these four poor Christians who, by means of his generosity, would be helped to fulfill the vow. Moreover, by this gesture, he would give the lie to the rumor that he was against Jewish observances.

21:25. The proposal made to Paul and presented in such a conciliatory manner was not extreme, but in order to render it more acceptable, the proposers cleverly insinuated a kind of *do ut des,* which covered the whole question. In the Council's decree — they recall — allusion was made to the

21:26. Then Paul took the men, and the next day after being
purified along with them he entered the temple and announced the
completion of the days of purification, when the sacrifice would be
offered for each of them.

Gentile believers, and on whom four prohibitions, listed here, had been
imposed (cf. 15:20 and 29). Let Paul then have a similar regard for the
Jewish Christians by accepting the proposal. In the Western Recension,
the *do ut des* is inferred in a more subtle way, since it appears to be concerned with Paul's peace of mind when faced with the eventual complaints
of the converted Gentiles. It reads thus: **But as for the Gentile believers,
they have nothing to say against thee; for we ourselves have written after
having decided that they need not observe any of these things, as long as
they abstain . . .** Undoubtedly this is a later emendation of the original text.

    21:26. Paul accepted the proposal. But did he do it with enthusiasm?
The contrary is to be suspected. He who shortly before had written the
epistle to the *Galatians* and in it had compared the Hebrew Law to a
severe **tutor** from which **faith in Jesus Christ** now sets them free (Gal.
3:24–26) could not relish returning to that tutor, even for a short time,
being without conviction and solely for the sake of others. Nevertheless,
it was not a question of doctrinal principle, but of individual free choice,
and involved charity which Paul himself had put before all charisms
(1 Cor. 13:1 sqq.) and which made him **become to the Jews a Jew that he
might gain the Jews to Christ** (*ibid.,* 9:20). Paul had acted in a similar
manner in the case of Timothy: cf. note on 16:1–3. — Having accepted
the proposal, Paul proceeded to carry it out on the **next day,** which was
the third after his arrival at Jerusalem (cf. vv. 18 and 26). Taking the four
Jewish Christians bound by the vow, he fulfilled the prescribed purification
ceremonies, which were intended especially for those who like him had
returned from pagan lands, and **entered the temple** to make the necessary
declaration as to when the vow would end (**he . . . announced, etc.**) and to
arrange with the priests on duty when the required **sacrifice would be**
offered for each of them. Having done that, Paul and the four men waited
to complete the offering, continuing to frequent the temple in the meantime. The following verse designates this period of waiting as **seven days**
with the article. This is obscure, especially as the article seems to refer to
a precise, known practice. The Mishna (*Nazir,* I, 3) fixed the shortest
duration of the Nazarite vow at thirty days (cf. the quotation of Flavius
Josephus in note on 18:18) during which time no fermented beverage might
be drunk nor might the hair be cut. At the end of thirty days, the person
under vow had to offer the prescribed sacrifices in the temple and shave

21:27. But when the seven days were almost over, the Jews from [the province of] Asia, seeing him in the temple, stirred up all the people and seized him,

21:28. shouting: "Men of Israel, help. This is the man who teaches all men everywhere against the people and the Law and this place, and moreover he has brought Greeks also into the temple and has desecrated this holy place."

21:29. For they had previously seen Trophimus, the Ephesian, in the city with him and they supposed that Paul had taken him into the temple.

---

the head, burning a lock of hair on the altar together with the sacrifice. It would seem from the present mention of **seven days** that shorter periods were also admissible for the vow, but we have no evidence from other documents. From the whole narrative, it cannot be concluded that Paul took the real "Nazarite" vow on this occasion. His part in the rite with the four men was that of a patron paying the costs of the sacrifices and perhaps performing some secondary rite connected with the vow, from personal devotion.

21:27-29. For the expression **seven days,** see preceding note. — The **Jews** from proconsular **Asia** had bitterly persecuted Paul during his stay at Ephesus (see notes on 19:10; 20:1) and they had not forgotten him. On one of the seven days, they had met him in the city with **Trophimus, the Ephesian** (for whom, see note on 20:4), and that had sufficed to make them keep an eye on him in the hope of finding some excuse for renewing their persecution against him. In Jerusalem, an essentially Jewish city, their intrigue would have better results than in the pagan city of Ephesus. A pretext was found shortly afterward when they again met Paul, this time in the temple. It was the moment to strike. As Jews, they felt that inside the temple they were masters of the situation, especially on a solemn feast day like Pentecost when the whole temple area, and in particular the "Court of the Gentiles" was thronged by pilgrims. For the Roman authorities in Jerusalem, the temple on the great feast days represented an erupting volcano which might explode at any moment. Therefore, on such days the Roman soldiers who were quartered in the nearby Fortress Antonia were armed and posted along the outside porticoes of the temple, so as to intervene immediately at any sign of a tumult (see note on vv. 31-32). It should be known that the "Court of the Gentiles" was accessible to pagans and therefore to Trophimus the Ephesian who, being an uncircumcised Christian, passed for a pagan in the eyes of the Jews. On the other hand,

21:30. And the whole city was thrown into confusion, and the people ran together, and seizing Paul, they proceeded to drag him out of the temple; whereupon the doors were immediately shut.

21:31. They were trying to kill him, when news reached the tribune of the cohort that all Jerusalem was in a tumult.

21:32. And he, immediately taking soldiers and centurions, ran down to them, and when they saw the tribune and the soldiers, they stopped beating Paul.

---

the same place was frequented by those who directed the vast secret movement of the Zealots-Sicarii, which a few years later led the revolt against the Romans and brought about the destruction of Jerusalem. This court was a kind of international information center from which the leaders of these insurgents followed the events of the Diaspora and Judea, and where they sent out orders to their followers in distant parts (cf. note on 20:3). These Sicarii, *particularly at the feasts, mix with the crowd, carrying small daggers* (called in Latin, *sica,* hence their name Sicarii) *hid under their clothes. With these they wound their adversaries, and when they have fallen, the murderers mix with the crowd and join in the outcry against the crime. Thus they passed unsuspected for a long time* (Flavius Josephus, *Wars of the Jews,* II, 255). Such was the background of the scene which now follows. Nevertheless it cannot be stated with certainty that the Sicarii took a direct part in it. — **Greeks** stands for "pagans" (cf. note on 11:20). The plural can be a "plural of category" (cf. note on 19:38), but it may be a hyperbole intended to emphasize the vastness of the crowd. — **He had taken him into the temple,** viz., into the "inner court" reserved exclusively for Jews, and entrance to which was forbidden to pagans under pain of death (cf. G. Ricciotti, *History of Israel,* II, pp. 339–340). The accusation was a most serious one, calculated to move the whole crowd to violence, as indeed happened as the following verses relate.

21:30. The shouts of verse 28 spread, for they excited the crowd gathered in the temple, and thence the confusion spread to **the whole city.** Paul was dragged **out of the temple,** i.e., from the "inner court," that they might proceed against him more freely. The Levites on duty, accustomed to these violent scenes, hurried to close **the doors** of the court so that the temple would not be desecrated, as it was easy to foresee that there might be bloodshed (cf. later, **they were trying to kill him**) which would involve profanation.

21:31-32. Reached, or **came up:** an expression which is topographically

21:33. Then the tribune came up and seized him and ordered him to be bound with two chains. He then inquired who he was and what he had been doing.

21:34. Some in the crowd shouted one thing, and some another, and as he could not learn anything certain on account of the tumult, he ordered him to be taken into the barracks.

21:35. And when he [Paul] came to the steps, he was actually being carried by the soldiers owing to the violence of the crowd;

21:36. for the mass of the people followed, shouting: "Away with him."

21:37. And as Paul was about to be taken into the barracks, he said to the tribune: "May I say something to thee?" He said: "Dost thou know Greek?

---

correct, since the level of the temple was lower than that of the Fortress Antonia, where the Roman garrison had its quarters. In this connection a passage from Flavius Josephus is very descriptive: *Where it* (the Fortress Antonia) *joined to the two porticos of the temple, it had passages down to them both, through which the guard (for there always lay in this tower a Roman legion) went several ways among the porticos with their arms on the Jewish festivals, in order to watch the people, that they might not there attempt to make any innovations. For the temple was a fortress that guarded the city, as was the Fortress Antonia a guard to the temple; and in that tower were the guards of those three* (those that guarded the city, the temple, and the Fortress Antonia) (*Wars of the Jews*, V, 243-245). See also note on 12:10. — The term **news** (φάσις) stands also for the person bringing it. As soon as the tumult began, a soldier was sent up from the "Court of the Gentiles" to the Fortress Antonia to warn **the tribune of the cohort.** For the duties of a tribune, see note on 22:28. The haste with which he ran showed how the Roman authorities feared such disturbances in the temple, while, on the other hand, the fact that those who were beating Paul ceased as soon as they saw the soldiers coming, showed how their violent manner of restoring order was feared by the crowd.

21:33. With two chains: just like Peter in 12:6; see note on 12:4.

21:34-36. A most vivid description of the scene, recalling the affair of the silversmiths' riot (19:29 sqq.). — For the **steps** spoken of here, see note on 12:10, and the passage of Flavius Josephus quoted above (vv. 31-32).

21:37. Dost thou know Greek? This question shows that Paul had

21:38. "Art not thou the Egyptian who recently stirred up to sedition and led out into the desert four thousand men of the Sicarii?"

21:39. But Paul said to him: "I am a Jew from Tarsus in Cilicia, a citizen of no mean city. But I beg thee, give me leave to speak to the people."

---

spoken in Greek to the tribune who had not understood the cry of the crowd because he did not understand their language which was Aramaic; cf. note on verse 40.

21:38. A little after the passage quoted in the note on verses 27–29, Flavius Josephus continues: *The false Egyptian prophet drew an even greater misfortune down upon the Jews. He was a charlatan come into the country, and having acquired the reputation of prophet, he gathered about 30,000 of those who were led astray (by him). Having led them round and round from the desert to the mountain called 'of Olives,' from there he would have been able to invade Jerusalem with force, and overcoming the Roman garrison, he would have set himself up as a ruler of the people supported by the armed mob which entered (with him). But his attempt was prevented by (the Roman procurator) Felix, who went to meet him with heavy Roman infantry, while the entire populace engaged in his defense. But when the conflict began, the Egyptian took flight with a certain few of his followers, while the greater number were killed or captured, and the rest of the crowd scattered to their homes (Wars of the Jews, II, 261–263).* Undoubtedly, this episode related by Flavius Josephus is the same as that spoken of here by the tribune. If the latter speaks of **four thousand men of the Sicarii** (for this name, see note on vv. 27–29), while Josephus speaks of *about 30,000,* the preference is to be given to the tribune, because, in the first place, Josephus frequently contradicts himself when he is dealing with numbers (see note on 5:36–37), and therefore should be accepted with reserve, and, in the second place, because he contradicts himself in this very instance. Josephus actually retells this episode in the *Antiquities of the Jews,* XX, 169–172, which is later than his other work, but he presents it with various divergences, among which is the statement that 400 of the Egyptian's followers were killed and 200 captured, but the total number is not given. But this 600 (400 + 200) men put out of action does not agree with the 30,000 of his account in the *Wars of the Jews,* of whom, *most* — a number certainly above 15,000 — are killed or captured. Therefore the *30,000* is one of the usual exaggerations of Josephus, while the *4000* of Luke's tribune is worthy of credence.

21:39. Paul replies indirectly to the tribune's question, telling him for the moment that he is not the Egyptian. That which will have more im-

21:40. And when [he] allowed it, Paul, standing on the steps, motioned with his hand to the people and when they had become quiet, he addressed them in Hebrew, saying:

22:1. "Brethren and fathers, listen to what I have to say to you in my defence."

22:2. And when they heard him speak to them in Hebrew, they became even more quiet. And he said:

---

portance for the tribune will come later (22:27). Now, all Paul wants is the chance to speak to the people, and he therefore asks for permission.

21:40. This discourse of Paul is paradoxical, but fully in keeping with the character of the speaker. He has been rescued from the violence of his fellow countrymen, worshipers of the God Jahveh, by pagan soldiers who had carried him out of Jahveh's temple. Yet in this bleeding and bruised condition, he wishes to speak to his fellow countrymen who do not want to hear his words, but only to seek his death. Paul here speaks as a **Hebrew of Hebrews** (Phil. 3:5) who not only wishes to show himself as a genuine compatriot of his hearers to make his *apologia before them* (cf. 22:1), but also to profess himself a sincere follower of the Messias Jesus and to draw his hearers to him. He is not, therefore, thinking of himself but of his fellow countrymen. He is not concerned with his own bleeding wounds, but with the perversity of the Jews concerning the Messias, their fellow countryman. It seems indeed that he is putting into action the words that he had written a few months before: **(in the hope) that I may provoke to jealousy those who are my flesh (my fellow countrymen) and may save some of them** (Rom. 11:14). Some have thought that all this was very unlikely and therefore have concluded that Paul's discourse was also fictitious. Indeed, it might seem so if the psychology of Paul were that of any ordinary man. — The **steps** (cf. note on v. 35) must have been a place from which Paul could speak and be safe from the reach of the mob. — **Motioned with his hand** (cf. note on 13:16) as best he could, since he was chained. — The *great silence* resulting from their **becoming quiet** was nothing extraordinary and could be explained by the fickleness and curiosity of the crowd. — **In Hebrew:** here is meant the "Aramaic" dialect of Palestine. Flavius Josephus also calls the "Aramaic" language, "Hebrew" (*Wars of the Jews*, VI, 96, and cf. I, 3; V, 272, 361). It was the ordinary language of daily life. However, the real ancient Hebrew language had not gone out as much as is commonly thought, for it was still used in learned circles though it had little place in public life.

22:3. "I am a Jew, born in Tarsus of Cilicia, but was brought up in this city and educated at the feet of Gamaliel according to the strict acceptance of the Law of our fathers, being zealous for God, just as all of you are today.

22:4. "[I am the one] who persecuted this way [of the Lord] even to the death, binding and committing to prison both men and women,

22:5. "as the high priest can bear me witness and all the elders. In fact, I received letters from them to the brethren, and I was on my way to Damascus to arrest those who were there, and bring them back to Jerusalem for punishment.

22:3. **Brought up:** the Greek verb (ἀνατρέφω) has been used twice before (7:20–21) in the physiological sense, viz., that of "being raised," "trained." Here it refers to cultural formation in the sense of "being instructed," "educated." This education took place **at the feet of Gamaliel** (mentioned in 5:34) in the sense that Paul frequented his lectures, but he also sat literally at the feet of Gamaliel, inasmuch as the pupils used to sit on the ground in a circle around the teacher who was seated on a stool. This custom is still practiced today in the Muslim university of al-Azhar in Cairo and elsewhere (cf. G. Ricciotti, *Paul the Apostle,* pp. 67–68). — **Educated ... according to the strict acceptance of the Law ... zealous,** etc. It is evident that by these words, Paul wishes to ingratiate himself with his hearers (cf. note on 21:40). Elsewhere also, he makes similar protestations, calling himself **a Pharisee, the son of Pharisees** (23:6; cf. Phil. 3:5) and one who **has advanced in Judaism above many of my contemporaries in my nation, showing much zeal for the traditions of my fathers** (Gal. 1:14).

22:4. **I who persecuted,** etc.: the events of 8:3. — **Way [of the Lord]:** see note on 18:25–26.

22:5. This unnamed **high priest** cannot be the one who was in office when Paul went to Damascus in the year 36 (see note on 9:12), but the high priest at the time of Paul's present discourse. Since here we are in A.D. 58, the high priest must have been Ananias, son of Nedebeus or Nebedeus, who held office from about A.D. 47 to 59 (cf. the notes on 4:5–6; 23:2). In fact, some documents of the Western Recension add the name **Ananias.** This high priest now in office and several members of the Sanhedrin could well have been part of the assembly in the year 36. The words which follow, **I received letters from them,** etc., do not disprove this, since the words **from them** — in the plural — do not refer to the high priest of the year 36 personally, but to the whole meeting of the Sanhedrin, which included the high priest and wielded the legislative power. — For

22:6. "And it came to pass that, as I was on my way and approaching Damascus, suddenly about noon, there shone round about me a great light from heaven;

22:7. "and I fell to the ground and heard a voice saying to me: 'Saul, Saul, why dost thou persecute me?'

22:8. "And I answered: 'Who art thou Lord?' And he said to me: 'I am Jesus of Nazareth whom thou art persecuting.'

22:9. "Now those who were with me saw indeed the light, but they did not hear the voice of him who was speaking to me.

22:10. "And I said: 'What am I to do, Lord?' And the Lord said to me: 'Get up and go into Damascus, and there thou shalt be told of all that thou art destined to do.'

22:11. "And as I could not see [anything] because of the dazzling light, my companions had to lead me by the hand, and so I reached Damascus.

22:12. "Now a certain Ananias, a devout observer of the Law, respected by all the Jews who lived [there],

22:13. "came to me and, standing beside me said to me: 'Brother Saul, regain thy sight.' And instantly I recovered my sight and looked at him.

22:14. "And he said, 'The God of our fathers has appointed thee

---

elders (or senate), the Greek has etymologically, the estate of the elders, the "presbyterium," but it means the Sanhedrin.

22:6 sqq. This is the second of the three accounts of the journey to Damascus: see note on 9:3 sqq.

22:9. Saw indeed the light, but they did not hear the voice: in 9:7, on the contrary, the men . . . were standing speechless, hearing indeed the voice but seeing no one: see note there.

22:12. This praise of Ananias which is not given to him in 9:10 sqq. was a fitting *captatio benevolentiae* for Paul's Jewish hearers here. But while previously he is called a Christian, here nothing is said about this fact.

22:13. This corresponds to 9:17, but the timidity expressed there by Ananias regarding Saul is here omitted.

22:14. The Just One: namely, Jesus Christ; see note on 3:14.

beforehand to learn his will and to see the Just One and to hear a voice from his mouth,

22:15. " 'for thou shalt be his witness before all men of what thou hast seen and heard.

22:16. " 'And now why dost thou delay? Get up and be baptised, and wash away thy sins, calling on his name.'

22:17. "And it came to pass that, when I had returned to Jerusalem and was praying in the temple, I was in an ecstasy,

22:18. "and saw him as he said to me, 'Make haste and go quickly out of Jerusalem, for they will not receive thy testimony concerning me.'

22:19. "And I said 'Lord, they themselves know that I used to imprison and beat in one synagogue after another, those who believed in thee;

22:15. This partly corresponds to 9:15, where, however, it is the Lord who speaks to Ananias announcing Paul's mission to him. But such a mission is more clearly announced to Paul, not by Ananias, but directly by the Lord himself in 26:16–18: see there.

22:16. Be baptised . . . calling on his name: here the question of "baptism in the name of Jesus Christ" occurs again, for which see note on 2:38.

22:17. This important episode is clearly a different one from Paul's conversion, since it happened later on, viz., when Paul, after his conversion and his baptism at Damascus, had returned to Jerusalem. While he was praying in the Hebrew temple there, he fell into an ecstasy with the results which he now relates. The only occasion known to us which we can assign for this episode is the visit Paul made to Jerusalem in A.D. 39, three years after his conversion (see note on 9:26). There is no foundation for identifying this ecstasy which Paul had in the temple at Jerusalem, with his being caught up into the third heaven, narrated by him in 2 Cor. 12:2 sqq. This last event actually took place fourteen years before Paul wrote this epistle and it must be assigned therefore to about A.D. 43, viz., when Paul was far away from Jerusalem.

22:18–21. The Lord orders Paul to leave Jerusalem because his apostolate among the Jews there will be fruitless. Paul replies, objecting that his own testimony as a former persecutor will be more efficacious. The Lord breaks off the discussion, telling Paul that he wishes to send him far away from Jerusalem and Judea to peoples or Gentiles who are distant (μακράν: an

22:20. " 'and when the blood of Stephen, thy witness, was shed, I was standing by and approved it, and took charge of the garments of those who killed him.'

22:21. "And he said to me: 'Go, for to the Gentiles far away I will send thee.' "

22:22. Now, till he said this, they were listening to him, but [then] they lifted up their voice and shouted, "Away from the earth with such a one, for it is not fit that he should live."

22:23. And as they were shouting and casting off their garments and throwing dust into the air,

22:24. the tribune ordered him to be taken into the barracks and to be scourged and tortured that he might find out why they shouted so against him.

---

adverbial expression meaning "afar off"). This conversation took place in the mystical realm of ecstasy, but, in the practical field, Paul's departure from Jerusalem was secretly desired by the local Christian community, for the reasons explained in the note on 9:30. The agreement between the mystical communication and the wish of the community, of which Paul must have had some report, induced him to depart immediately.

22:22. Till . . . this (literally, **unto this word**), i.e., the statement that he was sent to preach to the Gentiles. At this announcement the hearers exploded, even though they had been listening quietly when Paul was telling them of his vision in the temple. What now made them break out in protest was the announcement that the pagan peoples were judged a worthy substitute for the holy race of Israel and that they could be admitted to the following of the Messias, whom Paul preached, independently of the people of God. **Such a one,** a blasphemer and impious wretch, ought to be removed **from the earth.**

22:23. This is a scene accompanied by the usual Oriental histrionics, disorderly and noisy. It is useless to suppose, as some have done, that this action of casting off their garments was a symbol of stoning, or that throwing dust into the air had a superstitious meaning. Both were merely an outlet for their pent-up anger.

22:24. At this ugly turn of events, the tribune who had neither understood Paul's discourse in Aramaic nor the shouts of the crowd in the same language, judged that the situation was worsening, and he thought it best to question Paul, who was responsible for the tumult. In the tribune's view, since he had denied that he was the Egyptian rebel leader

22:25. But when they had bound him with the straps, Paul said to the centurion who was standing by, "Is it legal for you to scourge a Roman, and that without a trial?"

22:26. When the centurion heard this, he went to the tribune and reported, saying, "What art thou about to do? This man is a Roman citizen."

22:27. Then the tribune came and said to him: "Tell me, art thou a Roman?" And he said: "Yes."

22:28. And the tribune answered, "I obtained this citizenship at a great price." And Paul said, "But I am a citizen by birth."

(cf. 21:38), he must be some other agitator, of whom at that time there were many (see note on 21:27–29). But the cross examination of the prisoner must be at the same time quick and productive. If it were limited to questioning, much time would be lost with the lies, evasions, and dissimulations usual with this type of accused. So as to avoid delay, the tribune **ordered him to be taken into the barracks,** viz., into the Fortress Antonia adjoining the temple (see note on 21:31–32) and commanded him to be scourged and interrogated at the same time so that the truth might be wrung from him. Torture, as a means of inquisition, was practiced not only in the East, but also in Europe until only a few centuries ago.

22:25. Bound him with the straps, ἱμᾶσιν: viz., when they had *stretched* him forward by tying him *with the straps* so that he could not escape the blows. Some have translated **bound him for** (applying the blows of) **the straps,** interpreting these to mean the leather thongs of the scourge, as equivalent to μάστιξιν: see note on verse 29. — The **centurion** was the subordinate officer (cf. note on 10:1) detailed to superintend the prisoner after the superior officer had left.

22:26–27. The centurion was alarmed at Paul's question and the tribune was surprised and hurried to the prisoner. The episode at Philippi was being repeated (cf. note on 16:37–39). When Paul replied "Yes" it never entered the tribune's head that Paul might not be telling the truth. To have lied would have been an exceptionally reckless crime, and in rare instances when the claim had been fraudulently made, the offenders had been punished by death (Suetonius, *Claud.*, 25). — For the origins of Paul's Roman citizenship, see *Paul the Apostle,* pp. 183–185.

22:28. Finding himself before one who was a Roman citizen by birth, the tribune recalls with a certain tinge of sadness the heavy sum he has paid for that precious citizenship. He was called Claudius Lysias (cf. 23:26), namely, he had added to his original Greek name of Lysias the

22:29. At once therefore those who had been going to torture him left him; and the tribune himself was alarmed to find that Paul was a Roman citizen, and that he had bound him.

22:30. The next day, as he wished to find out the real reason why [Paul] was accused by the Jews, he loosed him and ordered the high priests and all the Sanhedrin to assemble; and bringing Paul down, he placed him in front of them.

Roman name of Claudius, probably because he had obtained his citizenship under that emperor. In fact, under this emperor there had been quite a trade, at various prices, in this matter (Dion Cassius, LX, 17). Perhaps Lysias had bought it at the beginning when the price was still high.

22:29. The tribune **was alarmed** at the mere responsibility for having **bound Paul.** The documents quoted in the note on 16:37-39 show that he had reason for his fear. The reference to **binding** him seems to confirm the fact that the **straps** of verse 25 were used for binding the prisoner and not for beating him. It should be noted how in the whole of this episode, Luke presents the Roman authorities in a favorable light with regard to Paul, which confirms what was said in the note on 3:13.

22:30. Wished to find out the real reason . . . This may have been one motive, though not the only one, that led the tribune to act as he did. In actual fact, he was not happy about what had happened and foresaw unpleasant consequences for himself. Besides the **alarm** at having **bound** (preceding verse) Paul, he had another attempted violation of Roman law on his mind, for he had ordered the prisoner to be scourged at the beginning of the interrogation, whereas the Emperor Augustus had decreed that a legal process could not begin with torture (*Digest,* XLVIII, 18, 1). It is true that this violation had not been carried out; nevertheless it had been begun and was a grave wrong done to a Roman citizen. All this made the tribune anxious and he very cleverly sought to implicate others so as gradually to withdraw himself from any personal responsibility in the matter. He therefore calls in the Sanhedrin, just as later he defers the whole matter to the Roman governor, not, however, without having given an account of it which was entirely to his own advantage (23:26 sqq.). — For a description of the Sanhedrin, see note on 4:5-6. Here it appears to have assembled outside the precincts of the temple, otherwise the pagan tribune would not have been able to take part in the proceedings. It certainly must have been a place below the Fortress Antonia where the tribune and Paul were standing, which overlooked the surrounding area, so that the expression **bringing Paul down** is correct. The tribune **loosed**

23:1. Then Paul, looking steadily at the Sanhedrin, said: "Brethren, I have conducted myself before God with a perfectly good conscience up to this day."

23:2. But the high priest Ananias ordered those who were standing by him to strike him on the mouth.

Paul to bring him before the Sanhedrin. Some codices add the words **from his bonds,** meaning the chains mentioned in 21:33. It was probably an act of deference to Paul on the part of the tribune (who had various reasons to ingratiate himself with him), so that a Roman citizen should not appear before his enemies of the Sanhedrin in that ill-becoming condition. Later on, however, Paul appears in public bound in chains (cf. 26:29). It is not only possible, but quite probable, that the tribune, in summoning the Sanhedrin to assemble, informed them briefly about Paul's case, so that when the proceedings began, Paul could commence speaking after a few words from the tribune. Naturally Luke omits these insignificant details, so much so that the impression is given that the meeting broke out into a tumult almost at once. In bringing Paul before the Sanhedrin, the tribune certainly did not intend to hand him over to the power of that tribunal, since the question concerned a Roman citizen protected by Roman law. But over and above that, he may have done it to show deference to those powerful Jews who could cause a lot of trouble for him if the Roman governor should go into the matter in any detail.

23:1. **Looking steadily at the Sanhedrin,** some members of which he may have known, and from whom he had received letters twenty-two years before for the persecution against the Christians in Damascus (cf. 9:2; 22:5). — **With a perfectly good conscience,** i.e., always with the approval of his conscience. The use of the term **conscience** is frequent in the letters of Paul (Rom. 2:15; 9:1; 13:5; etc.). — **Up to this day:** therefore not only before his conversion to Christ (26:4–5; Phil. 3:6), but also afterward, his conscience was clear before God.

23:2. The declaration made by Paul, while it was a clear statement of his own conviction, was also an appeal to the invisible judgment of his own conscience and God. This angered **the high priest Ananias** (cf. note on 22:5) who considered that Paul should acquit himself before him and the other visible judges gathered there. Therefore, in order to humiliate him, he gave the order **to strike him on the mouth.** The domineering and overbearing character of Ananias is partially confirmed by Flavius Josephus (*Antiquities of the Jews,* XX, 205–207) who describes him as an avaricious and violent man. He was assassinated in Jerusalem by the Zealots-Sicarii

23:3. Then Paul said to him: "God will strike thee, thou whitened wall! Dost thou sit there to try me by the Law, and in violation of the Law order me to be struck?"

23:4. But the bystanders said: "Dost thou insult God's high priest?"

23:5. And Paul said: "I did not know brethren, that it was the high priest, for it is written 'Thou shalt not speak evil of a ruler of thy people.'"

---

in July-August of A.D. 66, at the beginning of the revolt against Rome (*Wars of the Jews*, II, 429, 441).

23:3-5. When Paul heard the order that they should strike him, he reacted quickly and characteristically. The order was given by Ananias, the high priest, and Paul declared that he did not know that it was the high priest who spoke. This part of the narrative offers difficulties. It may well have been that Paul did not know Ananias personally, because when he was elected in A.D. 47 (cf. note on 22:5) Paul was traveling through Asia Minor on his first missionary journey. But even allowing that he did not know him by sight, he could have guessed his official position, either from the garments he wore or the place where he sat as president of the Sanhedrin or from some other detail. Several explanations have been given of this episode, some quite unconvincing and others little better. For example, Paul had weak sight (an explanation originating from mis-interpretations of some passages in his epistles) or that he was speaking ironically (that from the domineering behavior of Ananias, he would not have supposed him to be the high priest). Again, that the Sanhedrists did not sit in that assembly in order of precedence, and the high priest did not put on the special garments of his office; and suchlike. The most likely explanation is that Paul, warming up to his discourse, heard the words of Ananias but did not identify the person who had spoken them. So turning in the direction whence the words came, he made his spirited reply which was intentionally directed at the unknown Sanhedrist whom Paul thought was other than the high priest. In actual fact, Paul's reply fitted either of them since they were both sitting in judgment on him.— The epithet of **Whitened wall** comes from Ezech. 13:10 sqq., which was a text known to the Sanhedrists, and not from Mt. 23:27, which they did not know.— **In violation of the Law**: this alludes to Lev. 19:15; Deut. 25:1-2.— The construction of the words **will strike thee**, τύπτειν μέλλει, should be noted as not being an imprecation, but only an announcement regarding the future. Ananias was actually assassinated (see preceding note) but Paul's prophecy was directed in a general way to whoever had ordered him to be struck, and not to the high priest as such. Notwithstanding all

23:6. Then Paul, knowing that part of them were Sadducees and part of them Pharisees, cried out in the Sanhedrin, "Brethren, I am a Pharisee, the son of Pharisees; it is about the hope and the resurrection of the dead that I am on trial."

23:7. And when he said that, there arose a dispute between the Pharisees and the Sadducees, and the multitude was divided.

23:8. For the Sadducees say that there is no resurrection, and that there are no angels or spirits, whereas the Pharisees believe in both.

---

that, one cannot fail to make a comparison between the bearing of Paul and that of Jesus before the ex-high priest Annas (Jn. 18:22–23). At a reply of Jesus, Annas grew angry and a zealous servant obligingly struck Jesus for him, while the Lord with divine serenity asked him to show how he had offended (Ex. 22:28). Here Ananias is likewise angry and orders Paul to be struck, and even though it seems that the command was not obeyed, Paul's reaction was not a gentle one. In Paul's defense some have adopted explanations which are not to be despised, e.g., that he had to defend his dignity as a Roman citizen before the tribune, and that he did not curse Ananias but merely predicts his violent death. In the last analysis the best comment seems to be that of a man who had a character similar to Paul's, viz., Jerome, who says: *Where is that patience of the Saviour, who, led as a lamb to the slaughter, did not open his lips: rather he replied with all sweetness to the one who had struck him? . . . We do not belittle the Apostle, no, but we point out the glory of the Lord, who while suffering in the flesh, overcomes all insult and frailty of the flesh* (*C. Pelagianos*, III, 4; in Migne, *P. L.*, 23, 600).

23:6–8. It will be noted that Paul's discourse had only got as far as the few words of verse 1 when the incident with the high priest happened. But Paul did not limit himself to those few words only, and we gather that he spoke again and that his statements caused disagreement among the Sadducees, and approval among the Pharisees (see note on 4:1–2). Inasmuch as Paul was a follower of the Messias Jesus, both parties were opposed to him, but to break their hostile alliance, he shrewdly insisted on the differences between them. The seventy-one members of the Sanhedrin comprised three groups, of which that of the *high priests* and that of the *elders* were made up almost exclusively of followers of the Sadducean sect. That of the *Scribes* or *Doctors of the Law* consisted in great part of the followers of the Pharisean sect. This last group was the most powerful and authoritative with the ordinary people, while the other two were more of an aristocratic standing. Paul here leaned on the group of the Pharisees,

23:9. So there was a great uproar and some of the scribes belonging to the party of the Pharisees stood up and fought the question saying: "We find no evil in this man! What if a spirit has really spoken to him, or an angel?"

23:10. And as the dispute was becoming violent, the tribune, fearing lest Paul should be torn to pieces by them, ordered the soldiers

---

in the first place by proclaiming himself a Pharisee, son of Pharisees in a general way (cf. note on 22:3), and then by fastening on to the chief doctrinal question on which the Pharisees differed from the Sadducees, viz., the **hope** and the **resurrection of the dead.** The **hope** was that which was more fully called the **hope of Israel** (28:20; cf. 26:6–7), viz., the messianic hope, which according to the view then commonly held was intimately connected with the **resurrection of the dead,** inasmuch as the resurrection would take place at the time of the future messianic kingdom (cf. 24:15 and 21). Paul's declarations were true from his point of view. He continues to call himself a **Pharisee** later on (Phil. 3:5) when he refers to his past, as he probably does here. Moreover, he was now on trial because of his **hope** (in the Messias) **and the resurrection of the dead.** He was being persecuted because he had placed his hope in the Messias identified by him with Jesus, and he believed in the resurrection of the dead. If the non-Christian Pharisees rejected Jesus and were awaiting another Messias, the two doctrines remained true in spite of their attitude toward them. The respective doctrines of the Pharisees and Sadducees are given by Flavius Josephus (*Wars of the Jews,* II, 162–166; *Antiquities of the Jews,* XIII, 171–173, 288–298; XVII, 41–45; XVIII, 11–17), but only from this passage of the *Acts* do we know that the Sadducees believed in **no angels or spirits** (μήτε ἄγγελον μήτε πνεῦμα). It is unlikely that the two terms **angel** and **spirit** were equivalent collectively to "spiritual being" in general; they must mean two distinctive concepts in the terminology of the Bible and later Judaism (cf. v. 9). Nor does the fact that the word **both** refers to three things instead of two, present any difficulty, since there are other cases of similar references which are not numerically exact (see note on 19:16).

23:9. The fiery Oriental tempers broke out into an **uproar.** So as to prevail over their adversaries, some of the scribes openly defended Paul. Note should be taken of the interrogative, **what if** (εἰ δέ), etc., which remains unanswered. It corresponds more or less to the meaning, **it could be that . . .**

23:10. The tribune, being responsible for the safety of a Roman citizen, feared that Paul would **be torn to pieces.** This was not an exaggerated

to come down and take him by force from among them and bring him into the barracks.

23:11. But on the following night, the Lord stood by him and said: "Be steadfast; for just as thou hast borne witness to me in Jerusalem, so thou must bear witness also in Rome."

23:12. Now when day broke, the Jews assembled and bound themselves under a curse, saying that they would neither eat nor drink till they had killed Paul.

23:13. And there were more than forty who had made this conspiracy,

23:14. and they went to the chief priests and the elders and said: "We have bound ourselves under a great curse to taste nothing until we have killed Paul.

---

fear, because among the Orientals religious disputes often degenerated into fanatical quarrels, and that not only among Jews, but Christians also. Suffice to recall the Arian quarrels, the "latrocinium of Ephesus," and iconoclasm. — **To come down** from the Fortress Antonia, which was the soldiers' *quarters;* see note on 22:24 and 30.

23:11. **The Lord:** Jesus; as on other occasions of crisis, Paul was supernaturally guided or comforted: cf. 16:6–10; 18:9; 27:23–24. — **Rome:** where Paul for some time had planned to go; see note on 19:21.

23:12–13. The **Jews** here is a *nomen generis* because it does not refer to all of them, but to the **forty** referred to afterward. Whence some codices have more precisely altered it to **some of the Jews.** A similar **conspiracy** from nationalistic-religious motives plotted to kill Herod the Great, according to the detailed description of Flavius Josephus (*Antiquities of the Jews,* XV, 281–290), and so great was the fanaticism of the ten conspirators that there was even a blind man among them. In Paul's day fanaticism had increased, since the party of the Sicarii were very much at work (see notes on 20:3; 21:27–29 and 38). The imprecatory vow of **neither eating nor drinking** was more apparent than real, because if the object of the plot was not attained, the doctors of the Jewish Law could easily find a way to declare it invalid. Similar cases are considered in the Mishna, *Nedarim,* V, 6; IX, 1 sqq. In the present case, even though the aim of the plot was not achieved, we can be sure that none of the conspirators died of starvation!

23:14–15. Notice how **the chief priests** and **the elders,** i.e., the two Sadducean groups in the Sanhedrin, are named first (see note on vv. 6–8),

23:15. "Now therefore do you suggest to the tribune — together with the Sanhedrin — that he bring him down to you as though you mean to look into his case more carefully: but we are ready to kill him before he gets here."

23:16. Now the son of Paul's sister heard of the ambush, and he came and entered the barracks and told Paul.

23:17. Paul called one of the centurions to him and said, "Take this young man to the tribune; for he has something to report to him."

23:18. So he took him and brought him to the tribune and said, "The prisoner Paul called me and asked me to bring this young man to thee, for he has something to say to thee."

23:19. So the tribune took him by the hand and going aside with him asked him: "What is it thou hast to tell me?"

---

and then the **Sanhedrin** in general which included also the group of the Scribes and Doctors of the Law, who were mainly Pharisees. But the conspirators did not address themselves to these latter because they had sided with Paul (v. 9). The words, **together with the Sanhedrin,** are separated from **you** where one would expect to find them. Perhaps the reason for this is to make it appear that those who approached the tribune spoke in the name of the entire Sanhedrin, as though there were no disagreement among the three groups regarding Paul. — **Suggest:** thus the Greek verb, etymologically, ἐμφανίζω, which is used elsewhere as meaning "to present for denunciation" (24:1; 25:2 and 15), but here and in verse 22 it means rather "to show the opportunity of," "to inform someone so that he might do something." The whole question is resolved in some documents of the Western Recension which give the following reading: **Now therefore, we beg you to do this: when you have assembled the Sanhedrin, make it appear to the tribune (that it is opportune) that he should bring him, etc.**

23:16. The son of Paul's sister: this is the only reference we have to any of Paul's relatives. We do not know, however, either the age of this nephew (but he is called a **young man:** v. 18), or if he was a Christian, or if he lived in Jerusalem in order to follow his studies of the Hebrew Law as his uncle had done. Nor are we told whether Paul's sister then lived at Jerusalem or Tarsus or elsewhere. The young man revealed the plot just as another person unknown — probably a Christian — had revealed that other plot of 20:3.

23:18-19. The tribune's cordiality toward the young man sent by Paul

23:20. And he said: "The Jews have agreed to ask thee to bring down Paul to the Sanhedrin to-morrow, on the plea that thou shouldst have a more thorough investigation made into his case.

23:21. "But do not believe them, for more than forty of them are lying in wait for him, having bound themselves under a curse not to eat or drink until they have killed him; and they are now ready, only waiting for thy promise."

23:22. The tribune therefore let the young man go, charging him not to divulge to anyone that "thou hast made known to me this information";

23:23. then calling two centurions he said to them: "Get ready by the third hour of the night, two hundred soldiers to go as far as Caesarea, and seventy cavalry and two hundred spearmen;

23:24. "and provide beasts to mount Paul and take him in safety to Felix the governor."

---

was a consequence of his cordiality toward the prisoner himself; cf. note on 22:30.

23:20. That thou shouldst have a more thorough investigation, etc. (literally, as though thou wouldst inquire somewhat, etc.: this is the reading of the greater number of the uncial codices ὡς μέλλων τι, which would refer to the tribune. However there are variants such as μέλλοντες (the Sanhedrists), μέλλον (the Sanhedrin in general), etc. Probably the original reading was μέλλοντες, corresponding to the reading of verse 15, which then became μέλλον — τι: in verse 15 the τι is missing, resulting here from the division of the word.

23:21. The **promise,** or rather its fulfillment, which was to satisfy them by sending Paul down. Elsewhere in the New Testament, this term has a theological sense, the divine **promise.**

23:22. Thou hast made known to me this information: this is a change-over into direct speech. A similar case is found in 1:4. For the verb **made known,** see note on verse 15. The young man's information coincided with the tribune's vague wish to free himself of the whole troublesome business by passing the responsibility on to someone else (see note on 22:30). In this sense, he immediately makes his decision and proceeds at once to carry it out.

23:23-24. This language of the tribune is typical of a soldier. The superior officer gives the orders to two subordinates as he thinks them out

23:25. And he wrote a letter [besides] in these terms:

23:26. "Claudius Lysias to his excellency Felix the governor, greeting.

---

in accordance with his prearranged plan. The infinitive **to provide** or "have ready" does not depend on the preceding verb **said,** but on **you must** (δεῖ), which is understood, but omitted in keeping with the crisp military style of a command. In the same way the subject of **to mount** and **take him in safety** is omitted, but refers to the soldiers belonging to the company of the two centurions. The tribune is not satisfied with the first **two hundred soldiers** on foot, but adds **seventy cavalry,** able to move more swiftly being mounted. Finally, to be absolutely sure of the superiority of his escort, he includes another **two hundred spearmen.** This last word is in Greek δεξιολάβοι. It is not found elsewhere in any early Greek writings and appears only in the seventh century A.D. The Vulgate gives **lancearii** (lancers), while a Greek uncial codex gives δεξιοβόλοι (javelin throwers). At Antipatris, where the escort divides, the **soldiers** and **cavalry** are mentioned, but not the **spearmen** (vv. 31–32). A total of 470 soldiers as an escort might seem somewhat excessive, but the tribune, concerned at the number of the conspirators who were **more than forty men** (vv. 13 and 21), and preoccupied with the Zealots-Sicarii who were always on the prowl, especially around the countryside, wished the expedition to be able to overcome any attack. The last order given to the centurion concerned Paul. He and his personal bodyguard of soldiers must not go on foot but **mounted.** Such an arrangement would thereby provide that the Roman citizen Paul would not complain to the governor of the way in which he had been treated by the tribune from the start. The journey from Jerusalem **to . . . Caesarea,** passing through Antipatris (v. 31), was a little over 65 miles, of which the distance to Antipatris was 42 miles, the part most dangerous for the ambush (cf. Flavius Josephus, *Wars of the Jews,* II, 542–554). — The **third hour of the night** corresponded to our nine in the evening, thus darkness would better protect the march. — At the end of verse 24, the Vulgate, partly supported by documents of the Western Recension adds: **For he feared lest perhaps the Jews might take him away by force and kill him, and he should afterwards be slandered, as if he had taken money.**

23:25–26. The governor to whom this letter is addressed is Anthony Felix, who held office from the year 52 to 60. He was a freed slave and, as Tacitus says, he held his office with the mentality of a slave (*servili ingenio: Histor.,* V, 9), aiming solely at gain. He also had a mania, common among the *nouveaux riche,* for cultivating those in high places, so much so that he successively became the *husband of three queens* (Sue-

23:27. "Whereas this man had been seized by the Jews and was on the point of being killed by them, I came on them with the troops and rescued him, having learnt that he was a Roman.

23:28. "And wishing to know what charge they had preferred against him, I took him down into their Sanhedrin.

23:29. "I found him accused about questions of their Law, but not of any crime deserving of death or imprisonment.

23:30. "And when I was told of an ambush which they had prepared for him, I sent him to thee, directing his accusers also to state the case before thee. Farewell."

---

tonius, *Claud.,* 28). One of these wives was Drusilla, spoken of in 24:24, the sister of Agrippa II and Bernice named in 25:13, who had already been the wife of Azizus, king of Emesa (cf. note on 13:8). For an account of his governorship, see G. Ricciotti, *The History of Israel,* II, pp. 395–398. — The letter which follows was a typical Roman official document, a *eulogium* or presentation, which a magistrate was required to send to a higher authority when he referred a prisoner to him. With such a document, the subordinate officer informed his superior about the condemned man's case, and usually added his own personal opinion about it. The letter of Lysias has all the marks of authenticity, and Luke could easily have procured a copy of the original kept in the archives at Caesarea. A confirmation of the authenticity of the letter is the adroit way in which Lysias colors the facts to favor himself, slightly distorting some details and omitting others.

23:27. The assertions in this verse are true if taken literally (cf. 21:31–32; 22:27–28), but the connection between them is untrue, and, above all, much is left out. Here the tribune practically asserts that he acted on Paul's behalf because he knew he was a Roman, whereas in actual fact he learned this only incidentally after he had bound him and prepared him for torture. Naturally he kept quiet about these details which would be to his discredit.

23:30. Directing (literally, **having charged**), etc. This direction given to Paul's Jewish accusers does not appear in the preceding account. On the contrary, it would seem that Paul's dispatch to Caesarea was done secretly so as not to give any warning to the conspirators who wished to kill him. At most, the notice was given to them after Paul had left Jerusalem. On the other hand, according to 24:8, the order appears to have been given before Paul's departure, but much depends upon the authenticity of a passage which is not at all certain.

23:31. So the soldiers, in accordance with their instructions, took Paul and conducted him by night to Antipatris;

23:32. and the next day they returned to the barracks, leaving the cavalry to go on with him.

23:33. When [these others] reached Caesarea, they delivered the letter to the governor and also handed Paul over to him.

23:34. On reading it, he asked from what province he was; and learning that he [was] from Cilicia,

23:35. "I will hear thee," he said, "when thy accusers have come." And he ordered him to be kept under guard in Herod's palace.

23:31-32. By night: marching mostly at night. They must have arrived at Antipatris on the following day by reason of the distance (for which, see note on vv. 23–24). It was actually a forced march, necessitated by the circumstances. An even more forced march with the same goal, viz., Antipatris, was undertaken eight years later by the army of Cestius Gallus after he had been routed by the Jewish insurgents under the walls of Jerusalem (Flavius Josephus, *Wars of the Jews,* II, 542 sqq., 554). — **Antipatris** is the present-day Ras-el-Ain. There the open plain began and it was a good distance from Jerusalem, so that there was little fear of ambush. Consequently, Paul's escort was reduced to the **cavalry,** while the *foot soldiers* returned to Jerusalem. Of the *spearmen,* no mention is made (see note on vv. 23–24).

23:34-35. Of what province he was a native. The tribune's letter had given no indication of this. Really it was an unnecessary question, since from whatever province — senatorial or imperial — the accused came, he was for the present under the jurisdiction of the governor. When the governor said to Paul that he would wait for his accusers before trying his case, he was legally correct, but it is likely that he had some secret hope that in Paul's case there might be some financial gain (cf. 24:26) which would make it worth his while to draw the case out at length. — **Herod's palace** was the royal palace erected by Herod the Great when he completely rebuilt Caesarea, a project which took some twelve years. It was now called a *praetorium* because the highest Roman magistrate of Judea resided there, it being the custom of Roman officials to take up their headquarters in the royal palaces in the regions ruled by them (Cicero, *in Verrem.,* IV, 5, 30). Being a sumptuous and large building, it had cells for prisoners, in one of which Paul was kept, though otherwise he was treated with consideration.

24:1. Now five days later the high priest Ananias came down with some of the elders and one Tertullus, an attorney; and they presented their case against Paul before the governor.

24:2. When Paul had been summoned, Tertullus began to accuse him saying: "Whereas we live in much peace through thee, and whereas many reforms are in progress in this nation by thy foresight,

24:3. "we always and everywhere receive them, most excellent Felix, with all thankfulness.

24:4. "But not to detain thee too long, I entreat thee to be kind enough to grant us a brief hearing.

24:1. **Ananias**: cf. 23:2. — **Elders** of the Sanhedrin, therefore almost certainly Sadducees (cf. note on 23:6–8) and enemies of Paul. — We know nothing of this **Tertullus** who may have been a Greek or a Latin, but it is very unlikely that he was a Jew. If in this speech he seems to speak as a Jew (**this nation . . . we . . . receive**), he does so because he is following the usual custom by which an advocate identifies himself with his client for the purposes of the case, but that does not show that he was a Jew. The Greek text calls him a **public speaker**, or **orator**, which here corresponds to our **attorney**. The discussion of the case was certainly in Greek as was the practice also in Rome (Dion Cassius, LVII, 15; Suetonius, *Tiber.*, 71). The account of it given here is, as usual, only a short summary; this is true especially of the speech of Tertullus.

24:2–3. The *captatio benevolentiae*, obtained by means of praise for the hearers, was the oratorical convention of that age, but here Tertullus' eulogy is in such contrast to the actual facts as almost to suggest that he was speaking ironically. This exordium by Tertullus would be historically true if the word *not* were put before each verb in it. In truth we must say that Felix did deal severely with rebels who abounded in his territories (Flavius Josephus, *Wars of the Jews*, II, 253 sqq.), but that certainly did not produce **much peace**, as affirmed here, since the beginnings of the final insurrection against Rome started under Felix. In actual fact, he himself came to terms with the rebels when it suited him and made use of the Sicarii to kill the ex-high priest Jonathan (see note on 9:1–2) who was the very one who asked Claudius at Rome for him as Governor (*Antiquities of the Jews*, XX, 162–164). When Tertullus spoke of **all thankfulness**, that was belied by those Jewish leaders in Caesarea who went to Rome in A.D. 60 to accuse Felix before Nero (*Antiquities of the Jews*, XX, 182). — **Always and everywhere**: a play on words which is to

24:5. "[We are], in fact, those who have found this man a pest, a promoter of seditions among all the Jews throughout the whole world, and a ringleader of the sedition of the Nazarene sect,

24:6. "who even tried to desecrate the temple but we caught him;

24:7.

24:8. "by examining him thyself, thou wilt be able to discover all these things of which we charge him."

24:9. And the Jews also supported the charge saying that this was so.

---

be attributed more to Luke than to Tertullus, since the former uses it elsewhere (17:30; 21:28).

24:5-6. Tertullus' accusation against Paul is summarized in these two verses, the literary form of which is anything but readable and straightforward probably because they depend on brief notes taken down during or shortly after the trial. There are three charges preferred against Paul: he is a **promoter of seditions among all the Jews, etc.;** moreover he is a **ringleader** (πρωτοστάτην) of the . . . **Nazarene sect,** viz., the Christians (see note on 2:22); finally, in Jerusalem he **even tried to desecrate the temple.** The first two charges were serious, especially from the political viewpoint, since they bespoke a threat to that tranquillity of order which the Romans so jealously guarded. The third accusation was of a religious nature (see note on 21:27-29), but this also was an offense according to Roman law.

24:(7-8). After the words **we caught him,** a few minuscule codices and some documents of the Western Recension and the Vulgate add: **and wished to judge him according to our Law; ⁷but Lysias the tribune came upon us and with great violence took him away out of our hands, ⁸ordering his accusers to come to thee; by examining him etc.** Modern criticism in general is against accepting this addition, both because of the insufficiency of the documentation, and because of the difficulties which arise from it. In fact, Tertullus had every reason for ingratiating himself with the Roman authorities and would have been very unwise to extend his accusation to include the tribune Lysias, who incidentally was not brought into the discussion even by Paul in his reply (v. 10 sqq.). Furthermore, in the text without the addition, the words **by examining him** of verse 8 refer to Paul, just as the preceding **who (even tried)** . . . refers to him, but according to the inserted text, Tertullus says that the judge, by carefully **examining him,** will be able **to discover, etc.** But in the inserted text, Lysias is the subject of the sentence, and therefore the words **by examining him** should be referred to him. In such a case, there would be the incongruity of Lysias, against whom Tertullus is complaining in

24:10. Then when the governor nodded to him to speak, Paul answered: "As I know that for many years thou hast been a judge for this nation, I shall answer for myself with good courage.

24:11. "For thou canst ascertain that it is not more than twelve days since I went up to worship in Jerusalem,

24:12. "and neither in the temple did they find me disputing with anyone or creating a disturbance among the people, nor in the synagogues, nor about the city;

24:13. "neither can they prove to thee the charges that they now make against me.

24:14. "But this I admit to thee, that according to the Way, which they call a sect, so I serve the God of my fathers, believing all things that are written in the Law and the Prophets,

---

this insertion, making himself appear in the wrong. An able lawyer like Tertullus is not likely to have made such a gross tactical error. Probably the addition was occasioned by the assertion of 23:30, according to which Lysias had notified Paul's accusers to present themselves at the tribunal of the governor of Caesarea.

24:10. For many years was six years (see note on 23:25), but the term of the office of governors of Judea was usually shorter. From a passage in Tacitus (*Annal.*, XII, 54), it would seem that Felix had held the post of governor of Samaria and Judea at the same time that the procuratorship of Galilee was held by Ventidius Cumanus, who is ordinarily considered to have been Felix's predecessor in the governorship. But since this isolated statement of Tacitus is contradicted by the repeated and precise statements of Flavius Josephus (*Wars of the Jews*, II, 232–247; *Antiquities of the Jews*, XX, 118–137) which give Felix as the successor of Cumanus, in this instance the Jewish historian is to be preferred to the Roman. This is the only reference to the governor that Paul makes in his discourse, which is not a particularly laudatory one, but rather a statement of fact. Tertullus instead had to indulge in false adulation right from the start.

24:11. Twelve days complete, counting from the one referred to in 21:18, and adding the other indications of 21:26 (see note there); 21:27; 22:30; 23:11–12, 31–32; 24:1: but some of the days may overlap.

24:14. The Way: see note on 18:25–26. — **Which they call a sect:** as in verse 5, but the term (αἵρεσις) is used before also, for the Sadducees (5:17) and the Pharisees (15:5). — **God of my fathers:** the Greek has the adjec-

24:15. "having a hope in God which these men themselves also look for, that there is to be a resurrection of the just and the unjust;

24:16. "and in this I too strive always to have a clear conscience before God and before men.

24:17. "Now after several years I came to bring alms to my nation and to offer sacrifice,

24:18. "in which they found me engaged in the temple, after having been purified, with no crowd or disturbance at all.

24:19. "[These did not find me], but certain Jews from the province of Asia, who ought to have been here before thee and to have presented their charges, if they had any against me:

24:20. "or else let these men themselves say what they found wrong in me when I stood before the Sanhedrin,

24:21. "unless it be for the one thing I shouted out as I stood among them, 'It is about the resurrection of the dead that I am being judged by you this day.'"

24:22. Felix, however, having precise information about the Way [of the Lord], adjourned the trial, saying, "When Lysias the tribune comes down, I will decide your case."

---

tive **fatherly God** in the sense of "adored by our fathers." — **Law** . . . **Prophets:** the first two parts of the Hebrew Bible. In Lk. 24:44, the third part also is added, with the name of the "Psalms."

24:15. Hope: see note on 23:6–8.

24:17. To bring alms: see note on 20:3. — **Sacrifice:** Paul probably refers to the events of 21:26 sqq. Nevertheless, he had not come to Jerusalem expressly for those sacrifices, but for the feast of Pentecost (cf. 20:16) which entailed various offerings.

24:19. Jews from . . . Asia: these were the ones spoken of in 21:27. They had provoked the tumult and Paul's arrest, but had not presented themselves to prefer charges against him. It is of this that Paul complains.

24:22. Having precise information: the Greek has a comparative, but in a superlative sense. Felix's experience and his knowledge of Jewish customs and manners (cf. v. 10) made him *well informed* regarding Christianity (**the Way,** as in v. 14). This knowledge and Paul's convincing defense ought to have made Felix release him. Instead, he **adjourned the trial** (ἀνεβάλετο). It appears to have been the juridical term corresponding to the Latin one with which the presiding judge deferred sentence

24:23. And he instructed the centurion to keep Paul in custody but to allow him some liberty, and not to prevent any of his friends from looking after him.

24:24. Now some days later, Felix came with his wife Drusilla, who was a Jewess, and sent for Paul and heard what he had to say about the faith in Christ Jesus.

---

in a trial so as to obtain further evidence. In such cases, the assistant judges wrote on their tablets *N. L.* (viz., *non liquet*) and the presiding judge proclaimed the order *AMPLIUS,* from which comes the word *ampliare,* "to prorogue," "to defer" (cf. the phrase of Cicero, *causa septies ampliata*). If Felix deferred the sentence, on the pretext given in his next words, it was for a twofold reason; first, to avoid annoying the Sanhedrists overmuch, and, second to safeguard a Roman citizen; this in addition to the reason given in verse 26. Though Luke reveals the reprehensible conduct of Felix, he admits that the judge had fully recognized Paul's innocence. This bears out what was said in the note on 3:13, regarding the care taken in the *Acts* to put the Roman authorities in a favorable light.

24:23. To keep . . . in custody, etc. This kind of custody was the so-called *custodia militaris,* or "military custody," which was different from *custodia publica,* or "public custody," as was the case at Philippi (16:23 sqq.). The latter involved confinement in the common prison, while the former usually entailed being kept in a fortress or other guarded place in reasonable comfort and with some freedom. It was left to the discretion of the local authority to grant (*a certain*) *liberty* to the one detained in *custodia militaris,* allowing *his friends to look after him* and visit him, or even allowing him to lodge in a private house and go out for a short time (cf. note on 28:16; 23:30). Usually such a prisoner was bound by a chain to a soldier in such a way that one end of the chain was attached to the prisoner's right arm and the other end to the soldier's left arm (*eadem catena et custodiam et militem copulat:* "the same chain joins the prisoner and the soldier"; Seneca, *Epist.,* 5, 7). Thus joined, they could both go out together in public as is depicted on many monuments of the imperial age. However, when they were indoors, the chain could be removed. There was also another form of detention even more lenient, the *custodia libera,* or "free custody," permitting the prisoner to live in the house of some person of authority, who, by making a formal pledge or going bail, guaranteed the prisoner's whereabouts.

24:24. Drusilla (see note on 23:25) had Felix as her second husband, and although she did not arrive at the shamelessness of her sister Bernice

24:25. But as he talked of justice and chastity and the judgment to come, Felix became alarmed and answered: "For the present go thy way; but when I get an opportunity, I will send for thee."

24:26. At the same time he was hoping that money would be given him by Paul, and for this reason he would send for him often and talk with him.

---

and her brother Agrippa II (cf. 25:13), she followed the same way, which in any case was characteristic of the Herodian family. She was a Jewess, but more by race than by religion. At that time it was a kind of fad with noble Jewish ladies to interest themselves in the historical and philosophical aspects of religion not, however, with any intention of changing their spiritual loyalties. It is quite probable, therefore, that Drusilla herself had asked to meet Paul, being curious to know this "rebel" against her religion, about whom she had heard so much. This wish of Drusilla is explicitly stated in the margin of the Heraklean Syriac version, but it is obviously a gloss, inserted by an intelligent reader.

24:25-26. Felix had several conversations with Paul, at some of which Drusilla was also present. Right from the start, Felix was impressed by what Paul said **talking of justice and chastity and the judgment to come.** There was a gulf between the speaker and his two hearers, since **justice** for Felix consisted in his own personal gain (cf. notes on 23:25; 24:2-3), **chastity** (ἐγκράτεια) was almost a thing unheard of by both Felix and Drusilla, and as far as a future **judgment** was concerned, it was a bugbear that both of them would have willingly relegated to the world of dreams. Yet Paul dared to deal with such matters even with these two, as if he were applying his own rule: **Preach the word, be urgent in season, out of season, reprove, entreat, etc.** (2 Tim. 4:2). Even on this occasion, the effect, though incomplete, was there, and **Felix became alarmed and answered: "For the present go thy way; but when I get an opportunity, I will send for thee."** What really was wanting was not the time, for subsequently **he would send for him often and talk with him;** it was the good will that was lacking. If Felix were to accept the doctrine of Paul, it would necessitate his renouncing both the plunder he derived from his subjects and his possession of another man's wife. He preferred the plunder and the wife to Paul's teaching. He even hoped **that money would be given him by Paul.** In his strange prisoner, the governor sensed an opportunity for profit (cf. note on 23:34-35). Had Paul not just brought large sums of money to Jerusalem for alms (v. 17)? Might there not be among his innumerable disciples in various regions many wealthy followers ready to open their purses to help him? Everything, then, suggested that he should

24:27. But after two years, Felix was succeeded by Porcius Festus; and as he wanted to ingratiate himself with the Jews, Felix left Paul in prison.

---

prolong the trial and in the meantime treat the prisoner well, amusing oneself with him in religious-philosophic discussions. After a short time Paul must have understood very well what lay behind those talks and although he clearly saw their spiritual uselessness, he could not withdraw from them. There were no material riches to be gained from them, but the spiritual treasures which he was ready to bestow were not accepted, so that for **two years** (following verse) he had to bear this humiliation. But during those two years of inactivity, Paul could occupy himself in useful matters such as receiving disciples who would have come to visit him from various Mediterranean districts as soon as they knew of the master's imprisonment. He could also keep up an intense correspondence with the communities founded by him, to guide them in their new spiritual way of life. Luke almost certainly did not remain with him during these two years, but he must have frequently visited him. It is certain that when Paul left Caesarea, the faithful Luke reappeared at his side to accompany him (27:1 sqq.).

24:27. This period of **two years** runs from the beginning of Paul's imprisonment. Some have thought that it refers to the whole time that Felix was in office as governor. But though it is not stated here when Felix became governor, other data which we possess prevent us from restricting his governorship to two years (cf. note on v. 10). It has also been suggested that the new governor, **Porcius Festus,** succeeded Felix in A.D. 55. Such a suggestion is based on information supplied by Flavius Josephus (*Antiquities of the Jews,* XX, 182), according to which, Felix, being recalled to Rome, was put on trial by Nero for accusations leveled against him by the Jews of Caesarea who had come to Rome specially for this purpose. He was, however, acquitted through the intervention of his brother Pallas, who was very powerful at the emperor's court. But we know from Tacitus (*Annal.,* XIII, 14–15) that Pallas fell into disgrace under Nero a few months after the emperor's election, which took place on October 13 of the year 54, before the death of Britannicus in the middle of February of 55. Therefore, in this short period from mid-October to mid-February, in the depth of winter, all these events narrated by Josephus would have happened, viz., the summons from Rome to Judea for the recall of Felix, the voyage to Rome of Felix and the Jews of Caesarea, the preparation for the trial, its proceedings, the intervention of Pallas, and the acquittal of Felix. This is in the highest degree unlikely

25:1. Festus accordingly entered his province, and three days afterwards he went up from Caesarea to Jerusalem.

25:2. And the chief priests and Jewish leaders presented their charges against Paul, and begged him,

25:3. asking [it as] a favor against Paul, that he would have him fetched to Jerusalem. Meanwhile [they were] laying an ambush to kill him on the way.

---

during the season when sea voyages were practically suspended. We can rightly conclude, therefore, with the greater number of modern scholars, that Josephus has made one of his usual blunders, and that Felix was recalled in the year 60, as is suggested by other sources. — The new governor Festus belonged to the *gens Porcia,* of which the two Catos, the Greater and the Less, had been members. An upright man, he took office probably in the summer of 60 and remained governor until the year 62, when a premature death deprived Judea of a worthy governor who would have done much to improve the disastrous conditions he found there. — Felix, on relinquishing the governorship, discharged his Parthian shot by leaving **Paul in prison,** and he did this so as **to ingratiate himself with the Jews** (the same phrase as that used in 25:9). He feared that the reports of his bad government might reach Rome, as in fact happened, and that his obsequiousness to the Jews at Paul's expense might diminish their resentment. It may well have been that he also took this decision out of personal spite since he had failed to get any money out of the prisoner. One manuscript and a marginal note in the Heraklean Syriac version add another reason, viz., that **he left Paul in prison because of** (διά) **Drusilla.** This phrase recalls the account of John the Baptist's death, according to which, Herod Antipas put John in prison **because of** (διά) **Herodias** (Mk. 6:17). In the present case it would seem that Drusilla, irritated by Paul's discourses **on justice and chastity, etc.** (v. 25) took her revenge by demanding his continued imprisonment. She could not imitate Herodias by demanding his death because Paul was a Roman citizen. In the abstract this secondary reason has something to recommend it, but in actual fact there is very little documentary evidence for it.

25:1. **Festus** landed at **Caesarea,** the capital of his territory and the usual residence of the governor. Nevertheless, in some respects, **Jerusalem** was more important, and therefore the anxious governor went there after allowing himself only **three days** to rest and to take stock of the situation.

25:2-3. Preceding events are repeated here. Just as the Jews at Corinth

25:4. But Festus answered that Paul was being kept in custody at Caesarea, and that he himself would be going there shortly.

25:5. "Let, therefore, your influential men go down with [me]," he said, "and if there is anything wrong with the man, let them present charges against him."

25:6. After staying among them not more than eight or ten days, he went down to Caesarea, and the next day he took his seat on the tribunal, and ordered Paul to be brought in.

25:7. And when he was fetched, the Jews who had come down from Jerusalem surrounded him and brought many serious charges against him, which they were unable to prove.

---

had tried to influence Gallio as a *homo novus* (cf. note on 18:12), so here they attempt the same thing on Festus who was equally a *homo novus*. Just as a plot had been laid two years before, to capture and kill Paul during his removal in Jerusalem itself (cf. note on 23:12 sqq.), so now an attempt is made to kill him during his removal from Caesarea to Jerusalem. — The **chief priests and . . . leaders** are the same as the **chief priests and the elders** of 23:14. However, Ananias (23:2) was no longer the high priest. He had been deposed by Agrippa II (Flavius Josephus, *Antiquities of the Jews,* XX, 179) in the year 59, and had been replaced by Ismael, son of Fiabi or Fabi. — The phrase which follows is a little difficult, but means: **asking against him,** viz., Paul, as a **favor** to themselves, **that he would have him fetched,** etc. This was a favor which Festus, at the beginning of his governorship, ought to grant to his subjects, viz., the favor of concluding the trial of this **pest** (cf. 24:5), who for two years had been waiting for the penalty which he so richly deserved. — Here, also, the Heraklean Syriac version (see note on 24:27) gives a marginal note indicating that the persons detailed to kill Paul were still the forty conspirators of 23:13 sqq. This observation, besides being baseless, is extremely unlikely.

25:4-5. Festus' reply is an impartial appeal to the law then prevailing. Paul, as a Roman citizen, had been brought to Caesar's tribunal whither Festus also will shortly return. There is no reason then to transfer him to another tribunal in Jerusalem. In conclusion, let those Jews who are **influential** (οἱ δυνατοί) in preferring a charge in public, come down to Caesarea, and **let them present charges against him.**

25:6-8. Festus left for Jerusalem three days after his arrival in Caesarea (v. 1), and in the meantime may have gone to some place near Jerusalem

25:8. Paul said in his own defence: "Neither against the Law of the Jews, nor against the temple, nor against Caesar have I committed any offence."

25:9. But Festus wishing to do the Jews a favor, answered Paul and said, "Art thou willing to go up to Jerusalem and be tried before me on these charges?"

---

like Jericho. Luke, or the source he uses, includes the stay at Jerusalem or its neighborhood in the general statement **not more than eight or ten days.** After this, Festus returned to Caesarea and reopened Paul's trial the following day. From Paul's reply it appears that the charges preferred against him by the Jews were under three headings: crimes against **the Law of the Jews, against the temple,** and **against Caesar.** The first two had already been included in Tertullus' accusation (cf. 24:5-6), but the third — that **against Caesar** — was new, and particularly adapted to impress the Roman magistrate. The accusers of Jesus had adopted a similar plan (Jn. 19:12); but Jesus was not a Roman citizen, and Porcius Festus was of a different temperament to Pontius Pilate, so that this time the ruse did not work. We are not told under what guise this crime **against Caesar** was presented. It may have been like that preferred against Paul at Thessalonica (see note on 17:5-7).

25:9. The cautious Festus avoided contradicting the accusers outright, and **wishing to ingratiate himself with the Jews** (the phrase of 24:27) left open a way which might end in their favor, namely, he let Paul decide whether he wished to be tried in Jerusalem by the governor (**before me**). The proposal was a compromise, and the legal position was not clear for that reason. If Paul agreed to be tried in Jerusalem, by what tribunal would he be judged? If he was to be tried by the Roman court of the governor (**before me**), it was useless to go to Jerusalem, since Paul was arraigned before the Roman court in Caesarea. If it was to be by the Jewish court of the Sanhedrin it was hard to understand how the governor could say that Paul would be **tried before me on these charges.** But since it was a compromise, Festus included the three headings of the charges in his proposal (see preceding note), with the intention perhaps of leaving the Sanhedrin to judge the crimes against **the Law of the Jews** and **against the temple,** and of reserving to himself the crime **against Caesar** and the approval of the Sanhedrin's sentence. Paul's explicit assent was necessary for this proposal of Festus. This Roman citizen stood before the tribunal of the supreme magistrate, the emperor, represented by the governor of Judea. Nobody, therefore, could bring him to another tribunal without his consent.

25:10. But Paul said: "I am standing at the tribunal of Caesar, where I ought to be tried. To the Jews I have done no wrong, as thou thyself very well knowest.

25:11. "For if I have done any wrong, or committed a crime deserving of death, I do not refuse to die. But if there is no ground to their charges against me, no one can give me up to them. I appeal to Caesar."

25:12. Then Festus, after conferring with [those of] his council, answered: "Thou hast appealed to Caesar, to Caesar thou shalt go."

25:10–11. Paul quickly seizes on the distinction made mentally by Festus. He was standing before **the tribunal of Caesar,** and here the third charge should be tried, to find out whether he had committed any such crime **against Caesar.** As far as the other two charges were concerned, Paul is entirely innocent, as the governor himself **very well knows.** In view of this undeniable conviction of both judge and accused, nobody, even for the sake of doing the Jews a favor, **can give** him **up to them.** This last phrase, χαρίζομαι τινά τινι, which is repeated in verse 16,* signifies the delivering up of a person to the punitive power of another, but the idea of doing a favor to the one who has this power is not excluded. Paul, therefore, in so many words has stated where everybody's responsibility lies, and he cuts short the discussion by his own authority, declaring: **I appeal to Caesar.** — This solemn formula, uttered by a Roman citizen, had the effect of annulling all jurisdiction subordinate to the imperial power, leaving this alone in force. As soon as he heard this, the subordinate judge who was conducting the trial of a Roman citizen had to suspend it, even if the trial was about to be concluded with a condemnatory sentence. The accused had to be sent to Rome to the tribunal of the supreme magistrate, i.e., the emperor (except in very special and rare cases), and he could be neither convicted nor acquitted by a lower court.

25:12. Once the formula of appeal was pronounced, nothing remained to Festus but to put it into execution. There could be cases where the immediate and energetic intervention of a subordinate judge might be necessary, and then he could reject the appeal to the emperor, but such cases were extremely rare. Before deciding for or against the appeal, the lower magistrate had to listen to the views of his **council,** which assisted him in the discharge of his more important duties. These were generally young men starting their careers in the administration or *cursus honorum.* So Festus acted in this way, but it was a pure formality, since it was clear that Paul had the right of appeal. The brief conference over, Festus gave

25:13. And after an interval of some days, King Agrippa and Bernice came to Caesarea to pay their respects to Festus.

25:14. And as they were staying there several days, Festus laid Paul's case before the king saying: "There is a certain man left a prisoner by Felix,

25:15. "and when I was at Jerusalem, the chief priests and elders of the Jews presented their case against him, and asked for his conviction.

---

the decision: **Thou hast appealed to Caesar, to Caesar thou shalt go.** — The decision went against one of the parties concerned — the Jews — while the other two — Paul and Festus — benefited by it. The cause of the Jews suffered because of the decision, for they saw their prey escape them by being sent to Rome. It is true that there was always the possibility of following the accused to the court of the emperor, and maintaining their accusations against him there, but the practical difficulties of such a project were so many and so great as to dissuade any of them from undertaking it. Paul, on the other hand, was favored by the decision, since he was now sure of making the journey to Rome which he had had in mind for some time (cf. note on 19:21; 23:11). Festus also benefited by the decision, as he was able to extricate himself from the whole troublesome affair, and feel that his conscience was clear, without the Jews being able to complain against him.

25:13. To pay their respects, ἀσπασάμενοι: literally, **having saluted,** in the aorist tense, whereas one would expect the future tense, σόμενοι, as, in fact, some few less authentic codices have, probably as the result of a correction. It is possible that the aorist tense is used here to show the concomitance of the two actions **(they came . . . having saluted Festus):** others explain it in different ways. For information about this immoral couple, Agrippa and Bernice, see G. Ricciotti, *The History of Israel,* II, pp. 388–391. They were brother and sister, and Drusilla (24:24) was their sister. These two lived incestuously from the year 48 when Bernice at the age of 21 became the widow of her uncle, Herod, king of Chalcis, and went to live with Agrippa. She was subsequently married to Polemon, king of Cilicia, but soon left him and returned to Agrippa. The affair was known not only in Judea (Flavius Josephus, *Antiquities of the Jews,* XX, 145), but also at Rome, and provoked the sarcasm of Juvenal (*Sat.,* VI, 156 sqq.). During the war against Rome, Bernice began an affair with Titus (Tacitus, *Hist.,* II, 2). At the same time, she showed herself *magnificentia munerum grata,* "dear by the magnificence of her gifts" toward his father Vespasian

25:16. "But I told them that Romans are not accustomed to give any man up before the accused has met his accusers face to face, and has been given a chance to defend himself against the charges.

25:17. "Therefore, when they had assembled here, I lost no time, but on the following day I took my seat in the tribunal and ordered the man to be brought in.

25:18. "But when his accusers got up, they did not charge him with any of the crimes that I had expected.

25:19. "But they had against him certain questions about their [own] religion and about a certain Jesus who had died, but who Paul affirmed was alive.

(*ibid.*, II, 81). In the year 75, accompanied as usual by her brother, she came to stay with Titus at Rome and gained such a hold over him that the rumor spread that he had promised to marry her (Dion Cassius, LXVI, 15; Suetonius, *Tit.*, 7). Because of the bad impression that such a rumor produced at Rome, he was obliged to get rid of her. After the death of Vespasian, she came to stay with Titus again at Rome, but the new emperor *Berenicen statim ab Urbe dimisit, invitus invitam,* "dismissed Bernice from the city, *invitus invitam*" (Suetonius, *ibid.*). Agrippa II was her brother, son of Agrippa I who was the **king Herod** spoken of in 12:1. His full name was Marcus Julius Agrippa, and he is here called **king** because, in the year 50, Claudius had granted him the kingdom of Chalcis, whose territories in the years 53–55 were changed and enlarged at the same time as others of northern Palestine. Brought up in Rome at the court of Messalina, he pursued his studies and became a man of some culture. Although most faithful to Rome, even during the war with the Jews, he retained an attachment to his own nation, whose interests he supported several times with the emperor. He appears to have taken an interest also in Jewish religious questions, and rabbinical writings record several legal questions which he proposed. However, his purely intellectual ability was belied by the weakness of his character, for he was completely under the domination of his sister.

25:16. To give . . . up: the phrase used in verse 11. — The legal ruling here followed by Festus is found substantially in the *Digest,* XLVIII, 17, 1; Appianus, *Bell. civ.,* III, 45. — **To defend himself,** literally, **to take up a place of defence** (in the Greek), is used in the metaphorical sense of having the *possibility* or *opportunity,* in which sense it is employed in other cases; probably it was a legal expression.

25:18–19. They did not charge him . . . that I had expected: actually,

25:20. "Being at a loss as to how to investigate such matters, I asked [him] if he was willing to go to Jerusalem and be tried on these charges there.

25:21. "But when Paul lodged an appeal to have his case reserved for the decision of Augustus, I ordered him to be left in custody till I could send him to Caesar."

25:22. And Agrippa said to Festus, "I myself also could have wished to hear the man." "Tomorrow," said he, "thou shalt hear him."

---

the accusations leveled by the Jews had been under three distinct headings (see note on vv. 6–8). Here the Roman governor speaks from his own viewpoint, referring to political or moral charges which would interest him, and omitting religious questions which did not concern him. His attitude toward these questions was similar to that shown by Gallio (see note on 18:13–15). The indifference with which he speaks of the **questions about their [own] religion** (elsewhere called **superstition**, δεισιδαιμονία: see the corresponding adjective in 17:22) and of that **certain Jesus who had died, but who Paul affirmed was alive** is noteworthy. Festus does not so much as mention the charge of a crime **against Caesar**, which the Jews had preferred against Paul, being quite convinced that it was unfounded. If the political king preached by Paul was a **certain Jesus who had died**, Festus was not at all worried, as he was no longer alive, and in this his line of thought was probably the same as that of the Athenians of the Areopagus (cf. 17:32). Instead of **crimes** (wickedness) some codices have the adjective **wicked** (things). In this case, it would read: **they did not charge him with any wicked accusation that I had expected.**

25:20. Being at a loss (literally, **finding myself perplexed**). Here Festus puts forward this noble motive so as to cut a better figure before Agrippa. But his motive in verse 9, where he acted in favor of the Jews, is not so noble. Probably both motives had their share in influencing his actions.

25:21. Both **Augustus** and **Caesar** designate the emperor of the time, viz., Nero. The first title, **sebastòs** in Greek, had become an imperial title from the reign of Octavianus onward, and originally had a religious sense. Octavianus, who was already called **Caesar**, which was the name of his adoptive father, took the name **Augustus** in 27 B.C. (Suetonius, *Divus August.*, 7).

25:22. Agrippa most probably knew of Paul by repute, as indeed his sister Drusilla certainly did (see note on 24:24). Because of his inclination toward religious discussions (cf. note on v. 13), the king would be desirous

25:23. So the next day Agrippa and Bernice came with great pomp and entered the audience [hall] with the tribunes and principal men of the city, and, by order of Festus, Paul was brought in.

25:24. And Festus said: "King Agrippa, and all [you] men present here with us, you see this man about whom the whole multitude of the Jews pleaded with me at Jerusalem and here, crying out that he ought not to live any longer.

25:25. "But I, for my part, found that he had done nothing deserving of death, but as he himself made the appeal, I decided to send him to Augustus.

25:26. "Still I have nothing definite to write to my lord about him. So I have brought him forth before you, and especially before thee, King Agrippa, that after an examination of him has been made, I may have something to put in writing.

25:27. "For it seems to me unreasonable to send a prisoner without stating the charges against him."

---

to see and hear Paul (cf. also note on 26:26). Herod Antipas, his great-uncle, had similarly wished to meet Jesus (Lk. 9:9; 23:8).

25:23. The audience was invested with special solemnity, both to honor the visitors whom Festus wished to retain as his friends, and also so that a good impression should be carried to Rome and Jerusalem where Agrippa counted for much. Nevertheless, a more practical and simple reason might have been to provide a diversion from the monotonous life of a provincial city. — **Tribunes:** these were the commanders of the five cohorts of the garrison in Judea (see note on 10:1). The greater number of them were stationed at Caesarea, but one cohort was permanently based at Jerusalem (cf. note on 21:31-32) and another at Ascalon (Flavius Josephus, *Wars of the Jews,* III, 12). The article is left out before the word **tribunes,** which suggests that they were not all present.

25:24-27. These words of Festus do not pretend to be more than a brief presentation of the reason for the gathering. There is no question of passing sentence on Paul — says Festus — because such a judgment has been referred to the emperor by the wish of the prisoner himself. However, the prisoner must be sent to his judge with the usual presentation of the case, or *eulogium* (see note on 23:25 sqq.), but Festus is perplexed as to its form and contents. Therefore he will be grateful if the present company can suggest what he should write, especially **King Agrippa,** who was so well versed in Jewish matters (cf. note on v. 13). — In verse 26, the

26:1. Then Agrippa said to Paul, "Thou art permitted to speak for thyself." Then Paul stretched forth his hand, and began his defence.

26:2. "I think myself fortunate, King Agrippa, that I am to defend myself today before thee against all the accusations of the Jews,

26:3. "especially as thou art well acquainted with all the Jewish customs and controversies; I beg thee therefore to listen to me with patience.

26:4. "My life, then, from my youth up, the early part of which was spent among my own nation and at Jerusalem, all the Jews know;

---

title **(my) Lord,** signifying the emperor, should be noted (see note on 2:36). This title which was refused by Augustus and Tiberius (Suetonius, *Divus August.*, 53; *Tiber.*, 27; Tacitus, *Annal.*, II, 87), since it implied a state of slavery for the emperor's subjects, became a familiar term from the time of Caligula onward, and continued to take on a sacred character until Domitian ordered himself to be called *Lord and our god* (Suetonius, *Domit.*, 13). In A.D. 155, Polycarp the martyr would have escaped death if he had given the title of **lord** to the emperor of that time (cf. *Martyrium Polycarpi*, VIII, 2). For the view of the early Christians about this title, cf. 1 Cor. 8:5–6; 12:3; Rom. 10:9; Phil. 2:11.

26:1. The one who officially gave Paul permission to speak was Agrippa, which shows that Festus, out of deference, had given him the honor of presiding. But this favor of Festus is reciprocated by Agrippa, who by allowing Paul to speak, does so not in his own name, but impersonally, **Thou are permitted to speak.** — **Stretched forth his hand:** Paul was chained (cf. v. 29), and therefore could not raise his right hand much (cf. note on 21:40), but it was the gesture usual at the opening of a speech (cf. 13:16).

26:3. **Well acquainted:** cf. notes on 25:13; 26:26. The Greek construction is strange here, as the phrase is in the accusative which is not governed by any verb, while logically it refers to the preceding words, **before thee,** where the genitive is used. Perhaps it is an absolute accusative, or else the word **knowing** is to be understood (**knowing that thou art well acquainted . . .**), which is actually given in some codices.

26:4. **Life,** βίωσις, i.e., "the tenor of my life," "conduct." This is the only example of its use in the New Testament, and it is extremely rare anywhere else. — **Among my own nation,** viz., the Jewish nation, which was dispersed throughout the world, and at Tarsus, the native place of the speaker. This is in contradistinction to the following place, **Jerusalem.**

26:5. "for they have long known me, if only they are willing to give evidence, that according to the strictest sect of our religion I lived a Pharisee.

26:6. "And now for the hope in the promise made by God to our fathers, I am standing trial;

26:7. "to which promise our twelve tribes hope to attain as they worship night and day; and it is about this hope, O king, that I am accused by the Jews.

26:8. "Why is it deemed incredible with you if God does raise the dead?

26:9. "And I then thought it my duty to do mány things contrary to the name of Jesus of Nazareth.

26:10. "And this I did in Jerusalem, and many of the saints I shut up in prison, having received authority from the chief priests to do so; and when they were put to death, I cast [my] vote against them;

26:11. "and oftentimes in all the synagogues I punished them and tried to force them to blaspheme; and in my extreme rage against them I even pursued them to foreign cities.

26:5. Sect of the Pharisees; cf. note on 24:14.

26:6-8. Hope in the promise, i.e., of the Messias; see note on 23:6-8. The resurrection of the dead, of which the Messias Jesus was the first-fruits (1 Cor. 15:20), is linked up with this promise. — The twelve tribes, δωδεκάφυλον: the only time this expression is used in the New Testament. After the Babylonian captivity, only the memory of the twelve tribes remained, but a moral continuity was preserved in the tribe of Juda which carried on the Jewish religion, persevering in the hope in the promise. — For the placing of verse 8, see note on verses 22-23.

26:9-11. This is a summary of the events of 7:58-8:3. — I cast [my] vote. This does not seem to refer to an actual vote, but rather to consent and instigation: see note on 7:58 at the end. Seeing that the plural is used — they were put to death — whereas we read only of the death of Stephen, our information must be incomplete, and it is quite possible that there were other victims. In any case, the plural used here could be a "plural of category," of which there are other examples. The most obvious case is that of the two thieves, crucified with Christ, of whom only one blasphemed according to Luke (23:39-43), while Matthew (27:44) and

26:12. "But while I was journeying on this business to Damascus with authority and permission from the chief priests,

26:13. "at midday, O king, I saw on the way a light from heaven brighter than the sunshine round about me and my companions.

26:14. "We all fell to the ground, and I heard a voice saying to me in Hebrew, 'Saul, Saul, why dost thou persecute me? [It is] hard for thee to kick against the goad.'

26:15. "And I said: 'Who art thou, Lord?' And the Lord said: 'I am Jesus, whom thou art persecuting.

26:16. " 'But rise and stand up on thy feet; for I have appeared to thee for this purpose, to appoint thee to be a minister and a witness to those things wherein thou hast seen me, and to those things thou shalt yet see of me;

Mark (15:32) use the plural (they).— I . . . tried to force them: this expresses more the intention of the persecutor than the effect obtained by him. — The construction of the Greek text in verses 9–10 should be noted, where the μὲν is not followed by the customary δὲ, but is continued instead by the relative pronoun ὅ, just as in the much discussed prologue; see note on 1:2.

26:12 sqq. Here begins the third account of Paul's conversion, following that of 9:3 sqq. and 22:6 sqq.; see the notes there.

26:14. Fell to the ground: see note on 9:4 and 7. — A voice . . . in Hebrew, i.e., Aramaic; see note on 21:40. This detail of the narrative is given only in this account and not in the other two. — [It is] hard for thee to kick against the goad: these words are also exclusive to this account, although the Vulgate and other documents give them in 9:5 (and also in 22:7), taking them from here. The figure must have been a common one, almost a proverb, since it is found in various pagan writers such as Pindarus, *Pyth.*, 2, 94; Aeschylus, *Agam.*, 1624; Euripides, *Bacch.*, 795; Terentius, *Phormio*, 78, while a similar concept is expressed in Eccles. 12:11. In Palestine there was probably an Aramaic form of the saying, in which case, just as Jesus while on earth had taught by using popular parables and sayings, so the glorious Christ now uses a current proverb. It has been suggested that the literary form of this saying depends on a verse of Euripides (πρὸς κένλ λακκίζοιμι), but this dependence is by no means certain. If it were, then it must be attributed to whoever translated the words of Jesus into Greek, since they were pronounced in Aramaic.

26:16-18. Rise and stand: thus the Greek, ἀνάστηθι καὶ στῆθι. — Thou

26:17. " 'delivering thee from the people and from the Gentiles, to whom I am now sending thee,

26:18. " 'to open their eyes that they may turn from darkness to light and from the dominion of Satan to God; that they may receive forgiveness of sins and an inheritance among those sanctified by faith in me.'

---

hast seen me: in many documents the word me is omitted, but the sentence runs better with it. Insofar as it is a *lectio difficilior,* it is better to keep it. If it is omitted, it could be translated, to what thou hast seen, and to those things . . . — From the people, viz., the Jews. Jesus will deliver Paul from this people and from the Gentiles, both of them hostile to him (delivering thee from the people). — The whole period from the words to whom I am now sending thee up to by faith in me is overloaded with ideas tumbling after one another like certain of Paul's periods in his epistle to the *Ephesians.* For the sake of clarity, it is better to begin a new period after the word Gentiles, introducing it with the understood words to (these Gentiles) I am sending thee . . . After the words to God a new sentence should begin with the introductory words (and that) so they may receive forgiveness. . . . The final expression, by faith in me, can be linked up either with may receive or sanctified. — These three verses, 16–18, which foretell Paul's future apostolate, are substantially the same as in 22:14–15, where, however, it is Ananias who speaks to Paul, and not Jesus as is narrated here. Moreover, in 9:15–16, the Lord gives Ananias a similar message regarding Paul. It is a point of view which is different in the three accounts. In the first (9:15–16), Ananias is instructed by Christ to speak to Paul, and therefore when he does so, it will be in the name of Christ. In the second account (22:14–15), Ananias himself speaks, but in the name of Christ. But in this third account, Ananias is completely left out as the bearer of Christ's message, and the message is attributed directly to Christ. Paul had reason here to leave out mention of Ananias because the Apostle is speaking to the pagan Festus and the Romanized Agrippa, upon whom the reference to Ananias would make no impression, whereas a divine apparition which imparted orders would do so. On the other hand, in the second account, Paul does speak of Ananias because there he is addressing the rioting Jews in the temple who had regard for Ananias (cf. note on 22:12). For one like Paul, with a mentality essentially steeped in the Bible, it was entirely in keeping to leave out mention of Ananias, as he does in this third account, since in the Old Testament the words of God's messenger were regarded as equal to the words of God himself.

26:19. "Therefore, King Agrippa, I was not disobedient to the heavenly vision;

26:20. "but first to the people of Damascus and Jerusalem, and then all over Judea, and to the Gentiles, I set about declaring that they should repent and turn to God, doing works befitting their repentance.

26:21. "This is why the Jews seized me in the temple and tried to kill me.

26:22. "But aided to this day by the help of God, I stand here to testify to both high and low, saying nothing beyond what the Prophets and Moses said would come to pass:

26:23. "[regarding the question] that the Christ was to suffer, that he first by his resurrection from the dead, was to proclaim light to the people and to the Gentiles."

26:20. This list of the fields of Paul's apostolate is not clear, and is complicated as regards its chronology. The apostolate in **Damascus** and in **Jerusalem** offers no difficulty, as they refer respectively to the narrative in 9:22 (cf. Gal. 1:17) and 9:28–29 (see note there). But it is difficult to know to which period of Paul's activity the apostolate **all over Judea** should be assigned, because referring to A.D. 39, he affirms that he was **unknown by sight to the churches of Judea** (Gal. 1:22). We lack precise information about the following years, but the division of missionary labor between Peter and Paul, outlined in Gal. 2:7–9 does not in any way suggest that Paul labored **all over Judea,** since this region was the scene of Peter's activity. On the other hand, to interpret the whole phrase in the sense that Paul's apostolate aims at spreading throughout the whole world — as some scholars have done — is manifestly to force the sense of the words. Some have thought that the phrase **all over Judea** is an interpolation, but this hypothesis has no documentary foundation, and it seems to be excluded by the linking together of the whole period (**but . . . to the people . . . and . . . and then . . . and to . . .).** The hypothesis of Blass is quite likely, viz., to read with the minimum of correction, **in the whole country to the Jews and to the Gentiles . . .** — Repent . . . repentance, i.e., "to be sorry," "sorrow," terms already seen in 2:38; 3:19; 5:31, etc.

26:21. **To kill me:** this expression has been met with in 5:30.

26:22–23. **The Prophets and Moses:** namely, the second and first parts of the Hebrew Bible. These same testimonies were used by Jesus in his discussion with the disciples of Emmaus to show that the Messias had

26:24. While he was saying this in his defence, Festus said with a loud voice: "Paul, thou art mad; thy great learning is driving thee to madness!"

26:25. "I am not mad, excellent Festus," said Paul, "but I speak words of sober truth.

26:26. "For the king knows about these things, and to him also I speak without hesitation. For I am sure that none of these things escaped him; for none of them happened in a corner.

---

to suffer (Lk. 24:25-27). — The beginning of verse 23 has no clear link with what goes before, but, conceptually, the words added are to be understood **(regarding the question)**. It was one of the "questions" already referred to previously (25:19; 26:3), and one of the most important, joined with that other question of his Resurrection, that of knowing *if the Christ* (viz., the Hebrew Messias foretold by the Scriptures) *must undergo sufferings* ($\pi\alpha\theta\eta\tau\acute{o}\varsigma$). For both questions, see the notes on Peter's discourse in 2:23-32. — **First by his resurrection:** cf. 1 Cor. 15:20; Col. 1:18. — **Light . . . to the Gentiles:** cf. Isa. 42:6; 49:6; Lk 2:32. — It has been thought that verse 8 ought to be transposed here after verse 23, as the conclusion of the discourse. As far as the ideas go, such a transposition would fit in, but there is not the least foundation for it in the documentary evidence. In any case, since the discourse is an improvised one, it might well be that Paul anticipated the "conclusion," giving it as the "main theme" of the discourse.

26:24. The amiable Festus here confirms his completely alien attitude to religious questions, already pointed out in 25:19. His exclamation is one of good-natured teasing, rather like that of certain phrases in common use today among the people of Rome. At the same time, it shows his esteem for Paul, whose learning is acknowledged as being gained from *many sacred books* of the Hebrews. But precisely because the books were of that kind, they did not interest Festus, and he limited himself to admiring them from a distance.

26:26. If Festus the governor was **well informed** (24:22) about Christianity, much more did *King Agrippa know about these things*, seeing that he was interested in Jewish and religious questions (cf. note on 25:22; 26:3). The well-known facts of Christianity **(none of them happened in a corner)** were clear for all to see at the time Paul was speaking. This same assertion had been made also by Peter to his hearers at Pentecost, fifty days after the death of Christ **(as you yourselves know: 2:22)**.

26:27. "Dost thou believe the Prophets, King Agrippa? I know that thou dost."

26:28. But Agrippa said to Paul, "In a little thou wouldst persuade me to become a Christian."

26:29. And Paul answered: "I would to God that whether with little or with much, not only thou but also all who hear me today might become such as I am except for these chains."

26:27. Paul's question put Agrippa in two minds. The king believed in the **Prophets,** but with an abstract, theoretical faith. Paul instead expects a practical faith from him, one that sees in Jesus the historical fulfillment of the prophecies.

26:28. It is not unlikely that the term **Christian** here has a slightly ironical sense; see note on 11:26, toward the end. It will be observed how Agrippa uses the term **Christian** instead of "Nazarene" (*nazareo*) which was usual in Palestine (cf. 24:5), as if associating himself with the pagan ambit in which the term had sprung up, and to make himself better understood by his hearers, the majority of whom were pagans. However, the whole of the exclamation needs clarifying. The literal rendering is **In little thou art persuading me so as to make me a Christian.** The only variants worthy of notice are that of codex A, which has the first verb in the middle passive ($\pi\epsilon i\theta\eta$ instead of $\pi\epsilon i\theta\epsilon\iota\varsigma$) with the general sense of **in a little thou persuadest thyself** (or **thou art persuaded**) **to make me a Christian,** and that of the various codices and versions which, instead of the verb **to make,** have **to become.** If the phrase were meant to say **In a little thou persuadest me to make (myself) a Christian,** then it is not a Greek way of rendering it. Therefore, others have supposed that the last two words are a slavish translation of the Latin words, *Christianum agere,* i.e., "to play (the part of) a Christian." This opinion is very unlikely. There arises, however, another question. What is the real sense of **little** here? Is it in time or effort? In **little (time)** or with **little (effort)**? It would seem from Paul's reply, where he puts **much** in opposition to **little,** that the sense of effort is the one intended: **with little (effort) . . . with much (effort).** Whichever way Agrippa's reply is interpreted, as far as the individual words are concerned, it is not that of somebody impressed by Paul's words, to whom **little** remains to become a Christian. It seems rather to be the evasive answer of a skeptic who, with a certain courtesy, invites his questioner to stop deluding himself. A modern would have said in an ironic tone: "Oh yes, you don't think it would take much to convert me!"

26:29. Paul's reply seems to fit the sense of **with little or with much**

26:30. Then the king arose and the governor and Bernice, and those who had sat with them;

26:31. and after withdrawing they kept talking the matter over together, saying, "This man does nothing to deserve death or imprisonment."

26:32. And Agrippa said to Festus: "This man might have been set at liberty, if he had not appealed to Caesar."

27 **:1.** Now when it was decided that we should sail for Italy, they delivered Paul and some other prisoners to a centurion, named Julius, of the Augustan cohort.

(effort), unless one prefers to accept the sense of time; see preceding note. Agrippa does not take up Paul's reply, but rather seizes the opportunity to conclude the session which could become dangerous for him. In view of the incestuous intrigue in which he was engaged, and the presence of his accomplice at the meeting (cf. note on v. 25), the idea of conversion was too much.

26:30–32. The order of precedence of those present is worthy of note: first, **the king** (Agrippa), then the **governor** (Festus), then **Bernice,** and finally the others. It is the kind of exactness that would come from an eyewitness of the meeting. Equally natural are the remarks which the members of the party make as they leave the hall. — The use of the present tense in the words **does nothing** seems to refer to the habitual behavior of the prisoner. — **This man might have been set at liberty** before his appeal to Caesar, but once the appeal was made, it was no longer possible. The affirmation was legally correct; see note on 25:10–11.

27:1 sqq. We should set sail, etc.: here the first person plural shows the return of Luke, who embarks with Paul and accompanies him to Rome. During the two years that Paul passed at Caesarea, Luke was probably not with him all the time, but visited him frequently (see note on 24:25–26 at the end). The description of the sea voyage that Luke gives here is very detailed and reveals him not only as an eyewitness, but also as an attentive observer of events. Abounding in technical terms, this description has been judged by eminent historians to be one of the most important documents relating to the art of navigation among the Graeco-Romans, and modern nautical experts who have carefully examined both its historical and technical aspects, judge it an excellent piece of work (for the relative bibliography and other references cf. G. Ricciotti, *Paul the Apostle,* p. 435 sqq.). A similar journey from Palestine to Rome was made four

27:2. We went on board a ship of Adrumythium, which was bound for the ports of the province of Asia, and set sail; Aristarchus, a Macedonian from Thessalonica, being one of our party.

---

years later by Flavius Josephus in A.D. 64 (*Life,* 14–16), and he too was shipwrecked and landed at Pozzuoli. Of the 600 passengers on board, he was among the 80 who were saved. His account of it, however, takes only a few lines. Some have thought that Luke depended on Josephus, but there is no foundation for such a belief. — This **centurion, named Julius,** to whose custody the prisoners were assigned, proved during the voyage to be a man of fine sentiments, and he showed Paul special courtesy. We do not know which cohort is meant by the **Augustan cohort** or *cohort Sebastena* (Σεβαστῆς), to which we are told he belonged. It may have been one of the five cohorts then permanently garrisoned in Judea (see note on 10:1; 25:23). It is also possible that it was a cohort of the pretorian guard in Rome — called the *Augustiani* by Tacitus and Suetonius — which was often sent from Rome to the provinces for various duties. A likely theory is that Julius had been sent shortly before from Rome with a detachment, as an escort of honor for Porcius Festus when he came to the province as governor of Judea. In that case, since the detachment had to return to Rome, Festus might have taken this occasion to entrust Paul and the other prisoners to the centurion. These **other prisoners** may have been common criminals destined for the wild beasts in the circuses of Rome. It can be calculated from the chronological data given in the following verses that the embarkation from Caesarea took place toward the end of August. It was already late in the year for a Mediterranean crossing, and it was necessary to make haste so as to avoid the stormy season; see note on verse 9.

27:2. This **ship of Adrumythium** was based at Adrumythium, a Mysian harbor just below Troas (cf. 16:8; 20:5). The Vulgate mistakenly has **navem Adrumetinam,** which means a ship from Adrumetum, a harbor in proconsular Africa, just below Carthage. To reach its home port this ship had to turn northward, and then coast along **the ports of the province of Asia.** Julius hoped to find in one of these ports another ship which was going to Europe. This kind of coastal sailing along a great part of Asia Minor was neither speedy nor comfortable, and it would have been better to have sailed from Caesarea to Alexandria and there take one of the many grain vessels which carried supplies to Rome (cf. vv. 6 and 38) so as to reach Italy more directly. However, the service between Alexandria and Rome may have been suspended because of the winter season just begun (see preceding note), and Julius, to gain time, took advantage of

27:3. The next [day] we reached Sidon and Julius treated Paul kindly, allowing him to go to his friends and receive attention.

27:4. And putting to sea from there, we passed under the lee of Cyprus, as the winds were against us,

27:5. and sailing over the sea that lies off Cilicia and Pamphylia, we reached Myra in Lycia.

---

the ship at Adrumythium so as to get nearer to Rome. — Aristarchus is the one mentioned in 19:29; 20:4. It is not clear why he is referred to separately here after the "we-section." It is unlikely that he embarked with the idea of going as far as his native Thessalonica, while events later brought him to Rome against his will (Col. 4:10; Philemon 24). It is more likely that Luke wishes to give the exact number of the company, viz., the two who formed the subject of the "we-section" (Paul and the narrator) and Aristarchus. Paul's two companions boarded the ship, either as private passengers — since it was a commercial vessel — or, more probably, they were admitted on board through the kindness of Julius, who pretended they were Paul's slaves, for the law permitted a prisoner to be attended by a pair of slaves.

27:3. His friends, with the article, are certainly the Christians of the local community. It is really an unusual term to designate Christians, but it seems that Luke wishes to describe them from Julius' point of view. It was no surprise to find Christians at Sidon, because a Christian community already existed at Tyre (cf. 21:3-7), only about 20 miles south.

27:4. We passed under the lee: thus the Greek, in the nautical sense of keeping from the wind under the shelter of land, which in this case, was the island of Cyprus. The ship was coming from the south, and if it had taken a northwesterly course sailing west of Cyprus, it would have gone full into the contrary winds which blew from that direction, whereas sailing to the east of the island afforded some protection. On the preceding voyage, not only was the opposite course taken, but the ship then passed to the west of the island; see note on 21:1-3.

27:5. To the west of Pamphylia (for which, see note on 13:13) lay Lycia with its capital at Myra, situated a little east of Patara (see note on 21:1-3). The city was 20 stadia (2½ miles) according to Strabo (XIV, 3, 7) from the sea. The harbor, connected to the city by a canal, offered shelter for the ships which carried grain from Alexandria to Rome during the stormy season. There are several variants given in the codices for Myra which seem to be corruptions of a secondary name of that city. The most common is Lystra (cf. the Vulgate), which cannot possibly be

27:6. There the centurion found a ship of Alexandria bound for Italy and put us on board her.

27:7. For many days we made slow progress and had difficulty in arriving off Cnidus. Then as the wind kept us from going on, we sailed under the lee of Crete off Salmone,

27:8. and coasting along it with difficulty we came to a place called Fair Havens, near the town of Lasaia.

Lystra in Lycaonia (cf. 14:6 sqq.) which is very distant from the sea. After the words **and sailing** the Western Recension adds **for** (also **after:** διά) **fifteen days.** This chronological precision fits in well with the difficulties of navigation at that time and place, and it may, therefore, come from an authoritative source.

27:6. This **ship of Alexandria** must have been one of the grain vessels (see note on v. 2), as the generally accepted reading of verse 38 confirms. A long description of one of these ships and its eventful crossing from Alexandria to Pyhrreus is found in Lucianus, *Navigium,* I, 7. They were of different sizes. The one in which Paul sailed carried 276 passengers (v. 37) besides its cargo, and therefore was smaller than the one in which Flavius Josephus was shipwrecked, which carried 600 passengers. At a guess, one can say that it was 500 tons or a little more. It was broad and squat, like ships of that type, with a tall mast amidships and a smaller one forward (cf. v. 40). The bridge was situated above the hull and had hatchways or openings through which one could descend into the hold. Here the cargo was stowed and passengers took shelter in bad weather.

27:7. Cnidus lay on the southwestern point of Asia Minor opposite Rhodes. The distance from **Myra** was about 130 sea miles, which could be covered in fair weather in one day or a little more, since it is reckoned that these Alexandrian ships sailed at 5 to 6 knots. However it was only after **many days** that they arrived **off Cnidus.** This slow sailing was due to the wind, which, blowing from the northwest, caught the ship head-on. The violence of the wind was felt even more when the ship left the west coast of Asia Minor which partly sheltered it, and began to enter the open sea of the Aegean. Seeing that the going was difficult, the sailors sought to protect themselves from the wind by coming down southward and sailing under the shelter of the island of Crete. Therefore they sailed **under the lee of Crete** (the verb used in v. 4), after having rounded its eastern extremity formed by the promontory of Salmone, also referred to by Strabo (II, 4, 3).

27:8. Fair Havens: this place is still known by the same name today

27:9. But as much time had been spent and navigation was now unsafe, for the Fast was already over, Paul began to admonish them,

27:10. saying to them: "Men, I see that this voyage is threatening to bring disaster and heavy loss, not only to the cargo and the ship, but to our lives also."

(*Kalus Limniones*), and is about halfway along the west coast of Crete, a little east of Cape Matala (Litino). It is a little oval-shaped bay facing the southwest, partially protected at its opening by two small islets. The name **Lasaia** is given in the manuscripts with numerous variants, among which is that of **Alassa,** which then became **Thalassa** in the Vulgate. It was a small town of which some likely ruins have been discovered. At Fair Havens it was safe, but there was the inconvenience referred to in verse 12 which the sailors sought to avoid, but instead ran into something worse.

27:9. Much time had been spent: from the beginning of the voyage or from the stay at Fair Havens; the second is included in the first. — **Navigation was now unsafe:** if this was about the end of September to the beginning of October (cf. note on v. 1 at the end), it was considered a dangerous time for sailing in the Mediterranean, and, according to the common opinion, this period had already begun in the middle of September. The time known as the "closed sea" period followed shortly after the first ten days of November and lasted until the beginning of spring when the Favonian or westerly winds began to blow. During the "closed sea" period, navigation normally ceased altogether, although there were fearless men who defied the wintry season. Principal among these were the pirates, according to Pliny (*Nat. hist.,* II, 47), who observes that in his day, the avaricious followed their example. Herod the Great, anxious to save his throne, had also embarked at Alexandria for Rome in the middle of winter in 40 B.C., and had run into serious danger off Pamphylia (Flavius Josephus, *Wars of the Jews,* I, 279–281). — The **fast** is the Yom Kippur, or Day of Atonement, on which Jews were obliged to fast. Since this holy day fell on the tenth day of the month Tishri, viz., between the end of September and the beginning of October, it was at the time when navigation practically ceased, after which it was a serious risk to put to sea.

27:10. These words of Paul are conditioned by two openly contrasting facts. In the first place, by his own personal experience of the sea, since three years previously — namely in the year 57 — he had written of his having been thrice shipwrecked (2 Cor. 11:25), about which we know no details. Second, by the divine assurance that he would reach Rome (Acts

27:11. But the centurion gave more heed to the pilot and the captain than to what Paul had to say;

27:12. and as the harbor was unsuitable for wintering in, the majority favored sailing from there [to try] whether they could get to Phoenis, a harbor in Crete facing south-west and north-west, to winter there.

23:11). The first consideration prudently urged him to be a pessimist, the second suggested the general admonition which he gave here to the company as a whole, rather than to each individual. — The Greek has a difficult anacoluthon (ὅτι . . . μέλλειν: **that . . . is ready to become . . .**), which nevertheless does not suggest an interpolation, since other examples are found in classical writers (Xenophon, *Hellen.*, II, 2, 2; etc.).

27:11. By giving Paul's prudent opinion, it seems that Luke here makes a little anticipatory statement in the series of events. The contrary opinion expressed by the pilot and the captain must have resulted during the events narrated in the following verse, which presupposes a conference on board at which different views were expressed and discussed. — **Pilot** is in Greek, κυβερνήτης, from which comes the Latin *gubernator,* and the following term ναύκληρος, is used for **captain.** According to Plutarch (*Moral.,* 807 b), *the pilot chooses the sailors and the captain chooses the pilot,* so that the captain would be the superior officer. However, other texts show that in practice the meaning of the two terms was exchanged and widened, so that the owner of the ship (who frequently sailed with it) was also called the **captain,** or the person who had hired the ship or the officer in charge, and sometimes the **pilot.** At any rate, in the present case, the senior in charge was the **centurion** Julius, since the ship belonged to the imperial merchant fleet, and his decision was final in all questions on board. Now, the centurion had regard for Paul (vv. 3 and 43), but when it was a case of technical questions, it was natural that he should have more confidence in **the pilot and the captain,** if for no other reason than to exempt himself from all responsibility before his superiors, in case of misfortune. Some critics have thought that verses 9–11 are an interpolation added to the "Travel Diary" (just as in vv. 21–26); but the only reason given, that Paul appears there surrounded by supernatural light, does not merit discussion.

27:12. The expression **the majority** shows that a conference was held, presided over by the centurion, at which the pilot, the captain, some of the more expert sailors, and probably Paul took part. Paul must have expressed officially his opinion given in the preceding verse (which, in any case, he had probably expressed in private before). But in the

27:13. So when a light south wind sprang up, thinking they had attained their purpose, they weighed [anchor] and ran close along the coast of Crete.

27:14. But not long afterwards a violent wind called Euroaquilo burst against it;

---

discussion with those who were experts, the opinion of the one who was not so experienced in these matters was not accepted by **the majority** (*most of them*), and their decision to make the short run as described in the text was followed. Fair Havens, where the ship now lay, was a harbor **unsuitable for wintering in,** perhaps because it lacked warehouses in which to store the cargo for the winter and lodging for the passengers. These inconveniences would not be met with at **Phoenis** which was on the same western coast of Crete. The harbor of Phoenis looked **south-west** (κατὰ λίβα) **and north-west** (κατὰ χῶρον), but notwithstanding these details and the mention of it by Ptolemy (III, 17, 3) and Strabo (X, 4, 3), its identification is disputed. Most scholars identify it with the port of Lutro, situated about 40 miles northwest from Fair Havens, since this is the only natural harbor in those parts. But Port Lutro does not face southwest and northwest, but in the opposite direction. So others have interpreted the word **facing** as a nautical term, indicating the direction toward which the wind blows, and not the place from which it comes. In actual fact, Port Lutro faces northeast and southeast.

27:13. **A light south wind sprang up** (literally, **the south wind blew softly).** This is the verb ὑποπνέω, the diminutive of the verb "to blow." The wind was the well-known austro or south wind. This was the wind needed if the plan decided on in the conference on board was to be carried out. When the ship had sailed west and had covered the few miles from Fair Havens to Cape Matala (cf. note on v. 8), it would then have to veer northwest (cf. note on v. 12), sailing straight for Phoenis (or Port Lutro), and this wind was just what they needed to put them on that course. The circumstances were favorable, and the sailors thought **they had attained their purpose,** so, weighing anchor immediately, they sailed along Crete, **close along.** In this verse, the words, **close along** are given in the Greek as ἆσσον, a comparative of ἄγχι, meaning **nearer.** The Vulgate interprets it as a proper name, **Asson** (perhaps influenced by 20:13–14).

27:14. The rosy optimism of the sailors was doomed to sudden and tragic disappointment. One of those unexpected and violent changes of wind, characteristic of that part of the Mediterranean at that season, occurred and endangered the ship, blowing for several days. There **burst** (ἔβαλεν) **against it** (viz., the island of Crete last named) **a violent wind**

27:15. and when the ship was caught in it and could not face the wind, we gave way and were driven along.

27:16. And running under the lee of a small island called Cauda, we were able with difficulty to secure the boat.

27:17. After hoisting it on board, [the sailors] used supports to

---

called Euroaquilo. This name is made up of a Greek term, *euro,* viz., the east-southeast wind, and a Latin term, *aquilone* or the northeast wind. There are, however, variants of this name, such as εὑροκλύδων, "a stirring east wind," and εὑρυκλύδων, "an offward swinging." It is difficult to say which of these nautical terms (which are rarely found elsewhere) is the more probable. Perhaps the last mentioned is more likely. It is certain that the tempestuous wind or typhoon swept down suddenly from the mountains of Crete, blowing from the northeast (cf. v. 17).

27:15. The violent gusts of wind immediately caught the ship. **We gave way** (literally, **having yielded**) (ἐπιδόντες). The object of the verb is missing. It could be translated as an intransitive verb, in the sense of **having yielded, letting ourselves go,** viz., ceasing the attempt to maneuver against the contrary wind after having lowered the mainsail (cf. note on v. 6). The words **were driven along** (which return in v. 17) are to be understood in a similar sense.

27:16. **Cauda** (with **Clauda** as a variant) is a small island situated a little southwest of Fair Havens, called *Gavdos* in Greek, and *Gozo* in Italian (not, however, to be confused with *Gozo* above Malta). The ship, dragged onward by the typhoon, ran along the little island. The Greek has **ran under** in the same sense as the word "sailing under" (vv. 4 and 7), viz., under the wind. This circumstance allowed the carrying out of the action referred to presently, but **with difficulty.** Actually, sailing under the lee of Cauda, the ship was slightly protected from the force of the gale. The operation consisted in hauling on board **the longboat** (τῆς σκάφης), which the ship had been towing since its departure from Fair Havens. The crew, thinking that they would arrive at Phoenis in a short time, had left the longboat, used for landings, in tow. Now with the raging sea, there was not only the danger that the tow rope would break and the longboat be lost, but also that it would damage the hull by tossing against it. — **We were able:** notice the first person plural, which suggests that Luke and Paul, together with other passengers, also helped to draw in the longboat. In the following verse, the passengers' help is not spoken of, since it was a technical operation.

27:17. They **used supports,** βοηθείαις ἐχρῶντο: just what these **supports** were we do not know, but it is certainly a nautical term. Nor do we

undergird the ship, and as they were afraid of being driven on the
Syrtis quicksands, they lowered the gear and were driven along.

27:18. As we were being tossed about by the violence of the storm,
the next day they threw [some of the cargo] overboard,

27:19. and on the third day with their own hands, they threw the
ship's gear overboard.

---

know if they were part of the operation mentioned in the following
words. — **To undergird,** ὑποζωννύντες: etymologically, "to gird together" or
"to frap." We do not quite know just how this "binding together" of the
ship was accomplished. Probably it consisted in reinforcing it by strong
cables or hawsers which were drawn several times around the hull, which
they also shored up inside. However, the prefix ὑπο-, "under" **(undergird)** suggests that the cables went around under the keel of the ship from
side to side to hold it together. — **Being driven:** this is the verb ἐκπίπτω, "to
throw on," which reappears in verses 26 and 29. It is a nautical term for
"to run aground," "to run against." — **Syrtis** here is the Syrtis Major
(Syrtis Minor was farther west), viz., the Libyan Syrtis, an enormous
creek which is formed by the sea between Tripolitania and Cyrenaica,
completely silted up with sand and providing no entrance. It was the
terror of ancient sailors, since to fall into it meant the loss of the ship,
cargo, and everything. Even so, the ship driven onward by the northeast
wind headed straight for the Syrtis quicksands. Although the mainsail had
been lowered when they **gave way** (v. 15), that was not enough, since the
wind drove the ship itself forward. To prevent this disastrous course,
they lowered the gear. We do not know from any ancient document
exactly what was this so-called **gear,** σκεῦος (cf. note on 9:15; 10:11).
According to a hypothesis suggested by a passage from Plutarch among
others (*Moral.,* 507, a–b), it was a species of sea anchor, a large affair,
constructed of a beam or large plank held vertical in the sea by anchors
suspended beneath it, and fastened by rope tackle. When this was trailed
behind the ship, it helped to keep her on course by reason of the strong
resistance which it offered to the water. — **Were driven along:** cf. note on
verse 15.

27:18–19. The next day . . . the third day, i.e., counting from their
departure from Fair Havens. — **They threw . . . overboard:** the text only
has literally, **they made a casting overboard** (note should be made of the
third person plural in place of the first person used in v. 16). The text
does not say what was thrown overboard, but it must have been part of
the cargo. Not all of it, however, as more of it was jettisoned later in
verse 38. Probably here the deck cargo is meant, which might be washed

27:20. As neither sun nor stars were visible for many days and no small storm was raging, all hope of our being saved was in consequence given up.

27:21. Then, when they had eaten nothing for a long time, Paul got up in the midst of them and said, "Men, you should indeed have listened to me and not have sailed from Crete, thus sparing yourselves this disaster and loss.

27:22. "And now I beg you to be of good cheer, for there will be no loss of life among you, but only of the ship.

27:23. "For last night an angel of the God I belong to and serve, stood by me,

27:24. "saying, 'Do not be afraid, Paul; thou must stand before Caesar, and behold, God has granted thee all who are sailing with thee.'

27:25. "So, men, be of good cheer; for I have faith in God that it will be as it has been told me.

27:26. "But we are to reach a certain island."

---

away at any moment by the waves. In verse 38 the cargo was that in the hold of the ship, the openings of which could not now be opened as the sea would pour in and sink the ship. But seeing that the storm showed no sign of abating, on the third day the ship's **gear,** τὴν σκευήν, was thrown overboard. This would seem to have been not the mainmast which was without sail, and therefore not dangerous (cf. note on v. 38), but all the implements which were not strictly necessary. After all this, the ship remained a bare floating hulk, with little or no steering, and completely at the mercy of the waves.

27:20. Neither sun nor stars, etc.: sailors of that time, having no compasses, feared this very much, since with no guiding star, they completely lost all bearings. This was the chief reason for the "closed sea" during the winter season (cf. note on v. 9).

27:21. Eaten nothing: the Greek reads literally, **we being much in want of food** (ἀσιτίας). This was the effect both of seasickness and the general discouragement which had overtaken everybody as a result of their being in imminent danger for so long.

27:22-26: The fact that Paul was a charismatic and received frequent revelations is shown not only from the *Acts* (16:6–10; 18:9–10; 20:23; 22:17 sqq.; 23:11; etc.), but also from his writings, especially 2 Cor.

27:27. But when it was the fourteenth night and we were drifting in the Adria, about midnight the sailors began to suspect that they were drawing near to some land.

12:2 sqq. But these charisms of his, as in the case of other celebrated mystics, did not at all hinder his clear vision of material reality; on the contrary, sometimes they rendered it more vivid. Here we find that while the sailors and passengers lie on the deck exhausted and ill, or in the darkness of the hold amid the reek of vomit and filth, he alone concerned himself about the morrow and the material needs of the worn-out company (v. 34). — **An angel:** to Paul's hearers, nearly all of whom were pagans, this term was understood as *a messenger, one sent,* by the God of Paul. — **I belong to:** the Greek reads literally, **whose I am.** — **Before Caesar . . . :** cf. 23:11. — **Has granted thee . . . :** this is the Greek phrase, χαρίζομαι κτλ, referred to in the note on 25:11, but here it is used in an entirely favorable sense, viz., "to save someone's life to please another." Therefore, the reason why God promises to save the lives of Paul's fellow travelers is to grant a favor to him who had probably been praying for that intention on the very night of the apparition. The angel who appeared to Cornelius as he was praying is presented in a similar way, to tell him that his prayer was heard (10:3 sqq.). This exhortation of Paul must have made very little impression on the few who listened to him. When one has been for days in a state of complete prostration by seasickness, one desires nothing else but immediate relief from such torment. In any case, if the sailors themselves, with their experience, did not know where they were, how could this inexpert Jew know anything about it? The angel who had appeared to him must have been an hallucination, brought on by cramps in his stomach! However, a few, like the good Julius, may have thought that Paul was speaking with some authority. — Some critics have considered verses 21–26 as an interpolation in the "Travel Diary," like that of verses 9–11. The real reason is the one given in the note on verse 11, but here there is the added philological reason of the transition from the first person plural of verse 20 **(our being saved)** to the third person plural of verse 21 **(in the midst of them).** The value of this philological argument is proved by examining verses 15–20. In verses 15–16 the first person plural is used; in verse 17 the third person; in verse 18 the first person and then the third; in verse 19 the third; and in verse 20 the first person again. Would all these transitions from the first to the third persons suggest so many interpolations?

27:27. Fourteenth night: this clarifies the vague term **many days** of verse 20. — **The Adria,** for the ancients, was not only the present-day

27:28. On taking soundings, they found it twenty fathoms [deep],
and a little farther on they found fifteen fathoms:

27:29. then fearing that we might go on the rocks, they dropped
four anchors from the stern and longed for daylight.

27:30. But as the sailors were trying to escape from the ship and
had lowered the longboat into the sea, pretending that they were
going to cast anchors from the bow,

Adriatic Sea, but also the lower stretch from Sicily and Malta as far as
Greece and Crete (Ptolemy, III, 4, 1; III, 15, 1). Flavius Josephus also
(see note on v. 1) calls the sea in which he was shipwrecked the **Adria,**
although he was picked up by a Cyrenean ship and landed at Pozzuoli.
At any rate, the sailors did not know that night in which sea they were,
whether they were near Malta or the Syrtis, but after they had landed,
they soon learned. — **Drawing near,** προσάγειν (literally, **it approached**).
The expression is a typical nautical term, since land was said to *approach*,
when a ship drew near to it. Codex Vaticanus has προσαχεῖν, which appears
to be a doric form (or even a corruption) of προσηχεῖν, "to resound," a
reading which is confirmed by the codex *Gigas,* according to which the
sailors would have known land was near from the roar of the breakers
on the shore. However, this reading is not very well attested, and besides,
the sailors could have suspected by other means that land was near. They
would probably not have bothered to take a sounding (following verse)
if they had thought land was within a few hundred yards.

27:28. The old measure of a **fathom,** ὄργυια, was equivalent to the
length of the two arms with hands outstretched horizontally, or about
six feet. Therefore the **twenty fathoms** found by the first sounding was
a depth of water about 120 feet, and the **fifteen fathoms** of the second
sounding about 90 feet. Undoubtedly land was approaching fast, but
given the darkness of the stormy night, there was the risk of rushing
toward a hidden danger as is explained in the following verse. — **Little
farther on** (literally, **after a little space**), the words may apply either to
lapse of time or progress in distance which was practically the same here.

27:29-30. The fear of hidden rocks counseled fastening the ship where it
lay until daybreak. This was done by dropping **four anchors from the
stern.** The curve of the ship's hull in ancient times was not much different
at the bow or the stern, nevertheless the anchors were cast off from the
stern to keep the ship in the same position in which it faced the approaching invisible land, viz., shoreward, with the bow toward land and the
stern against the wind. This was the best position for a further approach

27:31. Paul said to the centurion and the soldiers, "Unless these men remain in the ship, you cannot be saved."

27:32. Then the soldiers cut away the ropes of the boat and let her drift off.

27:33. And when it began to grow light Paul begged them all to take food saying: "This is the fourteenth day that you have been constantly on the watch and fasting, without taking anything to eat.

27:34. "So I beg you to take some food for your safety: for not a hair from the head of anyone of you shall perish."

---

to the shore. However, the ship could be held more firmly by anchoring it forward, so that it would not swing around as it might otherwise do. But for this new casting of anchors it was not sufficient to throw them from the deck; it was necessary to take them in the **longboat** as far ahead of the ship as possible, and drop them into the sea. In this way the ship would be secure both fore and aft. The operation was a legitimate one, but the sailors proposed it only as a pretext for abandoning ship at that moment of great danger. The ship, in fact, was now anchored fast, and so had to take the full force of the waves. There was grave doubt whether the hull, already battered for fifteen days by storm, could stand up to it until morning. So, these sailors, men who were hired and picked up here and there from various Mediterranean ports, thought only of their own safety when they proposed to throw the anchors from the bow. Once in the longboat, they would make for the shore, abandoning the ship and its passengers to their fate. But as they were making their plans, Paul, or somebody who told him, overheard them, and so their real motive was discovered.

27:31-32. When Paul was informed of the plot that was being prepared, he passed on the information, not to the pilot, nor the captain, who in these circumstances had little authority over the sailors, but to the **centurion and the soldiers,** because the former was the superior officer on board (cf. note on v. 11), and both he and the others carried swords which alone could gain respect from the sailors. The swords, in fact, were used immediately, for as soon as they knew of the sailors' plot, **the soldiers cut away the ropes of the boat and let her drift off.** Thus all escape was cut off, and everyone on board would have to face the same plight.

27:33-34. And when it began to grow light: this phrase suggests the great trepidation which everyone on board felt in waiting for the daylight and the hope of safety that it might bring. Again the mystic Paul appears (cf. note on vv. 22-26) amid this feverish waiting, showing, by his

27:35. With these words he took bread and gave thanks to God before them all, and broke it and began to eat.

27:36. Then all became more cheerful and took food themselves.

---

exhortation, his deep appreciation of physical reality. It was easy to foresee that the salvaging of the ship, or at least of the passengers, would involve a difficult and toilsome day ahead, but no one had remembered that they were physically unprepared for these efforts, since after fourteen sleepless nights and days in which terror alternated with seasickness and nervous excitement, they could barely stand on their feet. Only the mystic Paul thought of it, and urged them all to strengthen themselves by taking food. It is also possible that the physician Luke suggested it to Paul. — **And fasting** (ἄσιτοι: cf. note on v. 21) **without taking anything to eat:** the sense of this phrase is to be taken widely and not too literally (cf. Mt. 11:18). — **Not a hair, etc.:** cf. Lk. 21:18.

27:35-36. The Greek has **and taking bread** without the article (see notes on 2:42 and 46; 16:34; 20:7). Theoretically speaking, some of the expressions used in this account could be applied to the Eucharistic rite. Such phrases as **taking bread . . . gave thanks** (εὐχαρίστησεν) **. . . broke** (κλάσας) are found in the various Gospel accounts of the institution of this rite. But the question here is a practical one, viz., did Paul intend, in this particular case, to celebrate the Eucharist? On the analogy of the expressions used, as mentioned above, some scholars — Catholics as well as Protestants and Rationalists — have replied in the affirmative. This view was shared already by the glossator of the Western Recension, who thought fit to add after the words, *to eat, having given it to us also,* with the avowed aim of making it resemble the Gospel accounts of the institution of the Eucharist. In actual fact, all that can be conceded regarding this view is that the early Christians performed the rite for comfort and consolation under stress, restricting it to the essential acts only (as in fact was done during World War II in certain concentration camps). But this is only a theoretical suggestion, and does not answer the question whether Paul here intended to celebrate the Eucharist. It would seem to us that he did not intend to do so. For whom would he have celebrated it? Obviously for the Christians present, of whom, so far as we know, there were only three, Paul, Luke, and Aristarchus (cf. note on v. 2). All the rest, including Julius, had not the remotest idea of the value and significance of that rite. The proportion of Christians to pagans was such — three Christians to two hundred and seventy-three pagans (viz., 276-3; cf. v. 37) — that certainly it was not the time to celebrate, in public, a rite which was so sacred and so incomprehensible to the bystanders. On the contrary, they

27:37. **Now, we were in all two hundred and seventy-six souls on board.**

27:38. **And after eating their fill, they proceeded to lighten the ship by throwing the wheat into the sea.**

27:39. **When day broke they could not make out the land, but they noticed a bay with a beach, and they proposed to run the ship ashore there if they could.**

---

had need of material food and physical nourishment before all else, as Paul himself well knew. The three Christians could celebrate the Eucharist privately in a few minutes. In conclusion, then, the food taken by Paul and all the others was an ordinary meal, and the prayers said before it (gave thanks), were the usual Jewish prayers of devotion which the Jews used to say before meals.

27:37. **Two hundred and seventy-six:** Codex Vaticanus reads, **about 76,** which is due to a copyist's error. For the tonnage of the ship, see note on verse 6.

27:38. For the first time, **wheat** is mentioned, which certainly must refer to the ship's cargo stowed in the closed hold. While it would have been the height of folly to open the hold during the stormy voyage, (see notes on vv. 18–19), now it could be opened, since the ship was anchored, and so lighten it in order to approach as near as possible to the shore. The mention of **wheat** suggests that it was a grain vessel, one of the many that plied between Alexandria and Rome (cf. notes on vv. 2 and 6). Since, however, this is the only reference to wheat in the whole narrative, some have thought that instead of **wheat,** σῖτον, originally the word was ἱστόν, **mast (of the ship)** which was mistakenly copied in writing. According to this theory, the mainmast of the ship, from which the mainsail had been lowered fourteen days before (cf. notes on vv. 15 and 18–19), was cut down on this occasion to lighten the ship. From the paleographical viewpoint, the theory is attractive, but there is nothing in the context to support it.

27:39. Nobody on board recognized the land close by, which need not surprise us, since the ordinary route from Alexandria to Pozzuoli (cf. 28:13) did not touch Malta. Even if any of the sailors had landed at Malta, they might not have recognized this particular point of the island. At first sight the beach seemed to offer a good landing. There was a creek (a certain **bay**) where, ordinarily, the sea is calmer than in the open water, and this creek had **a beach** running down to the water's edge, nice and open. This beach was ideal for landing. All that was needed was to steer the

27:40. So they slipped the anchors and left [them] in the sea, at the same time unlashing the fastenings of the rudders; and hoisting the foresail to the breeze, they made for the beach.

27:41. But we struck a place open to two seas, and they ran the ship aground. The prow stuck fast and remained immovable, but the stern began to break up under the violence [of the waves].

---

ship into the creek and then drive it on the beach and ground it in the sand. But the sailors suspected a danger, expressed here by the words **if they could.** The entrance to the creek was clearly free of rocks and other obstacles, but there might be hidden sandbars in shallow water, such as are frequently found at the entrance to bays or inlets. They are formed where two opposing currents, the waves of the outer sea and those of the inner water, meet, and because of the constant force of the waves there, they are always most dangerous to a ship stranded on them.

27:40. Seeing the wide bay apparently clear at the entrance, the sailors began to maneuver the ship in the manner here described to bring it ashore. They began by slipping the hawsers around the ship which tied the anchors to the stern, and they left them in the sea where they were lying. **At the same time** they loosened **the fastenings of the rudders,** viz., those ropes with which the rudders were tied to the hull during the storm. There were two rudders (as we see from ancient drawings of such ships) like large oars, one on either side of the hull. The ship, being now set free and maneuverable, began to move. As a breeze was blowing, the foresail was hoisted, and, carried onward by it, **they made for the beach.** The sail and its mast, called the **foresail** (ἀρτέμων), was near the prow and in ordinary times it served more to guide the ship than to carry it forward. It corresponded to what we would call today the foremast.

27:41. It seemed as though all was going well, when the danger foreseen by the sailors was upon them. They struck **a place open to two seas,** τόπον διθάλασσον, **and . . . ran the ship aground.** This expression is controverted. Etymologically, it signifies a place where the water is fairly deep on both sides, but is barely covered with water in the middle, though enough to hide the bottom. More than this cannot be gathered from the expression itself. The statement that **they ran the ship aground** is not clear either, because it does not say whether they did it by choosing a good place or were unable to prevent it. The second alternative seems to be the more likely as the sailors would not have deliberately taken such a dangerous decision, whose disastrous consequences appeared immediately. It is more probable that the sailors, despite their lookout for a landing spot, did not notice the sandbar because of bad

27:42. Now the soldiers planned to kill the prisoners lest any of them should swim ashore and escape,

27:43. but the centurion, wishing to save Paul, put a stop to their plan. He ordered those who could swim to jump overboard first and get to land,

27:44. and then the rest [to follow], some on planks and others on [various pieces] from the ship. And so it came to pass that all got safely to land.

28:1. After our escape we learned that the island was called Malta.

---

visibility (see note on v. 39) and struck it head-on. With the prow stuck fast in the sand, the ship **began to break up** at the stern, because of the force of the waves. This shows that the shipwreck happened near the shore, but in a raging sea.

27:42. As always happened on such occasions, everyone began to panic and to think only of themselves. The soldiers who were acting as escort to the prisoners thought of their own responsibility, which was very serious if any of the prisoners escaped (see notes on 12:18; 16:27). To make sure that this would not happen, they decided to kill them, and in that way they would be freer to think of their own safety.

27:44. On [various pieces] from the ship: ἐπί τινων τῶν ἀπό τοῦ πλοίου, interpreting the pronoun as neuter, viz., the pieces from the ship. Some have preferred to interpret it as masculine, **on those of the ship,** meaning on the shoulders of the sailors, who were capable of such a service. It seems very improbable, however, in view of the unhelpful attitude of the sailors toward the passengers, as noticed in verse 30.

28:1. **Malta,** Μελίτη, is certainly the present-day island of Malta. The name was of Punic, that is Semitic, origin, and the group of the two principal islands, Gozo to the north and Malta to the south, was called Gaudo-Melita. An attempt has been made to identify the island named here, not with Malta, but with Meleda (Greek, Μελίτη; Latin, *Melite;* Croatian, *Mljet*) which lay off the Dalmatian coast a little above Ragusa and opposite the Abruzzi on the Italian shore. Since this theory is prompted largely by local pride and has no serious evidence to substantiate it, no importance has been given to it by scholars. The distance from Cauda (27:16) to Malta is about 475 miles which involved fourteen days' sailing (27:27 and 33) until the shipwreck. On Malta, the place shown as that where the shipwreck took place is very probably authentic and has the support of

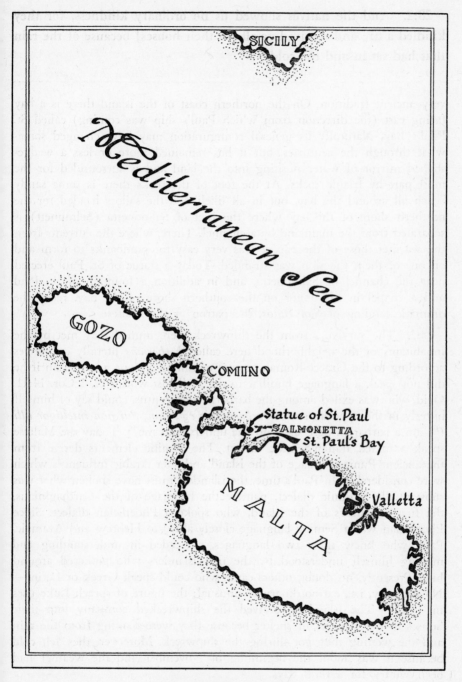

The Island of Malta

28:2. And the natives showed us no ordinary kindness, for they kindled a fire and received us all [in their houses] because of the rain that had set in and the cold.

---

very ancient tradition. On the northern coast of the island there is a bay facing east (the direction from which Paul's ship was coming) called St. Paul's Bay. Naturally its general configuration may have changed somewhat through the centuries, but it has remained more or less a wedge-shaped mirror of water pushing into the land and is surrounded for the most part by friable rocks. At the foot of the rocks there is some sandy beach all around the bay, but in all likelihood the sailors headed for the northern shore of the bay where the islet of Salmonetta (Selmunett) is separated from the mainland by a channel. There, where the currents from the sea met those of the bay, it was very easy for sandbanks to form and on one of them the ship was stranded. Today a statue of St. Paul erected near the channel of Salmonetta, and in addition a fountain of St. Paul and a chapel in his honor on the southern shore of the bay, recall the dramatic landing of *San Bulos,* the patron of the Maltese.

28:2. The survivors from the shipwreck were immediately met by the inhabitants of the neighborhood here called *barbarians* literally or **natives** according to the Graeco-Roman custom of calling anyone a barbarian if he did not speak a language familiar to the Hellenist world; cf. 1 Cor. 14:11. Ovid, who was exiled among the barbarians of Pontus, could say of himself bitterly in the opposite sense: *barbarus hic ego sum, qui non intelligor ulli* ("I am a barbarian here since no one understands me"). Today the Maltese speak a mixed Italian-Semitic dialect. The Semitic elements derive from the ancient Punic language of the island and later Arabic influences which were considerable. In Paul's time, the islanders must have spoken what was substantially a Punic dialect, namely the language of the Carthaginians, the first colonizers of the island, who spoke a Phoenician dialect. Since Phoenician was a Semitic language closely allied to Hebrew and Aramaic, Paul, who knew these two languages, succeeded in understanding and making himself understood by the first islanders who gathered around him. Presently, no doubt, others came who could speak Greek or Latin. — **No ordinary,** i.e., extraordinary or unusual: the figure of speech Luke uses in 19:11. — The islanders **received** the shipwrecked company into their houses or other places of shelter because they were soaking from the **rain** and the wetting they got during the shipwreck. Moreover, they felt **cold** because it was about the beginning of November and the weather had been wintry for several days.

28:3. Now Paul gathered a bundle of sticks and laid them on the fire, when a viper came out because of the heat and fastened on his hand.

28:4. When the natives saw the beast hanging from his hand, they said to one another: "Surely this man is a murderer, for though he has escaped the sea, Justice does not let him live."

28:5. But he shook off the beast into the fire and suffered no harm.

28:6. Now they were expecting that he would swell up and suddenly fall down and die, but after waiting a long time and seeing no harm come to him, they changed their minds and said that he was a god.

28:3. Paul, unable to keep still while others were working, now helped those who were tending the welcome fire. But a **viper** (ἔχιδνα), numbed by the cold and now awakened by the heat, came out of the bundle of sticks he had collected. It has been observed that today there are no poisonous snakes on the island of Malta, and this the islanders attribute to St. Paul. But though that may be true today, it does not follow that it was so in the past, and in actual fact some specialists have maintained that there were poisonous snakes on the island until a century ago. Today Malta has very little fauna at all, probably because of the density of population, since the island is one of the most densely populated in the Mediterranean. At the present day, only three species of serpents, all non-poisonous, are known there, but it is fair to suppose that the poisonous kind would have been killed off as the island became more thickly populated, until they disappeared altogether. In many other places, various other kinds of animals, especially if small and destructive, have become extinct. At any rate the experience of the islanders who were present and expected Paul to swell up and die from the poison (v. 6) is a clear argument that they recognized the viper for what it was. — **Fastened,** καθῆφεν: a common medical term. Luke will clearly appear as a physician in the description which follows.

28:4-6. The whole of this episode is a lively one in which the spontaneous reactions of the spectators are accompanied by the technical terminology of the medical narrator. The animal called at first a viper, is now called twice a **beast,** θηρίον, which could signify any kind of wild animal but was used by medical writers especially for serpents and vipers. Thus the medical cures for the bites of these beasts were called "theriaka medicines" from which comes the word "theriac." — The expression **swell**

28:7. Now in the vicinity there were estates belonging to the head man of the island, whose name was Publius, and he received us and entertained us hospitably for three days.

28:8. And it happened that the father of Publius was laid up with

---

up (literally, **to burn, to inflame** as a cause of the resultant **swelling up**), used of tumefactions produced by poisonous infections, and to **fall down,** used in connection with fainting and epilectic attacks, are likewise medical terms. The reactions of the Maltese are perfectly in keeping with their mentality at that time. They see a prisoner, as Paul was, who has just been saved from the sea, and is bitten by a poisonous snake as soon as he reaches land. He must be indeed, so they conclude, a ruthless criminal, a **murderer,** on whom "Dike" — **Justice** personified — is determined to inflict due punishment even after he has been saved from the sea. But when this imagined decree of Justice is not fulfilled, the islanders go to the other extreme and conclude that he is no ordinary man, for he can be neither drowned nor poisoned. He must, therefore, be a **god.** The Lycaonians of Lystra had come to a similar conclusion (14:11–13).

28:7. In the vicinity to where the shipwrecked company came ashore was the house of Publius to which they were welcomed. It was probably situated near the ancient capital of the island called Citta Vecchia or "Old City," about five or six miles from St. Paul's Bay (cf. note on v. 1). From this neighborhood came two inscriptions, a Greek one (*Corpus Inscr. Gr.,* III, 5754) and a Latin one (*Corpus Inscr. Lat.,* X, 7495) in which the title of *primus* or **head man,** given here to Publius, is found. It must have been the official title of the one who represented the Roman authority in the place, since the island depended administratively on the praetor of Sicily. It does not appear elsewhere as an official title, but it is typically Roman. (Even today in Rome, the head of a department is called *il principale* — the "principal" or "chief.") In Greek, **Publius** is Πόπλιος, which is, however, a "praenomen" like our Christian name, and not a full name. Therefore some have thought that the name **Popilius** is intended, but it seems unlikely. It has been pointed out that even Polybius (X, 2 sqq.) refers to the famous Publius Cornelius Scipio with the simple praenomen, Publius. It appears that the hospitality offered **for three days** was extended to **all** the survivors (cf. v. 2). Publius must certainly have had plenty of accommodation. In any case, as the supreme representative of the Roman authority, he was perhaps in duty bound to render assistance at least to the centurion and his group, among whom was Paul.

28:8–9. The narrator again appears as a medical man paying attention to cases connected with his profession. — **Fever:** the singular as well as the

fever and dysentery; but Paul went in, and after praying and laying his hands on him, he healed him.

28:9. After this all the sick on the island came and were cured;

28:10. and they honored us with many marks of honor, and when we sailed, they provided us with such things as we needed.

28:11. We set sail after three months in an Alexandrian ship with the Twins on her figurehead, which had wintered at the island.

---

plural is found in Greek to designate fever in general, but the plural here in the Greek implies in the context, the "fits of fever" which occur at intervals in such diseases. Even in Hippocrates, *fever* (or *fevers*) is more than once mentioned together with **dysentery**, the latter being used in the technical sense. The recurrence of the fever suggests the so-called "Maltese fever," but it would be difficult to diagnose it as such, owing to the lack of information here. — **Laying his hands:** for the imposition of hands in general, see note on 6:6; for its use in the curing of sickness, see note on 9:17. — **Were cured,** by whom? Certainly by Paul in particular, using his charisms, since the whole focus of the narrative is directed especially on him. But this does not rule out the possibility that Luke, too, as a doctor may have rendered his services.

28:10. This verse jumps the **three months'** stay (following verse) at Malta, during which many things must have happened. It is quite unlikely that a preacher of Paul's character would lose the opportunity of such a long stay to preach Christianity to the islanders. Nevertheless Luke says nothing of it, and the later Christian traditions (about *San Bulos* converting the Maltese, of Publius who became a bishop, etc.) do not supply for the silence of Luke. — **They provided us,** i.e., they loaded the ship with what would be needed by the passengers. These had in fact lost everything in the shipwreck and therefore needed everything. The generous gratitude of their well-wishers provided for all their needs.

28:11. **After three months,** i.e., at the beginning of February of A.D. 61. Actually, navigation was not usually resumed until a little later, toward the middle of March (cf. note on 27:9). But since the run between Malta and the southern shores of Italy was such a short one, it was hoped that time would be saved by departing earlier. — The new ship was an **Alexandrian** one, like that of 27:6, which carried the sign of the Dioscuri (or **Twins**), viz., the figureheads of Castor and Pollux, the two Dioscuri (cf. note on 8:9–11) who were the protectors of sailors (cf. Horace, *Carm.,* IV, 8, 31–32). It was a common custom for ancient ships to have a figure on the bow or, at least, the name of some divinity (cf. Lucianus, *Navigium,* I, 7).

28:12. We put in at Syracuse, and stayed there three days.

28:13. Then, following the coast, we reached Rhegium; and one day later a south wind sprang up, and on the second day we arrived at Puteoli,

28:14. where we found brethren and were entreated to stay with them seven days, and so we came to Rome.

28:12-14. The short run from Malta to Syracuse and thence to Puteoli (present-day Pozzuoli) across the Messina straits, went well. It is noticeable how Luke's "Travel Diary" becomes schematic like certain parts of Xenophon's *Anabasis* or Flavius Josephus' *Wars of the Jews,* based on personal notes by their respective authors. — At Syracuse, a stop of **three days** was made either for servicing the ship or to await a favorable wind to cross the strait. The words **following the coast** (περιελθόντες) can be interpreted either as "turning the ship about," by leaving the east coast of Sicily to head for Rhegium (modern Reggio), or "tacking" along the coast of Sicily, making a zigzag course, so as to keep in shelter from the wind which blew from the northwest. So they reached **Rhegium** to the east of the strait on the Calabrian peninsula (which corresponded to the Bruttium of the Romans, but not to the present-day Abruzzi). Fortunately, the next day a south wind sprang up (cf. note on 27:13) which was just what was needed, so much so that, on the day after, the long stretch from **Rhegium** to Pozzuoli was covered. Here they left the ship and made the journey overland to Rome. At Pozzuoli, previously called Dicearchia, Flavius Josephus had also landed after his shipwreck in the Adria sea (cf. note on 27:1 and 27). Here Paul found Christian **brethren,** and his party stayed **seven days.** Since this fairly long stay was made at the request of the **brethren,** it must be supposed that the centurion Julius must certainly have stopped at Pozzuoli for some formalities regarding the soldiers and the prisoners, but prolonged the stay for seven days to please Paul. The presence of Christians at Pozzuoli can easily be explained by the presence of a Jewish community there beforehand. Being a big commercial center and the chief port of the gulf of Naples, Pozzuoli at that time must have attracted many Jews from the whole Mediterranean region. According to Flavius Josephus, there were many wealthy Jews among them (cf. Flavius Josephus, *Wars of the Jews,* II, 104). A number of them had become Christians before Paul's arrival. There were certainly Christians in nearby Herculaneum and Pompeii at the time of the destruction of those cities (A.D. 79). — **We came to Rome:** here the verb **we came** stands for, **we pushed on toward, we set out for,** and implicitly indicates that as the sea voyage was now over, the short land journey to **Rome** began.

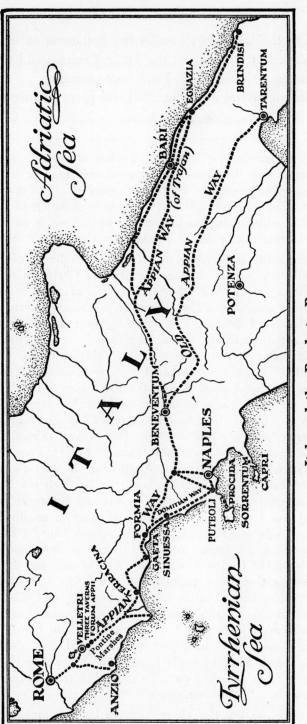

Italy and the Roads to Rome

28:15. And the brethren there, having had news of us, came as far as the Market of Appius and the Three Taverns; and when Paul saw them, he gave thanks to God and took courage.

28:16. On our arrival at Rome, Paul was given permission to live by himself with a soldier to guard him.

Some prefer the meaning for **Rome** to be taken in the wide sense of the **district of Rome,** *ager Romanus* (the Roman campagna or countryside), but in the following verse, the word **there** refers clearly to the city itself. **We came** could also be translated as a vague anticipation of the arrival at Rome which will be referred to precisely by the words **on our arrival** in verse 16. In this case, verse 15 would be a kind of parenthesis.

28:15. The Christians (**brethren**) of Rome knew already of Paul's imminent arrival, thanks to a message sent by the Christians of Pozzuoli during Paul's stay there. Wherefore representatives came to meet him, some of whom waited at the **Three Taverns,** while others went on to the Forum or **Market of Appius.** Paul, coming from the south along the Appian Way, met these latter first and then the others. The **Three Taverns** was a stopping place for travelers, mentioned also by Cicero (*Ad Attic.,* I, 13, 1; II, 10; II, 12) situated about 33 miles from Rome, where another road branches from the Appian Way in the direction of Anzio. The Forum or **Market of Appius,** a few miles farther south on the edge of the Pontine Marshes, took its name from its founder Appius Claudius, and had become a great gathering place for *sailors, tavern-keepers, and thieves,* as Horace described it after he had stopped there (*Sat.,* I, 5, 2-4). From Terracina, the ancient Anxur, to the Forum of Appius ran the *decemnovium,* that is, a straight stretch of road 19 miles long, beside which ran a navigable canal. This served for the transport of goods and passengers when the ordinary road was flooded by the Pontine Marshes as usually happened in spring. Since this was the time of Paul's present journey, he probably arrived at the Forum of Appius in a canal boat from Terracina, and there met the first group of Christians who had come to meet him from Rome. If Paul on seeing them **took courage,** we can gather that he had been worried in some connection. In his epistle to the *Romans,* 16:17-18, he had in fact warned them to **watch those who cause dissensions and scandals,** which words seem to refer to the Judaizing Christians, his old enemies. At the time of his arrival in Rome, he did not know whether these adversaries had made any progress by inciting the community there against him. On seeing those who had come to meet him from Rome, his fears disappeared and **he . . . took courage.**

28:16. After the stop at the Three Taverns, Paul's company began the ascent over the Alban hills which led past Velletri, but they must have made another stop, probably at Ariccia (Horace, *Sat.,* I, 5, 1), situated 16 miles from the city of Rome. From the top of the Alban hills, Paul looked on Rome for the first time. A few hours later, he entered the city following the Appian Way and passing through the Porta Capena (near the present-day Porta di S. Sebastiano). After the words, **at Rome,** the Western Recension adds **the centurion delivered the prisoners to the captain of the camp, but Paul was given permission, etc.** This title of *camp commander* (στρατοπεδάρχης) would correspond nominally to that of *praefectus castrorum* or camp prefect, among the Romans. Ordinarily it meant the camp commander of the praetorians situated near Via Nomentana and still called today Castro Pretorio. But the Latin text of the codex *Gigas* gives the title as *princeps peregrinorum,* namely the commander of the *milites peregrini* (foreign-service soldiers), who were billeted in a camp (*castra peregrinorum*) situated between the Coelian and the Palatine Hill, which was used for soldiers passing through, or for forage parties or special police services. If such were the case, Paul with the other prisoners would have been taken first to this camp of *milites peregrini,* where probably Julius and his soldiers were billeted. However, the existence of this camp at the time of Paul is not proved and there is only probable evidence of it in the second century, but quite certain proof in the third century. On the other hand, it is known that the barracks of the praetorians or Castro Pretorio, served as a place of detention for prisoners (cf. Flavius Josephus, *Antiquities of the Jews,* XVIII, 235). Therefore the solitary Latin reading of codex *Gigas* is not so authoritative as to make the title in question attributable to anyone other than the commander of the praetorian barracks. Besides, it is not impossible that at first Paul was handed over to the camp-commander of the *milites peregrini* (if such a barracks did actually exist), and shortly afterward transferred to the barracks of the praetorians. These latter were under the praetorian prefect who at that time was Afranius Burrus, a Stoic philosopher and friend of Seneca, and former tutor of the young Nero. Burrus, or one of his deputies, must have received Paul from Julius together with the official information regarding his trial. It is almost impossible that this information could have been given in the official document or *eulogium,* written and sent with the prisoner by Porcius Festus, since that document had almost certainly been lost at the bottom of the sea in shipwreck. There was nothing else to do, then, but accept the verbal presentation of the prisoner made by the centurion, always reserving the right to ask for another copy of the official *eulogium* from Judea if it should be necessary. We may be sure that the information about the prisoner given by the well-disposed centurion was couched in highly favorable terms, in keeping with the sentiments displayed by him toward Paul during the voyage. The outcome of the information, therefore, was

28:17. Now it happened that three days later he called together the leading Jews, and when they had assembled he said to them: "Brethren, although I had done nothing against the people or against the customs of our fathers, yet I was handed over to the Romans as a prisoner from Jerusalem.

28:18. "After an examination, they were ready to release me since I was innocent of any crime that deserved death;

---

excellent also: namely, **Paul was given permission** to remain outside the barracks (these last two words are explicitly added by a few documents), staying where he chose on the one condition of the continual supervision of **a soldier to guard him.** Paul was placed, then, under *custodia militaris* (military custody; for which, see note on 24:23) but of a very mild form, as will appear from verses 23 and 30.

28:17. After three days: Paul did not waste any time, nor did he think of resting after such an arduous voyage. In these three days, he must have sought to clarify his legal position as a prisoner in "military custody" before the Roman authorities. Moreover — helped no doubt by the Christians of Rome — he must have rented the house referred to in verses 23 and 30. Here this lodging place is not described, but this meeting with the Jews must have taken place in a private house. At this meeting, Paul wished to define his religious position before his own fellow countrymen. At Rome, the Jews were numerous and had some powerful protectors at the imperial court. So much so that Poppea, the wife of Nero, passed as an associate of Judaism (Flavius Josephus, **Antiquities of the Jews,** XX, 195). For a general presentation of contemporary Judaism, see G. Ricciotti, *The History of Israel,* II, pp. 183–190. A great number of the Jews present at the meeting must have known Paul by repute, since — even abstracting from other matters — his letter to the *Romans* written two years before, had circulated not only among Christians, but had been read also by the Jews who were relatives or friends of Christians, and no less interested than the Christians in the questions dealt with in the epistle. Perhaps they vaguely judged him to be an innovator of very extreme ideas, but were unable to form any clear judgment of him. They accepted Paul's invitation therefore, in order to make up their minds about him by hearing him speak. The exposition which Paul gives here and in the following two verses is a general one and rather cautious, perhaps because the first meeting was not opportune — perhaps also because of lack of time — for a long doctrinal discussion. — **People,** par excellence, Israel, the people of God.

28:18-20. This is a summary of the facts narrated from 21:27 up to 26:32. Naturally Paul here sticks to the ideas which he had already ex-

28:19. "but as the Jews objected I was forced to appeal to Caesar — not that I had any charge to bring against my own nation.

28:20. "This, then, is why I asked to see you and speak with you. For it is because of the hope of Israel that I am wearing this chain."

28:21. But they said to him, "We ourselves have received no letters about thee from Judea, and none of the brethren, upon arrival, has reported or spoken any evil of thee.

28:22. "But we want to hear from thee what thy views are: for as regards this sect, we know that everywhere it is spoken against."

---

pressed in his discourses reported on the previous occasions without descending too much to particulars (or so this summary would lead one to believe). — **Hope of Israel:** faith in Christ as the Messias: see notes on 23:6–8; 26:6–8.

28:21–22. This brief reply of the Jews, certainly shorter here than it must have been in actual fact, is very carefully thought out and not without a certain regard for Paul. They do not deny that they know of him by repute (cf. preceding note) but simply state that they have received no information about him, verbal or written, from Judea. Accepting this statement as true, we can conclude that the Jewish authorities at Jerusalem had not yet had time to notify the Jews in Rome of Paul's arrival in the city, either because of the sudden departure of Julius and his escort from Caesarea (cf. note on 27:1) or because of the difficulty of communications by reason of the "closed sea" (cf. note on 27:9). We gather from this, however, that there was a steady correspondence between the Jewish authorities in Jerusalem and Rome, otherwise the surprise expressed here at not having heard about Paul from Jerusalem would be unjustified. It should be noted also that the statement that nobody had spoken **any evil** against Paul, refers only to the **brethren** in Judea. As far as the Jews of Rome are concerned, we may well believe that Paul did not enjoy popularity among them. — **Sect**, i.e., of Christianity: see note on 24:14. These Jewish leaders here speak of knowing the sect by hearsay, as though they did not know it at firsthand. Here, in actual fact, the diplomatic acumen of the speakers appears to its best effect, for these Jews had personally experienced, or at least knew very well, the expulsion of the Jews from Rome, ordered by Claudius twelve years before (see note on 18:2) which was caused by the tumults against the incipient Christianity. But Paul's opponents very cleverly made a *tabula rasa* of such events, ignoring them completely. They simply want to **hear from** Paul **what** his **views are.** They are not interested in Paul's opinions about the tumults at the time of Claudius, but they want to know the theological arguments by reason of

28:23. So they fixed a day, and very many came to him at his lodging; and to them he explained the matter, bearing witness to the kingdom of God, and trying from morning till evening to convince them concerning Jesus [with arguments taken from] the Law of Moses and from the prophets.

28:24. And some believed what was said; and some disbelieved.

28:25. And as they could not agree among themselves, they began to depart when Paul added this one word: "Well did the Holy Spirit speak through Isaias the prophet to your fathers,

28:26. "saying: 'Go to this people and say:

with the ear you will hear the word and will not understand; and seeing, you will see and will not perceive.

---

which Paul figures as a ringleader of the . . . Nazarene sect (24:5). They do not show themselves as Paul's adversaries as yet, but they let him know that as for the sect which he represents, they have received information which is entirely unfavorable.

28:23. Paul's **lodging** was the house he had rented, referred to in verse 30. We have no way of determining where this house was. There have been several suggestions in the past as to the situation of this house in Rome, the chief one placing it at Santa Maria in Via Lata (near the modern Corso Umberto) where the buildings of the *gens Julia* stood, while another one sets it at San Paolo della Regola (near the present-day synagogue). Both, however, are very late and without foundation — especially the second one. We may rather suppose that it was some house near the Castro Pretorio, whence came the guards who took duty over him in turn (see note on v. 16; and cf. note on 24:23). This, however, is pure conjecture. The Jews of Rome came to this meeting to take part in the long discussion with Paul *in greater number* than at the previous session (v. 17), and this time it went on **from morning till evening.** From the start, Paul would have expounded his teaching concerning Jesus and have replied to the various questioners, clarifying their ideas and solving their difficulties. The general theme was to show that Jesus was the Messias foretold in the Old Testament, and to this end Paul adduced arguments **from the Law of Moses and from the Prophets,** his usual thesis before the Jews (see note on 13:16 sqq.), and his usual mode of presenting it (see note on 26:22–23).

28:25. **Well,** καλῶς: fittingly, rightly.

28:26–27. The passage from Isaias cited here follows the Greek Sep-

28:27. " 'For the heart of this people has been hardened,
and with their ears they have been hard of hearing,
and their eyes they have closed,
lest perhaps they see with their eyes,
and hear with their ears,
and understand with their heart and be converted,
and I (will) heal them' (Isa. 6:9–10).

28:28. "Be it known to you therefore that this salvation of God has
been sent to the Gentiles, and they will listen to it."

28:29.

28:30. And for two full years, he remained in his own hired lodging: and he welcomed all who came to him,

28:31. preaching the kingdom of God and teaching about the
Lord Jesus with all boldness, and unhindered.

---

tuagint and was quoted by Jesus (Mt. 13:14–15; cf. Mk. 4:12; Lk. 8:10)
to explain the result, mainly negative, of his parables. But it was also
quoted by the primitive Christian catechesis to explain the obstinacy of
the Jews against the teaching of the Messias Jesus, as appears from this
present passage as well as from Jn. 12:40 (and from Rom. 11:8 for which
cf. Isa. 29:10). The precise significance of lest has been discussed at great
length from antiquity. Its real meaning here, as well as in the Hebrew text,
is that of a threatened warning which makes the ruinous effect of their
obstinacy fall on those responsible (cf. G. Ricciotti, *Life of Christ*, pp.
372–375).

28:28. The substitution of the Gentiles for the stubborn Jews had
already been affirmed and put into practice by Paul at Antioch of Pisidia
(cf. note on 13:45–51) and at Corinth (cf. 18:6).

28:29. This verse, where it is given, reads thus: **And when he had said
these things, the Jews departed, having much argument among themselves.**
This passage is omitted in most authoritative Greek codices. It is found,
however, in a few Greek codices and various documents of the older
versions, including the Vulgate. The critical editions omit it altogether
and rightly so. It simply repeats, in other words, the information of
verses 24–25.

28:30–31. The period of **two full years** recorded here runs from the
spring of A.D. 61 (see note on v. 11) until well on into the spring of 63.
During this time Paul remained in *military custody* with much freedom of
action, viz., **preaching . . . and teaching . . . with all boldness, and un-**

hindered. We have occasional glimpses of such intense activity of Paul as a prisoner from his letter written from Rome to the *Philippians*. There we learn that he preached with good results both **throughout the praetorium,** i.e., among the soldiers who came from the Castro Pretorio barracks to guard him (cf. notes on vv. 16 and 23), and elsewhere. Moreover, **the greater number of the brethren in the Lord, gaining courage from my** (Paul's) **chains, dared to speak the word of God more freely and without fear** (Phil. 1:13-14). The outcome of this was that, at a certain point, Christians were found even in **Caesar's household** (*ibid.*, 4:22), i.e., in the imperial court on the Palatine, although it is not suggested that all these "august" Christians were converted by Paul. It is true that, in this flourishing evangelization of Rome, there were some who preached the Gospel out of **envy and contentiousness,** so as to spite Paul, **thinking to stir up affliction** at his imprisonment, while there were others who preached **out of good will** (*ibid.*, 1:15-17). But Paul calmly replies, **But, what of it? Provided only that in every way, whether in pretence or in truth, Christ is being proclaimed, in this I rejoice, yes and I shall rejoice (in the future)** (*ibid.*, 1:18). — The fact that Paul was able to carry on his preaching and teaching in Rome **unhindered** must be added to all the other points in favor of the Roman authorities already referred to in this book (see note on 3:13). With this final word of acknowledgment, the book of the *Acts* came to a close. It was like a last sad gaze on a rosy dream that had vanished forever, the dream of a peaceful coexistence of Christianity with the Roman Empire. We have already expressed our opinion that this abrupt ending of the *Acts* is to be linked with the burning of Rome in A.D. 64 and the consequent persecution of the Christians which quickly followed it (Introduction, Chap. VII). These cataclysmic events which marked the beginning of the struggle between the empire of Caesar and the kingdom of Christ, dispelled that rosy dream, and prevented the *Acts* from receiving its proper historical conclusion.

GENERAL INDEX

Aaron, 125, 138
Aberle, M., 28
Abraham, 118, 119, 120, 121 f, 126, 175, 283
Academians, 269
Acaicus, 282
Achaia, 27, 61, 282, 283, 284, 291, 302, 312
Acilii, 280
Acropolis, 268, 270
Actium, 251
Acts of Alexander, 1
Acts of Paul, 34, 147, 154, 161, 183, 193, 311
Acts of Paul and Thecla, 219
Acts of Peter, 36, 161, 189
Adalia, 228
Adria, 386 f, 398
Adriatic, 387
Adrumythium, 377
Aeneas, 161
Aeschylus, 371
Afranius Burrus, see Burrus
Agabus, 180 f, 326 f
Agape, 80
Agrippa I, 183 ff, 191, 331, 366
Agrippa II, 148, 154, 180, 189, 190, 191, 352, 359, 362, 365, 366 f, 374 f
Ain-Dirue, 145, 147
Albinus (procurator), 130
Alexander the Great, 1, 305
Alexander the Heretic, 322
Alexander the High Priest, 89
Alexander the Jew, 308 f
Alexandria, 114, 161, 182, 290, 291, 377, 378, 379, 390
Alexandrinus (Codex), 4
"Alms, journey of the," 182, 312 ff
Ambrosiaster, 6, 241
Amianus Marcellinus, 304
Ammonites, 125
Amos, 125
Amphipolis, 263
Ananias, husband of Sapphira, 17, 98 f
Ananias the High Priest, 338, 344 f, 354, 362
Ananias the Jew, 26, 152, 153, 154, 339 f, 372
Ananus, 130
Andrew, 51, 111
Andronicus, 312
Angelicus (Codex), 4, 6
Angels, 124, 128, 188
Annas, 89, 346

Antioch in Pisidia, 197, 201, 205 f, 217, 224, 226, 264, 272, 281, 405
Antioch in Syria, 8, 13, 23, 37, 38, 60, 176 f, 179, 180, 182, 184, 189, 190, 193, 194, 196, 205, 226, 228, 230 f, 239, 243, 244, 246, 289, 312
Antiochus IV, 193
Antipatris, 351, 353
Antonia, Fortress, 187, 333, 335, 342, 343, 348
Antonius Felix, 200
Antony, 251
Apollo, 254, 310
Apollonia, 263
Apollos, 290 ff, 294
Apostolic Council, 24, 35, 147, 182, 183, 190, 228, 232 f, 244 f, 288, 329
Appianus, 164
Appian Way, 251, 400, 401
Appius, Market of, 400
Apuleius, 153
Aquila and Priscilla, 190, 279, 280, 282, 287, 288, 290, 291, 307
Arabia, 25, 61, 157
Aramaic, language, 55, 109, 171, 337, 341, 371, 394
Aratus of Soli, 276
Arcadian Way, 303
Archons, 255
Areopagus, 39, 268, 270 f, 278, 279
Ares, 270
Aretas, 158
Ariccia, 401
Aristarchus, 23, 296, 303, 306 f, 310, 313 f, 378, 389
Aristeas, 119, 143
Aristobulus, 183
Aristotle, 269
Armenia, 63
Armenian Version, 5
Artapanus, 119
Artemis, see Diana
Ashdod, 147
Asia, 61, 113, 114, 204, 230, 249, 250, 290, 294, 297, 318, 333, 345
Asiarchs, 306 f
Asiatic Assembly, 307
Assos, 276, 317
Assuan, 142, 143

407

Athenians, 118, 269, 271, 273
Athens, 266, 267 ff, 272 ff, 278, 279
Attalia, 205, 228
Augustan cohort, 164, 377
Augustine, 5, 63, 100, 111, 241, 245, 254, 285
Augustus, 134, 142, 196, 251, 343, 367, 369
Azizus, king of Emesa, 202, 352
Azymes, 185

Babylon, 32, 125 f
Balaam, 255
Baptism, 58
Bar-Jesus, 197, 200, 201 f, 203
Barnabas, 15, 23, 27, 98, 159, 177, 178, 182, 188, 193 f, 195, 196, 197, 201, 205, 214 ff, 219 ff, 225 ff, 230 ff, 235 f, 244, 328
Bartholomew, 51
Baur, F. Ch., 34
Beirut, 186
Beisan-Scythopolis, 149
Benjamin, 209
Bernice, 287, 352, 358, 365 f, 376
Beroea, 263, 266, 267
Bethany, 47, 50
Bethlehem, 141
Beza (Codex), 5, 10, 222, 240, 241, 243, 252, 270, 290, 314, 317, 320
"Bishops," 318, 321
Bithynia, 250
Bithyniarchs, 308
Blass, F., 9 f
Blastus, 192
Bleck, 36
Bonsirven, J., 237
Bourget, E., 284
Brindisi, 251
Britannicus, 360
Burrus, Afranius, 28, 401

Cadbury, H. J., 39
Caesar, 32, 289, 363, 364, 365, 366, 385
Caesarea in Palestine, 13, 23, 28, 30, 38, 127, 147, 160, 164, 166, 176, 186, 189, 191 f, 288, 325, 351, 360, 361, 368, 376, 377
Caiphas, 89, 104, 148
Caligula, 93, 158, 161, 183, 369
Callisthenes, 1
Candace, 113, 142, 143
Cape Matala, 380, 382
Caponius, 108
Cappadocia, 61
Carmel, Mount, 161, 325
Cassian, 100
Castelrosso, 324
Castro Pretorio, 401, 404, 405
Catacombs (Priscilla), 78

Cato the Greater, 361
Cato the Less, 361
Cauda, 383, 392
Cenchrae, 282, 331
Cephas, see Simon Peter
Cestius Gallus, 353
Chalcis, 365, 366
Chaldeans, 213
Charisms, 63 f, 114, 194, 332
Chester Beatty papyrus, 4
Chios, 317
Chloe, 282
Christians, 150, 179, 180, 375, 378, 398
Cicero, 9, 205, 218, 219, 242, 262, 264, 266, 267, 270, 271, 353, 358, 400
Cilicia, 113, 114, 132, 160, 219, 239, 246, 247, 280, 336, 338, 365
Cis, 209
Citta Vecchia, 396
Claudius, Emperor, 181, 189, 191, 201, 280, 284, 343, 354, 403
Claudius Lysias, see Lysias
Cleanthes, 276
Clemen, C., 37
Clement of Alexandria, 4, 15, 36, 105, 111, 119, 135, 301
Clement of Rome, 15, 83, 112
Cleodemus, 119
"Closed sea," 380
Cnidus, 379
Colossae, 298
Coptic-Sahidic Version, 5, 6, 241
Copto-Bohairic Version, 4
Corinth, 35, 178, 190, 253, 263, 267, 278, 281, 282 ff, 291, 294, 302, 405
Cornelia Gens, 164
Cornelius the Centurion, 17, 27, 141, 154, 164 ff, 168, 190, 197, 229, 234
Cos, 324
Council of Jerusalem, see Apostolic Council and Jerusalem, Council of
Cretans, 63
Crete, 379 ff, 385, 387
Crispus, 282 f, 286
Cumanus, 356
"Curetes," 305
Custodia libera, 358
Custodia militaris, 358, 402
Custodia publica, 358
Cyprian of Carthage, 57, 146, 241
Cypriots, 177, 193, 195
Cyprus, 98, 159, 176, 178, 195, 197, 200, 205, 324, 378
Cyrenaica, 114, 384
Cyrenea, 177
Cyrenians, 113, 114, 177, 193

Damaris, 278

Vitruvius, 310
Vloten, von, 36
Vulgate, 4, 47, 53, 71, 78, 146, 148, 153, 212, 218, 231, 237, 240, 244, 252, 320, 322, 327, 351, 355, 371, 373, 379, 380, 382, 405

Weiss, B., 37
"We-sections," 3, 18 f, 22, 39, 181, 251, 314, 319, 376
Western Recension, 3, 4 ff, 11, 13, 47, 51, 53, 75, 78, 90, 132, 140, 169, 180, 202, 210, 214, 218, 219, 220, 222, 225, 231, 232, 240, 241 f, 243, 248, 250, 252, 259,

266, 270, 279, 282, 286, 288, 290, 294, 295, 296, 300, 313, 327, 332, 338, 349, 351, 355, 379, 389, 401
Wette, W. de, 34
Wilpert, G., 190
Windisch, H., 39

Xenophon, 22, 45, 218, 381, 398

Yom Kippur, 380

Zachary, 113
Zealots, 48, 108, 313, 334, 344; *see also* Sicarii
Zeigler, 36

INDEX OF SCRIPTURAL REFERENCES

Old Testament

New Testament